CONDITIONING FOR STRENGTH AND HUMAN PERFORMANCE

Fully revised and updated, the third edition of *Conditioning for Strength and Human Performance* provides strength and conditioning students with the clearest and most accessible introduction to the scientific principles underpinning the discipline. Covering bioenergetics and nutrition, a systematic approach to physiological and endocrinological adaptations to training and the biomechanics of resistance training, no other book provides such a thorough grounding in the science of strength and conditioning or better prepares students for evidence-based practice.

T. Jeff Chandler, CSCS, NSCA-CPT, FACSM, FNSCA has previously served as Professor and Department Chair at Marshall University, USA, and as Professor and Department Head at Jacksonville State University, USA. Dr. Chandler has 12 years of experience in a clinical sports medicine setting at the Lexington Clinic Sports Medicine Center, USA. He is the Editor in Chief of the *Strength and Conditioning Journal*, the professional journal of the National Strength and Conditioning Association, serving in that position since 1998.

Lee E. Brown, EdD, CSCS·D, FNSCA, FACSM was on the faculty at California State University, Fullerton, USA, from 2002–2017 and was the Director of the Center for Sport Performance and the Human Performance Laboratory. He was President of the National Strength and Conditioning Association (NSCA), the NSCA Foundation, and the Southwest American College of Sports Medicine (SWACSM). He also sat on the Board of Trustees of the national American College of Sports Medicine (ACSM) and is a Fellow of both the ACSM and the NSCA.

D0165141

CONDITIONING FOR STRENGTH AND HUMAN PERFORMANCE

THIRD EDITION

EDITED BY T. JEFF CHANDLER AND LEE E. BROWN

Routledge
Taylor & Francis Group

LONDON AND NEW YORK

Third edition published 2019
by Routledge
2 Park Square, Milton Park, Abingdon, Oxon OX14 4RN

and by Routledge
711 Third Avenue, New York, NY 10017

Routledge is an imprint of the Taylor & Francis Group, an informa business

First edition published by Lippincott Williams & Wilkins 2008
Second edition published by Lippincott Williams & Wilkins 2013

British Library Cataloguing-in-Publication Data
A catalogue record for this book is available from the British Library

Library of Congress Cataloging-in-Publication Data
Names: Chandler, T. Jeff, editor. | Brown, Lee E., 1956- editor.
Title: Conditioning for strength and human performance / edited by T. Jeff Chandler and Lee E. Brown.
Description: Third edition. | New York, NY : Routledge, 2018. | Includes index.
Identifiers: LCCN 2018004165| ISBN 9781138218062 (hbk) | ISBN 9781138218086 (pbk) | ISBN 9781315438443 (web pdf) | ISBN 9781315438429 (mobi) | ISBN 9781315438450 (ebk)
Subjects: LCSH: Physical fitness—Health aspects. | Exercise—Physiological aspects. | Physical education and training.
Classification: LCC RA781 .C43 2018 | DDC 613.7—dc23

ISBN: 978-1-138-21806-2 (hbk)
ISBN: 978-1-138-21808-6 (pbk)
ISBN: 978-1-315-43845-0 (ebk)

Typeset in Sabon
by Swales & Willis, Exeter, Devon, UK

Visit the companion website: www.routledge.com/cw/chandler
Printed in Canada

DEDICATIONS

For Theresa, you are the reason I am alive,
and you are my reason for living.

LEB, 2018

To my wife, Pam; my son Britt and his family; and
my daughter Kate and her family. With much love!

TJC, 2018

CONTENTS

CONTRIBUTORS

Clint Alley, MS
The Forge

C. Eric Arnold, PhD
University of Tampa

Saldiam R. Barillas, MS, CSCS, USAW, RYT
  200
Cardiff Metropolitan University

Travis W. Beck, PhD
University of Oklahoma

Matthew K. Beeler, MA, CSCS
The Ohio State University

Andy Bosak, PhD, EP-C, CSCS*D
Liberty University

Jake Bleacher, MSPT, OCS, CSCS
The Ohio State University

W. Britt Chandler, MS, CSCS, *D
Lexington, KY

Anthony B. Ciccone, PhD, CSCS
Utah Valley University

Jared W. Coburn, PhD, CSCS*D, FNSCA,
  FACSM
California State University, Fullerton

Kristen C. Cochrane-Snyman, PhD, CSCS*D
California State University, Fresno

Jaci N. Davis, BS
University of Mary Hardin-Baylor

Herbert A. deVries, PhD, FACSM
University of Southern California

Ian J. Dobbs, MS, CSCS*D
Cardiff Metropolitan University

Joan M. Eckerson, PhD
Creighton University

Todd S. Ellenbecker, DPT, MS, SCS, OCS, CSCS
Rehab Plus Sports Therapy, Scottsdale, Arizona

Tammy K. Evetovich, PhD, CSCS, ACSM
  EP-C, FACSM
Wayne State College

Andrew J. Galpin, PhD, CSCS*D, NSCA-
  CPT*D, FNSCA
California State University, Fullerton

Allen Hedrick, MA, CSCS*D, FNSCA
Colorado State University-Pueblo

Terry J. Housh, PhD, FACSM, FNSCA
University of Nebraska

Andy V. Khamoui, PhD, CSCS
Florida Atlantic University

Duane V. Knudson, PhD, FACSM, FISBS,
RFSA
Texas State University

William J. Kraemer, PhD, CSCS*D, FNSCA,
FACSM, FISSN, FACN
The Ohio State University

Scott K. Lynn, PhD
California State University, Fullerton

Moh H. Malek, PhD, FACSM, FNSCA,
CSCS*D
Wayne State University

Ryan T. McManus, MS, CSCS
California State University, Fullerton

Guillermo J. Noffal, PhD
California State University, Fullerton

Derek N. Pamukoff, PhD
California State University, Fullerton

Marie E. Pepin PT, DPT, MSPT, OMPT
Wayne State University

Tad Pieczynski, MSPT, OCS, CSCS
Rehab Plus Sports Therapy, Scottsdale, Arizona

Joseph A. Roche BPT, Dip. Rehab. PT, PhD
Wayne State University

Evan E. Schick, PhD, CSCS
California State University, Long Beach

Nathan Serrano, CSCS, USAW
California State University, Fullerton

Traci A. Statler, PhD, CMPC, CSCS
California State University, Fullerton

Lem Taylor, PhD, FACSM, FISSN
University of Mary Hardin Baylor

Anna Thatcher, DPT, SCS, OCS, ATC,
CSCS
AZ Sports Center Rehabilitation and
Pilates

Casey M. Watkins, MS, CSCS
Auckland University of Technology

Joseph P. Weir, PhD, FACSM, FNSCA
University of Kansas

Loree L. Weir, PhD
University of Kansas

Colin D. Wilborn, PhD, CSCS*D, FNSCA,
FISSN
University of Mary Hardin Baylor

Megan A. Wong, MS
Cardiff Metropolitan University

Michael C. Zourdos, PhD, CSCS
Florida Atlantic University

PREFACE

Welcome to the third edition of *Conditioning for Strength and Human Performance*. The field of strength and conditioning is growing exponentially along with an enormous increase in the science surrounding human adaptations related to training. This makes for a difficult task to stay abreast of new information. In this new edition, we have not only added the latest scientific published results but also new and expanded content related to the critical factors associated with human physiology systems, psychology, periodized training and neuromuscular adaptations to exercise.

This third edition retains the illustrative figures and photos of previous editions so vital to making the material inside come to life for students. In addition, laboratory activities have been enhanced to provide students with real hands-on experiences designed to highlight scientific theory and phenomena found in each chapter. Finally, all pedagogical elements remain including key points, case examples and real-world applications along with instructor slides and test questions.

The book is divided into four sections: Basic science, Organization and administration, Exercise prescription and Special topics. A new chapter has been added on Needs analysis to provide a foundation for determining the needs of the athlete and the demands of the sport and how these characteristics match. Following this chapter is another new addition on Program design which breaks down the systematic planning of resistance training into an easy to follow manageable task. Lastly, Age and gender have been combined and expanded as extraordinary issues of Special populations as they are two of the most important aspects affecting performance in strength and conditioning.

We hope the additional content of this third edition serves both instructor and student well. It has been our pleasure to write and compile this information into a unique educational textbook. We hope you will also enjoy reading and using it to maximize your own or your athlete's performance.

PART 1

BASIC SCIENCE

Contents

CHAPTER 1

BIOENERGETICS

T. Jeff Chandler, W. Britt Chandler, and C. Eric Arnold

OBJECTIVES

After completing this chapter, you will be able to:

- Identify the biological energy systems and explain their role in human athletic performance.
- Explain the concept of metabolic specificity and sources of energy as related to human athletic performance.
- Discuss the role of enzymes in catalyzing chemical reactions.
- Explain the role of lactic acid and lactate in human athletic performance.
- Demonstrate an understanding of the limiting factors in human athletic performance.

KEY TERMS

Activation energy
Anabolic
ATP
Bioenergetics
Blood lactate
Carbohydrate
Cardiorespiratory
    endurance
Catabolic
Chemical energy
Cytoplasm
Deaminated

Electron transport
    system (ETS)
Endergonic
Enzymes
Excess post-exercise
    oxygen consumption
Exergonic
Gluconeogenesis
Krebs cycle
Mechanical
    energy
Mitochondria

Oxygen consumption
Oxygen deficit
Phosphate
Phosphofructokinase
    (PFK)
Q10 effect
Rate limiting enzyme
Reactant
Specificity of training
Steady state
Substrate
Thermodynamics

INTRODUCTION

Human movement requires energy, and energy is vital for athletic performance. **Bioenergetics** is the flow of energy in biological systems and is a key consideration during exercise. For any physical activity, energy must be generated, and used by the body to accomplish the task.

The source of energy influences the ability of the sprinter to complete the 100-meter dash, the marathoner to complete a run, and the weightlifter to complete a lift. Understanding metabolism, specifically understanding the energy systems that are used during various types of exercise, is vital in developing effective activity-specific conditioning programs. With a basic knowledge of bioenergetics, the student can understand why specific chemical reactions that take place in skeletal muscles are turned on and how energy from these chemical reactions fuel muscles during exercise.

> Bioenergetics is the study of sources of energy in living organisms, and how that energy is ultimately utilized.

The food we eat contains energy in the form of **chemical energy**. We store this chemical energy in our body in the forms of glycogen, fat, and protein. Ultimately, the chemical energy stored can be released to provide energy to produce adenosine triphosphate (ATP). ATP is the primary source of energy to support muscle contraction during exercise. The structure of ATP is comprised of an adenine group, a ribose group, and three **phosphate** groups joined together (Figure 1.1).

The formation of the ATP occurs by combining adenosine diphosphate (ADP) and inorganic phosphate (Pi). This process requires a substantial amount of energy that must be captured from the food we eat.

> ATP is the high energy molecule responsible for muscular contraction and other life sustaining metabolic reactions in the human body.

ATP is a high energy molecule that stores energy in the form of chemical bonds. Energy is released when the chemical bonds that join ADP and Pi together to form ATP are broken (Figure 1.2). The chemical energy derived from the breaking of the chemical bonds provides energy to generate ATP, and thus energy to perform various types of exercise.

Metabolism is the total of **anabolic** and **catabolic** processes. A catabolic process breaks larger compounds into smaller compounds. In metabolism, this involves the breakdown of substances such as **carbohydrate** to provide fuel for the muscles during exercise. An anabolic reaction builds larger substances from smaller substances.

> METABOLISM = CATABOLISM + ANABOLISM.

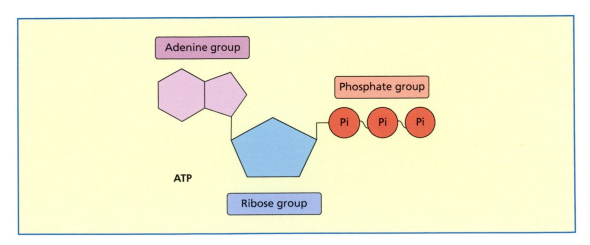

Figure 1.1 The basic structure of ATP. Energy is stored in the three phosphate bonds.

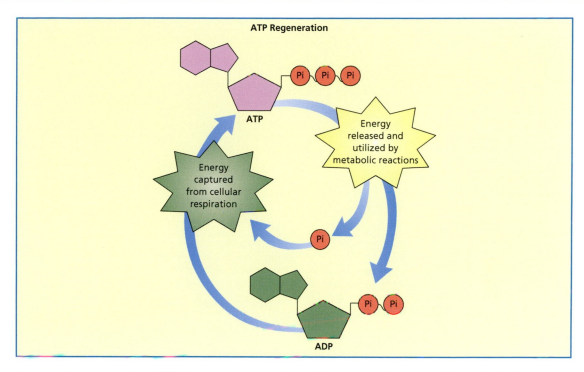

Figure 1.2 Regeneration of ATP. Energy is released when ATP is broken down into ADP and Pi. ATP is regenerated from ADP and energy captured from food.

ENZYMES

Enzymes are protein structured molecules that speed or facilitate certain chemical reactions by lowering the energy of activation of a chemical reaction (7). The energy of activation is considered an energy barrier that must be overcome for a chemical reaction to occur (Figure 1.3). Enzymes lower the **activation energy**, or the amount of energy needed to cause a specific chemical reaction to occur. In this way, enzymes facilitate metabolic chemical reactions. The enzyme does not become a part of the product, but remains intact as an enzyme.

A chemical reaction is classified as either an **exergonic** or an **endergonic** reaction. An exergonic reaction gives up energy and an endergonic reaction absorbs energy from its surroundings. During a 100-meter sprint, ATP is being broken down in the muscle and energy is being released (exergonic reaction) and utilized by the muscles (endergonic reaction)

that are being actively recruited during the activity. An exergonic reaction is illustrated in Figure 1.4 where A → B is a spontaneous

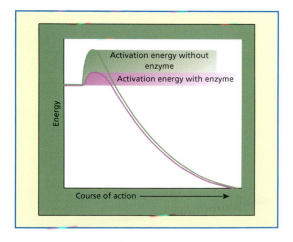

Figure 1.3 Energy of activation. An enzyme lowers the amount of energy that must be overcome for a chemical reaction to occur.

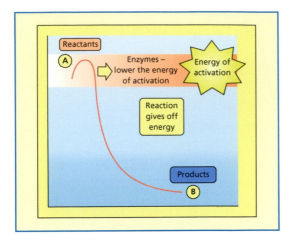

Figure 1.4 Exergonic chemical reaction. In an exergonic reaction, the energy level of the reactant(s) is greater than that of the product(s).

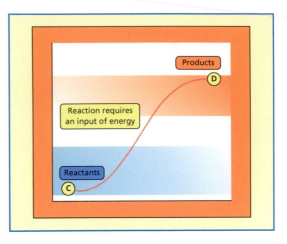

Figure 1.5 Endergonic chemical reaction. In an endergonic reaction, the energy level of the product(s) is greater than that of the reactant(s).

downhill reaction. In this example, the **reactant**'s (A) (ATP) energy level is greater than the product(s) (ADP + Pi) (7).

An endergonic reaction is illustrated in Figure 1.5 where C → D is a nonspontaneous uphill reaction (7). In this example, the energy level of the product(s) is greater than the reactant(s) (7). The C → D transition will not occur unless an enzyme is present to lower the energy of activation (7). The energy of activation serves as an energy barrier to the chemical reaction (7).

Metabolism is a series of enzyme controlled chemical reactions to store or use energy. Metabolism (Figure 1.6) begins with a substrate, which is the beginning material in the reaction. In each step, the substrate undergoes a chemical change catalyzed by enzymes.

At each step, the substrate is modified, and the modified compounds are referred to as intermediates. In the final step, the resulting compound is referred to as the product.

In a series of metabolic reactions, one enzyme is generally referred to as the **rate limiting enzyme**. A rate limiting enzyme is defined as an enzyme that catalyzes the slowest step in a series of chemical reactions (Figure 1.7). Generally, the rate limiting enzyme catalyzes the first step in the series of chemical reactions. To stimulate or inhibit a series of reactions, a substance must affect the rate limiting step. This is referred to as a negative feedback system, because the change that occurs is in the opposite direction from what was happening before the feedback.

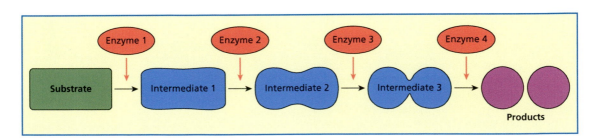

Figure 1.6 Metabolism. In this metabolic pathway, enzymes facilitate chemical reactions that change a substrate to intermediates and, finally, to a product.

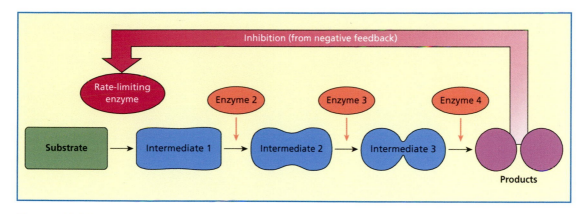

Figure 1.7 Inhibition of a chemical reaction. A rate limiting enzyme is inhibited by the final product of the reaction through negative feedback mechanism.

Enzymes are influenced by changes in both pH and temperature. Changes in pH can influence key enzymes that control metabolic pathways. During high-intensity exercise pH decreases within muscle which may affect enzyme function and could slow down glycolysis, reducing the amount of ATP available for muscle contraction.

Temperature can have an important effect on enzymatic reactions. This effect is studied by changing the temperature in multiples of 10° C and is referred to as the **Q10 effect**.

Increasing the temperature by 10° C doubles the speed of the enzymatic reaction. From a practical perspective, warming up the muscles prior to engaging in physical activity allows the athlete to take advantage of the Q10 effect.

THE "CREATION" OF CHEMICAL ENERGY

Where does energy come from? Energy is neither created nor destroyed but can be changed from one form to another. This concept reinforces the first law of **thermodynamics**, the physical science dealing with energy exchange, where energy is "changed" from one form to another. The first law of thermodynamics can be applied to muscle contraction. During exercise, chemical energy in the form of ATP is transformed into **mechanical energy** in the form of muscle contraction. Without chemical energy from the breakdown of ATP, mechanical energy in the form of muscle contraction could not occur.

The origin of the chemical energy that we take into our bodies is an anabolic process called photosynthesis. In photosynthesis, green plants, in the presence of sunlight and chlorophyll, take carbon dioxide and water and change it into carbohydrate (a carbon/hydrogen/oxygen compound) with oxygen given off into the atmosphere. It is this reaction that converts the sun's energy to chemical energy that we need to live and replenishes the oxygen supply in our atmosphere. These carbohydrate compounds formed in green plants are the basic form of energy needed by man. This carbon structure can be modified through anabolic reactions to form fats, which also contain carbon, hydrogen, and oxygen, and proteins, which contain carbon, hydrogen, oxygen, and nitrogen.

ENERGY SYSTEMS

There are three distinct yet closely integrated energy systems that operate together in a coordinated fashion to provide energy for muscle contraction: the phosphocreatine system, the anaerobic glycolytic system, and the oxidative system. The phosphocreatine and anaerobic glycolytic systems provide ATP at a high rate to support muscle contraction during short bursts of high intensity exercise such as a 200-meter sprint. However, the supply of ATP by the phosphocreatine and anaerobic glycolytic energy systems is limited.

> There are three energy systems that provide ATP for muscular work: the phosphocreatine system, the anaerobic glycolytic system, and the oxidative system.

The oxidative system predominates during low to moderate exercise intensity when oxygen is available to the muscle. At lower exercise intensities such as during walking, ATP demand is low and energy can be supplied at a high enough rate through the oxidative energy systems (20). At higher exercise intensities, ATP demand is high; energy cannot be supplied solely by oxidative metabolism (20). The anaerobic glycolytic system, therefore, must fill this gap between the phosphocreatine system and the oxidative system. During high intensity exercise, the supply of ATP must be derived from the phosphocreatine and anaerobic glycolytic energy systems.

It is important to note that all three energy systems are active at a given point in time, but one system will predominate based on the conditions at that time (Table 1.1). Each energy system operates like a dimmer switch in that they are not completely turned off but transitioned from one energy system to the next based on energy requirements of the muscle during exercise.

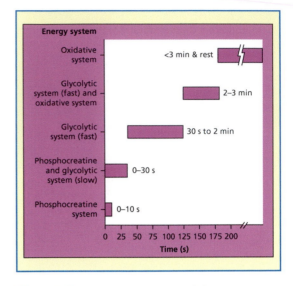

Figure 1.8 The energy systems and their approximate contributions to various durations of exercise at maximal intensity. Note the overlapping and timing of the various energy systems.

Figure 1.8 provides a graphic representation of the overlap and timing of the major energy systems. Box 1.1 provides a summary of the transition of energy systems from one to the next.

> Exercise intensity is the most important variable related to which energy system is activated to produce ATP for muscular work.

Box 1.1   Energy system transition

The recruitment and activation of energy systems during exercise are analogous to a dimmer switch in your dining room that controls the level of lighting. The phosphocreatine energy system is the first energy system recruited, followed by anaerobic glycolysis and oxidative phosphorylation (e.g., aerobic metabolism). The dimmer switch in your dining room provides more light to the room as you turn the dimmer switch up and less light as you turn it down. This dimmer switch relationship applies to all energy systems, the phosphocreatine system, anaerobic glycolysis, and the oxidative systems. As exercise progresses, the energy systems transition from one energy system to the next to provide the ATP needed to provide energy for the muscles to perform. As one system fades, the next system begins to take over the demand for the production of energy.

TABLE 1.1 The energy systems and their approximate contributions to various durations of exercise at maximal intensity (1)

Energy system	Duration
Phosphagen system	0–10 seconds
Phosphogen system and glycolytic system (slow)	10–30 seconds
Glycolytic system (fast)	30 seconds–2 minutes
Glycolytic system (fast) and oxidative system	2–3 minutes
Oxidative system	< 3 minutes and rest

Note: At submaximal intensity, each system can supply ATP for a longer time period.

Recovery from energy expenditure is aerobic.

Exercise intensity, duration, and the mode of exercise each play an instrumental role in determining which energy system will predominate during exercise. However, exercise intensity plays the most important role in dictating which energy system is activated.

Exercise intensity is prescribed using a percentage of maximal **oxygen consumption** (% VO_2 max). Maximal oxygen consumption is defined as the greatest amount of oxygen utilization that occurs during dynamic exercise and is measured in either mL/kg/min or l/min. For example, an individual may be prescribed exercise that requires 70% of his or her VO_2 max.

Understanding when a specific energy system is turned on during various activities and/or sporting events can assist the strength coach in developing programs that are metabolically specific.

The phosphocreatine system

ATP is broken down to release energy (a catabolic process) and can be regenerated from its component parts, an adenosine group and three **phosphate groups**. Conversely, energy is required to add a phosphate group to an adenosine group, which is an anabolic process.

Box 1.2 lists the characteristics of the phosphocreatine system.

When muscular energy is needed for a short period of time, the phosphocreatine system is capable of supplying most of the needed ATP. The phosphocreatine system will also supply energy in the beginning stages of all types of exercise. ATP is produced in the phosphocreatine system anaerobically (without oxygen present). There are three basic reactions in the phosphocreatine system (Figure 1.9). When physical activity is initiated, ATP stored in the muscles is utilized. All activities are initiated anaerobically, as it takes time to begin to produce ATP aerobically. The phosphocreatine system can regenerate ATP anaerobically, allowing anaerobic activity to proceed at a maximal or near maximal level, but only for a short period of time.

Myosin ATPase reaction

The first step in the phosphocreatine system is the breakdown of ATP to ADP + Pi in the presence of the enzyme myosin ATPase. This reaction produces energy for muscle contraction anaerobically. Some ATP is stored in the muscles to perform this task. As mentioned, the initiation of all activity depends on this

---

Box 1.2   Phosphocreatine system characteristics

1   Involves only one chemical step
2   Catalyzed by the enzyme creatine kinase (CK)
3   Very fast chemical reaction
4   One ATP generated per creatine phosphate molecule
5   Lasts for 5–10 seconds at maximal intensity
6   Anaerobic
7   Fatigue associated with creatine phosphate depletion
8   The dominant energy system in speed and explosive power events

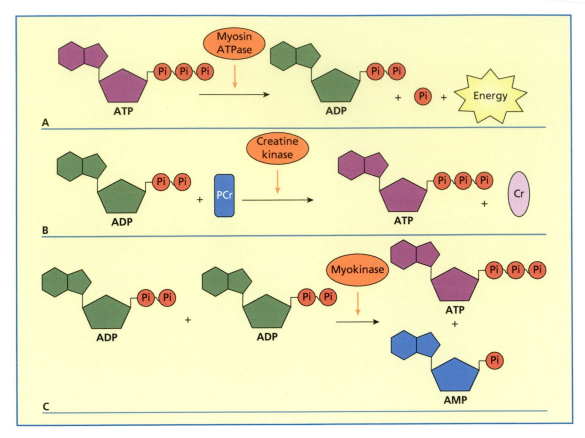

Figure 1.9 Reactions of the phosphagen system. (A) myosin ATPase reaction; (B) creatine kinase reaction; and (C) myokinase reaction.

stored ATP. Following the initial breakdown of ATP, there are two reactions that regenerate ATP anaerobically. These reactions are often named by the enzymes that catalyze the reactions: the creatine kinase reaction and the myokinase reaction.

Creatine kinase reaction

In the creatine kinase reaction phosphocreatine is combined with ADP in the presence of the enzyme creatine kinase to form new ATP.

Myokinase reaction

A second reaction that can regenerate ATP anaerobically over the short term is the myokinase reaction which regenerates ATP from two ADP. This reaction results in the production of one ATP and one AMP. The production of AMP is important to the control of metabolism, as AMP is a potent stimulator of glycolysis.

In summary, the ATP used in the phosphocreatine system starts with energy from carbohydrates (or fats or proteins) with the energy from the food stored in the chemical bonds between adenosine and phosphate (see Figure 1.1). ATP is broken down to provide energy and can also be "recharged" anaerobically. When ATP is regenerated, energy is stored. When ATP is used for energy, energy is released. ATP is the ultimate source of energy for muscular contraction.

Regulation of energy production

The **energy charge of the cell** (ATP/ADP ratio) plays an integral role in regulating the phosphocreatine system. The energy charge of the muscle cell provides information on how much energy (ATP) is available in the muscle to support the activity.

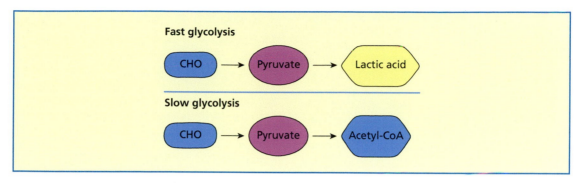

Figure 1.10 Reactions of fast and slow glycolysis. Pyruvate is converted to lactic acid if no oxygen is present, and to acetyl-CoA in the Kreb's cycle if oxygen is present.

Increased ADP concentration in the cell stimulates creatine kinase, the key regulatory control enzyme of the phosphocreatine system. An increase in intracellular ATP inhibits creatine kinase decreasing the rate of the enzymatic reaction. Therefore, high levels of ADP stimulate creatine kinase which accelerates the breakdown of PCr + ADP → ATP + Cr and provides energy for short-term high intensity exercise. High levels of ADP in the muscle would reflect that ATP is being extensively used by the muscle for providing energy for generating force as in a 200-meter run. Low levels of ADP in the muscle would reflect that ATP is not being used extensively as in, for example, walking at a slow pace.

Post-exercise phosphocreatine resynthesis occurs between 2 and 3 minutes of recovery (20) using the phosphocreatine energy shuttle. This process involves shuttling Cr and PCr between sites of utilization (e.g., myofibrils) and sites of regeneration (e.g., **mitochondria**).

When specifically training recovery of the phosphocreatine system, it may be advantageous for the athlete performing 40-meter sprints to allow for a 2–3 minute recovery to optimize phosphocreatine resynthesis (12). This would also apply to resistance training when an athlete is training for recovery of the phosphocreatine system. Allowing an adequate recovery time between sprints and resistance sets would provide more ATP availability through the phosphocreatine chemical reaction.

The glycolytic system

The glycolytic system, or anaerobic glycolysis, involves the breakdown of carbohydrate anaerobically to produce energy. Fats and proteins cannot be metabolized in the glycolytic system. The carbohydrate (the substrate) comes from either blood glucose or glycogen stored in the liver or muscles. There are two types of glycolysis, fast glycolysis and slow glycolysis (Figure 1.10). Slow glycolysis is sometimes referred to as "aerobic glycolysis" (7) because pyruvate is converted to acetyl-CoA if oxygen is present, and to lactic acid if no oxygen is present. Box 1.3 provides an analogy for the ATP investment and generation phases in glycolysis.

Box 1.3   ATP investment and generation phases in glycolysis

In the initial phases of anaerobic glycolysis, 2 ATP must be invested into the system, and 4 ATP are eventually produced for a net gain of 2 ATP. This investment of ATP is like an investment in a stock (e.g., IBM stock), and ATP generation is like a profit gained from a stock (e.g., IBM stock). So, there is a net total of 2 ATPs generated from the metabolism of 1 glucose molecule in glycolysis. Glycolysis is like investing in a stock where you invest $200 and gain $400 dollars at the end of a quarter. Therefore, you have a net gain of $200: double what you had when you initially invested in the stock.

Fast glycolysis breaks down glucose (CHO) to pyruvate and eventually to lactic acid anaerobically with the net production of 2 ATP. If glycogen is the substrate, 1 ATP is saved, and there is a net production of 3 ATP.

Slow glycolysis is the path the pyruvate takes if sufficient oxygen is present for aerobic metabolism. When oxygen is present, pyruvate is changed through a series of biochemical reactions to acetyl CoA, the first compound in the **Krebs cycle**. Slow glycolysis prepares the carbon compound (pyruvate) to enter the aerobic pathway. Glycolytic reactions take place for the most part in the **cytoplasm** of the cell, the watery medium between the cell membrane and the nucleus. The final step in slow glycolysis, pyruvate to acetyl CoA, takes place in the mitochondria.

> Anaerobic glycolysis produces a net gain of 2 ATP, but it is able to proceed when there is no O_2 present.

The control enzyme of the glycolytic system is **phosphofructokinase (PFK)**. PFK is the rate limiting enzyme that controls the rate of glycolysis. PFK is inhibited by high levels of ATP, phosphocreatine, citrate, free fatty acids, and a markedly decreased pH. PFK is stimulated by high concentrations of inorganic phosphate (Pi), ADP, phosphate, ammonia, and is strongly stimulated by AMP. Box 1.4 summarizes the basic characteristics of the glycolytic system.

The oxidative system

The oxidative system aerobically oxidizes or "burns" carbohydrates (or other carbon containing structures obtained from fat or protein). The preferred fuels for aerobic metabolism are carbohydrates and fats, but protein can be **deaminated** by removing the amino group, the nitrogenous component of the carbon/hydrogen/oxygen/nitrogen compound, and oxidizing the remaining carbon/hydrogen/oxygen compound aerobically. The oxidative system is a complex process that involves two parts: the Krebs cycle (citric acid cycle) (Figure 1.11) and the **electron transport system (ETS)** (Figure 1.12).

The **Krebs cycle** is a complex series of enzyme controlled metabolic reactions. The Krebs cycle takes place in the mitochondria, which is the site of aerobic ATP production. The Krebs cycle plays an integral role in oxidizing carbohydrates, fats, and proteins. The electron transport chain takes place in the inner membrane of the mitochondria and is responsible for the aerobic production of ATP. The Krebs cycle generates electrons in the form of hydrogen ions shuttled through the ETS by electron carriers (FAD+ or NAD+). It is in the ETS that many ATP molecules are generated. Aerobic metabolic reactions take place in the mitochondria, an organelle inside the cell membrane in the cytoplasm. One molecule of glucose oxidized aerobically produces approximately 38 ATP (7).

Skeletal muscle mitochondrial oxidative capacity declines with age and likely has a negative effect on activities of daily living including walking. Recent evidence indicates muscle

---

Box 1.4   Characteristics of the glycolytic system

1   18 chemical reactions, 6 are repeated
2   12 chemical compounds, 11 enzymes
3   Phosphofructokinase (PFK) is the rate limiting enzyme
4   Fast, but not as fast as creatine phosphate system
5   2 ATPs if glucose is the substrate, 3 ATPs if glycogen is the substrate
6   Anaerobic
7   1–2 minute duration at high (not maximal) intensity
8   Fatigue associated with decreased pH reflecting an increase in hydrogen ions
9   Predominant energy system in high intensity non-maximal exercise, e.g., 800 meter run

mitochondrial oxidative capacity affects both muscle strength and walking speed. Strength training may have a positive influence on this inefficiency in muscle bioenergetics and may improve functionality in older adults specifically related to walking speed.

> The aerobic system can produce many more ATP per molecule than the anaerobic system, but it cannot produce ATP rapidly, and the intensity must remain at or below a **steady state** (21).

Fats can also be oxidized aerobically to form ATP. First, fats are broken down into glycerol and free fatty acids. The free fatty acids then enter the mitochondria, and through a process called beta oxidation, they are degraded to acetyl CoA and hydrogen

atoms. The acetyl CoA enters the Krebs cycle directly as an intermediate compound.

Although it is not a preferred source of energy, protein can be broken down and oxidized aerobically. First, proteins are catabolized into their smaller components, amino acids. Amino acids can then be deaminated. The carbon/hydrogen/oxygen portion of the compound can be converted to glucose through **gluconeogenesis**, pyruvate, and other Krebs cycle intermediates.

The contribution of amino acids to energy production is minimal for anaerobic activities but may contribute up to 18% of the energy requirements for aerobic exercise (3). Branched chain amino acids are the major amino acids used by skeletal muscle for energy production. The nitrogenous waste, the amino portion of the amino acid, is eliminated from the body

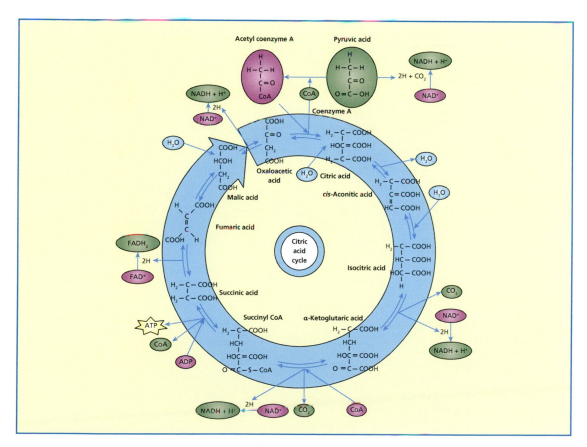

Figure 1.11 The Krebs cycle. Also known as the citric acid cycle, it is a complex series of enzyme-controlled metabolic reactions.

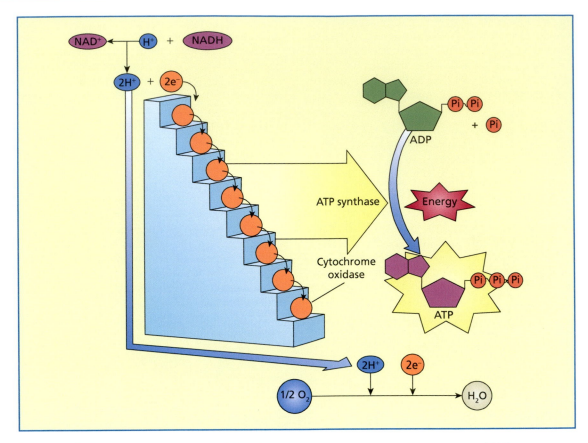

Figure 1.12 Electron transport system (ETS). ETS is responsible for the aerobic production of ATP.

as urea or ammonia. Ammonia is potentially a contributor to fatigue (19).

Control of the oxidative system is related to several factors. First, adequate amounts of FAD+ and NAD+ must be present to shuttle hydrogen ions into the ETS. A reduction in FAD+ and NAD+ leads to a decrease in the rate of oxidative metabolism. The ETS is inhibited by high concentrations of ATP and stimulated by high concentrations of ADP (7). Box 1.5 summarizes the characteristics of the oxidative system.

Box 1.5   Characteristics of the oxidative system

1   124 chemical reactions
2   30 compounds, 27 enzymes
3   Rate limiting enzymes, PFK, ID, CO
4   Slow
5   36 ATP generated from glucose, 37 via glycogen
6   Potentially limitless duration at lower intensity
7   Fatigue associated with fuel depletion (muscle glycogen)
8   Predominant energy system in endurance events, e.g., marathon

LACTATE

The lactic acid formed because of fast glycolysis is immediately buffered and changed into a salt called lactate. While lactic acid is certainly associated with fatigue, lactate becomes a substrate that can be converted back into pyruvate and used in the Krebs cycle, particularly in the heart and in slow twitch muscle fibers (3,8).

Q&A FROM THE FIELD

I have always heard that lactic acid makes you fatigued. Is that true?

Lactic acid is a byproduct of anaerobic metabolism. Anaerobic exercise is by definition high intensity, and the end product will be lactic acid. Also by definition, high intensity anaerobic exercise will lead to fatigue rather rapidly. In one sense, the production of lactic acid parallels fatigue. It may also be that molecules of lactic acid interfere with efficient muscle contraction. Lactic acid is also responsible for the immediate burning in muscle that is exercising at a high intensity. This burning is not to be confused with delayed onset muscle soreness (DOMS) that occurs over the next 24–48 hours. DOMS is not due to lactic acid. The lactic acid that is produced is quickly buffered to lactate. Lactate can be transported to the liver and converted to glucose. Lactate is a useful energy source for recovery from intense anaerobic exercise.

The lactic acid produced during heavy exercise is rapidly converted to lactate. Lactate is a useful metabolic compound that can be transported to the liver and changed to glucose in a process called "gluconeogenesis" in the liver. It can then be used by the body as fuel during recovery from exercise.

Lactate was once perceived as a metabolic waste product; however, lactate is now considered an important fuel source. The lactate shuttle hypothesis explained that lactate played a key role in the distribution of carbohydrate energy among various tissues and cellular compartments (6). The original lactate shuttle hypothesis was later renamed the cell-cell lactate shuttle (4). The cell-cell lactate shuttle involves the transportation of lactate produced by fast twitch muscle fibers (type IIx) during exercise to slow twitch muscle fibers (Type 1). The lactate produced by the fast twitch muscle fibers is shuttled directly to the adjacent slow twitch muscle fibers where oxidation occurs. Some 75 to 80% of lactate is disposed of through oxidation with the remaining converted to glucose or glycogen in a process called gluconeogenesis (5). **Gluconeogenesis** is a process that occurs in the liver and involves the formation of glucose from noncarbohydrate. Gluconeogenesis involves lactate leaving the fast twitch muscle fibers, circulating through the blood as **blood lactate**, and being delivered and taken up by the liver.

Blood lactate can be utilized as a laboratory test to predict endurance performance. The common laboratory test incorporated to estimate this maximal steady state speed is the lactate threshold. To determine the lactate threshold, a subject will run on a treadmill at various running speeds at different stages until they can't continue further. During each stage a blood sample will be obtained from the subject to provide a measure of the blood lactate concentration. The lactate threshold (LT) represents the point where blood lactate begins to increase in a non-linear fashion at a specific exercise intensity (Figure 1.13). During exercise above the anaerobic threshold, pulmonary oxygen uptake (VO_2) slowly increases (referred to as the slow component of VO_2). Recent evidence indicates that blood lactate accumulation decreases during this time without decreasing muscular efficiency (18).

Lactate threshold is an important factor in performance. If there are two athletes in an aerobic event with the same VO_2 max, the athlete with the highest lactate threshold will likely win the race.

The running speed at which the lactate threshold occurs is used as a predictor of performance (1). The measure of the maximal steady-state running speed is beneficial in predicting success in distance running events from two miles to the marathon (8–10,14–16).

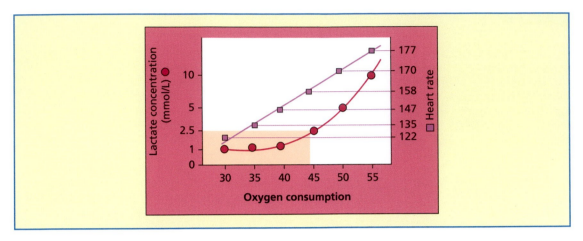

Figure 1.13 Lactate threshold. The lactate threshold represents the point where blood lactate begins to increase in a non-linear fashion at a specific exercise intensity (19). As exercise intensity increases, blood levels of lactic acid begin to accumulate in an exponential fashion.

SUMMARY OF CATABOLIC PROCESSES IN THE PRODUCTION OF CELLULAR ENERGY

Figure 1.14 summarizes the breakdown of food (catabolic process) to produce energy. The food we eat is composed of fats, carbohydrates, or proteins. Carbohydrates are broken down into blood glucose. The blood glucose can either be used for energy or stored as glycogen. When glycogen stores in the liver and muscles are full, the glucose is stored as fat.

The glucose, through glycolysis, is converted to pyruvic acid, then either lactic acid if no oxygen is present (fast glycolysis) or acetyl CoA if oxygen is present in the cell. The acetyl CoA then goes into the Krebs cycle and the electron transport system to produce ATP with the eventual end products of CO_2 and H_2O.

Q&A FROM THE FIELD

Is glucose and carbohydrate always stored as carbohydrate in the body?

There is a limit to the amount of glucose that can be contained in the blood, and there is a limit to the amount of glycogen that can be stored in the liver and muscles. When the amount of carbohydrate contained in the blood as glucose and in the liver and muscle as glycogen is maximal, excess calories consumed from carbohydrates can be converted to fat. You do not have to eat fat to store body fat.

Fats and proteins can both be used for energy. Fats are catabolized into glycerol and fatty acids. The glycerol can be converted to pyruvate and enter glycolysis. Fatty acids undergo beta oxidation and are converted to acetyl CoA and enter the Krebs cycle.

Proteins are catabolized into amino acids. The amino acids are deaminated with the amino group being secreted as urea. The resulting carbon compound can be converted to pyruvate, acetyl CoA, or other Krebs cycle intermediates.

EFFICIENCY OF THE ENERGY PRODUCING PATHWAYS

Efficiency of the energy producing pathways depends on the demands of the activity. At first glance, it may appear the aerobic pathway is the most efficient as it produces many more ATP molecules than the anaerobic pathways.

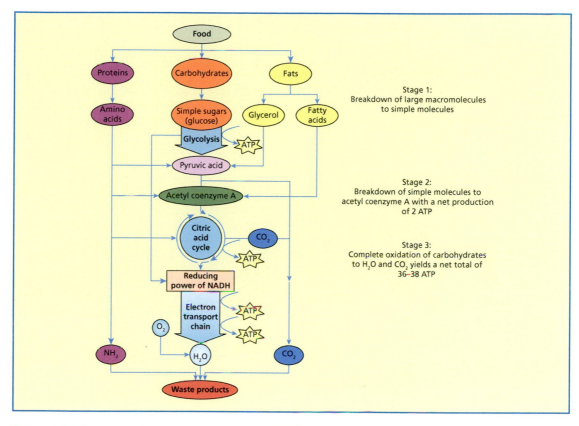

Figure 1.14 Summary of catabolic processes involved in breaking down food to energy.

There are, however, different ways to calculate efficiency. The simplest method of looking at the efficiency of each metabolic system is relative to the task at hand. If the task is a 100-meter sprint, the oxidative system is very inefficient as it does not have the time needed to produce ATP. Likewise, if the task is a marathon, the anaerobic pathways will be much less efficient as they lack the capacity to produce ATP over a long period of time. Using this logic, the anaerobic energy systems are the most efficient at producing ATP immediately. The aerobic energy system is the most efficient for producing ATP over a continuous period. Box 1.6 provides an analogy to further explain the efficiency of these systems.

Box 1.6 Efficiency of aerobic and anaerobic energy systems

Efficiency must be related to a specific task. For example, a gas-electric hybrid is more economical or efficient in terms of miles per gallon than a 4 x 4 "monster truck" for traveling cross country, but the truck is more efficient at carrying or pulling a heavy load, or climbing a steep hill. Efficiency must be viewed as task specific. The anaerobic energy systems are most efficient at producing ATP rapidly. The aerobic system is very inefficient at producing ATP if the demand is immediate. The aerobic energy system is more efficient at producing ATP over a longer duration and a lower workload. The anaerobic system, like the truck, is inefficient at performing low intensity work over a long period of time. The aerobic system, like the hybrid, is inefficient at performing at a high intensity such as pulling heavy loads or climbing a steep hill.

LIMITING FACTORS OF PERFORMANCE

Factors that limit performance from the metabolic standpoint (Table 1.2) will relate to the build up of metabolic byproducts (lactic acid and possibly ammonia), the depletion of PCr, or the depletion of substrate (fats, carbohydrates, or proteins). Obviously, the limiting metabolic factor in an activity will depend on the energy system involved in the activity which is determined, basically, by the intensity and duration of the activity. A low intensity activity such as a long distance run will result primarily in the depletion of muscle and liver glycogen.

High intensity activities that are not repeated without a great deal of rest have essentially no metabolic limiting factors. In repeated high intensity activities, muscle glycogen, ATP/PC, and a decrease in pH are all possible limiting factors. The hydrogen ions given off from the buildup of lactic acid have been shown to decrease force production in skeletal muscle (13), possibly by competing with the binding sites on troponin.

OXYGEN CONSUMPTION

Oxygen consumption is the ability of the body to take in and use oxygen to produce energy. Oxygen consumption can be estimated using a metabolic cart which can measure the oxygen content of the inspired and expired air. Maximal oxygen consumption is considered a measure of cardiorespiratory endurance.

TABLE 1.2 Metabolic factors that limit performance

Activity	Primary limiting factors
Marathon muscle	Glycogen, liver glycogen
High intensity repeated (10 × 40 m)	ATP, muscle glycogen, decreased pH
High intensity (400 m)	Decreased pH

Maximal oxygen consumption is also called VO_2 max, which can be measured in milliliters/kilogram/body weight (mL/kg/bw) or in liters/minute (l/min). Measuring VO_2 max in mL/kg/min is used when comparing two individuals because body weight influences maximal oxygen consumption. Liters per minute is used when just comparing an individual from one test to the second test. From a practical perspective, a coach develops a training program for his or her cross country athletes and desires to see the impact it has had on their VO_2 max. Prior to the training program the coach obtains a baseline measure of VO_2 max and then the training program begins. Therefore, the coach would have his or her athletes perform a second VO_2 max test to determine if any significant changes occurred in their respective values.

An important addition to the VO_2 max test would be the ability to obtain blood lactate levels during the test. The coach would have his or her athletes run on a treadmill at various speeds where a blood lactate sample would be obtained at each stage of the protocol. Information obtained from the VO_2 max would include:

1   At what VO_2 did the lactate threshold occur?
2   At what percentage of the VO_2 max did the lactate threshold occur?
3   At what running speed did the lactate threshold occur?
4   What heart rate (subjects would need a heart rate monitor) was achieved at the lactate threshold?

The information provided could assist both the coach and the athlete in tailoring a specific program based upon their VO_2 max, at what point and/or percentage of the VO_2 did the LT occur, and what maximal heart rate was achieved at the LT.

In the recovery from anaerobic work, energy (ATP) is supplied aerobically. Since it takes time for the oxidative system to begin to produce adequate ATP to support an aerobic activity, all exercise is supported initially by anaerobic metabolism. The initial portion of energy supplied anaerobically is termed the

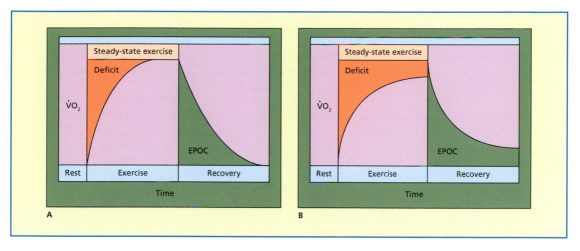

Figure 1.15 Oxygen deficit and EPOC (excess post-exercise oxygen consumption). (A) for aerobic exercise; (B) for anaerobic exercise.

oxygen deficit. After exercise, this "shortfall" must be replenished aerobically. This replenishment of the anaerobic system is termed the oxygen debt, or **excess post-exercise oxygen consumption** (EPOC). The term EPOC is more accurate than oxygen debt. The term debt implies a direct replacement of the deficit or initial shortfall. EPOC supports several metabolic processes that are in effect post-exercises.

EPOC must support the following:

1 Elevated HR during recovery
2 Elevated respiration rate during recovery
3 Elevated metabolism for heat dissipation
4 Elevated metabolism for the breakdown of hormones released during exercise
5 Resynthesis of ATP and CP stores
6 Resynthesis of glycogen from lactate
7 Re-saturation of body tissues (blood and muscle tissue) with oxygen (2,11,17).

Oxygen consumption, oxygen deficit, and EPOC are depicted for aerobic work in Figure 1.15A and anaerobic work in Figure 1.15B. Exercise where the oxygen supply is equal to the oxygen demand is termed steady state exercise. In aerobic exercise, anaerobic metabolism supplies energy for the first few minutes, creating an oxygen deficit. Although part of this deficit can be paid back during the activity, the deficit must be repaid post-exercise. Again, the energy for this post-exercise metabolic activity comes from aerobic sources. With anaerobic activity, note that the oxygen deficit is much larger because the demand for energy is greater than in the initial stage of aerobic activity.

METABOLIC SPECIFICITY

Specificity of training is a key concept in the field of training and conditioning. If training is to be specific to an actual sport or activity, then the training must focus on the same metabolic energy pathways used in the sport or activity. It is important to note that all energy systems are active to some degree all the time. Also, the intensity of the activity is a key determining factor in the energy system utilized.

Training energy systems involves manipulating both the intensity and the duration of the activity. Metabolic specificity does not mean that all training is the same intensity and duration as the activity. Most activities are difficult to classify exactly in terms of intensity and duration. Box 1.7 provides examples of specificity of training.

Box 1.7   Examples of specificity of training

1 If the average tennis point is six seconds, and the average intensity is 60% of maximum, it does not mean that all training should be done for six seconds at 60% of maximum intensity. Some points are shorter, and some are longer. Some points are more intense, and some points are less intense. Duration and intensity, then, should be used to determine a reasonable range within which a majority of the training should fall. Progression, from general training to metabolically specific training, is also a factor.

2 Football players predominately perform short bursts of high intensity. The short burst of activity requires the phosphocreatine and anaerobic glycolytic energy systems. Devising a conditioning program that includes sprint/agility activities at 5–10 seconds of sustained high intensity exercise would activate the phosphocreatine system. The anaerobic glycolytic energy system would be activated during the longer sprints (30 seconds to 2 minutes).

A basic understanding of metabolism and bioenergetics is a key to understanding the field of conditioning and applying that knowledge to improve human performance.

SUMMARY

The concepts of bioenergetics are keys to understanding human performance, as well as understanding exercise prescriptions that will enhance human performance. The source of energy for a specific sport or activity depends on the intensity and duration of the activity. The breakdown of food and changing it to the energy we need to move and live is a complex process.

Since human adaptation to training is specific to the type of training, we must learn to train athletes in a way such that the appropriate energy system is stressed at the appropriate time and peaks at the appropriate time.

MAXING OUT

1 Energy system training is sport specific, and may be specific to positions within a sport. Consider a soccer player. What are some things you need to consider when planning a metabolically specific training program for a soccer player?

2 What happens to the excess carbohydrate we consume in our diet when muscle glycogen stores are full?

3 What is the fate of lactic acid produced during exercise?

REFERENCES

1. Bassett DR Jr, Howley ET. Limiting factors for maximum oxygen uptake and determinants of endurance performance. *Med Sci Sp Exerc* 2000; 32:1;70–84.

2. Borsheim E, Bahr R. The effect of exercise intensity, duration, and mode on excess post oxygen consumption. *Sports Med* 2003; 33:14;1037–1060.

3. Brooks GA. Amino acid and protein metabolism during exercise and recovery. *Med Sci Sp Exerc* 1987; 19;S150–S156.

4. Brooks GA. Intra- and extra cellular lactate shuttles. *Med Sci Sp Exerc* 2000; 32:4;790–799.

5. Brooks GA. Lactate shuttles in nature. *Biochemical Society Transactions* 2002; 30:2;258–264.

6. Brooks GA. The lactate shuttle during exercise and recovery. *Med Sci Sp Exerc* 1986; 18;360–368.

7. Brooks GA, Fahey TD, Baldwin K. *Exercise Physiology: Human Bioenergetics and Its Applications*. Boston, MA: McGraw Hill, 2005.

8. Costill D, Thompson H, Roberts E. Fractional utilization of the aerobic capacity during distance running. *Med Sci Sp Exerc* 1973; 5;248–252.

9. Farrell P, Wilmore J, Coyle EF, Billing JE, Costil, DL. Plasma lactate accumulation and distance running performance. *Med Sci Sp Exerc* 1979; 11;338–44.

10. Foster C. Blood lactate and respiratory measurement of the capacity for sustained exercise. In: *Physiological Assessment of Human Fitness*, P. Maud and C. Foster, eds. Champaign, IL: Human Kinetics, 1995.

11. Gaesser GA, Brooks GA. Metabolic bases of excess post oxygen consumption. *Med Sci Sp Exerc* 1984; 10:1;29–43.

12. Harris RC, Edwards RHT, Hultman E, Nordesjo LO, Nylind B, Sahlin K. The time course of phosphocreatine resynthesis during recovery of the quadriceps muscle in man. *Pfluegers Arch – Eur J Physiol* 1976; 97;392–397.

13. Hermansen L. Effect of metabolic changes on force generation in skeletal muscle during maximal exercise. In: *Human Muscle Fatigue*, R. Porter and J. Whelan, eds. London: Pitman Medical, 1981.

14. Lafontaine T, Londeree B, Spath W. The maximal steady state versus selected running events. *Med Sci Sp Exerc* 1981; 13;190–192.

15. Lawler J, Powers S, Dodd S. A time saving incremental cycle ergometer protocol to determine peak oxygen consumption. *Br J Sports Med* 1987; 21;171–173.

16. Lehmann M, Burg A, Kapp R, Wessinghage T, Keul J. Correlations between laboratory testing and distance running performance in marathoners of similar ability. *Int J Sp Med* 1983; 4;226–230.

17. Mole P. Exercise metabolism. In: *Exercise Medicine: Physiological Principles and Clinical Application*, A. A. Bove and D. T. Lowenthal, eds. New York: Academic Press, 1983.

18. O'Connell JM, Weir JM, MacIntosh BR. Epub 2017 May 26. Blood lactate accumulation decreases during the slow component of oxygen uptake without a decrease in muscular efficiency. *Pflugers Arch* 2017 Oct; 469(10):1257–1265.

19. Smith SA, Montain SJ, Matott RP, Zientara GP, Jolesz FA, Fielding RA. Creatine supplementation and age influence muscle metabolism during exercise. *J of Appl Physiol* 1998; 85;1349–1356.

20. Spriet LL, Howlett RA, Heigenhauser GJF. An enzymatic approach to lactate production in human skeletal muscle during exercise. *Med Sci Sp Exerc* 2000; 32:4;756–763.

21. Zane A, Reiter D, Shardell M, Cameron D, Simonsick E, Fishbein K, Studenski SA, Specer RG, Ferrucci L. Muscle strength mediates the relationship between mitochondrial energetics and walking performance. *Aging Cell* 2017; 16:3; 461–468. Published online 2017 Feb 9. doi: 10.1111/acel.12568 PMCID: PMC5418194.

Contents

CHAPTER 2

THE CARDIORESPIRATORY SYSTEM

Andy Bosak

OBJECTIVES

After completing this chapter, you will be able to:

- Understand the function of the organs that comprise the cardiorespiratory system.
- Identify the components of the cardiac cycle and the specific patterns of the P-QRS-T complex.
- Understand the changes in cardiac output during exercise.
- Assess and analyze blood pressure readings.
- Discuss the importance of the respiratory system with the cardiovascular system.
- Analyze the distribution of blood flow in response to exercise.
- Discuss the impact the environment may have on the cardiorespiratory system.

KEY TERMS

Bohr effect
Bradycardia
Cardiac cycle
Cardiovascular drift
Cardiac output
Chronotropy
Concentric hypertrophy
Depolarization
Diastasis
Diastole
Diastolic blood pressure
Eccentric hypertrophy
Ejection fraction
Ejection phase

End-diastolic volume
End-systolic volume
Erythropoietin
Expiration
Fick equation
Frank-Starling mechanism
Hypertrophic
  cardiomyopathy
Hyperventilation
Hypervolemia
Hypohydration
Hypoxia
Inspiration
Intercalated discs

Interventricular
  septum
Inotropy
Myocardium
Partial pressure
P-QRS-T complex
Repolarization
Stroke volume
Systole
Systolic blood pressure
Tachycardia
Valsalva maneuver
Ventilatory equivalent
Ventilation

INTRODUCTION

The primary role of the cardiorespiratory system is to meet the energy demands of the body. During physical activity, as energy demands increase, the cardiorespiratory system can compensate by increasing the amount of necessary consumed oxygen and the volume of blood that can be pumped into the circulation. During prolonged exercise training, physiological systems can adapt to the increased demands that are placed upon it. Hence, these adaptations are specific to the type of exercise stimulus that is encountered by the body. After reviewing this chapter, students should understand the nuances of the cardiovascular and respiratory systems, as well as the changes that are seen during acute exercise and the adaptations that are seen during prolonged training. Furthermore, environmental factors that affect the function of the cardiorespiratory system will also be explored.

CARDIOVASCULAR SYSTEM

The cardiovascular system consists of an elaborate network of vessels that comprise the circulatory system and a pump, known as the heart, that is responsible for the delivery of oxygen and nutrients to active organs and muscles and in removing the waste products of metabolism. The heart is a four-chambered muscular organ that is located midcenter of the chest cavity. Its anterior border is the sternum, while posteriorly it borders the vertebral column. Of further importance, the lungs are situated on the heart's lateral borders and inferior to the heart is the diaphragm.

Morphology of the heart

The heart muscle, referred to as the **myocardium**, is similar in appearance to striated skeletal muscle. However, the fibers of the myocardium are multinucleated and interconnected end to end by **intercalated discs**. These discs contain desmosomes that maintain the integrity of the cardiac fibers during

contraction and gap junctions that allow for a rapid transmission of the electrical impulse that signals for contraction. The structure of the myocardium can be thought of as three separate areas: 1) atrial, 2) ventricular, and 3) conductive. The atrial and ventricular myocardium function quite similarly as skeletal muscle since they will contract in response to electrical stimuli. Yet, unlike skeletal muscle fibers, an electrical stimulus of only a single cell in either chamber will result in an action potential being rapidly spread to the other cells of the atrial and ventricular myocardium, resulting in a coordinated contractile mechanism. In addition, the cardiac fibers in each of these areas can function separately. The conductive tissue that is found between these chambers provides a network for the rapid transmission of conductive impulses allowing for coordinated action of both the atrial and ventricular chambers.

The structural detail of the heart can be seen in Figure 2.1. Notice the difference in the anatomy and physiology of the right and left sides of the heart as these differences specifically relate to their unique functions. The right side of the heart receives blood, via the right atrium, from all parts of the body, while the right ventricle pumps de-oxygenated blood to the lungs through the pulmonary circulation. The left side of the heart receives oxygenated blood, via the left atrium, from the lungs and pumps the blood from the left ventricle into the aorta and throughout the entire systemic circulation. The left ventricle is an ellipsoidal chamber surrounded by thick musculature which provides the power to eject the blood through the entire body, yet the right ventricle is crescent shaped with thin musculature that reflects the reduced ejection pressures seen specifically in this ventricle (25 mm Hg) compared to approximately 125 mm Hg in the left ventricle at rest. Notice that the **interventricular septum**, which is a thick muscular wall, separates the left and right ventricles.

Blood flow from the right atrium to the right ventricle goes through the tricuspid valve, which consists of three cusps or leaflets that allow only a one directional flow of blood. The bicuspid or mitral valve allows blood flow between the left atrium and left ventricle. The semilunar valves, located on the

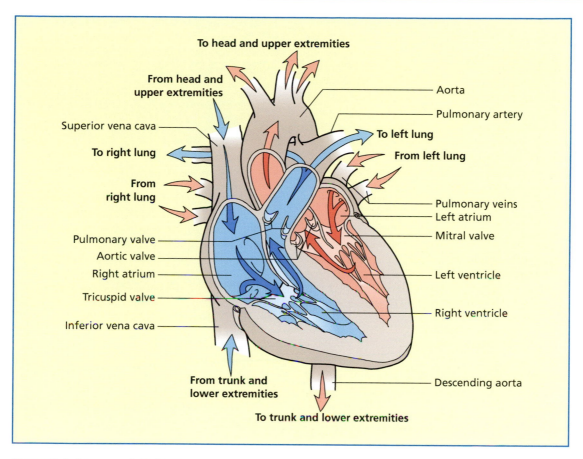

To head and upper extremities

From head and
upper extremities

Superior vena cava

To right lung

From
right lung

Pulmonary valve

Aortic valve

Right atrium

Tricuspid valve

Inferior vena cava

Aorta

Pulmonary artery

To left lung

From left lung

Pulmonary veins

Left atrium

Mitral valve

Left ventricle

Right ventricle

Descending aorta

From trunk and
lower extremities

To trunk and lower extremities

Figure 2.1 Anatomy of the heart.

arterial walls on the outside of the ventricles, prevent blood from flowing backwards into the heart between contractions.

Cardiac cycle

The contraction phase, where the atria or ventricles eject the blood in their chambers, is called **systole**, while the relaxation phase, in which the chambers refill with blood, is referred to as **diastole**. One complete revolution of systole and diastole is referred to as the **cardiac cycle**. At rest, the heart spends most of its time (approximately 60%) filling with blood and less time (approximately 40%) expelling the blood. However, during exercise this situation is reversed, with most of the cardiac cycle spent in systole. During systole, the tricuspid and mitral valves are closed, yet blood flow from

pulmonic and systemic circulation continues into the atria. As systole ends, the atrioventricular valves rapidly open and the blood that has accumulated in the atria flows quickly into the ventricles accounting for 70% to 80% of the ventricular filling. There are three specific periods occurring in diastole. The initial third is one of rapid filling; the middle third is characterized by very little blood flow into the ventricle and is referred to as **diastasis**; and during the final third, ventricle filling is completed with an additional 20% to 30% of blood pumped into the ventricle as the result of atrial systole.

The volume of blood in the ventricle at the end of diastole is called the **end-diastolic volume** (EDV). During systole, the pre-ejection and ejection phases occur. The pre-injection phase includes an electromechanical lag, which is the time delay between the beginning of ventricular excitation (depolarization) and the onset of ventricular contraction, and isovolumic contraction. Isovolumic contraction is the phase in which intraventricular pressure is raised prior to the onset of ejection. This part of the pre-injection phase occurs between the closure of the mitral valve and the opening of the semilunar valve (the aortic valve). During the **ejection phase** the blood within the ventricle will be pumped into the systemic circulation through the opening of the semilunar valve, and this phase will end with the closing of the semilunar valve. The blood remaining in the ventricle at the end of ejection is referred to as the **end-systolic volume** (ESV). The difference between EDV and ESV is called the **stroke volume**, which in simpler terms represents the amount of blood that is pumped out of the ventricles in one beat (1). The proportion of the blood pumped out of the left ventricle with each beat is called the **ejection fraction** (EF) and is determined by

SV/EDV. The ejection fraction averages about 60% at rest. This simply means that 60% of the blood in the left ventricle at the end of diastole will be ejected with the next contraction.

> The time spent in systole or diastole is dependent upon whether the individual is at rest or exercising.

Heart rate and conduction

A unique feature of the heart is its ability to contract rhythmically without either neural or hormonal stimulation. This autorhythmicity is due to a specialized intrinsic conduction system that consists of the sinoatrial node (SA node), internodal pathways, the atrioventricular node (AV node), and Purkinje fibers. The intrinsic conduction system of the heart can be seen in Figure 2.2.

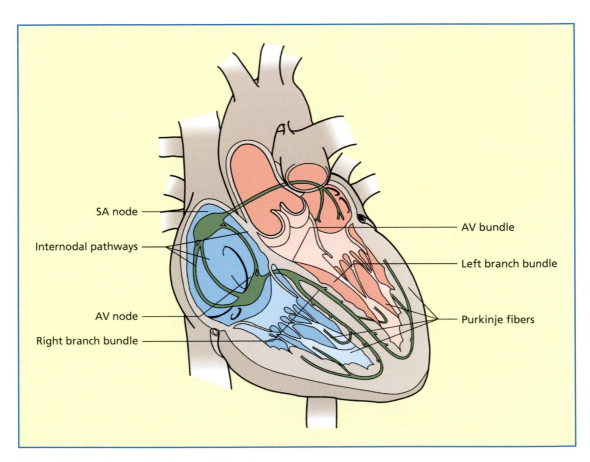

Figure 2.2 Intrinsic conduction system of heart.

The SA node located in the right atrium is a collection of specialized cells that can generate an electrical impulse. Because of this distinctive ability, it is appropriately nicknamed the pacemaker of the heart. Once an impulse leaves the SA node it propagates leftward and downward spreading through the atrial syncytium of the right and then left atrium through internodal pathways merging onto the AV node located toward the center of the heart on the lower right atrial wall.

The AV node, or the AV junction (comprised of the AV node and the Bundle of His), delay transmission of the impulse for a tenth of a second. This slight delay of ventricular excitation and contraction will allow for the atria to contract and permit a limitation in the number of signals that are transmitted by the AV node. This may serve as a protective mechanism for the ventricles from atrial tachyarrhythmias. The Bundle of His is found distally in the AV junction and divides into right and left segments, known as bundle branches, which transmit the electrical impulses to the right and left ventricles. The Purkinje fibers are found on the distal tips of the right and left bundle branches and extend their fibers into the walls of the ventricles accelerating the conduction velocity of the impulse to the rest of the ventricle. The conduction velocity of the Purkinje fibers may increase four-fold as compared to what is seen at the Bundle of His.

As previously stated, the SA node, AV node, and Purkinje fibers have the inherent ability for spontaneous initiation of the electrical impulse. But, the autonomic nervous system can also influence the rate of impulse formation, known as **chronotropy**, contractile state of the myocardium, known as **inotropy**, and the rate of spread of the excitation impulse. The sympathetic and parasympathetic nervous systems, as well as certain hormones, influence cardiac contractility. The atria are well supplied with both sympathetic and parasympathetic neurons, while the ventricles are primarily innervated by sympathetic neurons. Sympathetic stimulation releases the catecholamines epinephrine and norepinephrine from sympathetic neural fibers. These neural hormones will accelerate the heart rate by increasing SA node activity and increasing both atrial and ventricular contractile force. The increases in heart rate are referred to as **tachycardia**.

Parasympathetic stimulation through the vagus nerve will release acetylcholine, a neurohormone, which as a depressant effect on SA node activity and decreases atrial contractile force. A decrease in heart rate is known as **bradycardia**. Sympathetic stimulation may increase heart rate by over 120 beats per minute and the contraction strength by 100%, while maximal vagal stimulation may decrease heart rate by 20–30 beats per minute and lower contraction strength by approximately 30% (1,2).

Q&A FROM THE FIELD

My resting heart rate is about 45 beats per minute. I am a distance runner. Is that too low?

A low resting heart rate can be an indication of cardiac problems. In the case of a healthy athlete, the answer is probably not. Regular participation in aerobic exercise often results in a decreased resting heart rate: approximately 5 to 25 beats per minute. This is due to both the increased efficiency of the heart and the adaptations to the nervous system that affect heart rate. Also, a smaller reduction in heart rate may occur from resistance training, but the effects of resistance training on heart rate seem to be related to the volume and intensity of training.

The electrocardiogram (ECG)

The **P-QRS-T complex** is the typical pattern that is associated with ECG interpretation (Figure 2.3). Einthoven, a Dutch physician and scientist who was credited with the invention of the electrocardiogram in the early part of the 20th century, wanted to be mathematically correct with his description of ECG wave patterns. It is said that he admired the work of Descartes, the inventor of analytical geometry. Descartes labeled successive points on a curve starting with the letter "P". Therefore, Einthoven thought the letter "P" would be an appropriate means of labeling the first wave on an ECG (3).

By using ECG the practitioner is able to detect abnormalities of the electrical activity of the heart. Since a normal ECG is based on a nonathletic population, there is often concern about the athletic heart because of the similarities to an abnormal ECG. Unfortunately, this is an area that is often misunderstood due to the void in the research literature.

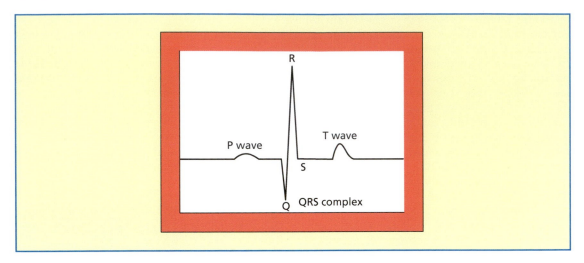

Figure 2.3 Normal ECG.

The ECG is comprised of 12 electrode leads that are placed on specific sites of the body. The sites of these leads are typically the arms, legs, and chest. The stimulation of the heart is recorded by these electrodes and the recorded electrical signal is presented by wave patterns known as the P-QRS-T complex. With the 12-lead ECG, the leads provide extensive data regarding the electrical activity of the heart as they transfer the information into the P-QRS-T wave complex which provides an indication of the normal or abnormal functioning of the heart.

Stimulation of cardiac tissue is a continuous sequence of processes referred to as **depolarization** and **repolarization**. The contraction of the atria and ventricles occurs when the cardiac cells are depolarized. As stated previously, this corresponds with the atria and ventricles pumping blood. The relaxation phase, which allows the cardiac cells to return to a normal resting state, represents repolarization. In the ECG, this is represented by the depolarization of the atria (P-wave) followed by the depolarization of the ventricles (QRS complex), and then a return to resting state or repolarization (ST, T, and U waves).

The P wave

The P wave is the depolarization of the atria beginning with the SA node and spreading from the right atrium to the left atrium. Some abnormal P wave ECG readings include:

- Prolonged P wave
  - Enlarged atria
- Absent or retrograde P wave
- Retrograde meaning the pacemaker of the heart is starting at the AV junction and the initiation of the heart beat is flowing backward (retrograde)
- Increased or decreased amplitude of P wave
  - Indicative of hypokalemia or hyperkalemia

Hypokalemia can be an issue for some athletes due to poor potassium intake, excessive perspiration, or gastrointestinal issues resulting in diarrhea. Muscle cramping and/or extreme fatigue represent other signs and symptoms of this condition.

QRS complex

The QRS complex represents the depolarization of the ventricles, where the blood is being ejected from the heart. Even though it appears to be a series of events in the making, the QRS represent a single event. The direction of the electrical impulse will indicate whether the deflection will be positive or negative. The first negative deflection is the Q wave, while the first positive deflection, the R wave, occurs next followed by the S wave, which is a negative deflection. Figure 2.4 shows examples of abnormal QRS wave readings.

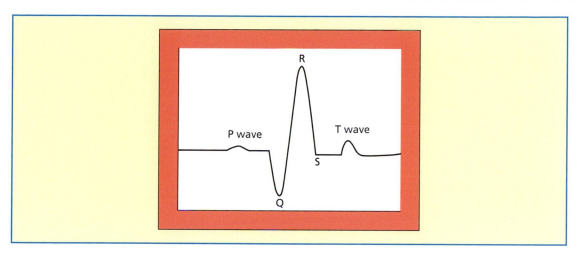

Figure 2.4 Conduction delay in wide QRS complex.

- Wide QRS complex
  - Bundle branch block
  - Electrolyte disturbance
  - Ischemia
- Decreased amplitude of complex
  - Chronic lung disease
  - Obesity
- Increased amplitude of R waves
  - Ventricular hypertrophy, known as the athletic heart, or hypertrophic cardio-myopathy (HCM)
- Abnormal Q waves
  - Myocardial infarction

Because of the fast response of the Purkinje fibers in the ventricles, the QRS complex depolarizes quite quickly. For this reason, we see delays in the QRS complex conduction resulting in an abnormal ECG. In the case of left and right ventricular hypertrophy, it is important to be aware that thin, young, and athletic individuals will demonstrate tall voltage in the R waves of the chest leads. However, it is often difficult to differentiate between someone that is a well-conditioned athlete versus someone that has ventricular hypertrophy. Therefore, it is usually recommended that the individual in question receive further testing in the form of an echocardiogram (i.e., an ultrasound test utilized to detect the sound waves of the heart) to attempt to make the differential diagnosis.

T wave

After the depolarization of ventricles and the resulting QRS complex, the T wave represents the beginning of ventricular repolarization. T waves are normally asymmetrical in shape with the asymmetry occurring towards the end of the wave in the form of a peak (Figure 2.5A).

A symmetrical T wave may reveal that a myocardial infarction has occurred. The S wave and T wave are looked at collectively, which represents the ST segment. Also, the Q wave and T wave provide the QT interval. Some T wave abnormal ECG findings include:

- T wave inversion
  - Myocardial ischemia
  - Myocarditis
  - Young patient
  - Arrhythmogenic right ventricular dysplasia (ARVD)
- Tall T wave
  - Acute myocardial ischemia "tombstones"
- ST segment depression
  - Right and left ventricular hypertrophy
  - Non Q wave MI
  - Subendocardial ischemia
- ST segment elevation
  - Pericarditis
- Conduction delay of the QT interval (Figure 2.5B)
  - Long QT syndrome

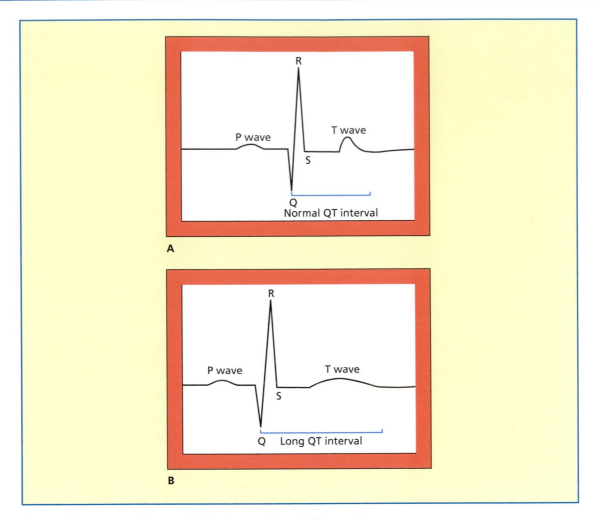

Figure 2.5 (A) Normal T wave; (B) Conduction delay of QT interval.

Many abnormalities are not limited to one lead or one ECG wave. Often, several leads and ECG waves are affected. For example, someone with hypertrophic cardiomyopathy might present a tall R wave in the QRS complex and an inverted T wave which are present in all lateral chest leads (4). Additionally, someone who is unhealthy may be suffering from several different cardiac issues making diagnosis more complicated.

> The ability to interpret the P-QRS-T complex may assist in the detection of abnormalities in the cardiac cycle.

Cardiac output

Cardiac output is the product of heart rate and stroke volume. It refers to the amount of blood pumped by the heart in one minute. Cardiac output is highly related to the energy demands of the body. In the average adult male, regardless of training status, the total volume of blood pumped out of the left ventricle per minute at rest is approximately 5 liters. If an individual's resting heart rate is 70 beats per minute, stroke volume would need to be approximately 71 mL per beat. In the endurance athlete, heart rate is generally much lower at rest due to a greater vagal tone and

TABLE 2.1 Cardiac output at rest in sedentary and endurance-trained men

	Cardiac output = (L)	Heart rate × (beats·minute⁻¹)	Stroke volume (mL)
Sedentary	5	70	71
Trained	5	50	100

reduced sympathetic drive. If the heart rate of this athlete was 50 beats per minute, stroke volume would be approximately 100 mL per beat. A comparison of the cardiac output in trained and sedentary males can be seen in Table 2.1. The mechanism that drives this particular adaptation is not entirely clear, but it is likely related to the increased vagal tone seen consequent to endurance training and to morphological adaptations of the heart.

Vasculature

The vascular system is composed of a series of vessels that carry oxygenated blood away from the heart to the tissues and return deoxygenated blood from the tissues back to the heart. Of great importance, the heart has its own coronary vascular system that is responsible for supplying the myocardium with oxygen and nutrients. The arterial system receives the blood from the left ventricle of the heart and distributes it throughout the body. Notice that blood is first ejected from the left ventricle into a thick, elastic vessel called the aorta. From the aorta, the blood is then circulated throughout the body via a network of arteries, arterioles (small arterial branches), metarterioles (smaller branches), and capillaries. The walls of the arteries are both strong and thick, which help withstand higher pressures associated with the rapid transport of blood to the tissues. The thickness of these vesicles prevents any gaseous exchange from occurring between them and the surrounding tissues. In addition, the arterial vasculature system is innervated by the sympathetic nervous system, allowing it to be effectively stimulated for regulating blood flow.

As blood reaches the tissues, it becomes diverted to smaller branches of the arterial system. At the end of the metarterioles (the smallest arterial vessel) are the microscopic capillaries.

The capillaries are approximately 0.01 mm in diameter and consist of a single layer of endothelial cells. Because of the small diameter, the rate of blood flow decreases as the blood circulates toward and into the capillaries. In addition, there is an extensive branching of the capillary microcirculation creating a large surface area between the capillary vasculature surrounding tissues. The combination of a large surface area, slow rate of blood flow, and a thin layer of endothelial cells make the capillaries an ideal place for gas exchange between the blood and the tissues.

As the blood leaves the capillaries, it enters the venous circulation. Similar to the arterial system, the venous system is comprised of vessels of various sizes that get larger as they get closer to the heart. Deoxygenated blood leaving the capillaries enters venules (small veins) that increase the rate of blood flow due to the smaller cross-sectional area of the venous system in comparison to the capillary system. The blood is transported back to the heart via the superior vena cava and the inferior vena cava. The deoxygenated blood then enters the right atrium, goes through to the right ventricle, and is pumped to the lungs to be reoxygenated and subsequently transported back into the left side of the heart to be circulated through arterial circulation once again.

During rest, blood flow is controlled by the autonomic nervous system and is primarily distributed to the liver, kidneys, and brain. However, during exercise there is a redistribution of blood flow to the exercising muscles. The muscles may receive 75% or more of the available blood at the expense of the other organs. In combination with a greater cardiac output, the exercising muscles may receive up to a 25-fold increase in blood flow. The flow of blood to the muscles and organs at rest and during exercise can be seen in Figure 2.6.

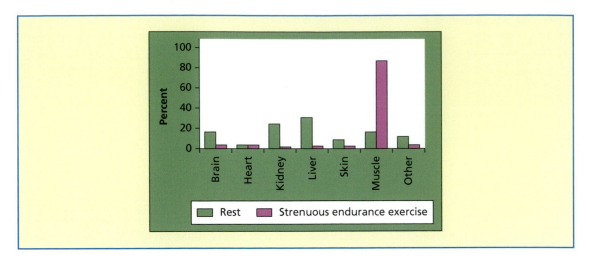

Figure 2.6 Distribution of cardiac output.

During exercise, blood flow will be diverted from organs to exercising muscles.

Blood pressure may reach unsafe levels during exercise. Therefore, it is important to understand both normal and abnormal changes in blood pressure as well as their relationship to various types of exercises.

Blood pressure

During each contraction, blood is pumped into the aorta from the left ventricle (systole). The pressure within the aorta under normal resting conditions reaches approximately 120 mm Hg. This measurement is referred to as the **systolic blood pressure**, which represents the strain against the arterial walls during ventricular contraction. Since the pumping action or contraction of the left ventricle of the heart is pulsatile in nature, the arterial pressure will fluctuate from an elevated level during systole to a lower level during the heart's relaxation phase known as diastole. **Diastolic blood pressures** are approximately 80 mm Hg at rest and provide an indication of the peripheral resistance or ease at which blood flows into the capillaries. As blood flows through the systemic circulation, pressure will continue to fall and reach approximately 0 mm Hg as it reaches the right atrium. The decrease in arterial pressure during each segment of the systemic circulation is directly proportional to the vascular resistance in that specific segment. Therefore, changes in the resistance of the systemic circulation are quite important in the regulation of blood flow.

RESPIRATORY SYSTEM

The coordination between the cardiovascular and respiratory system provides the body with an efficient means to transport oxygen to the tissues and remove carbon dioxide. During respiration, air is breathed in (**inspiration**) though the nasal cavity or mouth. The air then travels through the pharynx, larynx, trachea, and finally into the lungs. Once in the lungs, the air flows through an elaborate system comprised of branches termed bronchi and bronchioles that expand the surface area for gas exchange (see Figure 2.7). From the bronchioles, the air reaches the smallest respiratory unit, the alveoli. It is at the alveoli that gas exchange with the pulmonary circulation occurs (1). The lungs are located in the chest cavity (thorax), but do not have any direct attachment to the ribs or any other bony structure. Instead, they are suspended by pleural sacs that connect to both the lungs and thoracic cavity. Between the pleural sacs and lungs, a fluid is present to prevent friction from occurring during respiration.

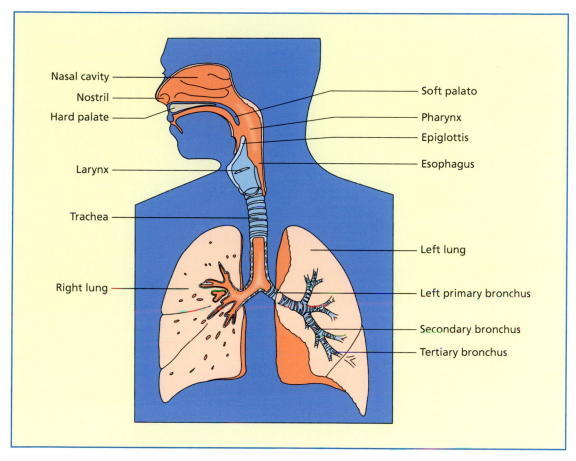

Figure 2.7 Anatomy of the respiratory system.

During inspiration, the muscles of the thoracic cavity (diaphragm and external intercostal muscles) contract causing the thorax to expand. As a result, the lungs stretch and initiate a reduction in air pressure within the lungs. As pressure within the lungs is reduced to levels below that seen on the outside, the pressure gradient will cause air to rush inside the lungs. During exercise, additional muscles, such as the pectoralis and sternocleidomastoid, can be recruited, causing a greater movement of the thorax and creating an even larger lung expansion.

When air is breathed out (**expiration**), the inspiratory muscles relax, or during forced expiration contraction of the internal intercostal and abdominal muscles will cause the thorax to return to its normal position. As a result, the pressure within the lungs expands to levels above that seen outside, causing expiration to occur.

A change in pressure is the primary mechanism in which air and gases flow into and out of the lungs and through the entire respiratory and circulatory systems. For **ventilation** to occur, only slight changes in pressure between the lungs and the outside environment need to occur. For instance, standard atmospheric pressure is 760 mm Hg and only slight changes in intrapulmonary pressure (i.e., pressure within the lungs) are needed to cause the air to be inhaled.

Pressure differentials in gases

In addition to changes in pressure that cause inspiration and expiration, pressure differentials in the gases within the air we breathe will be the primary impetus causing the exchange of oxygen and carbon dioxide. Each gas will exert a pressure in proportion to its concentration in the gas mixture, known as its **partial pressure**. The air that we breathe is comprised of 79.04% nitrogen, 20.93% oxygen, and 0.03% carbon dioxide. At sea level, in which atmospheric pressure is 760 mm Hg, the partial pressure of oxygen is 159.1 mm Hg (20.93% × 760 mm Hg) and carbon dioxide is 0.2 mm Hg (0.03% × 760 mm Hg).

As the air reaches the alveoli, the partial pressures of both the gases in the alveoli and the gases in the blood create a pressure gradient (see Figure 2.8). This is the basis of gas exchange. If the partial pressures of the gases on either side of the membrane were equal, no gas exchange would occur. The greater the pressure gradient, the faster the gases will diffuse across the membrane. As inspired air moves into the alveoli, the partial pressure of oxygen (Po_2) is between 100 and 105 mm Hg due to the mixing of the air within the alveoli. At the pulmonary capillary, blood has been stripped of most of its oxygen by the tissues. Typically, the Po_2 at the pulmonary capillary level is between 40 and 45 mm Hg. As a result, the pressure gradient favors oxygen going from the alveoli to the capillary. In addition, the pressure gradient of carbon dioxide favors exchange from the capillary to the alveoli where it can be exhaled from the body during expiration. The pressure gradient for carbon dioxide is not as great at the capillary–alveoli membrane as it is for oxygen. Nevertheless, carbon dioxide diffuses quite easily across the membrane, despite the low pressure gradient, due to greater membrane solubility than oxygen.

> Gas exchange occurring at the capillary and alveoli and between the capillary and the tissue is the result of pressure differentials that cause oxygen or carbon dioxide to diffuse from an area of high concentration to one of low concentration.

Oxygen and carbon dioxide transport

Oxygen is transported in the blood, either combined with hemoglobin (98%) or dissolved in the blood plasma (2%), and each molecule of hemoglobin can carry four molecules of oxygen. The binding of oxygen to hemoglobin is also dependent upon the Po_2 in the blood and the affinity between oxygen and hemoglobin. The greater the Po_2, the more saturated the hemoglobin molecules are with oxygen. In addition, the temperature and pH of the blood will also affect the affinity between oxygen and hemoglobin. As the pH of the blood decreases, the affinity that hemoglobin has to oxygen is decreased and oxygen is released. The rightward shift of the curve is known as the **Bohr effect** (see Figure 2.9) and is important during exercise when a greater amount of oxygen is

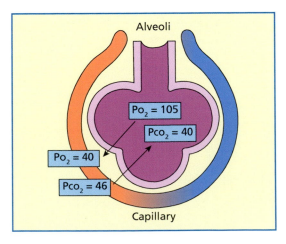

Figure 2.8 Pressure gradient between the capillary and alveoli within the lungs.

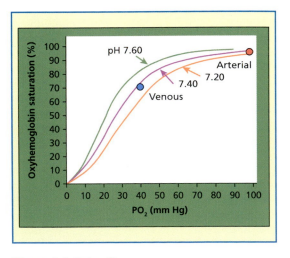

Figure 2.9 Bohr effect.

Increasing maximal oxygen consumption

Athletes of many sports aim to increase their level of maximal oxygen consumption. In the past, coaches have instructed their athletes to perform long slow distance (LSD) training with the goal of increasing VO_2 max. However, in recent years, it has been observed that interval training results in VO_2 increases similar to, or even greater than, traditional LSD training. Therefore, it may be beneficial to incorporate interval training into a conditioning program for athletes whose sports, such as soccer, lacrosse, field hockey, etc. rely on the ATP/CP and glycolytic systems, yet participate in competition for prolonged periods of time.

needed in the active musculature. On the other hand, when the pH is high, as it would be in the lungs, there is a greater affinity between oxygen and hemoglobin; this is important in order to saturate the hemoglobin molecules with oxygen (1).

Carbon dioxide transport in the blood occurs primarily in the form of bicarbonate ion (approximately 60–70%). Carbon dioxide will also be transported, dissolved in the plasma (7–10%), or bound to hemoglobin. However, it does not compete with oxygen since it has its own binding site on the globin molecule. In contrast, oxygen's binding site is on the heme molecule. As carbon dioxide diffuses from the muscle to the blood, it combines with water to form carbonic acid. This is a very unstable acid and it quickly dissociates, releasing a hydrogen ion (H^+) and forming a bicarbonate ion (HCO_3^-). This results in an increase in acidity, causing hemoglobin to lose its affinity for oxygen and increases oxygen's rate of diffusion into the tissues.

Gas exchange is affected by changes in pH and temperature.

BLOOD

Blood is a viscous fluid that is comprised of cells and plasma. More than 99% of the cells in the blood are red blood cells, the remainder being white blood cells. Plasma is part of the extracellular fluid of the body and is very similar in composition to interstitial fluid that is found between tissue cells. Yet these fluids differ regarding the amount of protein that is found between the two fluids where plasma contains approximately 7% protein, while interstitial fluid contains approximately 2% protein. The percentage of the blood that is cells is called the hematocrit and the average man has an approximate hematocrit level of 42, while the average female has a hematocrit level of approximately 38. Simply put, 42% of the blood is comprised of cells in an average male and 38% in an average female with the remaining component being plasma.

CARDIOVASCULAR RESPONSE TO ACUTE EXERCISE

Oxygen consumption (VO_2) is elevated during acute exercise to meet the higher energy needs of the exercising muscle and other associated tissues. It is important to note that as exercise intensity increases, a greater demand for energy is met by an increase in the cardiac output and/or by a greater oxygen extraction from the vasculature (a greater $(a-v)O_2$ difference). During the early stages of exercise, increases in both heart rate and stroke volume occur quite rapidly to bring about increases in cardiac output. Figure 2.10 demonstrates the effects of varying intensities of exercise on heart rate, stroke volume, and cardiac output.

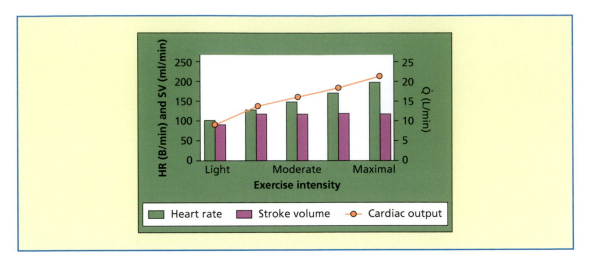

Figure 2.10 Effect of exercise intensity on heart rate, stroke volume, and cardiac output. HR = heart rate; SV = stroke volume; Q = cardiac output.

Cardiac output

Cardiac output at rest is approximately 5 L. However, during maximal endurance exercise, cardiac output may increase to as much as 20 L in young, sedentary men whereas in young, endurance-trained male athletes, cardiac output may reach 40 L. In examining this considerable difference in cardiac output, it is easy to notice that the maximal heart rate for both of these individuals (assuming that both men are 20 years old) will be approximately 200 bpm (maximal heart rate = 220 – age). Thus, a difference in stroke volume must account for the large differences in cardiac output. In our example, the stroke volume of the sedentary male would be approximately 100 mL per beat, while the stroke volume in the endurance trained athlete may reach 200 mL per beat.

The importance of a large cardiac output for the endurance athlete is reflected by the linear relationship seen between cardiac output and oxygen consumption (5). This relationship is seen not only in adults, but also reported in children and adolescents (6) and between trained and untrained individuals (7).

> Increases in cardiac output during exercise are the result of changes in stroke volume and heart rate. It is important to note that SV and heart rate respond differently to various types of training.

Heart rate

The increases in heart rate during exercise are primarily controlled by sympathetic stimulation from the brain's higher somatomotor centers. The heart rate response is directly proportional and linear to the intensity of exercise. Thus, as exercise intensity increases, heart rate will continue to increase until it reaches a plateau. Usually, at this specific point, the individual has apparently reached his or her maximal level.

Initial increases in heart rate are also related to a withdrawal of parasympathetic input. This occurs during low intensity exercise when, as the exercise session continues in duration or increases in intensity, a greater sympathetic stimulation is seen and becomes the driving force in increasing the heart rate. Sympathetic activation occurs from feedback mechanisms in peripheral, mechanical, and chemical receptors that monitor changes in pH, **hypoxia**, temperature, and other metabolic variables that can alter sympathetic drive.

As heart rate increases, the volume of blood that is pumped into circulation will also increase. However, there is a limitation to this effect as when the heart rate rises above a certain level, the strength of each contraction may decrease due to a metabolic overload. More importantly, the greater rate of contraction results in less time spent in the diastole phase.

Unfortunately, the time between contractions becomes so reduced that there is not sufficient time for the blood to flow from the atria to the ventricles. Thus, the total volume of blood made available to the circulation is reduced. For this reason, during artificial electrical stimulation, the heart rate will only increase to an approximate level of 100 to 150 beats per minute. However, elevations in heart rate from sympathetic stimulation will result in a heart rate between 170 and 250 beats per minute. Notice that sympathetic stimulation will also result in a stronger systolic contraction, decrease the time during systole, and thereby allow a greater time for filling during diastole.

> Decreases in resting heart rate likely reflect changes in sympathetic and parasympathetic stimulation.

Stroke volume

Increases in stroke volume occur early during exercise primarily through an increase in left ventricular end-diastolic volume (EDV). This rapid augmentation of stroke volume is due to the **Frank-Starling mechanism**, which is related to the increased volume of blood that returns to the heart during exercise. With a greater volume of blood returning to the heart, the ventricles will become stretched to a greater extent than normal and will respond with a more forceful contraction. This stronger contraction will result in a greater volume of blood entering the systemic circulation with each heart beat. This mechanism appears to occur in the early stages of exercise and at a relatively low exercise intensity level. The Frank-Starling mechanism may cause an approximate 30% to 50% increase in stroke volume (8). As exercise continues, increases in EDV will reach a plateau while exercise intensity is still at a submaximal intensity. Further increases in stroke volume are attributed to the enhanced left ventricular contractile function, which is controlled by enhanced sympathetic stimulation, thereby resulting in a greater decrease in end-systolic ventricular volume.

There are two mechanisms that appear to be responsible for the increase in EDV during exercise. The initial mechanism involves the use of the exercising muscles as a pump to increase the rate of return of the blood to the heart, and one would expect this to increase the pressures within the ventricular cavity during filling, thereby raising diastolic pressure. However, this does not occur in a healthy heart. Also, the relaxation seen in the left ventricle reduces the ventricular pressure below that of the left atrium, which in turn will cause the mitral valve to open and ventricular filling will occur. As mentioned previously in this chapter, the enhanced sympathetic response during exercise will increase the relaxation time during diastole. During this specific time, the increase in size of the left ventricle causes a further reduction in pressure creating a suction effect which draws additional blood into the chamber. This facilitation of the suctioning mechanism by sympathetic drive is the secondary mechanism that contributes to the increased stroke volume and is crucial in the recruitment of Frank-Starling mechanisms (8).

Cardiac drift

As exercise duration is prolonged, or when exercise is performed in a hot and potentially humid environment, a gradual increase in heart rate and a decrease in stroke volume may occur even when exercise intensity is maintained. This specific process is called **cardiovascular drift** and is thought to occur from a greater percentage of circulating blood being diverted to the skin attempting to dissipate body heat as a result of an increased core temperature in the exercising athlete. The greater concentration of blood in the periphery and a loss of some plasma volume, specifically water loss from the plasma which contributes to the composition of sweat, will result in a reduced blood volume (i.e., venous return) going back to the heart. The decrease in EDV will result in a reduced stroke volume, which will then cause the heart rate to increase in order to compensate for the change in stroke volume, and more importantly, to maintain cardiac output.

(a−v)O$_2$ difference

In an individual with a normal hemoglobin concentration, who is in a resting state, each liter of blood will contain approximately

200 mL of oxygen. Considering that a normal cardiac output is 5 L per minute at rest, approximately 1 L of oxygen is available to the body. However, only 250 mL, or 25% of the available oxygen, is extracted from arterial blood (the $(a-v)O_2$ difference) during rest, which will leave the remaining 750 mL of oxygen available as a reserve.

It is logical to assume that during exercise, oxygen extraction from the arterial blood is increased and up to 75% of the available oxygen may be used by the exercising muscles. The increase in oxygen extraction appears to be related to the intensity of exercise and may be further enhanced by participating in an endurance training program. The ability to extract oxygen from the blood and the total blood volume available to the muscles is critical in determining the aerobic capacity of the individual. This is reflected by the **Fick equation**:

$$VO_2 \; max = Maximal \; cardiac \; output \times Maximal \; (a-v)O_2 \; difference$$

Of major interest, there may be very little difference between moderately trained individuals and endurance athletes in the ability to extract oxygen, despite large differences in VO_2 max. Therefore, the primary factor determining aerobic capacity is likely cardiac output.

Distribution of cardiac output

During exercise, most of the circulating blood is diverted to the active muscles (see Figure 2.2). The magnitude of the shunting process will be dependent upon the environmental condition and possibly other factors including type of exercise and fatigue. The shunting of blood is generally accomplished by diverting blood flow from organs or areas of the body that can tolerate a reduction in blood flow to the exercising muscles, and this process is commonly referred to as autoregulation. However, certain organs such as the heart cannot function without a normal blood flow and will try strongly not to reduce their blood supply during exercise.

Blood pressure

Blood pressure typically increases in a linear fashion during dynamic exercise such as walking, jogging, or running. In a healthy individual, this increase is seen only in the systolic response. The systolic blood pressure response appears to be buffered to a large extent by the decrease in peripheral resistance caused by the vasodilation in the vasculature of the exercising muscles (9). The decrease seen in peripheral resistance appears to account for the minimal to non-existent change that is observed with diastolic pressures. It is also important to note that diastolic pressure may decrease during high intensity exercise bouts.

Q&A FROM THE FIELD

Can resistance training be harmful to the heart? Is it possible that this type of training can contribute to an enlarged heart?

The heart is a muscle, and exercise, including resistance training, increases the workload on the heart. The heart can hypertrophy just like any other muscle. Bodybuilders and weightlifters can get an enlarged heart, which by itself does not cause any heart problems. However, resistance training will cause your heart muscle to thicken without enlargement of its cavity, which enables the heart to work better under the increased intrathoracic pressure that occurs with anaerobic exercise. Other causes of an enlarged heart include certain diseases that are associated with specific heart problems.

During exercise that only involves the upper body, both systolic and diastolic blood pressures are higher than when exercise is performed with only the use of the legs (10). This is thought to occur because of the relatively smaller muscle mass and vasculature of the arms. Even when these vessels are maximally dilated it does not appear to have the same effect on peripheral resistance compared with lower body exercise. The higher pressor response seen with upper body exercise has important implications in determining the exercise prescription for individuals who have coronary heart disease.

During resistance training exercise, large increases in both systolic and diastolic blood pressures may occur (11,12,13). During maximal efforts that involve a large muscle mass, intra-arterial blood pressures exceeding

350/250 mm Hg in healthy young men have been reported (12). The large pressor response that occurs during resistance training is a combination of vascular compression within contracting muscles and a **Valsalva maneuver** (9). The magnitude of the pressor response is also related to the relative size of the muscle mass involved and the intensity of the effort. Note, blood pressure will increase with each repetition when an individual completes a set to failure, and then drops rapidly to below resting levels after the last repetition (12,13). This is a transient decrease and is likely related to the large vasodilation of the vasculature that was occluded during muscle contraction and may contribute to the dizziness that one may experience after an intense exercise session.

A major portion of the large pressor response seen during resistance training is attributed to a Valsalva maneuver. During a Valsalva maneuver, there is a rapid increase in intrathoracic pressure which results in an increase in both systolic and diastolic blood pressures (11). However, if the Valsalva maneuver is maintained, within several seconds, the systolic and diastolic pressures will begin to drop because of the reduced diastolic filling caused by an impaired venous return. Although often contraindicated during resistance exercise, the Valsalva maneuver may in fact be quite beneficial and have a protective effect in healthy resistance trained individuals (9,14). The increase in intrathoracic pressure seen during the Valsalva maneuver will provide stabilization to the spinal column, and reduce left ventricular transmural pressure, which is otherwise known as afterload (15). This contrasts to the high afterload that is normally expected when systolic pressures are elevated. In addition, the increase in intrathoracic pressure is also transmitted to the cerebral spinal fluid, which will reduce the transmural pressures of the cerebral vessels preventing vascular damage at the time of peak peripheral resistance (14).

> During exercise, systolic blood pressure is expected to increase relative to changes in exercise intensity; however, diastolic blood pressure will remain the same or decrease slightly.

PULMONARY VENTILATION DURING EXERCISE

During submaximal exercise, ventilation will increase linearly with oxygen uptake. The increase in oxygen consumption is primarily the result of an increase in tidal volume, which is the amount of air inspired or expired during a normal breathing cycle. As exercise intensity increases, the increase in oxygen consumption may rely more on increasing the breathing rate (i.e., the respiration rate). During steady state exercise, minute ventilation, which is the liters of air breathed per minute, will plateau when the demand for oxygen is met by supply. The ratio of minute ventilation to oxygen consumption is termed the **ventilatory equivalent** and is symbolized by V_E/VO_2. During submaximal exercise the ventilatory equivalent in healthy individuals is approximately 25:1 (16). In simple terms, this represents 25 L of air that is breathed in for every liter of oxygen. This ratio may be slightly higher in children (17) and may also be affected by the exercise mode such as swimming versus running (18). However, during maximal exercise, minute ventilation increases disproportionately in relation to oxygen uptake and this is important to consider since the ventilatory equivalent may reach as high as 35–40 L of air per L of oxygen consumed in a healthy adult.

CARDIOVASCULAR ADAPTATIONS TO TRAINING

When individuals are compliant to an endurance exercise program for a long period of time, this may result in numerous cardiovascular adaptations that are specific to the type of exercise program that the individual participates in. Endurance training and resistance training are modes of training that represent two distinctly different physiological demands that are placed on the cardiovascular system. Although many of the cardiovascular adaptations observed in these training programs are

TABLE 2.2 Cardiovascular adaptations to prolonged endurance and resistance training

	Endurance training		Resistance training	
	Rest	Exercise	Rest	Exercise
Heart rate	D	NC	D or NC	NC
Stroke volume	I	I	I or NC	I or NC
Cardiac output	NC	I	NC	I or NC
Blood pressure:				
Systolic	D or NC	D or NC	D or NC	D or NC
Diastolic	D or NC	D or NC	NC	D or NC
Morphological adaptations:				
Left ventricular mass	I		I	
Left ventricular diameter	I		I or NC	
Wall thickness:				
Left ventricle	I		I	
Septum	I		I	

I = increase, D = decrease, NC = no change

similar, others are quite different. A summary of these adaptations can be seen in Table 2.2 and are discussed in this section.

Cardiac output and stroke volume

Increases in VO_2 max are characteristic of compliance to an endurance training program. These increases are generally accompanied by increases in cardiac output and an improved extraction capability within skeletal muscle (increase in $(a-v)O_2$ difference). Improvement in oxygen extraction is related to the greater perfusion capabilities of exercising muscle. Since maximal heart rates are unaffected by training and will not differ between elite endurance athletes and age-matched sedentary individuals, increases in cardiac output are primarily the result of having an improved stroke volume.

Endurance training is a potent stimulus for increasing stroke volume both at rest and during maximal exercise, and the increases in stroke volume are related to an enlarged ventricular chamber (referred to as **eccentric hypertrophy**) caused by a chronic increased ventricular filling seen during endurance exercise. This increased preload seems to relate to the expanded plasma volume associated with such training (19,20).

It is important to note that resistance training results in little to no change in cardiac output. Yet, significantly greater stroke volumes have been reported in elite level weightlifters when compared to recreational lifters (21). However, the increase in stroke volume seen in these athletes appeared to be more a factor of a larger body size than a training adaptation (22).

Increases in cardiac output following prolonged endurance training are the result of an increased SV.

Heart rate

A decrease in resting heart rate, and a relative decrease in heart rate at any given submaximal VO_2 level, is a common adaptation to engaging in an endurance training program (23,24). The decrease in heart rate during submaximal exercise is likely subsequent to improved stroke volume and also is reflective of an improved exercise economy. The mechanism regulating training induced bradycardia (i.e., a low heart rate) is not thoroughly understood but is likely related to a change in the balance between sympathetic and parasympathetic activity. In addition, a decrease in the intrinsic rate of firing of the SA-node following long-term training has also been suggested to be a factor in the bradycardic response to long-term training (25).

Blood pressure

In normotensive individuals, resting systolic or diastolic pressures are generally unresponsive to endurance training programs. However, based on numerous epidemiological studies and other investigations examining exercise and hypertension, it appears that exercise is a potential stimulus for reducing both systolic and diastolic blood pressure in hypertensive individuals (26). The reduction in resting blood pressure appears to occur during endurance exercise programs that include training frequencies of between three and five sessions per week that are at least 30 minutes in duration and include an intensity level of 50% to 70% of VO_2 max (26,27).

During endurance exercise at a given exercise intensity level, the blood pressure response has been shown to decrease (9), but this may be related to the initial conditioning level of the individual. Therefore, well-conditioned endurance athletes will probably need to train at higher intensity exercise levels for a prolonged duration to see potential adaptations.

Resistance training appears to result in no change or a slight decrease in resting blood pressure (28), but a significant decrease in the blood pressure response during resistance exercise at the same absolute load tends to occur (29,30). However, a decrease in resting blood pressure subsequent to resistance training is likely the result of a decrease in body fat and possible reduction in the sympathetic drive to the heart (31).

> Changes in resting blood pressure are dependent upon the individual's initial conditioning level.

Cardiac morphology

An athlete's heart is quite large in comparison to a recreationally trained or sedentary individual. For many years, a debate was waged whether this enlarged heart in athletes was a consequence of pathological disease or physiological adaptation. However, the technological advances since the early 1980s have allowed for a much closer examination of the physiological adaptations of the heart in conjunction with prolonged training.

During prolonged training, the heart will adapt to match the workload placed on the left ventricle in order to maintain a constant relationship between systolic cavity pressure and the ratio of wall thickness to ventricular radius (32). Adaptations to the morphology of the heart are governed by the law of Laplace that states that wall tension is proportional to pressure and the radius of curvature (33). During a pressure overload, common to resistance exercise programs, the septum and posterior wall of the left ventricle increase in size to normalize myocardial wall stress. During a volume overload, common to endurance training programs, the increase is predominantly in the internal diameter of the left ventricle, which increases the size of the cavity, with a proportional increase in both the septum and posterior wall of the ventricle. Both endurance training and resistance training are at opposite ends of the spectrum concerning the volume and pressure stresses placed upon the heart. However, most sports have a parallel impact on both cavity dimension and wall thickness (34). In these specific sports, athletes perform a combination of aerobic and anaerobic training which results in cardiovascular adaptations associated with both an enlarged diastolic cavity dimension and a larger wall thickness. In sports that primarily emphasize a single form of training, such as distance running or road cycling, the morphological changes of the heart may be more extreme.

Endurance trained athletes have been shown to have a greater than normal left ventricular internal diameter, with normal to slightly thicker walls (34,35,36,37). This type of left ventricular hypertrophy is termed eccentric hypertrophy and is considered a normal physiological response to a volume overload consistent with prolonged endurance training.

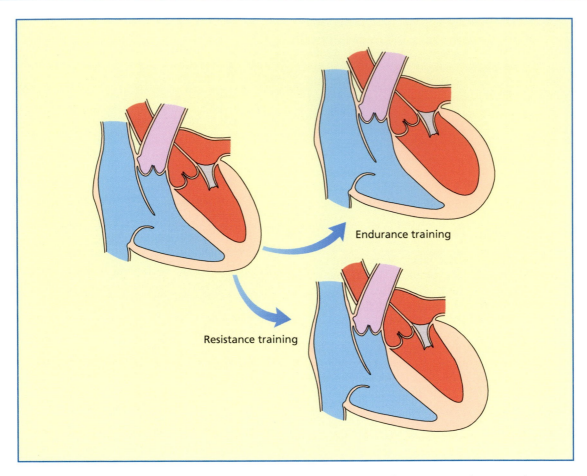

Figure 2.11 Caricature of morphological adaptations of the left ventricle subsequent to endurance and resistance training.

On the other hand, resistance trained athletes have normal internal diameters with significantly thicker ventricular walls (27,36,38,39). This type of hypertrophy is referred to as **concentric hypertrophy** and, at times, may approach levels that are seen in **hypertrophic cardiomyopathy**, which is a disease of the myocardium that is associated with large thickening of the septum and posterior wall at the expense of cavity size, which greatly impairs left ventricular function. Of major importance, the concentric hypertrophy seen in the resistance trained athlete does not impede on the internal diameter of the ventricle. In addition, the type of hypertrophy seen in cardiomyopathy is usually asymmetric, whereas in resistance trained or power athletes, the change in wall size is generally symmetrical.

Figure 2.11 compares morphological changes in the left ventricle between endurance and resistance trained individuals.

Left ventricular mass in highly trained athletes are on average 45% greater than in age-matched control subjects (35). This increase in mass is related to the increases in left ventricular internal diameter and ventricular wall thickness. When examined relative to changes in body mass or body surface area, the significantly greater ventricular mass is still present. Some studies have suggested that differences are more prevalent in elite athletes than in athletes of lesser caliber (22).

Morphological changes of the heart are dependent upon the type of training program performed.

RESPIRATORY ADAPTATIONS TO TRAINING

The respiratory system does not appear to be a major limiting factor in providing sufficient oxygen to the exercising muscles. However, similar to most other physiological systems in the body, the respiratory system can also adapt to physical exercise in order to maximize its efficiency. In general, lung volume and capacity will change very little from physical exercise. However, it appears that during maximal exercise vital capacity may increase slightly, but this may be related to the slight decrease seen in residual volume, which is the amount of air that remains in the lungs following maximal expiration (40).

> Respiratory capacity does not appear significantly affected by physical exercise.

Ventilatory equivalent and minute ventilation

Endurance training appears to reduce the **ventilatory equivalent** (i.e., the amount of air that is inspired at a particular rate of oxygen consumption) during submaximal exercise (41,42). As a result, the oxygen cost of exercise that is attributed to ventilation is reduced. This benefit may be realized by a reduction in fatigue of the ventilatory musculature and greater oxygen availability to the exercising muscles (43).

Minute ventilation also appears to decrease during submaximal exercise following prolonged endurance training. This yields an improved exercise efficiency resulting from such training. However, during maximal exercise, endurance training appears to cause minute ventilation to increase and this is thought to occur due to an increase in VO_2 max (44). In untrained subjects, minute ventilation can increase from 120 L·min^{-1} to about 150 L·min^{-1} after training (40). In addition, minute ventilation in highly trained endurance athletes may increase to 180 L·min^{-1} and elite rowers have been reported to reach as high as 240 L·min^{-1} (40).

BLOOD VOLUME ADAPTATIONS TO TRAINING

Endurance training appears to be a potent stimulus for causing **hypervolemia**, which is an increase in blood volume. This adaptation appears to occur within the initial two to four weeks of training and is thought to be the result of increases in plasma volume (45). However, as training progresses further, increases in blood volume appear to be the result of both continued plasma volume expansion and an increase in red blood cell number.

The increase in plasma volume is believed to be the result of increases in the fluid regulatory hormones antidiuretic hormone and aldosterone that bring about an increase in fluid retention by the kidneys. In addition, exercise causes an increase in plasma proteins, primarily albumin (46). This increase in plasma proteins within the blood will cause a greater osmotic pull causing fluid to be retained in the blood. Also, plasma volume expansion does appear to be a greater contributor to hypervolemia (47). Figure 2.12 shows the effect of prolonged endurance training on blood volume expansion and the contributions of both

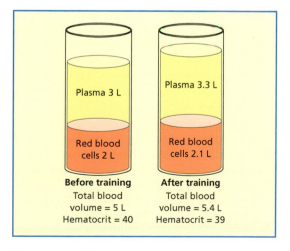

Figure 2.12 Effect of endurance training on blood volume, plasma volume and hematocrit.

Adapted from Hoffman JR. Physiological Aspects of Sport Training and Performance. Champaign, IL: Human Kinetics. 55, 2002.

plasma volume expansion and increases in red blood cell number. Although both plasma volume and red blood cell volume increase, they do not increase proportionally. Thus, hematocrit will decrease, which will lower the viscosity of the blood and facilitate blood flow through the circulation. However, the reduction in hematocrit does not appear to cause a concern for low hemoglobin concentrations. In fact, hemoglobin concentrations in endurance trained athletes are typically above normal and provide an ample capacity of oxygen to meet the body's needs during exercise.

> Increases in red blood cell number and plasma volume expansion as the result of endurance training will cause a reduction in hematocrit.

ENVIRONMENTAL FACTORS AFFECTING CARDIORESPIRATORY FUNCTION

Exercise performed under severe environmental conditions may cause a large strain on the cardiorespiratory system specifically in meeting the body's oxygen demands. In addition to potential performance limitations, exercise under such conditions poses significant risks to the health and well-being of the individual. This section will focus on the aspects of exercising in the heat and altitude and how this will impact cardiorespiratory function.

Cardiorespiratory response to exercise in the heat

During exercise in the heat, a large volume of circulating blood (up to 7 L·min^{-1}) is diverted to the skin to help dissipate the resulting body heat increases (48). As blood flow to the skin is increased, the peripheral vasculature becomes compliant and engorged with blood creating blood pools (49). Blood pooling in the periphery causes a reduction in venous return and subsequently a decrease in cardiac filling,

which in turn will result in further cardiovascular strain that is reflected by a decrease in stroke volume. To compensate for the decrease in SV, the heart rate must increase to maintain cardiac output and, as stated earlier, this process is known as cardiovascular drift. In addition, blood flow from splanchnic and renal areas are further reduced to compensate for the greater blood flow that is diverted to the exercising muscle and periphery for heat dissipation (48).

To combat elevations in body temperature resulting from exercising in the heat, sweat rate will increase to enhance evaporative cooling. This adds further to the cardiovascular strain by causing a greater reduction in blood volume (50). However, as blood volume becomes reduced, it will result in less blood being made available to the periphery and, as a result, sweat output will decline and the body's ability to dissipate heat will be reduced. Consequently, core temperature will rise, and in combination with a reduced blood volume, cardiovascular strain becomes elevated and the risk for heat illness is increased. When exercise in the heat is further complicated with a body water deficit, the resulting dehydration will exacerbate the physiological strain and in simpler terms, will cause the athlete to have a reduction in performance as he or she will have an inability to maintain the required exercise intensity.

An existing body water deficit, known as **hypohydration**, will have significant implications for cardiovascular function and results in a reduction of plasma volume. As a consequence, less blood is available to both exercising muscle and the skin. In addition, decreases in plasma volume are also associated with a reduction in stroke volume (51). To compensate, the heart rate will increase to maintain normal blood flow. However, depending upon the magnitude of the body water deficit, the increase in heart rate may be insufficient to fully compensate for the lower stroke volume. Unfortunately, cardiac output will also be reduced (51,52). However, one factor to consider is that cardiac output can be maintained at higher degrees of hypohydration if it occurs in the absence of a thermal strain (53).

During exercise in the heat, blood flow must be redistributed to accommodate the competing interests of thermoregulation and skeletal muscle. Furthermore, cardiovascular function can be compromised during exercise in the heat by a reduction in SV.

Effect of altitude on the cardiorespiratory response

As one ascends above sea level, the partial pressure of oxygen (Po_2) becomes reduced. Remember that the pressure gradient between arterial Po_2 and tissue Po_2 is approximately 64 mm Hg at sea level, which is the difference between an arterial Po_2 of 104 mm Hg and a tissue Po_2 of 40 mm Hg. This creates a pressure gradient causing oxygen to diffuse easily into the tissues. However, at altitude, a reduction in arterial Po_2 will cause a decrease in the pressure gradient reducing the diffusion capability of oxygen from the vasculature into the tissue. For instance, at an elevation of 2,500 m the arterial Po_2 drops to about 60 mm Hg, with the tissue Po_2 remaining at 40 mm Hg, creating a pressure gradient of only 20 mm Hg. This 70% reduction in the pressure gradient will cause a significant reduction in the speed at which oxygen moves between the capillaries and tissues. The reduction in the pressure gradient between the vasculature and the tissues has important implications in maintaining exercise performance during exercise at altitude. To compensate for the reduced Po_2 at altitude, breathing rate is increased. However, as breathing rate increases, known as **hyperventilation**, the partial pressure of carbon dioxide (Pco_2) in the alveoli becomes reduced. As a result, the stimulus to maintain a high rate of ventilation may be removed since Pco_2 is an integral part of the driving force behind hyperventilation.

To compensate for the reduced oxygen availability at altitude, increases in cardiac output occur at rest and during exercise. The primary mechanism that contributes to the increase in cardiac output appears to be an increase in heart rate. Heart rate has been shown to increase between 40 and 50% at rest

without any change in SV (54). Even during exercise, the increase in cardiac output appears to be primarily the result of an increase in heart rate. In contrast to what is normally seen during exercise at sea level, during exercise at altitude, stroke volume will decrease (54). The decrease in stroke volume is apparently from a reduction in plasma volume that is observed within a short time following arrival at altitude (55,56).

During initial exposure at altitude, observed at elevations above 3,000 m, decreases in plasma volume appear to be the result of both a diuresis and natriuresis, which is known as an increase in sodium excretion (57). The diuresis may be explained by the large evaporative heat loss caused by ventilation of dry inspired air at altitude. The natriuresis appears to be the result of a neural stimulation of the kidney to decrease the reabsorption of sodium due to the **hypoxic** (low oxygen) stimulus (57). Even during prolonged exposure to altitude, plasma volume will still remain below normal levels, and studies examining individuals that reside at altitude have reported lower plasma volumes in comparison to residents of sea level communities (58). Thus, acclimatization does not seem to have any significant effect on a return of blood volume to pre-exposure levels.

Changes in the partial pressure of oxygen as the result of ascending to altitude will impair gas exchange in the lungs and tissues.

Cardiorespiratory changes from prolonged exposure at altitude

During the first few days at altitude, changes in the respiratory response can be seen. Initially, breathing rate is increased while arterial Po_2 decreases. However, after a few days at altitude, arterial Po_2 begins to rise as Pco_2 values fall. The ventilatory rate will continue to rise from changes in the ventilatory response to CO_2 levels and in the sensitivity of the carotid body. The carotid body is situated above the bifurcation of the carotid artery and it serves as a sensor of oxygen saturation in the blood, and most notably, its location is ideal for this role since it receives a large blood supply allowing it to respond to oxygen saturation and not to oxygen content (59). The increased sensitivity of the carotid body appears to have a biphasic response. The initial response may be a decrease in the hypoxic ventilatory response during the first three to five days of altitude exposure, but following these initial days of exposure, an increase in the ventilatory response occurs (59).

In addition to changes in the ventilatory response, another component of respiratory adaptation to altitude may be the diffusion capacity of oxygen. After seven to ten weeks of altitude exposure, diffusion capacities are reported to increase between 15 and 20% (58). Although much of this improved diffusion capacity may be accounted for by increases in hemoglobin concentrations, other studies comparing individuals permanently residing at altitude to individuals residing at sea level have also reported significant differences in oxygen diffusion capacities between these population groups (60). These differences may be related to the larger lung volumes developed through exposure to chronic hypoxia and the subsequent development of greater surface area for oxygen diffusion (61).

> Altitude and temperature each elicit various physiological responses that are specific to the environment.

After several weeks of altitude exposure, cardiac output remains similar to those values observed at sea level. However, similar to what occurs during an acute exposure to altitude, increases in cardiac output following extended stays at elevation appear to be primarily attributed to increases in heart rate, yet stroke volume continues to remain reduced (62). One of the best-known adaptations to prolonged exposure to altitude is the increase in the number of red blood cells per unit volume of blood. Exposure to hypoxic conditions result in the release of the hormone **erythropoietin**. Erythropoietin is responsible for stimulating red blood cell (i.e., erythrocytes) production and is seen to increase within two hours of exposure to altitude and reaches a maximum rate of increase at about 24 to 48

hours (63). After three weeks of exposure to altitude, erythropoietin concentrations appear to return to baseline levels, but not until they have contributed to an approximate 20 to 25% increase in packed cell volume (64). Increases in red cell mass continue to increase even after erythropoietin returns to normal levels (64). However, the mechanism that underlies this continued increase is not known. This physiological adaptation to altitude is one of the reasons why many endurance athletes live at altitude and train at sea level.

Finally, as red cell volume increases, the blood's hemoglobin concentration will increase as well. This increase allows for a greater amount of oxygen to be carried per unit volume of blood. However, as red cell volume and hemoglobin concentration increase, the viscosity of the blood will also increase, presenting an inherent danger associated with these physiological adaptations that occur with altitude.

SUMMARY

In this chapter, the effect of acute exercise on cardiac function and how the heart will compensate for the increased energy demands of exercising muscles was discussed. This compensation is manifested by changes in cardiac output, regulated in part by enhanced sympathetic drive and increased venous return. In addition, blood flow is diverted from non-exercising muscles and non-essential organs to exercising muscles to provide for greater oxygen delivery. Differences in the acute cardiac response between endurance and resistance training programs were also reviewed. The coordinated relationship between the cardiovascular and respiratory systems and the effect both acute and prolonged training have on function was also discussed. In addition, the effects of prolonged training on both cardiovascular and respiratory adaptations were explored and a specific focus was placed on how these adaptations are dependent upon the type of training program employed. Finally, the effects of environmental stresses were also reviewed. Specific discussion was directed at acute exercise in the heat and at altitude with adaptation to prolonged exposure to altitude being briefly reviewed.

MAXING OUT

1   You are responsible for training a collegiate cross-country team in Park City, Utah, but most of the team members are traveling to southwest Georgia during the last few weeks of the summer break. The first competition of the cross-country season occurs in the second week of September. When do you advise your athletes to return to the mountains in Park City, and what physiological changes may happen when they are on vacation?

2   After an unusually hot and humid summer, one of your university age club level soccer players complains to you about having a higher heart rate than normal. After investigating this specific issue, you discover that many of the players have resting heart rates approximately ten beats higher than they did three months ago. What may have caused the problem and what methods will you employ to try to fix this problem?

3   You are the strength and conditioning coach for the junior Olympic (age 20 and under) track and field team. During an intense lifting session that consists of four sets of two to three repetitions of the dead lift, one of your throwing athletes loses consciousness. His teammates mention that his face turned very red during his final repetition of the third set. What was the likely cause of your athlete passing out in this manner?

REFERENCES

1.   Powers SK, Howley ET. *Exercise Physiology: Theory and Application to Fitness and Performance*, 10th ed. New York: McGraw-Hill. 2018; 224–255.

2.   Adamovich DR. *The Heart. Fundamentals of Electrocardiography, Exercise Physiology and Exercise Stress Testing.* Freeport, NY: Sports Medicine Books; 1984.

3.   Hurst JW. Naming of the waves in the ECG, with a brief account of their genesis. *Journal of the American Heart Association* 1998; 98;1937–1942.

4.   Dunbar C. *ECG Interpretation for the Clinical Exercise Physiologist.* Baltimore, MD: Lippincott Williams & Wilkins. 2009.

5.   Lewis SF, Taylor WF, Graham RM, et al. Cardiovascular responses to exercise as functions of absolute and relative work load. *J Appl Physiol* 1983; 54;1314–1323.

6.   Cunningham DA, Paterson DH, Blimkie CJ, et al. Development of cardiorespiratory function in circumpubertal boys: a longitudinal study. *J Appl Physiol* 1984; 56;302–307.

7.   Saltin B, Astrand PO. Maximal oxygen uptake in athletes. *J Appl Physiol* 1967; 23;353–358.

8.   Bonow RO. Left ventricular response to exercise. In: Fletcher GF, ed. *Cardiovascular Response to Exercise.* Mount Kisco, NY: Futura Publishing Co, Inc. 31–48. 1994.

9.   MacDougall JD. Blood pressure responses to resistive, static, and dynamic exercise. In: Fletcher GF, ed. *Cardiovascular Response to Exercise.* Mount Kisco, NY: Futura Publishing Co, Inc. 155–174. 1994.

10.   Toner MM, Glickman EL, McArdle WD. Cardiovascular adjustments to exercise distributed between the upper and lower body. *Med Sci Sports Exerc* 1990; 22;773–778.

11.   MacDougall JD, McKelvie RS, Moroz DE, et al. Factors affecting blood pressure response during heavy weightlifting and static contractions. *J Appl Physiol* 1992; 73;1590–1597.

12.   MacDougall JD, Tuxen D, Sale DG, et al. Arterial blood pressure response to heavy resistance exercise. *J Appl Physiol* 1985; 58;785–790.

13.   Sale DG, Moroz DE, McKelvie RS, et al. Effect of training on the blood pressure response to weight lifting. *Can J Appl Physiol* 1994; 19;60–74.

14.   McCartney N. Acute responses to resistance training and safety. *Med Sci Sports Exerc* 1999; 31;31–37.

15.   Lentini AC, McKelvie RS, McCartney N, et al. Assessment of left ventricular response of strength trained athletes during weightlifting exercise. *J Appl Physiol* 1993; 75;2703–2710.

16.   Wasserman K, Whipp BJ, Davis JA. Respiratory physiology of exercise: metabolism, gas exchange, and ventilatory control. *International Review of Physiology* 1981; 23;149–211.

17. Rowland TW, Green GM. Physiological responses to treadmill exercise in females: adult-child differences. *Med Sci Sports Exerc* 1988; 20;474–478.

18. McArdle WD, Glaser RM, Magel JR. Metabolic and cardiorespiratory response during free swimming and treadmill walking. *J Appl Physiol* 1971; 30;733–738.

19. Carroll JF, Convertino VA, Wood CE, et al. Effect of training on blood volume and plasma hormone concentrations in the elderly. *Med Sci Sports Exerc* 1995; 27;79–84.

20. Convertino VA, Keil LC, Bernauer EM, et al. Plasma volume, osmolality, vasopressin, and renin activity during graded exercise in man. *J Appl Physiol: Respiration Environmental Exercise Physiology* 1981; 50;123–128.

21. Pearson AC, Schiff M, Mrosek D, et al. Left ventricular diastolic function in weight lifters. *American Journal of Cardiology* 1986; 58;1254–1259.

22. Fleck SJ. Cardiovascular adaptations to resistance training. *Med Sci Sports Exerc* 1988; 20;S146–S151.

23. Blomqvist CG, Saltin B. Cardiovascular adaptations to physical training. *Annual Review of Physiology* 1983; 45;169–189.

24. Charlton GA, Crawford MH. Physiological consequences of training. *Cardiology Clinics* 1997; 15;345–354.

25. Schaefer ME, Allert JA, Adams HR, et al. Adrenergic responsiveness and intrinsic sinoatrial automaticity of exercise-trained rats. *Med Sci Sports Exerc* 1992; 24;887–894.

26. Seals DR, Hagberg JM. The effect of exercise training on human hypertension: a review. *Med Sci Sports Exerc* 1984; 16;207–215.

27. Fagard RH. Exercise characteristics and the blood pressure response to dynamic physical training. *Med Sci Sports Exerc* 2001; 33;S484–S492.

28. Goldberg L, Elliot DL, Kuehl KS. A comparison of the cardiovascular effects of running and weight training. *J Strength Cond Res* 1994; 8;219–224.

29. McCartney N, McKelvie RS, Martin J, et al. Weight-training-induced attenuation of the circulatory response of older males to weight lifting. *J Appl Physiol* 1993; 74;1056–1060.

30. Sale DG, Moroz DE, McKelvie RS, et al. Comparison of blood pressure response to isokinetic and weight-lifting exercise. *Eur J Appl Physiol* 1993; 67;115–120.

31. Fleck SJ, Kraemer WJ, 4th ed. *Designing Resistance Training Programs*. Champaign, IL: Human Kinetics. 2014.

32. Shapiro L. The morphological consequences of systemic training. *Cardiology Clinics* 1997; 15;373–379.

33. Ford LE. Heart size. *Circulatory Research* 1976; 39;299–303.

34. Spirito P, Pelliccia A, Proschan M, et al. Morphology of the "athlete's heart" assessed by echocardiography in 947 elite athletes representing 27 sports. *American Journal of Cardiology* 1994; 74;802–806.

35. Maron BJ. Structural features of the athletic heart as defined by echocardiography. *American Journal of Cardiology* 1986;7;190–203.

36. Morganroth J, Maron BJ, Henry WL, et al. Comparative left ventricular dimensions in trained athletes. *Annals of Internal Medicine* 1975; 82;521–524.

37. Pelliccia A, Maron BJ, Spataro A, et al. The upper limit of physiologic cardiac hypertrophy in highly trained elite athletes. *New England Journal of Medicine* 1991; 324;295–301.

38. Fleck SJ, Henke C, Wilson W. Cardiac MRI of elite junior Olympic weight lifters. *International Journal of Sports Medicine* 1989; 10;329–333.

39. Menapace FJ, Hammer, WJ, Ritzer TF et al. Left ventricular size in competitive weight lifters: an echocardiographic study. *Med Sci Sports Exerc* 1982; 14;72–75.

40. Kenney WL, Wilmore JH, Costill DL. *Physiology of Sport and Exercise*, 6th ed. Champaign, IL: Human Kinetics. 2015.

41. Girandola RN, Katch FL. Effects of physical training on ventilatory equivalent and respiratory exchange ratio during weight supported, steady-state exercise. *Eur J Appl Physiol Occup Physiol* 1976; 21;119–125.

42. Yerg II, JE, Seals DR, Hagberg JM, et al. Effect of endurance exercise training on ventilatory function in older individuals. *J Appl Physiol* 1985; 58;791–794.

43. Martin B, Heintzelman M, Chen HI. Exercise performance after ventilatory work. *J Appl Physiol* 1982; 52;1581–1585.

44. McArdle WD, Katch FI, Katch VL. *Exercise Physiology. Energy, Nutrition, and Human Performance*, 8th ed. Baltimore, MD: Williams & Wilkins. 253–456. 2014.

45. Convertion VA. Blood volume: its adaptation to endurance training. *Med Sci Sports Exerc* 1991; 23;1338–1348.

46. Yang RC, Mack GW, Wolfe RR, et al. Albumin synthesis after intense intermittent exercise in human subjects. *J Appl Physiol* 1998; 84;584–592.

47. Green HJ, Sutton J, Coates G, et al. Response of red cells and plasma volume to prolonged training in humans. *J Appl Physiol* 1991; 70;1810–1815.

48. Rowell LB. *Human Circulation Regulation during Physical Stress*. New York: Oxford University Press. 1986.

49. Sawka MN, Wenger CB, Young AJ, et al. Physiological responses to exercise in the heat. In: Marriott BM, ed. *Nutritional Needs in Hot Environments*. Washington, DC: National Academy Press. 55–74. 1993.

50. Sawka MN, Pandolf KB. Effects of body water loss on physiological function and exercise performance. In: Gisolfi CV, Lamb DR eds, *Fluid Homeostasis During Exercise. Perspectives in Exercise Science and Sports Medicine*. Vol 3. Indianapolis, IN: Benchmark Press. 1–38. 1990.

51. Nadel ER, Fortney SM, Wenger CB. Effect of hydration on circulatory and thermal regulation. *J Appl Physiol* 1980; 49;715–721.

52. Sawka MN, Knowlton RG, Critz JB. Thermal and circulatory responses to repeated bouts of prolonged running. *Med Sci Sports Exerc* 1979; 11;177–180.

53. Sproles CB, Smith DP, Byrd RJ, et al. Circulatory responses to submaximal exercise after dehydration and rehydration. *Journal of Sports Medicine and Physical Fitness* 1976; 16;98–105.

54. Vogel JA, Harris CW. Cardiopulmonary responses of resting man during early exposure to high altitude. *J Appl Physiol* 1967; 22;1124–1128.

55. Singh MV, Rawal SB, Tyagi AK. Body fluid status on induction, reinduction and prolonged stay at high altitude on human volunteers. *International Journal of Biometeorology* 1990; 34;93–97.

56. Wolfel EE, Groves BM, Brooks GA, et al. Oxygen transport during steady-state submaximal exercise in chronic hypoxia. *J Appl Physiol* 1991; 70;1129–1136.

57. Honig A. Role of arterial chemoreceptors in the reflex control of renal function and body fluid volumes in acute arterial hypoxia. In: Acher H, O'Regan RG, eds, *Physiology of the Peripheral Arterial Chemoreceptors*. 395–429. 1983.

58. West JB. Diffusing capacity of the lung for carbon monoxide at high altitude *J Appl Physiol* 1962; 17;421–426.

59. Ward MP, Milledge JS, West JB. *High Altitude Medicine and Physiology*. London: Chapman and Hall Medical. 1995.

60. Dempsey JA, Reddan WG, Birnbaum ML, et al. Effects of acute through life-long hypoxic exposure on exercise pulmonary gas exchange. *Respiration Physiology* 1971; 13;62–89.

61. Bartlett D, Remmers JE. Effects of high altitude exposure on the lungs of young rats. *Respiratory Physiology* 1971; 13;116–125.

62. Reeves JT, Groves BM, Sutton JR, et al. Operation Everest II: preservation of cardiac function at extreme altitude. *J Appl Physiol* 1987; 63;531–539.

63. Eckardt K, Boutellier U, Kurtz A, et al. Rate of erythropoietin formation in humans in response to acute hypobaric hypoxia. *J Appl Physiol* 1989; 66;1785–1788.

64. Milledge JS, Coates PM. Serum erythropoietin in humans at high altitude and its relation to plasma renin. *J Appl Physiol* 1985; 59;360–364.

Contents

CHAPTER 3

THE NEUROMUSCULAR SYSTEM

Jared W. Coburn, Travis W. Beck, Herbert A. deVries,
Terry J. Housh, Kristen C. Cochrane-Snyman, and Evan E. Schick

OBJECTIVES

After completing this chapter, you will be able to:

- Identify the structures in a neuron.
- Understand the feedback mechanisms of proprioception.
- Differentiate types of muscle fibers.
- Understand the timing of sliding filament theory of muscle contraction.
- Explain the neural and muscular adaptations to resistance training.

KEY TERMS

A band
Acetylcholine (Ach)
Actin
Action potentials
Adenosine diphosphate (ADP)
Adenosine triphosphate (ATP)
Afferent
Antagonist coactivation
Axon
Bilateral deficit
Concentric muscle action
Corpus striatum
Crossbridge recycling
Cross-education
Dendrites

Dynamic constant external resistance (DCER)
Eccentric muscle action
Efferent
Electromyography (EMG)
End bulb
Endolymph
Excitable membranes
Extrapyramidal system
H zone
Hyperplasia
Hypertrophy
I band
Intrafusal (IF) muscle fibers
Inverse myotatic reflex
Isokinetic muscle action
Isometric muscle actions

Lower motor neurons
Monosynaptic reflex
Motor endplate
Motor neuron
Motor nuclei
Myelin
Myofilaments
Myoneural junction
Myosin
Myosin ATPase
Myosin crossbridge
Myotatic
Neural adaptations
Neuromuscular junction
Neuron
Nodes of Ranvier
Peak torque

(continued)

(continued)

Power stroke	Red nucleus	Size principle
Proprioception	Reflex	Sliding-filament theory
Proprioceptive-cerebellar	Repetition maximum (RM)	Substantia nigra
system	Saltatory conduction	Synapse
Pyramidal system	Sarcomere	Transverse tubules
Pyramidal tracts	Sarcoplasmic	Tropomyosin
Rate coding	reticulum (SR)	Troponin
Rate of force	Satellite cells	Utricle
development (RFD)	Schwann cells	Vestibular receptors
Recruitment	Sensory	Z line

INTRODUCTION

The nervous system allows parts of the body to communicate rapidly with other parts of the body to regulate responses to internal and external stimuli. The nervous system can be divided anatomically into the central (brain and spinal cord) and peripheral (outside of the spinal cord) systems or functionally into the somatic (voluntary) and autonomic (involuntary) systems. The autonomic nervous system is composed of the sympathetic and parasympathetic systems, which control the involuntary functioning of various internal organs, the circulatory system (including vasoconstriction and vasodilation), and the endocrine glands. Voluntary human movement, however, is controlled by the somatic nervous system. When we decide to perform a muscle action, the electrical activity that eventually leads to muscle contraction originates in the motor cortex of the brain and travels through the central and peripheral systems to the muscle.

> The nervous system controls both voluntary and involuntary functions. Voluntary human movement is controlled by the somatic nervous system, while the involuntary functioning of internal organs, circulatory system, and endocrine glands is controlled by the autonomic nervous system.

THE NEURON

A nerve cell, or **neuron**, is the basic structural unit of the nervous system. Billions of neurons are in the nervous system; usually, several neurons are interconnected by **synapses** (junctions between neurons) to form pathways for conducting nervous impulses. The neurons that conduct sensory impulses from the periphery to the central nervous system are called **sensory** or **afferent** neurons. The neurons that conduct impulses from the central nervous system to the periphery are called **efferent** neurons, or **motor neurons** when directed at muscle. Although neurons are microscopic in diameter, one cell can be up to approximately 3 feet (1 m) in length, such as a motor neuron that extends from the spinal cord to a muscle of the foot.

The impulses directed from the central nervous system to the periphery and from the periphery to the central nervous system are transmitted via **action potentials**. Action potentials occur on **excitable membranes**, which are characterized by regions containing voltage-gated Na^+ and K^+ channels. An action potential is generated after the motor neuron cell body has reached its threshold for depolarization, which is usually approximately 15 mV greater than its resting membrane potential. A unique aspect of an action potential is that it has an "all-or-none" property. Thus, when an action potential is generated, the amplitude is constant, regardless of the magnitude of stimulus at the motor neuron cell body.

The typical motor neuron (Figure 3.1) includes a cell body, **dendrites** (which receive impulses and conduct them to the cell body), and an **axon** (which conducts the impulses, such as action potentials, away from the cell body). The cell body of the motor neuron,

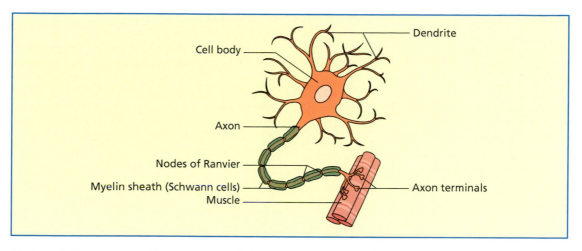

Figure 3.1 The neuron and its components. Each neuron consists of dendrites, a cell body, and an axon.

which innervates skeletal muscle, lies in the gray matter in the ventral horn of the spinal cord; its axon joins many axons from other motor neurons (and many sensory axons) to form a spinal nerve. Such a nerve is thick enough to be seen in gross dissection. From the ventral horn, the post synaptic motor neuron, which innervates skeletal muscle, branches and rebranches into many twigs, each of which innervates a single muscle fiber, also creating a motor unit, which will be discussed later.

One characteristic of many neurons is the presence of **myelin**, which surrounds the axon as a sheath. It is a fatty white substance produced by **Schwann cells** in the peripheral nervous system. Myelin functions as a powerful insulator, protecting the neuron from current (action potential) leakage across the membrane. In addition, due to its insulative properties, myelin reduces ion movement across the membrane and, therefore, conserves energy via reduced Na^+-K^+ ATPase pump activity. The myelin sheath is laid down in segments along the length of the axon, resulting in gaps called **nodes of Ranvier**. In myelinated axons, the velocity whereby the action potential is conducted is increased because it jumps from one node of Ranvier to the next. This is called **saltatory conduction**. Generally, the thicker the myelin sheath around an axon, the greater the conduction velocity of an action potential.

In addition to a greater conduction velocity due to axon myelination, the diameter of a neuron's axon has an effect on action potential propagation. As with neuron length, there are different axon diameters throughout the nervous system. Neurons with larger diameter axons also have increased conduction velocities compared to their smaller diameter counterparts. The conduction velocity across an axon increases by approximately the square root of the fiber diameter down which it travels.

> Neurons conduct electrical impulses to and from the central nervous system.

REFLEXES AND INVOLUNTARY MOVEMENTS

A **reflex** is most simply defined as an involuntary motor response to a given stimulus. An illustration is the automatic, unthinking leg extension response when a physician taps the patellar tendon with a rubber mallet. In this simplest form, a reflex consists of a discharge from a sensory (afferent) nerve ending, with the impulses traveling over the sensory nerve fiber to a synapse in the spinal cord with a motor (efferent) neuron. When the motor neuron is stimulated to discharge, impulses travel over its axon to the muscle, causing it to move. This simple reflex arc is called the **myotatic** or stretch reflex; because it involves only one synapse in the spinal cord, it is called a **monosynaptic reflex**. Other more complex reflexes (such as removing the hand from a hot surface) can involve multiple neurons and synapses.

> A reflex is an involuntary response to a given stimulus.

PROPRIOCEPTION AND KINESTHESIS

Optimal coordination of motor activity by the central nervous system depends on a constant supply of sensory feedback during the movement. This feedback of sensory information about movement and body position is called **proprioception**. The receptors for proprioception are of two types: vestibular and kinesthetic.

The **vestibular receptors** are found in the inner ear and respond to the movement of a fluid called **endolymph**. Indirectly, the inertia of the endolymph provides data to the brain regarding rotational acceleration or deceleration of movement, as in twisting or tumbling. Movement itself, however, is not recognized. For example, moving at almost the speed of sound in an airliner produces no sensation unless a change of direction or velocity occurs.

The vestibular system also includes an inner ear structure called the **utricle**, which provides data regarding positional sense. Specialized structures in the utricle respond to linear acceleration and tilting and thus are the source of data that inform us of our posture and orientation in space. For example, sensory information from the utricle is responsible for our ability to tell whether we are standing up or lying down, even with our eyes closed.

The kinesthetic or muscle sense is crucial to our ability to properly execute movement; it provides information about what our limbs or body segments are doing without our having to look. For example, most individuals have no difficulty touching their noses with their index fingers, even when blindfolded. Furthermore, one can usually make reasonably accurate guesses about the weight of an object by lifting it.

The two primary receptor structures that serve **kinesthesis** (sense of movement and body part location in space) are muscle spindles and Golgi tendon organs. Muscle spindles are large enough to be visible to the naked eye and are widely distributed throughout muscle tissue. Their distribution, however, varies from muscle to muscle. In general, muscles used for intricate movements (such as finger muscles) have many muscle spindles, while muscles involved primarily in gross movements have few.

In humans, each spindle includes from five to nine **intrafusal (IF) muscle fibers**. These IF fibers should not be confused with skeletal (extrafusal or EF) muscle fibers, which cause muscle contraction. The IF fibers of the muscle spindles are innervated by gamma motor neurons, while EF (skeletal) fibers are innervated by alpha motor neurons. Alpha motor neurons make up about 70% of the total efferent fibers; gamma motor neurons make up the remaining 30%. The structure of a muscle spindle is shown in Figure 3.2. It is important to note that the muscle spindles are oriented parallel to the EF fibers.

Because IF fibers lie lengthwise, parallel with the skeletal (EF) fibers, an externally applied stretch results in stretching the IF as well as the EF fibers. Thus, stretching results in a sensory afferent discharge from the muscle

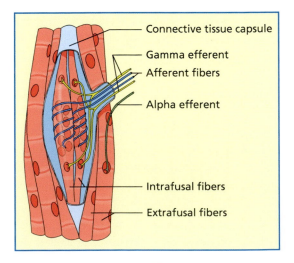

Figure 3.2 Muscle spindle. This sensory receptor is sensitive to stretch and helps to monitor muscle length.

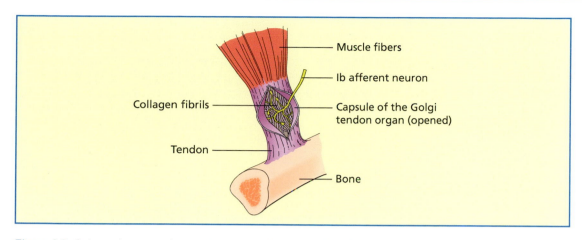

Figure 3.3 Golgi tendon organ. Located at the musculotendinous junction, this sensory receptor monitors tension.

spindles, which leads to contraction of the muscle that was stretched. This response underlies the stretch or myotatic reflex when a physician strikes the patellar tendon.

The Golgi tendon organ (Figure 3.3) is found in the musculotendinous junction and lies in series with the EF (skeletal) muscle fibers. Therefore, active shortening of the muscle (contraction) causes the Golgi tendon organ to discharge, while the muscle spindle discharges only when the muscle is stretched. The muscle spindle ceases to fire when contraction begins because it is in parallel with the EF muscle fibers and is thus unloaded as soon as the EF fibers shorten in contraction.

The primary functional difference between the muscle spindle and the Golgi tendon organ is that the muscle spindle facilitates contraction, whereas the Golgi tendon organ inhibits contraction, not only in the muscle of origin but also in the entire functional muscle group. Thus, the Golgi tendon organ may provide a protective mechanism that prevents damage to muscle tissue or a joint during extreme contractions. The activity of the Golgi tendon organ that prevents overstressing the tissues is called the **inverse myotatic reflex**.

> Proprioception involves sensory feedback about movement and body position. Kinesthesis is sometimes called muscle sense and involves the functions of muscle spindles and Golgi tendon organ.

HIGHER NERVE CENTERS AND VOLUNTARY MUSCULAR CONTROL

Voluntary muscular activity is controlled by three primary systems: the **pyramidal system**, the **extrapyramidal system**, and the **proprioceptive-cerebellar system**.

REAL-WORLD APPLICATION

The physiology of stretching

It has been theorized that stretching can improve performance and prevent injury. It is also important, however, to consider how to stretch. Specifically, we must consider the effect of the muscle spindle on flexibility and stretching.

(continued)

(continued)

A muscle that is stretched rapidly with a jerky motion will respond by contracting. The magnitude and rate of this contraction vary directly with the magnitude and rate of the movement that causes the rapid stretch. This contraction is a result of the myotatic or stretch reflex. The rapidly applied stretch causes activation of the muscle spindles located between the skeletal (extrafusal) muscle fibers. This rapid stretch causes an afferent impulse to be carried by a sensory neuron to the spinal cord, where the neuron synapses with a motor neuron. The motor neuron then carries an impulse back to the skeletal muscle, causing it to contract. The important point is that if, in an attempt to stretch the muscle, the stretch is applied with a bouncing, jerky motion, the result is activation of the myotatic reflex and a contraction of the very muscle that is the object of the attempted stretch. This can lead to less than optimal stretching at best and injury at worst.

Static stretching, on the other hand, in which the stretch is applied slowly, does not invoke the myotatic reflex. By moving slowly into the stretched position, activation of the muscle spindles is avoided. This allows the muscle to relax while being elongated, leading to a more effective stretch.

The pyramidal system

Electrical stimulation and clinical observations have been used to identify the functions of the various parts of the cerebral cortex. The most commonly used architectural map of the human cortex that relates location to function is that of Brodmann (Figure 3.4).

The **pyramidal system** originates in large "pyramid-shaped" neurons found mainly in area 4, often called the motor cortex, of the Brodmann map. The axons of the motor neurons with cell bodies in area 4 form large descending motor pathways, called **pyramidal tracts**, that go directly (in most cases) to synapses with the motor neurons in the ventral horn of the spinal cord. The neurons with cell bodies in the brain are called **upper motor neurons**, while those in the spinal cord are called **lower motor neurons**. Approximately 85% or more of the neurons of the pyramidal tract cross from one side to the other (decussate), some at the level of the medulla, others at the level of the lower motor neuron. The motor cortex is oriented by movement, not by muscle. That is, stimulation of the motor cortex results not in a twitch of one muscle but in a smooth synergistic movement of a group of muscles.

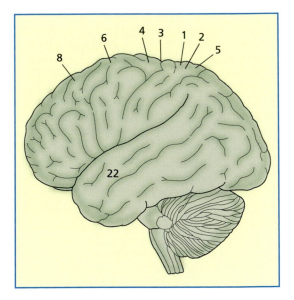

Figure 3.4 The areas of the human cerebral cortex involved in the pyramidal and extrapyramidal systems. The pyramidal system originates mainly in area 4 (motor cortex) of the brain and controls specific, voluntary movements. The extrapyramidal system (mainly area 6, but also areas 1 to 3, 5, and 8) is concerned with large, general movement patterns and posture control. In the temporal lobe, area 22 is concerned with the extrapyramidal pathways.

The extrapyramidal system

The **extrapyramidal system**, or the premotor cortex, originates primarily in area 6 of Brodmann's map. Some of the fibers descending in the extrapyramidal tracts, however, originate in other areas of the cortex, such as areas 1, 2, 3, 5, and 8.

The descending tracts from the premotor cortex are more complex than those from the motor cortex. These neurons do not synapse directly with the lower motor neurons but travel through relay stations called **motor nuclei**. The most important motor nuclei are the **corpus striatum**, **substantia nigra**, and **red nucleus**. Some neurons, however, also go by way of the pons to the cerebellum.

Important functional differences exist between the pyramidal and extrapyramidal systems. For example, electrical stimulation of area 4 produces specific movements, while stimulation of area 6 produces only gross movement patterns. Thus, it is likely that learning a new skill in which conscious attention must be devoted to the movements (as in learning a new gymnastic move, where every aspect of the movement is contemplated) involves area 4. As an individual becomes more skilled, the origin of the movement is thought to shift to area 6 (often, gymnasts do not have to concentrate on their feet but rather on very general patterns of movement). Area 4, however, still participates as a relay station, with fibers connecting area 6 to area 4.

The proprioceptive-cerebellar system

Kinesthesis and the vestibular system involve the sensory functions of the **proprioceptive-cerebellar system**. Typically, the pathway associated with vestibular proprioception leads directly or indirectly (via the medulla) to the cerebellum. Conscious sensory knowledge of movement from kinesthesis, however, travels via the thalamus, cortex, and cerebellum. The cerebellum is central to the gathering of sensory information on position, balance, and movement. The cerebellum receives sensory information from muscles, joints, tendons,

and skin as well as visual and auditory feedback. Thus, the loss of cerebellar function can lead to the impairment of volitional movements, disturbances of posture, and impaired balance control.

> Three primary systems control voluntary human movement: the pyramidal system, the extrapyramidal system, and the proprioceptive-cerebellar system.

GROSS STRUCTURE OF SKELETAL MUSCLE

A skeletal muscle is covered by a connective tissue sheath called the **epimysium**, which lies beneath the skin, subcutaneous adipose tissue, and superficial fascia. The epimysium merges with the connective tissue of the tendon, which allows the force produced by muscular contraction to be transmitted through the

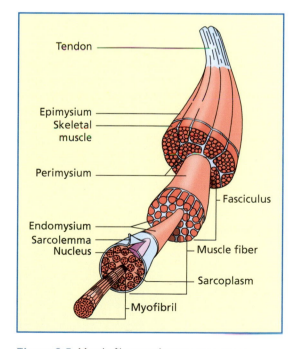

Figure 3.5 Muscle fibers and connective tissue sheaths. Each fiber, fasciculus, and whole muscle is surrounded by connective tissues called endomysium, perimysium, and epimysium, respectively.

connective tissues to the tendon and bone, resulting in movement.

Skeletal muscle cells or muscle fibers are oriented in bundles called fasciculi. Each fasciculus, which contains from a few muscle fibers to several hundred, is surrounded by a connective tissue sheath called the perimysium. Figure 3.5 illustrates these and other gross and microscopic structures of skeletal muscle.

> The gross structures of skeletal muscle are important for transducing the force of muscular contraction to the tendon and bone, resulting in movement.

MICROSCOPIC STRUCTURE OF SKELETAL MUSCLE

Surrounding each muscle fiber is a delicate connective tissue sheath known as the **endomysium**. Thus, the endomysium surrounds a single fiber, the perimysium surrounds a fasciculus, and the epimysium surrounds the whole muscle. The force produced within a muscle fiber is transferred in series to the endomysium, perimysium, epimysium, tendon, and then bone.

The diameter of individual muscle fibers may vary from approximately 10 to 100 μm (1,000 μm = 1 mm), while the length may range from 1 mm to the length of the whole muscle. The thickness of the fiber is related to the amount of force that the fiber can produce, and each muscle has fibers of characteristic size. For example, the eye muscles have fibers with a small diameter, while the fibers of the quadriceps femoris muscles are large.

Structure of the muscle fiber

Each skeletal muscle fiber is surrounded by a cell membrane known as the **sarcolemma**. Situated just inside the sarcolemma are many nuclei which direct protein synthesis within the cell. The fluid part, or cytoplasm, of the muscle cell is known as the **sarcoplasm**. Much of the sarcoplasm is occupied by column-like structures known as myofibrils. Alternating light and dark bands run the length of the myofibrils. The strict alignment of these bands

from one myofibril to another is what gives the muscle fiber its characteristic striated appearance under the light microscope.

> Muscle fibers may vary greatly in size and length yet have the same structures (i.e., cell membrane, cytoplasm) as other cells in the body.

Muscle fiber types

For nearly 200 years, scientists have recognized the heterogeneity of fiber types within skeletal muscle. To this day, a full appreciation for the assorted fiber types continues to evolve alongside developing identification and classification technologies. In the early 19th century, fiber color served as the basis by which scientists distinguished between muscle fiber types. Fibers appearing red were considered to be well suited for endurance activities, exhibiting remarkable fatigue resistance, whereas white fibers, considered to be specialized for high velocity and high force contraction, were susceptible to fatigue (63). Differences in intracellular levels of iron appear to account for the differences in color. Compared to white fibers, red fibers contain more myoglobin, an iron-containing oxygen transport protein which, along with imparting their red color, is partially responsible for their fatigue resistance (59). The technological age of the past half-century has given way to more modern methodological approaches to fiber type identification, allowing researchers to discriminate between the various fiber types based not only on their appearance, but also their mechanical, biochemical, and histochemical properties.

Though recent evidence indicates humans may display as many as eight different muscle fiber types, a consensus still supports the existence of three predominant fiber types (13). However, the older white versus red fiber-type classification system has become inadequate, since there are two subtypes of white fibers that are mechanically, biochemically, and histochemically different. Thus, in 1972, Peter et al. proposed a system that classified the three predominant muscle fiber types based on their mechanical and biochemical properties (62). According to this system, those primary fiber types in human skeletal muscle are slow-twitch oxidative (SO), fast-twitch oxidative

TABLE 3.1 Characteristics of muscle fiber types

Nomenclature			
Older systems	Red slow-twitch (ST)	White fast-twitch (FT)	
Dubowitz and Brooke	Type I	Type IIA	Type IIB
Peter et al.	Slow, oxidative (SO)	Fast, oxidative glycolytic (FOG)	Fast, glycolytic (FG)
Myosin heavy chain (MHC) content	Type I	Type IIA	Type IIX
Characteristics			
Speed of contraction	Slow	Fast	Fast
Strength of contraction	Low	High	High
Fatigability	Fatigue resistant	Fatigable	Most fatigable
Aerobic capacity	High	Medium	Low
Anaerobic capacity	Low	Medium	High
Size	Small	Large	Large
Capillary density	High	High	Low

glycolytic (FOG), and fast-twitch glycolytic (FG) (62). SO fibers possess a slow, fatigue resistant, low force twitch when stimulated with an electrical impulse and favor oxidative (aerobic) means of energy production; FOG fibers have a fast, high force twitch with intermediate fatigue resistance and are adept in both oxidative and glycolytic (anaerobic) forms of energy production; FG fibers are the fastest, highest force, yet most fatigable and favor glycolytic energy production. Table 3.1 compares the naming systems and lists the characteristics of muscle fiber types.

Developments in protein analysis techniques have continued to evolve fiber type nomenclature. Cutting edge protein identification and quantification methods reveal that the specific myosin heavy chain (MyHC) isoform expressed within a muscle fiber drives its unique biochemical and mechanical properties (Figure 3.6). Heavy chain protein, the largest sub unit of myosin, composes both its tail and head region and confers motor activity through its interaction with ATPase. The specific isoform of MyHC expressed in a muscle fiber determines the activity level of ATPase and, hence, the rate and force of contraction. In order of increasing ATPase activity and fatigability, the three distinct MyHC isoforms are: I, IIa and IIx (48). Furthermore, the heavy chain isoforms are encoded by the *MYH* genes: *MYH7* codes MyHC I, *MYH2* codes MyHC IIa, and *MHY1* codes MyHC IIx (8). Those fibers expressing MyHC I are referred to as type I muscle fibers, exhibiting the biochemical and mechanical

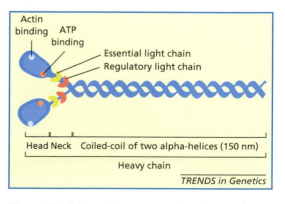

Figure 3.6 Schematic representation of a myosin filament: blue, the two coiled heavy chains, each containing an ATP and actin binding site in their heads.

properties of SO fibers (31). Type IIa muscle fibers express MyHC IIa and are FOG while type IIx fibers express MHC IIx and are FG. Thus, a more contemporary fiber classification scheme in humans is type I, IIa, and IIx. Not surprisingly, MyHC expression has been shown to be important for determining its performance in strength/power activities (67).

> The basic functional unit of the neuromuscular system is the motor unit, which consists of a motor neuron (nerve) and all the muscle fibers it innervates. All of the fibers within a particular motor unit are of the same type, although the fibers from different motor units are intermingled within the muscle belly. In small muscles, a single motor unit may consist of only a few fibers; in large muscles, each motor unit may comprise several hundred fibers.

The patterns of fiber type distribution in various muscles are related to the function(s) of the muscle. For example, postural muscles must be fatigue-resistant and therefore are usually composed mainly of type I fibers. In contrast, the ocular muscles do not contract for extended periods and therefore consist primarily of type IIa and IIx fibers. While muscles in non-athlete populations typically display a 1:1 ratio of type 1 to type IIa/x fibers, the same muscles in elite endurance or sprint/power athletes may display extreme patterns of fiber-type distribution (15). In fact, type 1 fiber composition may reach 60–70% in middle distance runners and nearly 90–95% in long endurance athletes. Conversely, elite weightlifters and powerlifters may exhibit 50% more type II fibers than endurance athletes, while type II composition in sprinters can reach 80% (1,9,32,77). Although each individual's fiber-type distribution pattern is genetically determined prior to adulthood, recent evidence (discussed below in 'Muscle fiber type transitioning') sheds light on the fascinating plasticity of muscle fibers.

Structure of the myofibril and the contractile mechanism

The **sarcomere** is the functional unit of the myofibril (Figure 3.7). It extends from one **Z line** to an adjacent Z line. The sarcomere comprises two **myofilaments** (contractile proteins), **myosin**, and **actin**, which lie parallel to one another. The myosin filament is approximately twice as thick as the actin filament and defines the length of the **A band**. It is the A band that forms the dark part of the striation effect. The actin filaments are longer than the myosin filaments and extend inward from the Z lines toward the center of the sarcomere. Within the A band is a lighter region known as the **H zone**, the area of the A band that does not contain actin filaments. The **I band** is the area between the ends of the myosin filaments. Because it is less dense than the A band, the I band is also lighter in color. These alternating areas of greater and lesser optical density are what give skeletal muscle its characteristic "striped" or "striated" appearance.

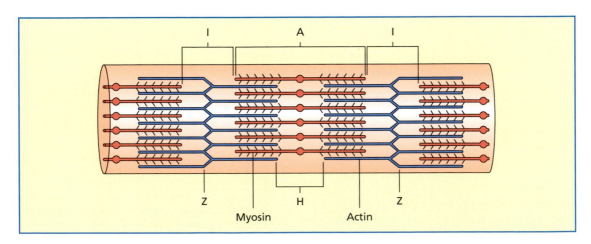

Figure 3.7 A sarcomere extends from Z line to Z line. The sarcomere is the functional unit of the myofibril.

THE SLIDING-FILAMENT THEORY OF MUSCLE CONTRACTION

The **sliding-filament theory** has been used to describe the mechanics of muscle contraction. It states the following:

1 Voluntary muscle contraction is initiated in the cortex of the brain.
2 Typically, the electrical current, or **action potential**, travels via an upper **motor neuron** and synapses with a lower motor neuron in the ventral horn of the spinal cord.
3 The action potential passes along to the end of a lower motor neuron (**end bulb**) and causes the release of the stimulatory neurotransmitter **acetylcholine (Ach)**. The intersection between a lower motor neuron and a muscle fiber is called the **myoneural junction**, or **neuromuscular junction**.
4 The Ach is released into a small gap between the motor neuron and the muscle fiber called the **synapse**. The Ach then binds to receptor sites on the muscle fiber membrane at a location called the **motor endplate**.
5 The binding of Ach with the receptors at the motor endplate causes an action potential to spread along the muscle fiber's sarcolemma.
6 The action potential travels along the sarcolemma and down channels that lead into the muscle fiber, called **transverse tubules**, or t tubules.
7 The action potential travels down the t tubules and intersects an intracellular structure called the **sarcoplasmic reticulum (SR)**. One function of the SR is to store calcium. When stimulated by the action potential, the SR releases calcium into the fiber's sarcoplasm.
8 The calcium binds to a protein called **troponin**, which is bound to another protein called **tropomyosin**. Under resting conditions, the contractile proteins actin and myosin are separated by the presence of tropomyosin. The binding of calcium to troponin changes the shape of the tropomyosin molecule and uncovers the binding sites on the actin molecule. Figure 3.8 illustrates these contractile proteins.
9 The myosin head then attaches to the binding site on the actin molecule, forming

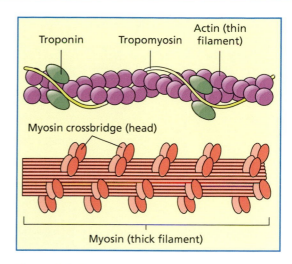

Figure 3.8 Contractile proteins actin, myosin, troponin, and tropomyosin. The interaction of myosin (thick filament) and actin (thin filament) allows muscle contraction to take place.

a **myosin crossbridge**. Prior to attaching to actin, the myosin head is "energized," storing the energy released from the breakdown of **adenosine triphosphate (ATP)** to **adenosine diphosphate (ADP)** and inorganic phosphate (Pi). Once attached to actin, the myosin crossbridge releases Pi and uses its stored energy to attempt to pull the actin filament toward the center of the sarcomere. This pulling action is referred to as a **power stroke**. Whether or not it is successful at shortening the sarcomere depends on the amount of force generated as well as the external force which opposes the crossbridges.

10 Once the myosin crossbridge has pulled actin and swiveled toward the center of the sarcomere, it releases ADP. A new ATP molecule then binds to the myosin head and causes the actin/myosin bond to be broken. After detaching, the enzyme **myosin ATPase** causes the splitting of the ATP molecule. This once again energizes the myosin head. This allows the myosin crossbridge to return to the upright position, attach to another actin binding site, and begin the contraction process again. This repeating process is called **crossbridge recycling**. Figure 3.9 summarizes the sliding-filament theory of muscle contraction.

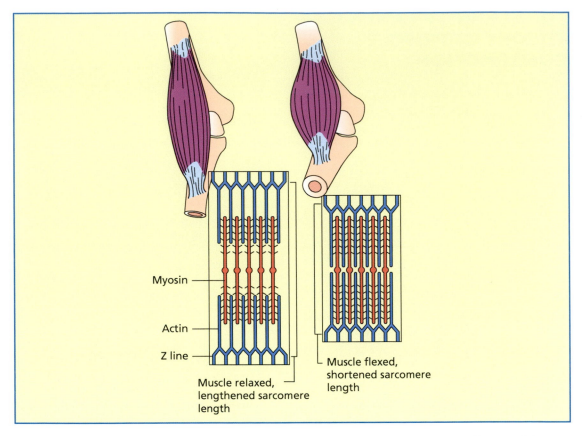

Myosin

Actin

Z line

Muscle relaxed, lengthened sarcomere length

Muscle flexed, shortened sarcomere length

Figure 3.9 The sliding-filament theory of muscle contraction. This theory proposes that the filaments slide past each other during muscle contraction without themselves changing in length.

> Muscle contraction is initiated by the central nervous system and generated at the molecular level through interaction of the contractile proteins actin and myosin.

GRADATION OF FORCE

Gradation of muscular force is achieved by varying the number of motor units activated, or motor unit **recruitment**, and by changes in the firing frequency of the active motor units, or **rate coding** (Figure 3.10). The recruitment of motor units generally follows what is called the **size principle**, according to which increasingly forceful contractions are achieved by the recruitment of progressively larger motor units. Smaller motor units are typically composed of SO fibers and have the lowest stimulus thresholds for contraction. Thus, smaller motor units are active during low-intensity contractions. Increasingly forceful contractions, however, require the recruitment of larger motor units containing fast-twitch fibers. In addition, active motor units can produce greater force by firing at higher frequencies (firing rates). The relative contributions of recruitment or firing rate to increasing force production vary from muscle to muscle. In general, large muscles with mixed fiber types, such as the quadriceps, tend to rely on recruitment to a greater degree than do small muscles, such as those in the hands, which rely more on rate coding.

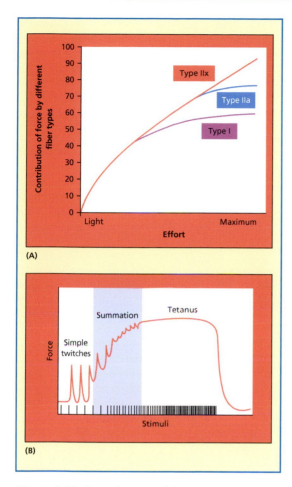

Figure 3.10 Contributions of A. motor unit recruitment and B. firing rate to force production. The nervous system uses these two methods to vary the force production of whole muscles.

Muscle force is modulated through two mechanisms: motor unit recruitment and rate coding. The relative contributions of these two mechanisms to force production vary in different muscles.

TYPES OF MUSCLE ACTIONS

The term *muscle contraction* implies muscle shortening. Muscles, however, can produce force while shortening, lengthening, or maintaining a given length. The term *muscle action* is therefore more accurate and descriptive. Muscle action types include isometric, **dynamic constant external resistance (DCER)**, isokinetic, concentric, and eccentric muscle actions.

Isometric muscle actions

Isometric muscle actions involve the production of force without movement at the joint or shortening of the muscle fibers. Even in sports characterized by dynamic movements, these muscle actions are important to stabilize joints or to resist an opponent. Isometric strength is joint angle–specific owing to varying degrees of overlap of the actin and myosin filaments as well as other biomechanical factors. In comparing isometric strength between individuals, the joint angle at which the isometric muscle action is performed is an important consideration.

Dynamic constant external resistance muscle actions

The muscle actions that occur during the lifting of free weights have traditionally been referred to as isotonic muscle actions. During a true isotonic muscle action, a muscle generates a constant amount of force throughout a range of motion. Force production by a muscle, however, rarely remains constant as the joint angle changes. Thus, the term dynamic constant external resistance (DCER) muscle actions more accurately describes the muscle actions occurring during this type of movement. Although the weight being lifted remains constant (constant external resistance) with changes in the joint angle, the force produced by the muscle is changing, or dynamic.

DCER strength is usually expressed in terms of a **repetition maximum (RM)** load. An RM load is the maximum amount of weight that can be lifted for a specified number of repetitions. For example, a 1RM load is the maximum amount of weight that can be lifted through the full range of motion for only one repetition, whereas a 6RM load is the maximum amount of weight that can be lifted for six repetitions but not seven. Typically, DCER strength testing involves a trial-and-error procedure where progressively heavier weights are attempted until the 1RM is determined. Because strength is joint angle–specific, DCER strength is limited by the weakest point in the range of motion; therefore, the 1RM load is the maximum weight that can be lifted at the weakest point in the range of motion.

Isokinetic muscle actions

An **isokinetic muscle action** is a dynamic movement that occurs at a constant velocity. Typically, isokinetic muscle actions are performed on a dynamometer, a device that accommodates the counterresistance based on the amount of torque being produced. This allows movement to occur at a constant velocity regardless of torque production. Isokinetic strength testing has advantages over both isometric and DCER testing because, during a maximal isokinetic muscle action, maximum torque (**peak torque**) is produced throughout the entire range of motion.

Concentric and eccentric muscle actions

A **concentric muscle action** occurs when a muscle produces torque (technically, the muscle produces force, resulting in torque around the joint) and shortens. When a muscle lengthens while producing torque, it is performing an **eccentric muscle action**. Both DCER and isokinetic muscle actions can be performed concentrically and eccentrically (Figure 3.11). The force produced concentrically decreases as velocity increases. When the velocity of a concentric muscle action is low, both slow- and fast-twitch fibers contribute to force production; at higher velocities, the

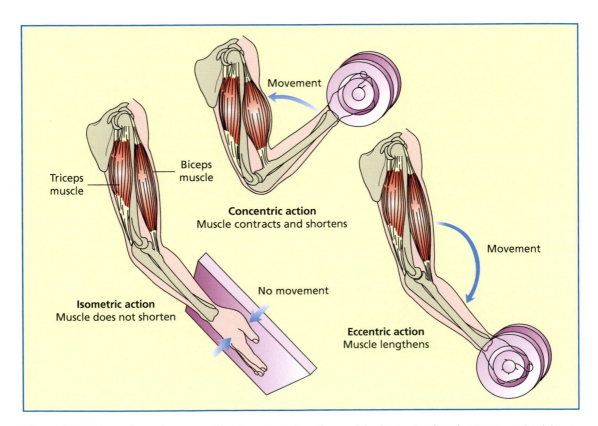

Figure 3.11 Types of muscle actions. Muscle may produce force while shortening, lengthening, or maintaining a constant length.

rate of muscle shortening is too great for the slow-twitch fibers to contribute to torque production. Because the slow-twitch fibers are "unloaded" at high velocities, fewer muscle fibers contribute to torque production; therefore, torque is decreased. On the other hand, eccentric strength changes little with increased velocity. During eccentric muscle actions, the myosin crossbridges are pulled apart from the actin molecules. In theory, the amount of force necessary to pull the myosin heads from the actin molecules is independent of the velocity.

> The three types of muscle action are isometric, dynamic constant external resistance (DCER), and isokinetic. Isokinetic and DCER muscle actions may be performed either concentrically or eccentrically.

NEUROMUSCULAR ADAPTATIONS TO RESISTANCE TRAINING

The following discussion focuses on neuromuscular changes resulting from prolonged resistance training.

Muscular strength adaptations

Training can lead to strength gains, regardless of the mode of resistance (30). Isometric, isokinetic, variable resistance, and DCER programs are all effective at eliciting strength gains assuming scientific principles of program design are applied. Strength gains, however, tend to be sensitive to the mode of training. For example, isometric training leads to greater gains in isometric strength than isokinetic strength (30). Even within a specific mode of training, there can be specificity. For example, in training with isokinetic muscle actions, greater gains in muscular strength tend to occur at velocities closest to the training velocity (16). Thus, specificity of training must be considered if the goal of a resistance training program is to transfer the newly developed strength to other activities, such as sport, recreational, or occupational pursuits.

> Strength gains resulting from resistance training tend to be specific to the type of training performed.

In terms of the absolute weight lifted, men tend to be stronger than women. This is because men are usually bigger and have more muscle mass. Women tend to be about 40% to 50% as strong as men in upper body movements and 50% to 80% as strong in lower body movements (30). When strength is expressed relative to muscle cross-sectional area, however, there are no sex-related differences in muscular strength (44) (Figure 3.12). Thus, for a given amount of muscle, men and women produce the same amount of force (54).

> The quality of muscle is the same for men and women. In addition, men and women respond to resistance training in a similar manner.

For many athletes, the ability to develop force rapidly is as important, if not more so, as developing maximal force. It usually takes in excess of 0.3 to 0.4 seconds to generate

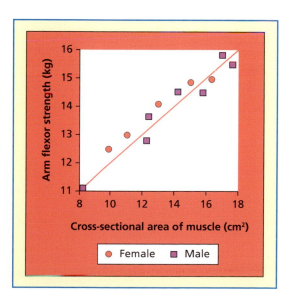

Figure 3.12 Muscle strength per unit of cross-sectional area of human muscle. There is no qualitative difference in strength per unit of muscle size between the genders.

maximal force (78). Because time is limited during many sport activities (i.e., 0.22 to 0.27 seconds during shot putting and 0.101 to 0.108 seconds during sprinting) (47,52), however, the activated muscles must exert as much force as possible in a short time. This capability can be measured by determining the **rate of force development (RFD)**. Performing "power" or "explosive" training exercises (plyometrics, cleans, pulls, weighted jumps, sprinting, etc.) can increase the RFD (37,64).

Muscle fiber adaptations

Resistance training typically results in increases in muscle size and strength. These adaptations may be partially explained by muscle fiber adaptations.

Hypertrophy and hyperplasia

Perhaps the most obvious adaptation to resistance training is enlargement of the trained muscles. Growth in muscle size can result from an increase in the size of existing muscle fiber (**hypertrophy**) or an increase in the number of muscle fibers (**hyperplasia**).

Substantial evidence supports muscle fiber hypertrophy as the primary mechanism of increasing muscle size (69) (Figure 3.13). This increase is primarily due to an increase in the number and size of actin and myosin

filaments (33). The actin and myosin filaments are added to the periphery of the myofibrils, resulting in enlargement of existing myofibrils. Once the myofibril reaches a critical size, it splits, yielding two or more daughter myofibrils (33). Although both slow- and fast-twitch fibers increase in size, the fast-twitch fibers appear to be more responsive to resistance training (33,46). The precise mechanism by which training leads to muscular adaptations is unknown, but it appears to be a complex interplay between mechanical, metabolic, and hormonal factors (18,19,20).

The role of **satellite cells** has been suggested to be a contributing factor to muscle growth in human and animal subjects in response to exercise and training (10). Satellite cells are precursor cells, like stem cells, which donate new myonuclei to a developing muscle fiber and are important for muscle development and regeneration. It has been suggested that these cells contribute to postnatal muscle growth in humans in response to both acute exercise and chronic training. The mechanism by which these cells are reactivated is thought to lie with a developmental gene which signals the satellite cells to re-enter the cell cycle and multiply. Although resistance training has been shown to be a potent stimulator of satellite cells (25,53), endurance exercise also has the capability of activating them (12). After acute periods of post-damaging (eccentric) exercise, satellite cells are likely involved

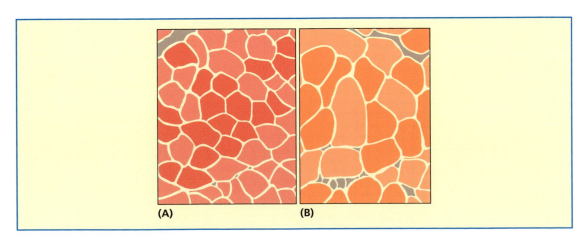

Figure 3.13 Muscle hypertrophy following resistance training. (A) pretraining; (B) posttraining. Hypertrophy results from an increased content of contractile protein (actin and myosin) in muscle.

in the repair and regeneration of damaged myofibrils, while at the end of chronic training (resistance or endurance), they appear as part of the adaptive remodeling of muscle, i.e., the hypertrophic response.

Although there is strong evidence supporting the role of satellite cells in mechanisms underlying hypertrophy, they may also play a part in regeneration, or hyperplasia, which would have important clinical applications. Evidence from studies of laboratory animals suggests that hyperplasia may contribute to resistance training–induced increases in muscle size (4,34). In regard to humans, there is conflicting information (22,74) but the general consensus is that evidence for hyperplasia is inconclusive, and therefore, may be of little significance (30). Thus, in humans, hypertrophy primarily accounts for the training-induced increase in muscle size.

It has been suggested that eccentric muscle actions are necessary to induce muscle hypertrophy. Hypertrophy, however, can occur following concentric-only training (42), suggesting that hypertrophy does not require eccentric muscle actions. Nonetheless, numerous studies have suggested that eccentric muscle actions may be more effective for inducing hypertrophy than concentric muscle actions (28). As with exercise action, accepted recommendations for inducing hypertrophy via resistance training programs have called for heavy loads, i.e., 67–85% 1RM (35). However, recent investigations have shown similar manifestations of hypertrophy from resistance exercise performed to failure at 30% 1RM and at 80–90% 1RM in both the upper and lower body (55,60). With regard to sexes, women respond to resistance training much like men (40). Although the absolute gains in muscle size are greater in men, the percentage increases are similar for the two sexes (11,21).

> Hypertrophy is the primary mechanism by which muscles increase in size.

Muscle fiber transitioning

As mentioned earlier, skeletal muscle fibers exhibit tremendous plasticity, i.e., ability to transition between types, in response to exercise training. Indeed, a wide range of research indicates that light and heavy resistance as well as aerobic training elicit rapid shifts in myosin heavy chain isoform expression from type IIx to type IIa (7,46,68,70,71). However, to date, most research has failed to show the existence of training-induced intertype transitioning, that is, type IIa to type I transitions and vice versa. Although limited, evidence on the subject suggests that if intertype transitioning is possible, high velocity training may promote type I to II transitioning and that sprint training may stimulate a consolidation of both type I and type IIx fibers to type IIa fibers (5,26,50,61). Interestingly, inactivity and unloading has been shown to induce a type I to type IIx transition (6,41,72). Research into the magnitude of muscle plasticity is still in its infancy, yet the current body of knowledge poses an intriguing question: How important to athletic performance is genetic fiber-type endowment in the face of training induced fiber plasticity?

Q&A FROM THE FIELD

The head coach of our women's volleyball team is hesitant to implement a resistance training program for our team. He doesn't believe that female athletes can gain strength and muscle size, like male athletes can. My previous experience is with conditioning male athletes. Is it true that females are less trainable than males when it comes to resistance training?
—Undergraduate student intern

There is every reason to believe that female athletes will adapt to resistance training in a manner similar to male athletes. The typical female athlete will be smaller, weaker, and have less muscle mass than her male counterpart. Her gains in size and strength will also be less than those of the male if expressed on an absolute basis, i.e., weight lifted in pounds. When size and strength gains are expressed as a percentage increase relative to initial values, however, the female will experience gains that are comparable to those of her male counterpart. Female muscle is of the same quality as male muscle and is just as trainable.

Nervous system adaptations

Although muscles produce force, it is the nervous system that provides for the activation of muscle tissue. It is not surprising, therefore, that resistance training programs lead to adaptations in both the nervous and muscular systems.

Evidence of neural adaptations

Several pieces of evidence point to the role of **neural adaptations** in resistance training. For example, increases in muscular strength may occur without accompanying increases in muscular size (38). If there is no increase in the size of the muscle fibers producing force, the logical conclusion is that adaptations within the nervous system are responsible for the observed strength gains.

It has been shown that the early gains in strength following initiation of a resistance training program often occur in the absence of muscle hypertrophy (56). Previously untrained subjects may have difficulty in fully activating their motor units, and strength gains resulting from the first several weeks of resistance training have been attributed to learning to recruit those units (56). Although neural adaptations are often associated with the early phase of resistance training (56), one study found that two years of training led to significant increases in strength and power despite minimal changes in muscle fiber size in competitive Olympic weightlifters (38). Weightlifters compete within body-weight categories and often want to develop increased strength without changes in muscle mass that might lead to changes in body weight (30). Thus, neural adaptations are an essential mechanism of strength increase among these athletes.

> Early gains in strength are due to neural factors, while long-term gains in strength are primarily due to hypertrophy.

Performing resistance training with one limb can lead to strength increases in the untrained limb on the opposite (contralateral) side of the body (27,48,57,79). This phenomenon is known as the **cross-education** or cross-training effect. The strength gain in the untrained limb is typically equal to or less than 60% of that in the trained limb (79). The cross-education effect demonstrates specificity of training. For example, unilateral resistance training for one leg will increase the strength of the contralateral leg but not the contralateral arm. There is also specificity regarding muscle action type. Training with concentric muscle actions leads to greater gains in the untrained limb when tested concentrically rather than eccentrically (79). Theories to explain this cross-education effect include (i) the concept that unilateral resistance training may activate neural circuits that modify motor pathways projecting to the opposite untrained limb, or (ii) that unilateral resistance training induces adaptations in motor areas that are primarily involved in the control of movements of the trained limb, but that may be accessed when activating the untrained limb. The latter would involve modification of neural circuits in ways similar to those that occur with motor learning (48). Whatever the mechanism for the cross-education effect, the site of the adaptation to training involves the brain and/or the spinal cord.

Force measured with both limbs concurrently (bilaterally) is typically less than the sum of the force developed by each limb independently (unilaterally) (17) (Figure 3.14). This **bilateral deficit** may be the result of less activation to each muscle group during bilateral

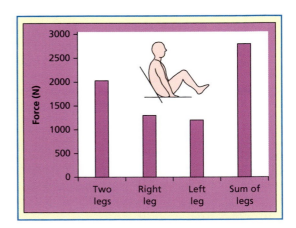

Figure 3.14 The bilateral deficit, showing that the bilateral force (two legs) is less than the sum of the left and right legs acting separately (sum of legs).

activation than to either muscle group activated maximally alone (43). This suggests that there is an inhibitory mechanism that limits maximal activation during bilateral muscle actions. Training with bilateral muscle actions reduces the bilateral deficit, bringing bilateral force production close to the sum of unilateral force production (23).

> Cross education and the reduction of the bilateral deficit provide evidence of neural adaptations to resistance training.

Electromyographic evidence of neural adaptations

Electromyography (EMG) records and quantifies the electrical activity in the muscle fibers of activated motor units (65) (Figure 3.15). It reflects the number of motor units activated

and their firing rates (65). Typically, isometric muscle actions are characterized by linear or curvilinear increases in EMG amplitude with torque (or force) (3). Therefore, an increase in maximal EMG activity would reflect an increase in motor unit activation (a neural adaptation). The increase in EMG activity may result from increased numbers of active motor units (i.e., high-threshold motor units), increased motor unit firing rates, or motor unit synchronization.

Numerous investigations have shown increases in EMG activity as a result of resistance training (2,39,58). Untrained individuals (those unfamiliar with resistance training exercises) may not be able to recruit the highest-threshold motor units (types IIa and IIx) (2). This is indicative of an inability to fully activate the agonist muscle(s). An increase in the ability to recruit these high-threshold motor units can increase the

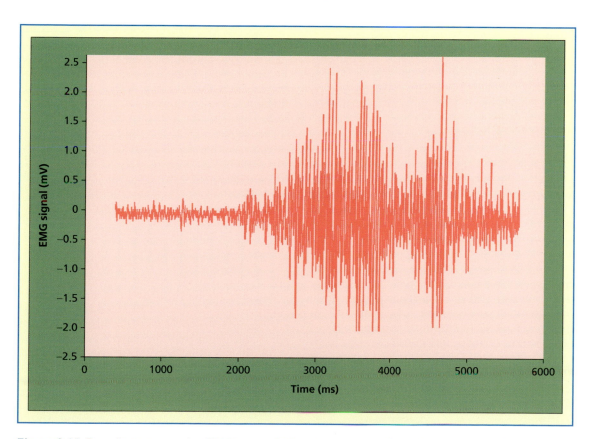

Figure 3.15 Raw electromyographic (EMG) signal. EMG is the recording of muscle action potentials.

expression of muscular strength. For example, the highest threshold motor units make up only about 5% of the total number of motor units of the triceps brachii, but these units contain approximately 20% of the total number of muscle fibers (65). Increasing the firing rate of motor units can also affect the force produced by activated motor units. Motor units can increase their force 10-fold by altering their firing rates (66). Not surprisingly then, resistance training has been shown to increase motor unit firing rates after training (45).

Increased synchronization of motor units has been observed after strength training (29). The more synchronous the firing of motor units, the more motor units will be firing at any given time. Theoretically, this might lead to an increase in maximal force production, although some evidence suggests that asynchronous firing of motor units may be more effective than synchronous firing in producing force during submaximal muscle actions (49). Thus, the role of synchronization of motor unit firing in force production remains unclear (30).

> Increased neural drive results from increased motor unit recruitment, increased motor unit firing rate, or synchronization of motor unit firing.

A maximal muscle action of an agonist muscle or muscle group is typically accompanied by simultaneous activation of the antagonist muscle or muscle group (65). This is known as **antagonist coactivation** (or co-contraction). For example, a maximal voluntary contraction of the elbow flexors (agonists) may also involve activation of the elbow extensors (antagonists). This coactivation reduces the net torque in the intended direction, reducing performance on the strength test. Coactivation may be a strategy used to help stabilize a joint, particularly if the individual is inexperienced or uncertain about lifting a load (24). Strength training reduces coactivation of antagonist muscle groups, leading to an increase in the expression of muscular strength (36).

Metabolic adaptations

Some evidence points to increased fuel availability following resistance training. One study showed increases in ATP (18%), phosphocreatine (PCr) (25%), and glycogen (66%) levels following five months of heavy resistance training (51). Another study showed increased activity levels of several key enzymes involved in anaerobic energy metabolism (creatine kinase, myokinase, and phosphofructokinase) (14). Others, however, concluded that strength training does not increase ATP or PC levels (75) or lead to increased activities of enzymes associated with the phosphagen, glycolytic, or oxidative energy systems (73). Differences between studies may be due to the pretraining status of subjects, muscles examined, and variations in the design of the training programs (30).

SUMMARY

The nervous system is complex; it may be divided into central (brain and spinal cord) and peripheral (motor and sensory neurons) components. Motor neurons conduct nervous impulses from the central nervous system (brain and spinal cord) to peripheral structures, such as skeletal muscles, while sensory neurons conduct nervous impulses from peripheral structures to the central nervous system. A reflex is an involuntary motor response to a given stimulus. Of the many types of reflexes, the myotatic (stretch) and inverse myotatic reflexes are especially important for those cultivating strength and conditioning.

The individual fibers comprising skeletal muscle are arranged into bundles called fasciculi. Each fiber, fasciculus, and whole muscle is surrounded by connective tissues called endomysium, perimysium, and epimysium, respectively. These connective tissues transmit the force of muscle contraction to the tendons, which are attached to bones and cause movement. The sliding-filament theory of muscle contraction describes how actin and myosin interact to cause contraction and thus force production.

The three muscle fiber types found in humans are slow oxidative (SO), fast oxidative glycolytic (FOG), and fast glycolytic (FG). These fiber types differ from one another based on their contractile and metabolic characteristics.

The relative proportions of each fiber type differ among people and are largely determined by genetics.

Resistance training increases muscle size and strength. Hypertrophy refers to an increase in cell size and is thought to be the primary mechanism by which muscles are enlarged with training. The nervous system also adapts to chronic heavy resistance training. Evidence of neural adaptations include the cross-education (cross-training) effect, reduction of the bilateral deficit, increased electromyographic (EMG) activity, and reduced antagonist coactivation.

MAXING OUT

1 You are working with a group of track athletes who want to estimate the percentage of fast-twitch muscle fibers in their quadriceps muscles, but you do not have access to the technology required for a muscle biopsy. You know that Thorstensson and Karlsson (76) developed a fatiguing isokinetic leg-extension test to estimate the percentage of fast-twitch fibers in the quadriceps muscles. In this test, the subject performs 50 consecutive maximal isokinetic leg extensions at 180° per second and the percent decline in peak torque is used to estimate the percentage of fast-twitch muscle fibers through the following equation:

Percent fast-twitch fibers = (percent decline − 5.2) ÷ 0.9
Percent decline = ([initial peak torque − final peak torque] ÷ initial peak torque) × 100
Estimate the percentage of fast-twitch muscle fibers for subjects with declines of 25, 40, 67, and 83%.

2 A previously inexperienced weight trainer has completed the first two weeks of a resistance training program designed to increase muscle size and strength. The athlete approaches you and expresses frustration that she does not see any sign of an increase in muscle size or fat-free body mass. Considering the time course of contributions from neural adaptations versus hypertrophy, explain to the athlete why this is normal following just two weeks of resistance exercise.

3 An athlete is intrigued that he is not able to exert as much force during higher- versus slower-speed concentric muscle actions despite making a maximal effort under each condition. Explain why there is a negative relationship between force and velocity for concentric muscle actions.

REFERENCES

1. Aagaard P, Andersen JL. Correlation between contractile strength and myosin heavy chain isoform composition in human skeletal muscle. *Med Sci Sports Exerc* 1998; 30(8):1217–1222.

2. Aagaard P, Simonsen EB, Andersen JL, Magnusson SP, Halkjaer-Kristensen J, Dyhre-Poulsen P. Neural inhibition during maximal eccentric and concentric quadriceps contraction: effects of resistance training. *J Appl Physiol* 2000; 89(6):2249–2257.

3. Alkner BA, Tesch PA, Berg HE. Quadriceps EMG/force relationship in knee extension and leg press. *Med Sci Sports Exerc* 2000; 32(2):459–463.

4. Alway SE, Winchester PK, Davis ME, Gonyea WJ. Regionalized adaptations and muscle fiber proliferation in stretch-induced enlargement. *J Appl Physiol* 1989; 66(2):771–781.

5. Andersen JL, Klitgaard H, Saltin B. Myosin heavy chain isoforms in single fibres from m. vastus lateralis of sprinters: influence of training. *Acta Physiol Scand* 1994; 151(2):135–142.

6. Baldwin KM, Haddad F. Effects of different activity and inactivity paradigms on myosin heavy chain gene expression in striated muscle. *J Appl Physiol* (1985) 2001; 90(1):345–357.

7. Bamman MM, Petrella JK, Kim JS, Mayhew DL, Cross JM. Cluster analysis tests the importance of myogenic gene expression during myofiber hypertrophy in humans. *J Appl Physiol* (1985) 2007; 102(6):2232–2239.

8. Beedle AM. Distribution of myosin heavy chain isoforms in muscular dystrophy: insights into disease pathology. *Musculoskelet Regen* 2016; 2.

9. Bergh U, Thorstensson A, Sjodin B, Hulten B, Piehl K, Karlsson J. Maximal oxygen uptake and muscle fiber types in trained and untrained humans. *Med Sci Sports Exerc* 1978; 10(3):151–154.

10. Blaauw B, Reggiani C. The role of satellite cells in muscle hypertrophy. *J Muscle Res Cell Motil* 2014; 35(1):3–10.

11. Brown CH, Wilmore JH. The effects of maximal resistance training on the strength and body composition of women athletes. *Med Sci Sports Exerc* 1974; 6(3):174–177.

12. Charifi N, Kadi F, Feasson L, Denis C. Effects of endurance training on satellite cell frequency in skeletal muscle of old men. *Muscle Nerve* 2003; 28(1):87–92.

13. Ciciliot S, Rossi AC, Dyar KA, Blaauw B, Schiaffino S. Muscle type and fiber type specificity in muscle wasting. *Int J Biochem Cell Biol* 2013; 45(10):2191–2199.

14. Costill DL, Coyle EF, Fink WF, Lesmes GR, Witzmann FA. Adaptations in skeletal muscle following strength training. *J Appl Physiol* 1979; 46(1):96–99.

15. Costill DL, Daniels J, Evans W, Fink W, Krahenbuhl G, Saltin B. Skeletal muscle enzymes and fiber composition in male and female track athletes. *J Appl Physiol* 1976; 40(2):149–154.

16. Coyle EF, Feiring DC, Rotkis TC, Cote RW, 3rd, Roby FB, Lee W, Wilmore JH. Specificity of power improvements through slow and fast isokinetic training. *J Appl Physiol* 1981; 51(6):1437–1442.

17. Cresswell AG, Ovendal AH. Muscle activation and torque development during maximal unilateral and bilateral isokinetic knee extensions. *J Sports Med Phys Fitness* 2002; 42(1):19–25.

18. Crewther B, Cronin J, Keogh J. Possible stimuli for strength and power adaptation: acute metabolic responses. *Sports Med* 2006; 36(1):65–78.

19. Crewther B, Cronin J, Keogh J. Possible stimuli for strength and power adaptation: acute mechanical responses. *Sports Med* 2005; 35(11):967–989.

20. Crewther B, Keogh J, Cronin J, Cook C. Possible stimuli for strength and power adaptation: acute hormonal responses. *Sports Med* 2006; 36(3):215–238.

21. Cureton KJ, Collins MA, Hill DW, McElhannon FM, Jr. Muscle hypertrophy in men and women. *Med Sci Sports Exerc* 1988; 20(4):338–344.

22. D'Antona G, Lanfranconi F, Pellegrino MA, Brocca L, Adami R, Rossi R, Moro G, Miotti D, Canepari M, Bottinelli R. Skeletal muscle hypertrophy and structure and function of skeletal muscle fibres in male body builders. *J Physiol* 2006; 570(3):611–627.

23. Enoka RM. Muscle strength and its development. New perspectives. *Sports Med* 1988; 6(3):146–168.

24. Enoka RM. *Neuromechanics of Human Movement*. Champaign, IL: Human Kinetics; 2002. xix.

25. Eriksson A, Kadi F, Malm C, Thornell LE. Skeletal muscle morphology in power-lifters with and without anabolic steroids. *Histochem Cell Biol* 2005; 124(2):167–175.

26. Esbjornsson M, Hellsten-Westing Y, Balsom PD, Sjodin B, Jansson E. Muscle fibre type changes with sprint training: effect of training pattern. *Acta Physiol Scand* 1993; 149(2):245–246.

27. Farthing JP, Chilibeck PD. The effect of eccentric training at different velocities on cross-education. *Eur J Appl Physiol* 2003; 89(6):570–577.

28. Farthing JP, Chilibeck PD. The effects of eccentric and concentric training at different velocities on muscle hypertrophy. *Eur J Appl Physiol* 2003; 89(6):578–586.

29. Felici F, Rosponi A, Sbriccoli P, Filligoi GC, Fattorini L, Marchetti M. Linear and non-linear analysis of surface electromyograms in weightlifters. *Eur J Appl Physiol* 2001; 84(4):337–342.

30. Fleck SJ, Kraemer WJ. *Designing Resistance Training Programs*. Champaign, IL: Human Kinetics; 2004. xiii.

31. Fry AC, Allemeier CA, Staron RS. Correlation between percentage fiber type area and myosin heavy chain content in human skeletal muscle. *Eur J Appl Physiol Occup Physiol* 1994; 68(3):246–251.

32. Fry AC, Schilling BK, Staron RS, Hagerman FC, Hikida RS, Thrush JT. Muscle fiber characteristics and performance correlates of male Olympic-style weightlifters. *J Strength Cond Res* 2003; 17(4):746–754.

33. Goldspink G, Harridge S. Cellular and molecular aspects of adaptation in skeletal

muscle. In: Komi PV, editor. *Strength and Power in Sport*. Oxford, UK: Blackwell Scientific; 2003. 231–251.

34. Gonyea WJ, Sale DG, Gonyea FB, Mikesky A. Exercise induced increases in muscle fiber number. *Eur J Appl Physiol Occup Physiol* 1986; 55(2):137–141.

35. Haff G, Triplett NT, National Strength & Conditioning Association (U.S.). *Essentials of Strength Training and Conditioning*. Champaign, IL: Human Kinetics; 2016. xvi.

36. Häkkinen K, Kallinen M, Izquierdo M, Jokelainen K, Lassila H, Malkia E, Kraemer WJ, Newton RU, Alen M. Changes in agonist-antagonist EMG, muscle CSA, and force during strength training in middle-aged and older people. *J Appl Physiol* 1998; 84(4):1341–1349.

37. Häkkinen K, Komi PV, Alen M. Effect of explosive type strength training on isometric force- and relaxation-time, electromyographic and muscle fibre characteristics of leg extensor muscles. *Acta Physiol Scand* 1985; 125(4):587–600.

38. Häkkinen K, Pakarinen A, Alen M, Kauhanen H, Komi PV. Neuromuscular and hormonal adaptations in athletes to strength training in two years. *J Appl Physiol* 1988; 65(6):2406–2412.

39. Higbie EJ, Cureton KJ, Warren GL, 3rd, Prior BM. Effects of concentric and eccentric training on muscle strength, cross-sectional area, and neural activation. *J Appl Physiol* 1996; 81(5):2173–2181.

40. Holloway JB, Baechle TR. Strength training for female athletes. A review of selected aspects. *Sports Med* 1990; 9(4):216–228.

41. Hortobagyi T, Dempsey L, Fraser D, Zheng D, Hamilton G, Lambert J, Dohm L. Changes in muscle strength, muscle fibre size and myofibrillar gene expression after immobilization and retraining in humans. *J Physiol* 2000; 524 Pt 1:293–304.

42. Housh DJ, Housh TJ, Johnson GO, Chu WK. Hypertrophic response to unilateral concentric isokinetic resistance training. *J Appl Physiol* 1992; 73(1):65–70.

43. Howard JD, Enoka RM. Maximum bilateral contractions are modified by neurally mediated interlimb effects. *J Appl Physiol* 1991; 70(1):306–316.

44. Ikai M, Fukunaga T. Calculation of muscle strength per unit cross-sectional area of human muscle by means of ultrasonic measurement. *Int Z Angew Physiol* 1968; 26(1):26–32.

45. Kamen G. Resistance training increases vastus lateralis motor unit firing rates in young and old adults. *Med Sci Sports Exerc* 1998; 30(Suppl.):S337.

46. Kraemer WJ, Patton JF, Gordon SE, Harman EA, Deschenes MR, Reynolds K, Newton RU, Triplett NT, Dziados JE. Compatibility of high-intensity strength and endurance training on hormonal and skeletal muscle adaptations. *J Appl Physiol* 1995; 78(3):976–989.

47. Lanka J. Shot putting. In: Zatsiorsky VM, editor. *Biomechanics in Sport: Performance Enhancement and Injury Prevention*. Oxford, UK: and Malden, MA: Blackwell Science; 2000. p 435–457.

48. Lee M, Carroll TJ. Cross education: possible mechanisms for the contralateral effects of unilateral resistance training. *Sports Med* 2007; 37(1):1–14.

49. Lind AR, Petrofsky JS. Isometric tension from rotary stimulation of fast and slow cat muscles. *Muscle Nerve* 1978; 1(3):213–218.

50. Liu Y, Schlumberger A, Wirth K, Schmidtbleicher D, Steinacker JM. Different effects on human skeletal myosin heavy chain isoform expression: strength vs. combination training. *J Appl Physiol* 2003; 94(6):2282–2288.

51. MacDougall JD, Ward GR, Sale DG, Sutton JR. Biochemical adaptation of human skeletal muscle to heavy resistance training and immobilization. *J Appl Physiol* 1977; 43(4):700–703.

52. Mero A, Komi PV. Force-, EMG-, and elasticity-velocity relationships at submaximal, maximal and supramaximal running speeds in sprinters. *Eur J Appl Physiol Occup Physiol* 1986; 55(5):553–561.

53. Mikkelsen UR, Langberg H, Helmark IC, Skovgaard D, Andersen LL, Kjaer M, Mackey AL. Local NSAID infusion inhibits satellite cell proliferation in human skeletal muscle after eccentric exercise. *J Appl Physiol* 2009; 107(5):1600–1611.

54. Miller AE, MacDougall JD, Tarnopolsky MA, Sale DG. Gender differences in strength and muscle fiber characteristics. *Eur J Appl Physiol Occup Physiol* 1993; 66(3):254–262.

55. Mitchell CJ, Churchward-Venne TA, West DW, Burd NA, Breen L, Baker SK, Phillips SM. Resistance exercise load does not determine training-mediated hypertrophic gains in young men. *J Appl Physiol* (1985) 2012; 113(1):71–77.

56. Moritani T, deVries HA. Neural factors versus hypertrophy in the time course of muscle strength gain. *Am J Phys Med* 1979; 58(3):115–130.

57. Munn J, Herbert RD, Gandevia SC. Contralateral effects of unilateral resistance training: a meta-analysis. *J Appl Physiol* 2004; 96(5):1861–1866.

58. Narici MV, Roi GS, Landoni L, Minetti AE, Cerretelli P. Changes in force, cross-sectional area and neural activation during strength training and detraining of the human quadriceps. *Eur J Appl Physiol Occup Physiol* 1989; 59(4):310–319.

59. Needham DM. Red and white muscle. *Physiol Rev* 1926; 6(1):1–27.

60. Ogasawara R, Loenneke JP, Thiebaud RS, Abe T. Low-load bench press training to fatigue results in muscle hypertrophy similar to high-load bench press training. *International Journal of Clinical Medicine* 2013; 4(2):114–121.

61. Paddon-Jones D, Leveritt M, Lonergan A, Abernethy P. Adaptation to chronic eccentric exercise in humans: the influence of contraction velocity. *Eur J Appl Physiol* 2001; 85(5):466–471.

62. Peter JB, Barnard RJ, Edgerton VR, Gillespie CA, Stempel KE. Metabolic profiles of three fiber types of skeletal muscle in guinea pigs and rabbits. *Biochemistry* 1972; 11(14):2627–2633.

63. Ranvier L. Propriétés et structures différentes des muscles rouges et des muscles blancs chez les lapins et chez les raies. *CR Acad Sci Paris* 1873; 77:1030–1034.

64. Ross A, Leveritt M, Riek S. Neural influences on sprint running: training adaptations and acute responses. *Sports Med* 2001; 31(6):409–425.

65. Sale DG. Neural adaptations to strength training. In: Komi PV, editor. *Strength and Power in Sport*. Oxford, UK: Blackwell Scientific; 2003. pp 281–314.

66. Sale DG, McComas AJ, MacDougall JD, Upton AR. Neuromuscular adaptation in human thenar muscles following strength training and immobilization. *J Appl Physiol* 1982; 53(2):419–424.

67. Schilling BK, Fry AC, Chiu LZ, Weiss LW. Myosin heavy chain isoform expression and in vivo isometric performance: a regression model. *J Strength Cond Res* 2005; 19(2):270–275.

68. Scott W, Stevens J, Binder-Macleod SA. Human skeletal muscle fiber type classifications. *Phys Ther* 2001; 81(11):1810–1816.

69. Shoepe TC, Stelzer JE, Garner DP, Widrick JJ. Functional adaptability of muscle fibers to long-term resistance exercise. *Med Sci Sports Exerc* 2003; 35(6):944–951.

70. Staron RS, Johnson P. Myosin polymorphism and differential expression in adult human skeletal muscle. *Comp Biochem Physiol* B 1993; 106(3):463–475.

71. Staron RS, Karapondo DL, Kraemer WJ, Fry AC, Gordon SE, Falkel JE, Hagerman FC, Hikida RS. Skeletal muscle adaptations during early phase of heavy-resistance training in men and women. *J Appl Physiol* 1994; 76(3):1247–1255.

72. Staron RS, Kraemer WJ, Hikida RS, Reed DW, Murray JD, Campos GE, Gordon SE. Comparison of soleus muscles from rats exposed to microgravity for 10 versus 14 days. *Histochem Cell Biol* 1998;110(1):73–80.

73. Tesch PA, Komi PV, Häkkinen K. Enzymatic adaptations consequent to long-term strength training. *Int J Sports Med* 1987;8 Suppl 1:66–69.

74. Tesch PA, Larsson L. Muscle hypertrophy in bodybuilders. *Eur J Appl Physiol Occup Physiol* 1982;49(3):301–306.

75. Tesch PA, Thorsson A, Colliander EB. Effects of eccentric and concentric resistance training on skeletal muscle substrates, enzyme activities and capillary supply. *Acta Physiol Scand* 1990;140(4):575–580.

76. Thorstensson A, Karlsson J. Fatiguability and fibre composition of human skeletal muscle. *Acta Physiol Scand* 1976;98(3):318–322.

77. Widrick JJ, Stelzer JE, Shoepe TC, Garner DP. Functional properties of human muscle fibers after short-term resistance exercise training. *Am J Physiol Regul Integr Comp Physiol* 2002;283(2):R408–416.

78. Zatsiorsky VM. Biomechanics of strength and strength testing. In: Komi PV, editor. *Strength and Power in Sport*. Oxford: Blackwell Scientific; 2003. p 439–487.

79. Zhou S. Chronic neural adaptations to unilateral exercise: mechanisms of cross education. *Exerc Sport Sci Rev* 2000;28(4):177–184.

Contents

CHAPTER 4

THE SKELETAL SYSTEM

W. Britt Chandler, T. Jeff Chandler, and Clint Alley

OBJECTIVES

After completing this chapter, you will be able to:

- Understand the living nature of bone tissue including the mechanisms for responding to load and stress.
- Recognize the types of tissue found in the human skeletal system.
- Discuss the functions of the skeletal system, specific joint classifications, and the various anatomical components that comprise the skeletal system.
- Discuss the role of Wolff's law in bone remodeling.
- Recognize the role of minimal essential strain for bone health, growth, and development.
- Discuss the key concepts of training to improve bone strength and bone.

KEY TERMS

Amphiarthrosis
Appendicular skeleton
Articular cartilage
Articulations
Axial skeleton
Canaliculi
Cartilage
Collagen
Cortical bone
Diaphysis
Diarthrosis

Distal insertion
Epiphyseal discs
Flat bones
Lacunae
Lever
Ligaments
Long bones
Minimal essential
    strain (MES)
Osteoblasts
Osteoclasts

Osteocytes
Osteonic canal
Osteons
Osteoporosis
Periosteum
Proximal insertion
Short bones
Synarthrosis
Tendons
Trabecular bone
Wolff's law

INTRODUCTION

The living skeleton is much more than the calcified bones we study in anatomy. It is a dynamic system with living cells that continually remodel bone and respond to the demands placed on it by training and conditioning. Specific protocols of loading and unloading bone tissues cause unique adaptations to bones, ligaments, tendons, and cartilage. **Ligaments** connect one bone to another. **Tendons** connect muscle to bone, and **cartilage** protects the ends of bones. This chapter discusses the anatomy, physiology, and response to training of the skeletal system.

The bones of the skeletal system provide the internal framework of the body. They comprise the levers and articulations that enable us to move. A **lever** is a rigid bar that moves around an axis of rotation. **Articulations**, where one bone meets another bone, allow movement and serve as the axes around which movement occurs. Bones function to protect our vital organs from trauma; they also produce blood cells, including the red blood cells that transport oxygen to our tissues. In addition to all this, bones serve as depositories for the minerals we need to remain healthy.

STRUCTURE OF THE SKELETAL SYSTEM

The human skeleton is divided into two major parts, axial and appendicular (Figure 4.1). The **axial skeleton** consists of the skull, vertebral column, sacrum, coccyx, ribs, and sternum. The **appendicular skeleton** can be subdivided into the pectoral and the pelvic girdles. The pectoral girdle includes the clavicle and scapula. The pelvic girdle is made up of the coxal bones of the hip. The bones of the appendicular skeletal system form articulations or joints that allow movement when forces are applied by muscles.

> The skeletal system is composed of an axial skeleton and an appendicular skeleton.

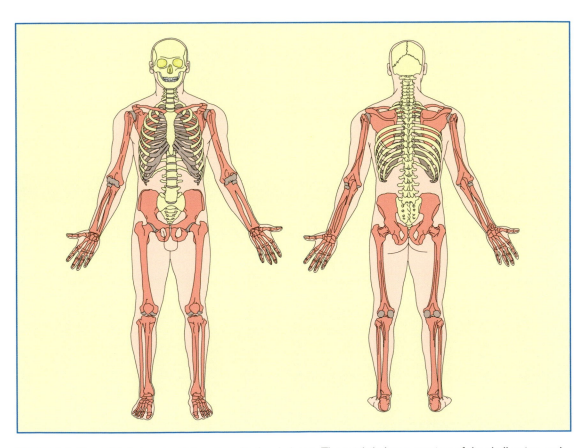

Figure 4.1 The axial skeleton and the appendicular skeleton. The axial skeleton consists of the skull, spine, and ribs. The appendicular skeleton consists of the appendages, shoulder girdle, and hip girdle.

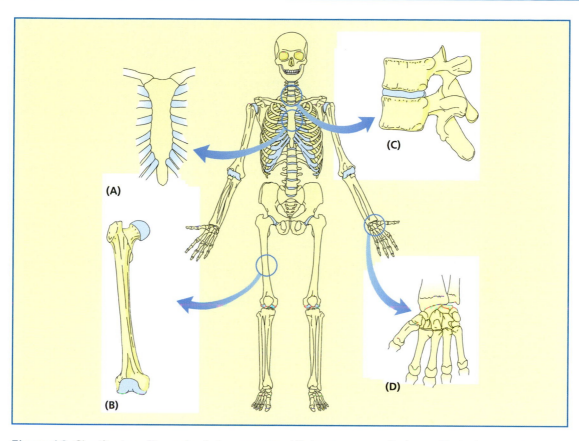

Figure 4.2 Classification of bones by their appearance. (A) the sternum is a flat bone; (B) the femur is a long bone; (C) the vertebrae are irregular bones; (D) the carpals are short bones.

The body's movement is general in nature (both angular and linear) and can range from locomotion and gross positioning to adept manipulations of the hands and feet.

Bone tissue

One way to classify bones is by their appearance (Figure 4.2). The **long bones** (femur, tibia, humerus, and radius) determine most of the length of the arms and legs, are responsible for most of our mature height, and provide one location for blood cell production. These bones are generally longer than they are wide. **Short bones** (carpals and tarsals) are more cubical in shape. Several adjacent short bones provide the hands and feet with a flexible base for dexterity at the distal articulations. The **flat bones** (ribs, scapula, bones of the skull and sternum) provide another site for blood cell production and protect the vital organs. Last, **irregular bones** (the vertebrae and maxilla) have different shapes depending on their functions. They may provide multiple facets for articulation and muscular attachment or unique leverage, depending on their location.

To better understand the function and nature of bone and its relation to physical activity, look first at its structures. Figure 4.3 illustrates these structures.

1   **Osteons**: Predominant structures found in cortical bone that compose the matrix.
2   **Osteocytes**: Bone cells. There are two types of bone cells, osteoclasts and osteoblasts, both located in the lacunae. **Osteoclasts** are responsible for reclaiming calcium for metabolic processes and removing damaged bone. **Osteoblasts** are responsible for depositing new bone matrix to replace the bone removed by osteoclastic activity.

3 **Canaliculi:** Small canals that allow the dissemination of nutrients and metabolites to osteocytes and surrounding tissue.

4 **Lacunae:** Small spaces at the centers of canaliculi, which house the osteocytes.

5 **Osteonic canal:** A longitudinal canal at the center of the osteon, which provides for the passage of nutrients and metabolic wastes. The osteonic canals house arterioles and venules, which carry blood and nourishment to the bone tissue. Osteonic canals are interconnected by perforating canals running perpendicular to them.

In a magnified cross-sectional view of a mature long bone, the osteonic canals run parallel to the shaft of the long bone and are surrounded by a calcified concentric matrix that fuses them together. Much like the annular concentric rings you see in a cross-cut tree, the concentric rings travel outward from the osteonic canal. Canaliculi are strategically placed to disperse fluid to the surrounding tissue. The osteocytes residing in the lacunae are distributed throughout the concentric rings to support the metabolism of specific portions of the bone. All the

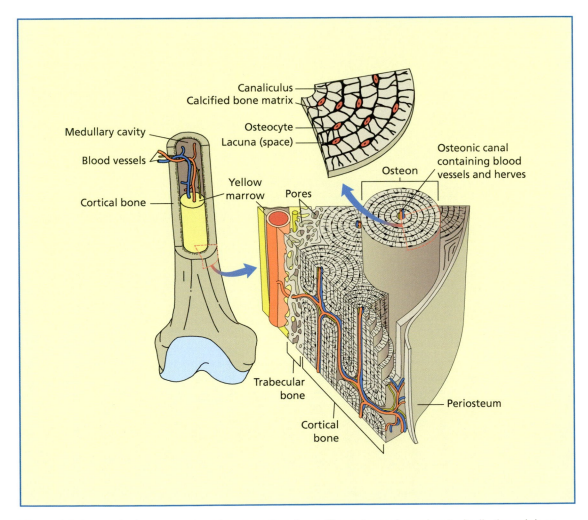

Figure 4.3 Longitudinal cross-section of a mature long bone. Osteonic canals run longitudinally through long bones. Osteocytes are arranged in concentric circles around the osteonic canal.

concentric rings surrounding an osteonic canal form an osteon.

There are two types of bone relative to porosity. **Cortical bone** is highly mineralized and dense, having a low porosity. This type of bone is found in the shafts of long bones and most small, short, irregular bones that are regularly subjected to compressive stresses. **Trabecular bone** is less mineralized, is more porous, and is therefore less dense. It is found at the ends of long bones and is encased in cortical bone, which provides certain advantages in enabling movement. Cortical bone is denser and thus contains more minerals, which add to its weight and rigidity. Because trabecular bone is located at the ends of long bones, the weight at the end of the bone is decreased, thus reducing the force that muscles must generate to move the lever. If the entire skeleton were composed of cortical bone, movement would be impaired due to the weight of the bones.

Bone tissue is continually being reabsorbed and reformed, and exercise is a key stimulus for this process. When bone is optimally stressed, osteoblasts deposit minerals, primarily calcium phosphate, on the collagen matrix. **Collagen** is a tough flexible protein found in other connective tissue as well as bone. Particularly in preadolescents and to some extent in adolescents, bone is more flexible because less calcium phosphate has been deposited on the collagen matrix. The **periosteum** is a tough, fibrous outer covering of bone. As we age, our bones continue to grow in circumference because new bone is being developed underneath the periosteum.

> Bone tissue is living tissue that is constantly being remodeled. Several factors, including hormonal status, nutritional status, and exercise, determine bone density.

Epiphyseal discs are the site at which bone increases in length. Long bones continue to grow in length up to the time of epiphyseal closure. Prior to epiphyseal closure, bone tissue in this region is more prone to injury from abnormal stresses. Injuries to the epiphysis prior to closure can cause cessation of longitudinal bone growth, which can lead to a limb-length discrepancy. Although resistance training is a concern in this regard, an appropriately designed resistance training program controls the stresses applied to the skeletal system more closely than does participation in many sports and activities.

> Training exercises performed properly and under proper supervision with spotters should minimize the risk of epiphyseal disc injuries during training.

Appropriately applied forces will strengthen the skeletal system. Building bone density in youth may help to maintain bone density throughout life. Many of the skeletal problems associated with aging are related to decreases in bone density. Some of these problems are related to hormonal or nutritional status. Some problems may be related to our failure to attain maximum bone density as we mature to adulthood.

Ligamentous tissue

Ligaments are composed of tough, fibrous tissue with little elasticity. Ligaments prevent joints from moving in abnormal patterns. By their arrangement, they may allow movement in one plane only or restrict movement in an abnormal direction. In a joint that is inherently lax, as in the shoulder, numerous ligaments function to stabilize the joint in various planes of motion. The ligaments may also serve to fix a bone to another bone where little or no movement is intended, as in the acromioclavicular joint.

Cartilage

Articular cartilage (Figure 4.4) covers the ends of long bones and reduces friction at the joint while it is moving under pressure. In basic composition, the structural components consist of a dense mesh of collagen fibrils, proteoglycan macromolecules (PGs), and water, creating a stiff gel-like substance. The tissue is semi-transparent, with four distinct layers:

1   The articular surface, which is super-slick. This layer greatly reduces friction between two articulating bone surfaces.

2   The middle zone, composed of collagen fibrils and fluid-swollen proteoglycans.

3 and 4   The deep zone and the tidemark region where the cartilage matrix meshes with the actual bone structure.

By maintaining the fluid content in the tissue at normal levels, the protective and friction-reducing properties of cartilage are retained (22).

If the friction-reducing properties of cartilage are lost, this may damage the cartilaginous tissue resulting in eventual deterioration of the joint increasing the potential for injury (14).

Articulations

Articulations are where bones join together. At articulations, contact is maintained by cartilage and forces associated with movement of the joint. This arrangement allows bone growth, conversion of angular to linear motion, and dexterity at distal extremities; it

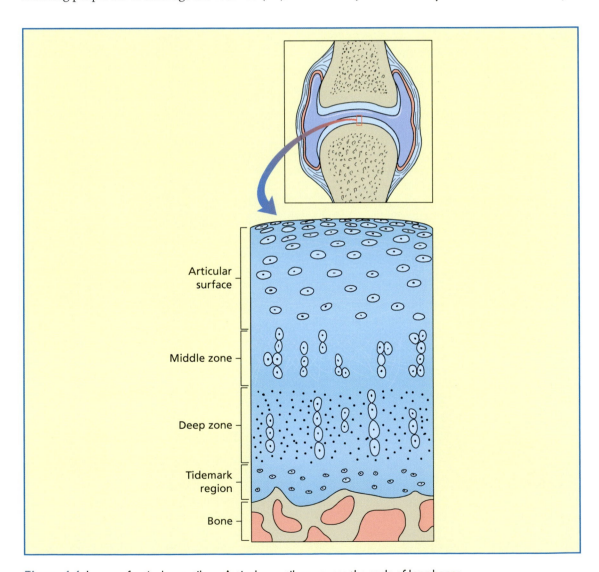

Figure 4.4 Layers of articular cartilage. Articular cartilage covers the ends of long bones.

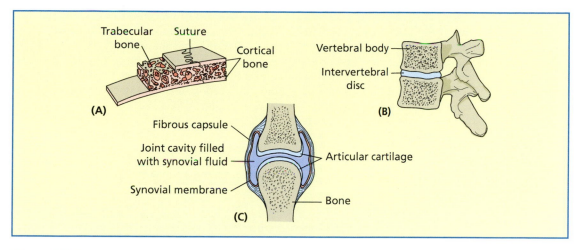

Figure 4.5 Types of articulations. (A) a cranial suture is a synarthrotic joint; (B) the shoulder is an amphiarthrotic joint; (C) the knee is a diarthrotic joint.

also provides for fusion, support summation, and motion as dictated by the location, type, and function of the articulation.

Articulations can be classified by the type of connective tissue used to form the articulation. There are three major classifications of joints: synarthrosis joints, amphiarthrosis joints, and diarthrosis joints. Each type of articulation has specific characteristics in terms of stability and mobility. A description of the classifications is as follows (Figure 4.5):

1 **Synarthrosis**: Immovable joints, bound tightly by fibrous tissue.
2 **Amphiarthrosis**: Slightly movable joints, cartilaginous.
3 **Diarthrosis**: Freely movable joints, synovial.

FUNCTIONS OF THE SKELETAL SYSTEM

The bones of the skeleton provide structure, allow movement, and provide protection for our organs as well as other physiological functions. We will examine each of these functions in more detail.

Structure and protection

Without bones, we would be incapable of standing, sitting, or moving in general. The length of our long bones determines the length of our body segments. For example, the talus, calcaneus, tibia, and femur make up the length of the leg and allow for ankle and knee flexion, extension, and gross compensation for surface irregularities so that we may stand erect. We can walk on an irregular or uneven surface because the foot can compensate for the slope with this adaptable base of support.

Movement

Bones provide both a proximal and distal insertion for muscles, allowing movement when sufficient tension is developed in the muscle that crosses a joint. The **proximal insertion** is closer to the trunk, and the **distal insertion** is farther from the trunk. The bones of the appendicular skeleton and to a lesser degree the axial skeleton are arranged as sets of levers with reciprocally shaped surfaces that allow maximal contact to be maintained at the joint during movement. Joints function as axes of rotation around which torque is generated by muscle force.

The structure of the skeletal system allows it to perform one of its essential functions: movement.

The bones of the skeleton act as a mechanical framework for movement and the attachment of muscles. The irregular bones of the spine (the vertebral bodies) are specifically engineered to bear the summed weight of the body superior to a specific vertebral articulation. Vertebral bodies distribute weight over a large surface area to distribute increasing pressures at each descending vertebral level. The legs, in particular the femur and tibia, are structured such that the cortical portion of the bone resists compressive forces from the weight of the entire body superior to them. The hips can experience as much as six times body weight during normal stair climbing (6). The bones support as much as five times their weight in soft tissue in the normal adult.

One function of the skull and vertebral column is to protect the brain and spinal cord from injury. The thoracic vertebrae have spinous processes that restrict hyperextension in the thoracic region. These processes provide additional surfaces for muscular attachment. The ribs and sternum protect the heart, liver, spleen, lungs, and large blood vessels in the thorax. The vertebral column and pelvis also mechanically protect the abdominal or visceral organs and to a lesser degree the genitalia.

Blood cell production

The spongy bone houses the red marrow, which produces the blood cells. The production of red and white blood cells is a result of differentiation of mature blood stem cells that reside primarily in the flat bones of the skull, ribs, sternum, and the ends of the long bones. As the spleen naturally destroys damaged red blood cells (RBCs), these cells must be continually replaced. Every second, the body produces over 2 million RBCs (17).

GROWTH OF THE SKELETAL SYSTEM

Bone changes in size and functional characteristics via two processes: 1) normal growth, and 2) remodeling due to applied loads. Normal growth is largely a function of migration of the epiphysis, resulting in an increase in bone length and diameter prior to skeletal maturity. Chondrocytes secrete a matrix of cartilage and minerals that then deposit themselves on the matrix, stiffening and strengthening it. This process is passive and takes time. Figure 4.6 depicts the epiphyseal region of a long bone.

The second mechanism, remodeling, is a result of the stresses and strains (or lack thereof) applied to the skeletal system through daily activity or planned exercise. In this process bone adapts to stresses due to osteoclastic and osteoblastic activity, which serves to strengthen bone to withstand the applied

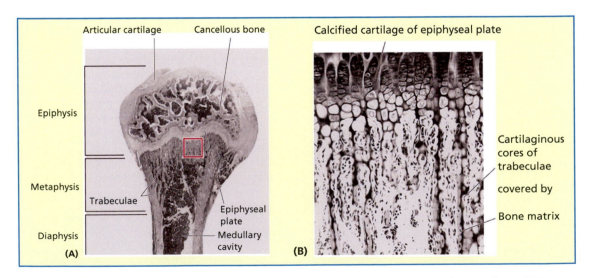

Figure 4.6 Epiphyseal growth region (A) the end of a long bone covered by cancellous bone and articular cartilage. The epiphyseal disc separates the epiphysis from the metaphysis; (B) a magnified section of the metaphysis undergoing calcification of the cartilaginous matrix. Adapted from Cormack DH. *Essential Histology*. 2nd ed. Philadelphia, PA: Lippincott Williams & Wilkins, 2001.

forces. Remodeling is more active in the maintenance of bone integrity; it increases and decreases the bone's circumference in relation to activity level. It is here that we have the greatest opportunity to generate bone adaptation to training. By loading in an exercise/training format, we can influence this adaptation and thus the strength of bone.

Primary bone growth in the epiphysis

At birth, the skeletal system is composed of a cartilaginous framework that has the general form of the skeleton but is not distinguished in proportion, specific structure, or definitive landmarks. In the first stage of growth, calcification of the cartilage framework begins. Development of the periosteum is evidenced by the periosteal bone collar along the center of the shaft and the development of **articular cartilage** at the ends of the femur. The collar appears as a ring of calcified bone around the shaft at approximately the midline. A short time later, the periosteal bone collar becomes the primary ossification center, and epiphyseal capillaries develop in the bone's proximal and distal ends.

Soon the ossification (calcium deposition) of the **diaphysis** or shaft of the bone becomes evident at the center of the shaft, and the epiphyseal plates or growth centers are apparent at the ends of the heavily mineralized centers. As the epiphyseal discs lay down new bone, they migrate toward the

distal ends. Still later, additional growth centers originate at both ends, forming the unique structural features of a long bone. The secondary ossification centers lay down spongy bone, which is covered by articular cartilage. As this growth in length is taking place, the layer on the surface just beneath the periosteum is adding to the circumference of the bone in response to the compression, shear, tension, and torsional loading imposed by movement and exercise. Long bones reach their final length in early adulthood, when the epiphyseal discs are completely closed. Figure 4.7 illustrates the transition of bone from cartilaginous to fully ossified.

Chondrocytes are active cells that specialize in the generation of the protein cartilage framework or matrix. In human growth, they synthesize and secrete matrix into the extracellular space (1). Chrondrocyte hypertrophy is an active process resulting in increased amounts of intercellular material, including mitochondria and endoplasmic reticulum. Increases in the height of the chondrocyte column height are responsible for 44% to 59% of longitudinal bone growth, the remainder being due to matrix synthesis and chondrocyte proliferation. The rate of differentiation of mesenchymal stem cells into chondrocytes is a factor that regulates the synthesis of the matrix and thus the rate of bone growth (1). In addition to the collagen matrix being laid down, osteoclasts and osteoblasts are being differentiated near the epiphysis, where there is a narrow band of cells called the "proliferating region" of the growth plate. Here,

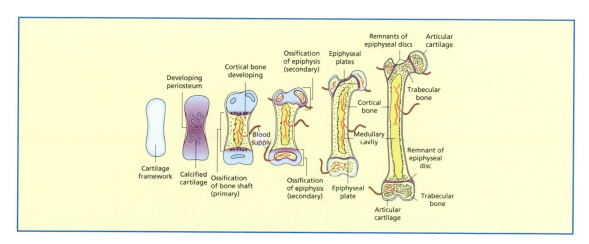

Figure 4.7 Prior to ossification, bone begins as a cartilaginous framework.

chondrocytes multiply and secrete matrix materials, causing migration of the active growth center toward the proximal and distal ends of the long bones. The matrix material is the template for ossification.

ADAPTATIONS OF THE SKELETAL SYSTEM TO LOADING

Loads applied to the skeletal system cause adaptations to occur that are specific to the type of load.

Wolff's law

Adaptation to training can be defined according to **Wolff's law**, which states that "the densities, and to a lesser extent, the sizes and shapes of bones are determined by the magnitude and direction of the acting forces applied to bone."

Growth in circumference acts to distribute the compressive forces over an increased cross-sectional area and thus reduces the amount of pressure per square unit of the bone's cross-sectional surface. In animal experiments, growth in regions of higher stresses and strain has been shown to occur (16). These adaptations can actually change the geometry of the bone and thus the response

to a repetitive movement or strain. Increased thickness in the direction of force application and bending serves to better accommodate repeated flexion. Bones, like muscles, adapt to progressive overload. If we increase the load, we increase flexion in the bone. Figure 4.8 demonstrates how bone under axial load "bends," stimulating the deposition of bone underneath the periosteum at the specific location where the bending occurred. Weight-bearing exercises are most effective in ensuring the overall health (size and density) of the skeletal system in a healthy individual.

> The response of bone tissue to stress is specific to the type of stress applied.

Because the diameter of the bone is enlarged through growth at the outer surface, the space in the center of the bone, required for the marrow, nerves, and blood supply, is not reduced. Since these functions are essential to healthy bone, hypertrophy on the external surfaces does not reduce the functional interior space but does allow increasing load accommodation.

Minimal essential strain

Minimal essential strain (MES) is the minimal volume and intensity of loading required to cause an increase in bone density. Approximately 10% of the strain required to fracture the bone

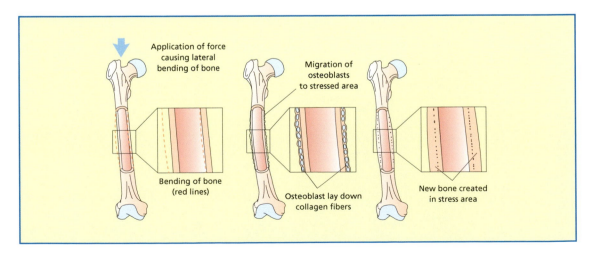

Figure 4.8 Wolff's law. If the load and speed of movement are high enough, bone will "bend" under an axial load. This stimulates the deposition of calcium in the specific location of the stress. Therefore, bone responds to "bending" by getting thicker in the direction of the load.

is considered the threshold at which new bone formation is triggered (8). The interaction of matrix strain and fluid flow may actually be the interacting source of the remodeling signal in bone tissue (12). Whether the stress comes from exercise or the work environment, bone remodeling will occur if the stress triggers the osteoblasts to migrate to the strained region of bone.

> An exercise program that does not reach the level of minimal essential strain will be ineffective at promoting bone density.

MES varies by age and individual. An obese person will have greater loads placed on the skeletal system in normal daily activities than his or her lighter peers. The obese individual, however, will also likely be less active.

Bone density decreases with age, beginning in the third decade. The amount of strain needed to start the remodeling process may occur in the elderly with a decreased load. In a younger, more active population, the requirements of MES should be higher based on higher individual levels of bone density. Therefore, more rigorous exercise may be required to achieve MES in a young, active population. Although stresses applied to bone and subsequent remodeling are ongoing, bone continues to increase in diameter. The total stress required to initiate new bone growth by remodeling is increased if the bone is stronger.

Training adaptations to the skeletal system

The response of bone to applied forces is specific to the applied forces. Strain activation changes a small section of exterior bone from the normal state to a state of remodeling. The location of the adaptation is underneath the outer layer of the bone – in the periosteum. The activated area of bone begins resorption, or the removal of the damaged bone by osteoclasts. This will take one to three weeks. Next is a reversal from primarily osteoclastic activity to osteoblastic activity, which takes another one to two weeks. Osteoblasts start forming new bone by producing matrix in the now cleared resorption area, which takes approximately three-and-a-half months.

Mineralization of bone takes place by the precipitation of calcium phosphate crystals, which bind to and fill in the protein matrix. Calcification increases the diameter of the bone and the thickness of the external cortical bone layer. Calcification of the matrix increases the rigidity of the bone. This adaptation can be stimulated by loading in exercise and can result in an increase in bone density during progress from a less trained to a more trained condition.

Studies in elderly females have shown no significant change in bone density in the femur and forearm after a resistance training period of five months or more (20). In animal studies, small changes in bone density result in a significant shift in bone strength (16). In all cases, care should be taken in training the elderly and the untrained so as to reduce the risk of injury. In these populations, acute loading may require less resistance than that perceived to result in the damage or failure of bone.

THE SKELETAL SYSTEM AND HEALTH

Although balanced growth, proper mineralization, and good training are important indicators of good health, pathologies can occur as a result of specific disorders of or stresses on the skeletal system. This section discusses loss of bone mass, improper alignment, structural damage, and repair of bone.

Imagine the strength of an I-beam increased proportionally by increases in thickness of specific portions of the beam. The increases in thickness of the vertical portion of the beam simulate an increase in rigidity from increased bone mineral density (BMD). As you can see there is an increased difficulty of bending the I-beam on the right versus the left. If bone strength is increased due to increased BMD as a result of remodeling, then the minimal essential strain (MES) would increase as the bone got stronger.

Bone density and health

Peak bone density is an indicator of long-term skeletal health. It is generally accepted that those who achieve a higher peak bone mass are less at risk for osteoporotic fracture later in life. **Osteoporosis** is a disease characterized by a loss of bone density; it is insidious in that it presents no signs or symptoms until the fracture of a bone that has lost its mineral density occurs. Three distinct populations are at higher risk for osteoporosis: (i) postmenopausal women after about age 50, (ii) both men and women after about age 70, and (iii) young female athletes who also have eating disorders, in whom it is a component of the female athletic triad (discussed later in this chapter).

We know that the appropriate dose of physical activity can increase bone mineral density (BMD) throughout our lives (13). Consider the person who achieves higher peak bone density and a larger calcium depot reserve to begin with. As he or she ages, the individual with higher bone density will likely be less prone to developing osteoporosis.

Q&A FROM THE FIELD

My mother and grandmother both have osteoporosis. Is there anything I can do to decrease my chances of having osteoporosis when I get older?

Heredity is certainly a risk factor. In females, the hormonal changes that accompany menopause are a risk factor. Several lifestyle factors increase the risk of osteoporosis: smoking, nutritional deficiencies, excessive alcohol consumption, and the lack of weight-bearing exercise. Everyone loses some bone density as they age. It is important to maximize bone density when you are younger with a weight-bearing exercise program designed to improve bone density.

If the bone mineral reserve was small to begin with, reductions in bone mineralization and decreases in strength would reach a critical state more rapidly. Reduced bone mineralization and thus the structural integrity of the bone makes the elderly more susceptible to bone breakage. A broken hip in an elderly individual can occur as a break at the neck of the femur under the normal load of locomotion, causing the person to fall. In normal locomotion, the stress on bone can be two to three times that of body weight. These breaks occur because the bone density and strength at a vital load-bearing point are diminished due to increased relative osteoclastic activity.

The higher the bone density achieved in the active years, the better the ability to maintain bone density through the aging process into the regression period. Attention given to diet and exercise in the early years may make the functional difference in the later years (19). Although new bone formation can occur at any time of life, the greatest gains are attained in the preadolescent and adolescent years. Adults who started engaging in load-bearing sports before puberty had 22% greater bone mineral content than did a control group. This is compared with a similar group of adults who first started participating in load-bearing activities in adulthood; although these individuals also had increased bone mineral content, it was only 8.5% greater than that in the control group (19). In the case of the female athletic triad, at the time in life when bone mineral density should be peaking, these athletes are intentionally starving their systems and thus greatly reducing their probability of good bone health in their later years.

Q&A FROM THE FIELD

I have heard that swimming is not a good activity to promote bone density. Is this true? Why? It seems like it would be a very good activity for bone density.

Swimming, or any activity in the water, takes place in a semi weightless environment. Astronauts lose bone density through prolonged exposure to a weightless environment. Because swimming is not a weight-bearing activity, it does not provide the minimal stimulus to bone to stimulate growth.

Q&A FROM THE FIELD

What is the best activity to promote bone density throughout the entire skeletal system?

At present, it would appear that moderate- to high-intensity resistance training using a variety of exercises and movement patterns would cause maximum adaptation of the skeletal system. Exercises should load the body axially, such as the bench press for the upper body or the squat for the lower body. Other activities do not stimulate bone density in the entire skeleton. Jogging causes some increase in bone density in the hips but not in the upper body. Tennis may stimulate increases in bone density in the dominant arm but not in the nondominant arm.

Spinal alignment maladies

The spinal maladies presented below are related to an improper or exaggerated spinal curve. An exaggerated thoracic curve, the curve of the vertebrae associated with the ribs and cervical area, is called kyphosis. This malady can result in a gross "head forward" posture or "hunchback." Another spinal deformity is the curvature of the lumbar vertebrae called lordosis. Both lordosis and kyphosis occur primarily in the sagittal plane.

A lateral curvature of the spine that can be life-threatening in extreme cases is scoliosis, which can occur simultaneously in the frontal and transverse planes (3), resulting in a far more complex diagnosis (Figure 4.9). This curve is not a mere exaggeration but rather should not exist and serves no function. In an exercising population, we should be aware of these maladies and the restrictions they may impose on the individual. Exercise programs that accommodate or minimize the effects of these disorders should be considered as much as possible.

Female athletic triad

The female athletic triad is a disease predominantly found in females whose sport, training, or competition is enhanced by a reduced ratio of body fat to lean body mass. Its components are osteoporosis, disordered eating (usually anorexia nervosa), and amenorrhea. Long-distance runners and gymnasts seem particularly susceptible to this malady, although it is also possible that young girls choose these sports to hide their disorder. Addiction to exercise caused by endorphin addiction has been also proposed as a cause of this behavior. Often these athletes attempt to improve their performance by reducing body fat. Reduced

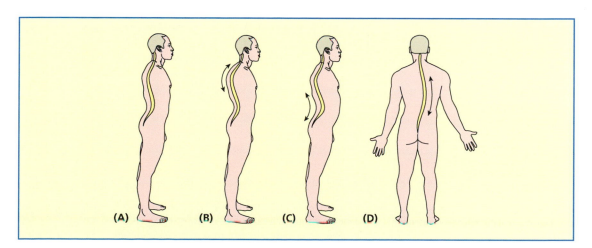

Figure 4.9 Skeletal abnormalities of the spine. (A) normal spinal alignment; (B) kyphosis; (C) lordosis; (D) scoliosis

body fat improves performance by modifying the strength-to-weight ratio, increasing power, and reducing total workload. When this process is carried to extremes, the female athletic triad can occur.

The three factors that make up this disorder are described as follows:

1   An eating disorder (normally anorexia nervosa) generally accompanied by a distorted body image. An anorexic athlete will see herself as fat even when she has starved herself to a dangerously low level.

2   Osteoporosis is the loss of bone mineral density and destruction of associated matrix materials. Loss of bone tissue can compromise health and make bone brittle. Competitive athletes generate much greater than normal forces in the body, and their bones may not hold up to these forces.

3   Amenorrhea (irregular or complete absence of menses). The athlete reduces nutritional intake to the point where not enough essential fat is left to produce sufficient female hormones. Estrogen is the major hormone responsible for the balance of osteoclastic and osteoblastic activity. If the athlete cannot produce enough estrogen, osteoclastic activity rises and bone tissue is lost.

A heavy training load (frequently self-imposed) is usually a part of a competitive athlete's training program. The female athlete triad is probably an interaction of overtraining, poor diet, and lack of adequate body fat from which to produce the required hormones to generate the menstrual cycle. It may also be driven by psychological factors, including the desire to be thin (2).

Different types of female athletes were compared in and out of season, looking at factors related to the female athletic triad. Long-term exposure to decreased estrogen levels was nearly associated linearly with decreased bone mineral density. A prolonged exposure to decreased estrogen locally generates compounds that cause an environment favoring the formation of osteoclasts and inhibiting apoptosis in osteoclasts when signaled (4). A lack of tone (normal resting muscle tension) in the muscles, in spite of a high-level training state, can be a key indicator of abnormality. In essence, these athletes starve themselves yet continue to train hard in an effort to improve their performance.

EXERCISE PRESCRIPTION TO PROMOTE BONE DENSITY

Considering the mechanisms of bone growth, the next step is creating training programs that will provide maximal bone growth, bone density, and overall health. To adequately test bone strength, we might remove the bone from the body and measure the forces that cause it to break. Because this is not possible, we have to depend on studies in animals and cultured bone cells to understand the characteristics and responses to stimuli exhibited in these situations. The current studies do not define the exact number of repetitions, sets, percentage of RM, speed, and frequency of loading, neither do they provide us with a "magic" combination or formula. Generally, when we examine a population of nonathletes compared with a population of athletes, we find major differences in bone mineral densities.

In racquet athletes, we find increased bone density in the dominant arm compared to the nondominant arm (11). Elevated activity levels in the athlete provide musculoskeletal stresses that improve BMD over that of the less active population (13). Currently, we cannot describe the best way to accomplish the desired goal. We can, however, provide some insight into the possible results of specific training programs and their effect on bone density.

Loading speed

Studies have been done to determine the effect of purposely slow training on bone density. Static loading has repeatedly been shown to produce little or no significant effect on new bone growth. Dynamic loading, on the other hand, has been shown to produce significant increases in new bone formation (9).

Bone cells are extremely sensitive to changes in hydrostatic pressure. Training movements and loads that maximize fluctuations in hydrostatic pressure within the bone cells will stimulate bone growth.

This occurs primarily because dynamic loading causes fluctuations in fluid pressure within the lacunar-canalicular system. Bone cells are very responsive to these fluctuations. We can presume that to stimulate new bone growth, our movements must be dynamic in nature.

Rate and frequency of loading

Bone responds most effectively to exercises that are dynamic and involve rapid loading (9). The frequency of an exercise also affects the rate of bone formation. A runner who runs with a stride frequency of 90 cycles per minute will form more bone in the pelvis and lower extremities than will someone who runs with a slower cadence of 60 cycles per minute.

Dynamic exercise at a high loading rate stimulates bone development. Deliberately slow movements probably will not promote bone adaptation to the same extent as dynamic movements.

Direction of loading and response

In animal experiments using rats, a process of loading the right ulna was applied to the right side of the animal, with the left side unstressed and used as the control (16). Data were gathered after a 16-week application of loading. Before and after, dual x-ray absorptiometry (DEXA) tests were conducted. A modest increase of 5.4% bone mineral density was found. After DEXA, the ulnae were removed and tested for strength in the direction of the loading protocol. It was determined that the increase in maximal amount of force that the bone could support before failing was 64%. So a relatively small increase in bone mineral density can translate into a much greater increase in strength to failure. The majority of bone growth took place consistent with the

direction of loading. In keeping with Wolff's law, the stimulus of loading actually changed the geometry of the bone.

Training programs that utilize a variety of movement and loading patterns will probably stimulate bone development to a greater extent.

Intensity of exercise

Load-bearing activities that place an axial load on the skeleton will induce greater bone formation. Along these lines, exercises such as running or jumping will elicit greater bone formation than walking (10). Dynamic weight-bearing exercises (such as the sport of weightlifting and the Olympic-style lifts) load more of the skeleton per repetition than do, say, arm curls. In animal experiments, the majority of new bone formation (greater than 95%) is stimulated by the first 40 repetitions of an exercise (23). Additional repetitions do not significantly increase the amount of bone that is formed.

Exercises that place an axial load on the skeletal system are probably superior, in terms of improving bone density, to exercises that do not place an axial load on the skeleton.

Short bouts of exercise followed by rest are better than prolonged workouts (18). The androgen receptors in the body that stimulate new bone growth experience desensitization after a period of time. They need a recovery period before they can be stimulated again to promote bone growth.

Bone takes about six to eight hours to recover its ability to stimulate new bone (18). After the androgen receptors that regulate new bone growth become saturated, they are again available after six to eight hours of rest. Because more receptors are available, full stimulation from the new bout of exercise may result. If a second training session starts before this recovery period, the formation of new bone may be compromised slightly. In another study, the femur and tibia of rats trained using only five jumps per day five days a week for eight weeks demonstrated significantly greater fat-free dry weights per body weight and maximum loads at the fracture tests than those in the control group (24).

Frequency of training

It appears it is better to add workouts to the training schedule rather than to extend existing workouts as long as there is enough rest between sessions. Rats that were trained to make 120 jumps five times a week experienced twice as much bone growth in their limbs as did another group that was trained to make 300 jumps twice a week (10). The same number of jumps distributed over a greater number of workouts significantly increased the development of new bone.

Vibration

With space travel, it was learned that astronauts lost bone density while in space (21). On the long-duration flights on Mir in the 1990s, cosmonauts lost as much as 20% of their bone density. In a weightless environment, as in space, axial loading of the skeletal system due to gravity does not occur. One of the contemplated remedies for this problem is vibration. Some information suggests the use of vibration as an alternative or supplemental method of training to maximize or maintain bone density.

When we look at the sensitivity of mature osteocytes to changes in hydrostatic pressure and increased osteoblastic activity, vibration would change the direction and flow of intracellular fluid at a rapid rate. Would the rate be adequate to inspire new bone growth and if so, what rate would be optimal?

Experimentation to combat the effects of microgravity using vertical vibrational loading to promote bone strength and BMD gains is ongoing (22). Therapeutic applications of vibration to improve or maintain bone density are being investigated in rehabilitation settings (5).

One study used a vibrating platform to manipulate rats with removed ovaries. Hormonal changes after menopause are thought to be at least partly responsible for bone loss in females. Over a 12-week period, the experimenters evaluated the effect of vibration in regard to bone loss and compared the experimental condition to a control condition (7). The results showed less bone loss over a five-week period in the vibration-trained group compared to the control group.

> Vibration as a stimulus for bone growth may promote bone density and prevent a loss of bone density under specific conditions.

Some important factors in vibration research include harmonic resonance dynamics, frequency modulation, consistent loading and stimulus application, and study length. Harmonic resonance occurs at certain frequencies of vibration. At some frequencies, tissue damage may occur. Frequency modulation is associated with the construction and application of sonic vibration. The mechanism of applying mechanical vibrational loading must be quantifiable and repeatable.

SUMMARY

Mechanisms within the human body cause adaptation of skeletal tissue in response to imposed stresses (15). The dynamic loading of bone stimulates bone growth. The rate and frequency of loading in animal models has a direct effect on bone growth. Designing conditioning programs to maximize bone growth and development should be specific to the demands of the sport and should include multidirectional loading.

Modest changes in BMD can represent large changes in bone strength. Short bouts with high-intensity loads are probably superior in promoting bone strength. Vibration will promote bone density in certain populations under specific conditions.

Frequent, short, dynamic exercises followed by a minimum of six to eight hours of rest appear to be optimal for the maintenance of bone health in athletes and others. The rest allows the osteoclastic activity to become more prominent than osteoblastic activity. This should be considered in planning training programs or practice sessions where multiple sessions are performed in one day.

MAXING OUT

1 A nonathletic female expresses concern to you that she may be at risk of bone density disorders as she gets older. Design a conditioning program to promote maximal bone density in this individual.

2 You believe that a female athlete on the track team is at risk for osteoporosis and that she may possibly have an eating disorder complicating the situation. What steps should you take to deal with this situation appropriately?

3 An athlete in a collision sport has a history of bone injuries, primarily stress fractures. He is accustomed to hard training and is experienced in a variety of lifting techniques. He is currently not injured. Plan a resistance training program for this athlete to promote maximal bone density.

REFERENCES

1. Ballock RT, O'Keefe RJ. Current concepts review: the biology of the growth plate. *J Bone Joint Surg* 2003; 85a(4):715–726,

2. Bemben DA, Torey D, Buchanan, et al. Influence of type of mechanical loading, menstrual status, and training season on bone density in young women athletes. *J Strength Cond Res* 2004; 8(2):220–226.

3. Burwell RG. Aetiology of idiopathic scoliosis: current concepts. *Pediatr Rehabil* 2003; 6(3–4);137–170.

4. Chan GK, Duque G. Age-related bone loss: old bone, new facts. *Gerontology* 2002; 48:62–71.

5. Cheung JT, Zhang M, Chow DH. Biomechanical responses of the intervertebral joint to static and vibrational loading: a finite elemental study. *Clin Biomech* 2003; 9:790–799.

6. Costigan PA, Deluzio KJ, Wyss UP. *J. Gait Posture* Aug 2002; 16(1):31–37.

7. Flieger J, Karchaolis T., Khaldi L, et al. Mechanical stimulation in the form of vibration prevents post-menopausal bone loss in ovariectomized rats. *Calcif Tissue Int* 1998; 63:510–514.

8. Frost H. From Wolff's law to the Utah paradigm: insights about bone physiology and its clinical applications. *Anat Rec* 2016; 262;398–419.

9. Hert J, Liskova M, Landa J. Reaction of bone to mechanical stimuli. 1. Continuous and intermittent loading of the tibia in rabbits. *Folia Morphol (Praha)* 1971; 19;290–300.

10. Hsieh YF, Turner CH. Effects of load frequency on mechanically induced bone formation. *J Bone Min Res* 2001; 16:918–924.

11. McClanahan BS, Harmon-Clayton K, Ward, KD, et al. Side-to-side comparisons of bone mineral density in upper and lower limbs of collegiate athletes. *J Strength Cond Res* 2002; 16(4):586–590.

12. Nauman E, Wesley C, Chang W, et al. Microscale engineering applications in bone adaptation. *Microscale Thermophys Eng* 1998; 2;139–172.

13. Nutter J. Physical Activity increases bone density. *NSCA J* 1986; 8(3):67–69.

14. Olsen S, Oloyede A. A finite element analysis methodology for representing the articular cartilage structure. *Comp Meth Biomech Biomed Eng* 2002; 5(6):377–386.

15. Platen P, Chae E, Antx R, et al. Bone mineral density in top level male athletes of different sports. *Eur J Sport Sci* 2001; 1:1–15.

16. Robling AG, Hinant FM, et al. Improved bone structure and strength after long term mechanical loading is greatest if loading is separated into short bouts. *J Bone Min Res* 2002; 17:1545–1554.

17. Rothenberg E, Lugo JP. Differentiation and cell division in the mammalian thymus. *Dev Biol* 1985; 112:1–17.

18. Rubin C, Lanyon L. Regulation of bone formation by applied dynamic loads. *J Bone Joint Surg* 1985; 66-A;397–402.

19. Silverwood B. *Pediatr Nurs* 2003; 15(5):27–29.

20. Simpkin A, Ayalon J, Leichter I. Increased trabecular bone density due to bone loading exercises in postmenopausal osteoporotic women. *Calcif Tissue Int* 1987; 40:59–63.

21. Shackelford LC, Oganov V, LeBlanc A, et al. *Bone Mineral Loss and Recovery after Shuttle-Mir Flights*. Available at www.hq.nasa.gov/osf/station/issphase1sci.pdf. Accessed June 24, 2006.

22. Teshima R, Nawata J, et al. Effects of weight bearing on the tidemark and osteochondral junction of articular cartilage. *Acta Orthop Scand* 1999; 70(4):381–386.

23. Torvinen S, Kannua P, Sievanen H, et al. Effect of 8-month vertical whole body vibration on bone, muscle performance, and body balance: a randomized controlled study. *J Bone Min Res* 2003; 18(5):876–884.

24. Umemura Y, Ishiko T, Yamauchi M, et al. Five jumps per day increase bone mass and breaking force in rats. *J Bone Min Res* 1997; 12:1480–1485.

Contents

CHAPTER 5

BIOMECHANICS OF RESISTANCE TRAINING

Scott K. Lynn, Guillermo J. Noffal, and Derek N. Pamukoff

OBJECTIVES

After completing this chapter, you will be able to:

- Comprehend units of biomechanical measurements.
- Apply velocity and joint angle specificity to training.
- Understand the length-tension and force-velocity-power relationships.
- Conceptualize Newton's laws of motion and apply them to training.
- Evaluate and compare different modes of resistance.
- Understand how to use a fundamental knowledge of biomechanics to progress or regress any exercise to the appropriate level for each individual.

KEY TERMS

Acceleration	Inertia	Stretch-shortening
Angular motion	Length	cycle (SSC)
Balance	Mass	Time
Biomechanics	Mechanical	Torque
Displacement	advantage	Velocity
Distance	Momentum	Velocity/speed
Force	Power	advantage
Friction	Rotary inertia	Weight
Gravity	Stability	Work

INTRODUCTION

Biomechanics has been defined as "the study of the structure and function of biological systems using the means and methods of mechanics" (10). This definition divides the word biomechanics into two parts: bio (biological system) and mechanics. In the field of strength and conditioning, the biological system that we are most concerned with is the human body. This includes all tissues directly involved with producing, preventing, or influencing movement (muscles, bones, ligaments, tendons, cartilage, the nervous system, etc.). Also, "mechanics" is defined as the study of the influence of force on bodies. Therefore, this chapter will be examining how we can manipulate forces in a strength and conditioning setting to produce the desired effect on the structures (tissues) and functions (movements) of the human body.

For the strength and conditioning specialist, a basic knowledge of biomechanics is essential in order to be able to evaluate human movement and then be able to design and prescribe appropriate movements (exercises) aimed at increasing the overall efficiency of movement. Forces are required to produce any type of human movement and there are various different types of forces and aspects of those forces that must be considered by the strength and conditioning specialist. A sound knowledge of basic mechanical principles will allow for the prescription of appropriate movements at the appropriate intensity to produce the desired movement outcomes without increasing the chance for injury (acute or chronic) of any of the movement structures/tissues.

It should be noted that many terms used in this chapter are not used according to their strict mechanical definition but have been simplified so that their applications in a strength and conditioning setting can be more clearly understood.

BASIC MECHANICS

Biomechanics can be simply defined as the effect of forces on the structure and function of living systems. In the field of strength and conditioning, there are several mechanical concepts that must be understood in order to fully comprehend how to most effectively and safely achieve our training goal. If we think of the simple example of someone lifting a barbell, some of the key mechanical concepts include force, distance, speed, inertia, mass, weight, velocity, acceleration, torque, power, and momentum. Many of these are derived from three basic variables – time, length, and mass (25). The basic unit of **time** is measured in either seconds, minutes, or hours; however, since many sporting or lifting movements are short in duration they are most often measured in seconds. The basic dimension of

length is measured in inches, feet, and yards in the USA, but the scientific community has adopted the metric system which utilizes centimeters, meters, kilometers, and so on. Lastly, the basic dimension of **mass** is commonly measured in kilograms.

To illustrate many of these biomechanical principles, we will examine one of the most basic of exercises, the bench press. Firstly, in the process of lowering the bar to your chest or pushing it back up, the bar moves through space in a fairly straight line. Naturally, if you are a tall individual with long arms you will be moving it a greater distance than someone with short extremities. Thus, **distance** is defined as the total path traveled by the bar. **Displacement** is defined as a straight line between where the movement started and where the movement ended. Although there is a difference between the two terms (distance vs. displacement), they are most often used interchangeably to describe how far the object has traveled. So, in the bench press example, if a beginner lifter struggles to push the weight up and it does not take a direct line from their chest to the finish position, they will have pushed the bar a greater distance than a more experienced individual who is able to push it straight up (Figure 5.1). For the more experienced lifter, the movement was much more efficient as the distance the bar traveled was much smaller to achieve the same displacement.

Similarly, if the beginner lifter took much longer to push the bar up, they would also have a lower bar **velocity** (often referred to as speed), which is defined as distance divided by time. Velocity can be measured in any unit that divides a measure of distance by a measure of time. The most common units used to measure velocity include meters/second, kilometers/hour, miles/hour. Therefore, in order to calculate velocity, you must measure the distance the object moved and the time it took to cover that distance. Distance and time can be measured in several different ways, which include the use of a tape measure and timing gates, video equipment, or electronic transducers.

Another illustration of velocity is the example of a sprinter finishing the 100 meter race in 10 seconds. This sprinter has achieved an average velocity of 10 m/s over the course

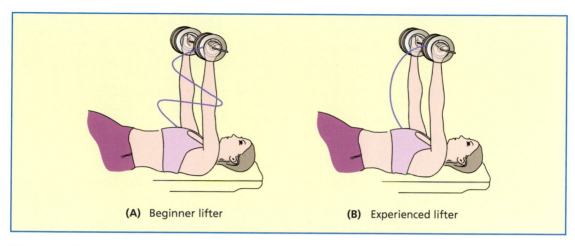

Figure 5.1 The path that the barbell travels for (A) a beginner; (B) an experienced lifter. Notice that the distance traveled is much greater for the beginner lifter; however, the displacements are the same.

of the race. This gives the strength and conditioning specialist some information, but in order to tailor appropriate training sessions to improve their time, more information is needed. If we obtained 10 meter split times for this race, we could calculate many velocities throughout the race and this would give us much more information regarding the portions of the race that need the most work. For example, if there is a large drop in velocity towards the end of the race, the strength and conditioning specialist may need to design a training program to work on the endurance of the athlete to ensure they are better able to maintain their velocity through the finish line. Thus, it becomes increasingly important to examine not just velocity, but how velocity is changing over time.

Acceleration is a measure of how velocity changes over time (defined as the change in velocity divided by time it took to make that change). An example that most are familiar with involves discussing how you would change velocities while driving your car (i.e., either speed up or slow down). In order to accelerate your car, or increase your car's speed, the accelerator pedal must be pressed. Conversely, in order to decelerate your car, or decrease the speed, you must press on the brakes. Thus, if while traveling at 40 mph you decide to increase your speed to 50 mph, an acceleration is needed. And if you are going

40 mph and you wish to stop your car (bring your car to a velocity of zero), a deceleration is needed. The rate at which these accelerations/decelerations happen become extremely important as well. Assume you are going 40 mph in your car and an animal jumps into the road directly in front of you. You need to decelerate from 40 mph to zero mph in a very short period of time to avoid hitting the animal. This scenario requires an extremely large deceleration as a large change in speed must happen over a short period of time. However, if you are going the same speed and you see the traffic light change to red 500 yards in front of you, you can press the brake more lightly and slow down gradually over a longer period of time. Thus, the same change in speed over a longer period of time requires a much smaller magnitude of deceleration. Good athletes generally have the ability to produce large accelerations and decelerations (quick changes in velocities). Therefore, training the ability to quickly and safely change speeds is important in most athletes.

Coming back to our bench press example, acceleration or deceleration of the bar is achieved through the application of force. **Force** is defined as a push or pull that moves or tends to move an object. The unit of force in the metric system is the Newton, while in the USA the pound (lb) is more commonly used. The amount of force being applied to an object can be calculated by multiplying the mass of the object by its acceleration. **Mass** is a measure of the quantity of matter within the object, and in the human body it would be the sum of all the tissues that make up our bodies (bones, muscles, fluids, etc.). Mass can be thought of as a measure of the linear inertia of a body. **Inertia** is defined as the resistance to changes in motion, and therefore an object with a larger mass will be more difficult to get moving and more difficult to stop once it has begun moving than an object with a smaller mass. Mass is often equated to **weight**; however, they differ in that weight is mass multiplied by the acceleration due to gravity (which we assume to be a constant value of 9.81 m/s^2 on the earth). Therefore, a person with a mass of 100 kg would weigh 981 Newtons while on earth, while in space in a zero gravity environment this person would be weightless, and while standing on the moon this person would weigh 162 Newtons (the acceleration due to gravity on the moon is approximately 1.62 m/s^2). Thus, while the weight will change depending on where the individual is standing, the mass will remain constant. It is fitting that the unit of force bears Isaac Newton's name as he has been credited with the discovery of gravity. **Gravity** is a mutually attractive force between two bodies that possess mass. Since the mass of the earth is much greater than that of anything on its surface, it will attract or pull all objects towards its core. Gravity is an important concept for strength and conditioning practitioners as weight training includes lifting and lowering objects against and with the force of gravity. It should be noted that gravity always pulls objects towards the center of the earth and thus only acts in the vertical direction.

Momentum is the product of mass and velocity and it is an important concept for the strength and conditioning specialist since momentum alone can continue the motion of an object. Unlike previous Aristotelian views that a constant force application was needed to maintain motion, Newton found that an object's inertia (mass) while on the move has a tendency to maintain that motion and only an external force acting on the object will slow it down and eventually stop its motion. Therefore, the greater the momentum of an object the greater the external forces needed to subsequently stop it.

There are many ways to increase the intensity of a workout session. Naturally, the most obvious is to increase the amount of weight being lifted. Another simple modification is to increase the number of repetitions to increase the workload. This introduces the concept of **Work**, which is defined as force times displacement and is measured in joules. As you increase the number of repetitions you also increase the displacement over which a force has been applied, therefore increasing the amount of work done. If there are two individuals lifting the same amount of weight over the same distance then these individuals are doing the same amount of work; however, if one of these

REAL-WORLD APPLICATION

Acceleration forces in lifting weights

One component of acceleration that is constantly acting on the human body and sports implements is acceleration due to gravity. In the example of arm curl with a dumbbell:

$$F = ma + mg$$

where F, force; m, mass of the dumbbell; a, instantaneous acceleration of the dumbbell; g, acceleration due to gravity (9.81 m/s^2); with a concentric muscle action in the dumbbell curl, gravity is a resistance force that results in negative acceleration. With an eccentric muscle action to lower the dumbbell, the force of gravity results in positive acceleration.

individuals is capable of producing the lift in a shorter period of time, then it is said that this person is more powerful.

Power is calculated two different ways: as work divided by time or as force multiplied by velocity, and it is measured in watts. Commonly used "slow-moving" exercises such as the bench press, squat, and dead lift only produce approximately half the power of the faster Olympic lifts (9). As can be seen from the formula, the optimization of both force and velocity is necessary for the greatest power output, and while large loads require large amounts of force to get moving, the movement speed is too low for optimal power. Conversely, lighter loads can be accelerated to high speeds but do not include the necessary force production to achieve greatest power.

Up to this point we have only been considering movements of objects or the body in a straight line, or what is generally called linear motion; however, many movements involve objects rotating about an axis or fulcrum and are defined as **angular motion**. In the human body these angular motions occur as our segments (foot, lower leg, thigh, etc.) rotate about axes created at the joints (ankle, knee, hip, etc.). Angular motion is measured in degrees, and in some instances can be described in radians (1 rad = approximately 57°) or revolutions (1 rev = 360°).

As discussed earlier, forces are needed to create linear motion. The angular equivalent of force is a **torque** (T), which is needed to create angular motion, and is expressed in foot-pounds (ft lb) or Newton-meters (N·m). In order to lift a dumbbell, the biceps brachii muscle must produce a torque in the upwards direction. How much torque is produced depends on the amount of force being utilized multiplied by the torque arm. The torque arm is defined as the perpendicular distance between where the force is being applied (the attachment of the biceps on the bone) and the axis of rotation (the elbow joint). In the example shown in Figure 5.2, lifting the dumbbell through concentric activity of the biceps requires a counterclockwise torque of greater magnitude than the clockwise torque being produced by the weight of the dumbbell. That is, the force of the biceps multiplied by

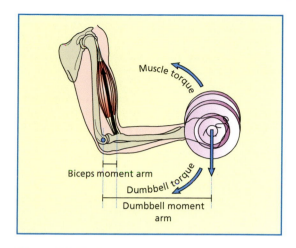

Figure 5.2 The biceps muscle torque (counterclockwise) and the torque produced by the dumbbell (clockwise), in an elbow flexion exercise.

the torque arm of the biceps has to be greater than the weight of the dumbbell multiplied by the distance this dumbbell is from the axis of rotation in order to produce concentric elbow flexion. If the opposite is true and the counterclockwise torque created by the dumbbell is greater than the clockwise torque created by the biceps brachii, eccentric elbow extension will be the resulting motion as the muscle will have allowed the dumbbell to "win." Isometric activity would occur when the magnitude of the torque produced by the muscle is equal to the torque produced by the dumbbell and there is no motion at the joint.

Q&A FROM THE FIELD

If the elbow flexors are strongest at 90° of flexion, why is the "sticking point" in the midrange of the movement?

The elbow is the strongest in flexion at 90° because the distance of the muscle force vector to the axis of rotation of the elbow is maximal here. This distance is a special kind of torque arm called the force arm (FA). This is the perpendicular distance from the muscle insertion to the axis of rotation at the elbow. However, the perpendicular distance from the point where the resistance is located to the axis of rotation, is also the greatest

(continued)

(continued)

in the midrange of the motion for an isotonic exercise. This distance is another kind of torque arm called the resistance arm (RA). Although the **mechanical advantage** of the elbow flexors is greatest at 90°, the increasing length of the RA in a heavy isotonic exercise overcomes this advantage. The sticking point will occur somewhere near 90°.

The concept of torque is very important for the strength and conditioning specialist to understand as modifying the placement of the weight or resistance from the axis of rotation can be an effective tool in either increasing or decreasing the muscular effort needed to successfully complete a movement. Figure 5.3 demonstrates this concept as picture (A) would require much more muscular torque than picture (B) to move the same mass. A real-life example of this would be having somebody do leg raises in the supine position with the legs straight and then with the legs bent at the knees. Bending the knees shortens the torque arm distance and decreases the amount of muscular torque needed to perform this exercise.

As mentioned earlier, **inertia** relates to an object's resistance to being moved or stopped from moving (in a linear sense); **rotary inertia** refers to an object's resistance to being spun (angular motion). Linear inertia can be easily

represented by the mass of the object; however, in order to calculate the rotary inertia, you need to measure both the mass of the object and how this mass is distributed relative to the axis of rotation. A simple example demonstrating this concept involves asking an individual to run without bending their knees. They will obviously not be able to run nearly as fast as when they are able to flex the knee during the swing phase of the running gait. While the legs themselves are not changing their mass as the hip flexes and extends, the outstretched leg is maintaining the mass of the lower leg and foot relatively far from the hip (axis of rotation). If instead the runner flexes the knee during the swing phase, this will bring the lower leg and foot closer to the hip (axis of rotation) and in so doing decrease the rotary inertia and allow the entire leg to now flex forward at a faster rate. This allows for the person to get through the recovery (swing) phase in a much shorter time and therefore run much faster (Figure 5.4).

Though this example demonstrates how bringing the mass closer to the axis of rotation promotes faster rotations, there are instances when rotation is not desired and the goal is then to increase the rotary inertia. Good examples of this are individuals walking along a tightrope. These daredevils often carry a long pole in their hands that is bent down from weights attached at its ends. The weights serve two purposes: it puts mass far away from the performer and brings the

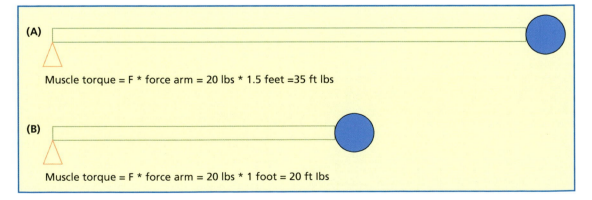

Figure 5.3 (A) a longer torque arm with the same mass = more torque required to move the object; (B) a shorter torque arm with the same mass = less torque required to move the object.

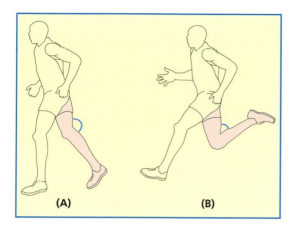

Figure 5.4 There is much more knee flexion during the swing phase of running than there is when walking. This allows the runner to decrease the rotary inertia of the swing leg and move it much faster.

center of gravity of the individual closer to the wire rendering them more stable and less likely to tip over (angular motion) to one side or the other due to the greater rotary inertia (Figure 5.5).

The term **balance** implies control of equilibrium, whereas **stability** is resistance to loss of equilibrium. One of the ways individuals increase their stability is by increasing the size of their base of support. This base of support is defined as the two-dimensional area formed by the supporting segments of the body (Figure 5.6). Coaches often ask their players to spread their feet shoulder-width apart rendering them more stable. Increasing the base of support enhances stability because it increases the distance your

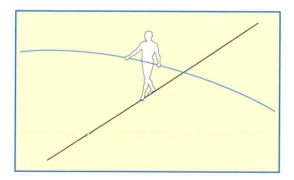

Figure 5.5 The pole used by a tightrope walker increases their rotary inertia.

line of gravity has to move before it ends up outside this base, causing a loss of balance. Once the line of gravity is outside the base of support, the body will experience a destabilizing torque from the pull of gravity that will tend to topple the body over. Lowering your center of gravity also increases stability by decreasing the magnitude of this destabilizing torque by reducing distance from your center of gravity to your axis of rotation (your feet on the ground). Olympic lifting competitions require not only for the athlete to lift the weight above their head, but they also need to demonstrate control of the weight by balancing it for three seconds. This balance is difficult due to the high center of gravity position since it is not uncommon for these athletes to be lifting more than twice their own body weight. Therefore, a shorter lifter would have a stability advantage over a much taller lifter as the same small movement of the load would produce a greater destabilizing torque in the taller lifter.

The most unstable foot position possible in a human being is standing on one foot. When standing on one foot our base of support becomes the length or width of the foot, and if the center of gravity falls outside of the dimensions of the foot, there will be a loss of balance. The strength and conditioning specialist can use this foot position during many different exercises to train stability. By training in this very unstable position, one can further develop the body's sensory and muscular recruitment strategies needed to maintain balance. Several pieces of equipment frequently in use in strength and conditioning facilities also have the goal of creating an unstable surface to allow for the training of the ability to maintain balance. One such recent invention is the BOSU® ball (Figure 5.7). If we stand on the platform side of this ball the base of support becomes the portion of the ball that is in contact with the ground. The stability challenge can then be altered by how much air you put in the ball. If the ball is pumped up with a lot of air, it will be very rigid and you will be balancing on a really small area of the ball. This makes maintaining balance more difficult as the base of support is extremely small. To make this challenge easier, you can remove air from the ball so that the ball becomes softer and more of it then comes in contact with the ground, increasing the base of support.

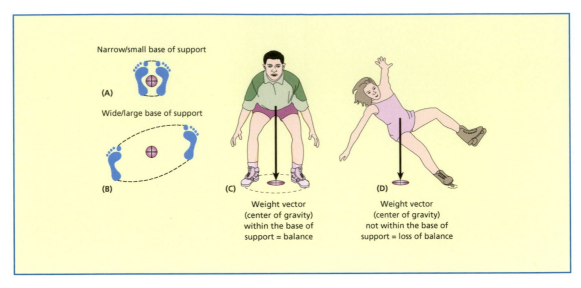

Figure 5.6 The position of the center of gravity relative to the base of support determines whole body stability and balance.

Friction can also be used in certain instances to increase the difficulty of a certain task or exercise. The two factors that determine the amount of friction are the nature of the two surfaces attempting to slide past one another (the coefficient of friction) and the amount of force pressing the two surfaces together (the normal force). Monarch cycle ergometers use increased tension of the belt around the wheel

Figure 5.7 Using a BOSU® ball to alter the size of the base of support during a squatting exercise.

to increase the friction and increase the resistance, this would be an example of altering the normal force or force pushing the two objects together. Football coaches stand on top of blocking sleds to increase the force pressing the sled to the ground and in so doing making it harder for football players to push the sled across the grass. This is another example of increasing the normal force in order to increase friction and make an exercise more difficult. Applying talcum powder to the hands in order to remove moisture and get a better grip while lifting is an example of changing the nature of the surfaces in contact and altering the coefficient of friction.

HUMAN MUSCULOSKELETAL MECHANICS

Length-tension relationship

There are two types of tissues that can create tension in a muscle: (i) the active component consisting of the acting and myosin muscle proteins, and (ii) the passive component consisting of the connective tissue within the muscle belly which comes together on either end to form the muscle tendon. The tension/force that can be created by these two different types of tissue changes as the length of the muscle changes throughout a movement (12,14).

The length-tension curve for the active component of muscle is an inverted "U" shape. The peak of this curve (where the maximum active tension/force can be produced) corresponds to the position where the muscle is in an optimal position to allow the most actin/myosin cross-bridges. As the muscle is increasingly stretched beyond this length, these cross-bridges are torn apart so the amount of tension/force the active component of muscle can produce decreases as the length of the muscle increases. Conversely, as the muscle is shortened from this optimal length, increasing numbers of the actin/myosin cross-bridges become overlapped and are no longer able to produce the power strokes that allow for the production of tension/force. Therefore, as the length of a muscle decreases so too does the amount of tension/force that the active component of muscle can produce.

The passive component of muscle only produces force/tension when the muscle is lengthened. You can think of this component of your muscles as elastic bands. If you shorten an elastic band beyond its resting length, it does not create any tension/force. The only way to produce tension/force of an elastic band is to stretch it beyond its resting length so that it then tries to snap back to its original shape. Therefore, when a muscle is shortened the total length tension curve involves only the inverted U shape of the active component as there is no passive contribution to force production. However, as the muscle is increasingly lengthened, the tendon and connective tissues are stretched beyond their resting length and produce an increasing amount of force with increased lengthening. Therefore, the total tension/force achieved when a muscle is stretched beyond its resting length is the sum of both the active and passive components (Figure 5.8).

Force-velocity-power relationship

Although the amount of force a muscle can produce is important, perhaps more important in many human movements is the velocity at which a muscle can develop this force. Often the terms "strength" and "power" are erroneously used interchangeably. Strength refers to a muscle's ability to produce force in isometric or slow velocity contractions; whereas power refers to a combination of force production and velocity (18). Training only force development at slow speeds (strength) may have negative implications for a wide range of individuals. Obviously, most sporting activities involve high velocity, high power movements and therefore, it may not be effective to train any athlete to only be able to slowly develop extremely large forces. Also, in order to train older adults to avoid falls, we must be concerned with the velocity of muscular contraction as well. If an individual loses their balance, they must move quickly and adjust the position of their center of gravity or take a step to widen their base of support to avoid falling. It has also been shown that as one ages, explosive strength or power decreases more than maximum isometric strength (16) which makes training these fast muscular contractions essential in older adults. Therefore, an understanding of the relationship between force, velocity, and power presented in Figure 5.9 (14) is essential for the strength and conditioning specialist.

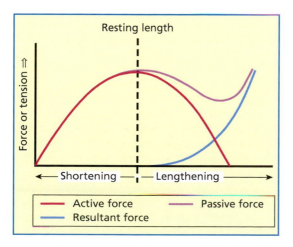

Figure 5.8 The active, passive, and resultant forces for the typical muscle length tension curve.

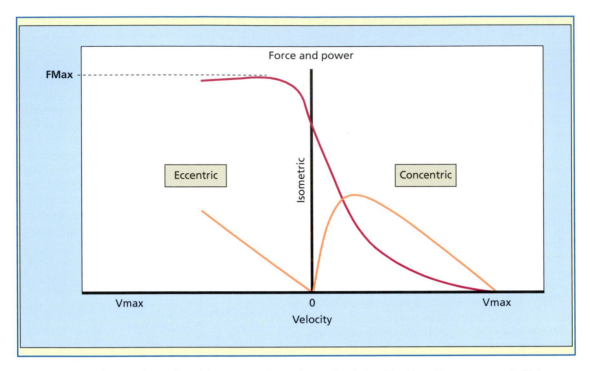

Figure 5.9 The force–velocity (purple), power–velocity (orange) relationship. Note: Recent research (2) has determined the eccentric force-power relationship.

If a muscle is maximally activated in an attempt to produce movements at different speeds, several important points must be observed:

1 As the speed of concentric contraction increases, the force that can be produced during those contractions decreases. Therefore, the minimum amount of force that a muscle can produce is during a fast concentric contraction.
2 Greater tension can be developed during an isometric contraction (velocity = 0) than during any speed of concentric contraction.
3 Muscles can generate their greatest forces while resisting motion during eccentric (lengthening) contractions. These eccentric or lengthening velocities are shown as negative velocities (x axis) in Figure 5.9. It should also be noted that forces generated during eccentric contractions also rise slightly and then remain relatively constant as velocity increases.
4 As was mentioned in the Basic mechanics section, Power = force × velocity. Since force and concentric velocity have an inverse relationship (i.e., as velocity goes up, force goes down), the point of peak concentric power will occur somewhere between an isometric and maximum velocity concentric contraction. The in vitro concentric power curve derived from the force-velocity relationship of skeletal muscle is highly dependent on the movement being tested. Izquierdo et al. (16) demonstrated that the best resistances (forces) for the development of peak power in the upper body were in the range of 30–45% of maximum isometric force. However, for explosive lower body movements peak power was observed at 60–70% of maximum isometric force.
5 Recent research (2) has demonstrated that as eccentric velocity increases, power increases as well in a linear relationship.

This force-velocity-power relationship can be readily observed in strength and conditioning settings. If we attempt to lift an extremely heavy load, the velocity of movement will be extremely small as we will need to produce maximal forces to move this load and will not be able to get it moving very quickly. When training with lighter loads we are much more able to get the resistance moving quickly; however, training with too light a load will necessitate extremely small forces from our muscles. Therefore, in order to achieve peak power we must choose an appropriate resistance to allow for adequate force productions and speed of movement.

Physiological cross-sectional area

The physiological cross-section area (PCSA) of a muscle is a measure of how many muscle sarcomeres are arranged in parallel in that particular muscle. This has been shown to determine the maximum force generating capacity of the muscle (8). Therefore, a bigger muscle (larger PCSA) can produce more force than a smaller muscle (small PCSA). This is logical as one of the main goals of resistance training is to increase the size, and hence the force producing capacity of our muscles.

One muscle with an extremely large PCSA in the human body is the gluteus maximus muscle (15). With the force generating capacity of this muscle being so large, many smaller muscles must compensate for it if it is not working efficiently. Therefore, it is important that we train it appropriately as extremely common pathologies such as low back pain have been associated with a loss of neural drive to this muscle – termed "gluteal amnesia" (24).

Stretch shortening cycle

Most human movements begin with motions in the opposite direction to the intended movement. For example, the vertical jump involves an initial flexion of the knees/hips and dorsiflexion of the ankles used to accelerate the center of gravity downwards. This causes an eccentric stretch of the knee/hip extensors and ankle plantarflexors that is quickly turned into a concentric contraction of these same muscles to produce the upwards motion of the center

of gravity resulting in the jump. This eccentric stretch followed closely by a concentric shortening has been termed the **stretch-shortening cycle of muscle (SSC)** of muscle. If there is a minimal time delay between the eccentric stretch and concentric contraction, it has been shown that there is an increase in the force produced as compared to an isolated concentric contraction (28). The magnitude of increase in concentric force depends on the movement performed and the resistance being moved but is generally thought to be in the magnitude of 10–20%. Therefore, the SSC is critical in producing high force and high power concentric muscular contractions.

Joint angle and muscular torque

Muscles pull on bones at a distance from the axis of rotation (joint) and therefore, they produce a torque that attempts to produce angular motion of the bones to which they are attached. The amount of torque can be calculated by multiplying the force by the torque arm distance. As a muscle causes movement of the bones, the length of the force arm changes. This means that with the same amount of muscular force, there are changes in the amount of torque generated as the muscle moves the joint through its range of motion. In a simple hinge joint like the elbow/knee, the flexors (biceps brachii/hamstrings) are at a mechanical advantage at a joint angle of 90° as the force arm is the longest in this joint position. As the joint angle increases or decreases, the force arm decreases in length, creating less torque with the same muscular force (Figure 5.10).

Levers

The arrangement of the bones, muscles, and joints in the human body create simple machines called lever systems. The anatomical levers of the body cannot be changed, but when the system is well understood, they can be used more efficiently to maximize the muscular efforts of the body (6). The three components of every lever system include the axis (joint), the resistance (weight of the

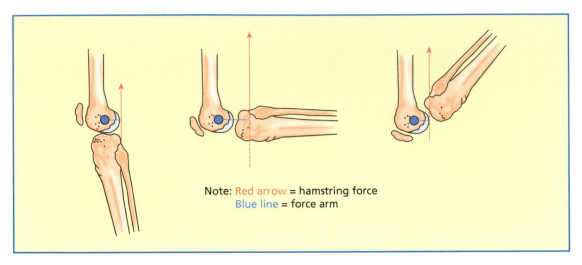

Note: Red arrow = hamstring force
Blue line = force arm

Figure 5.10 The change in the torque generating capacity (force arm distance) of the hamstring muscles as the knee joint angle changes.

segment being moved and any attached external weight), and the force (muscle force). The location of these three components with respect to one another will determine the type of lever and most importantly, the movement characteristics for which they are best suited. The lever type is determined primarily by which of the three components is located in between the other two. That is, a first class lever has the axis in the middle, while a second class lever has the resistance in the middle, and finally a third class lever has the force in between the axis and resistance (Figure 5.11).

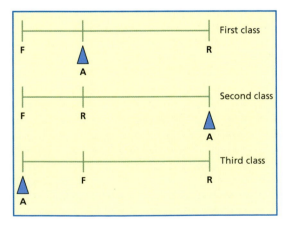

Figure 5.11 First class, second class, and third class lever systems.

The distances between the axis and the force (a special kind of torque arm called a force arm [FA]) and the axis and the resistance (a special kind of torque arm called a resistance arm [RA]) help determine the types of movements that each lever system is best designed to perform. Those levers with a short resistance arm and a long force arm are said to have a large mechanical advantage (calculated by dividing the FA by the RA). This is because large resistances can be moved over short distances with small forces if a lever is used that creates this mechanical advantage. For example, if a 180-pound person wants to move a 900 pound rock, they could do this most effectively by getting a board and wedging it under the rock and then balancing the board on an object really close to the rock (creating the axis of rotation). If the distance between the axis and the rock is two feet, this creates 1,800 ft-lbs of torque that must be overcome in order to move the rock. Therefore, the person would need to jump on the board ten feet from the axis to produce the required torque needed to move the large rock, but the resultant displacement and hence the velocity of the rock would not be large.

Human muscle bone levers have the muscles inserted really close to the joints creating extremely short FAs. By comparison, our limb segments are relatively long creating

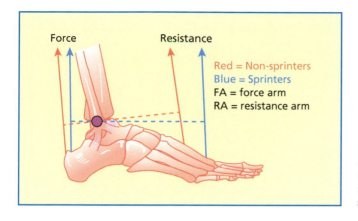

Figure 5.12 The differences in anatomy noted by Lee and Piazza (20) between sprinters and nonsprinters. Sprinters had a shorter force arm and a longer resistance arm, creating a speed advantage.

much longer RAs. This creates a mechanical disadvantage or a **velocity/speed advantage** (calculated by dividing the RA by the FA) in human muscle bone levers. This is due to the fact that it will take a lot of force to get the resistance moving (mechanical disadvantage), but once we get it moving it will have a much larger displacement and hence velocity/speed. This concept is displayed in research that examined the anatomical differences in the ankle/foot between a group of collegiate sprinters and a group of height matched non-athletes (20). It was discovered that the sprinters had longer toes and also had 25% shorter Achilles tendon FAs (Figure 5.12). Therefore, the sprinters had shorter FAs and were also able, with their longer toes, to get the force of the ground pushing back up on their foot further from the axis of rotation at their ankle, creating a longer RA. This creates a greater velocity/speed advantage that may be one mechanical reason why sprinters can run faster than non-sprinters.

BIOMECHANICS OF RESISTANCE

In strength and conditioning settings, various forms of resistance have been used to make movements/exercises more challenging. The extra stimulus provided by this resistance can help accomplish the goal of the training session, whether it is simply to make fundamental human movement patterns more efficient or to increase strength, speed, or both (i.e., power). The original and most commonly used form of resistance simply utilizes different forms of mass and the force of gravity. As various technologies have advanced, other forms of resistance have been developed that have certain biomechanical characteristics that are different from mass and provide a different stimulus to the human body during training. The following section will examine several different forms of resistance and discuss how the mechanics of these then produce different training stimuli. This information is important for the strength and conditioning specialist so that the appropriate form of resistance can be used to accomplish the specific functional goal of the training. It is important to tailor the training to the particular goal of the program to ensure success. An appropriate analogy can be drawn to the engines in our automobiles. A formula one car (designed for speed) will require a much different engine than a truck designed to haul and tow large loads (designed more for force production). The strength and conditioning specialist needs to choose the appropriate form of resistance to ensure that we are building the correct engines (muscles) to meet the goals of the individual.

The following section will examine the biomechanics of several different forms of resistance which will be divided into two main categories: (i) those that use mass and the force of gravity as the resistance, and (ii) those that do not use significant mass and generate the mechanical resistance using other means.

Q&A FROM THE FIELD

How can I alter the squat movement pattern to make it more "knee dominant" or more "hip dominant"?

In addition to external objects, other forces commonly place external torques on joints. For example, during weight bearing exercises, body weight acts downward toward the ground, and the ground pushes back upwards on the body to create a ground reaction force (GRF). This direction of the GRF is often positioned away from joint centers, and an external torque is created (Figure 5.13). In other words, the GRF is acting at a distance from the axis of rotation of the joint and this produces an external torque that is attempting to rotate the joint. Muscles must respond to this torque and produce the appropriate internal joint torques to achieve the desired movement. An example of this concept during a squatting motion is described in the Q&A 'From the Field' below and illustrates how the position of the ground reaction force influences relative contributions from the hip and knee joint musculature in producing the squat movement.

In Figure 5.13A, the ground reaction force is positioned much further posterior to the center of the knee joint and much closer to the center of the hip joint. This produces a relatively large external flexion torque on the knee joint that must be matched by the knee extensors (quadriceps). This individual could be considered "knee dominant"

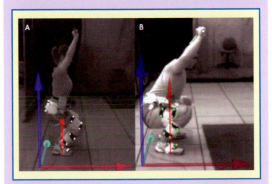

Figure 5.13 (A) The ground reaction forces (red arrows) are further from the knee joint than the hip joint indicating a "knee dominant" squat position; (B) the ground reaction forces (red arrows) are further from the hip joint than the knee joint indicating a "hip dominant" squat position.

because there is much larger knee joint torque relative to the hip joint torque. In contrast, the individual in Figure 5.13B has a ground reaction force that is acting much closer to the knee joint center and further anterior to the hip joint center. This produces a relatively larger external flexion torque on the hip that must be matched by the hip extensors. Therefore, this individual could be considered "hip dominant" because there is much larger torque on the hip than there is on the knee.

There are several ways to alter how much the knee and hip extensors contribute to producing this motion, but all utilize this basic mechanical principle. One simple way to shift the loading onto one joint or the other is to change where the mass of the body segments and resistance are located. Doing a counter-balanced squat, where you hold weights in your hands and raise them in front of you as you sit back in the squat, shifts the GRF anteriorly. This makes the exercise more "hip dominant" as it increases the load on the hip extensors and decreases the load on the knee extensors. Conversely, performing a squat where the weights remain on your shoulders keeps the GRF acting more posteriorly, which makes it more "knee dominant" (increases the load on the knee extensors and decreases the load on the hip extensors) (21).

Application: knee joint loading in osteoarthritis

In addition to external torques produced by objects such as dumbbells, external torques can also come from our body weight pushing into the ground. For example, during weight bearing activities, our body weight acts downward, and the ground pushes back up on our body creating a GRF. The position of the GRF relative to the center of our joints creates a torque (Figure 5.14). Notice the blue arrow representing the ground reaction force is positioned medial from the center of the left knee joint.

External torques can also influence internal joint loading with consequences for joint health and disease. For example, individuals with misaligned knees are at greater risk for knee osteoarthritis (27). In these individuals, the position of the ground reaction force vector is offset from the joint center in the frontal plane. This creates an external adduction torque on the knee joint and contributes to preferential loading of the medial side of the knee joint (1). Over time, excessive loading on the medial side of the knee joint may contribute to osteoarthritis by wearing of the

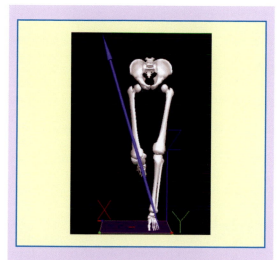

Figure 5.14 Notice the ground reaction force (blue arrow) acts medial to the left knee joint. This position places an external knee adduction torque on the joint.

joint articular surfaces (22). Interestingly, the vast majority of knee osteoarthritis cases occur in the medial compartment. Therefore, limiting excessive knee adduction torques may be useful in knee osteoarthritis prevention.

Application: strengthening hip abductors

In addition to chronic joint conditions, external torques can also cause acute injuries. For example, body position during landing activities

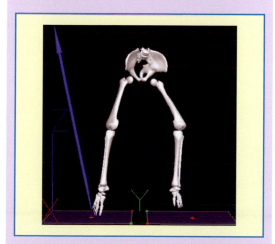

Figure 5.15 External abduction torque created by the position of the ground reaction force (blue arrow) relative to the position of the knee joint.

is implicated in traumatic knee injuries, such as anterior cruciate ligament (ACL) tear. For example, notice the position of the ground reaction force in Figure 5.15 and its lateral position relative to the right knee joint. This position creates an external knee abduction torque. An individual that lands with their knees caved inwards, often termed a "valgus collapse," is at greater risk factor for ACL injury (11). Importantly, these movement patterns highlight areas for conscious correction through muscle strengthening. For example, the described knee position also indicates excessive hip adduction. Therefore, strengthening and improving hip abductor function may be a focus for this individual, and the exercises described in the "Progressing/regressing movement" section may be useful.

Mass

When using any form of mass as resistance, the most important biomechanical concept that the strength and conditioning specialist must keep in mind is its inherent inertial properties. To be put another way, mass resists changes to its state of motion. So, if it is not moving, large forces must be applied to the mass to get it moving. Then, once it begins moving, less force must be applied to keep it moving than was needed to start it in motion. Most overlook the fact that, when performing a lift with a 20-pound dumbbell, the resistance provided to the human body throughout that lift can vary from much greater than 20 pounds to overcome the inertia of that mass, to almost zero if the mass is accelerated to a high enough speed during the lift.

The force the person is applying to the mass can best be calculated using the equation: $F = ma + mg$. The second part of this equation (mg) is constant as the acceleration due to gravity ($g = 9.81$ m/s^2) and the mass remain constant throughout a lift. However, the first half of this equation (ma) is not constant as the mass must be accelerated at the start of the lift and decelerated at the end of the lift. If a mass is moved extremely slowly through the range of motion, the effect of the "ma" term becomes negligible; however, for rapid movements with large changes in speed, this term becomes extremely important and can cause great variation in the resistance felt by the muscles throughout the range of motion. It has been shown that doing high speed lifts with free weight resistance requires in excess of 190% of the weight of the load in order to produce these high accelerations (4,26). That means that if doing a bench press with 130 lbs, the resistance at the beginning of the concentric phase can actually exceed 250 lbs as the momentum of the eccentric phase is quickly absorbed and the bar is accelerated concentrically to a high rate of speed. Then, once the weight is moving at a high rate of speed, the resistance provided to the muscles can decrease to almost zero if the weight is accelerated fast enough that the magnitude of the (m × a) term equals that of the (m × g) term. This gives the lifter the feeling that the bar is temporarily floating and almost thrown into the air, which can be dangerous in a bench press movement. This is demonstrated by studies showing that well trained athletes can spend up to 52% of the concentric phase of a high-speed lift attempting to decelerate and control the trajectory of the load (5), this leads to a decrease in the activity of the muscles producing the movement during this portion of the lift (26).

Two common forms of mass used as resistance in strength and conditioning settings include: (i) free weights and (ii) gravity-based machines.

Free weights

Free weights are often thought to include only barbells and dumbbells but can also come in many other forms. Any object that has a mass and allows for 6° of freedom movement of that mass can be considered a "free weight." Other common forms of free weight include: kettlebells, medicine balls, weight vests, weighted ankle/wrist straps, weighted sleds, training ropes, chains, and the simplest form of resistance of all, the individual's own body weight. The biomechanics of these forms of resistance follow the laws of inertia outlined earlier and always have the resistance acting vertically downward. Therefore, the force needed to move these weights vertically can be determined using the formula F = ma + mg. The force needed to move these weights horizontally does not need to overcome gravity and therefore can

be determined using F = ma. Therefore, adjusting how much a mass is moved horizontally/vertically can be a good method of progressing and regressing many different movements, as the amount of gravity that must be overcome during the movement can be altered. An example of this would be doing a push up with your hands on a bench rather than on the ground. With your hands on the bench, you will be moving your mass partially in a horizontal direction, making the movement much easier and requiring less muscular force to complete it.

Gravity-based machines

The resistance of any mass acts vertically downward, which limits our ability to train certain muscle groups. For example, using mass to train a vertical shoulder press movement is appropriate, but in order to train the antagonist movement (i.e., lat pull down exercise), the gravity force needs to be redirected. This is accomplished by machines that use cables and pulleys to allow us to direct the resistance of a mass/gravity upwards or horizontally (Figure 5.16). Older versions of these machines would have the user adjust the resistance by adding/removing weighted plates, but newer versions of these machines use pin-loaded weight stacks to make the adjusting of the resistance much easier.

Figure 5.16 Two gravity-based weight machines that allow the resistance of the mass to be redirected using pulleys.

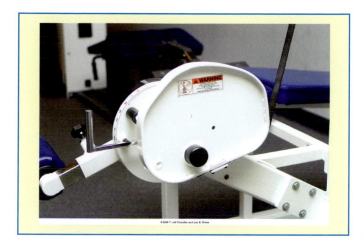

Figure 5.17 A variable radius cam.

Engineers have also attempted to design gravity-based machines so that the resistance delivered to the individual better matches our muscles' ability to produce force across the range of motion of the joint. For example, in the free weight bench press we are limited in resistance by the amount we are able to move through our weakest point (sticking point) near the bottom of the lift. Therefore, our muscles are not getting challenged appropriately in the upper part of the range of motion, as we must pick a resistance that allows us to get through the sticking point where our muscles are weakest. This was originally overcome by creating machines where the user would start the movement in their weakest position (i.e., the bottom position of the chest press movement) but with the machine lever arm to the weight stack extremely short. As the movement proceeded from bottom to top, the machine's lever arm to the weight stack would increase in length, thus also increasing the resistance felt by the user in the later stages of the lift. Various other gravity-based machines have also attempted to produce a variable amount of resistance throughout a lift using different designs. One common design uses a cable or chain that wraps over a variable-radius cam and alters the moment arm distance to the resistance (weight stack) as the user moves through the range of motion (Figure 5.17). Again, this allows for the user to feel more resistance at portions of the lift where the muscles are mechanically strongest and less resistance where the muscles are less optimally positioned. However, all of these machines use mass for the resistance and therefore the speed of movement becomes really important to determining the resistance felt by the muscles, as creating large accelerations of the mass could negate the effects of these variable resistance designs.

Other forms of resistance

Pneumatic resistance

In order to overcome the limitations associated with training at high speed using mass as the resistance, a technology was developed that creates the resistance with air pressure (17). It has been contended that this form of resistance does not have the inherent limitations of mass and its inertial properties. Therefore, high speed training involving large accelerations can be performed and the resistance can be kept relatively constant throughout the movement. The basic technology involves a compressor pumping air into a cylinder (Figure 5.18) (more air pressure = more resistance; less air pressure = less resistance) equipped with a piston that further compresses the air during the concentric phase and is pushed back out by the air during the eccentric phase of the movement. As the air is further compressed during the concentric phase of movement, the resistance increases, and this is thought to match the force producing capacity of our muscles during most movements. The user also has control of the resistance with hand

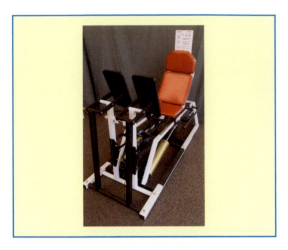

Figure 5.18 A Keiser pneumatic resistance machine showing the air cylinder (with the piston inside).

Figure 5.20 Adjustable pneumatic resistance machines that allow for the resistance to be focused in any direction and allow for much less control of the range of motion.

buttons or foot pedals that can increase (pump in more air) or decrease (let air out) the resistance throughout the movement.

There has been a wide range of exercise equipment designed using this pneumatic resistance technology. Some of these include machines designed for high stability that guide the user through the range of motion and train only specific movements (chest press, leg extension, leg press, etc.) – Figure 5.19. There are also cable machines that can be adjusted to

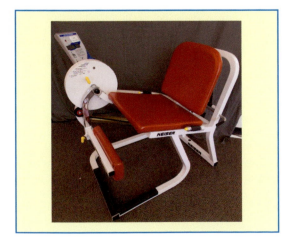

Figure 5.19 A pneumatic resistance machine designed for high stability by guiding the user through the range of motion.

provide the resistance in the desired direction for the exercise and allow for a less controlled range of movement – Figure 5.20. Finally, there have been power racks designed to be able to incorporate both mass and air resistance in a wide range of total body 6° of freedom movements (bench press, squat, deadlift, power clean, etc.). These can combine different amounts of mass and air resistance or can be used with negligible mass and only air resistance depending on the goal of the training session.

Research has shown that pneumatic resistance allows for greater movement velocities and also produces greater muscle activity at the end range of motion as compared to free weights in a bench press movement (7). This is due to the fact that pneumatic resistance contains limited mass and therefore does not develop momentum at high speeds. Athletic movements as well as many movements in everyday life (i.e., regaining equilibrium after a loss in balance) require high speed muscular contractions and velocity specific power production. Therefore, training with pneumatic resistance could provide some movement specific advantages over free weights. However, this work also suggests that pneumatic resistance reduces the forces required to use the stretch shortening cycle at the end of the eccentric and start of the concentric phase of motion (7). Therefore, further investigation is needed to identify the neuromuscular responses of the human body to this alternate form of resistance.

Hydraulic resistance

Another form of resistance similar to pneumatics uses fluid (generally oil) to create the resistance. This form of resistance has the movement drive a piston that forces the fluid through a small opening creating the resistance. The difference between pneumatic and hydraulic resistance comes in the compressibility of the fluid being used for the resistance. The air used in pneumatic resistance is compressible; therefore, the forces put into compressing it during the concentric phase are returned during the eccentric phase. The oil used in hydraulic resistance is essentially incompressible; therefore, hydraulic resistance does not provide any eccentric resistance during movement.

It has been shown that greater gains in peak torque can be achieved when movements are trained both concentrically and eccentrically (19). However, an examination of the differences between groups' subjects training with free weights (concentric-eccentric) and hydraulics (concentric only) revealed no differences in velocity, torque, power, or force between groups (13). Therefore, there is some controversy in the literature regarding the usefulness of hydraulic resistance in a training program. It can also be suggested that the elimination of the eccentric phase created with this equipment may have uses for special populations as it may also decrease the muscle soreness experienced by the user.

Elastic resistance

Various forms of elastic resistance have become extremely common in strength and conditioning settings recently. Elastics provide a variable amount of resistance throughout a movement as the elastic will produce more force the more it is stretched. It also provides an eccentric resistance as all the force that went into stretching the elastic will be returned as the individual's muscles control the speed at which the elastic is returned to its original length.

Studies comparing the effects of training with elastic resistance to training with mass as a resistance also provide contradictory results. In a sample of sedentary middle-aged women, there was found to be no differences in several functional and structural measures between training with elastic resistance versus training with a weight machine (3). Whereas, in a sample of recreationally trained college students, those who trained by simply doing depth jumps (using body weight) increased their vertical jump height, while those who trained with elastic resistance (VertiMax) did not change their jump height after training (23).

What form of resistance is best?

It should be clear from the sections outlined above that no single form of resistance is ideal for all training purposes. However, the strength and conditioning specialist must have a basic knowledge of all forms of resistance and how they can be combined and altered so that an appropriate stimulus can be selected to meet the goal of each individual training program.

PROGRESSING/ REGRESSING MOVEMENT

As a strength and conditioning specialist, an important skill is to be able to modify movements/exercises to (i) increase the difficulty of movement to further challenge those who have mastered the basic movement, and (ii) decrease the difficulty of movement to give those who are unable to perform the basic movement a chance to develop the proper strength and/or muscular recruitment strategies.

Progressing and regressing movements/exercises requires a good basic knowledge of many basic biomechanical principles. The simplest progressions and regressions can be performed by simply manipulating the variables of the equation presented in the previous section (F = ma). If we assume that progressions would generally involve creating movements that require more force production, this can be accomplished by either increasing the mass or increasing the rate of velocity change during the movement (acceleration or deceleration). Conversely, we could easily regress a movement/ exercise by decreasing the mass being moved or by moving more slowly (requiring less accelerations/decelerations). Although this sounds logical, there are other factors that must be kept in mind. For example, moving extremely slowly through a bench press movement may seem like a regression (less accelerations) when it may actually make the exercise more difficult. Newton's First Law (Law of Inertia) tells us that an object in motion wants to remain in motion; therefore, getting the bar moving quickly in certain phases of the lift would require less muscular effort to keep it moving in other phases. This becomes important in overcoming points in the range of motion where the muscle length tension relationship and angle of pull of muscle are at their least optimal (sticking point). Therefore, simply trying to manipulate the variables of that equation in order to progress/ regress movements is not enough. The strength and conditioning specialist needs a much more complete knowledge of biomechanics to be able to tailor movement/exercise difficulty to the level of each individual.

The following section will use the example of the single-leg Romanian dead-lift (RDL) in order to illustrate how biomechanical principles can be used to progress or regress a movement/exercise. We will begin with a biomechanical description of the basic movement.

Single-leg Romanian dead-lift (RDL)

This basic exercise (shown in Figure 5.21) has several main goals when used in a training program; some of these goals include: (i) training the hip abductors to increase frontal plane control of the pelvis, (ii) training the hip extensors to move us in the sagittal plane, (iii) training the balance and proprioceptive systems in single limb stance.

If we examine this movement in the frontal plane, we can see that the axis of rotation is created at the hip of the stance limb. Gravity then pulls on the rest of the body (person's left in Figure 5.21) and produces a torque that is attempting to spin our pelvis clockwise. Our hip abductors then produce a force on the other side of the axis of rotation to counter the body weight (clockwise) torque with the muscular (counterclockwise) torque needed to maintain a steady pelvis.

Figure 5.21 The basic single-leg Romanian dead-lift exercise.

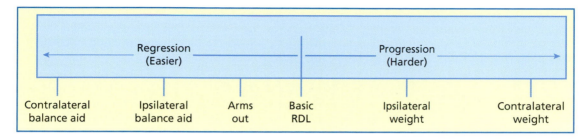

Figure 5.22 The single-leg RDL progression/regression continuum.

In the sagittal plane, tilting of the trunk anteriorly creates a clockwise torque attempting to produce flexion at the stance hip. We then have two counterclockwise torques acting on the other side of the axis of rotation attempting to produce hip extension: (i) the torque created by the weight of the contra lateral leg (which will be of smaller magnitude than the torque created by our trunk as the mass of a single leg will be much less than the mass of the trunk) and (ii) the muscle force created by your hip extensors that is needed to absorb the excess trunk torque in the eccentric phase and overcome it to produce the concentric hip extension needed to return to a standing position.

We will now examine how a good knowledge of biomechanics can be used to create three regressions and two progressions of the basic RDL exercise. The above continuum (Figure 5.22) shows each of the five exercise modifications that can be used to make the exercise less challenging (regressions) and more challenging (progressions). Note: The further the exercise is to the right, the harder the exercise is; and the further the exercise is to the left, the easier the exercise is.

Regressions

Arms out
The first basic regression involves doing the exercise with your arms out in a "T" position as shown in Figure 5.23. This simple modification of the exercise spreads your mass out over a larger distance, which increases your rotary inertia in the frontal plane. This increased resistance to angular motion makes it easier to keep your center of gravity within your base of support and maintain your balance.

Figure 5.23 The single-leg RDL exercise arms out regression.

Ipsilateral balance aid

In this middle regression, the client would use a balance aid in the same (ipsilateral) arm as the stance leg (Figure 5.24). In this regression, the client pushes the balance aid into the ground and, with our understanding of Newton's Third Law, the balance aid then pushes back up on them. This regression does not have an effect in the frontal plane as the force produced by the balance aid passes directly through the axis of rotation of the hip and therefore does not increase or decrease the torque required from the hip abductors. The effect of this regression occurs in the sagittal plane as there is another force to help fight the weight of the trunk that is pulling the stance leg hip into flexion. This decreases the force required from the hip extensors to both slow down the hip flexion in the eccentric phase and to create the hip extension in the concentric phase.

The ipsilateral balance aid would also increase the base of support in the anterior-posterior direction, therefore making it easier to maintain balance in this direction. However, it does not increase the base of support in the medial-lateral direction.

Contralateral balance aid

In the third regression, the client would use a balance aid in the opposite (contralateral) arm as the stance leg (Figure 5.25). This

Figure 5.24 The single-leg RDL exercise ipsilateral balance aid regression.

Figure 5.25 The single-leg RDL exercise – contralateral balance aid regression.

regression makes the exercise easier in both the sagittal and frontal planes. Since the mass is still the same distance from the axis of rotation of the hip in the sagittal plane, this regression would have the same effect on the hip extensors as would the ipsilateral balance aid. However, this regression decreases the challenge for the hip abductors in the frontal plane as the balance aid produces an extra counter clockwise torque to help balance the clockwise torque created by the body weight. This requires less force to be produced by the hip abductors in order to maintain pelvic stability in the frontal plane during the movement.

The contralateral balance aid also increases the base of support in both the anterior-posterior and medial-lateral directions. This makes it much easier to maintain the center of gravity within the base of support and maintain balance.

Progressions

Ipsilateral weight

The first progression involves adding a weight (generally a dumbbell) to the same hand as the stance leg (Figure 5.26). This progression is similar to the ipsilateral balance aid

Figure 5.26 The single-leg RDL exercise – ipsilateral weight progression.

Figure 5.27 The single-leg RDL exercise – contralateral weight progression.

regression except for now the weight is producing a force in the opposite direction (downward). This progression has no effect in the frontal plane as the line of action of the weight force passes directly through the axis of rotation of the hip and therefore does not increase or decrease the torque required from the hip abductors. The effect of this progression occurs in the sagittal plane as the weight produces an extra clockwise torque that must be absorbed by increasing the eccentric force created by the hip extensors.

Contralateral weight

The second progression involves adding a weight to the opposite hand as the stance leg (Figure 5.27). This progression makes the exercise more challenging for both the hip extensors and hip abductors. Now, the downward force produced by the weight is also producing a clockwise torque in the frontal plane and therefore the hip abductors must produce a much greater force to keep the pelvis stable. The effect of this contralateral weight in the sagittal plane is the same as with the ipsilateral weight, as the dumbbell is the same distance from the axis of rotation of the hip; therefore, the extra clockwise torque that must be absorbed by increasing the force created by the hip extensors is the same in both progression conditions.

SUMMARY

A good fundamental knowledge of biomechanics is essential for any strength and conditioning professional. This knowledge is imperative in order to ensure the prescribed exercises are tailored to the correct level, using the correct form and amount of resistance, and reinforcing the appropriate movement patterns to achieve the functional goals of the training session as quickly and safely as possible.

MAXING OUT

1 You want to incorporate some Olympic lifting into the strength and conditioning program for the volleyball team. However, a problem is that the athletes are having real trouble learning to perform the lifts correctly. How could biomechanics be used to assist you in teaching the athletes?

2 The football coach has told you that he only wants his players completing single joint exercise on pin-loaded resistance machines and at slow speed. His rationale is that he does not want the athletes injured in the weight room. From your biomechanics knowledge you do not believe such a program is optimal but you have to convince the coach. Write a discussion paper outlining the basis for including ground supported, multi-joint movements including high speed exercises once the athletes have developed the appropriate patterns of movement and muscle activation strategies.

CASE EXAMPLE

Extending the application of a simple contact mat timing system to derive more pertinent mechanical measurements

Background

You have just been employed as a strength and conditioning coach with a small college that has limited performance testing equipment and no current budget to purchase more sophisticated equipment. The program has a simple electronic timing system that can record contact time and flight time during vertical jumping. In the past, only the flight time has been recorded and provided to the athletes and coaches, but you would like to provide more extensive information that is both understandable and relevant.

Recommendations/considerations

One of the problems with just providing flight time is that the athletes cannot really relate to the measure. They want to know how high they have jumped. Also, in terms of quantifying leg power, flight time does not adequately quantify the explosiveness of the athlete or account for athletes of differing body weights. Based on your biomechanics knowledge you recommend to the coaches that the jumps be performed from an approach run, and that the athletes jump onto the mat then jump vertically upward for maximum height, landing back on the mat. You also recommend recording body mass. From these additional measures, jump height and power will be calculated.

Implementation

Each sporting squad is tested after a functional movement assessment and prior to a skills session. They are instructed beforehand to avoid strenuous activity for the previous 48 hours.

Measurement of body mass. Body mass is measured in kilograms for each athlete using an electronic scale.

Measurement of jump performance. As a group, the athletes are instructed in the correct technique for performing the test.

Stand approximately three strides back from the contact mat. Step into the mat area, landing with both feet on the mat, then jump vertically upwards for maximum height landing back on the mat. The hands are to be held on the hips throughout the test.

At the end of each trial, the contact time and subsequent flight time will be recorded.

Calculations

Flight to contact ratio. A useful and easily calculated measure is simply flight time divided by contact time.

Jump height. Jump height can be estimated based on the flight time and the assumption of simple projectile motion. The formula is:

Jump height = (g × flight time^2)/8

where g = 9.81 m^2

Work done. Once jump height has been determined, the work done during the concentric phase of the jump can be calculated as:

Work = Fd = mass × g × jump height

Absolute power output. As we have a measure of contact time prior to the jump, we have an estimate of the time over which the work calculated above was completed. We must assume that the duration of the concentric time is equal as we have no way of measuring this. So the

(continued)

(continued)

concentric time is equal to the contact time divided by 2. Absolute power is then calculated as the work done divided by the concentric time.

absolute power = work/(flight time/2)

Relative power output. Relative power output is calculated as absolute power output divided by body mass. This gives an indication of the power to weight ratio for the athlete.

relative power = absolute power × body mass^{-1}

Results

The following results were obtained on six athletes and the subsequent additional measure calculated. As you can appreciate, the use of biomechanics' principles has provided for a much more in depth and relevant analysis of vertical jump performance. This test could then be repeated at various intervals during a training program designed to improve vertical jump performance. This will provide invaluable quantitative feedback regarding whether or not your training is accomplishing its goal with every athlete.

Athlete	A	B	C	D	E	F
Mass (kg)	80	78	82	79	69	74
Contact time (s)	0.561	0.493	0.587	0.534	0.521	0.508
Flight time (s)	0.567	0.587	0.543	0.602	0.511	0.519
Flight: Contact ratio	1.011	1.191	0.925	1.127	0.981	1.022
Jump height (m)	0.394	0.423	0.362	0.444	0.320	0.330
Work done (J)	309	323	291	344	217	240
Absolute power (W)	1,103	1,312	991	1, 290	832	944
Relative power (W × kg^{-1}) 13.8	16.8	12.1	16.3	12.1	12.8	

REFERENCES

1. Bennell KL, Bowles KA, Wang Y, Cicuttini F, Davies-Tuck M, Hinman RS. Higher dynamic medial knee load predicts greater cartilage loss over 12 months in medial knee osteoarthritis. *Annals of the Rheumatic Diseases* 2011; 70:1770–1774.
2. Carney KR, Brown LE, Coburn JW, Spiering BA, Bottaro M. Eccentric torque-velocity and power-velocity relationships in men and women. *European Journal of Sport Science* 2012; 12:139–144.
3. Colado JC, Triplett NT. Effects of a short-term resistance program using elastic bands versus weight machines for sedentary middle aged women. *J Strength Cond Res* 2008; 22:1441–1448.
4. Cronin JB, McNair PJ, Marshall RN. Force-velocity analysis of strength-training

techniques and load: implications for training strategy and research. *J Strength Cond Res* 2003; 17:148–155.

5. Elliott BC, Wilson GJ, Kerr GK. A biomechanical analysis of the sticking region in the bench press. *Med Sci Sports Exerc* 1989; 21:450–462.

6. Floyd RT. *Manual of Structural Kinesiology*, 17th Ed. New York: McGraw Hill. 2009.

7. Frost MF, Cronin JB, Newton RU. A comparison of the kinematics, kinetics and muscle activity between pneumatic and free weight resistance. *Eur J Appl Physiol* 2008; 104:937–956.

8. Gans C. Fiber architecture and muscle function. *Exercise and Sports Sciences Reviews* 1982; 10:160–207.

9. Garhammer J. A review of power output studies of Olympic and Powerlifting: Methodology, Performance Prediction, and Evaluation Tests. *J Strength Cond Res* 1993; 7:76–89.

10. Hatze H. The meaning of the term: "Biomechanics." *Journal of Biomechanics* 1974; 7:189–190.

11. Hewett TE, Myer GD, Ford KR, Heidt RS, Jr., Colosimo AJ, McLean SG et al. Biomechanical measures of neuromuscular control and valgus loading of the knee predict anterior cruciate ligament injury risk in female athletes: a prospective study. *Am J Sports Med* 2005; 33:492–501.

12. Hof AL, Van den Berg JW. EMG to force processing II: Estimation of parameters of the Hill muscle model the human triceps surae by means of a calfergometer. *Journal of Biomechanics* 1981; 14:759–770.

13. Hortobagyi T., Katch FI. Role of concentric force in limiting improvement in muscular strength. *J Appl Physiol* 1990; 68:650–658.

14. Hill AV. *The First and Last Experiments in Muscle Mechanics*. Cambridge, UK: Cambridge University Press. 1970.

15. Ito J., Moriyama H., Inokuchi S., & Goto N. Human lower limb muscles: an evaluation of weight and fiber size. *Okajimas Folia Anatomica Japonica* 2003; 80(2–3):47–56.

16. Izquierdo M, Ibanez J, Gorostiaga E, Gaurrues M, Zuniga A, Anton A, Larrion JL, Häkkinen K. Maximal strength and power characteristics in isometric and dynamic actions of the upper and lower extremities in middle-aged and older men. *Acta Physiological Scand* 1999; 167:57–68.

17. Keiser DL. Pneumatic exercising device. USA patent: 4,257,593. 1981.

18. Knudson D. *Fundamentals of Biomechanics*, 2nd Ed. New York: Springer. 2007.

19. Lacerte M, deLateur BJ, Alquist AD, Questad KA. Concentric versus combined concentric-eccentric isokinetic training programs: effect on peak torque of human quadriceps muscle. *Archives of Physical Medicine and Rehabilitation* 1992; 73:1059–1062.

20. Lee SM, Piazza SJ. Built for speed: musculoskeletal structure and sprinting ability. *J Exp Biol* 2009; 212:3700–3707.

21. Lynn SK, Noffal GJ. Lower extremity biomechanics during a regular and counter-balanced squat. *J Strength Cond Res* 2012; 26:2417–2425.

22. Lynn SK, Reid SM, Costigan PA. The influence of gait pattern on signs of knee osteoarthritis in older adults over a 5–11 year follow-up period: A case study analysis. *Knee* 2007; 14:22–28.

23. McClenton LS, Brown LE, Coburn JW, Kersey RD. The effect of short-term VertiMax vs. depth jump training on vertical jump performance. *J Strength Cond Res* 2008; 22:321–325.

24. McGill S. *Low Back Disorders: Evidence Based Prevention and Rehabilitation*, 2nd Ed. Champaign, IL: Human Kinetics. 2007.

25. McGinnis PM. *Biomechanics of Sport and Exercise*, 2nd Ed. Champaign, IL: Human Kinetics. 2005.

26. Newton RU, Kraemer WJ, Häkkinen K, Humphries BJ, Murphy AJ. Kinematics, kinetics, and muscle activation during explosive upper body movements. *Journal of Applied Biomechanics* 1996; 12:31–43.

27. Sharma L, Chmiel JS, Almagor O, Felson D, Guermazi A, Roemer F et al. The role of varus and valgus alignment in the initial development of knee cartilage damage by MRI: the MOST study. *Annal of the Rheumatic Diseases* 2013; 72:235–240.

28. Wilson GJ, Elliott BC, Wood GA. The effect on performance of imposing a delay during the stretch-shorten cycle movement. *Med Sci Sports Exerc* 1991; 23:364–370.

Contents

CHAPTER 6

THE ENDOCRINE SYSTEM

Andy Bosak

(continued)

Enzymes	Messenger ribonucleic	Receptor
Exogenous	acid (mRNA)	Receptor density
Fight or flight response	Metabolism	Receptor specificity
Free hormone	Negative-feedback system	Salivary concentrations
Free testosterone	Neuroendocrine	Sex hormone-binding
GH-inhibiting hormone	Neurohormone	globulin (SHBG)
(GH-IH)	Neurotransmitter	Signaling pathway
Gluconeogenesis	Nocturnal urine measures	Steroid hormone
Half-life ($T_{1/2}$)	Noninvasive method	Stimulating G protein (G_s)
Hormone	Paracrine	Stress hormone
Hypothalamic-pituitary axis	Peptide hormone	Système Internationale (SI)
Influx	Plasma fluid shift	Total hormone
Inhibiting G protein (G_i)	Postreceptor activity	concentration
Invasive method	Posttranslational processing	Transcription
Leydig cells	Precursor molecule	Translation
Lipolysis	Pulsatile	Transport protein
Lipophilic	Quantal release	Trophic hormone
Lipophobic	Rate-limiting	Upregulation

INTRODUCTION

The human body is designed to provide amazing control of its physiological systems during physical exercise and sport performance. Each of these physiological systems is closely regulated and coordinated while the desired result is performance improvement. As similar to other physiological systems, the hormonal system is closely controlled and responds to exercise and physical activity to assure optimal results. The hormonal or endocrine system is very important as it can influence the other systems of the body. Most importantly, it is critical to understand how the endocrine system responds to the short-term requirements of a single bout of exercise and how it adapts to the chronic stresses of a long-term training program.

THE ENDOCRINE SYSTEM

The **endocrine** system helps to maintain homeostasis in the body by regulating hormonal functions. This occurs through the communication between chemicals in the body, called messengers, that regulate different physiological actions. The messengers are secreted into the bloodstream, travel to their respective binding sites, and promote changes in cellular functions upon arrival at the designated binding site.

Hormones defined

For the purposes of this chapter, a **hormone** is a chemical compound that is secreted into the circulation to regulate a biological function at a distant site in the body. A hormone is secreted directly into the bloodstream from a tissue known as an endocrine gland. These glands contain specialized cells designed to create and release their respective hormones. A **neurohormone** is very similar except that it is released from a nerve ending into the circulation. Regardless of the source, the hormones and neurohormones travel to various parts of the body until they reach their target tissues. Once arrived, they can bind to specialized receptors on or in the cells of the target tissues and they will influence how the target tissues function.

Hormones are chemical compounds secreted by endocrine tissues and are transported via the circulation.

Endocrine tissues

Numerous hormones and neurohormones are involved in the proper functioning of a healthy system. Hormones are chemical compounds that are produced by endocrine tissues and typically released into the circulation. Neurohormones are a type of hormone that also functions as a neurotransmitter in the nervous system. Of particular interest are those hormones that specifically respond to physical exercise and sport performance. Numerous endocrine tissues in the body participate in this process, whether it involves the short-term or sudden acute responses to a single bout of exercise or the long-term chronic adaptations to regular exercise and training. Figure 6.1 illustrates, in both a male and female, the endocrine glands and tissues responsible for the hormones and neurohormones discussed in this chapter. In general, these tissues release their hormonal products into the body's circulation where they are transported to their target sites. To fully understand the endocrine and neuroendocrine systems, it is important to be strongly familiar with the various endocrine tissues as well as the normal blood concentrations of the hormones, as listed in Table 6.1 (3,4).

Although those in the medical profession and the related health sciences often use conventional units of measure, scientific reporting requires the use of the measurements defined by the **Système Internationale (SI)**. The SI system is universally recognized by scientists all over the world and provides a logical and systematic method for quantification (4).

Hormonal transportation routes

Although most of the hormones discussed in this chapter are released into the circulation

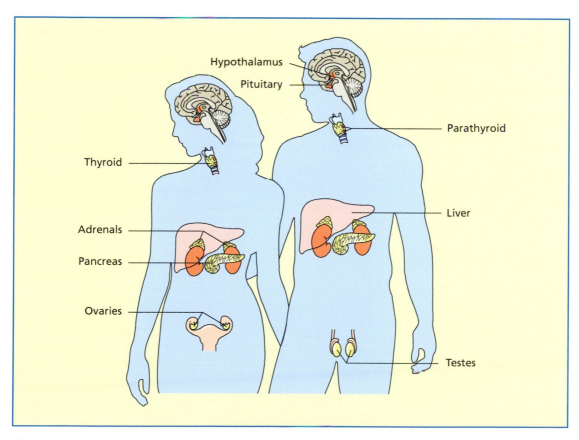

Figure 6.1 Anatomical location of the principal endocrine glands.

TABLE 6.1 Typical adult serum concentrations in both Système Internationale (SI) and conventional units (67,69)

Variable		SI Unit	Conventional Unit
Testosterone (4 p.m.)	Men	10–35 nmol·L$_{-1}$	3–10 ng·mL$_{-1}$
	Women	<3.5 nmol·L$_{-1}$	<0.1 ng·mL$_{-1}$
Cortisol (4 p.m.)		50–410 nmol·L$_{-1}$	2–15 µg·mL$_{-1}$
Growth hormone	Men	0–5 µg·L$_{-1}$	0–5 ng·mL$_{-1}$
	Women	0–10 µg·L$_{-1}$	0–10 ng·mL$_{-1}$
Insulin-like growth factor I	Men	0.45–2.2 kU·L$_{-1}$	0.45–2.2 U·mL$_{-1}$
	Women	0.34–1.9 kU·L$_{-1}$	0.34–1.9 U·mL$_{-1}$
Insulin (fasting)		35–145 pmol·L$_{-1}$	5–20 µU·mL$_{-1}$
Glucagon		50–100 ng·L$_{-1}$	50–100 pg·mL$_{-1}$
Epinephrine (resting, supine)		170–520 pmol·L$_{-1}$	30–95 pg·mL$_{-1}$
Norepinephrine (resting, supine)		0.3–2.8 nmol·L$_{-1}$	15–475 pg·mL$_{-1}$
Antidiuretic hormone		2.3–7.4 pmol·L$_{-1}$	2.5–8.0 ng·mL$_{-1}$
Aldosterone		< 220 pmol·L$_{-1}$	< 8 mg·mL$_{-1}$
Thyroxine (T$_4$)		51–42 nmol·L$_{-1}$	4–11 µg·mL$_{-1}$
Triiodothyronine (T$_3$)		1.2–3.4 nmol·L$_{-1}$	75–220 ng·mL$_{-1}$
Calcitonin		< 50 ng·L$_{-1}$	< 50 pg·mL$_{-1}$
Parathyroid hormone		10–65 ng·L$_{-1}$	10–65 pg·mL$_{-1}$

for transport to their respective targets, other methods of transport exist. Some hormones never leave their tissue while others never leave their cells. Figure 6.2 illustrates the autocrine, paracrine, endocrine, and neuroendocrine hormonal transport routes.

Autocrine

When hormones or neurohormones are synthesized in their respective cells, not all are released into the circulation. Certain chemical compounds never leave the cell and they can remain within the cell and influence the activity of the cell in some form or fashion. These types of chemical compounds are called **autocrine** hormones (5). An example of this is insulin-like growth factor-I (IGF-I). IGF-I is produced in many cells of the body and is responsible for many of the actions of growth hormone. IGF-I can be measured from the circulating blood, yet it is important to mention that some IGF-I never leaves the cell.

Paracrine

Some hormones leave their endocrine cells and never enter circulation, but they travel to adjacent cells, where they exert their influence on cellular activity. These are called **paracrine** hormones (6). As with an autocrine system, circulating amounts of these paracrine chemical compounds may be important, but they do not account for the portion that never enters the circulation.

Endocrine

The term endocrine refers to hormones that are released into the bloodstream or lymph

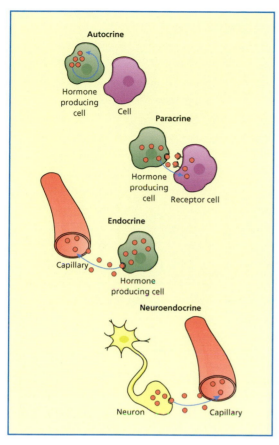

Figure 6.2 Autocrine, paracrine, endocrine, and neuroendocrine transport routes of hormones.

system to control growth, metabolism, mood, and reproduction. Also, the term **neuroendocrine** refers to hormones that are released into the bloodstream or lymph system following stimulation of the nervous system. Once the chemical compound is released, it travels via the circulation and eventually reaches its target tissue or is broken down into its metabolic by-products. Although many factors influence the concentrations of these hormones in the blood, it is still essential to measure their concentrations in the blood to fully understand their roles in physiological function.

Once produced, most hormones enter the circulation for transport (endocrine), some travel to adjacent cells (paracrine), and some never leave the cell (autocrine).

Types of hormones

Hormones come in different chemical forms (Figure 6.3) and three basic chemical structures account for the hormones that are of most interest (7).

Steroid hormones
The **steroid hormones** share the same four-carbon-ring structure and affect growth and the development of the sex organs. All steroid hormones are made from a cholesterol molecule, which is called a **precursor molecule**. Depending on the endocrine tissue involved, the cholesterol molecule is converted by **enzymes** (proteins serving as catalysts in mediating and speeding a specific chemical reaction) into the final steroid hormone that is to be released. Different endocrine glands have different hormonal enzymes that determine which steroid hormone will be produced. Since the steroid hormones are formed from cholesterol, they are **lipophilic**, which means that they can pass through the lipid membrane of a cell. Pharmaceutical forms of steroids, which are orally ingested or injected are called **exogenous** steroids, which means that they come from outside the body. These steroid types are typically variations of the hormones naturally produced by the body, which are known as **endogenous** steroids. Endogenous steroids will be the steroids that are focused on in this chapter.

Peptide hormones
A second group of hormones comprises the **peptide hormones**, which consist of chains of **amino acids**, the building blocks of protein. Small chains (of fewer than 20 amino acids) are simply termed *peptides* and larger chains are called *polypeptides*. These hormones can be quite long, as exemplified by growth hormone, which is 191 amino acids long. The shapes of these polypeptides are often determined by their amino acid sequences and by the existence of bonds between certain amino acids. These bonds cause the peptide to configure into the specific shape required for the hormone to function optimally. It is important to note that if any alteration occurs in the chain of amino acids, the hormone's function may be affected. This can occur when one or more of the amino acids in the chain is replaced with a different amino acid or if

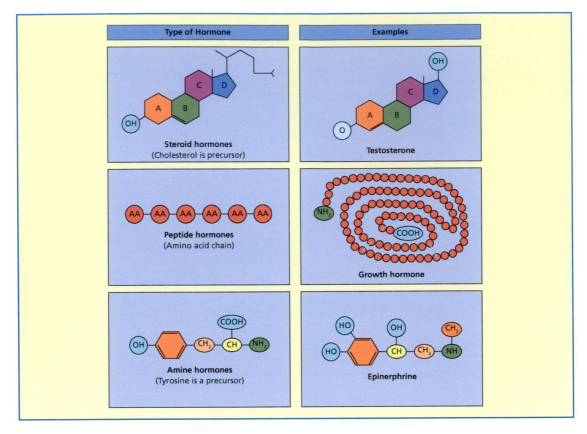

Figure 6.3 Different types of hormones include steroid, peptide, and amine.

the peptide chain is cut, which will result in a smaller peptide chain. Sometimes these altered forms of the hormone still have a function, but it is often different from that of the original hormone. Peptide hormones are more prone to **degradation** in the circulation than steroid hormones. Degradation is the breakdown of a complex compound into simpler compounds. Additionally, peptide hormones are **lipophobic**, which means they are repelled by lipids and cannot readily pass through the cell membrane. Hence, they will require a receptor at the membrane that will permit them to act.

Amine hormones

The last group of hormones are the **amine hormones**, characterized by an amine ring. Since amine hormones are derived from amino acids, they are sometimes classified as protein hormones. These hormones are found as either hormones or neurohormones and can be produced and secreted by either endocrine tissues or nerve endings. Some of these compounds also function as neurotransmitters in the nervous system. The typical precursor molecule of amine hormones is the amino acid tyrosine. In the event that tyrosine is not available in adequate quantities, phenylalanine can be converted to tyrosine and then used for the synthesis of an amine hormone. Some amine hormones, such as epinephrine (also known as adrenaline) and norepinephrine (noradrenaline), break down rapidly in the circulation and must therefore exert their influence on target tissues in a rapid manner. Amine hormones are lipophobic like peptide hormones, which means they will require a membrane receptor.

The three types of hormones, steroid, peptide, and amine are each synthesized differently. Therefore, each of the three types has a specific role during exercise.

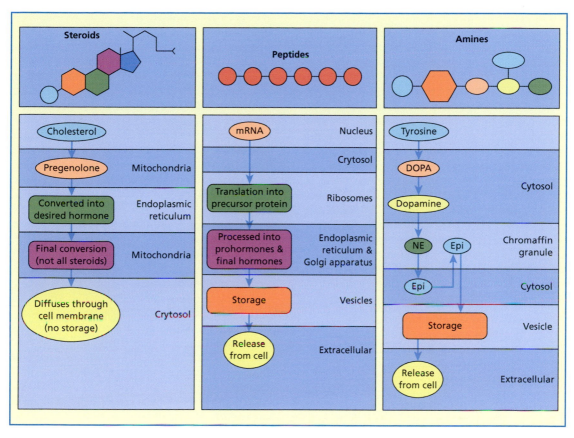

Figure 6.4 Synthesis of different types of hormones. mRNA = messenger RNA; DOPA = 3,4 dihydroxyphenylalanine; NE = norepinephrine; Epi = epinephrine.

Hormone production

As shown in Figure 6.4, each of the three types of hormones is produced in a different manner. Therefore, understanding how the human body makes these hormones can give us a greater appreciation of the complex role they play in human performance.

Production of steroid hormones

As mentioned earlier, the synthesis of the different types of steroid hormones is dependent on the various enzymes present in the particular endocrine gland (8,9). The first step is the conversion of cholesterol to pregnenolone in the mitochondria of the cell. This is called the **rate-limiting** step in the process, since the subsequent steps occur more readily. Once the stimulus for steroid hormone synthesis arrives at the endocrine cell, the process begins with this first step to pregnenolone. Pregnenolone is then transported to the endoplasmic reticulum where it is converted via several enzymatic steps into the desired steroid. For some of the steroid hormones, additional processing occurs in the mitochondria. Once the final hormone is completed, it can diffuse through the cell membrane, which consists of two lipid layers. Owing to the hormone's ability to exit the cell easily, these hormones are not stored, but instead produced as needed.

Production of peptide hormones

Peptide hormones are synthesized when the appropriate signal for hormone production results in **messenger RNA (mRNA)** being produced in the cell nucleus (9). The mRNA serves as the code indicating which amino acids are needed and in what specific order. The mRNA is transported to the ribosomes, where the appropriate amino acids are brought and assembled into a precursor molecule in a procedure called **translation**. The precursor molecules are then transported to the endoplasmic reticulum and the Golgi tendon organ for further modification. This very unique and detailed process is termed **posttranslational processing**, which often includes splicing the precursor amino acid chain into smaller molecules. Because peptide molecules are lipophobic, they cannot pass through the cell membrane. Therefore, to be released, they must enter storage vesicles in the cell, which can eventually release them to the surrounding environment. When a vesicle releases its contents, all the contents are released, but for more hormone to be released, additional vesicles must release their contents. This process is known as **quantal release**, since the amount of hormone secreted is always a multiple of the number of vesicles involved.

Production of amine hormones

Amine hormones are produced in **chromaffin cells** found in various tissues in the body (10). These cells are named based on their ability to take up chromium when stained. One family of amine hormones and neurohormones are the **catecholamines** which include examples such as epinephrine, norepinephrine, and dopamine. As previously stated, the precursor molecule tyrosine enters the cytosol of the cell, where enzymes ultimately convert it to dopamine. Dopamine will then enter the chromaffin granule found in the cell, where it is converted to norepinephrine. For norepinephrine to be converted to epinephrine, it must leave the chromaffin granule. After returning to the granule, epinephrine is stored in a vesicle, where it awaits quantal release from the cell. Depending on which enzymes are present or absent in the cell, the process of synthesis can stop at any of the preliminary hormones. Other amine hormones, such as the thyroid hormones, are produced in the follicular cells of the thyroid gland, and these hormones follow a different process for synthesis but are still characterized by amine rings.

Hormonal transport and binding proteins

Once hormones are released into the circulation, they must be transported in a timely fashion to the tissues where they are to act, but a problem the hormones encounter is the process of **metabolism,** or in other words, their degradation. Numerous factors can prevent hormone molecules from ever reaching their targets because of degradation. The time it takes for a hormone to be partially metabolized in the circulation, or for half of it to be degraded, is called its **half-life ($T_{1/2}$).** Some hormones have a half-life measured in seconds, while the half-lives of others are measured in minutes or hours. To preserve a hormone for longer periods, the hormonal molecule may be protected by becoming attached to a **binding protein** which will also assist in the hormone's transport, as illustrated in Figure 6.5 (11). Hormones such as steroid and thyroid hormones are bound to these **transport proteins**, while amines and protein hormones are not. **Albumin,** a binding protein made in the liver that helps to maintain blood volume in the arteries and veins, can bind numerous different hormones, but does not exhibit a high affinity to any of them. Regardless, the hormone-binding protein complex can move through the circulation without the hormone being degraded. The problem with this system is that the hormone is unable to bind to its target tissue until it is released from the binding protein. When this happens, the hormone is considered **biologically active,** which means it is available for use during metabolism. The portion of the hormone not bound to a binding protein is called the percent **free hormone**, while the **total hormone concentration** includes both the free and the bound portions. Typically, when binding proteins are used, most of the circulating hormone is bound to a transport protein. For example, only

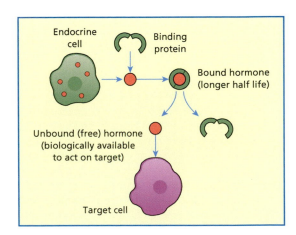

Figure 6.5 Binding proteins help protect circulating hormones.

approximately 1% to 2% of the total testosterone in the circulation is free testosterone, which suggests it is not bound to its binding protein.

> Binding proteins protect the hormone, but the hormone is biologically active only when it dissociates from the binding protein.

Factors affecting circulating concentrations

The concentration of hormones in the blood can be extremely variable, depending on the hormone and on a number of contributing factors (12).

TABLE 6.2 Factors affecting hormone concentrations

Site	Factor
Endocrine cell	Hormone synthesis
	Hormone release
Circulation	Method of transport to target tissue
	Binding proteins
	Hormonal concentration
	• Total
	• Free
	• Bound
	Fluid (plasma) shifts
	Venous pooling
	Hepatic (kidney) clearance rates
	Extrahepatic clearance rates
	Degradation of hormones
Target tissue	Binding affinity
Receptors	Maximal binding capacity
	Sensitivity
Intracellular	Second-messenger systems
	Nuclear receptor adaptations

Source: Reproduced with permission from Kraemer WJ. Endocrine responses and adaptations to strength training. In: Komi PV, ed. *Strength and Power in Sport.* Oxford, UK: Blackwell, 1992:291–304

Hormone production and release

It would initially seem that the primary factor would simply be how much hormone is being produced by the endocrine gland. Although this is certainly one factor, the process is much more complicated, as suggested in Table 6.2. Three sites in the body can contribute to the circulating concentrations and they include the endocrine cell, the circulating blood, and the target tissue. At the endocrine cell, it is not only the rate of hormonal synthesis that matters, but additional factors are how much hormone is released and how quickly this occurs.

Hormonal transport in the circulation

In the circulation, the binding proteins can affect the availability of a hormone at its target tissue (11). Additionally, hormones are degraded in various tissues, thus affecting how much hormone arrives at the target site. Other tissues are involved in this process, but hepatic clearance is a major factor. Concerning exercise, after a vigorous effort, blood may pool in the venous circulation, resulting in less of the hormones circulating to the target tissue. One of the largest factors during exercise is **plasma fluid shifts** (13). Plasma is the fluid portion of blood and during physical exercise, this fluid has a reduced volume within the blood which can result in a higher hormonal concentration. Factors that contribute to this specific change in plasma volume include fluid loss, specifically water, via sweating, and increased arterial pressures and postural changes. Plasma volume shifts of more than 15% have been reported for long-term endurance exercise as well as resistance training sessions. This response is augmented when the exercise occurs in a hot and/or humid environment.

Hormonal activity at the target cell

At the target tissue, the properties of the hormone receptors are critical factors (14). **Receptors** are the cellular structures to which the hormones bind and result in the appropriate action at the cell. The number of receptors available to bind to a hormone is known as **receptor density**. How readily the hormone attaches to the receptor, how sensitive the receptor is to the hormone, and **postreceptor activity** can vary. This can involve the role of the **signaling pathways** that instruct the cell how to respond once the hormone has bound to the receptor. Some of these signals are

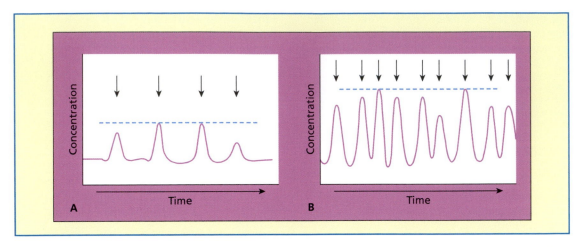

Figure 6.6 Pulsatility. Trophic hormones increase their signal by increasing the number and magnitude of pulses. Each arrow indicates a trophic hormone pulse. (A) A basal trophic signal. (B) An amplified trophic signal. Note that the signal is amplified by both increasing the frequency and the magnitude of pulses.

initiated at the receptors in the cell membrane and others are initiated in the cell nucleus, but this will depend upon the specific hormone.

> Hormones affect their target tissues by binding to hormone-specific receptors. Binding at these receptors initiates the specific cellular responses to the hormone.

Trophic hormones and pulsatility

In order for a hormone to be secreted by its endocrine gland, the gland must receive some type of signal, and the signal needed for many hormones is a **trophic hormone** from another endocrine gland or from the nervous system (15). When increased concentrations of a hormone are required, the body detects this need and causes the trophic hormonal signal to be increased. This signal is not based simply on the hormone's concentration, but also related to the trophic hormones that are released in a **pulsatile** fashion (i.e., periodic bursts) as illustrated in Figure 6.6 (16). The trophic signal is increased either by increasing the frequency of the pulses or by increasing their magnitude or amplitude. But, to properly study these signals, many blood samples must be taken to measure pulse frequency and amplitude. For example, the primary trophic hormone for testosterone in males is luteinizing hormone (LH), which

is released from the anterior pituitary gland. In turn, luteinizing hormone is regulated by LH-releasing hormone (LH-RH) from the hypothalamus. Thus, it is important to understand that the control of our hormones is very complex and highly dependent on the signaling pattern of the trophic hormones.

> Circulating concentrations are often regulated by trophic hormones that signal the synthesis and release of the hormones. This system is synchronized by a negative-feedback system that can detect the current blood concentrations.

HORMONAL RHYTHMS

Many hormones present different blood concentrations at different times of the day (17). In biological systems, hormonal variations occur over a number of time periods such as hourly, less than every 24 hours, every 24 hours, or at different times of the year (seasonally). Of particular interest to this chapter are the **circadian rhythms**, or daily cycles of physiological processes, also known as the **diurnal variation**. Figure 6.7 illustrates an example of the diurnal variation for cortisol. As shown, baseline concentrations can be quite high late in the typical sleep cycle and early in the morning. Therefore, any interpretation of the hormonal responses to exercise and sport must consider where the baseline values

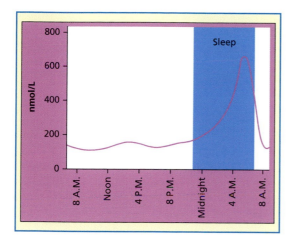

Figure 6.7 Examples of the variations of concentrations of cortisol during a typical day. The shaded area indicates a typical sleep cycle. (Modified from Goodman HM. *Basic Medical Endocrinology*. New York: Raven Press, 1998:103).

were prior to the physical activity (18,19). Yet, many researchers simply avoid the times of day when hormonal concentrations are elevated (e.g., early morning for cortisol). In addition, when hormonal levels are being studied over a long time, as in a training study, the time of day the blood samples are taken must be kept constant to minimize the effect of diurnal variations.

> Hormone concentrations are influenced by the time of day and by anticipation of an impending stressor, such as exercise or competition.

Anticipatory response

The hormonal response occurring in anticipation of impending exercise, sport, or physical activity is termed the **anticipatory response** (10). The body possesses a number of hormones collectively called **stress hormones** and these hormones help the body prepare for a stressful experience, whether it involves physical activity, cognitive stress, or both. They are part of the **fight or flight response** and all biological systems have methods of responding and dealing with stressful situations, whether they involve fighting the threat or fleeing from it (20). Experienced athletes are very familiar with the "pregame jitters" they encounter prior to an important competition, and similar feelings are also common in other scenarios,

such as taking exams, public speaking, and musical recitals. In examining the hormonal responses to physical activity, it is important to separate the responses due to stressful anticipation from those due to the actual physical activity. The catecholamine (i.e., epinephrine) that is particularly sensitive to an anticipatory response is illustrated in Figure 6.8. Yet, cortisol can also exhibit an anticipatory response. Therefore, blood sampling must be performed prior to the anticipatory response to determine the actual resting baseline value. It should be noted that some individuals will exhibit an anticipatory response to the actual process of taking a blood sample with a needle. Hence in these specific cases, the sample must be taken when the needle has previously been inserted (i.e., via an intravenous catheter) and after the individual has had time to relax and return to baseline.

Biocompartments

The typical method of measuring hormonal concentrations involves venous blood sampling. Most hormones of interest are released directly into the circulation, which indicates that this is often the most sensitive way to measure the endocrine responses. Information on hormonal

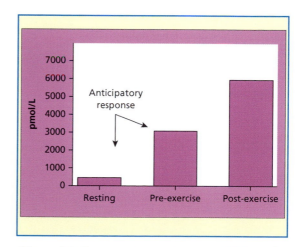

Figure 6.8 Example of the anticipatory response of epinephrine to a stressful lifting task. The difference between resting and preexercise concentrations represents the anticipatory response for the impending exercise. (Adapted from Fry AC, Kraemer WJ, van Borselen F, et al. Catecholamine responses to short-term high-intensity resistance exercise overtraining. *J Appl Physiol* 1994;77(2):941–946).

activity, however, can be collected from other sites, or **biocompartments**, in the body (21). Since hormones are ultimately degraded to their metabolic by-products, urine may be sampled to indirectly determine the quantity of hormone produced over a period of time. For example, when true baseline or resting levels are of interest, **nocturnal urine measures** are analyzed for the hormonal by-products. In this manner, the total amount of hormone produced during the sleep hours, when one is most at rest, can be estimated. Another common biocompartment is saliva, which may also be analyzed to determine hormonal concentrations, since **salivary concentrations** are related to blood concentrations. However, a limitation with salivary samples is that the measure is less sensitive to slight fluctuations in blood concentrations and it takes longer to respond to physical activity. On the other hand, both urine and saliva are obtained through **noninvasive methods**, meaning that they can be obtained without breaking the skin. Hence, both methods are easier to collect than biocompartment samples such as interstitial fluid, gathered by **invasive methods**, which necessitate an incision or puncture. See Figure 6.9 for further detail. It is important to consider that there is some interest in interstitial

fluid and intramuscular collection since this is the fluid that is surrounding the muscle. Thus, collection of interstitial fluid may provide information about the transport of hormones from circulation to the tissue (22).

Receptors and cell signaling

When a hormone molecule arrives at its target tissue, it interacts with the tissue by binding at a protein receptor. Receptors come in many different configurations, each hormone having a receptor specific to it. This is known as **receptor specificity** (8,14). This specificity has been described as being analogous to a lock and key. Just as the lock can be opened with only one particular key, one hormone can bind to only one type of receptor, resulting in the optimal desired response. In some cases, other similar hormones can also bind to the receptor, although the results may be slightly different or smaller in magnitude. This **cross-reactivity** exists when more than one hormone can bind at a particular receptor. Cellular receptors are a favorite site of action for many of the pharmaceutical drugs in use today, and these drugs act as **analogues** to the natural chemicals of the body, which means they are

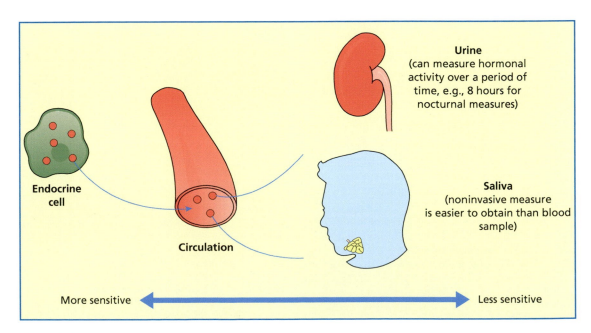

Figure 6.9 Hormonal levels can be determined by sampling from either blood (whole, serum, or plasma), or urinary or salivary biocompartments. Sensitivity of the sample to hormonal fluctuations decreases when not taken from the circulation.

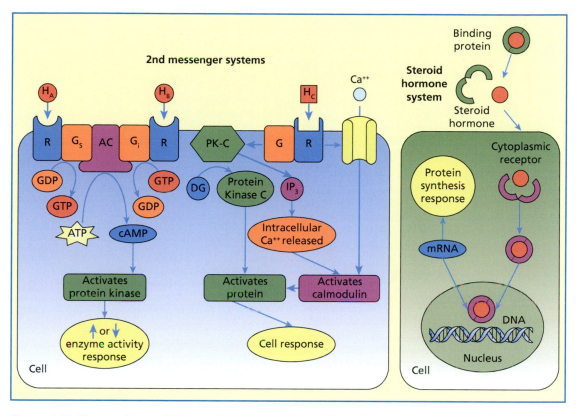

Figure 6.10 Hormonal intracellular signaling systems. Habc = different hormones; R = receptor; Gs = stimulating G protein; Gi = inhibiting G protein; AC = adenylate cyclase; GDP = guanosine diphosphate; GTP = guanosine triphosphate; ATP = adenosine triphosphate; cAMP = cyclic adenosine monophosphate; PK-C = protein kinase C; DG = diacyl glycerol; IP3 = inositol triphosphate.

similar enough that they are able to bind to their respective receptors. Since they are not identical to the body's endogenous hormones, neurohormones, and neurotransmitters, they can result in a number of unwanted side effects. Of particular interest, receptors are often located in the cell membrane, where the circulating hormones have ready access for binding, as illustrated in Figure 6.10. Steroid receptors, however, are located within the cell nucleus, since steroids can easily enter the cell due to their lipophilic nature, and regardless of the location of the receptor, the activity of the cell is modified in some fashion as soon as a hormone binds to its receptor.

Second-messenger systems

Figure 6.10 illustrates several of the second-messenger systems used by membrane-bound receptors, and it is abundantly clear that several different types of hormones can interact with the **adenylate cyclase–cyclic adenosine monophosphate (cAMP) system** (14,23). When hormone A (H_a) binds to its receptor, the **stimulating G protein (G_s)** activates adenylate cyclase to produce cAMP from adenosine triphosphate (ATP). This causes a kinase to modify an enzyme in the cell to either increase or decrease its activity. Yet, other hormones work in an opposite manner by activating an **inhibiting G protein (G_i)**, which turns off the adenylate cyclase activity. Also, other hormones (H_c) bind to receptors associated with a different second-messenger system, the **diacyl glycerol (DG)-inositol triphosphate (IP_3) system** (14,24). Activation of DG results in a protein-activated cell response, while production of IP_3 releases calcium from storage sites within the cell. This calcium activates **calmodulin**, which results in a protein-activated cell response. An alternative mechanism of action is a receptor-activated **influx** of calcium from outside the cell. As with IP$_3$, this activates calmodulin, which will produce the desired cell response.

Nuclear interactions

Steroid hormones work in a completely different manner, and since they can readily pass through the cell membrane, they are able to enter the **cytosol** where they are bound to a chaperone protein, sometimes called a **cytoplasmic receptor** (8,25,26). This protein escorts the steroid to the cell nucleus where it can bind to a site on the cell DNA. This initiates a process called **transcription**, which results in the coded signal for the production of a cellular protein. This signal leaves the nucleus in the form of messenger ribonucleic acid (mRNA), and at the ribosomes, the protein is assembled from the various amino acids, resulting in the desired cell response. Regardless of which system is used, each hormone binds to its target receptor, which activates many sequential events resulting in the proper cell response.

Regulating hormonal levels

As previously mentioned, the increase or decrease in production of many hormones depends on the signal of trophic hormones (15). When the central nervous system detects a need for increased or decreased hormonal levels, it signals a trophic endocrine gland to increase or decrease its signal to the target endocrine gland. The pulsatile nature of the trophic hormone release sends the appropriate signal to the endocrine gland of interest. Once the hormonal concentrations increase, both the regulating endocrine gland in the central nervous system (CNS) and the trophic endocrine gland detect these increased concentrations and decrease their signals. This regulatory mechanism is called a **negative-feedback system**. This regulatory mechanism is also known as **cybernetic regulation**, as displayed in Figure 6.11. The system for regulating testosterone in males is a good example of negative-feedback regulation as circulating concentrations of

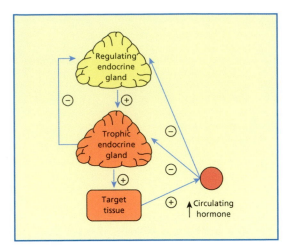

Figure 6.11 Example of negative-feedback regulation of circulating hormones. + = upregulation; − = downregulation; ↑ = increased.

testosterone are detected by both the hypothalamus, which produces LH-RH, and the anterior pituitary, which produces LH. This causes the signal to the testes to be altered, depending on whether more or less testosterone is needed. In this manner, the body is able to closely control the levels of hormones found in the circulating blood.

HORMONES VITAL TO EXERCISE

Although many hormones and neurohormones are responsible for the healthy functioning of the human body, the following section identifies the primary hormones of interest for this chapter.

Testosterone

Testosterone is a steroid hormone produced primarily by the **Leydig cells** in the male testes. Circulating testosterone in females is about 10% of that in males and is derived from the ovaries, (i.e., the female sexual glands, which produce estrogen, testosterone, and progesterone), and the adrenal cortex. During maturation, testosterone contributes to many of the male sexual characteristics associated with development. Testosterone is regulated by the **hypothalamic-pituitary axis**. In this regulatory structure, the hypothalamus detects circulating concentrations of testosterone and secretes LH-RH. This stimulates the release of LH from the anterior pituitary, which functions as the primary stimulus for the release of testosterone from the testes. This process takes up to 15 minutes to occur, so faster responses are probably due to direct innervation of the testes or to sympathetic nervous activity via circulating epinephrine or norepinephrine. Once released, testosterone is bound to its binding protein known as **sex hormone-binding globulin (SHBG)**.

Cortisol

Cortisol is a steroid hormone secreted by the outer layer of the adrenal glands (i.e., the **adrenal cortex**), and it is sometimes called a **stress hormone** since it is released when the individual experiences either physical or psychological stresses. Cortisol's principal role is to ensure the availability of energy. In this role, cortisol increases the production of glucose from either fat or protein in the liver (a process called **gluconeogenesis**), decreases glucose uptake, increases glycogen production in skeletal muscle, and causes amino acids to be mobilized from skeletal muscle. Because of this breakdown of protein into amino acids, cortisol is often termed a **catabolic hormone**. Circulating levels of cortisol are detected by the hypothalamus, which secretes **corticotropin-releasing hormone (CRH)**, a polypeptide hormone involved in the stress response. CRH then stimulates the anterior pituitary to release **adrenocorticotropic hormone (ACTH)**, which in turn signals the adrenal cortex to produce and release cortisol.

Testosterone/cortisol ratio

The ratio between testosterone, an **anabolic hormone** that causes the synthesis of molecules into more complex molecules, and cortisol, a **catabolic hormone**, has been used as a hormonal indicator of training stress (27). This can be considered for both a single aerobic training session and/or a long-term training phase. With a single stressful exercise session, testosterone initially increases or decreases, but cortisol increases to a greater extent. The net result is that the ratio decreases. Thus, the more stressful the session is then the more the ratio decreases. The ratio will also decrease over time in performing a stressful phase of training involving multiple sessions. As the individual tapers or backs off the training, the ratio returns to initial levels. As such, this ratio has been used as a marker of training stresses and is thought to be very useful when monitoring recovery status of athletes. Also, using the ratio between **free testosterone** (the portion of circulating testosterone not bound to SHBG) and cortisol could be a more sensitive indicator for monitoring an athlete's recovery status. This idea is based on the fact that free testosterone is the actual hormone that is biologically available to exert its actions at the target tissue.

Growth hormone

Growth hormone is a polypeptide hormone consisting of 191 amino acids and 2 disulfide bonds. It is produced and secreted from the anterior pituitary gland in a pulsatile fashion. Concentrations of growth hormone are increased by its trophic hormone, GH-RH, and decreased by **GH-inhibiting hormone (GH-IH)**, both from the hypothalamus. Many variations of growth hormone appear to exist because various forms of the original peptide are produced, but this makes growth-hormone data difficult to interpret at times. Many of the actions of growth hormone occur because of its effect on insulin-like growth factors. Although growth hormone is most often associated with its growth properties (including skeletal muscle), it also exerts tremendous influence on the metabolic system and energy availability as it increases muscle uptake of amino acids as well as the breakdown of lipids via **lipolysis**. The net result is that amino acids are preferentially used for anabolic purposes by muscle, and glycolytic energy sources are spared in favor of lipid energy sources.

Insulin-like-growth factor I (IGF-I)
The IGF-I system is composed of the IGF-I ligand (a 7.6-kD 70 amino acid polypeptide secreted from the liver), six binding proteins,

an acid labile subunit, and two receptors. The synthesis of IGF-I has been reported to be under the regulation of GH release, but exercise-related IGF-I responses, especially at the local tissue level, appear to be independent of GH (28,29). Similar to GH, IGF-I has multiple metabolic and hypertrophic actions, including insulin-like activity and direct stimulation of protein synthesis pathways.

Insulin and glucagons

Insulin and glucagons are considered together, since their actions are so closely associated. Insulin is a 51-amino-acid peptide hormone produced by the **beta cells** of the pancreas, the organ that secretes both insulin and glucagon. Insulin consists of a 21–amino acid A-chain and a 30–amino acid B-chain connected by two disulfide bonds. Glucagon is also a polypeptide chain, yet it is only 29 amino acids long and is produced by the **alpha cells** of the pancreas. Insulin and glucagons are released in response to increasing or decreasing blood glucose levels. Increasing concentrations of insulin prompt circulating glucose to be taken up by the following:

1   Adipose cells for conversion to triglycerides
2   Liver cells for conversion to glycogen
3   Skeletal muscle cells for conversion to glycogen

The net result is control of rising blood glucose levels and storage of energy for future use. Glucagon, however, results in the exact opposite responses. Triglycerides are metabolized in adipose tissue whereas amino acids and glycogen are metabolized in the liver. These collectively increase circulating glucose during times of high energy needs, such as during exercise, sport, and physical activity. Both insulin and glucagon are also under control by epinephrine and norepinephrine from the sympathetic nervous system (SNS), causing insulin to decrease and glucagon to increase.

Epinephrine

Epinephrine, sometimes referred to as adrenaline, is an amine neurohormone. Although it serves as a **neurotransmitter** in the CNS and transmits signals between the synapses of nerve cells, its role in the circulation is of major interest in this chapter. Blood-borne epinephrine comes from chromaffin cells in the center portion (i.e., medulla) of the adrenal glands. Upon neural stimulation, the adrenal medulla dumps its contents into the renal vein, which contributes to a very fast epinephrine response. Furthermore, the adrenal medulla is completely surrounded by the adrenal cortex and therefore, the medulla is constantly exposed to cortisol. This specific interaction with cortisol is critical for maintaining resting levels of epinephrine. When it is released into the circulation, epinephrine interacts with a variety of **alpha** and **beta receptors** in many different tissues of the body. Epinephrine is responsible for many of the "fight-or-flight" responses, and the physiological responses to stress prepare the body to either fight or flee from an impending threat and include increased arousal and cardiac output, altered blood-flow patterns, enhanced muscle contractions, and greater energy availability.

Norepinephrine

Norepinephrine, also known as noradrenaline, is an amine neurohormone. Unlike epinephrine, which is derived primarily from the adrenal medulla, most of the circulating norepinephrine comes from spillover from the SNS synapses. Hence, norepinephrine is sometimes considered an indicator of SNS activity. The adrenal medulla also produces some norepinephrine, but this is usually less than 20% of the epinephrine released.

Aldosterone

Aldosterone is a steroid hormone secreted by the adrenal cortex and is a key player in fluid regulation as it responds to a decrease in blood pressures due to lowered blood fluid volumes. To counter this problem, aldosterone acts in the kidneys to keep sodium from being excreted. When sodium is retained, fluid is also retained, which helps counter the previously detected fluid loss. It is important to note that this response is not rapid and requires 30 minutes or more to go into effect.

Antidiuretic hormone

Antidiuretic hormone (ADH) is a peptide hormone secreted by the posterior pituitary under hypothalamic control. Also known as arginine vasopressin, ADH responds to hydration status as does aldosterone, yet the mechanisms behind ADH are somewhat different. The concentration of proteins in the blood is known as the blood's osmolality, and this increases when fluid leaves the plasma portion of blood. The change in osmolality is readily detected in the arterial and venous circulation, which will yield a rapid ADH response. With ADH stimulation, the kidneys readily take up more fluid, which otherwise might have been excreted. ADH is also a strong vasoconstrictor which helps maintain blood pressure even when blood fluid levels have been reduced.

Thyroid hormones

The thyroid hormones thyroxine (T_4) and triiodothyronine (T_3) are secreted by the thyroid gland. They are derived from tyrosine and contain either four or three iodine molecules respectively. They are regulated by thyrotropin, also known as thyroid-stimulating hormone (TSH), from the pituitary gland. T_4 is secreted in greater quantities than T_3, but much of T_4 is converted throughout the body to the more potent T_3. The thyroid hormones are basically responsible for increasing the body's metabolic rate and enhancing the action of other hormones.

Calcium-regulating hormones

Calcitonin, from the thyroid gland, and parathyroid hormone, from the parathyroid gland, are both responsible for regulating calcium concentrations in the circulation. As calcium levels in the blood are detected, calcitonin is released to stop calcium from being taken from bone and to increase the excretion of calcium in the kidneys. Parathyroid hormone, however, works in an opposite manner. When blood calcium levels are low, release of parathyroid hormone stimulates bone to release calcium and inhibits excretion of calcium in the kidneys. Since the largest pool of calcium in the body is found in the skeletal system, it has been speculated that alterations of these hormones may be critical for the proper skeletal adaptations to exercise and physical activity.

EFFECTS OF EXERCISE ON THE ENDOCRINE SYSTEM

The endocrine system responds and adapts to the stresses placed on it, which include exercise, physical activity, and training for sports performance. The body will adapt to stress and produce enhanced performances or at least a tolerance for current activity levels (30). Although the hormonal response is not the only adaptation the body makes to exercise, it is of major importance as these hormones interact with so many other tissues and systems of the body.

REAL-WORLD APPLICATION

Maximizing your endocrine response

Athletes perform resistance training for a variety of reasons. One of the most common goals is skeletal muscle hypertrophy. In order to optimize anabolic hormone responses, the training program must be designed to do so. A resistance training session with the goal of increasing anabolic hormone responses, and in turn, inducing muscle hypertrophy, should meet the following criteria: 1) target large muscle groups; 2) be comprised of complex, multi-joint movements; 3) intensity of effort should be high; 4) volume should be high with intensity of load being moderate-to-heavy; and 5) rest period should be low (around 60 seconds).

Acute and chronic training adaptations

Regular training and physical activity result in an adaptation of the body to accommodate the stress. Hormonally, this can lead to the upregulation or downregulation of different hormones, depending on the types of physical activity and the physiological system involved. **Upregulation** refers to an increase in the number of receptors on the surface of target cells which make the cells more sensitive to a hormone or other molecule. Conversely, **downregulation** is a decrease in the number of receptors on the surface of target cells which make the cells less sensitive to a hormone or other molecule. On the one hand, these changes can be quite simple as they either increase or decrease the circulating concentrations found in the blood, but the changes can also be more complex. Figure 6.12 illustrates an example of how some hormones can both increase and decrease in response to long-term training (31,32). Prior to engaging in a chronic training program, individuals can exercise only up to a certain work rate due to their untrained status. But, as they increase their exercise intensity, the hormonal response increases accordingly. After long-term training has resulted in an increased capacity to exercise, they can exercise at a higher work rate. Also, when they exercise at the same absolute work rate as they did before participating in the chronic training program, they now will require less hormonal response to complete the same activity. On the other hand, when they exercise at their maximal capacity, they can produce a greater hormonal response which yields a greater work rate. Essentially, the individual will become more efficient during submaximal exercise while at the same time being capable of functioning at much higher intensities. It is important to note that acute responses to exercise are determined immediately or shortly after completing the exercise as these values represent the hormonal response to a single exercise session. On the other hand, chronic hormonal responses are often determined from changes in resting hormonal concentrations. These values represent the long-term concentrations that are continuously exposed to the target tissue.

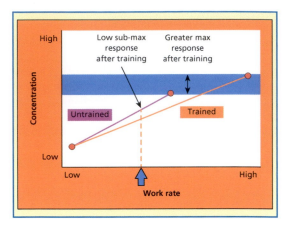

Figure 6.12 Common long-term training adaptations for hormonal responses to an exercise session. Note the decreased hormonal response at an absolute submaximal work rate after long-term training (indicated by the large arrow) but the increased hormonal response at maximal work rates. The trained individual is capable of exercising at higher work rates.

Responses and adaptations of hormones to endurance exercise

The following section addresses the primary hormones of interest and how they acutely respond to different intensities and durations of aerobic exercise. Where available, the chronic responses to long-term training are also included. It is very important to notice that the figures for each hormone indicate representative values and responses and these may vary between individuals and with different testing conditions.

> During aerobic activities, most hormones increase as intensity and duration increase. Some important exceptions, however, should be noted.

Testosterone and endurance exercise

Acute responses to endurance exercise
During aerobic exercise, testosterone increases in an intensity-dependent manner. Meaning, low intensities of exercise elicit little or no response and maximum or near-maximum intensities result in a significant elevation, as noted in Figure 6.13. During prolonged

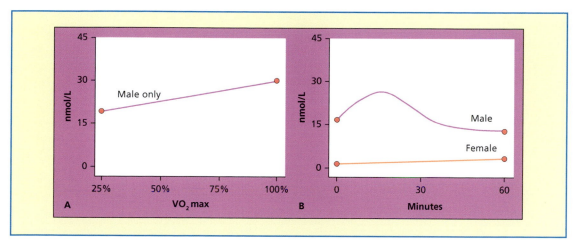

Figure 6.13 Responses of circulating concentrations of total testosterone to aerobic activities (33,34). A. Typical responses for men at different aerobic intensities (% <adV>O₂ max). B. Testosterone concentrations during 60 minutes of high-intensity endurance exercise for both men and women.

aerobic exercise, testosterone exhibits a biphasic response (35). Provided that the intensity is great enough, testosterone concentrations increase initially. If the duration of the exercise is long enough, concentrations decrease, which suggests that the decline in glucose levels may blunt the testosterone response. An example of this is the depressed testosterone levels that are reported after a runner completes a marathon. Also, of further importance, since the amounts of testosterone in females are small, little to no responses are usually observed (36).

Chronic responses to endurance exercise
Long-term endurance training has often been associated with lower concentrations of testosterone, but this may be simply due to the effects of the huge volumes of training reported for these individuals. Testosterone is inversely related to training stress where once the training stress increases, the testosterone levels will decrease. However, the observed lower concentrations are not enough to be medically significant. In addition, the fraction of testosterone measured in the blood and its other physiological roles may affect concentrations. Testosterone can be measured as a bound fraction (bound to SHBG), free, or total. Some researchers will only report the free testosterone concentrations, theorizing

that it is the only one that is biologically available to the individual. Also, testosterone has a potent chronic metabolic role which increases the production of red blood cells, yielding an increase in oxygen carrying capacity.

Gender differences
Instead of testosterone, the primary sex-related hormones of interest in females are progesterone and the estrogens such as estradiol, estrone, and estriol. As with testosterone, these hormones increase somewhat in an intensity-dependent manner (37). The phase of the menstrual cycle and energy balance can influence the acute and chronic responses. Plus, it is important to note that the use of hormonally based oral contraceptives can alter these responses. Given these factors, it is hard to determine the sole effects of endurance exercise on sex-related hormones.

Cortisol and endurance exercise
Acute responses to endurance exercise
During aerobic exercise, cortisol increases mostly in an intensity-dependent manner (38,39). Hence, at very low intensities, cortisol is not increased and may actually decrease slightly due to the very low stress on the metabolic systems at these intensities.

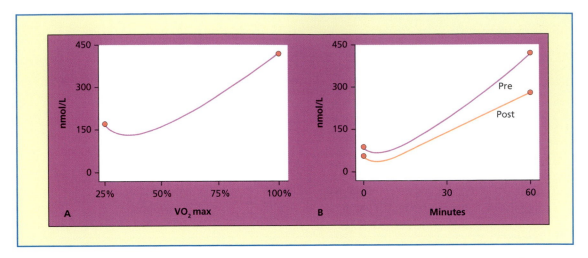

Figure 6.14 Responses of circulating concentrations of cortisol to aerobic activities (25,40,41,42). A. Typical responses at different aerobic intensities (%<adV>O$_2$ max). B. Cortisol concentrations during 60 minutes of endurance exercise at = 60% <adV>O$_2$ max. Pre and post refer to before and after long-term training.

As illustrated in Figure 6.14, intensities greater than 50% of Vo$_2$ max result in elevations of cortisol due to the energy requirements needed to perform at these levels. A similar response is observed for prolonged aerobic exercise, with elevations in cortisol levels occurring as the duration of exercise increases (43).

Chronic responses to endurance exercise
The long-term training response includes lower cortisol concentrations (32), and these reflect the body's ability to utilize the energy substrate available in a more efficient manner. However, no long-term differences and transient increases have been reported (14). Short-term high-intensity training may temporarily increase resting levels, but as with testosterone, this may be indicative of the nature of the training stressors.

Testosterone/cortisol ratio and endurance exercise

Because of the extremely high volumes of training that endurance athletes often perform, this hormonal ratio is often depressed among endurance athletes (45–47). This does not have to be the case, however, since this ratio can rebound when training volume is reduced.

The ratio between testosterone and cortisol is extremely important for strength adaptations. The body will be in a catabolic state if cortisol levels are greater than testosterone levels. However, when testosterone levels are higher than the cortisol levels, the body will be in an anabolic state which yields adaptations to strength training.

Growth hormone and endurance exercise

Acute responses to endurance exercise
Since growth hormone is closely tied to energy availability, circulating concentrations are positively related to exercise intensity and are highly correlated with lactate response (38,39). During aerobic exercise completed at maximal intensities, very large increases in growth hormone levels can be observed. Also, as displayed in Figure 6.15, the levels of growth hormone increase with increasing durations of aerobic exercise (49).

Chronic responses to endurance exercise
Few data exist describing the chronic resting adaptations of GH to endurance exercise, but it appears that chronic training has no effect on resting GH concentrations. Women do exhibit higher resting concentrations versus their male counterparts, but this occurs regardless of their training status.

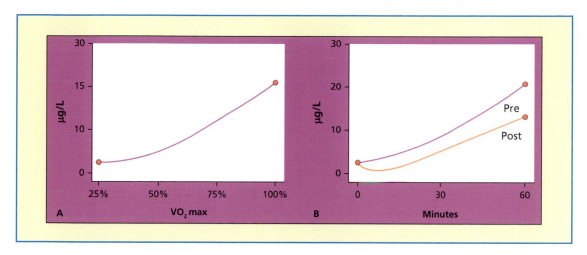

Figure 6.15 Responses of circulating concentrations of growth hormone to aerobic activities (40,41,48). A. Typical responses at different aerobic intensities (%<adV>O₂ max). B. Growth hormone concentrations during 60 minutes of high-intensity endurance exercise. Pre and post refer to before and after long-term training.

During exercise, long-term training results in a lesser acute response to a given submaximal workload, which appears to be the result of a more efficient metabolic system in trained individuals (50). However, maximal exercise efforts result in a greater growth hormone response in trained individuals (38).

Gender differences
Few studies exist that have evaluated gender differences in GH in response to endurance training. However, a prior study in trained endurance runners reported that GH concentrations increased in men, but not women after prolonged moderate intensity running (96). Conversely, other studies have reported no differences (52,53).

IGF-I and endurance exercise

Acute responses to endurance exercise
Increases, decreases, and no change in IGF-I concentrations during exercise have been reported, yet the majority of the studies suggest a transient increase in an intensity-dependent fashion, but then a return to resting values occurs within 30 minutes of exercise (44). As previously indicated, exercising IGF-I levels are not under the control of GH and increases may be due to the release of a muscle isoform of IGF-I (29). Also of

importance, IGF-I is highly dependent on nutritional status and this may account for the disparate results.

Chronic responses to endurance exercise
Chronic training produces a biphasic response of IGF-I, decreasing in the initial few weeks of training, followed by an increase that is above pretraining values (52). In addition, cross-sectional studies have suggested that IGF-I is highly correlated with VO₂ max values, which may suggest that this is a possible biomarker for fitness status (54). However, the completion of more research studies is needed concerning the role that IGF-I may play in endurance training adaptations.

Gender differences
Similar to GH responses, gender differences in IGF-I response to endurance exercise are conflicting, with few differences being reported (51).

Insulin, glucagon, and endurance exercise

Acute responses to endurance exercise
During aerobic exercise, insulin decreases, which will maximize the uptake of blood glucose when it is needed for energy. However, glucagon increases, which will permit glucose

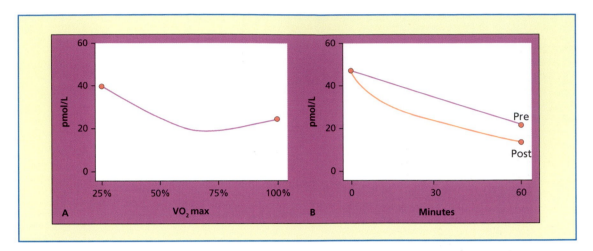

Figure 6.16 Responses of circulating concentrations of insulin to aerobic activities (23,57). A. Typical responses at different aerobic intensities (%<adV>O$_2$ max). B. Insulin concentrations during 60 minutes of high-intensity endurance exercise. Pre and post refer to before and after long-term training.

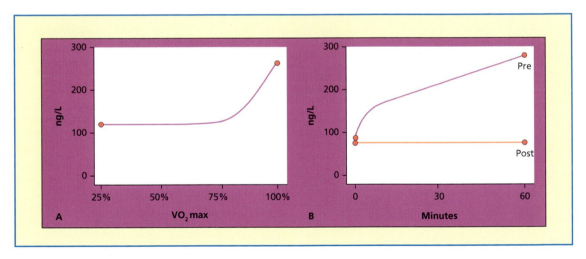

Figure 6.17 Responses of circulating concentrations of glucagon to aerobic activities (40,41). A. Typical responses at different aerobic intensities (%<adV>O$_2$ max). B. Glucagon concentrations during 60 minutes of high-intensity endurance exercise. Pre and post refer to before and after long-term training.

to become available for energy. In this manner, these two hormones work together to properly regulate glucose availability during physical activity (38,39). Figure 6.16 illustrates the responses of insulin to aerobic activities, and Figure 6.17 shows the responses of glucagon to aerobic activities.

Chronic responses to endurance exercise
After long-term training, the decrease in insulin is less pronounced, which is most

likely due to the almost nonexistent change in glucagon. Glucose uptake becomes less dependent on insulin, since chronic training results in increased activation of membrane glucose transport proteins, which regulate the transport of glucose across the plasma cellular membrane. In addition, chronic training results in a decreased response of the sympathetic nervous system; thus, levels of insulin are decreased, and glucagon increases to a lesser extent.

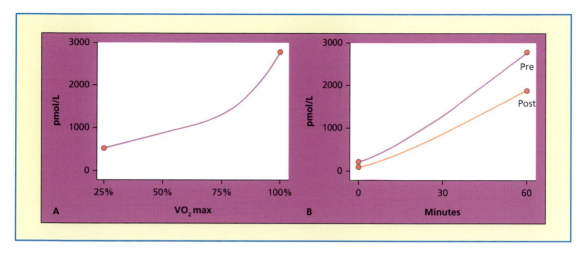

Figure 6.18 Responses of circulating concentrations of epinephrine to aerobic activities (18,40,43,59). A. Typical responses at different aerobic intensities (%<adV>O$_2$ max). B. Epinephrine concentrations during 60 minutes of high-intensity endurance exercise. Pre and post refer to before and after long-term training.

Gender differences

Women exhibit greater increases in insulin in response to submaximal endurance exercise compared to men (51,55). Researchers speculate that this difference is due to either autonomic nervous system regulation differences and/or substrate utilization differences.

Epinephrine and endurance exercise

Acute responses to endurance exercise

Compared to other hormones, the catecholamines exhibit extremely large responses to physical exercise. Epinephrine is particularly susceptible to an anticipatory response (56,57). In response to aerobic exercise, concentrations of epinephrine increase in an intensity-dependent manner (41,58) as suggested in Figure 6.18, yet the responses at low intensities are sometimes minimal. Furthermore, concentrations will increase with increasing duration of aerobic exercise (38,60).

Chronic responses to endurance exercise

As illustrated in Figure 6.12, long-term aerobic training results in an increased ability to secrete epinephrine at maximal intensities. On the other hand, absolute submaximal intensities result in lower concentrations after training, indicative of a more efficient system. The receptors for epinephrine are very sensitive to circulating concentrations and will readily decrease in number or responsiveness if epinephrine levels remain elevated for too long a time (33).

Gender differences

Males exhibit greater concentrations of epinephrine during exercise when compared to females (61,62). This differential response may be related to the fact that men utilize more carbohydrates during prolonged exercise, while women rely primarily on fat oxidation. Data concerning the training effect on chronic epinephrine concentrations is limited and it is unclear whether women exhibit the same chronic effects as men (63).

Norepinephrine and endurance exercise

Acute responses to endurance exercise

Although epinephrine and norepinephrine appear to respond similarly, they are primarily derived from different sources and their responses to exercise are not absolutely identical. As such, they represent different physiological phenomena. Norepinephrine increases in an aerobic intensity-dependent manner, with greater intensities eliciting larger responses (41,58). As displayed in Figure 6.19, similar to epinephrine, norepinephrine

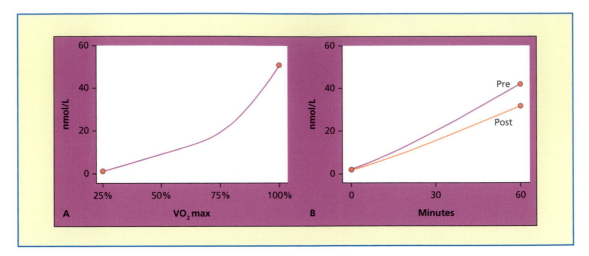

Figure 6.19 Responses of circulating concentrations of norepinephrine to aerobic activities (18,40,43,59). A. Typical responses at different aerobic intensities (%<adV>O₂ max). B. Norepinephrine concentrations during 60 minutes of high-intensity endurance exercise. Pre and post refer to before and after long-term training.

increases with longer duration aerobic exercise (38,60).

Chronic responses to endurance exercise
Long-term training will result in greater norepinephrine concentrations with maximal exercise, yet submaximal exercise will produce smaller concentrations, but this is dependent upon a more efficient system, as suggested in Figure 6.12. If exercise results in excessive elevation of the catecholamines for extended periods of time, the physiological system responsible (SNS) can become exhausted and lead to an impaired performance (27).

Gender differences
The gender difference of norepinephrine in response to exercise is equivocal, with

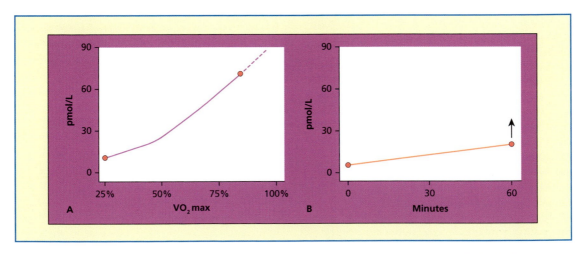

Figure 6.20 Responses of circulating concentrations of aldosterone to aerobic activities (35,65). A. Typical responses at different aerobic intensities up to 80% <adV>O₂ max. The dotted line indicates expected values for greater intensities. B. Aldosterone concentrations during 60 minutes of high-intensity endurance exercise. Note that the aldosterone response is highly dependent on the exercise intensity and the existing hydration status of the individual.

increased responses in men being reported (61) and no differences also being reported (53,55).

Aldosterone and endurance exercise

Acute responses to endurance exercise

As with many hormones, aldosterone increases during aerobic exercise in an intensity-dependent manner (64). Although aldosterone will increase during long-duration aerobic exercise, the extent of this increase is highly dependent on the environmental conditions (40). For example, conditions where sweat rates are high will eventually result in lowered plasma fluid levels and a concomitant decrease in blood pressure. As displayed in Figure 6.20, in extreme conditions, the aldosterone response can be quite large.

Chronic responses to endurance exercise

Chronic endurance training may enhance aldosterone response and sensitivity during exercise leading to an expansion in plasma volume. This may explain the greater stroke volumes and lower heart rates with a given exercise intensity observed in trained athletes (66).

ADH and endurance exercise

Acute responses to endurance exercise

At low aerobic exercise intensities, ADH exhibits little or no response, but at greater intensities, the increase in ADH is quite substantial (64).

Chronic responses to endurance exercise

As with aldosterone, long-duration aerobic exercise increases ADH, but these responses are very dependent on the environmental conditions (40). As shown in Figure 6.21, long-term aerobic training results in lowered ADH responses at the same absolute exercise intensity, while the response increases at the same relative intensity.

Thyroid hormones and endurance exercise

Acute responses to endurance exercise

Although the thyroid hormones are undoubtedly critical for health, their responses to exercise are reportedly quite variable (67), and little is known concerning their responses and adaptations to acute and chronic exercise. However, a prior study suggested that exhaustive endurance exercise decreases thyroid hormones for 24 hours into recovery and that cortisol responses are inversely related to the reduction, which illustrates the important role that thyroid hormones play in energy balance during and after exercise (68).

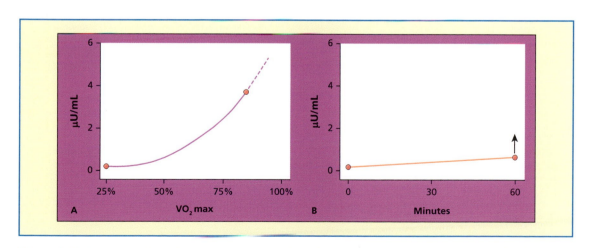

Figure 6.21 Responses of circulating concentrations of anti-diuretic hormone to aerobic activities (35,65). A. Typical responses at different aerobic intensities up to 80% <adV>O$_2$ max. The dotted line indicates expected values for greater intensities. B. Antidiuretic hormone concentrations during 60 minutes of high-intensity endurance exercise. Note that the aldosterone response is highly dependent on the exercise intensity and the existing hydration status of the individual.

Chronic responses to endurance exercise

Some evidence exists that the thyroid hormones decrease chronically during stressful phases of training, but this is not conclusive. Given the acute data, it is possible that chronic decreases would result from lower hypothalamic-pituitary signaling and may be indicative of energy conservation in athletes undergoing high-intensity training (69,70).

Calcium-regulating hormones and endurance exercise

To date, it has been difficult to tie calcium regulating hormones in with the exercise-induced responses of the skeletal system. Although acute exercise can increase circulating concentrations of these hormones, no definitive pattern has been identified concerning acute or chronic exercise responses (67).

Responses and adaptations of hormones to resistance exercise

One of the problems with studying the endocrine responses to resistance exercise is the tremendous variety that exists with the various training stimuli. This is best illustrated by the five acute training variables for resistance exercise (71,72). They are as follows:

1   Choice of exercise
2   Order of exercise
3   Volume of exercise
4   Intensity (or load) of exercise
5   Interset rest intervals

These five variables represent all of the possible variables for a single weight-training session. Needless to say, each of the variables

TABLE 6.3 Known effects of the acute weight training variables on several hormonal responses to a single exercise session (8,29,31,48,56,73–79)

Acute training variable	Testosterone	Cortisol	Growth hormone	Lactate
Choice of exercise	↑ With large-muscle-mass exercises and high-power exercises, moderately high volumes necessary	↑ With large-muscle-mass exercises and high-power exercises, ↑ usually with full body training session	↑ With large-muscle-mass exercises and high-power exercises, ↑ with free weights > ↑ with machines	↑ With large-muscle-mass exercises and high-power exercises
Volume of exercises	Variable responses, depends on other factors	↑ With increasing volume. Note: volume can be low if intensity is high enough	↑ With increasing volume. Note: GH response related to total work	↑ With increasing volume
Intensity of exercise	↑ With increasing relative intensity (% of 1RM)	↑ With increasing relative intensity (% of 1RM). Note: cortisol ↑ > testosterone ↑	↑ With increasing relative intensity (% of 1RM). Note: volume must be high enough	Too high an intensity → smaller HLa response
Interset rest intervals	↓ Rest may ↑ testosterone (responses are variable)	↑ With decreasing rest intervals	↑ With decreasing rest intervals	↑ With decreasing rest intervals

↑ = increases, ↓ = decreases, RM = repetition maximum, > = greater than includes many options. When all five variables are considered, the number of possible combinations becomes exponentially large, thus representing the huge number of stimuli resistance exercise can present. When the long-term program is added to this, the characteristics of the training program can almost be overwhelming. Regardless, much progress has been made concerning the effect of the acute training variables on the subsequent hormonal responses. Unfortunately, many questions remain unanswered concerning the hormonal responses to each of these acute training variables. For example, little is known about how changing the order of exercise influences the hormonal responses and adaptations. Furthermore, little is known about how numerous hormones respond to resistance exercise. Nevertheless, Table 6.3 summarizes much of the research on several hormonal responses to a single resistance exercise training session and the roles of the acute training variables.

> During heavy resistance training exercise, the specific hormonal response is rather dependent upon the acute training variables which include: the choice of exercise, order of exercise, total repetitions, load or intensity, and interset rest.

Q&A FROM THE FIELD

Hormonal responses to resistance exercise seem to be very specific to the type and intensity of exercise. Can this specific hormonal response be planned based on specific goals and phases of a periodized strength training and conditioning program?

Yes. Specific hormonal responses help to determine the training effect on muscle tissue. In a hypertrophy phase of training, the male athlete would want to stimulate the body's own production of testosterone. This can best be accomplished by large-muscle-mass exercises, heavy resistance, and a moderate to high volume with short (about 60-second) rest intervals. The testosterone response in male athletes is greatest with two or more years of resistance training experience.

> To stimulate the body's production of growth hormone, use resistance training protocols that stimulate high lactic acid production (high-intensity, 10RM, short rest periods). The appropriate use of carbohydrate and protein supplements before and after the workout can also help with endogenous production of growth hormone.
>
> To optimize the adrenal response to resistance training, the athlete should use high-volume, large-muscle-mass exercises with short rest periods. Exposing the athlete to a variety of resistance training stimuli at a high intensity allows the adrenal response to take an active role in recovery. In a high-intensity protocol such as this, always monitor the athlete for signs of overtraining.

Testosterone and resistance exercise

Acute responses to resistance exercise

Testosterone readily increases during a weight-training session, but this requires at least a moderate training volume as measured by the total repetitions completed (79–82). Sessions that utilize large-muscle-mass multi-joint exercises appear to elicit larger responses than those using just small-muscle-mass exercises (83,84). Additionally, exercise sessions that incorporate high-power exercises such as the Olympic weightlifting movements that include the snatch, and clean and jerk, can also produce considerable increases in testosterone (84). These types of exercises (e.g., squats, bench presses, cleans, dead lifts, etc.) have large energy requirements and activate the body's endocrine and neuroendocrine systems to a greater extent than other types of resistance exercises (e.g., arm curls, leg extensions, leg curls, etc.). The relative intensity, as expressed as a percent of one-repetition maximum, or % of 1RM, is critical, with greater relative intensities producing the largest increases (79). It is important to note that the intensity may be so high (e.g., 100% of 1RM) that an adequate training volume cannot be performed. Hence, the net result is little to no testosterone response (77). When very low relative intensities are used, such as 40% of 1RM, acute responses of testosterone are also minimal (83). Some evidence also exists that decreasing the rest between sets may increase the testosterone response slightly (79). Again, it should be pointed out that too short a rest interval may mean that the loads have to be decreased below the critical level for a significant testosterone response.

Chronic responses to resistance exercise

Observations in resting testosterone concentrations during resistance training are inconsistent in both men and women with increases, no differences, and reductions being reported (85). Furthermore, resting levels may depend on the current volume and intensity of training (85). In a study where resting increases were reported during short-term high-volume training, subsequent reductions were observed when volume was reduced and intensity was increased over seven weeks (86). Thus, substantial changes in volume and intensity may elicit transient changes in resting testosterone concentrations and values, which then return to baseline during normal training.

Cortisol and resistance exercise

Acute responses to resistance exercise

Compared to testosterone, cortisol tends to exhibit a larger acute response to resistance exercise (79). As with testosterone, cortisol responds most when large-muscle-mass, multi-joint exercises are performed and when high-power exercises are utilized (84). Due to the metabolic requirements, cortisol levels will increase when total-body training sessions are performed. Cortisol responds in a relative intensity- and volume-dependent manner (79). When interset rest intervals are decreased, cortisol responses are also increased, again most likely due to the metabolic requirements of the session (79). It should be noted that some dietary supplements have been promoted with claims that they decrease the cortisol response to exercise. Although cortisol is a catabolic hormone, it also serves an important role in the remodeling of muscle tissue. As such, decreasing or eliminating the cortisol response may not be desirable.

Chronic responses to resistance exercise

Despite the role cortisol has in remodeling muscle, chronically elevated levels can be deleterious. Chronic resistance training produces inconsistent patterns of cortisol secretion and studies have reported in men and women (i) no change (18,48,87,88), (ii) reductions (42,89,90), and (iii) increases (59) during training and short-term overreaching. Also, when compared to untrained individuals, highly resistance trained individuals appear to have less of a cortisol response to intense resistance training, yet this adaptation may be of little importance as a trained individual may not be undergoing the same extreme muscular adaptations as someone who is untrained.

Growth hormone and resistance exercise

Acute responses to resistance exercise

The fact that acute resistance exercise stimulates a potent GH release in both men and women is well documented (1). However, the magnitude of acute release in response to resistance exercise depends upon several variables, which include: rest time between sets, volume, load, exercise selection, training status, muscle actions used, amount of muscle mass recruited, time of day, and total work. Thus, it is extremely difficult to isolate the individual variable effects on GH release. The use of large-muscle-mass, multi-joint exercises as well as high-power exercises is critical for a large growth hormone response (1,79). Research evidence suggests that free weights may produce a larger response than machine exercises, but this may simply be related to the muscle mass involvement (91). The relative intensity and the volume of exercise are positively related to the growth hormone response as well (79,92). The interset rest interval is extremely important as very short rest intervals elicit extremely large acute growth hormone responses (79,86).

Chronic responses to resistance exercise

Chronic training may increase the GH response to acute exercise in both men and women (90). However, this response is likely due to their ability to perform more work and utilize heavier loads, as resting values do not change.

Gender differences

Women have higher resting values when compared to men, but the data is conflicting as to whether there are differences in the acute exercise response, with no differences being consistently reported (78,93). A heavy loading protocol has been reported to elicit a GH response in men versus women, yet both genders have an equal response to a higher rep, lower rest interval protocol (42). This data suggests that factors such as lean body mass, total body mass, fat mass, nutritional intake, training status, and the menstrual cycle may all play a role in the resistance exercise induced GH response.

IGF-I and resistance exercise

Acute responses to resistance exercise

The response of circulating IGF-I to an acute resistance exercise bout is variable, with some investigations showing no change (20,65) and some reporting increases (78,90,92). These reported differences may be due to the differences in protocols, subjects' trained state and age, gender, and nutritional status. In 1991, Kraemer et al. (78) compared the responses of eight men and eight women to two different full body acute resistance exercise protocols. Protocol one utilized a 5RM load, 3-minute rest period. Protocol two utilized a 10RM load, 1-minute rest period and had a higher total work than the first protocol. Both protocols were designed to control for load, rest period length, and total work (each protocol contained a secondary workout surrounding the primary protocol to equalize total work). IGF-I increased in response to both exercise protocols in both genders, but there were no significant differences between men and women.

Chronic responses to resistance exercise

Well-trained men are reported to have higher concentrations of IGF-I at rest compared to untrained men, despite no differences between these two groups in circulating concentrations of GH (92). Temporal changes in IGF-I levels were reported in both men and women in response to different exercise protocols that differed in volume and rest periods (94). In addition, increased resting levels of IGF-I were reported after the supplementation period, suggesting that dietary manipulation played a role in IGF-I dynamics (2).

Gender differences

Similar to GH, women have significantly higher resting values of IGF-I and the higher values at rest are reflective of the GH mediated control of IGF-I. However, some researchers speculate that the significant increases at rest in women gives further support to the concept that women may rely upon the IGF/GH axis to a greater extent than men as an anabolic signaler for strength gains, while men probably rely more on testosterone.

Lactate: acute response to resistance exercise

Although not a hormone, lactate provides insight on the metabolic characteristics of different weight-training sessions. In general, protocols that use large-muscle-mass, multi-joint, and high-power exercises, with large training volumes and short interset rest intervals, produce the largest lactate responses (78,84,95). However, if the relative intensity is too great, the volume that can be performed becomes too low, which compromises the lactate response.

Long-term adaptations to resistance exercise

The long-term (chronic) responses to heavy resistance exercise are found in Table 6.4 (18,89,97,98). In general, resting concentrations of these hormones are not always altered, but differences in the acute responses to a resistance training session can occur. In some cases, the response increases, which suggests an enhanced capacity of the involved endocrine glands. In other cases, the response decreases, indicating greater efficiency of those hormones. At present, the responses of a number of hormones are not known.

> Long-term hormonal adaptations to training are more subtle than the acute response to a single session, but they can provide an important training adaptation.

TABLE 6.4 Hormonal effects of long-term normal resistance exercise training (15,23,38,57,69,87,95,96)

Hormone	Effects
Testosterone	Slight increase
Cortisol	Slight decrease
Growth hormone	Slight decrease
Insulin	Increase
Glucagon	Decrease
Epinephrine	Max intensity: increase
	Submax intensity: decrease
Norepinephrine	Max intensity: increase
	Submax intensity: decrease
Antidiuretic hormone	Slight decrease (depends on the environmental conditions)
Aldosterone	Slight decrease (depends on the environmental conditions)
Thyroxine	No known change
Triiodothyronine	No known change
Calcitonin	No known change
Parathyroid hormone	No known change

Overtraining and the endocrine system

Although a properly designed training program is desirable for optimal results, sometimes the exercise program is improperly prescribed, resulting in maladaptations or overtraining. Overtraining occurs when training volume and/or intensity is excessive and results in prolonged decreases in performance (27,72). Short-term performance decrements are sometimes referred to as overreaching and are often part of a planned training program (e.g., two-a-day training sessions for many sports). As one might expect, the endocrine system has been implicated in the maladaptations occurring during overtraining. It has been suggested that monitoring certain hormones may permit monitoring of the training stresses, which may help avoid the onset of an overtrained state (73). However, different types of overtraining appear to elicit different hormonal responses, and this has often been overlooked (27).

Overtraining occurring from activities that emphasize aerobic endurance is often characterized by very high training volumes (45–47). As seen in Table 6.5, most hormonal responses eventually decrease except for the stress hormone cortisol. The decrease in catecholamines appears to be reflective of exhaustion of the sympathetic nervous system. High volumes of resistance exercise exhibit many of the same endocrine characteristics (27,72,96). Perhaps the most commonly cited variable for monitoring overtraining is the testosterone/cortisol ratio (73). In general, this appears to be indicative of the collective training stresses, but it is very important to notice that changes in this ratio can often occur when overtraining is not present. Therefore, one cannot diagnose overtraining using this variable alone. It appears that subsequent exposures to high-volume resistance exercise overtraining may permit the body to adapt to the stress, resulting in an avoidance of overtraining (57,96).

Contrary to many of the common characteristics of aerobic overtraining or high-volume resistance exercise, high-intensity resistance exercise overtraining exhibits a much different endocrine profile. In general, the steroid hormones and growth hormone are often unaffected. In fact, some studies have shown an increase in testosterone which is the exact opposite to other types of overtraining (74). In this case, the catecholamines actually exhibit increased responses to exercise (56,57). It is believed that the SNS is still attempting to preserve performance and has not yet reached a state of exhaustion as previously described for other types of overtraining.

Although many factors can contribute to overtraining and the accompanying decreases in performance, several easily administered training variables can help (72). When training volumes and volume loads have been high, small but critical decreases in either volume or relative intensity can result in the avoidance of overtraining. Although not always

TABLE 6.5 Endocrine responses to overtraining (17,24,28,61,73,99)

Hormone	Aerobic overtraining	High-volume RE overtraining	High-intensity RE overtraining
Testosterone	Decrease	Decrease	NC or slight Increase
Cortisol	Increase	Increase	NC
Tes/Cort	Decrease	Decrease	NC
Growth hormone	Increase → decrease	NC	NC
Epinephrine	Decrease	Decrease?	Increase
Norepinephrine	Decrease	Decrease?	Increase

RE = resistance exercise, NC = no change

the case, high volumes of resistance exercise typically depress resting testosterone and the testosterone/cortisol ratio. Simply providing a day of recovery each week, or at least a sharp decrease in volume (and usually intensity), may avoid such a problem. It is not hard to fathom that an alteration in training volume is easy to administer, yet this particular recovery method is overlooked and often ignored.

> As similar to skeletal muscle adaptations, hormonal adaptations occur as a result of short- and long-term training. As training continues, the amount of hormones needed will increase or decrease.

Using the endocrine system to monitor training

A major issue for many coaches and athletes that must be addressed is monitoring the physiological effects of a training program. This can be relevant for either the individual training session or for the longer-term effects of a phase of the training cycle. Obviously, obtaining blood samples from an athlete is often easier said than done, and having the blood analyzed may be even more difficult. An alternative approach might be to collect salivary or urine samples, but the analyses are still time-consuming and expensive. Regardless, much

valuable information may be attainable if this information is accessed.

> It has been proposed that levels of fatigue, recovery, and overtraining may sometimes be monitored by tracking hormonal responses and adaptations to training.

Training effect of a single session
The hormonal response to a single training session can help the coach determine whether the desired training stimulus is being applied (21). The responses of testosterone, cortisol, and growth hormone can help determine the anabolic characteristics of the training stimulus. It is also logical to assume that the thyroid hormones and insulin be also monitored for this very reason, since they have also been associated with anabolic responses of muscle.

Training intensity of a single session
It has been suggested that supporting information on whether proper training intensities have been applied can be deduced from the acute hormonal profiles. If hormonal responses are typically monitored, then it may be possible to evaluate whether the prescribed intensity is appropriate based on the responses of intensity-dependent hormones (21).

A training session may be designed that optimizes or minimizes the anabolic hormonal responses.

Diagnosing fatigue

All coaches and athletes would like to know how well the training program is being tolerated (21,27,72). When the training becomes excessive, it is critical to detect this problem before it turns into a long-term overtraining syndrome. To properly do this, hormonal variables must be measured on a regular basis to determine normal values for each individual. Possible variables to monitor include: testosterone, cortisol, the testosterone/cortisol ratio, and the catecholamines. It is also important to remember that just because some of the endocrine variables change, it does not mean that overtraining has occurred or that excessive fatigue exists. Yet, it may serve as a warning of impending problems.

Monitoring recovery

Once normal hormonal levels have been determined for an individual, it is possible to determine when a fatigued individual returns to a prefatigue state (21). Any hormone or neurohormone that responds to training stress may have to return to normal levels for that individual before physiological recovery is considered complete. This may be a critical step in assessing whether a periodized training program has been designed to adequately permit recovery during certain phases of the training.

OPTIMIZING THE TRAINING PROGRAM

The ultimate challenge for the reader of this chapter is to utilize the information provided in designing a strength and conditioning program. Such a program will, of course, depend on the desired goals determined for the specific purpose of the training. Although numerous physiological systems of the body must be considered, insight on the development of training programs can be deduced from the endocrine data available.

Goal: muscle hypertrophy

In designing a program where muscle hypertrophy is a primary objective, it will be important to design the training stimulus to optimize the anabolic hormone response. For example, growth-hormone responses are optimized when large-muscle-mass exercises are used with approximately 10RM loads, while rest intervals are kept fairly short (1 minute or less). In addition, some work with relatively heavy loads is necessary to optimize the acute testosterone response.

Goal: no muscle hypertrophy

Some sports may require an individual to maintain a certain body weight (e.g., weight-class sports such as wrestling, or activities where a large body mass may not be desired such as figure skating, distance running, or climbers in professional cycling). In designing a program for such individuals, it may be wise to minimize the anabolic hormone response. For example, avoiding large-muscle-mass exercises may minimize some of the growth-hormone response to a training session. Of course, this is also dependent on the intensities and rest intervals prescribed. In some cases, large-muscle-mass, multi-joint exercises are necessary for the purposes of the training. In such instances, allowing longer rest intervals will definitely minimize the growth-hormone response.

Goal: high-power performance

It has been suggested that optimal power performances occur when resting testosterone concentrations are relatively high (100). If this is the case, the training program must permit a long-term elevation in resting testosterone levels. One method of doing this is by decreasing the training stresses (i.e., decreasing volume and/or intensity) during the taper phase (76). In addition, chronic utilization of high relative intensities using high-power, large-muscle-mass exercises may contribute to slight elevations of long-term resting levels of testosterone (98).

Goal: peak performance

If a performance peak is desired, the preceding training taper must permit the resting concentrations of certain hormones to be adequately recovered. In this case, decreasing the volume-load (i.e., reps times weight) can result in elevations of resting testosterone and increases in the testosterone/cortisol ratio (76).

Goal: avoiding overtraining

Although many factors can contribute to overtraining and the accompanying decreases in performance, several easily administered training variables can help (72). When training volumes and volume loads have been high, small but critical decreases in either volume or relative intensity can result in the avoidance of overtraining. Although not always the case, high volumes of resistance exercise typically depress resting testosterone and the testosterone/cortisol ratio. Simply providing a day of recovery each week, or at least a sharp decrease in volume (and usually intensity), may avoid such a problem.

SUMMARY

The endocrine system comprises complex interactions of hormones and neurohormones with each other and other physiological systems. Thus, proper responses of the endocrine system are essential for optimal adaptations to a training program. Although it may be hard to measure and analyze these variables, a thorough understanding of how the body responds and adapts to the stresses applied is imperative for developing truly effective training programs and understanding why they are effective. Finally, understanding how the endocrine system responds to the various acute training variables assists in the ability to design a training prescription that provides an optimal hormonal environment for the desired results.

MAXING OUT

1 You are interviewing to become a strength and conditioning coach for collegiate track and field throwers. The head coach asks if resistance training the men and women the same way will result in exactly the same results pertaining to hormonal adaptations. Please explain to your prospective head coach how the hormonal response to resistance training for the male and female throwers will be different and therefore contribute to potentially different training outcomes.

2 One of your 5 km distance runners mentions to you that they would like to become an ultra-marathon runner when their collegiate athletic career is over, but they are concerned about maintaining their current muscle mass as well as their ability to train every day of the week. Please explain to your athlete how the hormonal response to prolonged endurance exercise, as in the case as to when they begin training like an ultramarathon runner, may impact their ability to maintain their current muscle mass and discuss how their ability to recover may be jeopardized with making the change to becoming an ultramarathon athlete.

3 One of the head coaches in your athletic department approaches you with a concern that one of their athletes complains of always feeling like they are tired and that their performance appears to be declining. Please explain to the coach that the condition that the athlete may be experiencing is overtraining and discuss how this relates to the hormone levels in the body. Also, discuss with the coach how monitoring hormonal levels may be able to be used to predict overtraining in the "under-recovered athlete" in question.

REFERENCES

1. **Kraemer WJ and Ratamess NA.** Hormonal responses and adaptations to resistance exercise and training. *Sports Med* 2005; 35:339–361.
2. **Kraemer WJ, Volek JS, Bush JA, Putukian M, and Sebastianelli WJ.** Hormonal responses to consecutive days of heavy-resistance exercise with or without nutritional supplementation. *J Appl Physiol* 1998; 85(4):1544–1555.
3. **Wilson JD, Foster DW, eds.** *Williams Textbook of Endocrinology*. Philadelphia, PA: Saunders, 1992: inside front cover.
4. **Young DS.** Implementation of SI units for clinical laboratory data. *Ann Intern Med* 1987; 106:114–128.
5. **Sporn MB, Todaro GJ.** Autocrine secretion and malignant transformation of cells. *N Engl J Med* 1980; 303:878–880.
6. **Feyrter F.** Ueber die These von den peripheren endokrinen Druesen. *Wien Zeitschr Inn Med* 1946; 27:9–38.
7. **Ojeda SR, Griffin JE.** Organization of the endocrine system. In: *Textbook of Endocrine Physiology*, Ojeda SR, Griffin JE, eds. New York: Oxford University Press, 1988:3–16.
8. **Clark JH, Schrader WT, O'Malley BW.** Mechanisms of action of steroid hormones. In: *Williams Textbook of Endocrinology*, 8th ed., Wilson JD, Foster DW, eds. Philadelphia, PA: Saunders, 1992:35–90.
9. **Hebener JF.** Genetic control of hormone function. In: *Williams Textbook of Endocrinology*, 8th ed., Wilson JD, Foster DW, eds. Philadelphia, PA: Saunders, 1992:9–34.
10. **Landsberg L, Young JB.** Catecholamines and the adrenal medulla. In: *Williams Textbook of Endocrinology*, 8th ed., Wilson JD, Foster DW, eds. Philadelphia, PA: Saunders, 1992:621–705.
11. **Mendel CM.** The free hormone hypothesis: a physiologically based mathematical model. *Endocr Rev* 1989; 10:232–274.
12. **Kraemer WJ.** Endocrine responses and adaptations to strength training. In: *Strength and Power in Sport*, Komi PV, ed. Oxford, UK: Blackwell, 1992:291–304.
13. **Wilkerson JE, Gutin B, Horvath SM.** Exercise-induced changes in blood, red cell, and plasma volumes in man. *Med Sci Sports* 1977; 9:155–158.
14. **Kahn CR, Smith RJ, Chin WW.** Mechanism of action of hormones that act at the cell surface. In: *Williams Textbook of Endocrinology*, 8th ed., Wilson JD, Foster DW, eds. Philadelphia, PA: Saunders, 1992:91–134.
15. **Houk JC.** Control strategies in physiological systems. *FASEB J* 1988; 2:97–107.
16. **Veldhuis JD, Johnson LM.** Cluster analysis: a simple, versatile, and robust algorithm for endocrine pulse detection. *Am J Physiol* 1988; 250:E486–E493.
17. **Czeisler CA, Klerman EB.** Circadian and sleep-dependent regulation of hormone release in humans. *Rec Progr Horm Res* 1999; 54:97–130.
18. **Häkkinen K, Pakarinen A, Alen M, et al.** Daily hormonal and neuromuscular responses to intensive strength training in 1 week. *Int J Sports Med* 1988; 9:422–428.
19. **Thuma JR, Gilders R, Verdun J, Loucks A.** Circadian rhythm of cortisol confounds cortisol responses to exercise: implications for future research. *J Appl Physiol* 1995; 78(5):1657–1664.
20. **Cannon WB.** *Bodily Changes in Pain, Hunger, Fear, and Rage*. New York: Appleton, 1922.
21. **Viru A, Viru M.** *Biochemical Monitoring of Sport Training*. Champaign, IL: Human Kinetics, 2001:61–65.
22. **Nindl BC, Pierce JR.** Insulin-like growth factor I as a biomarker of health, fitness, and training status. *Med Sci Sports Exerc* 2010; 42:39–49.
23. **Gilman AG.** G-proteins and regulation of adenyl cyclase. *JAMA* 1989; 262:1819–1825.
24. **Hokin LE.** Receptors and phosphoinositide-generated second messengers. *Annu Rev Biochem* 1985; 54:202–235.
25. **Borer K.** *Exercise Endocrinology*. Champaign, IL: Human Kinetics, 2003:45.
26. **Glass CK.** Differential recognition of target genes by nuclear receptor monomers, dimers, and heterodimers. *Endocrinol Rev* 1994; 15:391–407.
27. **Fry AC, Kraemer WJ.** Resistance exercise overtraining and overreaching: neuroendocrine responses. *Sports Med* 1997; 23(2):106–129.
28. **Eliakim A, Nemet D, and Cooper DM.** Exercise, training, and the GH-IGF-I axis. In: *The Endocrine System in Sports and Exercise*, WJ Kraemer and AD Rogol, eds. Malden, MA: Blackwell, 2005:165–179.
29. **Goldspink G, Yang SY, Hameed M, Harridge S, and Bouloux P.** The Role of MGF and Other IGF-I Splice Variants in Muscle Maintenance and Hypertrophy. In: *The Endocrine System in Sports and Exercise*, WJ Kraemer and AD Rogol, eds. Malden, MA: Blackwell Publishing Ltd, 2005:180–193.

30. Selye H. *The Stress of Life*. New York: McGraw-Hill, 1956.

31. Kjaer M, Galbo H. Effect of physical training on the capacity to secrete epinephrine. *J Appl Physiol* 1988; 64:11–16.

32. Winder WW, Hickson RC, Hagberg JM, et al. Training-induced changes in hormonal and metabolic responses to submaximal exercise. *J Appl Physiol* 1979; 46:766–771.

33. Atgie C, D'Allaire F, Bukowiecki LJ. Role of beta1 and beta3 adrenoceptors in the regulation of lipolysis and thermogenesis in rat brown adipocytes. *Am J Physiol* 1997; 273:C1136–C1142.

34. Chandler RM, Byrne HK, Patterson JG, and Ivy JL. Dietary supplements affect the anabolic hormones after weight-training exercise. *J Appl Physiol* 1994; 76:839–845.

35. Cumming DC, Brunsting LA III, Strich G, et al. Reproductive hormone increases in response to acute exercise in men. *Med Sci Sports Exerc* 1986; 18:369–373.

36. Baker ER, Mathur RS, Kirk RF, et al. Plasma gonadotropins, prolactin, and steroid hormone concentrations in female runners immediately after a long-distance run. *Fertil Steril* 1984; 38:38–41.

37. Bonen A, Ling WYU, MacIntyre KP, et al. Effects of exercise on the serum concentrations of FSH, LH, progesterone, and estradiol. *Eur J Appl Physiol* 1979; 42:15–23.

38. Galbo H. *Hormonal and Metabolic Adaptation to Exercise*. New York: Thieme-Stratton, 1983.

39. Sutton JR, Farrell PA, Harber VJ. Hormonal adaptations to physical activity. In: *Exercise, Fitness, and Health*, Bouchard C, Shephard RJ, Stephens T, et al, eds. Champaign, IL: Human Kinetics, 1990:217–257.

40. Francesconi RP, Sawka MN, Pandolf KB, et al. Plasma hormonal responses at graded hypohydration levels during exercise-heat stress. *J Appl Physiol* 1985; 59:1855–1860.

41. Kotchen TA, Hartley LH, Rice TW, et al. Renin, norepinephrine, and epinephrine responses to graded exercise. *J Appl Physiol* 1971; 31:178–184.

42. Kraemer WJ, Staron RS, Hagerman FC, et al. The effects of short-term resistance training on endocrine function in men and women. *Eur J Appl Physiol Occup Physiol* 1998; 78:69–76.

43. Brandenberger G, Follenius M. Influence of timing and intensity of muscle exercise on temporal patterns of plasma cortisol levels. *J Clin Endocrinol Metab* 1975; 40:845–849.

44. Consitt LA, Copeland JL, Tremblay MS. Hormone responses to resistance vs. endurance exercise in premenopausal females. *Can J Appl Physiol* 2001; 26:574–87.

45. Lehmann M, Foster C, Netzer N, et al. Physiological responses to short- and long-term overtraining in endurance athletes. In: *Overtraining in Sport*, Kreider RB, Fry AC, O'Toole ML, eds. Champaign, IL: Human Kinetics, 1998:19–46.

46. Lehmann, M, Gastmann U, Petersen KG, et al. Training-overtraining: performance, and hormone levels, after a defined increase in training volume vs training intensity in experienced middle- and long-distance runners. *Br J Sports Med* 1992; 26:233–242.

47. Lehmann M, Gastmann U, Baur S, et al. Selected parameters and mechanisms of peripheral and central fatigue and regeneration in overtrained athletes. In: *Overload, Performance Incompetence, and Regeneration in Sport*, Lehmann M, Foster C, Gastmann U, et al, eds. New York: Kluwer Academic/Plenum, 1999:7–26.

48. Häkkinen K, Pakarinen A, Kyrolainen H, et al. Neuromuscular adaptations and serum hormones in females during prolonged power training. *Int J Sports Med* 1990; 11:91–98.

49. Lassare C, Girard F, Durand J, Reynaud J. Kinetics of human growth hormone during submaximal exercise. *J Appl Physiol* 1974; 37:826–830.

50. Wideman L, Weltman JY, Hartman ML, Veldhuis JD, Weltman A. Growth hormone release during acute and chronic aerobic and resistance exercise: recent findings. *Sports Med* 2002; 32(15):987–1004.

51. Vislocky LM, Gaine PC, Pikosky MA, Martin WF, Rodriguez NR. Gender impacts the post-exercise substrate and endocrine response in trained runners. *J Int Soc Sports Nutr* 2008; 26:5–7.

52. Eliakim A, Portal S, Zadik Z, Rabinowitz J, Adler-Portal D, Cooper DM, Zaldivar F, Nemet D. The effect of a volleyball practice on anabolic hormones and inflammatory markers in elite male and female adolescent players. *J Strength Cond Res* 2009; 23(5):1553–9.

53. Friedmann B, Kindermann W. Energy metabolism and regulatory hormones in women and men during endurance exercise. *Eur J Appl Physiol Occup Physiol* 1989; 59(1–2):1–9.

54. Nindl BC. Insulin-like growth factor-I as a candidate metabolic biomarker: military relevance and future directions for

measurement. *J Diabetes Sci Technol* 2009; 3(2):371–376.

55. Tarnopolsky LJ, MacDougall JD, Atkinson SA, Tarnopolsky MA, Sutton JR. Gender differences in substrate for endurance exercise. *J Appl Physiol* 1990; 68(1):302–308.

56. Fry AC, Kraemer WJ, van Borselen F, et al. Catecholamine responses to short-term high-intensity resistance exercise overtraining. *J Appl Physiol* 1994; 77(2):941–946.

57. Fry AC, Kraemer WJ, Stone MH, et al. Endocrine responses to over-reaching before and after 1 year of weightlifting training. *Can J Appl Physiol* 1994; 19(4): 400–410.

58. Christensen NJ, Galbo H, Hansen JF, et al. Catecholamines and exercise. *Diabetes* 1979; 28:58–62.

59. Häkkinen K, Pakarinen A. Serum hormones in male strength athletes during intensive short term strength training. *Eur J Appl Physiol* 1991; 63:191–199.

60. Kinderman W, Schnabel A, Schmitt WM, et al. Catecholamines, growth hormone, cortisol, insulin, and sex hormones in anaerobic and aerobic exercise. *Eur J Appl Physiol* 1982; 49:389–399.

61. Horton TJ, Pagliassotti MJ, Hobbs K, Hill JO. Fuel metabolism in men and women during and after long-duration exercise. *J Appl Physiol* 1998; 85(5):1823–32.

62. Mendenhall LA, Sial S, Coggan AR. Gender differences in substrate metabolism during moderate intensity cycling (Abstract). *Med Sci Sports Exerc* 1996; 27: S213.

63. Zouhal H, Jacob C, Delamarche P, Gratas-Delamarche A. Catecholamines and the effects of exercise, training and gender. *Sports Med* 2008; 38(5):401–423.

64. Tidgren B, Hjemdal P, Theodorsson E, et al. Renal neurohormonal and vascular responses to dynamic exercise in humans. *J Appl Physiol* 1991; 70:2279–2286.

65. Kraemer WJ, Aguilera BA, Terada M, et al. Responses of IGF-I to endogenous increases in growth hormone after heavy-resistance exercise. *J Appl Physiol* 1995; 79:1310–1315.

66. Convertino VA. Blood volume: its adaptation to endurance training. *Med Sci Sports Exerc* 1991; 12:1338–1348.

67. McMurray RG, Hackney AC. Endocrine responses to exercise and training. In: *Exercise and Sport Science*, Garrett WE, Kirkendall DT, eds. Philadelphia, PA: Lippincott, Williams & Wilkins, 2000:135–164.

68. Hackney AC, Dobridge JD. Thyroid hormones and the interrelationship of cortisol and prolactin: influence of prolonged, exhaustive exercise. *Endokrynol Pol* 2009; 60:252–257.

69. Baylor LS, Hackney AC. Resting thyroid and leptin hormone changes in women following intense, prolonged exercise training. *Eur J Appl Physiol* 2003; 88(4–5):480–484.

70. Simsch C, Lormes W, Petersen KG, Baur S, Liu Y, Hackney AC, Lehmann M, Steinacker JM. Training intensity influences leptin and thyroid hormones in highly trained rowers. *Int J Sports Med* 2002; 23:422–427.

71. Fleck SJ, Kraemer WJ. *Designing Resistance Exercise Programs*. 4th ed. Champaign, IL: Human Kinetics, 2014.

72. Fry AC. Overload and regeneration during resistance exercise. In: *Overload, Performance Incompetence, and Regeneration in Sport*, Lehmann M, Foster C, Gastmann U, et al, eds. New York: Kluwer Academic/Plenum, 1999.

73. Adlercreutz H, Harkonen M, Kuoppasalmi K, et al. Effect of training on plasma anabolic and catabolic steroid hormones and their response during physical exercise. *Int J Sports Med* 1986; 7:S27–S28.

74. Fry AC, Kraemer WJ, Ramsey LT. Pituitary-adrenal-gonadal responses to high-intensity resistance exercise overtraining. *J Appl Physiol* 1998; 85(6):2352–2359.

75. Goodman HM. *Basic Medical Endocrinology*. New York: Raven Press, 1988:103.

76. Häkkinen K, Pakarinen A, Alen M, et al. Relationships between training volume, physical performance capacity and serum hormone concentrations during prolonged training in elite weight lifters. *Int J Sports Med* 1987; 8(Suppl):61–65.

77. Häkkinen K, Pakarinen A. Acute hormonal responses to two different fatiguing heavy-resistance protocols in male athletes. *J Appl Physiol* 1993; 74(2):882–887.

78. Kraemer WJ, Gordon SE, Fleck SJ, et al. Endogenous anabolic hormonal and growth factor responses to heavy resistance exercise in males and females. *Int J Sports Med* 1991; 12:228–235.

79. Kraemer WJ, Marchitelli L, McCurry R, et al. Hormonal and growth factor responses to heavy resistance exercise. *J Appl Physiol* 1990; 69(4):1442–1450.

80. Fahey TD, Rolph R, Moungmee P, et al. Serum testosterone, body composition, and strength of young adults. *Med Sci Sports* 1976; 8:31–34.

81. Gotschalk LA, Loetbel DD, Nindl BC, et al. Hormonal responses of multi-set versus single-set heavy resistance exercise protocols. *Can J Appl Physiol* 1997; 22(3): 244–255.

82. Weiss LW, Cureton KJ, Thompson FN. Comparison of serum testosterone and androstenedione responses to weightlifting in men and women. *Eur J Appl Physiol* 1983; 50(3):413–419.

83. Harber MP, Fry AC, Rubin JC, et al. Skeletal muscle and hormonal adaptations to circuit weight training. *Scand J Med Sci Sports* 2004; 14(3):176–185.

84. Kraemer WJ, Fry AD, Warren BJ, et al. Acute hormonal responses in elite junior weightlifters. *Int J Sports Med* 1992; 13(2):103–109.

85. Kraemer WJ, Ratamess NJ, Hatfield DL, and Vingren JL. The endocrinology of resistance exercise and training. In: *Essentials of Sports Nutrition and Supplements*, J Antonio, ed. Totowa, NJ: Humana Press, 2008.

86. Ahtiainen JP, Pakarinen A, Alen M, Kraemer WJ, Häkkinen K. Short vs. long rest period between the sets in hypertrophic resistance training: influence on muscle strength, size, and hormonal adaptations in trained men. *J Strength Cond Res* 2005; 19(3):572–582.

87. Häkkinen K, Pakarinen A, Kraemer WJ, et al. Basal concentrations and acute responses of serum hormones and strength development during heavy resistance training in middle-aged and elderly men and women. *J Gerontol A Biol Sci Med Sci* 2000; 55:B95–B105.

88. Potteiger JA, Judge LW, Cerny JA, Potteiger VM. Effects of altering training volume and intensity on body mass, performance, and hormonal concentrations in weight-event athletes. *J Strength Cond Res* 1995; 9:55–58.

89. Häkkinen K, Pakarinen A, Alen M, Komi PV. Serum hormones during prolonged training of neuromuscular performance. *Eur J Appl Physiol* 1985; 53:287–293.

90. Marx JO, Ratamess NA, Nindl BC, et al. Low-volume circuit versus high-volume periodized resistance training in women. *Med Sci Sports Exerc* 2001; 33(4):635–43.

91. Schilling BK, Fry AC, Ferkin MH, Leonard ST. Hormonal responses to free-weight and machine exercise [abstract]. *Med Sci Sports Exerc* 2001; 33(5 Suppl):S270.

92. Rubin MR, Kraemer WJ, Maresh CM, et al. High-affinity growth hormone binding protein and acute heavy resistance exercise. *Med Sci Sports Exerc* 2005; 37:395–403.

93. Taylor JM, Thompson HS, Clarkson PM, Miles MP, and De Souza MJ. Growth hormone response to an acute bout of resistance exercise in weight-trained and non-weight-trained women. *J Strength Cond Res* 2000; 14:220–7.

94. Kraemer WJ, Fleck SJ, Dziados JE, et al. Changes in hormonal concentrations after different heavy-resistance exercise protocols in women. *J Appl Physiol* 1993; 75(2):594–604.

95. Guezennec Y, Leger L, Lhoste F, et al. Hormone and metabolite response to weight-lifting training sessions. *Int J Sports Med* 1986; 7:100–105.

96. Fry AC, Kraemer WJ, Stone MH, et al. Endocrine and performance responses to high volume training and amino acid supplementation in elite junior weightlifters. *Int J Sport Nutr* 1993; 3(3):306–322.

97. Häkkinen K. Neuromuscular and hormonal adaptations during strength and power training. *J Sports Med Phys Fit* 1989; 29:9–24.

98. Häkkinen K, Pakarinen A, Alen M, et al. Neuromuscular and hormonal adaptations in athletes to strength training in two years. *J Appl Physiol* 1988; 65(6):2406–2412.

99. Hoffman J. *Physiological Aspects of Sport Training and Performance*. Champaign, IL: Human Kinetics, 2002:15–26.

100. Bosco C, Tihanyi J, Viru A. Relationship between field fitness test and basal serum testosterone and cortisol levels in soccer players. *Clin Physiol* 1996; 16:317–322.

Contents

CHAPTER 7

NUTRITION

Colin D. Wilborn, Lem Taylor, and Jaci N. Davis

OBJECTIVES

After completing this chapter, you will be able to:

- Provide dietary recommendations to a variety of athletic populations.
- Draw your own conclusions about commercially available diets.
- Determine whether or not an athlete's diet appropriately corresponds to his or her training.
- Understand the importance of timing the intake of nutrients.
- Identify the composition and quality of nutrients within different foods.

KEY TERMS

Carbohydrates	Macronutrient	Trans fats
Empty calorie	Magnesium	Triglycerides
Energy balance	Nutrient density	Vitamin C
Essential fatty acids	Nutrient timing	Vitamin E
Glycemic load	Overtraining	Zinc
Glycemic index	Protein	

INTRODUCTION

Nutritional intake is essential for optimizing the performance adaptations initiated in the gym, on the track, or on the field. Of the modifiable factors contributing to optimal exercise performance, nutritional intake is one of the most easily adaptable and often overlooked. There are many important facets of proper dietary regulation of athletes including energy balance, macronutrient type, and timing of ingestion. Consistent consumption of appropriate macro- and micronutrients during periods of heavy training can improve muscle protein turnover (the breakdown of old tissue and the rebuilding of new, more functionally adapted tissue) (44,63) as well as augment the function and recovery of the nervous system (20), immune system (41), and musculoskeletal system (29). Strength and conditioning professionals must impress on their athletes the importance of understanding how to appropriately fuel the body for the demands of specific training. Coaches who neglect the nutrition component of training limit their own efficacy in terms of helping their athletes and team to improve.

ENERGY BALANCE

Energy balance is the relationship between energy ingested and energy expended. It is an important determinant of exercise performance, body composition, training adaptation, and

optimal physiological functioning in athletes. Unfortunately, many hold a simplistic view of energy balance suggesting it is as simple as the equation: calories in = calories out. It is often incorrectly assumed that total energy intake is predominantly related to weight gain or loss, ignoring **macronutrient** composition and timing. Our body absorbs 90% to 95% of the calories taken in, so caloric intake is not 100% efficient. More so, many factors relate to energy expenditure, some of which are not affected by diet and exercise. For example, if an athlete wants to lose body fat or overall mass, eating less will produce a negative energy balance; however, the athlete may not experience the changes that they are expecting. Figure 7.1 lists the details regarding glycemic index, one aspect concerning caloric intake.

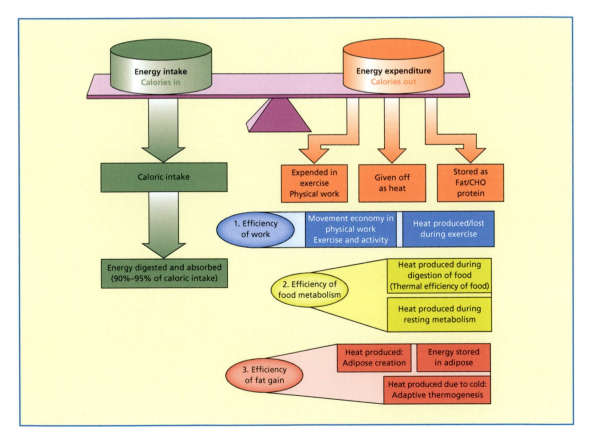

Figure 7.1 Factors related to the efficiency of energy intake and expenditure. (Adapted from Rampone AJ, Reynolds PJ. Obesity: thermodynamic principles in perspective. *Life Sci* 1988;43:93–110.)

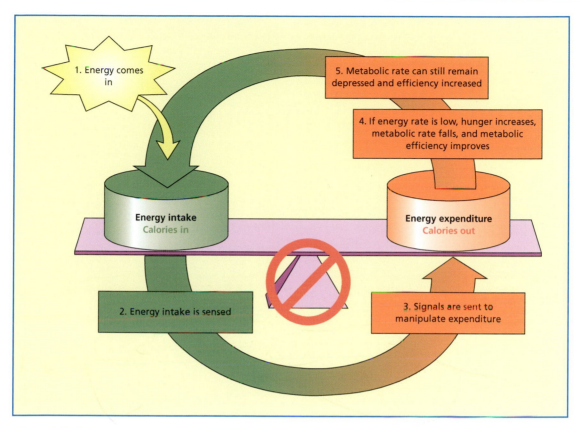

Figure 7.2 The relationship between energy intake and expenditure. This relationship determines how energy intake will affect body mass and composition.

Figure 7.2 demonstrates the relationship between energy intake and energy consumption, comparing common diets which modify macronutrient ratios. This relationship between macronutrients and energy demands determines how energy intake will affect body mass and composition. Creating a hypocaloric intake will cause the athlete's metabolic rate to slow and muscle mass will be compromised, resulting in a negative effect on performance. Optimal performance and health are related to total energy intake, metabolic rate, tissue turnover, and muscle mass.

Since the micronutrient content of the diet is closely related to energy intake, decreases in energy consumption may lead to nutrient deficiencies. Nutrient deficiencies can lead to impaired performance through fatigue, immune suppression, lethargy, and potentially lead to overtraining. **Overtraining** is a physiological and psychological condition that occurs when the volume and intensity of an individual's training exceeds their recovery capacity. Dietary factors play a large role in the body's ability to recover from intense training and avoid overtraining. Therefore, athletes should eat nutrient-dense foods to increase the ratio of nutrients ingested to energy ingested. **Nutrient density** is the amount of nutrients (carbohydrate, protein, fat, vitamins, minerals) per unit of energy (kcals) in a given food. For example, athletes who habitually eat sugary breakfast cereals in an attempt to increase carbohydrate intake would benefit from exchanging these cereals for a combination of fruits, vegetables, and a whole grain like oatmeal, increasing the nutrient composition of their meal. These latter foods are not only more nutrient-dense, but they also have more fiber and a lower glycemic index, which means that they cause less of an increase in blood sugar than more refined carbohydrates. **Glycemic index** (GI) is a term that describes how rapidly and how long a specific carbohydrate increases blood glucose. Foods with a glycemic index greater than 100 raise blood glucose levels more rapidly, whereas foods with a glycemic index of less than 100 raise blood glucose more slowly. In addition, high-fiber and low-glycemic carbohydrates play a role in improving health and body composition. In recent years sports nutritionists have begun to rely on the glycemic load of food as opposed to the glycemic index alone. The **glycemic load** takes into account the amount of carbohydrates eaten multiplied by the GI. So a large volume of carbohydrate that has a moderate GI may in fact be worse for the athlete than a food that is high on the GI but low in grams of carbohydrate. Table 7.1 lists the glycemic indexes of common sources of carbohydrates.

TABLE 7.1 The glycemic index of common sources of carbohydrates

Glycemic Index	Source
Extremely high (greater than 100)	Cake, doughnut
	Waffles
	Gatorade
	Bagel
	Pretzels
	Cornflakes cereal
	Cheerios
	Rice Chex cereal
	Rice Krispies cereal
	Watermelon
	Popcorn
	Jellybeans
Glycemic standard = 100%	Bread, white
High (80–100)	Angel-food cake
	Pound cake
	Bran muffin

Glycemic Index	Source
	Pastry
	Coca-Cola (250 mL)
	Orange juice
	Pineapple juice
	Corn chips
	Oat bread
	Pitta bread
	Special K cereal
	Pineapple
	White rice
Moderately high (60–80)	Cranberry juice cocktail
	Tomato juice
	Vanilla ice cream
	Banana
	Grapes
	Orange
	Baked beans
	Chicken nuggets
	Spaghetti
	Chocolate milk
	Power bar
Moderate (40–60)	Apple
	Apple juice
	Super supreme pizza (Pizza Hut)
	All-Bran cereal
	Skimmed milk
	Yogurt
	Peanut M&Ms
	Butter beans
	Split peas
Low (less than 40)	Chickpeas
	Kidney beans
	Peanuts

Source: Adapted with permission from Foster-Powell K, Holt SHA, Brand-Miller JC. International table of glycemic index and glycemic load values: 2002. *Am J Clin Nutr* [Special Article] 2002;76:5–56.

> The glycemic index tells us which carbohydrates will have the greatest impact on blood sugar. Avoid or limit foods high on the glycemic index. However, keep in mind that high GI carbohydrates may be warranted pre-, during, and/or post-exercise.

Athletes must find ways to consume more calories from food while maintaining an optimal body composition and body mass for their specific activity. Although it may seem counterintuitive to suggest that an individual can lose fat mass while eating more food, taking advantage of appropriate food selection and strategic nutrient timing can accomplish both goals (49). Examining each macronutrient (i.e., carbohydrate, protein, and fat) and how to optimize times of feeding will allow individuals to develop a better understanding of how these strategies affect strength athletes.

> Total energy intake combined with appropriate timing is the most important dietary factor governing the adaptive response of strength-power athletes to exercise training.

Carbohydrate intake

Carbohydrates are foods that are commonly referred to as sugars, starches, cellulose (fiber), and gums. Carbohydrates are converted to glucose, which is the primary source of energy for physical activity and are the only source of energy for the brain and nervous system. Structurally, they can be classified as mono-, di-, tri-, and polysaccharides. The smallest carbohydrates are the single-unit monosaccharides, like glucose and sucrose (i.e., table sugar). Polysaccharides such as starch, cellulose, and glycogen are long chains of saccharide molecules and can be quite large.

Dietary carbohydrate intake has become a controversial topic. Carbohydrates have been demonized in the media, with some challenging the paradigm set forth by the U.S. Food Guide Pyramid and the Canadian Food Guide and instead suggesting low-carbohydrate diets as a better option. Some short-term studies have demonstrated that a lower carbohydrate intake leads to better overall weight loss, losses in body fat, and better preservation of muscle mass. Moreover, favorable changes in triglycerides and high-density lipoprotein (HDL) cholesterol typically occur when carbohydrate intakes are decreased. Very low carbohydrate diets (i.e., ketogenic diets), however, will reduce an athlete's total energy intake, impair intense exercise performance, reduce work capacity, suppress immune function, and increase perception of effort during normal exercise tasks. Although athletes could potentially benefit from a slight reduction in carbohydrate intake during rest periods and training periods of low volume/intensity, it is generally not recommended that strength-power athletes restrict carbohydrate to less than 10% of total energy intake.

Although some authors recommend that as much as 70% of the diet come from carbohydrates, this amount may displace dietary protein and fat and also make fat loss more difficult, particularly if more refined carbohydrates are chosen rather than whole grains. Instead of a chronic high-carbohydrate diet, a better strategy might be to emphasize carbohydrate type (e.g., whole grain versus refined carbohydrates) and timing (before, during, and after a workout).

The data are clear that carbohydrates are important in an athletic population. Higher-carbohydrate diets can lead to increased concentrations of muscle glycogen and may therefore delay fatigue, prevent exercise-stress-induced immunosuppression (8), and – when combined with protein during the exercise and post-exercise periods – stimulate an increase in muscle protein synthesis and glycogen resynthesis (46). Athletes, however, often consume the wrong types of carbohydrates at the wrong times. Rather than simply ingesting large amounts of "empty" calories during the day, athletes should replace their high-glycemic-index, nutrient-devoid carbohydrate choices with lower-glycemic, high-fiber carbohydrate choices. The term **empty calorie** refers to a food that offers no nutritional value other than energy itself. Foods such as legumes; whole grains; minimally processed breads, pastas, and other grains; fruits; and vegetables are digested more slowly and provide more continuous energy throughout the day acting as better carbohydrate choices. By substituting lower-glycemic, high-fiber foods and timing carbohydrates appropriately, athletes will be better able to manage daily energy fluctuations, ingest their daily recommendation of fiber, lose fat while preserving muscle mass, and reduce the chances of developing the micronutrient deficiencies that are common in athletic populations. On the contrary, higher-glycemic carbohydrates can be ingested after exercise to promote recovery and glycogen storage – a source of rapid energy when it is most needed (during training and competition). This is the time when the large insulin response that accompanies the ingestion of high-glycemic carbohydrates may lead to an improvement in muscle recovery. By following these recommendations, athletes may be better able to manage body composition while enhancing recovery.

> Different types of carbohydrates confer different physiological responses. The majority of one's caloric intake should be derived from the consumption of unprocessed, high-fiber carbohydrates.

Protein intake

Protein is composed of individual amino acids which join together to form peptide chains. Although the structure of each peptide chain is unique, the overall peptide structures collectively are known as proteins. Of the 20 common amino acids, 9 are indispensable or **essential** (the term *essential* as it relates to nutrition describes nutrients that you must consume, because your body does not make them endogenously); that is, they must come from the diet. As a result of the essentiality of these amino acids, protein, unlike carbohydrate, must be present in the diet. The recommended dietary allowance (RDA) for dietary protein in sedentary individuals is 0.8 g of protein per kilogram of body mass. Very few athletes are at risk for a true protein deficiency; however, it is likely that 0.8 g/kg is not sufficient to offset the oxidation of amino acids with exercise and provide enough amino acids for lean tissue accretion (14). Thus, many sports nutrition scientists have suggested that athletes may need more protein

than their sedentary counterparts (1.5 to 2.0 g/kg body mass) (35).

Other populations will have higher protein needs as well: young athletes who are still growing, athletes training for strength and muscle mass, athletes in contact sports, endurance athletes, and women who are pregnant. At times, more than one of these situations may be present in the same athlete, thus further increasing his or her protein needs.

Athletes will often self-select a protein intake that is higher than conventionally recommended. In seeking to optimize an athlete's protein intake, a simple rule of thumb is to plan the athlete's diet from the foundation of 1 g of protein per pound of body mass (2.2 g/kg body mass). This is easier for the athlete to understand and monitor and provides a small safety factor to ensure adequate protein intake. Once the protein intake is fixed, carbohydrate and fat intakes must be added to meet total daily energy needs. The best way to optimize an athlete's protein intake would be to experiment with a variety of levels of dietary protein and assess outcomes in terms of personal performance and body composition to determine which intake leads to the best response. Nutritional strategies should always be evaluated using an outcome-based approach.

In addition to experimenting with overall protein intake, it is important to make sure that a large percentage of daily protein comes from complete protein sources (proteins that contain all the essential amino acids). Even if an adequate total daily protein intake is ingested, if the protein is from an incomplete protein source (e.g., rice, grains, and other plant sources, etc.), the athlete may experience suboptimal adaptations to training. This situation can be improved by either ensuring that most of the dietary protein is from complete protein sources (e.g., animal proteins, including eggs and dairy products) or by consuming enough total energy with sufficient amounts of incomplete proteins. Animal proteins are important not only as sources of complete protein but also because they provide a number of highly bioavailable nutrients, such as B vitamins, zinc, and iron, of which deficiency is more prevalent in an athletic population. While it has often been argued that increased protein intake may have harmful side effects, no current evidence shows that healthy individuals would experience harm due to a higher-protein diet (36).

A complete food source such as eggs, chicken, fish, and lean beef are a preferred source of protein; however, there are many dietary supplements (discussed in more detail in Chapter 23) that may be added to the diet. The two most common types of supplementary protein are whey and casein. While both protein types are derived from milk, casein is a slower acting protein better utilized in the evening and whey is a faster acting protein better utilized in the morning or post-workout.

The International Society of Sports Nutrition has adopted a position stand on protein that highlights the following points (14): 1) exercising individuals need approximately 1.4 to 2.0 g of protein per kilogram of body weight per day; 2) concerns that protein intake within this range is unhealthy are unfounded in healthy, exercising individuals; 3) an attempt should be made to obtain protein requirements from whole foods, but supplemental protein is a safe and convenient method of ingesting high-quality dietary protein; 4) the timing of protein intake in the time period encompassing the exercise session has several benefits including improved recovery and greater gains in fat-free mass; and 5) exercising individuals need more dietary protein than their sedentary counterparts.

> Strength-power athletes need more protein (1.5–2.0 g/kg/day) than the RDA (0.8 g/kg/day). Moreover, no evidence exists that the consumption of protein at levels two to three times the RDA is harmful to otherwise healthy individuals.

Fat intake

It is becoming increasingly clear that dietary fat is essential to the athlete's nutrition program. The three main types of dietary fatty acids are saturated, monounsaturated, and polyunsaturated fatty acids (omega-3 and omega-6 fats are both types of polyunsaturated fatty acids). **Triglycerides** are the main storage form of fat. Triglycerides are formed from a glycerol skeleton with three **fatty acids** attached. Each of the three types of fats offers unique benefits. In the past, a simplistic view of fat was adopted because coaches and athletes believed that dietary fat made you fat; however, research has demonstrated this to be false. In fact, some fats (known as **essential fatty acids**) are absolutely necessary for survival. In addition, the right kinds of dietary fat can improve body composition by promoting fat loss (57). Furthermore, certain fats can improve training hormonal status (22), increase the body's ability to store glycogen, increase the body's ability to burn fat (57), and improve overall health by providing anti-inflammatory, anticarcinogenic, antioxidant, and antithrombotic effects (56). Although the American Dietetic Association recommends that less than 30% of the diet of a sedentary individual should come from fat, research suggests that athletes should ingest approximately 30% of the diet as fat as long as the individual proportions of fatty acids are distributed appropriately. For optimal health and performance, a balanced approach toward fat consumption is warranted; approximately 10% of dietary energy should come from saturated sources (e.g., whole-fat dairy, animal fats, etc.), approximately 10% from monounsaturated sources (many vegetable fats, especially olive oil), and approximately 10% from polyunsaturated sources (predominantly vegetable fats, especially flaxseed and fish oils). Of the polyunsaturated fats, approximately 50% should come from omega-6 fatty acids and approximately 50% from omega-3 fatty acids. It is important to realize that the distribution of fatty acids in the diet is as important as the absolute amount of fat. Therefore, athletes should pay attention to both.

A final consideration related to fat consumption is trans fat. **Trans fats** are artificial fats created when polyunsaturated vegetable oils (high in omega-6 fatty acids) are combined with hydrogen molecules to increase shelf life and stabilize the polyunsaturated oil. This process makes nonhydrogenated fat similar to saturated fat (which is naturally saturated with hydrogen), which can produce "bad" LDL cholesterol and potentially lead to heart disease. Consumption of trans fats leads to the inhibition of several critical enzymatic processes in the body, blood lipid abnormalities, and an increased risk of cardiovascular disease. Unfortunately, trans fats are found in many processed foods. Any food that lists hydrogenated or partially hydrogenated fats on the ingredient list contains trans fats.

> It is important that athletes consume predominantly unsaturated fats. Both athletes and the general population should limit (but not eliminate) saturated fats in their diets.

TRAINING NUTRITION

During and after training and competition, the energy demands of the body are high, fluid needs increase (42), insulin sensitivity and glucose tolerance are dramatically improved (28), and skeletal muscle is primed for anabolism as long as amino acids are provided (47,61,63). Nutrition during and after exercise should focus on providing carbohydrate energy, preventing dehydration, stimulating glycogen resynthesis, and stimulating increases in skeletal muscle protein synthesis. As indicated, during the workout and post-workout periods, insulin sensitivity and glucose tolerance are improved, and the efficiency of glycogen storage is highest. This makes the post-workout period the best time to ingest a larger amount of carbohydrate. In addition, since a large increase in insulin can facilitate greater glycogen resynthesis and muscle protein synthesis, higher glycemic index carbohydrates (i.e., sports drinks containing glucose or glucose polymers) should be ingested during these times. By providing a large amount of carbohydrate during this critical period, fewer carbohydrates should be ingested during the remainder of the day in order to achieve better control of body composition and to promote maximal recovery. As a starting point, athletes could begin by ingesting liquid carbohydrate-protein supplements immediately prior to (61) or during exercise (42) as well as immediately after exercise (46,61) so as to promote recovery. To facilitate fluid replacement as well as rapid energy delivery, the two beverages should be diluted to 8% to 12% concentrations (80 to 120 g of substrate (carbohydrate) per 1000 mL of water) and should provide approximately 0.8 g of carbohydrate and 0.4 g protein per kilogram of body mass. It

is important to experiment with differing amounts of energy to determine the best composition for each individual athlete.

Q&A FROM THE FIELD

How does dehydration affect the strength-power athlete and what recommendations would you give to prevent the harm caused by fluid loss?

Dehydration refers to both hypohydration (being dehydrated prior to exercise) and to exercise-induced dehydration (i.e., that which develops during exercise). Inadequate fluid intake can adversely affect muscle metabolism, the regulation of body temperature, cardiovascular function (increased heart rate), and perceived exertion (more rapid development of fatigue).

Negative effects on performance have been demonstrated with modest (< 2% of body weight) dehydration. In one investigation, college wrestlers were actively dehydrated (4.9% of body weight), after which their upper body isokinetic performance was measured (65). There was a decrease in strength of 7.6% for lat pulldowns, 6.6% in chest push, and 12% in shoulder-press repetitions. In contrast, lower body musculature was not significantly affected by the 4.9% loss.

Many athletes are reluctant drinkers during exercise and do not ingest fluid at rates equal to their fluid loss. To promote proper hydration for athletes' optimal health and performance, follow these recommendations (17):

1 Athletes are advised to drink 14 to 22 oz of fluid two hours prior to exercise to promote adequate hydration and allow time for the excretion of excess ingested water.
2 During exercise, athletes should start drinking early into the workout and at regular intervals. If training continues for over one hour, a carbohydrate-containing beverage should be ingested at a rate of 30 to 60 g/hour to maintain oxidation of carbohydrates and delay fatigue.
3 Immediately after exercise, athletes should consume 16 to 24 oz of fluid for every pound of body weight lost during exercise. All athletes (strength, power, or endurance) need to maximize their fluid intake and employ behavioral strategies before, during, and after exercise to enhance their training and competitive performances. (Courtesy of Jennifer Hofheins, MS, RD, LD, of the Center for Applied Health Sciences.)

Post-workout consumption of carbohydrate combined with protein and/or essential amino acids are critical in enhancing the adaptive response to exercise (i.e., greater gains in lean body mass, greater loss of fat mass, improved performance, etc).

NUTRIENT TIMING

An exciting avenue of research is the area of **nutrient timing**, the specific time at which you consume certain nutrients to enhance the adaptive response to exercise. Certainly, we know that the composition of the food you ingest is important for promoting gains in muscle protein; however, the timing of nutrient consumption may be just as important.

In a 2007 study by Willoughby and Colleagues (67), researchers examined the effects of pre- and post-workout protein supplementation on markers of strength, mass, and anabolism. Researchers found that 20 g of protein by subjects taken before and after resistance training workouts resulted in greater gains in fat-free mass and strength than the placebo group that consumed 20 g of dextrose. In addition, the subjects consuming protein had a significantly greater expression of muscle specific proteins.

In another study, subjects cycled intensely for 2.5 hours to fully deplete the muscle glycogen levels in their thigh muscles (29). Subjects supplemented immediately and two hours post-exercise with the following:

- Group 1: carb-pro-fat (80 g carb, 28 g pro, 6 g fat)
- Group 2: carb-fat (108 g carb, 6 g fat)
- Group 3: carb-fat (80 g carb, 6 g fat)

Note that the beverages groups 1 and 2 consumed were isocaloric, meaning they contained the same number of calories. After four hours of recovery, the investigators found that the greatest amount of muscle glycogen was replenished in group 1. Thus, the replacement of some carbohydrate with protein may expedite muscle glycogen repletion post-exercise.

Other investigations have yielded similarly interesting results. Post-exercise supplementation with added protein improved time to exhaustion

during a test of endurance (49). Older men who consumed a protein supplement (10 g protein, 7 g carbohydrate, 3 g fat) immediately after training (12-week resistance training program, three days per week), had greater gains in strength, muscle fiber size, and lean body mass compared to the group who ingested the supplement two hours after training (23). It has been suggested that the availability of amino acids is more important than the availability of energy immediately post-exercise to promote the repair and synthesis of muscle protein (7).

Other health benefits may accompany the ingestion of protein immediately post-exercise. In a study of healthy male recruits in the U.S. Marine Corps, subjects received a post-exercise supplement during their 54-day basic training period, which was either a placebo (0 g carbohydrate, 0 g protein, 0 g fat), control, or protein supplement (24). The protein-supplemented group had an average of 33% fewer total medical visits, 28% fewer visits due to bacterial/viral infections, 37% fewer visits due to muscle/joint problems, and 83% fewer visits due to heat exhaustion compared with the placebo and control groups. Muscle soreness immediately post-exercise was significantly reduced on both days 34 and 54 by protein supplementation but not by the placebo or control supplements.

Some evidence suggests that nutrient timing affects body composition (21). In one study, 17 slightly overweight men were put on a 12-week program consisting of mild caloric restriction (17% reduction) and a light resistance-exercise training program utilizing dumbbells. One group ingested a protein supplement (10 g protein, 7 g carbohydrate, 3.3 g fat, and 33% of the RDA for vitamins and minerals) immediately after exercise. The other group did not consume a supplement. Protein and energy intake were the same for both groups, and protein intake met the RDA. Both groups lost an equal amount of fat; however, the protein-supplemented group maintained fat-free mass (FFM), while the group that did not supplement lost FFM.

Although most studies have examined post-workout nutrition, some data are available that compare pre-workout supplementation as well (63). Researchers compared the anabolic response of consuming a combination of an essential amino acid (6 g) plus carbohydrate (35 g sucrose) before versus after heavy resistance exercise (11). Phenylalanine uptake across the leg (a measure of muscle protein anabolism) over a three-hour period was 160% greater when the amino acid/carbohydrate supplement was taken before versus after a workout. A 2007 study (62) by the same group found that if the pre vs. post ingestion was an intact protein such as whey, there does not appear to be a differential effect. Thus, consuming the proper nutrients before exercise may be more anabolic and facilitate recovery better than a post-exercise consumption strategy.

A 2008 Position Stand (JISSN) by Kerksick et al. (33) found the following in regard to nutrient timing: 1) prolonged exercise of moderate to high intensity exercise will deplete stores of energy, and prudent timing of nutrient delivery can help offset these changes; 2) ingestion of 6–20 g of EAAs and 30–40 g of high-glycemic CHO within three hours after an exercise bout and immediately before exercise have been shown to significantly stimulate muscle PRO synthesis; 3) daily post-exercise ingestion of a CHO+PRO supplement promotes greater increases in strength and improvements in lean tissue and body fat % during regular resistance training; 4) dietary focus should center on adequate availability and delivery of CHO and PRO; however, including small amounts of fat does not appear to be harmful, and may help to control glycemic responses during exercise; and 5) irrespective of timing, regular ingestion of snacks or meals providing both CHO and PRO (3:1 CHO:PRO ratio) helps to promote recovery and replenishment of muscle glycogen.

A 2017 study (52) investigated the effects of pre vs post protein intake on strength and body composition. Subjects were 21 college age resistance-trained men (>1 year RT experience). After baseline testing, participants were randomly assigned to one of two experimental groups: a group that consumed a supplement containing 25 g protein and 1 g carbohydrate immediately prior to exercise or a group that consumed the same supplement immediately post-exercise. The RT protocol consisted of three weekly sessions performed on non-consecutive days for ten weeks. A total-body routine was employed with three sets of 8–12 repetitions for each exercise. Results showed that pre- and post-workout protein consumption had similar effects on all measures studied ($p > 0.05$). These findings refute the contention of a narrow post-exercise anabolic window to maximize the muscular response and instead lends support to the theory that the interval for protein intake may be as wide as several hours or perhaps more after a training bout depending on when the pre-workout meal was consumed.

A meta-analysis published in the *Journal of the International Society of Sport Nutrition* (50) shed some interesting light on this topic. The strength analysis comprised 478 subjects and 96 effect sizes, nested within 41 treatment or control groups and 20 studies. The hypertrophy analysis comprised 525 subjects and 132 effect sizes, nested within 47 treatment or control groups and 23 studies. The researchers sought to determine the best approach to the timing of ingestion of protein and/or carbohydrate to optimize recovery and gains. The idea of nutrient timing post-workout or the "anabolic window" is based on the idea that the athlete is in a fasted state. Thus, there seems to be less clarity if the athlete is not. The findings of the meta-analysis are inconclusive in identifying one particular feeding time as being superior to another. What appears to be most important is that the athlete is adequately fed, and the peri-workout window is important. According to Aragon and Schoenfeld (2), due to the transient anabolic impact of a protein-rich meal and its potential synergy with the trained state, pre- and post-exercise meals should not be separated by more than approximately three to four hours, given a typical resistance training bout lasting 45–90 minutes. If protein is delivered within particularly large mixed-meals (which are inherently more anticatabolic), a case can be made for lengthening the interval to five to six hours.

> To optimize the adaptive response to exercise, all strength-power athletes should consume a carbohydrate-protein post-workout beverage. This strategy would also be helpful for the recreational athlete or fitness enthusiast seeking to improve his/her body composition.

Carbohydrate-protein ratio

Controversy exists as to the correct or ideal combination of carbohydrate and protein consumed post-workout. It is difficult to make direct comparisons between investigations due to differences in subject population, treatment duration, the type of exercise performed, nutrients ingested, etc. One can extrapolate from these studies, however, to suggest that timing may be as important (if not more so) as nutrient composition. For instance, you will find a carbohydrate-to-protein ratio of about 3:1 (approximately three times more carbohydrate than protein) and as low as 0.7:1 (30% less carbohydrate than protein) comparable for promoting recovery. Furthermore, the energy content of recovery supplements varies from 500 kcal to as little as 100 kcal. Therefore, sports nutritionists should consider each athlete individually to determine the most effective nutrient combinations for that person.

MEAL FREQUENCY AND CONTROLLED FASTING

To understand the impact that meal timing might have on body composition change it is important to first understand how energy balance is derived. Many clinicians, dieticians, and scholars have subscribed to the theory of calories in vs. calories out mentioned earlier. While simplistic in nature and good for instructional purposes, this theory continues to receive a wide array of criticisms, such as food type, timing, amino acid intake/protein quality, and metabolic rate as factors that individually and collectively may result in more favorable changes in weight loss and body composition. In addition, the concept is further challenged when individuals (such as athletes) hope to lose only adipose tissue as opposed to losing body mass. Therefore, it is vital that weight loss occurs at a rate that allows for optimal fat loss, but effectively preserves skeletal muscle in the process. Singly, this complex paradigm has initiated decades of research studies, debates, and position stands.

Likely the most profound aspect of nutrient timing for weight loss is the frequency of meals. This topic is quite popular in the mainstream media as a number of reports suggest that an increased meal frequency favorably impacts metabolism and weight loss outcomes. In recent years, dieticians, nutritionists, and exercise enthusiasts have taken this theory to suggest that if one is to eat more frequently, resulting metabolic activity will be increased and sustained at these higher levels throughout the day. This concept, in essence, is where recommendations are commonly made to eat five or six smaller meals in a day rather than two or three meals. It is important to note that this theory would be based on consuming the same amount of calories regardless of the number of meals. Many people believe that if the body is fed at regular intervals, continual feedback is received that energy is available to the body and as a result doesn't have to store calories. In contrast, when we skip meals we trigger a nutrient sparing mode where metabolism is negatively affected, resulting in a decrease in calorie burning. However, research is conclusive that it does not appear to matter if you eat two meals or six if the calories and macronutrients are right. A 1997 review of the existing literature found that many of the studies done prior to 1997 failed to find any significant relationship between meal frequency and body composition as most of these studies utilized 24-hour recall, which is known to be inaccurate. They concluded that the epidemiological evidence is at best very weak. They further concluded that any effects of meal pattern on the regulation of body weight are likely to be mediated through effects on the food intake side of the energy balance equation (5).

A study done on free living subjects had some contrasting results to the previous work done in free living subjects. A study done in pre and post menopausal women found eating more frequently had no effect on pre menopausal women and had a negative effect on the post (69). Dallosso and colleagues investigated the effects of eating two versus six meals on energy balance as measured by whole body calorimetry (19). These researchers did not find that meal frequency had any impact on energy expenditure. Similar findings were observed in 1987 using indirect calorimetry and comparing two versus six meals (68). Most recently and also in support of these data, 16 obese (34.6 ± 9.5 years and 37.1 ± 4.5 kg/m2) men and women were instructed to reduce their energy intake by 700 kcals/day and were randomized into two treatment groups. In an energy-matched fashion, one group consumed six meals each day (three traditional meals and three snacks) and the other group consumed three meals per day. Before and after the eight-week intervention, obesity indices, body mass, appetite, and ghrelin were measured and no significant differences were found (13). This last study is particularly important because it is one of the few studies to utilize a true experimental approach, and under more rigorous conditions it is consistently reported that an increased meal frequency exhibits no pattern of relationship with being overweight, increased adiposity, etc.

In addition, it has been hypothesized for many years that you should not eat before you do cardio to burn for fat. In addition, it has been suggested that you should not eat several hours prior to bed so that you fast longer and burn more fat. Then in recent years the idea of intermittent fasting has come up, which has you fast at different times of the day. This idea involves training after an overnight fast to accelerate the loss of body fat. In theory, low glycogen and insulin levels cause the body to shift energy utilization away from carbohydrates, allowing greater mobilization of stored fat for fuel. Findings from several acute studies appear to support this contention (27,1,16). Despite an apparent theoretical basis, evidence is scant as to whether fasted aerobic exercise results in greater fat loss over time compared to exercising in a fed state. In a recent study researchers investigated changes in fat mass and fat-free mass following four weeks of volume-equated fasted versus fed aerobic exercise in young women adhering to a reduced calorie diet. They found that body composition changes associated with aerobic exercise in conjunction with a reduced calorie diet are similar regardless of whether or not an individual is fasted prior to training (51). In addition, it is very possible and quite likely that you will not only be burning fat in a fasted state, but that you may burn protein too, which could impact lean tissue. To spare protein, a small number of calories are helpful. Not to mention the benefit of fueling exercise to be able to operate at a high intensity.

It has been hypothesized that late night feeding leads to weight gain and obesity. However, it is also true that late night eaters are typically eating processed simple sugars. While there may been some scientific rationale for this line of thinking, it is actually contrary to research. In fact, research over the last several years has actually showed that eating before bedtime actually increases protein synthesis, increases muscle mass, boosts metabolism, and improves recovery (38,43,34).

The rationale of the experimental fasting is based on the idea that only eating in an 8-hour window would cause the body to use fat storages over the course of the 16-hour fast. Principally this makes a little bit of sense because in a fasted state we are likely to burn more stored fuel such as fat. This is similar to the idea theorized by fasting cardio and fasting while sleeping. While there is some interesting hypothesis, there is little literature to support these findings. There are several models of intermittent fasting that have been hypothesized. One of the most common forms of fasting is the whole-day fasting or 24-hour fasting model. This model has been researched the most as it is associated with many religious practices. However, given the rigorous training schedule of athletes, this is likely not a wise approach. The most recent and intriguing model is the one mentioned above that employs various fasts within a 24-hour period. An 8-week trial by Tinsley et al. examined the effect of a 20-hour fasting/4-hour feeding protocol done four days per week on recreationally active, but untrained subjects (60). No limitations were placed on the amounts and types of food consumed in the four-hour eating window. The fasting group lost body weight, due to a significantly lower energy intake. Cross-sectional areas of the biceps brachii and rectus femoris increased similarly in both the fasting and normal diet group. No significant changes in body composition were seen between the groups. A study by Moro et al. found that in resistance-trained subjects on a standardized training protocol, a 16-hour fasting/8-hour feeding cycle resulted in significantly greater fat mass loss in fasted vs normal diet control groups with no significant changes in fat-free mass in either group (40). Seimon et al. recently published the largest systematic review of intermittent fasting research to date, comparing the effects of intermittent energy restriction to continuous energy restriction on body weight, body composition, and other clinical parameters (53). Their review included 40 studies in total. They found that overall, the two diet types resulted in apparently equivalent outcomes in terms of body weight reduction and body composition change.

OPTIMAL DIET TO PREVENT OVERTRAINING

Overtraining is a physiological and psychological phenomenon that occurs as a result of under-recovery. The signs and symptoms of overtraining are decreased performance, impaired immune system, lethargy, sleeplessness, depression, hormone imbalance, prolonged muscle soreness, psychological stress, and injury. It is estimated that 10% of athletes will experience overtraining. Proper periodization and nutrient intake is paramount to preventing overtraining. A diet that can address the physiological needs of an athlete that is training at the high end of the training paradigm needs to increase energy, support recovery, reduce inflammation, reduce oxidative stress, hydrate, and reduce the overall catabolic environment.

There is a strong link between hydration and overtraining. The research says that as little as a water deficit of 2% can negatively affect exercise. In fact, one study showed that when resistance-trained athletes were slightly dehydrated, their repetitions dropped significantly over what they could do when they were properly hydrated (32). Through normal processes we excrete over half a gallon of water a day, so add in exercise and that could quickly reach a gallon. So we should drink at least that much to make sure we are hydrated adequately to do work. The research also suggests that athletes do not eat enough calories (54). Athletes tend to over analyze what they eat in terms of sugar, carbs, fats, protein, and a million other things that media suggest they should be eating. However, caloric sufficiency is the basic fundamental of repair and recovery. Thus, athletes would benefit from not only increased protein, but overall calories as well. As discussed previously, adequate protein intake is paramount at offsetting the oxidation of amino acids associated with exercise. In addition, total calories being at or exceeding basic needs is paramount during heavy training. Athletes should strive to not lose weight during training by monitoring their weight and increasing calories as needed.

The next thing an athlete needs is antioxidant rich foods. These center around fruits and vegetables. Foods rich in antioxidants can improve both immunity and reduce inflammation (discussed later). It is possible that this would allow the athlete to limit days missed and train harder. This is an important category as it is one that athletes commonly miss. Adequate carbohydrate intake is needed to optimize fat burning, and the natural vitamin content can improve performance if an athlete is at a deficit in any area. The final area is adequate fat intake. It was hypothesized for years that dietary fat makes us fat, but that is misleading in that it is a positive calorie balance that makes us gain weight regardless of the source. The research shows that adequate fat intake has anticatabolic effects and reduces muscle damage. In addition, the caloric content of fat can be exactly what we need to push us over the calorie barrier.

VITAMIN AND MINERAL INTAKE

Few studies have examined the micronutrient (vitamins and minerals) intakes of strength-power athletes. Clearly, however, suboptimal consumption of certain vitamins and minerals may predispose the individual to a number of diseases. For instance, according to one study, suboptimal folic acid levels, along with suboptimal levels of vitamins B_6 and B_{12}, are a risk factor for cardiovascular disease, neural tube defects, colon and breast cancer; low levels of vitamin D contribute to osteopenia and fractures; and low levels of the antioxidant vitamins (vitamins A, E, and C) may increase risk for several chronic diseases. Many people do not consume an optimal amount of all vitamins by diet alone. Subsequently, it appears prudent for all adults to take vitamin supplements.

At this moment it is not clear that consuming extra or supplemental vitamins can improve athletic performance. Some intriguing data on nutrient intakes in strength-power athletes, however, suggest a potential benefit of supplementing with specific micronutrients. Some research has suggested that strength and power athletes are deficient on basic nutrient requirements (4,48). Furthermore, deficiencies in basic nutrient requirements can lead to illness, injury, and detriments in performance (37). There is currently a lack of conclusive evidence that exercise performance or recovery would benefit in any significant way from vitamin or mineral supplementation, unless of course a deficiency exists.

Regardless of what the composite data may be regarding the average macro- or micronutrient intakes of athletes, one could certainly argue that these data are unimportant in counseling individual athletes. To assess whether an individual athlete is meeting his or her dietary needs, it is of no utility to draw conclusions based on the scientific literature. This is because each individual must have his or her food intake separately analyzed to determine whether alterations in a particular nutrition program may be of benefit.

> It is impossible to determine an individual's macro- or micronutrient needs based on a composite picture derived from survey studies in the scientific literature.

Vitamin E

Vitamin E is a fat-soluble vitamin that may have beneficial effects in athletes. For example, in one study, 12 weight-trained men were divided into two groups: one group received 1200 IU of vitamin E once per day for two weeks while the control group received a cellulose-based placebo pill (39). Plasma creatine kinase (CK) levels (an indirect marker of muscle fiber injury) increased significantly in both groups after 24 and 48 hours; at 24 hours, however, the increase in CK was less in the vitamin E supplemented group than in the placebo group. Plasma malondialdehyde (MDA), an indicator of free-radical interaction with cellular membranes, was elevated in both groups; however, MDA levels remained higher for a longer time in the placebo group. Thus, vitamin E may lessen the injury sustained by skeletal muscle fibers as a result of heavy resistance exercises; moreover, its antioxidant effects may be of potential benefit to athletes.

Alternatively, no effects of vitamin E supplementation (1200 IU for three weeks in non-resistance-trained men) were found on recovery responses to repeated bouts of resistance exercises. According to the investigators, "Vitamin E supplementation was not effective at attenuating putative markers of membrane damage, oxidative stress, and performance decrements after repeated bouts of whole-body concentric/eccentric resistance exercise" (3).

Vitamin C

Vitamin C is a water-soluble vitamin that is needed for collagen formation and may have beneficial effects for active individuals through its effects on cortisol and via an antioxidant effect.

Twenty-four physically active young subjects who ingested either vitamin C (400 mg), vitamin E (400 mg), or a placebo for 21 days before and 7 days after performing 60 minutes of box-stepping exercise were examined (30). The investigators tested the function of the triceps surae muscles and found that, compared to the placebo group, no significant alterations in maximal voluntary contraction (MVC) were found immediately after exercise; however, the recovery of MVC was superior in the vitamin C group during the first 24 hours after exercise. According to the study's authors, "prior vitamin C supplementation may exert a protective effect against eccentric exercise-induced muscle damage." No effects were observed in the vitamin E supplemented group (30).

One study had 16 male subjects randomized to a placebo or vitamin C group (58). These subjects performed a prolonged 90-minute intermittent shuttle-running test, and supplementation commenced after the cessation of exercise. That is, immediately after exercise, the subjects drank a 500 mL beverage containing 200 mg of vitamin C (or placebo) dissolved in solution. Later that same day and for the next two days, the subjects again consumed their treatment drinks. As a result, vitamin C supplementation had no effect on post-exercise CK concentrations, muscle soreness, or muscle function of the leg extensors and flexors. Certainly, longer or prolonged consumption of vitamin C must be further examined. In one study, 16 male subjects consumed either vitamin C (200 mg twice daily for two weeks) or placebo. Subjects performed 90 minutes of intermittent shuttle running 14 days after supplementation commenced. As a result, it was found that vitamin C did have beneficial effects on muscle soreness, muscle function, and plasma concentrations of serum malondialdehyde (59).

Based on the very limited data on vitamins C and E, one can reasonably conclude that supplementation may have beneficial effects on a subset of individuals that have dietary or exercise induced deficiencies. There appear to be no deleterious effects on any of the parameters measured in published studies.

Minerals

Magnesium is an essential mineral that regulates neuromuscular, cardiovascular, immune, and hormonal function (9). Exercise may deplete magnesium, which – combined with inadequate intake – may impair energy metabolism. In a study investigating the effects of magnesium supplementation on strength development during a double-blind, seven-week strength training program, both groups involved gained strength; however, the magnesium-supplemented group demonstrated significantly better performance compared to the control group in absolute torque, relative torque adjusted for body weight (T/BWT), and relative torque adjusted for lean body mass (T/LBM) when "before" values were used as the covariate.

Zinc is a mineral required for the activity of more than 300 enzymes. Recently, it has been recognized that zinc may play an important role in thyroid hormone metabolism. The effects of zinc supplementation in athletes have been studied previously. Moreover, chronic exercise can have long-term effects on zinc metabolism (18). It has been reported that runners have lower plasma zinc levels than controls. One consequence of low serum zinc levels could be a reduction in muscle zinc concentrations, possibly resulting in a reduction in endurance capacity. Zinc may also be acting directly at the membrane level; changes in extracellular zinc levels have been reported to influence the twitch-tension relationship in muscle. If one consumes an adequate diet rich in zinc, it is likely that zinc supplementation may be of no consequence to skeletal muscle or hormonal function. If one's diet is inadequate (e.g., vegetarians or individuals on low-energy diets), however, zinc supplementation may be considered. A 2004 study (66) found that the combination of zinc and magnesium had no effect in resistance-trained subjects.

An examination of the scientific literature shows that vitamin and mineral supplementation either has a neutral or positive effect on various health and performance indexes in exercising individuals. As a strategy, it would make sense to consume a multivitamin as an "insurance policy" against poor eating habits. Eating a diet rich in unprocessed, high-fiber carbohydrates, lean meats, and other high-quality protein sources should form the basis of one's energy intake.

DIETS

Little research is available regarding dietary manipulation to improve performance relative to strength and size in comparison to improving performance in the endurance athlete. A number of different theories, beliefs, and recommendations from health professionals are available regarding the proper way to fuel the body for better performance. Although an infinite number of dietary prescriptions are available, essentially they fall into four overall categories: diets very high in carbohydrate and very low in fat (e.g., Pritikin or Ornish); high in carbohydrate and low in fat (e.g., the USDA MyPyramid food guide system, Figure 7.3); very low in carbohydrate and high in protein and fat (e.g., Atkins or South Beach diets);

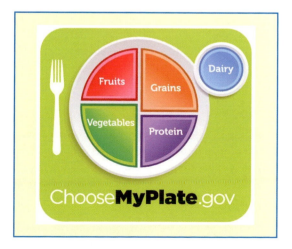

Figure 7.3 The USDA MyPyramid food guide system.

and moderate in carbohydrate and higher in protein (e.g., Zone diet). Table 7.2 compares these approaches. Most people have their own dietary beliefs that may have worked for them or the athletes they train; significant scientific support exists, however, for each of these approaches.

Eating disorders are a major concern with athletic and exercising populations. As exercise professionals, we must be aware of these disorders and be able to address the issue appropriately. This includes a basic understanding of the disorders and of the team approach to treatment (Box 7.1).

Box 7.1   Eating disorders

Eating disorders are often related to disorders of self-image, self-concept, and self-esteem. They are not uncommon among athletic and exercising populations. Disordered eating is one component in the female athletic triad (discussed in Chapter 4). Additionally, compulsive exercise can be a component of some eating disorders.

Three eating disorders are discussed briefly below.

Compulsive overeating

Compulsive overeating is an "addiction" to food. Compulsive overeaters use food and eating to help with daily stresses and problem solving. Individuals who are compulsive overeaters tend to be overweight. They are aware of their inability to control their eating and may be particularly sensitive to comments about their weight or diet. Because obesity is a major health concern in today's society, we should be aware of the potential role compulsive overeating may play in this disorder.

Anorexia nervosa

The person with anorexia may perceive him/herself as fat or may be afraid of becoming fat. This individual probably has an emotional disorder and reacts by controlling his or her eating behaviors.

Signs of anorexia may include obsessive exercise; calorie counting or fat-gram counting; self-induced vomiting and the use of diet pills, laxatives, or diuretics; and a persistent concern with body image. Individuals with anorexia may go through periods of bulimia and their body weight is generally below average.

Bulimia nervosa

The primary symptoms of bulimia are episodes of binging and purging. The individual will eat a large quantity of food in a relatively short time and then induce vomiting or take laxatives, often related to the guilt of overeating. The episodes of binging and purging may be related to feelings of anger, depression, stress, or anxiety. Individuals suffering bulimia may be aware of their eating disorder and usually enjoy discussing food and diet. They may also be overweight, or their weight may fluctuate greatly.

Summary

Similarities can be found among various eating disorders, the most common being some form of emotional disorder. With anorexia and bulimia, it may seem to be nothing but an obsessive concern over body image. For many of these individuals, deeper emotional issues may need to be resolved.

Young female athletes in sports such as gymnastics are considered to be at high risk for eating disorders, specifically anorexia or bulimia. Rather than causing the disorder, it may be that some sports attract anorexic/bulimic athletes, enabling them to hide their condition. A team approach to treatment should be considered that potentially involves the coach/exercise professional, the parents, a physician, a nutritionist, a psychologist, and perhaps others. This is not a disorder the exercise professional can or should try to handle alone.

VERY HIGH CARBOHYDRATE, VERY LOW-FAT DIETS

Carbohydrates are primarily sugars and starches and represent the primary macronutrient consumed by Americans. When we consider the dietary needs of a strength athlete, carbohydrates should be the basis of a sound nutritional program. Carbohydrates provide the major source of energy for the athlete through the breakdown of glycogen (the storage form of carbohydrate) during exercise (6). Moreover, increased carbohydrate intake may delay fatigue and can enhance post-exercise protein synthesis alone (10) (though not to the same extent as amino acids) or synergistically when combined with protein during recovery (46). Although carbohydrates are a crucial part of a sound nutritional program for the strength athlete, they do not play the same role with the endurance athlete who uses up glycogen stores more rapidly through lower-intensity, continuous aerobic activities. Some scientific evidence suggests that carbohydrate supplementation prior to and during high-volume resistance training results in the maintenance of muscle glycogen concentration, which potentially could result in the maintenance or increase of performance during a training bout (26). Additionally, the ingestion of carbohydrates following resistance exercise may enhance muscle glycogen resynthesis, which may result in a faster time of recovery from resistance training, thus possibly allowing for a greater training volume. It is unlikely that resistance training depletes muscle glycogen to the same extent as endurance training.

As is seen in Table 7.2, very high carbohydrate, very low-fat diets, such as those developed by Pritikin and Ornish, recommend a macronutrient composition of approximately 80% carbohydrate and 10% protein while advocating less than 10% fat. Both of these approaches are supported by a number of scientific studies in terms of positively modulating health outcomes (e.g., heart disease, lipid values, blood pressure, etc.); no direct research, however, supports their applicability to strength athletes. In fact, these diets may be contraindicated if the goal is to cause hypertrophy or increase speed or another variable that an athlete participating in a high-intensity sport may desire, since these diets are low in both protein and fat. It has been posited that diets very high in carbohydrate and low in both protein and fat may suit the needs of a patient with heart disease, owing to the increased intake of fibrous carbohydrates and reduced intake of saturated fat; the limited amounts of protein and fat recommended will not benefit the strength athlete. However, recent work published in the *American Journal of Clinical Nutrition* states that "there is no significant evidence for concluding that dietary saturated fat is associated with an increased risk of CHD or CVD" (55).

Macronutrient manipulation is commonly used by strength athletes to positively influence the hormonal milieu (testosterone, growth hormone, insulin, etc.), with the intention of favoring hypertrophy. As discussed earlier, dietary fat has been shown by a number of studies to correlate with serum sex hormones (22,64), improve body composition by promoting fat loss (57), improve overall health by providing anti-inflammatory effects (56), and even increase the body's ability to store glycogen. These facts, together with the known health benefits and increases in hormone concentrations from resistance training itself, demonstrate the importance of consuming adequate amounts of dietary fat (i.e., > 10% recommended with these plans).

Let's use the example of a 150 lb strength-trained athlete who needs 2,500 kcal/day. Using the 80%/10%/10% (carbohydrate/protein/fat, respectively) model of Ornish or Pritikin, this individual would be getting approximately 500 g of carbohydrate per day or about 7.3 g of carbohydrate per kilogram per day and about 63 g of protein and fat per day (that is, about 0.9% of protein and 0.4% of fat per kilogram per day). Obviously consuming a diet that replaces much of the dietary fat and protein with carbohydrate makes it impossible to obtain adequate levels of either fat or protein. As discussed earlier, the strength-trained athlete needs more than the RDA for protein each day (from 1.5 to 2.0 g/kg per day) (20), which is clearly much higher than the 0.9 g/kg per day the individual in our example would consume. Similarly, considering that glycogen is not depleted to the same extent in a strength athlete as it is in an endurance athlete, such a high intake of carbohydrate on a regular basis is unnecessary. Consequently, such a diet is not recommended for the otherwise healthy strength-training athlete.

TABLE 7.2 Comparison of popular diets

Meal plan	Dietary recommendations	Comments
Ornish's and Pritikin's plans	≥ 80% carbohydrate 10% protein ≤ 10% fat	Strength athletes do not need such a high carbohydrate intake. Fortunately, there is at least a distinction made and high-quality carbohydrates are recommended with these two plans. Both the protein intake and fat intake are too low to elicit the positive benefits that these two macronutrients provide, which has been demonstrated through various research studies.
The Food Guide Pyramid (FGP)	55% to 60% carbohydrates 12% to 15% protein <30% fat	Also a bit too high in carbohydrates for the strength athlete. Without the guidance of a nutrition professional, one might assume that all carbohydrates are created equal and therefore overconsume refined carbohydrates by following the FGP. The FGP also places fat in the limited category, when we know that different types of fats are clearly linked to health benefits and positive changes for the strength athlete. Another problem with the FGP is that it does not differentiate between protein sources high in saturated fat (e.g., ground beef) versus those that are lean (e.g., whey protein powders) or contain healthy fat (e.g., salmon).
Zone diet	40% carbohydrate 30% protein 30% fat	Following this diet will not provide the strength athlete with adequate energy to build lean body mass. This diet was not originally intended for strength-power athletes. However, if the energy intake is increased following a 40:30:30 plan, it should provide adequate protein, healthy carbohydrate, and unsaturated fat.
Atkins diet	Low-carbohydrate (25 to 90 g/day; the typical recommendation is 35 to 40 g). Fat and protein make up the rest of the diet. No types of fat are out of the question.	Strength athletes do not have the same macronutrient needs as endurance athletes; however, performance will be shortchanged by almost eliminating regular consumption of carbohydrates, particularly the high-fiber, low-glycemic variety. In addition, although consensus exists in much of the scientific community about strength athletes' increased protein needs above the RDA, increasing protein at the expense of unprocessed carbohydrates is not warranted. Unprocessed carbohydrates should make up the bulk of one's nutrition program.

HIGH-CARBOHYDRATE, LOW-FAT DIETS

Coming on the heels of the very high carbohydrate plans described above, high-carbohydrate, low-fat diets, such as that of the Food Guide Pyramid (FGP), recommend a macronutrient composition of approximately 55% to 60% carbohydrates, 12% to 15% protein, and less than 30% fat. Table 7.3 lists recommended foods that contain each macronutrient. The quantity of foods recommended from each block of the FGP is dependent on the activity level of an individual; however, again, no specific energy recommendation is provided. Using the FGP model, the same 150 lb athlete from above who needs 2,500 kcal/day would have to consume approximately 340 to 375 g of carbohydrate (~5–5.5 g CHO/kg per day), 75 to 90 g of protein (about 1.1 to 1.3 g/kg per day) and 83 g of fat (~1.2 g/kg per day).

Like the diet prescriptions described earlier, one shortcoming with the USDA FGP is that we have an individual in this example who would find it difficult to obtain adequate levels of protein (1.5 to 2.0 g/kg protein per day for most strength training athletes) by following the USDA's guidelines. Another limitation of the FGP is its lack of specificity when it comes to carbohydrate and fat recommendations. There is no argument that carbohydrates are used as a form of energy. In fact, they are the primary source of energy of your brain and skeletal muscles. Not all carbohydrates are alike, however. Although the FGP does emphasize a carbohydrate-based diet, it stops short of differentiating among the various types of carbohydrate. Processed carbohydrates such as white rice and pasta should be limited (not eliminated). Knowing the benefits of the other macronutrients during strength training, namely protein and fat, it would be wise to replace the refined carbohydrates in the diet with lean proteins and healthy fats. Separating the various types of proteins (e.g., red meat versus salmon) and fat (e.g., butter versus olive oil) is the best approach to developing a sound nutritional program for athletes.

TABLE 7.3 Recommended selections for each macronutrient

Carbohydrate	Protein	Fat
Oatmeal	Lean red meat	Fish oil
Oat bran	Poultry (skinless, white meat)	Olive oil
Brown rice	All seafood	Flax oil
Wholewheat pasta	Low-fat/fat-free cottage cheese	Nuts (e.g., almonds, peanuts, etc.)
Yams/sweet potatoes	Eggs	Peanut butter
Red potatoes	Protein powders composed of whey, casein, or combinations thereof	Avocado
All vegetables		
All fruits		
Quinoa		
Legumes		
Lentils		
Whole-grain bread		
(e.g., pumpernickel, rye)		
Low-fat/fat-free dairy		
Buckwheat		

Note: some foods, such as legumes, lentils, dairy, and peanut butter cross over into other categories (i.e., lentils also have protein). They are placed in the category of the macronutrient that is most abundant.

LOW-CARBOHYDRATE, HIGH-PROTEIN DIETS

A number of diets fall into this category. The one most commonly discussed and researched is the Zone. Barry Sears, its originator, recommends a 40/30/30 ratio (carbohydrates/protein/fat, respectively), which he states will support even the most competitive athletic endeavors. The intention of this specific ratio of macronutrients is to control the body's ratio of insulin to glucagon, ultimately enhancing performance and the ability to mobilize body fat. Although no specific studies used this particular diet with strength athletes, one review (15) and one short-term study measured endurance performance utilizing the Zone diet (31). Both publications came to similar conclusions: athletes should not implement the Zone diet in their practices.

Energy intake is the most important component of any dietary strategy. Without adequate energy the body cannot rebuild, repair, or recuperate from training. One study demonstrated, through diet records, that at the end of the seven-week study period, subjects following the Zone diet consumed 1994 ± 438 kcal/day (25). Considering that these were active male subjects with a mean age of 26 years, this energy intake is much too low to support any type of athletic endeavor. It is impossible to enhance strength and performance if the body is not being fed what it needs. Going back to our previous example of the 150 lb athlete needing 2,500 kcal/day, he would take in 250 g of carbohydrate per day (3.7 g CHO/kg/day), about 188 g of protein per day (about 2.75 g of protein per kilogram per day), and about 83 g fat (about 1.2 g of fat per kilogram per day).

One positive aspect of this plan is that it provides a bit more protein than the previously mentioned diets. With this low-energy diet, the protein is particularly important so as to prevent the loss of muscle tissue. In addition, the Zone recommends consuming most carbohydrates as wholegrain carbohydrates to reduce the insulin surge associated with refined carbohydrates. Finally, Sears also separates fats into their various components and recommends increasing the intake of more healthy fats over saturated fats. This macronutrient model is closer to what we would recommend on a daily basis for strength athletes; energy needs, however, must be met first to optimize the training adaptations of the strength-power athlete.

LOW-CARBOHYDRATE, HIGH-FAT, HIGH-PROTEIN (KETOGENIC) DIETS

Carbohydrates were recently demonized with a resurgence of books on low-carbohydrate diets. These types of diets are essentially intended for weight loss; they are, however, increasing in popularity in athletes as well. Looking at the Atkins diet (one of the most popular low-carbohydrate plans) as a model, it recommends that a person consumes 25 to 90 g of carbohydrate each day, with the low end of the scale as the "induction phase" when they first begin the program, and then works up to the higher end of the scale as time progresses and they ultimately reach their goal. With this plan, both fat and protein make up the remaining energy, meaning that intakes of both macronutrients are unlimited and rather high. Our previously mentioned 150 lb athlete who consumed 2,500 kcal/day in the induction phase would have an intake of 25 g of carbohydrate. By dividing protein and fat equally to meet the remaining energy needs in this example, we would provide 300 g of protein (about 4.5 g/kg per day) and about 133 g of fat (about 1.95 g/kg per day). This amount of protein is not only extremely high but unnecessary. The amount of fat in this diet plan is relatively high (e.g., no limit on intake), particularly since Atkins claims that saturated fats are no more hazardous to your health than unsaturated and polyunsaturated fats.

Scientists have begun to measure the effects of low-carbohydrate, high-fat diets on exercise performance (12). The assumption here is that although glycogen is the storage form of dietary carbohydrates, drastically reducing carbohydrates will cause only a transient negative effect on energy levels, since fat and protein metabolites can ultimately be used as sources of energy. All of the research in this area has been conducted on endurance athletes, because carbohydrates and glycogen are more crucial in terms of endurance performance. Eliminating or drastically reducing carbohydrates is more likely to be detrimental to endurance activity than it is to strength activities.

With strength training, the ultimate goal is typically hypertrophy, speed, and/or power. As discussed, protein is necessary for building muscle mass, and dietary fat is correlated to the production of serum sex hormones. It is obvious that the Atkins diet will provide an abundant amount of both protein and dietary fat. Unfortunately, with this diet, the purpose of high intakes of protein and fat is to displace dietary carbohydrate. Although not as important in short-duration, high-intensity activities, the drastic reduction of dietary carbohydrate and subsequently glycogen stores will hinder performance. Furthermore, the Atkins diet, and other similar diets, are low in total energy. No matter what the macronutrient ratio or combination, total energy is ultimately the most important factor in an athlete's diet.

Another consideration for many strength trainers is the effect of the diet on body composition, whether with regard to esthetics and/or performance. Research has demonstrated that a diet lower in carbohydrate and higher in protein and fat may in fact have positive effects on body composition, stimulating greater changes in weight loss while maintaining lean body mass. Supporters of the low-carb strategy suggest that this positive change (e.g., loss of body fat) is due to the elimination of gross changes in plasma insulin concentrations caused by the excessive consumption of dietary carbohydrates. As yet, no long-term data demonstrate the superiority of one diet of this type over another, and the studies to date supporting high-fat diets were all of short duration (aside from one 12-month study, which showed no significant changes in body weight versus the higher-carbohydrate diet at the completion of the 12 months). It should be noted that it is virtually impossible to scientifically study the effects of a diet in the long term (i.e., more than one year). Thus, comparisons between and among diets are relegated to short-term studies that represent small windows of time.

Another limiting factor to regularly displacing dietary carbohydrate with fat and protein is the lack of variety in the foods allowed, making a low-carbohydrate lifestyle difficult to follow for a long time. The lack of variety also limits the intake of micronutrients, phytochemicals, antioxidants, and other beneficial components of food, which are all correlated with a lower incidence of various diseases. A healthy athlete is an athlete who can continually train harder and ultimately perform better. Also consider the previously discussed studies demonstrating that carbohydrates at specific times before, during, and after workouts may enhance protein synthesis, recovery, and ultimately growth (29,23,63). Drastic reductions in carbohydrate intake will not allow athletes to take advantage of this window of opportunity, when insulin levels are high from resistance exercise and muscle cells are in exact need of the nutrients that are shuttled in more rapidly with the ingestion of high-glycemic carbohydrates. Consequently, the suggestion that a low-carbohydrate, high-fat diet can enhance performance is unsound and not based on science.

> It is virtually impossible to make blanket dietary recommendations for high-performance athletes without first determining their current food intake. The placement of severe restrictions on certain macronutrients, however, is probably not the best approach.

1 Eat about six or seven meals each day. For instance, this would include breakfast, a mid-morning meal, lunch, a mid-afternoon meal, a post-workout meal, dinner, and another meal before bedtime.
2 The bulk of your food should come from unprocessed carbohydrate foods and whole grains (e.g., vegetables of all kinds, oatmeal, brown rice, yams, sweet potatoes, etc.).
3 Protein should be consumed: approximately 2 g of protein per kilogram of body weight; a more practical and easy-to-remember method is 1 g of protein per pound of body weight.

(continued)

(continued)

4 The majority of dietary protein should come from lean sources such as chicken, fish, and turkey. Supplementing with whey or casein can also be beneficial.
5 Unsaturated fats such as fish fat, fats from nuts and legumes, and olive oil are to be emphasized, but you still need to consume saturated fat (e.g., from beef, eggs, etc.) on occasion.
6 Always consume a post-workout carbohydrate-protein shake that consists of a high-glycemic carbohydrate and fast-absorbing protein (e.g., whey).
7 Limit your intake of processed carbohydrates. Simple or high-glycemic carbohydrates, however, should be consumed as part of your pre-, during-, and/or post-workout beverage.
8 Not including the window before, during, and after a workout, try limiting your consumption of liquid calories (e.g., soda, beer, etc.).
9 Avoid fast food and excessive condiments. Fast food is typically high in sugar and fat and lacking in nutrient value.

REAL-WORLD APPLICATION

Avoiding overtraining with dietary intervention

1 Eat nutrient dense foods. Calories are king when it comes to training intensely. Athletes should ensure they have an adequate calorie intake.
2 Get plenty of fluids. Dehydration can lead to a number of performance-related issues. This can lead to fatigue and contribute to overtraining. Athletes should strive to consume at minimum one gallon of water per day when training.
3 Post-workout nutrition is key. Eating a meal immediately after you train or compete will replenish glycogen stores and support protein synthesis.
4 Take a multivitamin every day. Many athletes are known to be slightly low in some vitamins and minerals. A multivitamin will ensure that the athlete is not deficient.

SUMMARY

Various experts on sports nutrition may provide different answers to the same question based partly on science, anecdote, and personal experience. Blanket dietary recommendations are difficult to make because so many factors affect the optimal diet. Not only is resistance training itself important, but training history, performance goals (e.g., hypertrophy versus power versus changes in body composition), program design, individual responses to training and diet, and acute versus chronic adaptations to training will all play a role in nutritional recommendations.

A few basic nutritional principles can apply to all athletes. First, athletes must try to ingest as much energy as possible while achieving optimal body mass and composition for their respective sports. To do so, they should focus on ingesting approximately 1 g of protein per pound of body weight. This recommendation simplifies the calculations necessary to determine needs, and the value can be adjusted based on established outcome measures. Dietary carbohydrate and fat energy should balance out the remainder of the diet with a higher proportion of carbohydrate than fat. The primary sources of carbohydrates should be primarily unprocessed low-glycemic-index carbohydrates, which provide sufficient fiber and abundant nutrients. The intake of high-glycemic-index carbohydrates should be limited to the periods before, during, and after exercise. Fat intake should be substantial (approximately

30% of total energy), with special attention to balancing saturated, monounsaturated, and polyunsaturated fats. Finally, nutrient timing through the consumption of energy (preferably in liquid form to facilitate absorption and ease of use) during and after exercise is critical to improving training response and recovery.

Dietary recommendations should be specific to the current training modality and should be regularly adjusted to meet an athlete's changing needs. Seeking the assistance of a qualified registered dietitian or sports nutritionist will allow the athlete to achieve the desired goals in a healthy but timely manner.

MAXING OUT

1   A two-sport female athlete coming out of the basketball season goes straight into the golf season. The athlete is having trouble getting her energy levels up. She complains to you of trouble sleeping, lack of appetite, lethargy, and poor performance. You fear the athlete is suffering from overtraining. What type of nutritional advice would you give this athlete?

2   A coach at your school has been telling athletes that high protein content in the diet will cause liver failure and that athletes should limit their intake. In addition, he tells them that there is no benefit to increased intake of protein. How will you approach this issue with the coach and the athletes?

3   Being the strength coach at a small school you are often approached by faculty and staff about diet and exercise advice. Knowing that most faculty and staff would have different energy requirements than the athletes you normally deal with, what advice would you give them? Give the faculty and staff three nutrition keys that will help them obtain their general health goals.

4   A novice long-distance runner who has participated in three half-marathons and one marathon (26.2 miles) asks for your advice regarding her nutrition program. She currently eats two to three meals per day with an emphasis on proteins, healthy fats, and low carbohydrate. What questions would you ask her and what nutrition advice might she need that is simple yet effective?

5   An 18-year-old collegiate strength athlete who is 5'11" and 198 lbs has come to you for some nutrition advice. The athlete is consuming about 4,000 kcal per day, but he is on a meal plan at school and can only eat twice a day at the cafeteria. He feels like he is gaining weight, but fat weight. His funds are limited, but he needs dietary help. What advice would you give this athlete? How can his diet help him gain the lean muscle that he wants within his limited budget?

REFERENCES

1. Ahlborg G, Felig P. Influence of glucose ingestion on fuel-hormone response during prolonged exercise. *J Appl Physiol* 1976; 41(5 Pt. 1):683–688.

2. Aragon A and Schoenfeld B. Nutrient timing revisited: is there a post-exercise anabolic window? *J Int Soc Sport Nutr* 2013; 10:5. https://doi.org/10.1186/1550-2783-10-5.

3. Avery NG, Kaiser JL, Sharman MJ, et al. Effects of vitamin E supplementation on recovery from repeated bouts of resistance exercise. *J Strength Cond Res* 2003; 17(4):801–809.

4. Bazzarre TL, Kleiner SM, Ainsworth BE. Vitamin C intake and lipid profiles in competitive male and female bodybuilders. *Int J Sport Nutr* 1992; 2(3):260–271.

5. Bellisle F, Mcdevitt R, Prentice AM. 1997. Meal frequency and energy balance. *Br J Nutr* 1997; 77(Suppl 1):S57–S70.

6. Bergstrom J et al. Diet, muscle glycogen and physical performance. *Acta Physiol Scand* 1967; 71:140–150.

7. Biolo G, Tipton KD, Klein S, et al. An abundant supply of amino acids enhances the metabolic effect of exercise on muscle protein. *Am J Physiol* 1997; 273:E122–E129.

8. Bishop NC, Blannin AK, Walsh NP, et al. Nutritional aspects of immunosuppression in athletes. *Sports Med* 1999; 28:151–176.

9. Bohl CH, Volpe SL. Magnesium and exercise. *Crit Rev Food Sci Nutr* 2002; 42:533–563.

10. Borsheim E, Cree MG, Tipton KD, et al. Effect of carbohydrate intake on net muscle protein synthesis during recovery from resistance exercise. *J Appl Physiol* 2004; 96:674–678.

11. Borsheim E, Tipton KD, Wolf SE, et al. Essential amino acids and muscle protein recovery from resistance exercise. *Am J Physiol Endocrinol Metab* 2002; 283:E648–E657.

12. Burke LM, Kiens B, Ivy JL. Carbohydrates and fat for training and recovery. *J Sports Sci* 2004; 22(1):15–30.

13. Cameron JD, Cyr MJ, Doucet E. Increased meal frequency does not promote greater weight loss in subjects who were prescribed an 8-week equi-energetic energy-restricted diet. *Br J Nutr* 2010; 103(8):1098–1101.

14. Campbell B, Kreider RB, ZiegenfussT, et al. International Society of Sports Nutrition position stand: protein and exercise. *J Int Soc Sport Nutr* 2007; 4:8.

15. Cheuvront SN. The zone diet and athletic performance. *Sports Med* 1999; 29(4):213–228.

16. Civitarese AE, Hesselink MK, Russell AP, Ravussin E, Schrauwen P. Glucose ingestion during exercise blunts exercise-induced gene expression of skeletal muscle fat oxidative genes. *Am J Physiol Endocrinol Metab* 2005; 289(6):E1023–E1029.

17. Convertino VA, et al. American College of Sports Medicine position stand. Exercise and fluid replacement. *Med Sci Sports Exerc* 1996; 1:i–vii.

18. Cordova A, Alvarez–Mon M. Behaviour of zinc in physical exercise: a special reference to immunity and fatigue. *Neurosci Biobehav Rev* 1995; 19:439–445.

19. Dallosso HM, Murgatroyd PR, James WP. Feeding frequency and energy balance in adult males. *Hum Nutr Clin Nutr* 1982; 36C(1):25–39.

20. Davis JM, Alderson NL, Welsh RS. Serotonin and central nervous system fatigue: nutritional considerations. *Am J Clin Nutr* 2000; 72:573S–578S.

21. Doi T, Matsuo T, Sugawara M, et al. New approach for weight reduction by a combination of diet, light resistance exercise and the timing of ingesting a protein supplement. *Asia Pacific J Clin Nutr* 2001; 10:226–232.

22. Dorgan JF, Judd JT, Longcope C, et al. Effects of dietary fat and fiber on plasma and urine androgens and estrogens in men: a controlled feeding study. *Am J Clin Nutr* 1996; 64(6):850–855.

23. Esmarck B, Andersen JL, Olsen S, et al. Timing of postexercise protein intake is important for muscle hypertrophy with resistance training in elderly humans. *J Appl Physiol* 2001; 535:301–311.

24. Flakoll PJ, Judy T, Flinn K, et al. Postexercise protein supplementation improves health and muscle soreness during basic military training in marine recruits. *J Appl Physiol* 2004; 96:951–956.

25. Fleming J, Sharman MJ, Avery NG, et al. Endurance capacity and high-intensity exercise performance responses to a high fat diet. *Int J Sport Nutr Exerc Metab* 2003; 13(4):466–478.

26. Haff GG, Lehmkuhl MJ, McCoy LB, Stone MH. Carbohydrate supplementation and resistance training. *J Strength Cond Res* 2003; 17:187–196.

27. Horowitz JF, Mora-Rodriguez R, Byerley LO, Coyle EF. Lipolytic suppression following carbohydrate ingestion limits fat oxidation during exercise. *Am J Physiol* 1997; 273(4 Pt 1):E768–E775.

28. Ivy JL. Glycogen resynthesis after exercise: effect of carbohydrate intake. *Int J Sports Med* 1998; 19(Suppl 2):S142–S145.

29. Ivy JL, Goforth HW, Jr., Damon BM, et al. Early postexercise muscle glycogen recovery is enhanced with a carbohydrate–protein supplement. *J Appl Physiol* 2002; 93:1337–1344.

30. Jakeman P, Maxwell S. Effect of antioxidant vitamin supplementation on muscle function after eccentric exercise. *Eur J App Physiol* 1993; 67(5):426–430.

31. Jarvis M, Seddon A, McNaughton L, et al. The acute 1-weed effects of the zinc diet on body composition, Blood lipid levels, and performance in recreational endurance athletes. *J Strength Cond Res* 2002; 16(1):50–57.

32. Judelson DA, Maresh CM, Farrell MJ, Yamamoto LM, Armstrong LE, Kraemer WJ, Volek JS, Spiering BA, Casa DJ, Anderson JM. Effect of hydration state on strength, power, and resistance exercise performance. *Med Sci Sports Exerc* 2007; 39(10):1817–1824.

33. Kerksick C, Harvey T, Stout J, et al. International Society of Sports Nutrition position stand: nutrient timing. *Int J Sport Nutr* 2008; 5:18.

34. Kinsey AW, Cappadona SR, Panton LB, Allman BR, Contreras RJ, Hickner RC, Ormsbee MJ. The effect of casein protein prior to sleep on fat metabolism in obese men. *Nutrients* 2016; 8(8):452. doi: 10.3390/nu8080452.

35. Lemon PW, Berardi JM, Noreen EE. The role of protein and amino acid supplements in the athlete's diet: does type or timing of ingestion matter? *Curr Sports Med Rep* 2002; 1:214–221.

36. Lowery LM and Devia L. Dietary protein and resistance exercise: what do we really know? *J Int Soci Sport Nutr* 2009; 6:3.

37. Lukaski H. Vitamin and mineral status: effects on physical performance. *Nutrition* 2004; 20(7):632–644.

38. Madzima T, Panton L, Fretti S, Kinsey A, Ormsbee M. Night-time consumption of protein or carbohydrate results in increased morning resting energy expenditure in active college-aged men. *Br J Nutr* 2014; 111(1): 71–77.

39. McBride JM, Kraemer WJ, Triplett-McBride T, et al. Effect of resistance exercise on free radical production. *Med Sci Sports Exerc* 1998; 30:67–72.

40. Moro T, Tinsley G, Bianco A, Marcolin G, Pacelli Q, Battaglia G, et al. Effects of eight weeks of time-restricted feeding (16/8) on basal metabolism, maximal strength, body composition, inflammation, and cardiovascular risk factors in resistance-trained males. *J Transl Med* 2016; 14(1):290.

41. Nieman DC. Exercise immunology: nutritional countermeasures. *Can J App Physiol* 2001; 26(Suppl):S45–S55.

42. Noakes TD. Fluid replacement during exercise. *Exerc Sport Sci Rev* 1993; 21:297–330.

43. Ormsbee MJ, Gorman KA, Miller EA, Baur DA, Eckel LA, Contreras RJ, Panton LB, Spicer MT. Nighttime feeding likely alters morning metabolism but not exercise performance in female athletes. *Appl Physiol Nutr Me* 2016; 41(7):719–727.

44. Phillips SM, Tipton KD, Aarsland A, et al. Mixed muscle protein synthesis and breakdown after resistance exercise in humans. *Am J Physiol* 1997; 273:E99–E107.

45. Rampone AJ, Reynolds PJ. Obesity: thermodynamic principles in perspective. *Life Sci* 1988; 43:93–110.

46. Rasmussen BB, Tipton KD, Miller SL, et al. An oral essential amino acid–carbohydrate supplement enhances muscle protein anabolism after resistance exercise. *J Appl Physiol* 2002; 88:386–392.

47. Rennie MJ and Tipton KD. Protein and amino acid metabolism during and after exercise and the effects of nutrition. *Annu Rev Nutr* 2000; 20:457–483.

48. Rokitzki L, Sagredos, AN, Reuss F, et al. Assessment of vitamin B6 status of strength and speedpower athletes. *J Am Coll Nutr* 1994; 13(1):87–94.

49. Roy BD, Luttmer K, Bosman MJ, et al. The influence of post-exercise macronutrient intake on energy balance and protein metabolism in active females participating in endurance training. *Int J Sport Nutr Exerc Metab* 2002; 12:172–188.

50. Schoenfeld B, Aragon A, and Krieger J. The effect of protein timing on muscle strength and hypertrophy: a meta-analysis. *J Int Soc Sport Nutr* 2013; 10:53. https://doi.org/10.1186/1550-2783-10-53.

51. Schoenfeld B, Aragon A, Wilborn C, Krieger J, Sonmez G. Body composition changes associated with fasted versus non-fasted aerobic exercise. *J Int Soc Sport Nutr* 2014; 11:54.

52. Schoenfeld BJ, Aragon A, Wilborn C, Urbina SL, Hayward SE, Krieger J. (2017) Pre- versus post-exercise protein intake has similar effects on muscular adaptations. *PeerJ5*:e2. https://doi.org/10.7717/peerj.2825.

53. Seimon R, Roekenes J, Zibellini J, Zhu B, Gibson A, Hills A, et al. Do intermittent diets provide physiological benefits over continuous diets for weight loss? A systematic review of clinical trials. *Mol Cell Endocrinol* 2015; 418(Pt 2):153–172.

54. Short SH, Short WR Four-year study of university athletes' dietary intake. *J Am Diet Assoc* 1983; 82(6):632–645.

55. Siri-Tarino PW, Sun Q, Hu FB, Krauss RM. Meta-analysis of prospective cohort studies evaluating the association of saturated fat with cardiovascular disease. *Am J Clinc Nutr* 2010; 91(3):535–546.

56. Stark AH and Madar Z. Olive oil as a functional food: epidemiology and nutritional approaches. *Nutr Rev* 2002; 60:170–176.

57. Terpstra AH. Effect of conjugated linoleic acid on body composition and plasma lipids in humans: an overview of the literature. *Am J Clin Nutr* 2004; 79:352–361.

58. Thompson D, Williams C, Garcia-Roves P, et al. Post-exercise vitamin C supplementation and recovery from demanding exercise. *Eur J Appl Physiol* 2003; 89:393–400.

59. Thompson D, Williams C, McGregor SJ, et al. Prolonged vitamin C supplementation and recovery from demanding exercise. *Int J Sport Nutr Exerc Metab* 2001; 11(4):466–481.

60. Tinsley G, Forsse J, Butler N, Paoli A, Bane A, La Bounty P, et al. Time-restricted feeding in young men performing resistance training: A randomized controlled trial. *Eur J Sport Sci* 2017; 17(2):200–207.

61. Tipton KD, Borsheim E, Wolf SE, et al. Acute response of net muscle protein balance reflects 24-h balance after exercise and amino acid ingestion. *Am J Physiol Endocrinol Metab* 2003; 284:E76–E89.

62. Tipton KD, Elliott TA, Cree MG, et al. Stimulation of net protein synthesis by whey protein ingestion before and after exercise. *Am J Physiol Endocrinol Metab* 2007; 292(1):E71–E76.

63. Tipton KD, Rasmussen BB, Miller SL, et al. Timing of amino acid–carbohydrate ingestion alters anabolic response of muscle to resistance exercise. *Am J Physiol Endocrinol Metab* 2001; 281:E197–E206.

64. Volek JS, Kraemer WJ, Bush JA, et al. Testosterone and cortisol in relationship to dietary nutrients and resistance exercise. *J App Physiol* 1997; 82(1):49–54.

65. Webster S, et al. Physiological effects of a weight loss regimen practiced by college wrestlers. *Med Sci Sports Exerc* 1990; 22(2):229–234.

66. Wilborn CD, Kerksick CM, Campbell BI, et al. Effects of zinc magnesium aspartate (ZMA) supplementation on training adaptations and markers of anabolism and catabolism. *J Int Soc Sport Nutr* 2004; 1(2):12–20.

67. Willoughby DS, Stout JR, Wilborn CD. Effects of resistance training and protein plus amino acid supplementation on muscle anabolism, mass, and strength. *Amino Acids* 2007; 32(4):467–477.

68. Wolfram G, Kirchgessner M, Muller HL, Hollomey S. Thermogenesis in humans after varying meal time frequency. *Ann Nutr Metab* 1987; 31(2):88–97.

69. Yannakoulia M, Melistas L, Solomou E, Yiannakouris N. Association of eating frequency with body fatness in pre- and postmenopausal women. *Obesity (Silver Spring)* 2007; 15(1):100–106.

PART 2

ORGANIZATION AND ADMINISTRATION

Contents

CHAPTER 8

FACILITY ADMINISTRATION AND DESIGN

Allen Hedrick

OBJECTIVES

After completing this chapter, you will be able to:

- Understand all aspects of managing a strength and conditioning facility.
- Identify the primary duties involved in strength and conditioning maintenance and safety for both the equipment and the facility.
- Demonstrate an understanding of the legal duties and concepts associated with facility design and management.
- Identify potential areas of legal concern in the operations of a strength and conditioning facility and the steps that can be taken to minimize risk.
- Demonstrate an understanding of the policies and procedures associated with developing and managing a strength and conditioning facility.

KEY TERMS

Assumption of risk	Mission statement	Pre-operation phase
Construction phase	Negligence	Product liability
Design phase	Performance team model	Risk management
Liability	Pre-design phase	Standard of care

INTRODUCTION

Strength and conditioning professional responsibilities extend beyond designing and implementing well designed training programs to also include managing the strength and conditioning facility. Among the more critical administrative considerations include the number of athletes training in the facility, the size of the strength and conditioning coaching staff and the amount of equipment available, and the amount of time available for each team/athlete to train (1). The purpose of this chapter is to discuss facility development and management in a typical weight room along with legal responsibilities and concepts, liability exposure, and policies and procedures.

Working as a strength and conditioning coach requires competencies in sport/exercise science, administration, management, teaching/coaching, while also complying with various laws and regulations. This combination of requirements creates remarkable challenges in terms of facility design and administration, requiring considerable experience, expertise, and resources. Strength and conditioning coaches, and those who hire them, are responsible both for addressing these needs and meeting the standard of care in providing safe and effective programs and training facilities.

> A safe training environment requires that employees avoid any negligent supervision with a client and/or while setting up a facility, understand the standard care that is required, and recognize the risks that may occur.

FACILITIES AND EQUIPMENT

Most architects believe the design of a structure should be based on its purpose. While this approach seems straightforward, many strength and conditioning facilities were originally designed for another purpose. In addition, sometimes these facilities contain less than ideal equipment. Even in facilities that can be considered state-of-the-art, regular upgrades to equipment can be advantageous because equipment manufacturing companies continue to offer improvements in the equipment they manufacture. Because the design of the facility and administering the program are entwined, equipment selection and layout should allow the training program to be implemented safely and effectively. While this concept seems simple, it may be complex in application.

> Policies of a facility may require employees to have specific experiences and/or certifications. Also, as an employee, understanding the safety procedures of the facility is of utmost importance.

> Conduct your programs in such a way that you are proud to let a knowledgeable visitor observe your athletes training.

Layout and scheduling

The initial step in planning and designing a new facility is to form a committee to assist in each step of the process. This can be subdivided into **pre-design**, **design**, **construction**, and **pre-operation phases** (2).

The practitioner should evaluate existing equipment based on the program needs of all athletic teams using the facility (2). This will involve multiple considerations, including the number of athletes using the facility, types of strength training required by each group, age groups, and the training experience of athletes training in the facility.

When building a new facility, the design of the room should be based on arranging equipment to be placed in the room(2). Considerations include access to the room, location of the coach's office(s), ceiling height, type(s) of flooring, placement of electrical outlets, mirrors, and the location of such things as drinking fountains, rest rooms, telephones, signs, bulletin boards, storage, and repair areas.

Safety is the most important consideration when arranging equipment. Figure 8.1 shows an example of a well-designed strength/power area. Thought should be given to creating specific areas to meet distinct needs (e.g., stretching/warm-up, circuit training, free weights, Olympic lifting). For example (3):

- When performing standing exercises from a rack, consider the bar length plus a 6 ft safety cushion, then multiply this by a suggested user space width of 8 to 10 ft [e.g., if using a 7 ft Olympic bar for the back squat exercise, (7 ft + 6 ft) × (10 ft) = 130 sq ft].

Figure 8.1 Diagram depicting appropriate layout for strength/power area. A strength/power area must be designed with regard to facility layout and arrangement as well as equipment safety and function.

- During performance of weightlifting exercises (e.g., cleans, jerks, snatches), consider the platform/lifting space length plus a 4 ft perimeter walkway and multiply this by the platform/lifting space width plus another 4 ft perimeter walkway safety space (e.g., [8 ft + 4 ft] × [8 ft + 4 ft] = 144 sq ft).

Regardless of training philosophies, it is a priority that conditioning coaches supervise the facility. Often this must be accomplished with limited staff and a high number of athletes in the facility at the same time. Depending on training methods and movements utilized, the challenge is to equip and arrange the facility to maximize capacity without negatively affecting efficiency or safety.

Although equipment selection in any facility is a matter of matching training philosophies and the clientele of the facility, guidelines can be applied to help direct choices. Practitioners should carefully consider both the benefits and drawbacks of the equipment being considered and make purchasing decisions based on what equipment best matches their training beliefs and philosophies.

When selecting equipment, consideration should be given to practical issues, including the following:

- Versatility
- Coaching/teaching requirements (and corresponding staffing/spotting responsibilities)
- Safety
- Cost, space/time efficiency

When training for strength and power, and enhancing athletic performance, literature suggests that unguided-resistance equipment (e.g., free weight training) is superior to emphasizing machine training, especially when there is qualified instruction and supervision in place (4–7). There seems to be a variety of reasons for this superior training effect that free weight training provides, which in turn can make the equipment selection process easier. In general, the facility design and equipment should match the program's goals and objectives, and the needs of those training in the facility, enabling athletes to perform a variety of multiple joint, multi-plane movements that challenge their coordination and movement skills. Much of the equipment selected should be appropriate for exercises that involve accelerating the resistance over a long range of motion allowing for high-power levels and rates of force development as well as different types of muscular contractions (concentric, eccentric, isometric, and stretch-shortening cycle).

Maintenance and safety

One of the primary responsibilities of the strength and conditioning coach is to provide a safe training environment while emphasizing performance enhancement and injury prevention (2).

Practitioners also have a responsibility to maintain and clean the facility and equipment (2). Establishing maintenance and cleaning schedules, and keeping the required supplies, tools, and other items on hand, helps ensure safety, maintain the equipment at a high level, and keep appearance, cleanliness, and functionality at a high level.

Environmental factors within the strength and conditioning facility also need to be considered for participants' health and safety. Some specific environmental factors to consider include (2,8):

- Volume on sound and video systems need to be set to allow clear communication between coach and athletes and spotters and lifters at all times
- Air temperature kept within a range of 72° to 78°F (22° to 26°C)

- Ventilation systems providing a minimum 8 to 10 air exchanges/hour with no strong odors in the room
- Equipment and floor not wet and slick due to humidity
- Facility well illuminated and free of dark areas
- Exit sign well lighted
- Extension cords large enough for electrical load; properly routed, secured, and grounded
- Safety, regulation, and policy signs posted in clear view

Within these areas of responsibility, it is important to understand litigation issues (3,9–15). By doing so, practitioners can manage, but not eliminate, the risk of injury among participants. It is also important for practitioners to understand the concept of **product liability**. Product liability is defined as a manufacturer's and/or vendor's legal responsibilities if someone using their equipment sustains injury or damage due primarily to a defect or deficiency in design or production (2), as well as actions that can place one at risk for litigation. Product liability issues are discussed in further detail later in this chapter. Box 8.1 provides basic guidelines for planning and designing a new facility.

> An important consideration when planning the facility is to evaluate the needs of the athletes and teams who will be training in the facility.

Box 8.1 Facilities and equipment

Select a committee of professionals to accomplish the following:

- Assess equipment currently in the facility based on the needs of all athletic teams using the room.
- Evaluate the design of the facility and arrange existing equipment with safety and function as top priorities in determining equipment arrangement.
- Consider seasonal athletic team priorities (i.e., in-season vs. out of season), staff-to-athlete ratios, and equipment availability relative to the number of athletes in the room at any given time.
- Establish frequent maintenance and cleaning schedules to ensure safety, protect equipment, and maintain the facility's appearance, cleanliness, and functionality.

REAL-WORLD APPLICATION

Funding a training facility

Weight rooms are often filled with obsolete and nonfunctional equipment, and the budget is too small to reequip many facilities on a regular basis. This is a common situation, and not one commonly addressed in an academic setting. Suggestions for creative opportunities for funding are provided here.

Create a priority list of the equipment that needs to replaced first. Be specific with how many of each item you will need and what the cost will be. Remember that many equipment vendors do provide discount incentives for buying multiple pieces of equipment. Schedule the upgrade in phases, starting with those items most needed and progress from there. If a piece of equipment is still functional, no matter how old or worn, defer replacing it until later. For example, barbells and plates that are old and rusted may not be aesthetically pleasing but will suffice temporarily. Spend available funds on high-priority equipment that cannot be donated or built on site that will most increase the ability to effectively train those using the facility.

Once you have completed planning the upgrade, consider possible resources to fund the project. There may be creative funding opportunities available. Ask your athletic director (e.g., administrator who oversees the work of coaches and staff working in an athletic department or facility) for permission to approach local boosters or businesses for "gifts in kind." Often boosters will exchange services and/or products for tickets or other incentives. Many athletic directors set aside reserve money in their budget until late in the fiscal year to cover unforeseen expenses. Ask them to consider directing a portion of that to a weight room upgrade, emphasizing how it can benefit every team's performance and recruiting. With approval, consider approaching a development officer for the institution. Possibly there is a list of boosters who can provide products or services, such as building-supply centers that might donate lumber for platforms, welders who can fabricate equipment, and the like. Boosters are generally gratified to know that you're giving them first consideration and that you have seen their advertisements in media guides, game-day programs, stadium signage, and so on.

If you have a specific company in mind for your new equipment, ask about their design capabilities to show different options for laying out the equipment in the weight room. They may be able to provide various floor plan options, elevations, or other drawings that will help visualize the various choices which help in making the final decision easier.

One important note: when pursuing the services of welders, carpenters, or other contractors, be sure to provide them with the required information to build to industry specifications. If the equipment should fail at some point, the facility may be liable for any resulting injuries or damages.

LEGAL DUTIES AND CONCEPTS

Practitioners and their employers share legal responsibility to provide an appropriate level of supervision and instruction to accomplish the following: meet a reasonable standard of care, provide and maintain a safe environment for athletes, inform users of the risks inherent in and related to their activities, and prevent unreasonable risk or harm resulting from negligent instruction or supervision (10–13). In fact, these legal duties and concepts define the organizational and administrative tasks of the profession.

> The strength and conditioning practitioner's primary responsibility is to provide a safe training environment for all athletes.

A strength and conditioning professional should understand the following legal terms (2):

- **Assumption of risk**. Voluntary participation in activity with knowledge of the inherent risk(s). Practitioners must thoroughly inform participants of the risks involved in athletic and conditioning activities. Ideally, athletes should be required to sign a statement indicating their understanding and acceptance of the risk.
- **Liability**. A legal responsibility. Practitioners must take reasonable steps to ensure safe participation in conditioning activities, prevent injury, and act prudently when an injury occurs (9).
- **Negligence**. Failure to exercise the care a prudent person would under similar circumstances. For a practitioner to be guilty of negligence, there must be duty, breach of duty, proximate cause, and damages (15). He or she is negligent if proven to have a duty to act and to have failed to act with the appropriate standard of care, proximately causing injury or damages to another person.
- **Standard of care**. What a prudent and reasonable person would do under similar circumstances. A practitioner is expected to act according to his or her education, training, and certification status.

> Practitioners and their employers share a legal duty to provide an appropriate level of supervision and instruction.

Types of standards

In addition to standards for desired operational practices published by professional organizations such as the National Strength and Conditioning Association (NSCA), standards for technical/physical specifications have been published by independent organizations. In a negligence lawsuit, established standards of care can be used to gauge a practitioner's professional competence by comparing his or her actual conduct with written benchmarks of expected behavior. In addition to standards and guidelines established by allied organizations such as the American College of Sports Medicine (ACSM) (16,17), American Heart Association (AHA) (16,18), and National Athletic Trainers Association (NATA), other associations have also delineated standards of practice (Aerobics and Fitness Association of America, American Physical Therapy Association, National Association for Sport and Physical Education). Moreover, relevant technical/physical specifications have been published by the U.S. Consumer Product Safety Commission and the American Society for Testing and Materials (19,20).

Applying standards of practice to risk management

Risk management is a proactive administrative process meant to help minimize legal liability while also limiting the frequency and severity of injuries and subsequent claims and lawsuits (10,21). It may not be possible to eliminate all risk of injury and liability exposure, but these can be effectively minimized with risk-management strategies. Although the coordinator is ultimately responsible for risk management, all practitioners should be involved in various aspects of the process. Eickhoff-Shemek (22) proposes a four-step procedure (adapted from Head and Horn [23]) for applying standards of practice to the risk-management process:

1 *Identify and select standards of practice as well as all applicable laws*. There are several standards of practice published by various organizations. As a result, it is challenging for the practitioner to be aware of all of them and decide which one to apply when implementing the risk-management plan. As far as participant safety, normally the most stringent standards in an industry should be adhered to.

2 *Develop risk-management strategies reflecting standards of practice and all applicable laws*. This involves writing procedures defining specific responsibilities

and/or duties that staff will carry out in specific situations. The procedures must be written clearly, succinctly, without excessive detail. Once the written procedures are completed, include them in the staff policies and procedures manual.

3 *Implement the risk-management plan.* Implementing the risk-management plan involves staff training to ensure that the practitioner's daily conduct is consistent with written policies and procedures and applicable laws and standards of practice. The policies and procedures manual is to be used in conjunction with initial training of new employees as well as during regular in-service training where all employees practice specific procedures. From a legal perspective, it is important to explain to staff the necessity of carrying out such duties appropriately.

4 *Evaluate the risk-management plan.* Standards of practice are not static and must be updated periodically to reflect change. The risk-management plan should be stringently evaluated annually, if not sooner, as well as after any accident or injury to determine if emergency procedures were performed correctly and what steps could be taken, if any, to prevent a similar incident occurring.

> Application of standards of practice to the risk-management process is a four-step process: identify and select standards of practice as well as all applicable laws; develop risk-management strategies reflecting standards of practice and all applicable laws; implement the risk-management plan; and evaluate the risk-management plan.

DUTIES AND RESPONSIBILITIES: LIABILITY EXPOSURE

Although every program and facility is unique, it is beneficial to examine the duties and responsibilities of the practitioner in terms of common areas of liability exposure (14). For example, proper instruction and supervision are related to both personnel qualifications and facility layout and scheduling. Noncompliance in one area can affect other areas, thereby increasing the risk of negligence and potential litigation. Practitioners and their employers share the corresponding duties and responsibilities.

The NSCA's *Strength and Conditioning Professional Standards and Guidelines* (14) identifies nine areas of liability exposure:

REAL-WORLD APPLICATION

Policies and procedures

The following is a sample policy for a strength and conditioning facility:

> *Work with an attentive spotter and use appropriate safety equipment (e.g., power racks) for performing movements where free weights are supported on the trunk or moved over the head/face. Olympic lifts are an exception to the spotter rule and should be performed on an 8 ft by 8 ft platform that is clear of people and equipment.*

When writing a policy, consider how it will be enforced. To carry out a policy and ensure it is enforced, several steps should be taken: (i) the staff must be trained on expectations both in terms of teaching athletes to spot and dealing with athletes who neglect to use a spotter; (ii) the athletes must be trained in spotting, what lifts need a spotter, and the number of spotters required for specific exercises; it will be a necessity to train incoming athletes as they enter the program, and it may be necessary to reinforce this training each year; and (iii) determine the consequences in advance for not following policy; be fair and consistent when enforcing policy; consider the legal implications if an athlete who has not followed policy is injured.

pre-participation screening and clearance; personnel qualifications; program supervision and instruction; facility and equipment setup, inspection, maintenance, repair, and signage; emergency planning and response; records and record keeping; equal opportunity and access; participation by children; and supplements, ergogenic aids, and drugs. Within these areas of liability exposure, a total of 11 standards ("must do's") and 13 guidelines ("should do's") are proposed. These further define the tasks involved in facility organization and administration.

Pre-participation screening and clearance

A physical examination (ideally conducted by a licensed physician) is a necessity for all athletes prior to participating in a program. This should include a comprehensive health and immunization history (as defined by current guidelines from the Centers for Disease Control and Prevention) as well as relevant physical exam, including an orthopedic evaluation. Cardiovascular screening, as discussed later, is also recommended. The practitioner does not need a copy of the results, but a signed statement verifying proof of medical clearance to participate must be obtained. Often this will occur through the athletic trainers responsible for each sport. Athletes who are returning from an injury or illness or have special medical requirements must be required to show proof of medical clearance before beginning or returning to participation.

Currently, no universally accepted standards are available for screening athletes, neither are there approved certification procedures for health care professionals who perform such examinations. The joint Pre-Participation Physical Evaluation Task Force of five organizations has published a widely accepted monograph, including detailed instructions on performing a pre-participation history and physical exam and determining clearance for participation, and a medical evaluation form to copy and use for each examination (24). The American Heart Association and American College of Sports Medicine have also published statements on pre-participation

screening for those involved in fitness-related activities (16,18,25). Relevant issues can be summarized as follows:

Educational institutions have ethical, medical, and possible legal obligations to implement cost-efficient pre-participation screening strategies (including a complete medical history and physical examination), thereby ensuring that high school (e.g., typically students in the age range of about 14 years of age to about 18 years of age) and college (typically students in the age range of about 18 to about 22 years of age) athletes are not subject to unacceptable risks. Support for such efforts, especially in large athletic populations, is mitigated by cost-efficiency considerations, practical limitations, and awareness that it is not possible to achieve zero risk in competitive sports.

A properly qualified health care provider (with requisite training, medical skills, and background to reliably perform a physical examination, obtain a detailed cardiovascular history, and recognize heart disease) should perform the pre-participation athletic screening. A licensed physician is preferable, but an appropriately trained registered nurse or physician assistant may be acceptable under certain circumstances in states where non-physician health care workers are permitted to perform pre-participation screening. In the latter situation, a formal certification process should be established to demonstrate the examiner's expertise in performing cardiovascular examinations.

The best available and most practical approach to screening populations of competitive sports participants involves a complete and careful personal and family medical history and physical examination designed to identify (or raise suspicion of) cardiovascular risk factors known to cause sudden death or disease progression. Such screening is a realistic and obtainable objective and must be mandatory for all athletes. A complete medical history and physical examination should be performed before participation in organized high school athletics (grades 9 to 12). An updated history should be obtained in intervening years. For collegiate athletes, a comprehensive personal/family history and physical examination should be performed by a qualified examiner initially upon entering the institution, before beginning training and competition. Screening should be repeated every two years thereafter unless more frequent examinations are indicated. An updated history and blood pressure measurement should be obtained each subsequent year to determine if another physical examination, and possible further testing, is required (e.g., due to abnormalities or changes in medical status).

To assist in assigning a level of risk in terms of likelihood of injury, health appraisal questionnaires should be completed prior to participation in any exercise testing and/or training. Written and active communication between facility staff, including athletic trainers and team physicians, and the participant's personal physician or health care provider, should ideally occur when a medical evaluation/recommendation is advised or required. Athletes should be educated regarding the importance of the pre-participation health appraisal and medical evaluation/recommendation (if indicated) and should not be allowed to participate without them.

Personnel qualifications

To properly supervise and instruct athletes utilizing facilities and equipment, qualified personnel must be in place. A three-pronged approach is recommended:

1   *The practitioner should acquire expertise, and have a degree from an accredited institution in one or more of the topics comprising the "scientific foundations" domain identified in the Certified Strength and*
   Conditioning Specialist (CSCS) Examination Content Description (26) or a relevant subject. He or she should also make an ongoing effort to continue to acquire knowledge and competence throughout the duration of his or her career.

2   *Professional organizations within the area of strength and conditioning offer certifications with continuing education requirements as well as a code of ethics for practitioners interested in acquiring the necessary competencies.* Depending on one's specific duties, responsibilities, and interests, relevant certifications offered by other governing bodies may also be appropriate.

3   *The **performance team model**, which involves developing a staff composed of qualified professionals with interdependent areas of expertise and shared leadership roles, can enhance practitioners' knowledge and skill development and improve their ability to provide high quality instruction to their athletes (27,28).* The profession's scope of practice has expanded and diversified to an extent where it is very challenging and often impossible for one individual to acquire proficiency in all areas.

The importance of putting qualified staffing in place to fulfill the institution's and practitioner's shared legal duties for safety, supervision, and standard of care cannot be overstated. A lack of qualified instruction and supervision can be identified as a causative factor in the available literature on injuries and litigations associated with strength and power training. In some cases, this causative effect is obvious (29–31), while in other situations it can be inferred. For example, despite the technical and athletic requirements of weightlifting, the relatively high coach-to-athlete ratio and corresponding standard of care are likely reasons for its low incidence of injury (32,33).

Program supervision and instruction

About 80% of all court cases concerning injuries to athletes are related to supervision (9). Although serious accidents are rare in supervised exercise programs, the liability costs associated with inadequate or lax supervision are significant; plaintiffs' recovery rate in such negligence lawsuits is almost 56% (34). Poor facility maintenance, defective equipment, and inadequate instruction and/or supervision are the main causes of these incidents. The importance of staffing is obvious in each circumstance. For example, in a review of 32 litigations resulting from negligent weight training supervision, three issues were raised by the plaintiff's attorneys in each case (35): poor instruction or instructor qualifications; lax/poor supervision; and failure to warn of inherent dangers in the equipment, facility, or exercise. The issue of professional instructors' qualifications, as discussed in the previous section, is a prevalent trend in such litigations.

> As a strength and conditioning practitioner, one should fully be able to properly use the equipment within the facility, while also being able to recognize when the equipment is no longer safe to use.

Athletes must be properly supervised and instructed all the time to ensure maximum safety. Bucher and Krotee (36) recommend the following principles:

- Always be there
- Be active and hands-on
- Be prudent, careful, and prepared
- Be qualified
- Be vigilant
- Inform athletes of safety and emergency procedures
- Know athletes' health status
- Monitor and enforce rules and regulations
- Monitor and scrutinize the environment

In addition to the qualified practitioners being present, effective instruction and supervision involves several practical considerations (13,34,37,38).

- A clear view of all areas of the facility, or at least the areas being supervised by each practitioner, and the athletes in it. This issue is significantly related to facility design and layout; including equipment placement with respect to visibility, versatility, and accessibility.

- A practitioner's proximity to the group of athletes under his or her supervision. This includes the ability to see and communicate clearly with one another and easy access to athletes in need of immediate assistance or spotting.
- The number and grouping of athletes to make optimal use of available equipment, space, and time.
- The athletes' age(s), experience level(s), and need(s).
- The type of program being conducted (i.e., skillful/explosive free weight movements versus guided-machine resistance training) and associated need for coaching and spotting.

Ideally, practitioners should achieve an optimal training environment by scheduling teams and athletes throughout the day. Even with careful planning, however, most facilities have times of peak use based on both team practices and athletes' class schedules. Realistically, it is not possible to schedule activities over a wide range of times to achieve an acceptable professional-to-athlete ratio. The primary concern is to provide adequate facilities and qualified staff so that all athletes have a safe place to train and are properly instructed and supervised during peak usage times (17,39,40). Practitioners should emphasize proper exercise technique, movement mechanics, and safety, and utilize instructional methods, procedures, and progressions consistent with accepted professional practices to minimize injury risk and liability exposure.

Even when reasonable steps are taken to make optimal use of facility space and staff, a potential inequity exists between available resources and demand for programs and services in many settings. The combined effects of rapid growth in collegiate/scholastic athlete participation (especially among women), corresponding liability exposures, and equal opportunity/access laws create a significant standard-of-care load and liability challenge for practitioners and their employers. A two-pronged approach can thus be recommended:

1   *During peak use times, activities should be scheduled, and the required number of qualified staff should be in place so*

recommended guidelines are achieved. These guidelines include the minimum average floor space required per athlete (100 ft²), and coach-to-athlete ratios at the following levels: practitioner-to-athlete ratios of 1:10 junior high school; 1:15 high school; and 1:20 at the college level. Further, the number of athletes per barbell or training station should be kept at ≤3 (33,37,39,41). Ideally, this results in one practitioner supervising three to four training stations and/or 1,000 ft² area (junior high school); five training stations and/or 1,500 ft² area (high school); or six to seven training stations and/or 2,000 ft² area (college), respectively. Professional discretion can be used to adjust these guidelines with respect to the practical considerations discussed earlier.

2 *Practitioners and their employers should strive toward a long-term goal of achieving the professional-to-athlete ratio in the facility to each sport's respective coach-to-athlete ratio.* This is relatively straightforward at the college level, where the NCAA limits the number of coaches per sport and compiles sports participation data. In the absence of similar information in other settings, such determinations can be made on an individual-institution basis (or possibly according to trends within a district, division, or state).

Facility and equipment setup, inspection, maintenance, repair, and signage

In some instances, practitioners are involved in all phases of facility design and layout. More commonly, they assume responsibility for an existing facility, in which case the opportunities to plan or modify the facility are often limited. Either way, the practitioner and his or her employer are jointly responsible for maximizing the facility's safety, effectiveness, and efficiency such that available space and time can be put to optimal use.

Practitioners should establish written policies and procedures for equipment/facility selection, purchase, installation, setup, inspection, maintenance, and repair. These should be included in the policies and procedures manual (as discussed in the next section). Safety checks and periodic inspections of equipment, maintenance, and repair should be conducted and status reports issued. Manufacturer-provided user's manuals, warranties, operating guides, and other relevant records regarding equipment operation and maintenance (e.g., selection, purchase, installation, setup, inspection, maintenance, and repair) should be kept on file and adhered to (36).

As mentioned previously, practitioners must understand the concept of product liability. Although this applies to manufacturers and vendors, certain actions and/or behaviors by the practitioner can increase the practitioner's responsibility, increasing the risk for claims or lawsuits. The following steps can minimize equipment-related liability exposure (9,36):

- Buy equipment only from reputable manufacturers and be certain that it meets standards and guidelines for professional/commercial (not home) use.
- Use equipment only for the purpose intended by the manufacturer. Modifying equipment from the condition in which it was originally sold should be avoided unless such adaptations are clearly designated and instructions for doing so are included in the product information.
- Post any signage provided by the manufacturer on or close to the equipment.
- Do not allow unsupervised athletes to utilize equipment.
- Regularly inspect equipment for damage and wear that may place athletes at risk for injury.

Emergency planning and response

An emergency response plan is a written document describing the proper procedures of care for injuries that may occur during activity. While all facilities should have such a document, the document itself does not prevent injuries. In fact, the document may provide a false sense of security if not supported with appropriate training and preparedness by a concerned, professional staff. Therefore, practitioners must:

- Know the emergency response plan and the proper procedures for dealing with an emergency (i.e., location of phones, activating emergency medical services, designated personnel to care for injuries, ambulance access, and location of emergency supplies) (42,43).
- Review and practice emergency policies and procedures regularly (i.e., at least quarterly).
- Maintain current certification in cardiopulmonary resuscitation (CPR). First aid training and certification may also be necessary if sports medicine personnel (e.g., certified athletic trainer [ATC], physician) are not immediately available.
- Adhere to universal precautions for preventing exposure to and transmission of blood-borne pathogens (44,45).

Records and record keeping

Documentation is a critical part of program and facility management. A variety of records should be kept on file (36,46–48).

- Policies and procedures manual (as discussed in the next section).
- Manufacturer-provided user's manuals, warranties, and operating guides as well as equipment selection, purchase, installation, setup, inspection, maintenance, and repair records.
- Personnel credentials and certifications.
- Professional standards and guidelines.
- Safety policies and procedures, including a written emergency response plan.
- Training logs, progress entries, and/or activity instruction/supervision notes.
- Injury/incident reports, pre-participation medical clearance, and return to participation clearance documents (after the occurrence of an injury, illness, change in health status, or an extended period of absence) for each participant under the practitioner's care.
- In collegiate and scholastic settings, athletes may be required to sign protective legal documents covering all athletically related activities. In contrast, in other settings, the practitioner should consider having participants sign similar legal documents.

Legal and medical records should be kept on file in the event an injury claim or lawsuit is filed. It is good practice to maintain files for a duration recommended by a legal authority. This period is based on the statutes of limitations, which varies from state to state (48). As is the case with other organizational and administrative tasks, adequate staff are necessary to properly keep and maintain such records.

> To ensure proper medical care is given, it is important to obtain consent to treat as well as a record of any previous medical history of the client prior to any physical activity within a facility.

Equal opportunity and access

In the majority of organizations, institutions, and professions, discrimination or unequal treatment (e.g., according to race, creed, national origin, gender, religion, age, handicap/disability, or other such legal classifications) are prohibited by federal, state, and potentially local laws and regulations. For example, practitioners working in federally funded educational settings must comply with civil rights statutes, including Title IX of the Education Amendments of 1972, which requires gender equity in providing opportunity and access to athletic facilities, programs, and services. Practitioners must obey the letter and spirit of these laws when working with athletes and staff.

Participation in strength and conditioning activities by children

Resistance training can be an important component of youth fitness, health promotion, and injury prevention (49,50). Facility administration and design should allow for total supervision and the complete safety of children when using the facility. More information on conditioning for children will be presented in Chapter 20.

> Despite children's physical ability to train, they must be supervised at all times.

The role of the strength and conditioning practitioner and supplements

Strength and conditioning practitioners share in the responsibility for educating athletes regarding supplements and banned substances. The issue of nutritional supplement and drug use is complicated by several factors. According to the Dietary Supplement Health and Education Act of 1994, supplements are regulated as foods rather than drugs. This raises concerns about quality control/assurance and possible consequences for consuming these supplements.

Practitioners are often approached for advice on nutrition and supplementation and need to be aware of the following: The Federal Trade Commission has primary responsibility for advertising claims. Put simply, advertising for any product, including dietary supplements, must be truthful, substantiated, and not misleading. The U.S. Food and Drug Administration has primary responsibility for product labeling claims. The legislation enforced by this agency includes "Current Good Manufacturing Practices" and selected portions of the Federal Food, Drug and Cosmetic Act related to dietary supplements. Manufacturing practices for nutritional supplements established by the U.S.

Pharmacopeia and National Formulary are cited as primary resources in this legislation.

The distinctions between dietary supplements, drugs, and conventional foods are not clear. This is especially challenging for competitive athletes and coaches, because such products may contain substances that are banned by one or more sport governing bodies, despite a manufacturer's or vendor's use of terms such as *herbal, legal, natural, organic, safe and effective*, etc. Furthermore, supplement manufacturers are constantly developing new products with different combinations of ingredients, making it more challenging to identify those that may be problematic.

Banned-substance policies differ among sport governing bodies. A compound that is banned according to one governing body may not be banned according to another.

> Standards and guidelines can be applied across nine areas of liability exposure: pre-participation screening and clearance; personnel qualifications; program supervision and instruction; facility and equipment setup, inspection, maintenance, repair, and signage; emergency planning and response; records and record keeping; equal opportunity and access; participation by children (if applicable); and supplements, ergogenic aids, and drugs.

REAL-WORLD APPLICATION

Mission statement

A **mission statement** is a brief statement of an organization's purpose that provides both scope and direction for the organization. Here is an example of a mission statement for a strength and conditioning program:

> *The strength and conditioning program will empower athletes and coaches to optimize their capabilities, and thereby achieve excellence through learning and applying fundamentally sound principles.*

This is a very broad statement, so including a list of goals and objectives helps professionals adhere to the mission statement. Mission statements will vary by facility and should relate to the goals and objectives of the facility. The mission statement should be a product of the core beliefs of the administration and staff. Periodically the mission statement should be reevaluated to make sure that it still reflects the core beliefs of the program.

POLICIES AND PROCEDURES

Strength and conditioning professionals must develop policies and procedures that allow them to provide safe and effective programs and services and meet the optimal standard of care for their athletes. This requires a working understanding of facility and equipment considerations, legal concepts, and duties and responsibilities dictated by liability exposures, as described in previous sections.

It is important that the strength and conditioning program has a well-defined mission along with identifiable goals and objectives (47). Safety, performance enhancement, and injury prevention are, of course, fundamental goals in every program. These should be complemented with specific objectives as part of a holistic mission statement.

It is important to clearly define and distinguish job titles and duties for each position within the strength and conditioning program (47). These job duties should be developed for the director, associate(s) and/or assistant(s), facility supervisor(s), and other staff members including interns, administrative assistants, and others.

Staff members must be required to maintain a professional code of conduct and work cooperatively as a team. This encompasses a wide range of issues, including staff meetings, athlete orientation, annual planning, budgeting, staff facility use, relationships with athletes and other staff, professional goals, posted information, visitor tours, coaching and spotting procedures, testing, record keeping, athlete incentives, and so on.

A written policies and procedures manual is essential to implementing a safe and effective program (47). In addition to the issues discussed earlier, the manual should address facility access, daily operation, telephone/music system use, rules and regulations, and emergency procedures as well as equipment/facility selection, purchase, installation, setup, inspection, and maintenance and repair. This type of documentation may seem mundane but is fundamental to managing programs or facilities involved in serving people.

Policies and procedures should be clearly explained to all staff and athletes using the facility. These policies and procedures should not be rigid or static. Instead, they should be compiled with insight and discretion and revised periodically as circumstances dictate. Box 8.2 provides basic guidelines for writing policies and procedures.

> Sound policies and procedures should be developed to ensure the safety of the athlete and guide administrative decisions.

SUMMARY

Facility administration and facility design are important in every aspect of the strength and conditioning program. The design of a facility is related to functionality, which is vitally important to training athletes successfully. Facilities and equipment often must be designed for specific groups of athletes.

The legal responsibilities of managing a strength and conditioning facility often exceed expectations and training. It is important for the strength and conditioning practitioner to understand the liability aspects of providing a safe training environment for athletes.

Many opportunities in strength and conditioning will provide challenges that reach beyond programing sets and reps. Budgets, equipment, facilities, and staff can often be severely limited

---

Box 8.2   Guidelines for writing policies and procedures

- Safety, performance enhancement, and injury prevention are fundamental goals in developing and clarifying the program's mission, goals, and objectives.
- Job titles, descriptions, and duties should be clearly defined and distinguished for each staff position.
- Practitioners must maintain a professional code of conduct and work cooperatively as a team.
- Understand the administrative decisions involved in safe and effective program implementation.
- Create a policies and procedures manual.

or lacking altogether. This results in a mismatch between demand for and the opportunity to provide safe and effective programs and services. Professionals and their employers share a legal duty to meet the standard of care for athletes. The individual practitioner is not solely responsible for fulfilling this standard (unless he or she is self-employed); the individual and his or her employer are jointly responsible for doing so.

The NSCA's *Strength and Conditioning Professional Standards and Guidelines* document (38) is one of the main resources cited in this chapter. Its implementation will present significant challenges and involve ambitious changes in many programs. Resistance to change can be expected from some athletic directors/employers because it will require them to allocate more resources to the strength and conditioning program. Nonetheless, the employing institution or business has a legal responsibility to help practitioners provide or obtain the resources needed to fulfill their standard of care.

MAXING OUT

1 You are the strength and conditioning coordinator at a college program. A team coach approaches you with a program obtained from another university, asking you to implement that program with her team instead of the one you have developed. Explain what your policy is in this situation, including how it will affect the team's programming and scheduling opportunities in the varsity weight room.

2 You are the strength and conditioning coordinator at a college program, and your athletic director is expressing concern that the facility looks like a "football weight room" equipped primarily with free weights. He feels that this is causing multiple problems, including compromising the programs and services provided to other teams, discouraging other teams' recruits from attending the school, and placing the university at risk of a Title IX lawsuit. As a result you are instructed to develop a proposal on how to reequip the weight room emphasizing machine training and fewer free weights to make it more accommodating for all sports. Develop and explain your policy regarding equipment selection with respect to performance enhancement and injury prevention.

3 As the Head Strength and Conditioning Coach for a competitive institution, you are given two possible locations for new weight rooms. Your primary needs are a weight room specifically for football, and a weight room specifically for women's sports. You have the space and money to equip both weight rooms with only a few renovations necessary in the existing weight rooms to accommodate the remainder of the sports. Location one is under the seats of the football stadium. The space is climate controlled and has adequate space for either group. The second space is on the second floor of the athletic building with coaches' offices, which is climate controlled and has adequate floor space for either group. What are the pros and cons of each location? Which group of athletes would you locate where? List all factors you may need to take into consideration.

CASE EXAMPLE

Program scheduling, supervision, and instruction

Background

You coordinate a strength and conditioning program that is responsible for programming and servicing a total of 362 student athletes in 16 sports:

(continued)

(continued)

TABLE 8.1 Facility schedule

Day Time	Mon	Tue	Wed	Thurs	Fri
7:00 am	M. Soccer (26) W. Soccer (23)			M. Soccer (26) W. Soccer (23)	M. Basketball (16) Softball (18) W. Tennis (10)
8:00	V. Football (10)	J.V. Football (10)	V. Football (10)	J.V. Football (10)	J.V. Football (10)
9:00	V. Football (10)	J.V. Football (10)	V. Football (10)	J.V. Football (10)	J.V. Football (10)
10:00	V. Football (10) M. Golf (3)	J.V. Football (10)	V. Football (10)	J.V. Football (10)	J.V. Football (10)
11:00	V. Football (10)	J.V. Football (10)	V. Football (10)	J.V. Football (10)	J.V. Football (10)
Noon	closed	closed	closed	closed	closed
1:00 p.m.	V. Football (10) M. Golf (5)	J.V. Football (10)	V. Football (10)	J.V. Football (10)	J.V. Football (10)
2:00	2:45 W. Basketball (14)		2:45 W. Basketball (14)		W. Basketball (14) 2:30 W. Golf (8)
3:00	3:30 Baseball (31)	W. Tennis (10)	3:30 Baseball (31)	M. Golf (10)	3:30 Baseball (31)
4:00	Softball (18)		Softball (18)		
5:00	Track and Field (60)	M. X-Country (13) W. X-Country (13)	Track and Field (60)	M. X-Country (13) W. X-Country (13)	Track and Field (60)
6:00	M. Basketball (16) Volleyball (14)	W. Golf (8) M. Tennis (10)	M. Basketball (16) Volleyball (14)	M. Tennis (10)	

Explanation of abbreviations

M: Men
W: Women
V: Varsity
J.V.: Junior varsity

Including yourself, you have a three-person staff and a 6,000 ft² weight room equipped with eight Olympic lifting platforms, eight self-contained power stations, four plyometric stations, and various secondary equipment. It is the first week of September; fall sport athletes have completed preseason camp and classes have begun. Your task is to schedule team workouts for the first six weeks of the fall semester such that in-season sports (cross-country, football, soccer, volleyball) train two days per week, whereas off-season sports train three days per week. Your programs involve periodized multi-set free weight training, including explosive movements.

Recommendations/considerations

Begin by contacting team coaches regarding which days and times they prefer their teams to train. Make it clear that in-season sports have priority in the scheduling of the weight room because their schedules are less flexible due to practices, meetings, and games.

The advantage of morning training sessions is that they reduce the demand for weight room time during peak (afternoon) hours. The disadvantages are that they can conflict with athletes' sleep and/or meals and lengthen the staff's workday. Limiting staff hours can probably be alleviated to a degree by allowing flex time for those staff working the early shift (e.g., leaving work after morning sessions are completed and returning in the afternoon).

Some team coaches may allow some or all of their athletes to train during off-peak times individually or in small groups (e.g., between 8 a.m. and 3 p.m.). Further, there may be athletes who have academic commitments during their team workouts and need to use this option. Again, this has the effect of reducing demand on the weight room during peak hours.

Some coaches may also be willing to train varsity (typically students 16 to 18 years of age) and junior varsity athletes (typically students 13–15 years of age) on different schedules. This can be extremely useful with large teams in sports such as football. Finally, it is helpful to recruit qualified interns to assist with program implementation, especially during busy times.

Implementation

With a 6,000 ft² facility and three-person staff, there may be the opportunity to schedule multiple teams concurrently during peak usage times, depending on the size of the team. With smaller teams, it may be feasible to start two sessions simultaneously; in larger-group situations, it may be advisable to stagger their starting times every 20 to 30 minutes. Since most of these sports have common demands in terms of total-body power and rate of force development (RFD) and can benefit from similar exercises/equipment, it is helpful to designate specific training stations for each group to minimize congestion. In any case, workouts should be planned to meet the following recommended guidelines:

(continued)

(continued)

- 100 ft² average floor space allowance per athlete = maximum capacity of 60 athletes
- 1:20 professional-to-athlete ratio = up to three-group capacity, with each practitioner supervising one group and up to 6 or 7 training stations (or 2,000 ft² area)
- ≤ 3 athletes per barbell or training station = equipment capacity of 60 athletes (if distributed between platforms, power stations, and plyometric stations)

Results

Here is an example facility schedule (**boldface** indicates in-season teams).

Keep in mind that each time the fall, winter, or spring sports' in-season phases begin or end, you may have to adjust the facility schedule. As a result, a variety of schedules for the facility may be in place during the year.

TABLE 8.2 Squad size

Sport	Squad size (Men)	Squad size (Women)
Baseball	31	—
Basketball	16	14
Cross-country	13	13
Football	96	—
Golf	10	8
Soccer	26	23
Softball	—	18
Tennis	10	10
Track & field	32	28
Volleyball	—	14
Total athletes	234	128

ACKNOWLEDGMENTS

The author wishes to thank Steven Plisk and N. Travis Triplett, the first two authors respectively of this chapter in editions one and two of this book, and the source for the material presented within.

REFERENCES

1. Kraemer WJ, Dziados J. Medical aspects and administrative concerns in strength training. In: Kraemer WJ, Häkkinen K, eds. *Strength Training for Sport*. Oxford, UK: Blackwell Science, 2002:163–175.
2. Greenwood M, Greenwood L. Facility organization and risk management. In: Baechle TR, Earle RW, eds. *National Strength and Conditioning Association. Essentials of Strength Training and Conditioning*. 3rd ed. Champaign, IL: Human Kinetics, 2008:543–568.
3. Kroll B. Structural and functional considerations in designing the facility: part I. *NSCA Journal* 1991; 13(1):51–58.
4. Morrissey MC, Harman EA, Johnson MJ. Resistance training modes: specificity and effectiveness. *Med Sci Sports Exerc* 1995; 27(5):648–660.
5. Nosse LJ, Hunter GR. Free weights: a review supporting their use in rehabilitation. *Athletic Training* 1985; 20(4):206–209.
6. Stone MH, Borden RA. Modes and methods of resistance training. *Strength Cond* 1997; 19(4):18–24.
7. Stone M, Plisk S, Collins D. Training principles: evaluation of modes and methods of resistance training-a coaching perspective. *Sports Biomechanics* 2002; 1(1):79–103.
8. Armitage-Johnson S. Providing a safe training environment: part II. *Strength Cond* 1994; 16(2):34.
9. Baley JA, Matthews DL. *Law and Liability in Athletics, Physical Education and Recreation*. Boston, MA: Allyn & Bacon, 1984.
10. Eickhoff-Shemek J. Standards of practice. In: Cotten D, Wilde J, Wlohan J, eds. *Law for Recreation and Sport Managers*, 2nd ed. Dubuque, IA: Kendall/Hunt Publishing, 2001:293–302.
11. Halling DH. Liability considerations of the strength and conditioning specialist. *NSCA J* 1990; 12(5):57–60.

12. **Halling DH.** Legal terminology for the strength and conditioning specialist. *NSCA J* 1991; 13(4):59–61.

13. **Herbert DL.** Supervision for strength and conditioning activities. *Strength Cond* 1994; 16(2):32–33.

14. **National Strength and Conditioning Association.** *Strength and Conditioning Professional Standards and Guidelines.* Colorado Springs, CO: National Strength and Conditioning Association, 2009.

15. **Rabinoff MA.** Weight room litigation: what's it all about? *Strength Cond* 1994; 16(2):10–12.

16. **Balady GJ, Chaitman B, Driscoll D, et al.** American Heart Association and American College of Sports Medicine. Recommendations for cardiovascular screening, staffing and emergency policies at health/fitness facilities. *Circulation* 1998; 97(22):2283–2293; *Med Sci Sports Exerc* 1998; 30(6):1009–1018.

17. **Tharrett SJ, Peterson JA, eds.,** for the American College of Sports Medicine. *ACSM's Health/Fitness Facility Standards and Guidelines*, 2nd ed. Champaign IL: Human Kinetics, 1997.

18. **Maron BJ, Thompson PD, Puffer JC, et al.** American Heart Association. Cardiovascular pre-participation screening of competitive athletes. *Circulation* 1996; 94(4):850–856; *Med Sci Sports Exerc* 1996; 28(12):1445–1452.

19. **American Society for Testing and Materials.** *ASTM Standard Consumer Safety Specification for Stationary Exercise Bicycles: Designation F12508–9.* West Conshohocken, PA: ASTM, 1989.

20. **American Society for Testing and Materials.** *ASTM Standard Specification for Fitness Equipment and Fitness Facility Safety Signage and Labels: Designation F17499–6.* West Conshohocken, PA: ASTM, 1996.

21. **Eickhoff-Shemek J.** Distinguishing protective legal documents. *ACSM Health and Fitness Journal* 2001; 5(3):27–29.

22. **Eickhoff-Shemek J, Deja K.** Four steps to minimize legal liability in exercise programs. *ACSM Health and Fitness Journal* 2000; 4(4):3–18.

23. **Head GL, Horn S.** *Essentials of Risk Management, vol. I*, 3rd ed. Malvern, PA: Insurance Institute of America, 1995.

24. **Pre-participation Physical Evaluation Task Force.** American Academy of Family Physicians, American Academy of Pediatrics, American Medical Society for Sports Medicine, American Orthopaedic Society for Sports Medicine and American Osteopathic Academy of Sports Medicine. *Pre-participation Physical Evaluation*, 2nd ed. New York: McGraw-Hill, 1996.

25. **Maron BJ, Thompson PD, Puffer JC, et al.** American Heart Association. Cardiovascular pre-participation screening of competitive athletes: addendum. *Circulation* 1998; 97(22): 2294.

26. **NSCA Certification Commission.** *Certified Strength and Conditioning Specialist (CSCS) Examination Content Description.* Lincoln, NE: NSCA Certification Commission, 2000.

27. **Katzenbach JR, Smith DK.** *The Wisdom of Teams.* Boston, MA: Harvard Business School, 1993.

28. **Katzenbach JR, Beckett F, Dichter S, et al.** *Real Change Leaders.* New York: Times Books/Random House, 1995:217–224.

29. **Jones CS, Christensen C, Young M.** Weight training injury trends: a 20-year survey. *Physician and Sportsmedicine* 2000; 28(7):61–72.

30. **Reeves RK, Laskowski ER, Smith J.** Weight training injuries: part 1. Diagnosing and managing acute conditions. *Physician and Sportsmedicine* 1998; 26(2):67–96.

31. **Reeves RK, Laskowski ER, Smith J.** Weight training injuries: part 2. Diagnosing and managing chronic conditions. *Physician and Sportsmedicine* 1998; 26(3):54–63.

32. **Hamill BP.** Relative safety of weightlifting and weight training. *J Strength Cond Res* 1994; 8(1):53–57.

33. **Stone MH, Fry AC, Ritchie M, et al.** Injury potential and safety aspects of weightlifting movements. *Strength Cond* 1994; 16(3):15–21.

34. **Morris GA.** Supervision-an asset to the weight room? *Strength Cond* 1994; 16(2):14–18.

35. **Rabinoff MA.** 32 reasons for the strength, conditioning, and exercise professional to understand the litigation process. *Strength Cond* 1994; 16(2):20–25.

36. **Bucher CA, Krotee ML.** *Management of Physical Education and Sport.* 11th ed. New York: McGraw-Hill, 1998.

37. **Armitage-Johnson S.** Providing a safe training environment: part I. *Strength Cond* 1994; 16(1):64–65.

38. **Herbert DL, Herbert WG.** *Legal Aspects of Preventive, Rehabilitative and Recreational Exercise Programs*, 3rd ed. Canton, OH: PRC Publishing, 1993.

39. Hillmann A, Pearson DR. Supervision: the key to strength training success. *Strength Cond* 1995; 17(5):67–71.

40. Kroll B. Liability considerations for strength training facilities. *Strength Cond* 1995; 17(6): 16–17.

41. Jones L. *USWF Coaching Accreditation Course: Club Coach Manual*. Colorado Springs, CO: U.S. Weightlifting Federation, 1991.

42. Anderson JC, Courson RW, Kleiner DM, et al. National Athletic Trainers' Association Position Statement: Emergency Planning in Athletics. *Journal of Athletic Training* 2002; 37(1):99–104.

43. Schluep C, Klossner DA, eds. National Collegiate Athletic Association. *2003–04 NCAA Sports Medicine Handbook*, 16th ed. Indianapolis, IN: NCAA, 2003.

44. Centers for Disease Control and Prevention/ U.S. Department of Health and Human Services. *Perspectives in disease prevention and health promotion update: universal precautions for prevention of transmission of human immunodeficiency virus, hepatitis B virus, and other bloodborne pathogens in health-care settings.* MMWR 1988; 37(24):377–388.

45. Occupational Safety and Health Administration. U.S. Department of Labor. *OSHA Regulations (Standards-29 CFR) 1910.1030: Blood-Borne Pathogens.* Washington, DC: OSHA, 1996.

46. Cotten DJ, Cotten MB. *Legal Aspects of Waivers in Sport, Recreation and Fitness Activities*. Canton, OH: PRC Publishing, 1997.

47. Epley B, Taylor, J. Developing a policies and procedures manual. In: Baechle TR, Earle RW, eds. National Strength and Conditioning Association. *Essentials of Strength Training and Conditioning*. 3rd ed. Champaign, IL: Human Kinetics, 2008:569–588.

48. Herbert DL. A good reason for keeping records. *Strength Cond* 1994; 16(3):64.

49. Faigenbaum AD, Kraemer WJ, Cahill B, et al. National Strength and Conditioning Association. Youth resistance training: position statement paper and literature review. *Strength Cond* 1996; 18(6):62–75.

50. Faigenbaum AD, Micheli LJ. *Current Comment from the American College of Sports Medicine: Youth Strength Training*. Indianapolis, IN: American College of Sports Medicine, 1998.

Contents

CHAPTER 9

WARM-UP AND FLEXIBILITY

Duane V. Knudson

OBJECTIVES

After reading this chapter, you will be able to:

- Explain the difference between warm-up and stretching and the purpose of each.
- Identify the different warm-ups based on individual needs.
- Define and explain the term flexibility.
- Recall the ways to measure flexibility and understand the basic advantages and disadvantages of each.
- Describe ways to increase flexibility by using various stretches and understand the benefits and limitations of increased ROM.
- Design an appropriate and recommended exercise prescription for stretching.

KEY TERMS

Active warm-up	Hypermobility	Static stretching
Ankylosis	Hysteresis	Stiffness
Ballistic stretching	Mechanical strength	Stress relaxation
Dynamic stretching	Muscle spindles	Thixotropy
Elasticity	Passive stretching	Viscoelastic
Flexibility	Passive warm-up	Warm-up
Golgi tendon organs	Static flexibility	

INTRODUCTION

Athletes looking to improve sport performance or lengthen their athletic careers by reducing the risk of injury – as well as the exercising public – often focus on warm-up and flexibility routines in their training. Considerable research has been conducted on both issues, and with a rapid expansion in the number of studies in the last several decades a new picture is emerging on these important fitness issues. The consensus of the current research is supportive of performance and injury-prevention beliefs related to warm-up. Traditional hypotheses about flexibility and stretching, however, are changing. This chapter summarizes what is known about the performance and injury-prevention benefits of warm-up and flexibility. These two important fitness concepts have complex relationships to performance and the risk of musculoskeletal injury that influence the strength and conditioning professional. The chapter concludes with general recommendations for prescribing stretching exercises and programs.

WARM-UP

It is important to realize that warm-up and stretching are two different activities. Warm-up is designed to elevate core body temperature and stretching is primarily performed to increase the range of motion (ROM) at a joint or group of joints. It is well accepted that generalized warm-up movements are important to maximizing sport performance and reducing injury risk in physical activity. **Warm-up** consists of active or passive warming of body tissues in preparation for physical activity. **Active warm-up** consists of low-intensity movements that are effective in elevating body temperature, warming tissue, and producing a variety of improvements in physiological function. **Passive warm-up** includes external heat sources like heating pads, whirlpools, or ultrasound. Prior to vigorous exertion, athletes should perform several minutes of general body movements (general warm-up) of progressively increasing intensity. These movements should emulate the actual movements of the sport or exercise to follow. Submaximal intensity movements specific to the sport or activity of interest are often included in the final phase warm-up.

Warm-up benefits performance through thermal, neuromuscular, and psychological effects. In some people, warm-up may also decrease the occurrence of dangerous cardiac responses from sudden strenuous exercise. Active warm-up activities mobilize metabolic resources and increase tissue temperature. Much of the benefit of warm-up

comes from the increased body temperature. Moderate-intensity active warm-up (general movements) and passive warm-up (e.g., diathermy, heating pads, whirlpool) can increase muscular performance by between 3% and 9% (10,11). Large-muscle-group motor tasks generally benefit from warm-up more than fine motor tasks.

Another reason for warm-up is to prepare the tissues for the greater stresses of vigorous physical activity and thus to lower the risk of muscle-tendon injury. Biomechanical evidence supports this "injury-protective" hypothesis, since warmed-up muscle in animal models has been found to elongate more, absorbing more energy before failure compared to no warm-up. This, combined with prospective studies of warm-up, supports the theory that general warm-up prior to vigorous activity may decrease the risk of musculotendinous injury compared to no warm-up. More direct evidence of this relationship would be helpful (18), but it is not ethically possible to design studies that put subjects at risk of injury.

> Warm-up activities are important to prepare the body for vigorous physical activity because they increase performance and may decrease the risk of muscular injury.

Athletes and other exercisers should therefore warm-up prior to competition, practice, and physical conditioning. Recommendations for effective warm-up routines vary depending on the nature and duration of the exercise to be performed. In general, warm-up routines should use general, whole-body movements up to 40% to 60% of aerobic capacity and gradually increasing intensity, focusing on the muscles and joints to be used in training or competition for five to ten minutes followed by five minutes of recovery (11). The American College of Sports Medicine recommends five to ten minutes of progressive, light to moderate cardiorespiratory and muscular endurance activities in warm-up (3) and a recent review describes < 15 minutes of aerobic activity followed by four to five minutes of specific warm-up and transition (52). There has also been initial work on the gradual decline of warm-up performance enhancements with rest (1,19), consequently some teams provide passive and rewarm-up to try and maintain performance benefits for inactive athletes (15,52).

Dynamic movements and muscular contractions commonly used in active warm-up create decreases in passive tension (56,64) and increases in ROM as large as or larger than those due to **passive stretching** (26,57). Recent research to optimize dynamic warm-up protocols have focused on manipulating movements and additional resistance to take advantage of contraction history-dependent neuromuscular factors like stretch-shortening cycles and post-activation potentiation (6,7,51,65,66,75), as well as warm-ups for individual athletes (49). Much more work is necessary to equate dosages for good comparisons for evidence-based recommendations, but in the future there may be a consensus of specific warm-up protocols for different athletes, movements, and activities.

Recent active warm-up protocols have been sometimes called **dynamic stretching**. This terminology should be avoided because it creates confusion with well-defined terms like **ballistic stretching** and **static stretching** that are not beneficial as warm-up activities. Static stretching currently is not recommended during most warm-up routines (31,44). The reasons for this change from traditional practice are explored in the following sections on flexibility and stretching.

> Warm-up and stretching are not synonymous, but both do belong in a strength and conditioning program. Warming up elevates core temperature and blood to the working muscles. Optimal warm-up protocols for specific activities have yet to be established; however, general warm-up of whole body movements beginning at a low intensity that progressively increases over time, followed by specific warm-up movements that mimic the upcoming sport or activity is recommended.

FLEXIBILITY

Flexibility is an important component of fitness and physical performance. Inconsistent use of terminology related to the term *flexibility*

by a variety of health and exercise science professionals has led to confusion. There is a distinct difference between flexibility and joint laxity. **Flexibility** is "the intrinsic property of body tissues which determines the range of motion achievable without injury at a joint or series of joints" (25). The ability to move a joint through an ROM without causing injury usually refers to the major anatomical rotations at joints rather than the joint laxity or accessory motion tests that orthopedists, physical therapists, and athletic trainers often evaluate to test joint and/or ligament integrity. Flexibility can be measured a variety of ways, and several variables of interest have emerged.

One variable is the common clinical measure of the limits or maximum ROM referred to as **static flexibility**. This is estimated by linear or angular measurements of the limits of motion in a joint or joint complex. For example, it might be of clinical interest to know the static flexibility of areas of the body that tend to lose ROM with inactivity, like the lower (lumbar region) back or hamstring muscle group. Many professionals employ a sit-and-reach test (Figure 9.1), using a linear measurement that provides a good field measure of hamstring static flexibility. These tests are limited by the rise in passive tension as the muscle and connective tissue are stretched.

Figure 9.1 Since its development in the 1950s, the sit-and-reach test and several variations have become popular field tests of hamstring static flexibility.

Tests of static flexibility, although easy to administer, have several limitations. A major weakness of these tests is that the measures obtained are subjective and largely related to the subject's stretch tolerance (46), as well as the way in which the endpoint of the ROM is determined. Accurate measurements also depend on strict adherence to testing methodology. Variations in instruments, body positioning, instructions, or the protocol used all heavily influence results. Another problem is the variety of conditions in which the measurements are made. For example, physical therapy uses both active ROM (unassisted) and passive ROM (therapist-assisted) tests. The ROM achievable with the assistance of the tester (passive) is usually greater than that obtained with unassisted ROM. A great deal of information must be known about testing conditions to interpret data on static flexibility.

In a research setting, we can measure mechanical properties of the muscle groups, fibers, and connective tissue components of some muscles in addition to ROM. Research laboratory measurements of flexibility using computerized dynamometers, ultrasound, and imaging have allowed the measurement of new biomechanical variables related to the mechanical properties of muscle and tendon. Two of these variables that may be related to performance and injury risk are stiffness and hysteresis. These terms are used in physics to describe properties of materials. Since the human body is composed of living materials that react to external forces in a similar fashion, the terms are also applicable to the human body.

The term **stiffness**, sometimes referred to as dynamic flexibility, refers to how quickly tissue resistance rises during a movement requiring the muscle-tendon unit to stretch. With passive stretching, the stiffness of the muscle-tendon unit measures how quickly the passive tension rises right before damage occurs. Studies show that the rise in tissue resistance (stiffness) shares only about 44% to 66% of common variance with static flexibility (46,54). Therefore, these variables are related but probably represent different functional properties of the musculature.

One problem in discussing the stiffness of muscles and tendons is the difference in the scientific and lay meaning of *stiffness* and *elasticity*. In biomechanics, stiffness and **elasticity** are synonymous, so a muscle with a quick rise in tension during stretch has the potential to recover rapidly when the stretch is released, returning more stored energy than a compliant muscle. This conflicts with the colloquial meaning of the term *elasticity*, which some people relate to a low resistance to elongation.

Figure 9.2 illustrates a schematic of a torque-angle curve of the elongation phase of repeated passive stretches of a muscle group. These angular variables approximate well the load-deformation (linear) curve of the muscle and provide an *in vivo* (in the living animal) functional estimate of the passive stiffness of muscle groups (43). Scientists normally use linear measurements of load and deformation to define the mechanical properties of materials. Note in Figure 9.2 the torque, and therefore the tension in the muscle, rises in a complex (non-linear) fashion, slowly at first and then more rapidly.

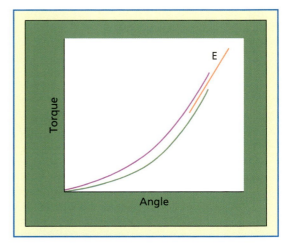

Figure 9.2 Schematic of a torque-joint angle plot during repeated passive stretches of a muscle group. Stress relaxation makes the passive torque at a given joint angle in subsequent stretches (green line) less than in the first stretch (purple line). The stiffness (E) of the muscle group in these stretches (slope), however, is not different.

Also note that the stiffness (E) of the muscle group does not change with repeated static stretching. Sometimes the initial response of tissues (short-range stiffness) is of interest, so the slope of the curve early in the range of motion is used, but the term stiffness is usually reserved for the rise in tension late in a stretch, just before permanent damage. Short-range stiffness is that tightness in muscles when sitting in a fixed position for a long time, which is quickly reduced with just a few movements. More on the immediate and long-term biomechanical responses to stretching are covered later in this chapter.

Biological tissues have other complex behaviors that influence their function. The muscle-tendon unit resistance to stretch is **viscoelastic**. This means that tension developed during a stretch depends both on the amount of deformation and the rate of deformation (timing). A slow stretch of muscle will result in lower tension in the muscle and tendon for a particular joint angle compared to a fast stretch. A faster stretch would have a similar load-deformation shape curve, but will have a higher stiffness because of viscoelasticity.

Although the application of materials science to the human body may seem complex, it is important to realize that the human body is a living material that responds to stress in a predictable manner. Materials science defines stiffness as the slope of the stress-strain curve in the elastic (linear) region, which is how quickly the tension rises late in elongation before the elastic limit. The elastic limit is the point on the graph depicting the lengthening of the muscle-tendon unit just before the material begins to fail (the beginning of permanent damage). Beyond the elastic limit is the plastic region, so called because this is where the deformation and damage are not immediately recoverable in materials. Fortunately, normal vigorous physical activity rarely gets near the elastic limit for muscles or tendons and small stretches near the elastic limit may be repaired by the body if it is given enough rest. An unusually severe or unexpected elongation can, however, cause rupture or complete failure of the tissue. Materials scientists call the maximum force or energy absorbed before complete failure the **mechanical strength** of the material.

When a muscle is stretched, but not beyond its elastic limit, it will return to resting length and recover some of the energy stored in it as it was stretched. Some of the energy, however, is lost as heat. The energy lost in the return to normal length from a deformed material is termed **hysteresis**. This represents the energy lost and can be visualized as the area (loop) between the loading (elongation) and unloading (restitution) phases in Figure 9.3. Figure 9.3 illustrates a schematic of a torque-angle curve of the elongation phase (purple line) and the restitution phase (blue line) of a static stretch.

From Figure 9.3, note that in static stretching exercises, about 40% to 50% of the energy stored in the stretch is lost as the muscle returns to normal length (40). Much of this energy loss is in the contractile and connective tissue components within the muscle. To the contrary, studies of long tendons in normal vigorous physical activity show that they recover most (80% to 90%) of the energy stored in them in the

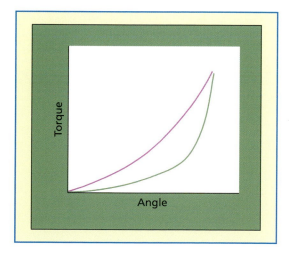

Figure 9.3 Schematic of a torque-joint angle plot of the elongation (purple) and restitution (green) phases of a passive stretch of a muscle group. The energy lost (hysteresis) is the area of the loop between the loading and unloading phases.

quick stretch-shortening actions common in movement (36).

Measuring energy or other biomechanical variables may be better for examining the effect of stretching on muscle performance, as opposed to stiffness or ROM, because muscle tissue often does not reach the elastic region of the stress/strain curve in typical hamstring stretches (43). Stretching and other passive movement can have a greater effect on hysteresis than on the stiffness of muscle. Research on the biomechanical effects of warm-up movements and stretching are important because it could result in practical applications in improving muscular performance.

> The ability to move the joints of the body freely without injury is known as flexibility, and several mechanical properties and variables can be used to document important aspects of flexibility.

Normal static flexibility

The wealth of research on static flexibility measurements provides a general picture of what is normal static flexibility for most joints and populations. Normal static flexibility is the typical joint movement allowed between two extremes (Figure 9.4): ankylosis and hypermobility. **Ankylosis** is pathological loss of ROM, whereas **hypermobility** is excessive ROM. Static flexibility is not a whole-body characteristic but, like fitness, is specific to joints and directions of movement. People may tend to have low static flexibility in one part of the body and normal or high flexibility in another. It is also clear that, in general, females have greater static flexibility than males (22), and some of these differences are related to anthropometric differences.

Fitness professionals can access data on normal ranges of static flexibility for most joints from several professional sources (see online references). Several reviews of flexibility have been published (see online references) and provide more information on static flexibility. It is unclear, however, whether an "optimal" level of static flexibility for muscle groups or areas of the body exists. If this is the case, it is likely that different sports would require different optimal levels of static flexibility. Future research studies should be designed to focus on determining "normative" static ranges of motion at joints in athletes participating in specific sports, as well as documenting anomalies in athletes and active people who are outside of this normative range. It is too early to make a definitive

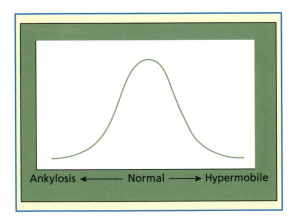

Figure 9.4 Schematic of a continuum of static flexibility. There is considerable research documenting the normal limits of static flexibility but little prospective research that links specific levels of static flexibility to increased risk of injury at either extreme.

Figure 9.5 Repetitive work or body positions (like wearing high heels) can create tight muscles and decrease ankle static flexibility.

statement, but it is possible that an athlete or active person whose muscles are too tight is more prone to *muscle* injuries and that one whose muscles are too loose is more prone to *joint* injuries as well as decreased performance in maximal effort activities.

Common deviations from normal static flexibility are present in many joint(s). Some people lose ROM from physical inactivity. People may also lose static flexibility with aging, from workplace or sport-specific positions, and/or repetitive movements. For example, the repetitive motion in several sports with overhead throwing patterns (baseball, tennis, etc.) without specific stretching intervention can result in glenohumeral internal rotation deficit (GIRD). Persistent wearing of high heels can decrease ankle dorsiflexion ROM (Figure 9.5).

> Several resources provide normative data on the typical static flexibility of most major joints of the body, but current research does not identify an optimal level of static flexibility.

Flexibility and injury risk

The literature on clinical and basic science provides a different view of the role of flexibility in injury risk and performance than what is commonly believed by many people, athletes, and coaches. What appears to be desirable, based on data on the incidence of muscle-tendon injuries, is to avoid the extremes in static flexibility. Athletes and exercisers at both extremes of static flexibility may be at a higher risk for musculoskeletal injuries (27,30). This section focuses on the association between flexibility and injury risk: the sections on stretching, further on, discuss the association between stretching and changes in muscular performance and injury risk.

Low levels of hamstring flexibility have been related to a higher risk of muscular injury in soccer (76). The common belief that greater static flexibility will always decrease the risk of muscular injury, however, appears not to be valid. This may be explained by the stability-mobility paradox. The mechanical stability and ROM at a joint or joints are inversely related. It is possible that as static flexibility increases beyond the normal range, the potential benefits of greater motion and less tissue resistance are offset by the greater instability of the joint. For example, static stretching and soccer play significantly increase knee joint laxity compared to controls (8). More research is needed to begin to define the ranges of motion for various joints, so that the best compromise of stability and mobility may be provided, along with a lower risk of injury.

A good example of the lack of an association between high levels of static flexibility and lower injury risk is provided by low back fitness testing. Although it seems logical that less flexible back or hamstring muscles would be related to the incidence of low back pain, little evidence supports this association. Despite a large body of the research, there is limited support (mixed results) for an association between lumbar/hamstring flexibility and the occurrence of low back pain. One of the largest prospective studies on this topic found no relationship between static flexibility and subsequent low back pain in adults. Therefore, the field tests of hamstring static flexibility commonly used in fitness test batteries may not be useful in predicting future low back injury.

People also commonly believe that less "stiff" muscles result in greater flexibility and a lower risk of injury. This belief is often based on a misunderstanding of stiffness and people's common experience of short-range stiffness. Unfortunately, there is still not adequate research on the association between muscle stiffness and injury risk. Less stiff muscles may be less susceptible to muscle strain injury (74), but few studies have been conducted in this area (53). It appears that muscle with greater stiffness is more susceptible to eccentrically induced muscle damage. Currently, the evidence is insufficient to conclude that decreased muscular stiffness will provide an injury-protective benefit. Combined with the unclear nature of the exact levels of static flexibility that decrease injury risk, this means that strength and conditioning professionals must educate athletes on the complexity of flexibility and injury risk.

REAL-WORLD APPLICATION

The stability-mobility paradox

Static flexibility is like exercise in that more is not always better. Joint motion (mobility) is inversely proportional to the stability of the joint. Decreasing muscle passive tension around a joint increases the joint's ROM but also makes it easier for the joint to be pulled out of normal position. This presents the fitness professional with a paradox. What is the right amount of static flexibility? How much motion is necessary for normal and safe movement without adversely affecting the joint or ligaments? It is not possible to give universal or optimal answers to these questions. The amount of motion depends on the joint, the requirements of the sport/activity a person engages in, and other factors. Given that the lowest injury rates seem to correspond to normal flexibility and higher injury rates with the extremes in flexibility (inflexible and hypermobile), maintenance of normal or moderate amounts of static flexibility should be the goal for most people. Unless a person participates in an activity requiring extreme flexibility (dance, gymnastics, diving), most exercise prescriptions should focus on maintaining normal levels of static flexibility.

> A complex relationship exists between static flexibility and risk of muscular injury. Higher injury rates seem to be related to the extremes (very flexible or very inflexible) of range of motion.

Assessing flexibility

Exercise prescriptions to modify flexibility should be based on valid measurements using standardized testing procedures. Static flexibility tests are based on both linear and angular measurements of the motion of a joint or group of joints. These tests can focus on single joints or compound movements of many body segments and joints.

Single-joint static flexibility tests are commonly used clinically in the medical professions; they often involve angular measurements (with goniometers or inclinometers) rather than linear measurements. Single-joint tests are considered better measurements of static flexibility than compound tests because they better isolate specific muscles and are less affected by anthropometric differences (13). The straight-leg-raise and active-knee-extension tests are the common hamstring flexibility tests used in physical therapy. The many variations of the sit-and-reach test are compound flexibility tests and are often validated with the straight leg raise or active knee extension.

Sit-and-reach scores are primarily associated with hamstring flexibility, but not with low back flexibility (50). Although the sit-and-reach test has been shown to be a moderately valid measure of hamstring flexibility which is only slightly affected by anthropometric variations, the prescriptive value of these measurements is limited. One study reported that 6% of children falsely passed and 12% falsely failed the sit-and-reach test relative to the straight-leg-raise test (13). If these data are consistent across all ages, athletes or clients failing the sit-and-reach field test should be retested with the straight-leg-raise or active-knee-extension test to make sure that they have limited hamstring static flexibility.

Current health-related norms for sit-and-reach or other static flexibility tests should be used only to identify individuals at the extremes who may be at higher risk for muscle injuries. Not enough data are available to provide specific static flexibility goals beyond the maintenance of normal flexibility. Fitness professionals must also remember that in measuring static flexibility, exacting attention to testing details is necessary. Static flexibility scores are subjective and highly dependent on the subject's tolerance of the high muscle tension (discomfort) during testing. The clinical measurement of dynamic flexibility variables like passive tension, stiffness, or hysteresis is not practical; it is limited to research settings because of problems related to expensive equipment, insufficient standardization, and the time needed.

DEVELOPMENT OF FLEXIBILITY

Normal levels of flexibility can be maintained by regular physical activity and through specific programs of stretching and strengthening exercises. Strength and conditioning professionals should assess a client's flexibility, and based on these data and the client's history, develop a program to improve flexibility. Although poor flexibility can be treated with a combination of stretching and strengthening exercises (4), this section focuses on general recommendations for stretching in mass exercise prescription. Regular stretching exercises are usually recommended for most people often because of their limited physical activity and also because regular participation in some activities is associated with sport-specific flexibility imbalances. In general, stretching recommendations should be limited to the maintenance of normal levels of static flexibility because of the complex nature of flexibility and the lack of data linking specific levels of flexibility to lower injury risk or better performance. This section concludes with recent evidence on the effect of stretching on muscular performance, which has implications for the typical placement of stretching in the training cycle.

Stretching exercises are usually classified into four types: passive, static, ballistic (dynamic), and proprioceptive neuromuscular facilitation, or PNF. Passive stretching uses an external force, usually another person, to stretch muscle groups (Figure 9.6). Static stretching involves a slow increase in muscle group length and holding the stretched position at that length for a short time (usually 15 to 30 seconds). Ballistic stretching traditionally has meant fast, momentum-assisted, and bouncing stretching movements. These stretches should be avoided because of the viscoelastic nature of muscle. For a given elongation, a fast stretch results in a higher force in the tissue and a greater risk of injury.

Figure 9.6 Passive stretching often uses external force from another person to produce a greater stretch of a muscle group.

Some refer to the active warm-up movements mentioned earlier as dynamic stretching. These "stretches" may be acceptable if they are performed in a slower manner than violent, ballistic stretching. Moderate intensity active warm-up/dynamic stretching creates muscle elongation without imposing high levels of force on the tissue. This is probably how regular physical activity and weight training can usually maintain normal levels of static flexibility.

The last group of stretching exercises focuses on PNF. PNF stretch routines use a specific series of movements and contractions to utilize neuromuscular reflexes to relax the muscles being stretched. PNF stretches can be performed with or without assistance. A simple PNF procedure is a "contract-relax" stretch where a person performs an isometric contraction of a muscle to be stretched, which is immediately followed by a static stretch of that muscle. This strategy takes advantage of the inhibitory effects of **Golgi tendon organs** as the muscle is slowly stretched. Assisted stretching procedures like PNF should be performed with care by trained subjects or sports medicine personnel. The practice of having athletes passively stretch partners should be used with caution until the athletes have been carefully trained in correct procedures and understand the risks of incorrect or high-force stretches.

TABLE 9.1 Stretching recommendations for group exercise prescription

Fitness variable	Recommendation
Frequency	At least three times per week, preferably daily and after moderate or vigorous physical activity
Intensity	Slowly elongate muscle and hold with low level of force to the person's perception of tightness without discomfort
Time	Up to 4 to 5 stretches held from 15 to 30 seconds. Stretch normally during the cool-down phase. Be sure to stretch only muscles that have been thoroughly warmed up from physical activity. Warning: stretching in the warm-up prior to physical activity may weaken muscles and decrease performance
Type	Static or PNF stretches for all major muscle groups

Source: Adapted with permission from Knudson D, Magnusson P, McHugh M. Current issues in flexibility fitness. *PCPFS Res Digest* 2000;3(10):1–8 (31).

> Increasing ROM takes time and can be achieved by using various methods of stretching: static, dynamic, and proprioceptive neuromuscular facilitation (PNF).

The recommendations for stretching procedures are based on reviews of the basic science studies of the viscoelastic response of muscle to stretching. These recommendations (Table 9.1) are designed for group exercise prescription with most persons (i.e., not hypermobile or with ankyloses). Static or PNF stretching should normally be performed at least three times per week, preferably daily and after moderate or vigorous physical activity (in the cool-down phase of training). Exacting technique in stretching is recommended to safely focus tension on a muscle group or groups without systematic stress on other joint stability structures (ligaments, joint capsules, cartilage). Some experts have hypothesized, based on functional anatomy, that some stretching exercises are contraindicated because of potentially dangerous ligament and tissue loading (39). While there is no prospective evidence of these injuries, it would be desirable for professionals to select alternative stretches than these contraindicated stretches.

Stretching programs should include up to 4 or 5 stretches for each major muscle group, with each stretch held for 15 to 30 seconds. The intensity (force) of each stretch should be minimized, slowly elongating and holding the stretched position just before the point of discomfort. Slow elongation of muscles creates less reflex contraction through the action of **muscle spindles**. These tissues sense muscle length and are responsible for the contraction of a stretched muscle (myotatic reflex). This reflex contraction is most sensitive to fast stretches, so slow muscle elongation in stretching exercises helps maintain relaxation in the muscle groups being stretched.

Static stretching will create a short-term increase in ROM and a decrease in passive tension in the muscle at a specific joint angle due to **stress relaxation**, which is the gradual decrease in stress (force per unit area) in a material stretched and held at a constant length. Most people can feel the decrease in passive tension in a muscle group held in a stretched position. This stress relaxation following stretching provides an immediate 10% to 30% decrease in passive tension (41,47,56), but the effect will have dissipated after about an hour (45). Holding stretches for 15 to 30 seconds is a good guideline, because most of the stress relaxation in passive stretches occurs in the first 20 seconds (40,55).

> Stretching to increase static flexibility in a muscle group should normally use 4 to 5 static stretches held for 15 to 30 seconds.

Stretching should normally be performed during the cool-down period because of four lines of evidence:

1 Warmed-up tissues are less likely to be injured.
2 The placement of stretching within the workout does not affect gains in static flexibility.
3 Stretching creates immediate decrements in muscle strength expression.
4 Stretching likely has no effect on the immediate risk of muscle tendon injury.

Programming static stretching during the cool-down period is also logical because stretching tends to relax or inhibit muscle activation (5,67). For example, static stretching is commonly used for the acute relief from muscle cramps or delayed-onset muscle soreness (DOMS). The former is indicated, but research on the latter indicates no effect of stretching before or after activity (70) on the DOMS that occurs after unaccustomed exercise. Static stretching routines in the cool-down period primarily serve to help maintain normal levels of static flexibility (23).

Q&A FROM THE FIELD

Our track-and-field athletes often want to stretch before their events. I know that flexibility is an important component of performance, but I have heard rumblings in the running community for the last few years that stretching before racing is a bad idea. Is it true that stretching prior to high-intensity track and field events is a bad idea? Will it have a negative effect on our athletes' performance?

Athletes stretch in the warm-up for track events because they believe that it decreases their risk of injury and improves their performance. Unfortunately, research has shown that this practice is probably not justified for most athletes. Unless an athlete has a major deficit in ROM, stretching prior to vigorous exertion decreases most forms of maximal muscular performance for about 30 minutes to an hour. In addition, stretching prior to vigorous activity has also been shown to have no acute effect on the risk of muscular injury. The most important thing a coach can do is teach athletes that proper warm-up is essential

for maximum performance and decreasing the risk of injury. Focus their precompetition routine around a progressive and specific active warm-up with movements related to their event. If there is a delay before competition, strive to use passive warming or re-warm-up to maintain preparation for intense activities. Most athletes with normal flexibility should perform their stretching routines after practice or competition.

Biomechanical effects of stretching

Stretching exercises are prescribed routinely to increase static flexibility. Considerable research has reported that stretch training can increase ROM (4), although much of this increase may be also due to stretch tolerance (16). Stretch tolerance is primarily an analgesic effect that allows a person to accept higher tensions associated with a greater stretch of a muscle group. What is also less well known is that these long-term training effects can be different than the short-term immediate effects (62). This section will summarize the short-term effects of stretching on the muscular performance variables like strength, stiffness, and hysteresis.

Passive stretching can create large tensile loads in the muscle, so it is possible to weaken and injure muscle with vigorous stretching programs. Stretching exercise is like any other training stimulus in that it results in temporary weakening before the body recovers and supercompensates for that activity. A 4% to 30% decrease in muscular performance following static or PNF stretching has been reported in over 100 studies in all kinds of people and fitness levels. This research on acute performance decrements from stretching are so extensive there have been several narrative and systematic reviews published recently (9,29,63).

Stretch-induced decrements in muscular performance appear to be equally related to neuromuscular inhibition and decreased contractile force and can last 30 to 60 minutes (17,45). The minimum dose of static stretching to create a physiologically meaningful decrease (5%) in strength is 20 to 30 seconds (32,63). Most stretching should be performed in the cool-down phase of training and usually avoided in the warm-up period for athletic competition. Only athletes who require extreme static flexibility for performance (dancers, gymnasts, divers) might need to stretch at the middle of a warm-up routine. Several studies have reported that stretch-induced weakness in warm-ups can be eliminated if followed up by additional dynamic warm-up activities (9). The logic of this strategy of a longer warm-up for no or lower performance benefits must be questioned unless the athletes test inflexible or they compete in high-flexibility activities.

> Stretching should normally be performed in the cool-down phase of conditioning because stretching before activity decreases muscular performance for about 30 minutes.

Stretching can create a short-term increase in ROM, but this improvement quickly (5 to 30 min) disappears (58,71). This greater static flexibility is a result of lower passive tension (stress relaxation) at equivalent joint angles and increased stretch tolerance. This lower passive tension and greater range of motion that people feel, however, is not the same as stiffness.

Studies of the immediate effect of stretching on muscle group stiffness have reported both no effects and small reductions (12,24,58,59,71). The lack of consensus may result from the use of different measurements and calculations of stiffness over different portions of the range of motion. Some researchers incorrectly defined stiffness as the change in tension over the change in angle at the beginning of the load-deformation curve, not as the true mechanical stiffness (the slope in linear region) of the tissue near the end of the tolerable ROM. If stretching can create a decrease in muscle stiffness, the effect is short (15 to 20 minutes) and it is unclear where the change resides (58,71) or how it may affect performance. Because we do not clearly know the immediate effects of stretching on muscle stiffness, strength and conditioning professionals should instruct athletes and other exercisers that the primary benefits of stretching are maintenance of ROM and a decrease in the passive tension of the muscles at similar joint angles.

While the evidence is mixed that static stretching immediately affects muscle stiffness, passive motion exercise can create significant reductions in muscle stiffness (56). Cyclic movements that create a slow stretch of muscle groups, just like the active warm-up described earlier, also decrease the energy lost (hysteresis) in subsequent stretches (42). Static stretching has also been observed to significantly reduce hysteresis (34,35,42). More research on muscle hysteresis is needed, but currently it appears that active or passive movement is an effective strategy to make muscles more compliant and recover more energy following a stretch. These properties likely have immediate benefits to many kinds of performance and may help reduce the risk of injury.

The relationship between stretching performance is complex for many reasons. Stretch training can have different effects on the various fiber and connective tissue components of the muscle-tendon complex (28,34,48,58,59). Second, muscles have history-dependent or a **thixotropic** response, where differences in previous muscle status (rest, concentric, active, or passive stretch) have an immediate effect on the mechanical response of subsequent muscle actions. Overall performance of a multi-segment biomechanical system will be even more difficult to predict because of the different kinds of performance variables, as well as the interaction of technique, neuromuscular, muscle, and tendon effects. For example, lower levels of static flexibility have been associated with better running economy (14,21); however, less stiff musculature may be more effective in utilizing elastic energy in stretch-shortening cycle movements (37,38,68,72,73). It is likely that the effects of stretching and flexibility on muscular performance are complex, both muscle (33) and activity-specific (20). Considerable future research is needed to outline the best matching of the immediate and training effects of stretching to the many kinds of muscular performance in sport and exercise.

Prophylactic effects of stretching

The other traditional rationale for prescribing preactivity stretching is a hypothesized reduction in the risk of injury. The logic was that if there were greater static flexibility from stretching, the chance that stretching the muscle beyond this point might lead to injury would be reduced. In the case of flexibility, this logic has not been supported by scientific evidence. Muscle strains (pulls) occur more often in eccentric muscle actions rather than passive elongation.

The larger and better-designed prospective studies have shown little or no effect of stretching on injury rate (2,60,61,69). The studies with larger samples and better controls (60,61) and the consensus of the research (9) support the conclusion that flexibility and stretching may be unrelated to injury risk. Currently the data are insufficient to support the common prescription of stretching programs to modify flexibility based on the hypothesis of reducing the risk of muscle injury. Much more research on the effects of stretching and the associations between various flexibility levels and injury rates are needed before specific guidelines on stretching will be available.

> Research has not confirmed the belief that stretching decreases the risk of muscular injury, so general stretching prior to physical activity probably confers no protective effect.

SUMMARY

Both active and passive warm-up are common preparatory activities before exercise and athletic competition. Several lines of research have supported the beneficial effects of warm-up on improving performance and reducing injury risk. Typical warm-up should consist of general and future activity-specific movements of gradually increasing intensity. The intensity of warm-up should be moderate (up to 40% to 60% of aerobic capacity) and sustained (5 to 10 minutes) to increase the tissue temperature.

Flexibility is an important property of the musculoskeletal system that determines the ROM and resistance to motion at a joint or group of joints. This property can be examined by measuring the limits of the achievable motion (static flexibility) or several other biomechanical variables of passively stretched muscle group. Normal ranges of static flexibility are well documented for most joints through a variety of tests. There is some evidence that extremes in static flexibility (top or bottom 20% of the distribution) may be associated with a higher incidence of muscle injury. Sport science research and prospective studies of flexibility and stretching indicate that stretching should not normally be performed in warm-ups. Stretching prior to physical activity decreases muscular performance and does not reduce the risk of musculoskeletal injury. Currently, little scientific evidence is available on which to base precise, individualized prescriptions of stretching development beyond the maintenance of normal levels of static flexibility. Static or PNF stretching should normally be performed during the cool-down phase of physical activity. Stretches should slowly elongate and hold muscles with low levels of force for 15 to 30 seconds. Four to five stretches per muscle group or area of the body are usually recommended. Athletes with poor flexibility or in sports that demand extreme flexibility may stretch in the warm-up if they conclude the warm-up sport-specific active muscle actions. Future research on history-dependent properties and muscle mechanical variables may identify more specific ways to optimize warm-up and stretching for specific activities.

MAXING OUT

1 Dancer – A dancer/cheerleader requests your help in increasing hip flexion and abduction ROM to facilitate the split position for a variety of stunts. What stretching program would you recommend? Design a ten-week progressive flexibility program to improve hip flexion and abduction ROM to improve the ability of the cheerleader to perform in the split position.

2 Personal training client – A manager seeks relief from neck and shoulder pain from long days on an office computer. What stretching and strengthening exercises would you recommend? Design a progressive ten-week stretching and strengthening program for your client

3 Athlete – An athlete who has undergone acute rehab wants to return to play and increase plantarflexion ROM following an ankle sprain. What assessments would you use to document progress and what stretching program would you utilize?

CASE EXAMPLE

Postmatch flexibility routine in tennis

Background

You are a strength coach working with the university medical staff and a 20-year-old male collegiate tennis player. The player has limited internal shoulder rotation ROM in the dominant shoulder, which is common in repetitive overarm sports like tennis.

Recommendations/considerations

Following matches, practice, and conditioning sessions, the cool-down phase will consist of a static stretching routine. This will be a typical whole-body routine but will focus extra stretching on sport-specific imbalances common in tennis players: reduced shoulder internal rotation and flexibility of the lower back and hamstrings.

Implementation

Three 20-second wrist flexor and extensor stretches.
Four 20-second standing pectoralis major stretches
Four 20-second shoulder internal rotation stretches

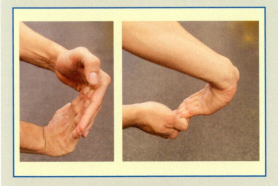

Figure 9.7 Wrist flexor and extensor stretches.

Figure 9.8 Standing pectoralis major stretch.

Four 20-second knees to chest low back stretches
Three 20-second trunk twists both directions

Figure 9.9 Shoulder internal rotation stretch.

Figure 9.10 Knees to chest low back stretch.

Three 20-second butterfly hip internal rotator stretches
Four 20-second seated hamstring stretches

Figure 9.11 Butterfly hip internal rotators stretch.

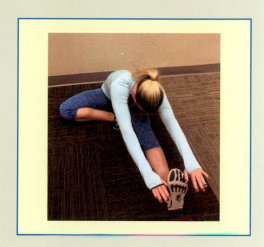

Figure 9.12 Seated hamstring stretch.

Three 20-second seated calf stretches
Three 20-second seated dorsiflexor stretches

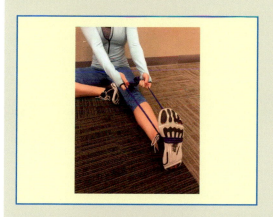

Figure 9.13 Seated calf stretch.

Figure 9.14 Seated dorsiflexor stretch.

Results

Results before and after (a ten-week flexibility program) indicate an improvement in ROM over the period of the training program in specific movements. Tests included shoulder internal rotation ROM, hip flexion ROM, and sit-and-reach.

Shoulder internal rotation ROM

Initial: dominant, 33°; nondominant, 66°.

(continued)

(continued)

After training: dominant, 48°; nondominant, 70°.

As is typical with overhead throwing athletes, shoulder internal rotation was decreased in the dominant extremity. The prescribed program caused a change in the ROM of the dominant arm in internal rotation in the direction of normal. Because of the demands of the sport, it is unlikely that the dominant arm would ever reach the same ROM as the nondominant arm.

Hip flexion ROM with knee extended

Initial: dominant, 40°; nondominant, 39°.

After training: dominant, 51°; nondominant 50°.

In hip flexion, a dominant-to-nondominant difference is not as pronounced as it is in the upper extremity. Both extremities demonstrated a small increase in ROM related to hamstring extensibility from the prescribed flexibility program.

Sit-and-reach flexibility

Initial: + 1 cm

After training: + 3 cm

The flexibility program resulted in a slight increase in ROM in trunk flexion. These increases in ROM related to hamstrings extensibility could, in theory, maintain this athlete in a lower injury risk to hamstring and lower back compared to players with reduced or excessive flexibility. These tests support the efficacy of the training program and should be maintained and monitored in this athlete.

REFERENCES

1. Alberti G, Annoni M, Ongaro L, et al. Athletic performance decreases in young basketball players after sitting. *Int J Sports Sci Coach* 2014; 9:975–984.

2. Amako M, Oda T, Masuoka K, et al. Effect of static stretching on prevention of injuries for military recruits. *Mil Med* 2003; 168:442–446.

3. American College of Sports Medicine. *ACSM's Guidelines for Exercise Testing and Prescription*, 10th ed. Philadelphia, PA: Lippincott Williams & Wilkins, 2017.

4. Aquino CF, Fonseca ST, Goncalves GGP, Silva PLP, Ocarino JM, Mancini MC. Stretching versus strength training in lengthened position in subjects with tight hamstring muscles: a randomized controlled trial. *Man Ther* 2010; 15:26–31.

5. Avela J, Kyrolainen H, Komi PV. Altered reflex sensitivity after repeated and prolonged passive muscle stretching. *J Appl Physiol* 1999; 86:1283–1291.

6. Ayala F, Moreno-Perez V, Vera-Garcia FJ, et al. Acute and time-course effects of traditional and dynamic warm-up routines in young elite junior tennis players. *PLoS ONE* 2016; 11(4), e0152790. doi:10.1371/journalpone.0152790.

7. Barnes KR, Hopkins WG, McGuigan MR, Kilding AE. Warm-up with a weighted vest improves running performance via leg stiffness and running economy. *J Sci Med Sport* 2015; 18:103–108.

8. Baumgart C, Gokeler A, Donath L, et al. Effects of static stretching and playing soccer on knee laxity. *Clin J Sports Med* 2015; 25:541–545.

9. Behm DG, Blazevich AJ, Kay, AD, McHugh M. Acute effects of muscle stretching on physical performance, range of motion, and injury incidence in health active individuals: A systematic review. *Appl Physiol Nutr Metab* 2016; 41:1–11.

10. **Bishop D.** Warm up I: potential mechanisms and the effects of passive warm up on exercise performance. *Sports Med* 2003a; 33:439–454.

11. **Bishop D.** Warm up II: performance changes following active warm up and how to structure the warm up. *Sports Med* 2003b; 33:483–498.

12. **Cabido CET, Bergamini JC, Andrade AGP et al.** Acute effect of constant torque and angle stretching on range of motion, muscle passive properties, and stretch discomfort perception. *J Strength Cond Res* 2014; 28:1050–1057.

13. **Cornbleet SL, Woolsey NB.** Assessment of hamstring muscle length in school-aged children using the sit-and-reach test and the inclinometer measure of hip joint angle. *Phys Ther* 1996; 76:850–855.

14. **Craib MW, Mitchell VA.** The association between flexibility and running economy in sub-elite male distance runners. *Med Sci Sports Exerc* 1996; 28:737–743.

15. **Edholm P, Krustrup P, Randers MB.** Half-time re-warm up increases performance capacity in male elite soccer players. *Scand J Med Sci Sports* 2015; 25:e40–e49.

16. **Flopp H, Deall S, Harvey LA, Gwinn T.** Can apparent increase in muscle extensibility with regular stretch be explained by changes in tolerance to stretch? *Aus J Physiother* 2006; 52:45–50.

17. **Fowles JR, Sale DG, MacDougall JD.** Reduced strength after passive stretch of the human plantar flexors. *J Appl Physiol* 2000; 89:1179–1188.

18. **Fradkin AJ, Gabbe BJ, Cameron PA.** Does warming up prevent injury in sport: The evidence from randomized controlled trials. *J Sci Med Sport* 2006; 9:214–220.

19. **Galazoulas C, Tzimou A, Karamousalidis G, Mougios V.** Gradual decline in performance and changes in biochemical parameters of basketball players while resting after warm-up. *Eur J Appl Physiol* 2012; 112:3327–3334.

20. **Gleim GW, McHugh MP.** Flexibility and its effects on sports injury and performance. *Sports Med* 1997; 24:289–299.

21. **Gleim GW, Stachenfeld NS, Nicholas JA.** The influence of flexibility on the economy of walking and jogging. *J Orthop Res* 1990; 8:814–823.

22. **Harris ML.** *Flexibility. Phys Ther* 1969; 49:591–601.

23. **Herbert RD, Gabriel M.** Stretching before and after exercise: effect on muscle soreness and injury risk. *Br Med J* 2002; 325:468.

24. **Herda TJ, Cosley PB, Walter AA et al.** Effects of two modes of static stretching on muscle strength and stiffness. *Med Sci Sports Exerc* 2011; 43:1777–1784.

25. **Holt J, Holt LE, Pelham TW.** Flexibility redefined. In: Bauer T, ed. *Biomechanics in Sports XIII*. Thunder Bay, ON: Lakehead University, 1996:170–174.

26. **Hubley CL, Kozey JW, Stanish WD.** The effects of static stretching exercises and stationary cycling on range of motion at the hip joint. *J Orthop Sports Phys Ther* 1984; 6:104–109.

27. **Jones BH, Knapik JJ.** Physical training and exercise-related injuries. *Sports Med* 1999; 27:111–125.

28. **Kay AD, Blazevich AJ.** Moderate-duration static stretch reduces active and passive plantar flexor moment but not Achilles tendon stiffness or active muscle length. *J Appl Physiol* 2009; 106:1249–1256.

29. **Kay AD, Blazevich AJ.** Effect of acute static stretch on maximal muscle performance: A systematic review. *Med Sci Sports Exerc* 2012; 44:154–164.

30. **Knapik JJ, Jones BH, Bauman CL, et al.** Strength, flexibility, and athletic injuries. *Sports Med* 1992; 14:277–288.

31. **Knudson D, Magnusson P, McHugh M.** Current issues in flexibility fitness. *PCPFS Res Dig* 2000; 3(10):1–8.

32. **Knudson D, Noffal G.** Time course of stretch-induced isometric strength deficits. *Eur J Appl Physiol* 2005; 94:348–351.

33. **Kubo K, Miyazaki D, Shimoju S, Tsunoda N.** Relationship between elastic properties of tendon Structures and performance in long distance runners. *Eur J Appl Physiol* 2015; 115:1725–1733.

34. **Kubo K, Kanehisa H, Fukunaga T.** Effect of stretching on the viscoelastic properties of human tendon structures in vivo. *J Appl Physiol* 2002a; 92:595–601.

35. **Kubo K, Kanehisa H, Fukunaga T.** Effect of transient muscle contractions and stretching on the tendon structures in vivo. *Acta Physiol Scand* 2002b; 175:157–164.

36. **Kubo K, Kanehisa H, Fukunaga T.** Gender differences in the viscoelastic properties of tendon structures. *Eur J Appl Physiol* 2003; 88:520–526.

37. **Kubo K, Kanehisa H, Kawakami Y, et al.** Elastic properties of muscle-tendon complex in long-distance runners. *Eur J Appl Physiol* 2000; 81:181–187.

38. **Kubo K, Kawakami Y, Fukunaga T.** Influence of elastic properties of tendon structures on

jump performance in humans. *J Appl Physiol* 1999; 87:2090–2096.

39. Liemohn W, Haydu T, Phillips D. Questionable exercises. *PCPFS Res Digest* 1999; 3(8):1–8.

40. Magnusson SP. Passive properties of human skeletal muscle during stretch maneuvers: a review. *Scand J Med Sci Sports* 1998; 8:65–77.

41. Magnusson SP, Aagaard P, Nielson JJ. Passive energy return after repeated stretches of the hamstring muscle-tendon unit. *Med Sci Sports Exerc* 2000; 32:1160–1164.

42. Magnusson SP, Aagard P, Simonsen E, et al. A biomechanical evaluation of cyclic and static stretch in human skeletal muscle. *Int J Sports Med* 1998; 19:310–316.

43. Magnusson SP, Aagaard P, Simonsen EB, et al. Passive tensile stress and energy of the human hamstring muscles in vivo. *Scand J Med Sci Sports* 2000; 10:351–359.

44. Magnusson P, Renstrom P. The European College of Sports Sciences Position statement: The role of stretching exercises in sports. *Eur J Sport Sci* 2006; 6:87–91.

45. Magnusson SP, Simonsen EB, Aagaard P, et al. Biomechanical responses to repeated stretches in human hamstring muscle in vivo. *Am J Sports Med* 1996; 24:622–628.

46. Magnusson SP, Simonsen EB, Aagaard P, et al. Determinants of musculoskeletal flexibility: viscoelastic properties, cross-sectional area, EMG and stretch tolerance. *Scand J Med Sci Sports* 1997; 7:195–202.

47. Magnusson SP, Simonsen EB, Aagaard P, et al. Visocoelastic response to repeated static stretching in human skeletal muscle. *Scand J Med Sci Sport* 1995; 5:342–347.

48. Mahieu NN, McNair P, De Muynck M, Stevens V, Blanckaert I, Smits N, Witvrouw E. Effect of static and ballistic stretching on muscle-tendon tissue properties. *Med Sci Sports Exerc* 2007; 39:494–501.

49. Mandengue SH, Miladi I, Bishop D, Temfemo A, Cisse F, Ahmaidi S. Methodological approach for determining optimal active warm-up intensity: predictive equations. *Sci Sports* 2009; 24:9–14.

50. Martin SB, Jackson AW, Morrow JR, et al. The rationale for the sit and reach test revisited. *Meas Phys Ed Exerc Sci* 1998; 2:85–92.

51. McCray JM, Ackermann BJ, Halaki M. A systematic review of the effects of upper body warm-up on performance and injury. *Br J Sports Med* 2015; 49:935–942.

52. McGowan CJ, Pyne DB, Thompson, KG, Rattray B. Warm-up strategies for sport and exercise: mechanisms and applications. *Sports Med* 2015; 45:1523–1546.

53. McHugh MP, Connolly DAJ, Eston RG, et al. The role of passive muscle stiffness in symptoms of exercise-induced muscle damage. *Am J Sports Med* 1999; 27:594–599.

54. McHugh MP, Kremenic IJ, Fox MB, et al. The role of mechanical and neural restrains to joint range of motion during passive stretch. *Med Sci Sports Exerc* 1998; 30:928–932.

55. McHugh MP, Magnusson SP, Gleim GW, et al. Viscoelastic stress relaxation in human skeletal muscle. *Med Sci Sports Exerc* 1992; 24:1375–1382.

56. McNair PJ, Dombroski EW, Hewson DJ, et al. Stretching at the ankle joint: viscoelastic responses to holds and continuous passive motion. *Med Sci Sports Exerc* 2000; 33:354–358.

57. Medeiros JM, Smidt GL, Burmeister LF, et al. The influence of isometric exercise and passive stretch on hip joint motion. *Phys Ther* 1977; 57:518–523.

58. Mizuno T, Matsumoto M, Umemura Y. Viscoelasticity of the muscle-tendon unit is returned more rapidly than range of motion after stretching. *Scand J Med Sci Sports* 2013; 23:23–30.

59. Morse CI, Degens H, Seynnes OR, et al. The acute effect of stretching on the passive stiffness of the human gastrocnemius muscle tendon unit. *J Physiol* 2008; 586: 97–106.

60. Pope RP, Herbert RD, Kirwan JD. Effects of flexibility and stretching on injury risk in army recruits. *Aust J Physiother* 1998; 44:165–172.

61. Pope RP, Herbert RD, Kirwan JD, et al. A randomized trial of preexercise stretching for prevention of lower-limb injury. *Med Sci Sports Exerc* 2000; 32:271–277.

62. Shrier I. Does stretching improve performance? A systematic and critical review of the literature. *Clin J Sport Med* 2004; 14:267–273.

63. Simic L, Sarabon N, Markovic G. Does pre-exercise static stretching inhibit maximal muscular performance? A meta-analytical review. *Scan J Med Sci Sports* 2013; 23:131–148.

64. Taylor DC, Brooks DE, Ryan JB. Viscoelastic characteristics of muscle: passive stretching versus muscular contractions. *Med Sci Sports Exerc* 1997; 29:1619–1624.

65. Thompsen AG, Kakley T, Palumbo MA, Faigenbaum AD. Acute effects of different warm-up protocols with and without weighted vest on jumping performance in

athletic women. *J Strength Cond Res* 2007; 21:52–56.

66. Turki O, Chaouach A, Behm DG, et al. The effect of warm-ups incorporating different volumes of dynamics stretching on 10- and 20-m sprint performance in highly trained male athletes. *J Strength Cond Res* 2012; 26:63–72.

67. Vujnovich AL, Dawson NJ. The effect of therapeutic muscle stretch on neural processing. *J Orthop Sports Phys Ther* 1994; 20:145–153.

68. Walshe AD, Wilson GJ, Murphy AJ. The validity and reliability of a test of lower body musculotendinous stiffness. *Eur J Appl Physiol* 1996; 73:332–339.

69. Weldon SM, Hill RH. The efficacy of stretching for prevention of exercise-related injury: a systematic review of the literature. *Manual Ther* 2003; 8:141–150.

70. Wessel J, Wan A. Effect of stretching on the intensity of delayed-onset muscle soreness. *Clin J Sports Med* 1994; 4:83–87.

71. Whatman C, Knappstein A, Hume P. Acute changes in passive stiffness and range of motion post-stretching. *Phys Ther Sport* 2006; 7:195–200.

72. Wilson GJ, Elliott BC, Wood GA. Stretch shorten cycle performance enhancement through flexibility training. *Med Sci Sports Exerc* 1992; 24:116–123.

73. Wilson GJ, Wood GA, Elliott BC. Optimal stiffness of series elastic component in a stretch-shorten cycle activity. *J Appl Physiol* 1991; 70:825–833.

74. Wilson GJ, Wood GA, Elliott BC. The relationship between stiffness of the musculature and static flexibility: an alternative explanation for the occurrence of muscular injury. *Int J Sports Med* 1991; 12:403–407.

75. Wilson JM, Duncan NM, Marin PJ et al. Meta-analysis of postactivation and power: Effects of conditioning activity, volume, gender, rest periods, and training status. *J Strength Cond Res* 2013; 27:854–859.

76. Witvrouw E, Danneels L, Asselman P, et al. Muscle flexibility as a risk factor for developing muscle injuries in male professional soccer players: a prospective study. *Am J Sports Med* 2003; 31:41–46.

Contents

CHAPTER 10

TEST ADMINISTRATION AND INTERPRETATION

Megan A. Wong, Ian J. Dobbs, Casey M. Watkins, and Lee E. Brown

OBJECTIVES

After completing this chapter, you will be able to:

- Understand the purpose of testing.
- Differentiate between validity and reliability.
- Perform a needs analysis.
- Determine appropriate testing protocols for specific performance variables.
- Familiarize yourself with statistical measures.

KEY TERMS

Assessment	Maximum	Range
Bimodal curve	Mean	Ratio scores
Central tendency	Measurement	Reliability
Concurrent validity	Median	Subpopulation
Construct validity	Mode	Standard deviation (SD)
Content validity	N	Standardized scores
Criterion	Negatively skewed	Sum
Evaluation	Normative	Test
Face validity	Ordinal	T-score
Interval scores	Population	Validity
Intraclass correlation	Positively skewed	Variance
coefficient (ICC)	Predictive validity	Z-score

INTRODUCTION

Test and measurement is at the heart of any resistance-training program. This is the point where initial decisions are made regarding the exercise prescription and involve such topics as frequency, intensity, and volume. However, testing is not a one-time task, but rather an ongoing method of evaluation throughout the prescribed program. In this sense, it is the beginning, the middle, and the end of a true individual periodized regime. The results can be used to evaluate performance and make decisions regarding the future of a program or individual. They may also be used to predict future performance in much the same way that college entrance exam scores are used to predict an individual's probability of graduating. Lastly, test scores may be used in a research environment as part of an in-depth analysis of an important question. Ultimately, the outcome of this entire process is the individualized exercise prescription that will best serve each athlete or client.

> Physical testing is an ongoing task to assess the status of both the athlete and the program.

PURPOSE OF TESTING

The main reason test and measurement is at the heart of resistance training is that it determines where an individual currently stands regarding his or her training status and, more importantly, where he or she is headed. The final outcome of any training program is to arrive at a peak level of performance or to achieve some predetermined goal (12). Therefore, having goals is of no consequence if neither the exerciser nor the strength and conditioning professional knows the present state of the athlete. In short, before we can plan for a trip to go somewhere, we must first know where we currently are. In this way a cogent strategy can be designed and implemented based on the individual and unique demands of the athlete which have been determined through test and measurement.

Using the results of a properly designed and implemented test and measurement protocol will enable the tester or coach to make objective rather than subjective decisions regarding their client's or athlete's program. The ultimate assessment will be based on hard data collected through judicious use of appropriate tests gathered under the scrutiny of a well-prepared tester. In this way, individual bias can be reduced, and the tester's prejudice can be eliminated when measuring an attribute on a test. There is, however, still a place for subjective reasoning during an evaluation process,

but it is better utilized in the overall synergy of how the athlete's skills may be able to coordinate with the sport requirements rather than on the independent collection of raw data.

The purpose of this chapter is to lay the framework for a neat and concise assessment procedure when evaluating clients or athletes. Before proceeding it is important to understand the nomenclature used during this process.

- **Population**: an entire group of individuals sharing some common characteristic. This might be all third graders in America or all NCAA Division I female pole-vaulters. This group is nearly always too large in number to test every member, so a smaller sample is chosen as representative.
- **Sub-population**: the sample group mentioned above, which contains a manageable number of people in which to obtain performance measures. The results of this sub-population will be used to infer to the total population.
- **Test**: a tool used to measure performance. This may take the form of a vertical jump test, a one-repetition maximum (1RM) strength test, or a timed muscular endurance test. The test is just a tool used to collect data in the course of the assessment procedure.
- **Measurement**: the quantitative score derived from the test. It will be in the units described by the individual test such as inches or feet or pounds. Alone it has very little meaning since different tests have different scales, making comparisons difficult if not impossible.
- **Evaluation**: placing a value on the measurement derived from the test. This is the point where the score must be compared to a scale and given worth. This part of the procedure requires a professional trained to choose the proper ranking scale and mindful of the intricacies involved in making decisions in the face of extraneous variables as well as individual differences associated with age, gender, and training status.
- **Assessment**: putting all three of the aforementioned events together. Choose a test, measure the score, then make an evaluation based on a scale comparison.
- **Normative**: a post-measurement scale derived from the scores of a peer group. When

comparing within a sub-population, placing the greatest score at the top then listing the descending scores in order of magnitude generally determines this scale. In other words, if scores on a vertical jump test ranged between 28 and 12 inches, then all the other scores would be ranked between them and some value placed on each performance. Breaks in the scale can be established according to statistical rules such as central tendency, standard deviation, or natural breaks.

- **Criterion**: an a priori scale whereby the break points are known prior to testing and each person must meet an established level of performance to achieve that value level. It is important to understand that this scale is usually derived from many bouts of normative testing. When a considerable amount of data is collected on enough sub-populations to constitute a logical inference of the results to the total population, then a criterion scale can be established and used for evaluation of subsequent scores. This scale requires participants to perform at a standard level of achievement. It may be reaching a specific height during the vertical jump for a basketball team, or lifting a specific amount of weight as in a pre-employment screening exam, or attaining a particular height before being allowed to enjoy an amusement park ride.

> Testing data can be useful in justifying a program or a training method.

TEST SELECTION

To accurately evaluate athletes, proper tests must be chosen which allow an in-depth view of an individual's performance level. This is best accomplished by choosing specific tests designed to measure only one aspect of human performance (13,18). Often many separate tests will be required to precisely measure an athlete's state of training, and each test should be chosen with risks and outcomes in mind. Sport coaches sometimes make choices based on anecdotal evidence or use insensitive tests that are incapable of discriminating variable human performance. The proper procedure is to first determine what the desired outcome is, then design a test and measurement protocol around those outcomes (5).

> Tests chosen should be specific to the sport and to the population being tested.

Physical tests include measurements of cardiovascular and respiratory function, strength, power, endurance, and anthropometry just to name a few. Each of these categories consists of a myriad of choices, every one of which is intended to measure a single factor of that performance characteristic within specific and detailed guidelines (11). Violation of these guidelines will result in spurious data, which is of no use whatsoever.

REAL-WORLD APPLICATION

Calculating average velocity during sprint running

The example is an athlete completing a 40-meter sprint. We have electronic timing lights at 10, 20, and 30 meters from the starting light gate. The average speed over the last 10 meters might be used as an indication of maximum running speed. Let's assume the times and distances are as follows:

Distance	10	20	30
Time	1.741	2.890	3.995

Velocity is change in distance over change in time. Therefore:
velocity = $(30 - 20) / (3.995 - 2.890) = 10 / 1.105 = 9.05$ m/sec.

Making decisions about an individual's physical state of being is not a trivial task and carries with it severe consequences for both the evaluator and the client. The utilization of spurious data will ultimately result in drawing erroneous conclusions. The severity of prescribing exercise for an individual that is beyond their capacity or returning an athlete to play prior to their being able to participate without undue risk of danger cannot be over emphasized. Remember, bad data is worse than no data at all because it may offer an unstable foundation on which to build further training.

Validity

Validity is the most important aspect of any assessment procedure. In order for a test to be valid it must test what it purports to test (14). That is, if one wishes to measure leg strength, then a valid test might be the squat, leg press, or deadlift. Each test would result in different scores and care would need to be exercised when choosing the proper test for a unique sub-population, but each is a valid test of leg strength. In contrast, the vertical jump test includes leg strength as a component but is a test of leg power. Therefore, the vertical jump test is not a valid test of leg strength because it measures an individual's ability to produce power. However related strength and power might be, they are still distinct mechanisms of physical performance. Again, this is the sensitive nature of test selection.

Validity is historically measured against a "gold standard" of performance. For instance, if someone has designed a new device to test leg strength, then the procedure would be to obtain measures using the new device and compare those with the "gold standard" method (7). Using statistical techniques, it is possible to determine whether the two tests are conceptually similar and to what degree their results differ. A correlation analysis such as the Pearson product moment (r) may answer the conceptual question by determining the association of the two scores, while an analysis of variance

(ANOVA) may answer the degree to which the tests' scores differ. These techniques are beyond the scope of this chapter, but the concept should not be lost on the reader. The concept is that a test must measure what it has been designed to measure in order for the results to be a valid quantification of that physical component.

There are five major types of validity:

1 **Face validity** states that the test is logical on the surface, as when having a person lift a weight to measure strength.
2 **Content validity** states that the test includes material that has been taught or covered; for instance, testing speed after training for speed.
3 **Predictive validity** states that test scores can accurately predict future performance. An example would be the NFL measuring college football players prior to the draft to determine their potential.
4 **Concurrent validity** states that the test is a measure of the individual's current performance level. This happens when the test occurs shortly after training is completed.
5 **Construct validity** states that the test measures some part of the whole skill, such as measuring bench press strength for football linemen.

Reliability

Reliability is loosely defined as repeatability. That is, the ability of a test to arrive at or near the same score upon repeated measurements in the absence of any intervention strategy. A reliable test should result in consistent scores. To accomplish this (using the new device scenario stated previously), the procedure would be to measure individuals using the new device, then allow a time delay of approximately 48 to 72 hours so no significant training effects could interfere with the results, and then measure each person a second time using the identical procedures as the first measurement. If reliability is high then people scoring well on the first test should also score well on subsequent tests (6,7).

REAL-WORLD APPLICATION

Reproducing physical test results in training and conditioning

Reproducing test results of physical tests is important to maintain the validity and reliability of a test. Testing athletes in the weight room or on the field presents special challenges in terms of reproducing test data.

Why is reproducibility important in training and conditioning? It is important for a number of reasons, even though the data may not be used for research purposes.

You will make a decision about the type of program you use based on the results you obtain. If your results are not accurate, then you may be making the wrong decision, choosing a program that is not producing the results you seek. Pre-testing and post-testing must use reproducible testing procedures so you can accurately make that decision.

Conditioning programs should focus on specific areas of weakness in a particular athlete. Those areas of weakness must be monitored on a regular basis using reproducible tests. If the tests used are not reproducible, then once again, the incorrect decision will be made.

Inconsistent test results may not motivate the athlete to improve. We know that hard work pays off with improved scores, but if the scoring is inconsistent, we are providing bad information to the athlete. Documenting improvement in the athletes you train is an indication you as a conditioning coach are doing your job. Providing your administrators with accurate testing records obtained using reproducible tests is an important step in justifying your position.

Are there steps the conditioning professional can take to improve the reproducibility of the test results? Of course!

- Standardize the testing procedures for every test. Have the procedures in writing and provide a copy to each data collector.
- Train the data collectors to collect the test results accurately and consistently.
- Use the same data collectors as much as possible.
- Allow the same number of trials for each test.
- Test in the same environmental conditions as much as possible. Environmental conditions are best controlled indoors, so test indoors as much as possible and practical.
- Standardize the amount and type of external motivation provided to the athlete and keep it consistent from one testing session to the next.
- Test at the same time of day if possible.
- Always test after a day of rest if possible. Strenuous training of specific muscle groups may decrease performance on some tests.
- Maintain the same order of testing.

Control diet as much as possible. You may not be able to control diet to a great extent but remember that it can have an effect on performance, both positive and negative.

The rank order of participants should remain relatively constant as in back-to-back days of handgrip strength testing. A perfect rank order between tests would mean that each person kept his or her spot in the ordinal sequence relative to all others. This almost never occurs with human testing. Employing the statistical techniques of Pearson r would establish this rank order of the two measurements and establish reliability on a continuum ranging between 1.0 and –1.0. Reliability is not an either/or proposition, but rather a floating scale of different levels.

Table 10.1 depicts one strategy to use to categorize the level of reliability between two measurements taken at two different times using the same population. Remember that a negative correlation still represents reliability but simply states that as one score increases another score decreases thereby inverting the rank order of participants. This may occur when comparing two different tests such as vertical jump height and percent body fat. Figure 10.1 shows graphical representations of the scores as they appear when scatter plotted. The trend line (sometimes referred to as the "line of best fit") has been added to illustrate positive, negative, and null relationships respectively.

Although the Pearson r correlation can be used to determine the relationship between subsequent tests in our new device scenario, it is no longer the gold standard when determining reliability. Instead, an **intraclass correlation coefficient (ICC)** can be used to better establish reliability. A Pearson r score close to 1 or –1 will denote that an individual has scored similarly with respect to his/her peers, but does not take into account any changes in the mean test score. What would happen if the group of athletes we tested on our new device all finished in the same rank order on the second test, but each scored several points higher? This would be a case in which Pearson r correlation would

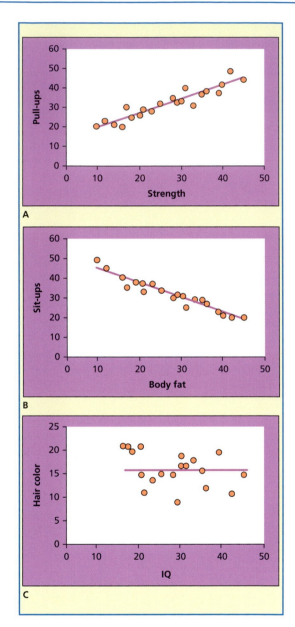

Figure 10.1 Graphical representation of scores when scatter-plotted. (A) Positive relationship between strength and number of pull-ups. (B) Negative relationship between body fat and number of sit-ups. (C) No relationship between IQ and hair color.

TABLE 10.1 Category system to determine level of reliability

r-value	Relationship
1.0–0.8	Very high
0.79–0.6	High
0.59–0.4	Moderate
0.39–0.2	Low
0.19–0	Very low

be high, because all of the athletes performed similarly with respect to their peers, on both tests. The test would not be reliable, however, because the mean score was higher on the second test. Therefore, the results are not repeatable. The ICC takes into account any difference that may be present, not only in the rank of each athlete, but the overall difference in the value of the scores (10). It is important to remember that the ICC, like the Pearson r, does not determine the reliability of a test in a yes or no fashion, but rather places the reliability on a theoretical continuum which allows us to state the degree to which a test is reliable.

It should be evident then that a test may be reliable but not valid, while a valid test must always be reliable. It is always important to remember that each of these procedures assumes complete cooperation of the athlete and 100% maximum effort during every test session. That is not always the case and should be carefully monitored by the individual responsible for test administration or sub-maximal testing should be performed (26).

> Tests chosen must be valid and reliable and must be administered using a reliable protocol.

ASSESSMENT

The first thing that should be done is a full assessment, including medical and exercise history, obtaining a physician release if necessary, performing physiological testing, determining baseline nutritional status (to determine if referral to an RD/LD is necessary), and determining program goals. The objective of the assessment is to provide a comprehensive view of the athlete, what they are capable of, what their limitations are, and any special needs that may need to be addressed. This initial assessment may be done the first time you meet but will be ongoing as you work with and learn about the person's needs.

Medical history and PAR-Q

The medical history should begin with a few basic questions, such as those found on the PAR-Q form. The PAR-Q is a limited tool that should not be considered to encompass all the information that you will need to know. It is a quick and easy way to determine whether a

potential client is at risk for any major complications during low to moderate, but not vigorous, exercise. In addition to the PAR-Q, it is appropriate to determine the following:

- Is the person diabetic? If so, are they able to control their blood glucose levels, and how do they monitor blood glucose? Additionally, have they ever been on a regular exercise program while diabetic?
- Do they have asthma? If so, is their asthma exercise induced, and at what levels? Do they use a fast-acting inhaler or other medication to control attacks?
- Do they smoke? If so, how much and how often?
- Is there a family history of heart attack, coronary artery bypass surgery, or sudden death before age 55 in men, or age 65 in women?
- Do they have a history of hypertension (systolic pressure ≥140, or diastolic pressure ≥90), or are they on antihypertensive medications?
- Do they have a total cholesterol level greater than 200 mg/dL?
- Are they obese, defined as a body mass index of ≥30, confirmed with a waist measurement of >100cm?

You will also need to know about any previous injuries that might interfere with their ability to perform certain exercises. Ask about such things as sprains and strains, arthritis, athletic injuries, unusual pain or swelling in any of the joints, and any tightness that limits their ability to move with ease.

> Understanding an individual's medical and exercise history will help you make an informed decision regarding exercise prescription, or whether referral to a medical professional for additional testing is indicated.

Physician release

The words "please consult with your physician before beginning an exercise program" are often found on the control panels of cardiovascular equipment. No matter how thorough a medical history you obtain, a physician will

TABLE 10.2 Various strength, power, endurance, and agility tests

Tests	Muscle groups and joints used	Muscle actions	Time limits	Kinetic chain	Energy system
Wingate Anaerobic Cycle	Hips, quads, ankles	Concentric	30 s	Closed	Anaerobic
Margaria-Kalamen Stair Climb	Hips, quads, ankles	Concentric & eccentric	2 s	Closed	ATP-PC
Isokinetic velocity spectrum	Each one individually	Concentric & eccentric	5 s to 60 s	Open	ATP-PC & Anaerobic
Overhead medicine ball throw	Entire body	Concentric & eccentric	2 s	Closed	ATP-PC
Counter movement vertical jump	Hips and ankles	Concentric & eccentric	2 s	Closed	ATP-PC
1RM power clean	Arms, shoulders, back, hips, quads, ankles	Isometric & concentric & eccentric	5 s	Closed	ATP-PC
1RM squat	Entire lower body	Isometric & concentric & eccentric	5 s	Closed	ATP-PC
1RM bench press	Entire upper body	Isometric & concentric & eccentric	5 s	Closed	ATP-PC
Bench press body weight for total reps	Entire upper body	Isometric & concentric & eccentric	30 s to 60 s	Closed	Anaerobic
Push-up test	Upper body	Concentric & eccentric	30 s to 60 s	Closed	Anaerobic
40-yard dash	Entire lower body	Concentric & eccentric	5 s	Closed	ATP-PC
T-test	Entire body	Isometric & concentric & eccentric	10 s	Closed	ATP-PC & Anaerobic
5–10–5 shuttle	Entire body	Isometric & concentric & eccentric	5 s	Closed	ATP-PC & Anaerobic
Standing long jump	Entire lower body	Concentric & eccentric	2 s	Closed	ATP-PC
5–0–5 test	Entire lower body	Isometric & concentric & Eccentric	5 s	Closed	ATP-PC

Source: Lockie RG, Jalilvand F, Orjalo AJ, Giuliano DV, Moreno MR and Wright GA. A methodological report: Adapting the 505 change-of-direction speed test specific to American football. *J Strength Cond Res* 2017; 31(2): 539–547.

be better able to assess the medical ability of a person to begin an exercise program, and may have information that can help you to determine the best course of action for that person. It is a good idea to have a medical release form that describes each of the exercise components, including the levels of intensity and duration.

Nutrition

It is important to get a basic understanding of the person's nutritional status. Nutritional programming should only be performed by a registered or licensed dietician. However, you can obtain basic information, such as choice of foods, quantity, and timing of meals from a simple three-day recall. Having the client recall everything ingested for the past three days will allow you to decide if more specific dietary interventions are necessary, in which case a referral to an RD/LD is necessary.

Needs analysis

Two main concerns when choosing proper tests to be administered to athletes are the needs of the individual and the needs of the activity. Each of these brings specific requirements to the task of test selection and should be treated with equal diligence.

> A needs analysis should be performed to evaluate the needs of the athlete and the demands of the sport.

First, individual needs may be assessed through traditional physiological methods such as body fat, cardiovascular, muscular strength/power, and flexibility testing. These tests are designed to evaluate the individual's present state of readiness to participate in the activity of choice. Not all tests will be required for each person as not all physiological variables are equally required across sporting activities. Furthermore, each category may compel the investigator to pick appropriate ways to measure the individual.

Second, the needs of the particular sport or activity are unique and require different physiological performance levels of the athlete or client. Some sports require maximal isometric upper body movements such as wrestling while others require sub-maximal continuous lower body movements such as cycling or running. Once again, the need to be specific with a test and measurement scheme is vital for the success of the program.

In short, preparation for a comprehensive test and measurement system requires time and diligence of the tester at the onset of the program in order to choose tests that measure the requisite needs of both the participant and the activity. These needs should consider all aspects of human performance including, but not limited to, energy systems, duration of each repetition, duration of the entire event, muscle used, muscle actions used, range of motion involved, and speed of movement (22,23).

Table 10.2 displays a myriad of tests designed to measure strength, power, muscular endurance, and agility, yet each is unique in that it requires different muscles, muscle actions, time limits, kinetic chain limitations, and energy systems. The tests presented in this chapter are by no means the only available methods of evaluating strength, power, muscular endurance, and agility. Instead, they have been selected as a representation of the vast array of choices one has in assessing an athlete's training needs. Table 10.3 presents normative data for many of these tests.

Warm up protocol

Warming up prior to performance testing is essential for assessing muscular strength. General warm-ups are intended to increase muscle temperature, whereas specific warm-up tends to increase neuromuscular activation. For improved short-term performance activity, a moderate intensity warm-up is sufficient to cause only minimal fatigue (4). Performing an active dynamic warm-up has been shown to be effective for preparing the body before explosive tests (30). In contrast, static stretching reduces strength and power and has been shown to have little effect on reducing injury risk (15). Therefore, coaches should warm up athletes appropriately to the battery of tests being performed. For testing guidelines, it is

TABLE 10.3 Calculated ratios for female/male comparisons of absolute (N·m) and relative (N·m·kg-1) peak torque for knee extension and flexion

Female/male ratio for torque values										
	Joint motion	60°·s⁻¹		180°·s⁻¹		300°·s⁻¹		Average	
		Abs	Rel	Abs	Rel	Abs	Rel	Abs	Rel
Men	Knee extension	0.77	0.81	0.84	0.88	0.83	0.87	0.81	0.85
	Knee flexion	0.88	0.93	0.93	0.99	0.86	0.91	0.89	0.94
Women	Knee extension	0.76	0.77	0.85	0.86	0.83	0.85	0.81	0.83
	Knee flexion	0.88	0.88	0.95	0.96	0.86	0.86	0.9	0.9

Sources: Beam WC, Bartels RL, Ward RW, Clark N and Zuelzer WA. Multiple comparisons of isokinetic leg strength in male and female collegiate athletic teams. *Med Sci Sports Exerc* 1985; 17(2):Abstract #20, 269.

Wyatt MP and Edwards AM. Comparison of quadriceps and hamstring torque values during isokinetic exercise. *Journal of Orthopaedic and Sports Physical Therapy* 1981; 3:48–56.

recommended to perform a moderate general warm-up in addition to a specific warm-up prior to maximum strength assessments (1).

Instructional cues

Providing verbal instructions to athletes before administering tests may influence performance. Directing attention towards the bodily movements and muscles (internal focus of attention) may hinder performance. Focusing on directing attention to an external object or toward the movement outcome (external focus of attention) tends to enhance motor learning and overall performance (3,16,17). Testers should display confidence and explain the expectations of the test in simple terms. If applicable, it is strongly encouraged for testers to instruct athletes using external objects or devices to focus on when cueing, which has been shown to enhance performance testing (31,32). Examples of external cues include "Break the bar" during a bench press, or "Push the ground away" during a vertical jump test. Finally, testers should clearly answer any questions that athletes have before testing begins.

Wingate anaerobic cycle test

The Wingate anaerobic cycle test was designed as a means to measure overall anaerobic lower extremity power. The athlete is made to cycle as fast as possible for 30 seconds with a predetermined resistance (Figure 10.2). This resistance is derived by multiplying the athlete's body weight (kg) by the constant 0.075 (2,19).

Specialized cycle ergometers will record the athlete's peak power and mean power during the 30-second test. This test is a good overall assessment of lower extremity power

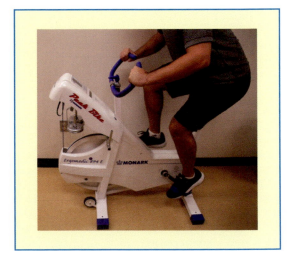

Figure 10.2 Wingate anaerobic cycle test. This test is a good indicator of overall anaerobic lower extremity power.

TABLE 10.4 Comparative data for Wingate Anaerobic Cycle Test

Comparative data for Wingate Anaerobic Test						
Group	Peak anaerobic power			Mean anaerobic power		
	Force (%wt)	Absolute (W)	Relative (W_kg⁻¹)	Work (kJ)	Absolute (W)	Relative (W_kg⁻¹)
Men						
Non-athletes (18–28y)	7.5	700	9.2	16.9	563	7.3
Non-athletes (18–24y)	7.5	540	8.2	13.5	450	7.0
Non-athletes (25–34y)	7.5	700	9.2	16.2	540	7.2
Non-athletes (35–44y)	7.5	660	8.6	15.0	500	6.6
Cyclists (Category I–II)	10.0	1125	14.7	27.1	903	11.8
Cyclists (Category II–IV)	9.5	963	13.3	23.5	783	10.8
Women						
Non-athletes (18–28y)	7.5	454	454.0	11.4	381	6.3
Active women	7.5	561	561.0	13.6	453	7.2

Sources: Inbar O, Dotan R and Baro-Or O. Anaerobic characteristics in male children and adolescents. *Med Sci Sports Exerc* 18, 264–269, 1986.

Jacobs I. The effects of thermal dehydration on performance of the Wingate Anaerobic Test. *International Journal of Sports Medicine* 1, 21–24, 1980.

Maud PJ and Schultz BB. Norms for the Wingate Anaerobic Test with comparison to another similar test. *Research Quarterly for Exercise and Sport* 60(2), 144–151, 1989.

Tanaka H, Bassett DR, Swensen TC and Sampredo RM. Aerobic and anaerobic characteristics of competitive cyclists in the United State Cycling Federation. *International Journal of Sports Medicine* 14, 334–338, 1993.

as it requires contributions from all major muscle groups of the lower extremities. Also, it can be used to measure not only peak power, but mean power over a 30-second period as well. For this reason, it is a good test to include with sports that require maximal effort for bouts that last longer than just a few seconds. One negative aspect of this test is the need for a specialized cycle ergometer that will derive the athlete's peak and mean power. These ergometers are costly and are used primarily for research purposes (Tables 10.4 and 10.5).

Margaria-Kalamen Stair Climb Test

This test of lower extremity power is easy and quick to perform. It is performed on a staircase and is a good measure of lower body power and explosiveness, which is important to athletes requiring speed, agility, and quickness. First, measure the subject's body weight and calculate the height of each step. The test is performed by beginning in front of a flight of at least a dozen stairs. Each step height is approximately 17.5 cm (7 in) high. Timing mats are placed on the third and ninth steps, which are connected to a timing device and are activated by the subject's body weight. The subject begins 6 meters from the first step then runs toward and up the steps, taking them three at a time (Figure 10.3). The result (power) is the product of body weight and the step vertical distance and gravity divided by the total time from the third to the ninth step. Results of this

TABLE 10.5 Category for absolute and relative peak and mean anaerobic power and fatigue index by gender

Category	%ile	Peak anaerobic power Men Absolute (W)	Men Relative (W_kg⁻¹)	Women Absolute (W)	Women Relative (W_kg⁻¹)	Mean anaerobic power Men Absolute (W)	Men Relative (W_kg⁻¹)	Women Absolute (W)	Women Relative (W_kg⁻¹)	Fatigue index Men (%)	Women (%)
Well above average	95	867	11.1	602	9.3	677	8.6	483	7.5	21	20
Above average	90	822	10.9	560	9.0	662	8.2	470	7.3	23	25
	85	807	10.6	530	8.9	631	8.1	437	7.1	27	25
	80	777	10.4	527	8.8	618	8.0	419	7.0	30	26
	75	768	10.4	518	8.6	604	8.0	414	6.9	30	28
Average	70	757	10.2	505	8.5	600	7.9	410	6.8	31	29
	60	721	9.8	480	8.1	577	7.6	391	6.6	35	34
	50	689	9.2	449	7.6	565	7.4	381	6.4	38	35
	40	671	8.9	432	7.0	548	7.1	367	6.2	40	38
	30	656	8.5	399	6.9	530	7.0	353	6.0	43	40
Below average	25	646	8.3	396	6.8	521	6.8	347	5.9	45	42
	20	618	8.3	376	6.6	496	6.6	337	5.7	47	44
	15	594	7.4	362	6.4	485	6.4	320	5.6	47	44
	10	570	7.1	353	6.0	471	6.0	306	5.3	52	47
Well below average	5	530	6.6	329	5.7	453	5.6	287	5.1	55	48

Source: Maud PJ, and Shultz BB. Norms for the Wingate Anaerobic Test with comparison to another similar test. *Research Quarterly for Exercise and Sport 60(2)*, 144–151, 1989.

test have shown a moderate correlation to the Wingate Cycle Test (21). The normative ranges for the Margaria-Kalamen Stair Climb Test are shown in Table 10.6.

Isokinetic velocity spectrum

Isokinetic testing involves controlling the velocity of a given movement rather than the force or power with which it is performed. A computerized dynamometer is set to a specified velocity at which the lever arm of the machine can be moved. The athlete then attempts to move the lever arm as fast as he or she can through a preset range of motion. Torque (rotational force) and power produced during the movement are then recorded by the dynamometer. These measurements can be expressed as maximal values or averaged over several repetitions to derive mean torque and power values. This testing is often performed at a range of velocities, or spectrum, so that the tester can get a better indication of whether potential deficits exist during slow or fast velocity movements (29).

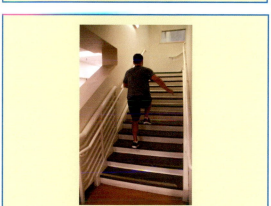

Figure 10.3 Margaria-Kalamen Stair Climb Test. This test is a good indicator of lower extremity power.

Figure 10.4 Isokinetic testing. Using a computerized dynamometer, this test measures torque and power at various velocities.

TABLE 10.6 Margaria-Kalamen Stair Sprint Test normative ranges

Classification	Men's age groups (years)				
	15–20	20–30	30–40	40–50	50+
Excellent	2,197+	2,059+	1,648+	1,226+	961+
Good	1,844–2,197	1,726–2,059	1,383–1,648	1,040–1,226	814–961
Average	1,471–1,824	1,373–1,716	1,098–1,373	834–1,030	647–804
Fair	1,108–1,461	1,040–1,363	834–1,088	637–824	490–637
Poor	Under 1,108	Under 1,040	Under 834	Under 637	Under 490
Classification	Women's age groups (years)				
	15–20	20–30	30–40	40–50	50+
Excellent	1,785+	1,648+	1,226+	961+	736+
Good	1,491–1,785	1,383–1,648	1,040–1,226	814–961	608–736
Average	1,187–1,481	1,098–1,373	834–1,030	647–801	481–598
Fair	902–1,177	834–1,089	637–824	490–637	373–471
Poor	Under 902	Under 834	Under 637	Under 490	Under 373

Source: Fox EL, Bowers RW, and Foss ML. *The Physiological Basis of Physical Education and Athletics* (5th ed.). Dubuque, IA: Wm. C. Brown, 1993

Isokinetic dynamometers can be used to test a variety of joints in either seated or reclined positions. These machines can only test each joint in isolation, and not as part of a dynamic movement. Therefore, they are limited in their application to the movement patterns specific to an individual sport. They do, however, provide precise, highly reliable data which can easily be compared between athletes, injured and uninjured limbs, or agonist and antagonist muscle groups (8,27,28).

Overhead medicine ball throw

This test requires explosive total body movement to throw a medicine ball for maximum distance. The overhead medicine ball throw test (Figure 10.5) is suitable specifically for athletes involved in sports where total body power is important. This test requires a 2 or 3 kg rubber medicine ball (men use 3 kg, women use 2 kg), tape measure, and clear open area.

The athlete begins by facing their back towards the direction they are throwing. Feet must be shoulder width apart with heels on the start line (zero distance mark). The athlete will then start with the ball in both hands held extended over their head. While keeping the arms extended, the athlete will swing the ball down between their legs while flexing the knees, hips, and trunk. This serves as the countermovement. After the countermovement, the athlete will thrust the hips forward, extend the knees and trunk, flex the shoulders, while in one motion, throwing the ball back overhead. At the end of the throw, the feet can leave the ground as in a vertical jump to minimize any deceleration in the movement. These procedures should allow the muscles involved to generate power similar to the countermovement vertical jump test. The examiner is encouraged to allow the athlete several warm-up throws prior to the test.

Displacement of the medicine ball during this test strongly correlates with the power index for the countermovement vertical jump test, which has been shown to be a reliable

Figure 10.5 Overhead medicine ball throw.

test for muscular power. This suggests that the overhead medicine ball throw test is reliable for assessing total body muscular power (26).

Countermovement vertical jump
The vertical jump is performed, primarily, utilizing the hip extensor and ankle plantar flexor muscle groups. The athlete is instructed to jump as high as he or she can following a quick downward squatting movement. The athlete's jump height can be recorded simply by measuring the difference between chalk markings placed on a wall while standing on the ground and reaching and the highest point that athlete can reach while performing the countermovement jump. Commercial products involving a series of plastic sticks that rotate about a vertical axis when touched are also available to measure vertical jump height (Figure 10.6).

This test is often a good choice with athletes as it is an essential skill in many sports. Therefore, the movement pattern and metabolic demands are similar to what the athlete might encounter in a game situation. Furthermore, improvement on a test such as this may have a direct effect on sport performance. One limitation of the counter movement vertical jump test is the fact that technique often differs between athletes. Thus, the examiner must be careful that differences in scores on subsequent tests are due to training and not variations in the athlete's jumping technique.

One-repetition maximum power clean
The power clean is an exercise performed using several upper extremity, lower extremity, and core muscle groups (Figure 10.7). Because the exercise is designed for the athlete to lift the weight as quickly as possible, it is a good

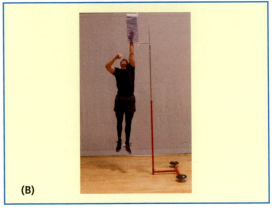

Figure 10.6 Countermovement vertical jump. (A) first, determine the athlete's reach while standing on the floor; (B) then, have the athlete jump to determine maximum height.

indication of ballistic strength. The repetition maximum power clean is considered to be the greatest load with which the athlete can perform one repetition of the movement with proper form. This test is useful for power athletes who are required to move explosively for short durations.

One-repetition maximum squat

The one-repetition maximum squat is considered the greatest load with which an athlete can perform the exercise in good form (Figure 10.8). This test is a good indication of overall lower body strength as the movement requires contributions from all of the major muscle groups of the lower body. It is an important test for athletes whose sports require high

Figure 10.7 Power clean. (A) starting position; (B) first pull; (C) catch.

amounts of lower extremity strength such as basketball and volleyball.

The guidelines for one-repetition maximum testing are set out in Box 10.1.

Figure 10.8 Squat. (A) starting position; (B) downward movement.

Box 10.1   One-repetition maximum testing guidelines

Prior to prescribing a resistance training program, baseline performance values must be obtained for each exercise. One-repetition maximum (1RM) tests are frequently employed by strength and conditioning professionals to assess an athlete's initial strength level. This information is then used to prescribe training intensity for a given exercise as a percentage of 1RM. The following are guidelines for conducting a 1RM test:

1 Ensure the athlete is proficient in the exercise to be assessed for 1RM.
2 Ensure that pre-testing precautionary issues have been addressed (e.g., appropriate number of spotters; correct spotting technique).
3 Instruct the athlete to perform a general warm-up (low intensity aerobic exercise) to raise core body temperature and reduce the risk for injury.
4 Instruct the athlete to perform a specific warm-up (1 set of 5–10 repetitions of the exercise to be assessed using a light to moderate load [50% estimated 1RM], followed by one additional heavier but sub-maximal set [~70% 1RM]).
5 Instruct the athlete to lift a weight corresponding to approximately 3RM.
6 Provide 3–5 minutes of recovery.
7 Instruct the athlete to attempt their first 1RM trial.
8 Based on trial outcome, make load adjustments based on athlete feedback and the following guidelines:

   a   If the trial was successful, add 5–20 pounds for upper body exercises and 10–30 pounds for lower body exercises
   b   If the trial was unsuccessful, remove 5–10 pounds for upper body exercises and 10–20 pounds for lower body exercises

9 Provide 3–5 minutes of recovery between trials.
10 Repeat steps 8 and 9 until 1RM is achieved.

Source: Brown LE and Weir JP. ASEP procedures recommendation I: Accurate assessment of muscular strength and power. *Journal of Exercise Physiology online* 4(3), 2001.

One-repetition maximum bench press

Like the squat test for the lower body, the one-repetition maximum bench press is often used to estimate an athlete's overall upper body strength (Figure 10.9). Again, this value is obtained by determining the greatest load with which the athlete can perform the movement with good form. It is a particularly useful test for sports requiring upper body strength such as football. Since all athletes can benefit from improving their overall strength base, a general upper body test such as this is good to include for all athletes.

Finding a true one-repetition maximum may be both difficult and unnecessary in some cases. As with other repetition maximum tests, the bench press test can be time consuming to conduct (9). Long periods of rest are required between trials and several trials are necessary for each test. Therefore, repetition maximums are often derived using prediction equations. Many prediction equations exist and are based on the mass lifted and the amount of repetitions performed.

Bench press body weight for total reps

This test is another good indicator of general upper body strength and muscular endurance. It may be a more valid measure than the one-repetition maximum test, because it takes into consideration individual differences in mass. Using this test would allow the strength coach to compare an athlete to his or her peers more appropriately.

Although this test provides for variations in strength due to mass, it does not consider differences in training age. Athletes who have greater training ages may be able to bench press their body weight several times without much difficulty. As such, this test may provide a base line of strength for some and muscular endurance for others. Deciding on an appropriate test for upper body strength should take both differences in mass and training age into account.

Push-up test

The push-up test aims to assess an athlete's general upper body muscular endurance. This test (Figure 10.10) is suitable for athletes whose sport requires them to endure repeated muscular contractions. To perform this test, a flat surface, optional mat, and an assistant are required. To start this test, the athlete will lie face down on the mat with hands shoulder width apart with fully extended arms. The athlete will lower their body until the elbow reaches 90° and subsequently return to the starting position. The push-ups are to be continuous with no rest between repetitions. The athlete will complete as many successful push-ups as possible. The examiner will record the total number of successful repetitions.

40-yard sprint

The 40-yard sprint is another highly functional test to gauge total lower body power. Sprinting at top speed is a skill required in many sports. Therefore, the 40-yard sprint is

Figure 10.9 Bench press. (A) starting position; (B) downward movement.

Figure 10.10 Push-up.

often a good test to include, as its performance may have direct application to many athletes' sports. Although many highly accurate timing devices are available, the test can easily be performed using a stop watch.

To assess 40-yd sprint speed, obtain the appropriate space necessary to perform the test (e.g., a straight section of track). As usual, a general and specific warm-up consisting of light aerobic activity and a few submaximal trials, respectively, should be performed by the athlete. After completing the trial runs, have the athlete get into the starting position by assuming a four-point stance. On the tester's cue or following some other auditory stimulus, the athlete will sprint the pre-marked 40-yard distance, with the best of two trials recorded for later assessment.

One negative aspect of this test, however, is its potential to be over emphasized.

In fact, such importance is placed on this test that highly competitive athletes often spend a great deal of time and effort practicing form drills in the hopes of running a few tenths of a second faster. Although this is a very functional and useful test, its results should be used in conjunction with other tests to identify an athlete's strengths and weaknesses. It should not be used as a direct predictor of how he or she will perform on the field.

T-test

The T-test assesses change of direction ability in the forward and lateral planes. This test (Figure 10.11) requires four cones placed in the shape of a "T." The athlete will begin the test at the base of the "T" in the standing position. The athlete will then sprint 10 yards forward to the first cone, shuffle laterally 5 yards to

Figure 10.11 T-test.

Figure 10.11 (continued)

Figure 10.11 (continued)

the left cone without crossing his or her feet, shuffle laterally 10 yards to the far right cone, shuffle 5 yards left back towards the center cone, and end with a 10-yard backpedal to the starting point.

5–10–5 shuttle

The 5–10–5 shuttle (Figure 10.12), or pro agility test, is another frequently employed agility test. The NFL combine administers the 5–10–5 shuttle as part of its test battery to assess potential draftees. This test assesses change of direction ability in a linear plane and it only requires three cones placed in a straight line 5 yards apart. The athlete will begin the test behind the center cone in a two-point stance. The test begins when the athlete initiates movement on their own and sprints 5 yards to the left, touches the cone, 10 yards to the right, touches the cone, and finally 5 yards left across the starting position.

Figure 10.12 5–10–5 shuttle.

Figure 10.12 *(continued)*

Figure 10.12 *(continued)*

The 5–0–5 test measures an athlete's ability to change direction while sprinting in a linear direction. To begin the 5–0–5 test, the athlete will sprint 10 meters to timing gates and a further 5 meters past the timing gates where the athlete will decelerate on a chosen leg. They will then accelerate back past the timing gates and a change of direction score will be recorded.

Standing long jump

The standing long jump is also a good functional test that measures total lower body power (Figure 10.13). Though the vertical jump is used to measure vertical power, the long jump is used to measure horizontal power. Being another test of lower body power, it too is a good choice for athletes requiring speed, agility, and quickness. The test is very easy to conduct; a tape measure and an open space with a flat surface are the primary requirements. First, place a piece of masking tape or other heavy-duty tape on the testing surface to serve as a starting line. Then have the athlete get into the starting position by standing with their toes behind the line. Instruct the athlete to jump as far as possible using a single countermovement. For the jump to be considered successful, the athlete must land with both feet without any disturbances to his or her balance. If the jump is deemed successful, the distance between the starting line and the point behind the athlete's heels constitutes the jump distance. Have the athlete complete three trials with the best score recorded for later assessment.

(A)

Figure 10.13 Standing long jump. (A) starting position; (B) jump; (C) landing.

(B)

(C)

Figure 10.13 *(continued)*

Although this is a valid measure of lower body power, the standing long jump is a movement pattern that is not specific to many sports. Therefore, other field tests, such as the 40-yard sprint test and vertical jump may have more specific applications for many athletes.

Q&A FROM THE FIELD

The head S & C coach for the football team at our university only uses 4 tests for the players: the 40-yard dash, vertical jump, 1RM squat, and 1RM bench press. We had such a great season last year, winning our conference championship, so the tests seem adequate, but should we be doing more?
—*graduate student intern*

Certainly we must take many things into consideration when designing a testing program. A mature, well-trained group of players might be able to continue to perform well with minimal testing. In order to determine the appropriate tests, we need to review the basic rationale for testing athletes. Remember the primary reasons for testing:

1 to determine the fitness base of the athlete
2 to determine the performance characteristics of the better players in the sport, and
3 to motivate the athletes to continue to train hard.

There are other possible reasons for testing. One reason might be that the S & C coach is in the process of justifying his position on the coaching staff. Good solid data demonstrating improvement in a number of performance characteristics in the teams he trains would provide solid evidence that he is performing an important service for those athletes.

To get a total picture of the fitness base of the athlete, you will likely need tests in a number of areas of performance. These areas might include:

1 upper body strength
2 lower body strength
3 upper body endurance
4 lower body endurance
5 upper body power
6 lower body power
7 aerobic capacity
8 speed
9 speed endurance
10 maximal anaerobic capacity.

You may choose some tests that overlap two of these characteristics, or you may determine that a test is not appropriate for a particular sport. Maximal anaerobic capacity tests that cause a dramatic rise in lactic acid production might not be appropriate for a golfer, for example. Do recall, however, that aerobic capacity is used in recovery, even in anaerobic sports.

Remember also that we base our decisions about the type of training program needed on the testing results. In a mature, highly performing group of athletes, it is possible that the training protocols are well established and the testing data will not greatly affect the program. Thus, a minimal testing program might work in some specific situations. Spending less time testing allows more time for conditioning or practice of the sport, which might be an advantage in some situations.

In summary, there are several reasons to consider adding tests to the testing program described above. It is also possible to spend too much time and energy testing, taking away from training time and practice time. The correct answer to your question depends on the goals of that particular testing program. Do the athletes need more motivation to train hard? Additional tests may provide the additional motivation the athletes need. Is it important for the S & C coach to provide data to justify his value to the team? Additional tests may prove his importance. Do the chosen tests adequately represent the physical requirements of the sport? If not, additional tests may provide the missing data. Are the tests position-specific? In football, physical demands of different positions can vary. A 40-yard dash may be appropriate for backs, while a 10- or 20-yard dash may be more appropriate for lineman. Matching testing to position-specific physical requirements will provide useful information. The training program should provide position-specific benefits to the individual athlete.

Every group of athletes will be different to some extent, and the philosophy of conditioning programs will vary from school to school as well. An S & C coach is constantly thinking about what he can do to keep motivation high, to keep the athletes working hard, and to keep a positive attitude toward the training. The testing program should evaluate improvement in performance that is specific to the sport of football as well as to the athlete's position. A properly designed testing program can be a key component of the program!

Test interpretation

Administering a test and recording a measurement are the simple portions of any assessment routine. The final and most complicated portion is making an evaluation of those scores. This involves placing a value on the recorded score so it may be used to help design a program of training specific to the individual. In order to accomplish this the scores must be put into a logical order and analyzed for practical significance. Once the scores have been collected they must be compared to a proper criterion or normative scale based on the subpopulation (20,24,25). The scope of this book does not allow an in-depth discussion of statistical significance and therefore this discourse will focus on practical uses of test scores.

> Once the test data is collected, it should be accurately interpreted to the coach and the athlete in terms of norms and expected improvement.

Order scales

Test scores fall into three main categories. Nominal scores are those that are coded for entry into a spreadsheet or statistical computer program. They represent the "real" item through the use of numbers. An example is coding gender as 1 for men and 2 for women or vice versa. One might also use a code for positional differences on an athletic team such as 1 for outside hitters and 2 for setters and 3 for middle blockers on a volleyball team. This procedure allows the tester to add up the number of participants who possess similar characteristics but not to perform mathematical calculations on those values.

Interval scores are those that do not possess an absolute zero, meaning that zero does not represent the absence of that variable, but that it sometimes contains negative scores and there is no standard unit of difference between scores. The most popular form of interval scoring is temperature expressed in Fahrenheit degrees. Freezing is expressed as 32°; zero does not constitute no temperature; negative numbers are used to express colder temperatures; and 66° is not twice as warm as 33°.

Ratio scores possess all the traits not held by interval. They have an absolute zero, meaning a zero score is an absence of that variable, as in an elderly person's vertical jump score of zero inches. They contain no negative numbers and there is an absolute scale of measurement between scores, such that lifting 50 pounds is exactly half as much as lifting 100 pounds. This is the most popular form of physiological measurement and is predominantly used in physical activity literature and testing.

Sometimes a fourth form of scoring order is expressed as **ordinal**, which is more accurately described as a ranking system rather than a scoring scale. An ordinal system ranks scores from top to bottom or highest to lowest or greatest to least. All the other scales of measurements can be listed in ordinal rank, but it does not change them from their original scaling form.

Mathematical measures

There are a few variables associated with central tendency that need to be discussed so the investigator may draw conclusions from the collected data. They are fundamental in nature and require little mathematical skill but will provide the tester with valuable information regarding the data as a whole and each individuals' relationship to the overall group.

- **Minimum** and **maximum** refer to the least score and the greatest score respectively.
- **Range** is the difference between the minimum and maximum and represents the overall spread of scores as a whole number. The formula is max – min.
- **Sum** is the total of all scores combined and added together. The formula is $x_1 + x_2 + x_3 + x_4$, etc.
- **N** is the symbol used to denote the number of people in the test group and is used in conjunction with the sum to arrive at other important variables.
- **Mean** is simply the arithmetic average derived from the sum divided by N. It is the most sensitive of all measures of central tendency and is also used most often. It considers every score in the group and is pulled away from the middle by extreme scores. The formula is sum/n.
- **Median** is the exact middle of the total number of scores. It is not affected by outliers, shows a position only and is rarely used for any statistical calculations. To find the

median, the scores should first be placed in an ordinal ranking, then if there is an odd number of scores the median will be the middle score (e.g., if 11 scores then median is score #6 since 5 scores are greater and 5 scores are less). If there is an even number of scores then the median will be an average of the two middle scores (e.g., if 12 scores then median is the average of scores 6 and 7).

- **Mode** is the score that occurs most frequently. There may be multiple modes or there may not be a mode at all. It is also not affected by extreme scores, neither is it used frequently in statistical calculations.

Distribution of scores

Once all the scores have been collected it is beneficial to determine their measures of central tendency. **Central tendency** is the measure of the middle of a distribution of scores. The measurement community relies on scores following a few basic rules, which causes them to take familiar shapes when presented graphically. The scores can then be analyzed using basic statistical assumptions. Figure 10.14 displays a normal bell curve, the basic element and starting point of many statistical techniques. The bell curve is a frequency histogram which plots the number of times a score occurs on the vertical, or Y axis, against the raw number

itself on the horizontal or X axis where scores increase as they move from left to right. The conventional hump in the middle demonstrates that the greatest number of scores fall in the middle range with fewer and fewer scores out to either side. Most tests will produce a graph that is at least in part similar to a bell curve. In other words, there will be a few very low and very high scores with the majority of scores being very similar. It is of paramount importance to remember that while many statistical calculations are based on the bell curve, *it almost never occurs in real life data*. Therefore, there is a bit of error built into all statistics and they should always be read with this in mind. The only true bell curve is when the mean, median, and mode are exactly the same number.

The hump in the bell curve shows the likeness of scores. If many of the athletes scored similarly, then the hump would be tall and thin, whereas a group with many varied scores would be short and flat. In some instances, the curve does not follow such a symmetrical shape as that of the bell curve. Figure 10.15A displays a **positively skewed** curve with a long tail on the right and a hump near the left side of the graph. Figure 10.15B displays a **negatively skewed** curve with a long tail on the left and a hump near the right side of the graph. There are even times when a group of scores may produce multiple humps. Figure 10.15C displays a **bimodal curve** where the frequency of scores was greatest in two different portions of the final outcome. Since the hump exhibits similarity of scores, a bimodal curve may reveal that the group contains two like groups of people (e.g., two genders, two athletic teams, etc.).

Variability

The most commonly used measure of variability in scores is the **standard deviation (SD)**. It describes the scatter of scores about the mean and is used to show inclusion of scores for different percentages of the population and can be used as a measure of homogeneity when compared to the mean. It is derived through a few simple mathematical steps:

1   Calculate the deviation of each score from the mean by subtracting the mean from each raw score. Half of the deviation scores will be negative since half the scores will

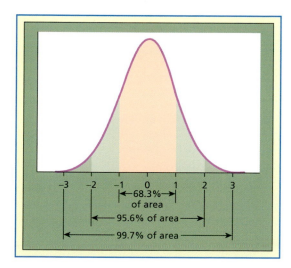

Figure 10.14 Normal bell curve. This commonly occurring frequency histogram demonstrates that the greatest number of scores falls in the middle range, with fewer scores at the extremes.

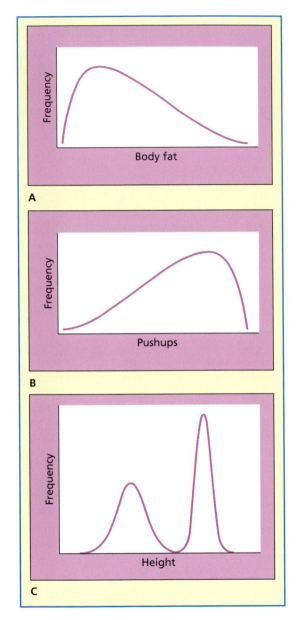

Figure 10.15 Likeness of scores shown by humps on graphs. (A) positively skewed curve; (B) negatively skewed curve; (C) bimodal curve.

4   Divide the sum of the squared deviations by N – 1 (e.g., if N = 11 then divide by 10) the answer is termed the **variance**. By eliminating one participant from the group it will better assist the tester in using the resultant data to predict the performance of other similar groups that were not tested.

5   Take the square root of the variance to counter-balance the squaring process performed earlier in the second step. The answer is the SD.

Now the SD can be used to explain the variability of scores previously displayed in the bell curve. Figure 10.14 shows how the mean and SD can be used to calculate group inclusion numbers. Simply stated, the mean plus or minus 1-SD includes approximately 68% of the total group population. In other words, if following a test the scores revealed a mean of 25 and an SD of 10 then it could be stated that approximately 68% of the group population had scores between 15 and 35 (e.g., 25 – 10 = 15 and 25 + 10 = 35). If N = 75 then 68% of that population would be 51 (i.e., 75 × 0.68). Likewise, the mean plus or minus 2-SD includes approximately 95% of the population while the mean plus or minus 3-SD includes approximately 99% or almost everyone in the test population. Remember that since the bell curve almost never occurs (mean, median, and mode must be exactly the same number), there is always some error in the system. Therefore, the percentages rarely fall directly on those numbers but are most often close.

Standardized scores

Another important use for the SD is to calculate **standardized scores**. These are scores that express each individual score as an SD making it easier to determine each score's standard distance from the mean. This procedure allows tests with different units of measurement to be compared without confusion (e.g., vertical jump in inches vs 1RM in pounds). They are therefore very popularly used with standardized tests of knowledge or for large population groups following administration of a test battery.

Standardized scores are divided into two types. First are **Z-scores**, which range between –3 and +3 and are expressed out to 2 decimal places. They are calculated by subtracting the mean from the raw score then dividing by the SD. If a

fall below the mean. Do not let this concern you as it will be remedied in the next step.

2   Square each deviation score by multiplying it by itself. This will convert all negative scores to positive scores.

3   Add all the squared deviations together to arrive at a sum.

raw score were 35 and the mean 25 with an SD of 10, then the equation would be $(35 - 25)/10 = 1$. The resultant Z-score of 1 means that the raw score of 35 is exactly 1-SD greater than the mean. Consequently, the average Z-score is zero and all positive Z-scores are raw scores greater than the mean while all negative Z-scores are raw scores that are less than the mean.

Second, **T-scores**, which range from 30 to 80, are almost identical to Z-scores. They are the same because they are derived from Z-scores. The procedure for T-scores is to multiply the Z-score by 10 then add 50. T-scores are always positive whole numbers (i.e., no decimal places). Consequently, the average T-score is 50 and all T-scores greater than 50 are raw scores greater than the mean, while all T-scores less than 50 are raw scores that are less than the mean. T-scores are used because the resultant value is always positive and easy to understand by the lay person.

SUMMARY

A valid and reliable evaluation and assessment program begins with a careful needs analysis of both the client/athlete and the activity/sport. Appropriate tests are then chosen based on the individual needs of the situation and the results are carefully analyzed using the basic mathematical calculations of central tendency and variability. By performing these simple calculations, assumptions can be made regarding the value of each score for each participant. Scores can then be compared to population specific normative values or a criterion scale developed from those norms. In the final analysis the well-prepared and knowledgeable tester will be able to evaluate each individual's needs and subsequently prescribe an appropriate training program to meet the derived client-specific goals.

MAXING OUT

1 A graduate student wanted to know something about the vertical jump of her classmates. She tested each one in the class and came up with the data set below: 19.5, 20, 21.5, 18, 17.5, 16, 22.5, 25, 24.5, 17.5. Find the mean, median, and mode of the data set and explain how to use these numbers to describe a team to a coach.
2 The basketball coach comes to you and wants an assessment of the team. You plan to do a "needs analysis" looking at both the individual player and the game of basketball. List the tests you will need to perform to answer the coach's query regarding the state of his team.
3 A colleague of yours has just developed a new assessment tool and has come to you in order for you to establish the validity and reliability of the new tool. What would you do to establish both validity and reliability of this tool? How are the two different?

CASE EXAMPLE

Designing a performance testing program for an elite junior tennis athlete

Background

You are employed in a major, well equipped sports facility with all testing equipment available to you. You are told to prepare for a complete fitness evaluation of a 16-year-old, nationally ranked male tennis player preparing to turn pro. The player is the current national champion in the 16-and-under age group. He was first runner-up in the Junior U.S. Open this year.

(continued)

(continued)

The athlete is experienced in all areas of training and conditioning. He uses free weight resistance training regularly in his program, and performs a variety of multi-joint and Olympic-style lifts. He participates in a variety of speed and agility training exercises.

The athlete does participate in clay court tournaments from time to time, but his primary surface, and the surface his game is expected to excel on, is a hard court surface.

Using a needs analysis of the sport of tennis and a typical tennis athlete, design a complete fitness testing session to evaluate this athlete.

Recommendations/considerations

Begin with a needs analysis of the sport of tennis. Professional tennis is an explosive fast game, particularly on hard court surfaces. The tennis athlete is required to change directions rapidly several times in a point. The ability to generate ground reaction force and transfer that force to the upper body is a key component of success in tennis. The testing program for this athlete will likely include tests for the following: muscular endurance, lower extremity muscular strength, lower extremity power, upper extremity muscular strength, upper extremity power, speed, agility, cardiorespiratory endurance, and joint range of motion. Injuries should be noted, and the musculoskeletal adaptations to those injuries should be considered.

Implementation

Maximal treadmill test with metabolic cart

Although tennis is primarily an anaerobic sport, recovery between points is aerobic. Moderate to moderately high levels of oxygen consumption are desirable in the tennis athlete. This test will provide information on the athlete's ability to work aerobically and to recover between points.

Bench press

Since the athlete trains using free weights, the bench press is a good measure of upper body strength.

Squat

Again, since the athlete trains with free weights, the squat is a good choice for measuring overall lower extremity strength. The ability of a tennis player to generate ground reaction force is a key component of tennis performance.

Vertical jump

The vertical jump is an excellent choice to measure lower body power. Performance on this test is relevant to tennis as it is an indicator of the ability of the athlete to get a quick start and may also be an indicator of the athlete's ability to generate power in the service motion.

Seated medicine ball push

This test is a measure of general upper body power.

20-yard dash

Speed in tennis is limited to short distances, and 20 yards would be the maximum a player would have to run all out without stopping or changing direction.

Hexagon

This test is used to measure footwork and agility.

"T" test

This test measures lateral, backward, and forward movement over a short distance, and the ability to transition among each form of locomotion.

5–0–5 test

This test measures changes-of-direction speed by running 10 meters to timing gates, decelerating through 5 meters, changing direction on one leg and accelerating back through the timing gates.

5-point agility run

This test measures the ability of the athlete to move in diagonal patterns, changing direction, gaining speed, decelerating, and stopping.

Underwater weighing

Measuring body composition using underwater weighing techniques is an accurate way to determine body composition.

Push-ups in 60 seconds

In this athlete, push-ups are a test of upper body muscular endurance. In the athlete who can only perform a few push-ups, it becomes a test of muscular strength.

Sit-ups in 60 seconds

Sit-ups are a general measure of core body strength and endurance. The trunk is very important in tennis as it transfers forces from the ground to the upper extremity.

Results

Results are reported by percentile rank using a database of over 100 16-year-old male tennis athletes.
   Maximal treadmill test with metabolic cart: 90th percentile
   Bench press: 96th percentile
   Squat: 91st percentile
   Vertical jump: 60th percentile

(continued)

(continued)

Seated medicine ball push: 88th percentile
20-yard dash: 88th percentile
Hexagon: 85th percentile
"T" test: 89th percentile
5-point agility run: 87th percentile
Underwater weighing: 90th percentile
These results should be reported to the athlete, the coach, and/or the parents of the player. The one area of athletic fitness that obviously needs the most work is lower body power. Remember when conveying results to the player to point out needed areas of improvement and prescribe appropriate exercise regimens to correct the identified deficits.

REFERENCES

1. Abad CCC, Prado ML, Ugrinowitsch C, Tricoli V, Barroso R. Combination of general and specific warm-ups improves leg-press one repetition maximum compared with specific warm-up in trained individuals. *J Strength Cond Res* 2011; 25(8):2242–2245.

2. Bar-Or O. The Wingate test: An update on methodology, reliability and validity. *Sports Med* 1987; 4:381–394.

3. Benz A, Winkelman N, Porter J, Nimphius S. Coaching Instructions and Cues for Enhancing Sprint Performance. *Strength Cond* 2016; 38(1):1–11.

4. Bishop, D. Warm up II-performance changes following active warm up and how to structure the warm up. *Sports Med* 2003; 33(7):483–498.

5. Brown LE, Weir JP. ASEP procedures recommendations for the accurate assessment of muscular strength and power. *J Exerc Physiol* [serial online]. 2001; 4(3):1–21. Available at: http://faculty.css.edu/tboone2/asep/August2001JEPonline.html. Accessed October 16, 2003.

6. Brown LE, Whitehurst M, Bryant JR. A comparison of the LIDO sliding cuff and the tibial control system in isokinetic strength parameters. *Isokinetics and Exercise Science* 1992; 2(3):101–109.

7. Brown LE, Whitehurst M, Bryant JR. Reliability of the LIDO active isokinetic dynamometer concentric mode. *Isokinetics and Exercise Science* 1992; 2(4):191–194.

8. Brown LE, Whitehurst M, Bryant JR, Buchalter DN. Reliability of the Biodex system 2 isokinetic dynamometer concentric mode. *Isokinetics and Exercise Science* 1993; 3(3):160–163.

9. Chapman PP, Whitehead JR, Binkert RH. The 225-lb reps-to-fatigue test as a submaximal estimate of 1-RM bench press performance in college football players. *J Strength Cond Res*, 1998; 12:258–261.

10. Chinn S, Burney PGJ. On measuring repeatability of data from self-administered questionnaires. *Int J Epidemiol* 1987; 16:121–127.

11. Conway DP, Decker AS. Utilizing a computerized strength and conditioning testing index for assessment of collegiate football players. *Strength Cond* 1992; 14(5):13–16.

12. Dolezal BA, Thompson CJ, Schroeder CA, et al. Laboratory testing to improve athletic performance. *Strength Cond* 1997; 19(6):20–24.

13. Enoka RM. *Neuromechanical Basis of Kinesiology*. Champaign, IL: Human Kinetics, 1988.

14. Graham J. Guidelines for providing valid testing of athletes' fitness levels. *Strength Cond* 1994; 16(6):7–14.

15. Haddad M, Dridi A, Chtara M, Chaouachi A, Wong DP, Behm D, Chamari K. Static stretching can impair explosive performance for at least 24 hours. *J Strength Cond Res* 2014; 28(1):140–146.

16. Halperin, I, Williams KJ, Martin DT, Chapman DW. The effects of attentional focusing instructions on force production during the isometric midthigh pull. *J Strength Cond Res* 2016; 30(4):919–923.

17. Halperin I, Chapman DW, Martin DT, Abbiss, C. The effects of attentional focus instructions on punching velocity and impact forces among trained combat athletes, *J of Sports Sci* 2016; 35(5):500–507.

18. Magill RA. *Motor Learning: Concepts and Applications*, 5th edition. Madison, WI: Brown & Benchmark Publishers, 1998.

19. Maud PJ, Shultz BB. Norms for the Wingate Anaerobic Test with comparison to another similar test. *Res Quart for Ex and Sport* 1989; 60:144–151.

20. Mayhew JL, Ware JR, Prinster JL. Using lift repetitions to predict muscular strength in adolescent males. *Strength Cond* 1993; 15(6):35–38.

21. Patton JF, Duggan A. An evaluation of tests of anaerobic power. *Aviation Space Environ Med* 1987; 58:237–242.

22. Plisk SS. Anaerobic metabolic conditioning: A brief review of theory, strategy and practical application. *J Strength Cond Res* 1991; 5(1):22–34.

23. Plisk SS, Gambetta V. Tactical metabolic training: Part 1. *Strength Cond* 1997; 19(2):44–53.

24. Schweigert D. Normative values for common preseason testing protocols: NCAA division II women's basketball. *Strength Cond* 1996; 18(6):7–10.

25. Semenick D, Connors J, Carter M, et al. Rationale, protocols, testing/reporting forms and instructions for wrestling. *Strength Cond* 1992; 14(3):54–59.

26. Stockbrugger BA, Haennel RG. Validity and reliability of a medicine ball explosive power test. *J Strength Cond Res* 2001; 15(4):431–438.

27. Swank AM, Adams K, Serapiglia L, et al. Submaximal testing for the strength and conditioning professional. *Strength Cond* 1999; 21(6):9–15.

28. Taylor NAS, Sanders RH, Howick EI, Stanley SN. Static and dynamic assessment of the Biodex dynamometer. *Eur J Appl Physiol* 1991; 62:180–188.

29. Timm KE, Fyke D. The effect of test speed sequence on the concentric isokinetic performance of the knee extensor muscle group. *Isok Exerc Sci* 1993; 3(2):123–128.

30. Turki O, Chaouachi A, Behm DG, Chtara H, Chtara M, Bishop D, Chamari K, Amri M. The effect of warm-ups incorporating different volumes of dynamic stretching on 10- and 20-m sprint performance in highly trained male athletes. *J Strength Cond Res* 2012; 26(1):63–72.

31. Winkelman, N. Attentional focus and cueing for speed development. *Strength Cond* 2017; 40(1):13–25.

32. Wu WFW, Porter JM, Brown LE. Effect of attentional focus strategies on peak force and performance in the standing long jump. *J Strength Cond Res* 2012; 26(5):1226–1231.

Contents

CHAPTER 11

RESISTANCE EXERCISE TECHNIQUES AND SPOTTING

Ryan T. McManus and Andrew J. Galpin

OBJECTIVES

After reading this chapter, you will be able to:

- Apply general physiological adaptations to resistance training.
- Explain the proper technique for specific free weight, machine, and trunk exercises performed at both slow and explosive speeds.
- Provide safe and effective spotting assistance for specific exercises.
- Understand the importance of wearing proper clothing and footwear in the weight room.
- Understand the basic components of resistance-training exercise technique.
- Identify specific exercises that can have carryover to other activities.

KEY TERMS

Absolute muscular strength	Intermuscular adaptation	Periodization
Alternated grip	Intramuscular adaptation	Pronated grip
Common grip	Muscle recruitment	Relative muscular strength
Energy intake	Narrow grip	Spotter
Five-point contact position	Neutral grip	Sticking point
Hook grip	Osteopenia	Supinated grip
Hyperplasia	Osteoporosis	Valsalva maneuver
Hypertrophy	Overload	Wide grip
	Overtraining	

INTRODUCTION

This chapter provides an explanation of the physiological benefits, safety, equipment, and techniques of resistance training. It also includes detailed descriptions of 25 free weight, 7 machine, and 8 trunk exercises. These exercises are categorized into the following classes: total-body (power/explosive), multi-joint lower-body, single-joint lower-body, multi-joint upper-body, and single-joint upper-body exercises. Total-body exercises emphasize loading the spine directly or indirectly. Multi-joint exercises involve two or more joints that change angles during the movement of a repetition. Single-joint exercises involve only one joint changing its angle during the completion of a repetition. Each exercise described in this chapter is accompanied by a detailed explanation of the type of exercise, muscles utilized, body and limb alignment, ascending and descending movement, safety points, and variations of exercise technique.

The benefits of resistance training are provided and include positive adaptations to muscles, nerves, and bones. Safety is important in resistance-training exercises, particularly considering the increased loads placed on the body during specific lifts. Spotters should be utilized in resistance training when appropriate. Exercise technique is important for safe execution of each lift and to understand the musculature affected in each exercise.

BENEFITS OF RESISTANCE TRAINING

Muscles adapt to resistance training by strengthening and growing. This process, called **hypertrophy** (4,5,10,15), involves an increase in the cross-sectional area of muscle fibers, not the splitting of the muscle into additional muscle fibers, which is called **hyperplasia**. A muscle will develop more force and power as it increases in cross-sectional area (5). Hypertrophy has been demonstrated to occur from an increase in the thickness and number of myofibrils (4,5,10,15,16). It is believed to be the primary mechanism governing muscle growth. Many factors generally are responsible for muscle hypertrophy (4,5,10,15,16):

> By varying exercises, volumes, and intensities, safe and well-planned resistance training can have positive effects on skeletal muscle growth, neuromuscular coordination, and bone mineral density in both men and women (13).

- **Overload**/mechanical tension. The resistance should be greater than the muscle's previous ability.

- **Muscle recruitment.** The maximal numbers of muscle fibers should be recruited.
- **Metabolic stress.** The resistance and volume should combine to cause muscular fatigue.
- **Energy intake.** An adequate amount of carbohydrate and protein should be consumed.

Resistance training can enhance absolute and relative muscle strength (4,5,10,15,16). **Absolute muscular strength** is the strength an individual can develop regardless of body weight. **Relative muscular strength** is defined by absolute muscular strength divided by body weight in either kilograms or pounds. Increases in muscle and explosive strength are generally tied to inter- and intramuscular adaptations and muscle hypertrophy. The term **intermuscular adaptation** refers to the proper execution of technique for exercises performed at both slow and explosive speeds. As an individual acquires proper technique, less energy is required to perform the exercise; therefore, the resistance utilized can be increased. **Intramuscular adaptation** refers to how many motor units are recruited during the effort, how quickly they are recruited, and whether antagonistic motor units interfere with the movement (4,5,10,16). By undergoing resistance training, individuals can expect an increased number of motor units to be recruited at an accelerated speed along with an increased inhibition of antagonistic muscle(s).

> Increases in strength from resistance training are due to both hypertrophic and neurological adaptations.

Other benefits of resistance training include improvements in bone density, energy utilization, and substrate storage. The lack of weight-bearing activity with aging has often been linked to **osteopenia** (lowering of bone mineral mass to 1 standard deviation below young-normal levels) and **osteoporosis** (lowering of bone mineral mass to more than 2.5 standard deviations below young-normal levels). As discussed in Chapter 4, bone adapts to resistance training by increasing mineralization in a particular region of the bone. This results in increases in strength and ability to handle the stress (5,13,14). This may be accomplished through exercises using loads at greater than 75% of an individual's 3RM (the maximum weight an individual can utilize for three repetitions) that are weight-bearing in nature (multi-joint, closed-chain-kinetic exercises, such as leg presses, squats, and Romanian deadlift). If the resistance training includes light to moderate loads (40% to 60% of 1RM), higher repetitions (12 to 25), and shorter rest periods (30 to 60 seconds), moderate increases of 5% in VO_2 (oxygen uptake) may be expected (2,5). With resistance training, individuals will utilize and store energy more efficiently. This will result in the muscle's ability to train at higher resistances and for longer periods of time. Resistance training performed with good technique through a full range of motion (ROM) can also enhance muscle flexibility and reduce the likelihood of injury (2,5).

> The effects of a resistance-training program depend on how training variables such as repetitions, intensities, and rest periods are modified.

Although males are typically stronger than females, the differences in muscle strength are not tied to the quality of the muscle tissue or its ability to produce force or power. In these respects, no difference exists between genders. A significant difference does exist, however, in the quantity of muscle tissue in the average male (40%) versus female (23%), which is largely responsible for the male strength advantage. It is this difference that also helps to explain why women are typically 43% to 63% weaker in upper-body strength and 25% to 30% weaker in lower-body strength (2,5). Conditioning programs for male and female athletes for the same sport should be essentially the same, as the physiological demands of the sport are the same.

> Males generally have a greater absolute strength than females, but males and females are similar in relative strength when cross-sectional area is equated.

Overtraining is characterized by a decline in performance over a time. This occurs when an individual's body is not given enough time to recuperate from training prior to the next training session (2,4,5,10,16). Symptoms of overtraining include but are not limited to the following:

- An increase in morning resting heart rate
- An unintentional decrease in body weight
- Inability to perform in a training session at the same level of strength, power, or endurance as had been achieved earlier
- An increase in muscle soreness from one training session to the next
- Extreme muscle soreness and stiffness on the day immediately following a training session
- A decrease in appetite

Once an individual becomes overtrained – that is, by exhibiting two or more of the warning signs listed above – the frequency, intensity, and duration of activity should be reduced until the symptoms dissipate. Obviously, it is more effective to prevent overtraining than to recover from it. Guidelines for preventing overtraining include increasing training intensity and duration gradually (< 5%), following sound nutritional guidelines, and devoting adequate time to sleep and recovery. The risk of overtraining may be increased in training the multisport athlete (see the case study further on). Additionally, utilization of **periodization** when designing resistance-training programs is essential for both avoiding overtraining and maximizing benefits. Periodization is the planned variation of training variables (volume, intensity, choice, rest intervals, etc.) to achieve peak levels of performance and/or fitness at a designated time (5,6).

> Proper planning using a periodized resistance-training program will help prevent overtraining and maximize results.

REAL-WORLD APPLICATION

Training male and female athletes for the same sport

You are asked to evaluate the conditioning program for both the boys and girls on your high school's basketball teams. You are asked to make recommendations to the coaches as to changes that they could consider.

Observed: After observing the training program you note the girls' team uses only body-weight exercises while the boys' team is using only machines.

Recommendations: The boys' and girls' teams should not be using separate programs, since they are training for the same sport. It is recommended that both teams use free weight exercises that focus on lower-body strength and power. Areas of muscular weakness or imbalance should be identified and targeted with specific assistance training.

SAFETY

Training equipment and facilities can provide a safe environment for exercise as long as basic safety guidelines are utilized.

Spotting

Probably the most critical aspect of safe training (once the facility and equipment utilized have been inspected) is the use of a spotter(s), particularly with free weight exercises. A **spotter** is a knowledgeable individual who assists in the proper execution of an exercise (2,5,6). His or her responsibility is to ensure the exerciser completes all repetitions with good technique, assist the exerciser with completion of a repetition when needed (or to help complete forced repetitions), and summon help when necessary (2,5,6). This responsibility should be taken very seriously, as failure to do so may result in serious injury not only to the exerciser, but to the spotter as well. Since the following maneuvers are the most potentially harmful to the athlete, exercises involving free weights either over the head (standing barbell press), with the barbell resting on the back (barbell lunge or back squat), racked at the front of the upper shoulders (barbell front squat), or over the face (barbell bench press or supine triceps extension) necessitate the use of one or more skilled spotters. Power exercises, as well as any exercise involving raising the barbell or dumbbell to the side or front of the body below shoulder level generally do not require a spotter.

> Spotting must be taken seriously to ensure safe lifting practices are taking place. The focus of the spotter must be solely on the lifter throughout the entire exercise. Communication between the lifter and the spotter is essential. For example, the spotter must know the intensions of the lifter (i.e., repetition goals and when to provide aid).

> Barbells should always be loaded evenly on both sides and the weights secured with collars.

Exercises performed overhead and with the barbell on the front or back of the shoulders should be performed inside a power rack with the safety bars placed at an appropriate height. Individuals who are not spotting or performing the exercise should remain at a safe distance. Because the loads utilized in these exercises can be substantial, spotters should ideally be nearly as strong and as tall as the exerciser. All additional barbells, collars, plates, weight trees, and other equipment should be outside the immediate exercise area. Collars should be utilized regardless of the load to prevent weight plates from sliding off the barbell. For maximum safety, three spotters (one directly behind the exerciser and one on each side of the barbell) should be present. All three should assist with removing the load from the rack as well as returning the load to the rack on completion of the repetitions. When multiple spotters are being used, a lead spotter should be designated. It is this person's job to direct the other spotters and make the call on when assistance should be given to the exerciser.

Q&A FROM THE FIELD

You notice that a particular exerciser in your program looks fatigued. What questions might you ask him? What possible causes of the fatigue should you consider?

How much sleep he is getting? What are his eating habits? Is he getting enough recovery between training sessions? Is there enough variety in his exercises? You should consider overtraining, disease, psychological problems, and normal emotional stresses as possible causes.

For exercises performed over the face, the spotter should hold the barbell with an alternated grip inside the exerciser's grip to ensure the barbell does not leave the exerciser's hands and land on the exerciser's face, neck, or chest. In the case of an exercise where the athlete's grip is narrow, the spotter may grasp the barbell immediately outside the exerciser's grip. Spotters should be conscious of body alignment (flat back, feet shoulder-width apart in a solid base, and a bent-knee position), as they may be called on quickly to help the exerciser by catching the barbell or by helping to lift the load. Dumbbell exercises may pose a different challenge to the spotter as they require more skill to assist. For the safety of the exerciser, it is important for spotters to spot by standing as close to the dumbbells as possible and spotting near the wrists so that the spotter can quickly support the exerciser if his or her elbows collapse, preventing the dumbbells from falling inward toward the exerciser's chest or face. For exercises in which one dumbbell is used, such as seated overhead triceps extension or supine dumbbell pull-over, it is important to spot with the hands directly on or slightly below the dumbbell.

In selecting the number of spotters for a given exercise, an exerciser should consider the load being lifted, the physical strength and height of the spotters, and the experience level of both the exerciser and spotters. The heavier the load, the greater the risk for injury and the severity of injury to both the exerciser and the spotter should the exerciser fail to complete a repetition and an inadequate spot be provided. For most exercises that involve overhead lifting with a barbell, a barbell on the back or shoulders with heavier loads, and over-the-face exercises with

heavier loads, a lead spotter should be placed immediately behind the lifter to direct the other spotters placed on each side of the barbell. As the number of spotters increases, so does the potential for errors in timing. Prior to the first lift, the exerciser should tell the spotter(s) how the barbell will be lifted from the rack, how many repetitions will be performed, and how the barbell will be returned to the rack. This ensures the exercise can be performed safely and the spotters do not disrupt the exercise.

Exercises that require explosive power should not utilize a spotter. Spotting these exercisers places both the exerciser and the spotter at increased risk for injury. Exercisers performing these explosive lifts should be taught the proper technique for missing a lift. To miss a lift when the barbell is in front of the body, the proper technique is to push the barbell forward and release it as the lifter moves backward. To miss a lift with the barbell behind the body, the lifter should release the barbell and jump forward. For the safety of not only the exerciser but also other exercisers in the surrounding area, power exercises should be performed on a segregated power platform clear of other exercisers and equipment (5).

Exercise apparel

Proper clothing when exercising with resistance equipment is critical for two major reasons: safety and etiquette. It is important to wear a workout shirt that covers the chest, upper back, and shoulders to avoid losing control of a barbell on exercises where the barbell rests on the upper shoulders (e.g., barbell back squats). Without a shirt that covers those areas, a barbell may slip off the body, putting the exerciser, spotters, and other exercisers nearby at risk for injury. Covering the upper body with a T-shirt is also important on exercises that require the exerciser to lie prone or supine on a bench. Not doing so is poor etiquette and may also cause damage to the equipment's upholstery.

Footwear is also important in resistance training. Closed-toe training shoes that provide a solid, stable base should be used at all times. The proper shoes will ensure that the exerciser has a stable lifting base, which is critical for all explosive lower-body, squatting, overhead lift, or lifting from the floor exercises. Closed-toe shoes also provide some protection against dropped plates, barbells, and dumbbells. Sandals and bare feet should not be permitted in the resistance-training area for reasons of safety and hygiene.

> Clothing provides a layer of protection from exercise equipment and provides friction between the lifter and the bar. For example, the bar does not slide off the back during a squat as easily while clothed as it would on a bare back. Shoes protect the feet from foreign objects lining the floor and provide a stable base, encouraging proper lifting technique.

Safety is extremely important in a resistance-training program, and proper precautions should be taken at all times.

RESISTANCE-TRAINING TECHNIQUE

Every resistance-training exercise provides its own unique benefits and challenges. Understanding the similarities and differences between exercises is essential for the proper design of a resistance-training prescription. The proper execution of a resistance-training exercise has eight basic components:

1 Objective for exercise selection
2 Equipment alignment
3 Body alignment
4 Stabilization of body
5 Movement of body during exercise
6 Speed of movement
7 Breathing
8 Initiation and return of exercise equipment

In selecting an exercise, it is essential to ensure the exercise matches the objective of the program. For example, exercisers often perform numerous sets of chest exercises while not balancing them with an appropriate number of upper back exercises, or failing to perform leg exercises. Spot enhancement or reduction of a given section of the body is not achievable (1,5,10). It is important for exercisers to recognize the importance of balance in a resistance-training exercise prescription. You are only as good as your weakest link.

As a general rule, select equal amounts of exercises that work opposing muscle groups. This reduces the likelihood of asymmetrically stressing joints, which can lead to injury of muscles, joints, and cartilage over time.

Equipment alignment means setting the equipment up properly so the exercise can be performed safely and with maximum benefit. The proper resistance should be set on a machine exercise, the barbell should have equal resistance on each side, or dumbbells of identical resistance should be selected. Collars should be placed securely on each side of the barbell to make sure weights do not slide or fall off the barbell, causing the barbell to tip. Hooks for barbell exercises in which the barbell is placed on the shoulder should be set 3 to 4 in. below shoulder level so the exerciser can drop under the barbell to remove it from the rack to initiate the set and then return it to the rack above the hooks before sliding it back down on the hooks at the completion of the set. Safety bars on the power rack should be set slightly below the end ROM on squat or power exercises performed within the rack. Cams, seats, and arm and leg lengths on machines should be adjusted to the exerciser's optimal safe ROM.

In positioning the body during resistance training, the axial skeleton and its immediate attachments are of the highest priority (1,5,10). This means particular attention should continuously be paid to the positioning of the pelvis, spinal column, and shoulder girdle before and during any resistance-training exercise. The spinal column is in its most stable and therefore strongest position when it, the pelvis, and the neck are all in neutral positions with a slight thoracic kyphosis and lumbar lordosis. To place the torso in an ideal resistance-training position, the athlete should pull the shoulder blades back slightly and down, lift the sternum slightly out and up, and pull the chin slightly back and down, creating or maintaining the natural arch in the thoracic and lumbar regions of the spine (1,5,10). Be careful to not over arch, or hyperextend the lumbar spine. Positioning of the hands is also important. The two primary handgrip positions are the **pronated grip** (palms down and knuckles up) and **supinated grip** (palms up and knuckles down). A variation of either grip is the **neutral grip** (knuckles point laterally). Other grips include the **alternated grip** (one hand supinated and the other pronated). In performing exercises that require a stronger grip (Olympic-style lifts), a **hook grip** (wrapping the index and middle fingers around the thumb, which is placed against the bar first), designed to add at least 10% to any pulling motion, is used (5). Along with the handgrip, grip width must be considered. The three grip widths are a **common grip** (shoulder width), a **wide grip** (outside of shoulder width), and **narrow grip** (inside shoulder width).

> Before performing any exercise, it is important to know the correct grip choice and grip width. The proper grip to use can be determined by the choice of exercise, load, and/or target musculature.

Regardless of whether the exercise is performed utilizing a barbell, dumbbell, or machine, stabilization of the body is critical (9,11,12). A stable position enables an exerciser to maintain proper body alignment during an exercise, which in turn ensures that the appropriate stress is placed on the intended muscles and joints. Exercises that call for a standing position require the feet to be positioned shoulder-width, with all parts of the feet securely in contact with the floor. Whether the exerciser is seated, prone (lying face down), or supine (lying face up), his or her head, shoulders (front or back), chest or upper back, lower back, and buttocks or pelvis should be in contact with the bench or machine. The feet must remain in contact with the floor unless the height of the machine does not permit or require the feet to be in contact with the floor or the exercise is a lower-body open-chain exercise. When the head, back, pelvis, and both feet are in contact with the bench and floor, it is known as the **five-point contact position**.

The movement of the body differs during different exercises. Although exercises generally have a maximum ROM, the ideal ROM depends on variations in the exerciser's musculoskeletal, neurological, and biomechanical systems, and purpose of the exercise selection.

Modern exercise machines are often designed with a range of controls for both the eccentric and concentric muscle actions. Additionally, power racks allow the exerciser to control ROM in barbell exercises.

Speed of motion with exercises depends on the type of exercise being performed. Exercises should always be performed in a controlled manner. Explosive power exercises are intended to maximize movement speed. Other exercises are generally performed more slowly with an emphasis on ROM, technique, and movement quality. The eccentric muscle action of these exercises should generally be performed over a 2- to 4-second period, with a 1-second hold at completion before initiating the concentric movement. The concentric movement is generally performed over a 1- to 3-second period with a 1-second hold at the completion before initiating the eccentric muscle action. If movement speed is increased, do not compromise exercise technique, body alignment, stability, or general movement quality.

Exercisers should breathe at some point during every repetition. The most strenuous portion of a repetition, typically where the lifter is most likely to fail, is referred to as the **sticking point** (5). This is the point in the ROM of any joint where the mechanical advantage of the lever system is the lowest. The exact angle of the sticking point will depend on the mechanical properties of a specific joint. A general rule is for exercisers to inhale before initiating an exercise or at the less stressful phase of the repetition and to exhale after passing the sticking point. The use of the **Valsalva maneuver** (expiring against a closed glottis, which when combined with contracting the abdomen and rib cage muscles, creates rigid compartments of fluid in the lower torso and partially braces the spine) may be necessary to maintain proper vertebral alignment and support (6,9,10,11,12). Emphasis should be placed on firstly filling the abdomen (not the thoracic chest) with air. This bracing should be accomplished prior to starting the movement or placing the load on the body. However, implement with caution as movements exceeding 2 to 4 seconds may cause dizziness, lightheadedness, or in extreme cases, blackouts.

As a final aspect of resistance-training technique, it is very important exercisers properly lift the resistance to initiate a set and return the resistance to its starting position at the completion of a set. At least one spotter should be assisting when using a barbell with a power rack or bench to perform exercises that require loading of the vertebral column or overhead or over-the-face exercises. For the safety of the exerciser and others in the immediate area as well as for equipment maintenance, exercise should be initiated with the resistance being lifted from its resting position and returned to its starting position slowly.

RESISTANCE-TRAINING EXERCISES

Power exercises (1,5,6,7)

Power clean
High pull
Push jerk
Kettlebell swing
Medicine ball slam
TRX sprinter's start

Hip/thigh exercises (1,3,5,6)

Back squat
Front squat
Deadlift
Barbell split squat
TRX rear foot elevated split squat (RFESS)
Romanian deadlift (RDL)
Single-leg Romanian deadlift (single-leg RDL)
Leg press
Leg extension
Leg curl
Standing calf raise

Chest exercises (1,5,14)

Bench press, dumbbell
Bench press, barbell
Incline press, barbell
Dumbbell fly

Upper back exercises (1,5,14)

Dumbbell one-arm row
Lat pull-down
Seated cable row

Shoulder exercises (1,5,14)

Dumbbell seated shoulder press
Machine shoulder press
Barbell upright row

Triceps exercises (1,5,14)

Supine triceps extension
Triceps pushdown

Biceps exercises (1,5,14)

Barbell bicep curl
Seated dumbbell bicep curl

Abdominal and lower back exercises (1,4,5,8)

Abdominal crunch
Back extension
Stability ball jack knife
Stability ball roll-out
Prone plank
Side plank
Paloff press
Hollow position

Box 11.1   Power exercises

Power clean

Type of exercise

Total body/power (explosive) exercise

Muscles used

Gluteals, hamstrings, quadriceps, soleus, gastrocnemius, trapezius, and deltoids

Starting position (A)

(A)

1. Approach the barbell on the floor and take an approximately shoulder-width overhand grip on the bar.
2. Keep the arms straight, the wrists slightly flexed, and the elbows locked and rotated outward.
3. Stand with feet hip-width apart.
4. Pull the shoulders back and down, elevate the chest, keep the eyes looking forward.
5. Squat down, while keeping the shoulders in front of the barbell and the weight on the forward half of the feet.

First pull (B)

(B)

(continued)

(continued)

6   Keep the back flat and the arms straight, extend the hips and knees to lift the barbell off the ground to mid-thigh. Avoid jerking the bar, rounding the back, or locking out the knees when moving the barbell from below knee height to mid-thigh height.

7   Look straight and raise the shoulders and hips at the same speed.

Second pull (C)

(C)

8   Keeping the arms straight and the wrists slightly flexed, explosively extend the hips, rise up on the toes, and elevate the shoulders, moving the bar vertically and not away from the body.

9   Continue looking straight ahead as you elevate the barbell as high as possible, to chest level, without using the muscles in the arms.

Receiving position (D)

10 When the bar has reached its maximum height, drop under it into a quarter squat, lifting the elbows up and under the bar. If this is done properly, the bar is received on the front of the shoulders at the same time that you reach quarter squat. The shoulders should not slump forward.

(D)

Ending position

11 Keeping the elbows high and the chest elevated, stand straight up.

High pull

Type of exercise

Total-body/power (explosive) exercise

Muscles used

Gluteals, hamstrings, quadriceps, soleus, gastrocnemius, trapezius, and deltoids

Starting position (A)

1 Approach the barbell on the floor and take an approximately shoulder-width, pronated grip on the bar.
2 Keep the arms straight, the wrists slightly flexed, and the elbows locked and rotated outward.
3 Stand with the feet hip-width apart.

(continued)

(continued)

4 Pull the shoulders back, elevate the chest, and keep the eyes looking forward.
5 Squat down, while keeping the shoulders in front of the barbell and the weight on the forward half of the feet.

First pull (B)

6 Keeping the back flat and the arms straight, extend the hips and knees to lift the barbell off the ground to the mid-thigh in a slow and controlled manner. Avoid jerking the bar off the ground, which will cause the back to round. Avoid locking out the knees when moving the barbell from below knee height to mid-thigh height.
7 Look straight ahead and raise the shoulders and hips at the same speed.

Second pull (C)

8 Keeping the arms straight and the wrists slightly flexed with the bar at mid-thigh

level, violently extend the hips, rise up on the toes, and elevate the shoulders explosively, keeping the bar close to the body.

9   Continue looking straight ahead as you elevate the barbell to about chest level, without using the muscles of the arms.

Ending position

10   When the bar has reached its maximum height, around the level of the chest, let the bar return to a resting position on the thighs.

11   Once the bar is on the thighs return it to the floor by squatting down with the back flat and the spine in neutral position.

Push jerk

Type of exercise

Total-body/power (explosive) exercise

Muscles used

Gluteals, hamstrings, quadriceps, soleus, gastrocnemius, trapezius, and deltoids

Starting position (A)

(A)

(continued)

(continued)

1   Begin by standing straight with the feet hip-width apart and the bar on the front of the shoulders.
2   Take a shoulder-width grip on the bar, with the palms facing upward.
3   Elevate the chest, pull the shoulders back, and tuck the chin.

The dip

4   Keeping the weight on the heels, the barbell on the shoulders, and the chest up, quickly move into a quarter squat by pushing the hips back and flexing the knees.

The drive

5   Without pausing at the bottom of the squat, explosively reverse directions, driving straight up with the legs until rising up onto the toes. The act of driving up will force the bar up off the shoulders.

Ending position (B)

(B)

6   When the bar has reached its greatest height from the drive, continue to press it until the arms are extended and the barbell is in line with the hips (slightly behind the head).

Safety: technique on how to miss

If the lifter loses control of the barbell or cannot complete a rep for any reason, he or she should quickly get out from underneath and let it drop (without trying to save it on the way down). Use the barbell's downward momentum to move out of the way (the lifter is told to "keep your grip and push yourself away from the barbell as it falls"). Stay between the plates (this does not mean that the lifter should remain under a falling barbell but rather should move backward or forward, not sideways, to escape).

Kettlebell swing

Type of exercise

Total body/power (explosive) exercise

Muscles used

Gluteals, quadriceps, hamstrings, rectus abdominis, erector spinae, lattisimus dorsi, and deltoids

Starting position (A–D)

(A)

(continued)

(continued)

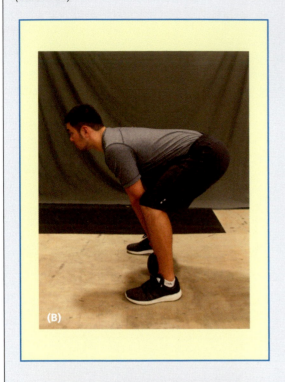

(B)

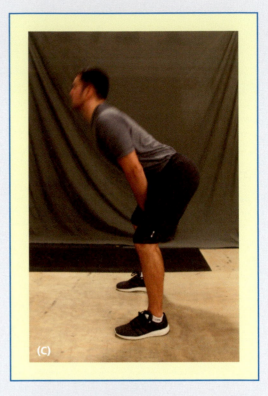

(C)

(D)

1 Stand over the kettlebell with feet flat, shoulder-width apart, toes facing forward, chest up, shoulders back.
2 With a neutral spine, squat down and grab the kettlebell with both hands, with a firm, closed, pronated grip.
3 Grip the kettlebell and stand up maintaining a neutral spine, keeping the elbows fully extended with the shoulders back engaging the torso muscles.
4 Shift the body weight slightly towards the heels and soften the knees and hips to a quarter squat position with the kettlebell hanging between the thighs, ready to swing.

Action (E–H)

5 Flex at the hips to allow the kettlebell to swing backwards between the legs. Keep the knees in the same starting flexed position with the back neutral and arms extended.

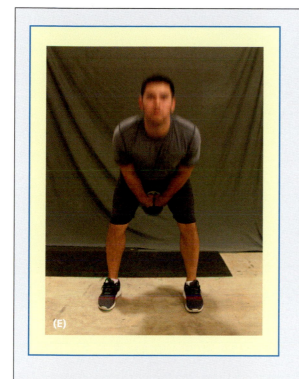

(E)

(F)

(G)

(H)

(continued)

(continued)

6   Allow the kettlebell to swing backward until the torso is nearly parallel to the floor. The kettlebell should be past the vertical line of the body.
7   Push through the heels, engage the gluteal muscles, and extend the hips and knees to swing the kettlebell upward. Allow momentum to swing the kettlebell up to eye height keeping the arms extended. At the top of the movement, engage the torso muscles.
8   Let the weight descend passively (while still maintaining control of the kettlebell) and flex at the hips and knees to absorb the weight.
9   Prepare the body for the next swing by shifting weight back towards the heels while bending at the hips, loading the hamstrings and glutes.
10 Allow the kettlebell to swing back between the legs and continue.
11 Drive through the heels, gluteals, and hips as the kettlebell swings backward to forward.

Medicine ball slam

Type of exercise

Total-body/power (explosive) exercise

Muscles used

Gluteals, hamstrings, quadriceps, soleus, gastrocnemius, rectus abdominus, and deltoids

Starting position

1   Stand with feet slightly wider than shoulder-width apart holding a medicine ball with both hands directly in front of the chest; palms facing each other, and elbows bent pointing toward the floor.

The action

2   Lift the medicine ball above the head, fully extending the body, while standing on the forefoot.
3   Reverse the motion, slamming the ball onto the ground as hard as possible.

Ending position

4   Catch the ball with both hands on the bounce.
5   Return to the standing position.

Suspension sprinter's start

Type of exercise

Lower-body/power (explosive) exercise

Muscles used

Gluteals, hamstrings, quadriceps, soleus, and gastrocnemius

Starting position (A)

1   Begin by standing facing away from the suspension trainer with a neutral grip on the handles.
2   The arms are positioned over the straps and bent at the elbows with hands tucked close to the body.
3   Stagger the feet, one stride length in front of the other, approximately hip-width apart.

The action (B)

4   Slightly flex the ankles, knees, and hips.
5   Rapidly extend the ankle, knee, and hip of the forward leg while forcefully driving the rear knee upward while flexing the ankle and hip of the rear foot, and maintaining a neutral spine.

Ending position

6   Land on flat feet with slight flexion of the ankles, knees and hips while returning to the starting position. Complete the desired number of repetitions, and then switch foot position.

To choose appropriate exercises, the lifter or coach must understand how to select the proper exercises. Selection of exercises, proper alignment, movement, and speed of movement are all components of resistance training.

Box 11.2   Hip/thigh exercises

Back squat

Type of exercise

Lower-body/multi-joint

Muscles used

Gluteals, quadriceps, and hamstrings

Starting position (A)

1   Position the rack so that the bar is approximately at shoulder height.
2   Step under the bar to place it on the upper portion of the back and shoulders. The bar should
     not rest on your vertebrae.
3   Grip the bar at a comfortable position, about a thumb's length from the knurling (the rough
     part of the bar) or slightly wider than shoulder-width.
4   Lift the bar off the rack by extending the hips and knees, then step back, placing legs about
     shoulder-width apart and toes pointed slightly outward.

Action (B)

5   Brace the spine and pelvis while gripping the floor with your feet before initiating a backward movement with the hips.
6   Allow the body to descend by flexing at the hips and knees. Keep knees in a path that aligns with the toes.
7   As the body descends, maintain an upright torso and a neutral spine.
8   Depending on the desired ROM, descend until the thigh and calf contact each other, the spine loses neutrality, or the tops of the thighs are parallel to the ground.
9   Return to starting position using the same path used for the downward movement.

Only squat as deep as can be performed with proper form (spine neutral, knees tracking toes, feet completely in contact with the ground and facing forward).

Avoid excessive forward lean of the torso.

Spotter (C, D)

(C)

(continued)

(continued)

(D)

1   Ask the lifter if they would like to be spotted from the bar, chest, or arms.
2   Load the bar evenly and use collars to secure the weight.
3   Ask the lifter how many reps they are intending to complete.
4   Step behind the lifter while the bar is still placed in the rack.
5   As the lifter steps back from the rack, position the arms in ready position, under the lifter's arm pits. Move as close to the individual as possible without touching them or disrupting the movement.
6   Squat down in unison with the lifter so support may be provided throughout the entire movement if needed.
7   Help the lifter back into the rack when the set is completed or when they need assistance.

Q&A FROM THE FIELD

In observing an exerciser in the squat, you note that she has too much forward trunk lean during the descent. Additionally, you notice that she has her heels on blocks of wood to raise them off the floor. What advice would you consider for this lifter?

This lifter should lower the bar position and focus on keeping her chest up during the lift. She should also work on gastrocnemius ROM so as to allow the heels to be flat during the lift.

Front squat

Type of exercise

Lower-body/multi-joint

Muscles used

Gluteals, quadriceps, and hamstrings

Starting position (A)

(A)

1   Position the rack so that the bar is approximately at shoulder height.
2   Grip the bar approximately a thumb's length from the knurling (or slightly wider than shoulder-width), and rotate elbows upward from underneath the bar. Using your fingers to help stabilize, allow the bar to rest across the top of the shoulders and clavicle. Fully flex the elbows to position the upper arms parallel to the ground.
3   Lift the bar off the rack by flexing the hips and knees, then step back, placing legs about shoulder-width apart and toes pointed slightly outward.

(continued)

(continued)

Action (B)

(B)

4 Brace the spine and pelvis while gripping the floor with your feet and keeping the elbows high before initiating a backward movement with the hips.
5 Allow the body to descend by flexing at the hips and knees. Keep knees in a path that aligns with the toes.
6 As the body descends keep an upright torso, neutral spine, and elbows high.
7 Depending on the desired ROM, descend until the thigh and calf contact each other, the spine loses neutrality, or the tops of the thighs are parallel to the ground.
8 Return to starting position using the same path used for the downward movement.

Only squat as deep as can be performed with proper form (spine neutral, knees tracking toes, feet completely in contact with the ground and facing forward).

Avoid excessive forward lean of the torso. The torso should remain in a more upright position compared to the back squat.

This variation of the squat typically elicits higher quadriceps activation compared to the back squat.

Spotter (C, D)

(C)

(D)

(continued)

(continued)

1   Ask the lifter if they would like to be spotted from the bar, chest, or arms.
2   Load the bar evenly and use collars to secure the weight.
3   Ask the lifter how many reps they are intending to complete.
4   Step behind the lifter while the bar is still placed in the rack.
5   As the lifter steps back from the rack, position the arms in ready position, under the lifter's arm pits. Move as close to the individual as possible without touching them or disrupting the movement.
6   Squat down in unison with the lifter so support may be provided throughout the entire movement if needed.
7   Help the lifter back into the rack when the set is completed or when they need assistance.

Deadlift

Type of exercise

Lower-body/multi-joint

Muscles used

Gluteals, erector spinae, hamstrings, quadriceps, trapezius, rhomboids, deltoids, and finger flexors.

Starting position (A)

(A)

(B)

1   Start with the bar on the floor and position the feet under the bar so that the bar is over the laces of the shoe and toes pointed forward. The legs should be about hip-width to shoulder-width apart.
2   Hinge hips backward, lean torso forward over the bar, and flex at the knees to get into the proper starting position. The shoulders should be over or slightly in front of the bar. Be sure to maintain a neutral spine by depressing and retracting the shoulder blades and keeping the chest up.
3   Grip the bar about a thumb's length from knurling and extend the arms at the elbows.

Action (B)

4   Keeping the feet flat on the floor and weight distributed slightly toward the heels, brace the spine and pelvis before beginning to pull the bar off the ground.
5   Raise the bar by bringing the hips forward and extending at the knees. Focus on pushing through the ground with the legs and do not allow the hips to rise before the shoulders. Keep the bar close to the body, arms straight, and spine in a neutral position.
6   The shoulders should remain over or slightly ahead of the bar until the bar reaches the knees. Continue the movement until the knees and hips are fully extended.
7   Return to starting position using the same path used for the downward movement. Keep the spine in a neutral position.

   If the individual is not strong enough to lift standard plates, bumper plates or blocks can be used to maintain the ideal starting position.
   A "snatch grip" or "wide grip" can be used.

Compound, multi-joint exercises can be broken down into simple, single-joint movements. For example, dead lifts and front squats can benefit the power clean. Different exercises can also activate the same muscle groups as other exercises, providing a large carryover between them. Dumbbell flies and the incline bench press activate the same muscles that are being used during the barbell bench press, thereby assisting the bench press.

Barbell split squat

Type of exercise

Lower-body/multi-joint

Muscles used

Gluteals, iliopsoas, quadriceps, hamstrings, soleus, and gastrocnemius

Starting position (A)

1   Position the rack so that the bar is approximately at shoulder height.
2   Step under the bar to place it on the upper portion of the back and shoulders.
3   Grip the bar at a comfortable position, about a thumb's length from the knurling or slightly wider than shoulder-width.
4   Lift the bar off the rack by extending the hips and knees, then step back. Create a "split stance" by placing one leg in front of the torso and the other behind the torso. Keep legs about hip-width apart.

(continued)

(continued)

Action (B)

5   Brace the spine and pelvis while keeping the front foot flat on the floor and the torso in an upright position, allow the body to descend by initiating movement through knee flexion of the rear leg.
6   Descend the body straight down and resist "lunging" forward with the hips. The front leg should be allowed to flex at the knee as the body descends.
7   As the body descends keep an upright torso and neutral spine.
8   Descend until the back knee is just above the ground.
9   Return to starting position using the same path used for the downward movement.
10   Perform the desired number of reps, switch the front and rear leg, and repeat.

Avoid excessive forward lean of the torso.

   The same exercise can be performed holding dumbbells at the sides in order to limit spinal loading, or with the bar in the "front rack position" to increase activation of the quadriceps.

Spotter

1   Ask the lifter if they would like to be spotted from the bar, chest, or arms.
2   Load the bar evenly and use collars to secure the weight.
3   Ask the lifter how many reps they are intending to complete.
4   Step behind the lifter while the bar is still placed in the rack.
5   As the lifter steps back from the rack, position the arms in ready position, under the lifter's arm pits. Move as close to the individual as possible without touching them or disrupting the movement.

6   Position the body in the same "split position as the lifter."
7   Squat down in unison with the lifter so support may be provided throughout the entire movement if needed.
8   Help the lifter back into the rack when the set is completed or when they need assistance.

Variation (split squats with dumbbells)

If balancing a barbell is too difficult for the lifter, dumbbells held at the sides may be substituted as an alternative.

Suspension rear foot elevated split squat (RFESS)

Type of exercise

Lower-body/multi-joint

Muscles used

Gluteals, iliopsoas, quadriceps, and hamstrings

Starting position (A)

(A)

(B)

(continued)

(continued)

1   Adjust the suspension trainer so the handles are about mid-shin height.
2   Place one foot in the lower loop of the suspension trainer. Position the foot so the loop is around the laces of the shoe and the heel is resting on the hard handle.
3   Step out with the other foot into a "split" position.

Action (B)

4   Maintain a neutral spine and lower the body straight down by pushing the rear hip back and flexing the front leg at the knee joint.
5   Descend until the top of the thigh is parallel to the ground and the knee is over the toe. Allow the elevated leg to swing back.
6   Return to starting position using the same path for the downward movement.
7   Perform the desired number of reps, switch the front and rear leg, and repeat. This movement can be increased in intensity by holding a kettlebell at the chest to add resistance.

Romanian deadlift (RDL)

Type of exercise

Lower-body/single-joint

Muscles used

Gluteals, erector spinae, and hamstrings

Starting position (A)

(A)

1 Position the rack so that the bar is slightly above knee height.
2 Grip the bar approximately a thumb's length from knurling or slightly wider than shoulder-width. Extend the arms at the elbows. Extend the hips and knees to lift the bar off the rack and step back.
3 Position feet about shoulder-width apart with knees slightly bent.

Action (B)

(B)

4 Brace the spine and pelvis while gripping the floor with your feet before hinging at the hips (flex and push the hips backwards) to decrease the angle between the torso and thigh. Be sure to maintain a neutral spine.
5 Lower the bar until it is in line with the patella tendon or slightly below the knee.
6 Return to starting position by extending the hips and using the same path used for the downward movement. The knees should remain static and keep the same amount of flexion throughout the entirety of the movement.

Avoid flexion through the spine and rounding of the back.

The same exercise can be performed holding dumbbells in front of the body in order to limit spinal loading.

(continued)

(continued)

Variation

This movement may also be performed with a pair of dumbbells of equal weight or specially designated plate-loaded equipment.

Single-leg Romanian deadlift (single-leg RDL)

Type of exercise

Lower-body/single-joint

Muscles used

Gluteals, erector spinae, and hamstrings

Starting position

1   Position the rack so that the bar is slightly above knee height.
2   Grip the bar approximately a thumb's length from knurling or slightly wider than shoulder-width. Extend the arms at the elbows, lift the bar off the rack by extending the hips and knees, then step back.
3   Position feet about hip-width apart with knees slightly bent.

Action

4   Brace the spine and pelvis while gripping the floor with your feet.
5   Simultaneously, allow one leg to rise off the floor, extending behind the body. Be sure to maintain a neutral spine and keep hips parallel with the floor.
6   Lower the bar until it is in line with the patella or slightly below the knee, with the chest parallel to the floor.
7   Return to starting position by extending the hips and using the same path used for the downward movement.

Avoid flexion through the spine and rounding of the back.

Only allow the torso to fall as far as the back leg can rise. The body should act like a teeter-totter with the planted leg serving as the fulcrum.

The same exercise can be performed holding a dumbbell in contralateral arm of the planted leg to increase activation of gluteus medius.

Leg press

Type of exercise

Lower-body/multi-joint

Muscles used

Gluteals, quadriceps, and hamstrings

Machine setup (A)

(A)

1   Adjust the starting position so that the knees are bent to approximately 90° when placed upon the foot plate.
2   Position the feet on the foot plate approximately hip-width apart with the toes slightly pointed out.
3   Choose the appropriate resistance on the weight stack.

Action (B, C)

4   Push the foot plate away from the body by extending the hips and knees until fully extended.
5   Return to the start position in a controlled manner.

(continued)

(continued)

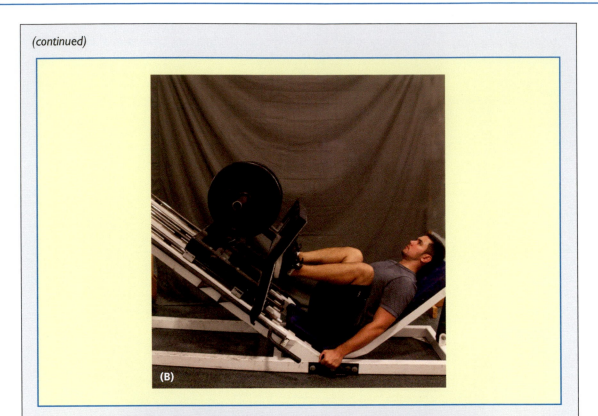

(B)

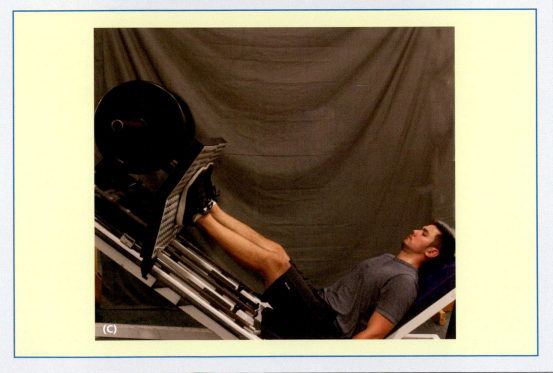

(C)

Leg extension

Type of exercise

Lower-body/single-joint

Muscles used

Quadriceps

Machine setup (A, B)

1 Position the back pad so that the knee joints align with the machine's axis of rotation.
2 Adjust the starting position so that the leg pad rests on, or directly above, the shins while the knees are bent to 90°.
3 Adjust the leg pad so it rests in a comfortable position just above the ankles.
4 Select the appropriate resistance on the weight stack.
5 Sit straight up with the back firmly against the back rest and head in a neutral position; grasp the handles at the side.

Action (C–E)

6 Extend the knees in a smooth and controlled manner until they reach full extension.
7 Return to the start position in a controlled manner.

(A)

(B)

(continued)

(continued)

(C)

(D)

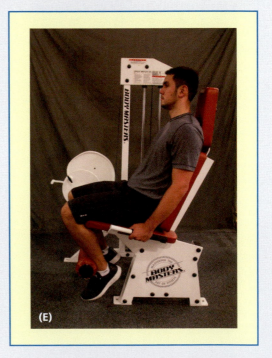

(E)

Leg curl

Type of exercise

Lower-body/single-joint

Muscles used

Hamstrings

Machine setup (A)

1   Position the back pad so that the knee joints align with the machine's axis of rotation.
2   Adjust the leg pad so it is positioned just under the ankles while the knees are extended.
3   Select the appropriate resistance on the weight stack.
4   Sit straight up with the back firmly against the backrest and head in a neutral position; grasp the handles at the side.

(A)

(continued)

(continued)

Action (B)

(B)

5 Flex the knees in a controlled motion to move the pad until the heels are fully flexed.
6 Return to the start position in a controlled manner.

Standing calf raise

Type of exercise

Lower-body/single-joint

Muscles used

Gastrocnemius and soleus

Starting position

1 Position the rack so that the bar is approximately at shoulder height.
2 Step under the bar to place it on the upper portion of the back and shoulders.

3   Grip the bar at a comfortable position, about a thumb's length from the knurling or slightly wider than shoulder-width.
4   Lift the bar off the rack and step back, placing legs about hip-width apart.

Action

5   Elevate the body by extending the ankles and allowing the heels to come off the ground.
6   Fully extend the ankles, while still remaining on the balls of the feet.
7   Return to the starting position using the same path as the upward movement.

The same exercise can be performed holding dumbbells at the sides of the body in order to limit spinal loading. Additionally, the balls of the feet can be placed on a flat lying plate to increase the range of motion of the exercise.

To achieve greater activation of the soleus, the same exercise can also be performed in a seated position with knees at 90°. Use plates or dumbbells positioned on the thighs to add resistance.

Box 11.3   Chest exercises

Bench press, dumbbell

Type of exercise

Upper-body/multi-joint

Muscles used

Pectoralis major, pectoralis minor, deltoid, serratus anterior, and triceps brachii

Starting position

1   After selecting the appropriate dumbbells, sit on the edge of the bench with the dumbbells resting on thighs above the knee.
2   Firmly grasp the dumbbells with a closed grip and carefully lie back onto the bench, bringing the dumbbells into position near the shoulders.

Action

3   While maintaining the five-point contact, press the dumbbells up in a controlled manner until the arms are fully extended over the chest.
4   Lower the dumbbells back down to the resting position in a controlled manner to complete the repetition.
5   Repeat this movement until the desired number of repetitions has been completed.

(continued)

(continued)

Spotter

1   Clear the area in case the lifter needs to drop the weight.
2   Ask the lifter how many repetitions they intend to complete.
3   Stand at the head of the bench ready and prepared to assist the lifter.
4   Assist the lifter with getting the dumbbells into the starting position by lifting near the wrists.
5   Keep hands placed near the forearms throughout the lift.
6   Assist the lifter in sitting up and removing the dumbbells once the lift is completed.

Bench press, barbell

Type of exercise

Upper-body/multi-joint

Muscles used

Pectoralis major, pectoralis minor, deltoid (anterior), serratus anterior, and triceps brachii

Starting position (A, B)

1   Lie on the bench, maintaining a five-point contact.
2   Grasp the bar with a firm, closed, pronated grip with hands slightly wider than shoulder-width apart.
3   With spotter assistance, remove the bar from the rack and support directly over the chest.

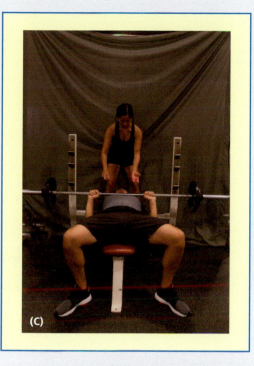

(C)

Action (C)

4   While maintaining the five-point contact position, lower the bar to the chest in a controlled manner. Avoid bouncing the bar off the chest.

5   Press the barbell up to the starting position until the elbows are fully extended, using a complete range of motion. Repeat motion for desired number of repetitions.

6   Once the desired number of repetitions is completed, return the bar to the rack with the assistance of your spotter.

Spotter

1   Before the exercise begins, ensure the bar is evenly loaded and collars are in place.

2   Ask the lifter how many repetitions they intend to complete.

3   Stand at the head of the bench, behind the bar and grasp the bar with an alternated grip inside the lifter's hands. Assist the lifter with the bar off the rack.

4   When the lifter is ready, slowly transfer the weight of the bar to the lifter's hands.

5   Stand back out of the lifter's line of sight, ready to assist in case the movement cannot be completed at any point.

6   Once the desired number of repetitions has been completed, assist the lifter with returning the bar to the rack.

Q&A FROM THE FIELD

A lifter states she has reached a plateau in the bench press and is unable to increase in weight. What variations can you suggest to the program to help?

Alternate exercises such as flies, incline press, or decline press can be used to add variety. Dumbbells can be used to require the lifter to balance the load, and lighter weights can be used explosively to increase power. The lifter may be overtraining, and some time off or a period of active rest may be necessary.

Incline press, barbell

Type of exercise

Upper-body/multi-joint

(continued)

(continued)

Muscles used

Pectoralis major, pectoralis minor, deltoid (anterior), serratus anterior, and triceps brachii

Starting position (A, B)

1   Lie on the bench, maintaining a five-point contact position.
2   Grasp the bar with a firm, closed, pronated grip with hands slightly wider than shoulder-width apart.
3   With spotter assistance, remove the bar from the rack and support directly over the chest.

Action (C)

4   While maintaining the five-point contact position, lower the bar to the chest in a controlled manner. Avoid bouncing the bar off the chest.
5   Press the barbell up to the starting position until the elbows are fully extended, using a complete range of motion. Repeat motion for desired number of repetitions.
6   Once the desired number of repetitions is completed, return the bar to the rack with the assistance of your spotter.

Spotter

1   Before the exercise begins, ensure the bar is evenly loaded and collars are in place.
2   Ask the lifter how many repetitions they intend to complete.

(A)

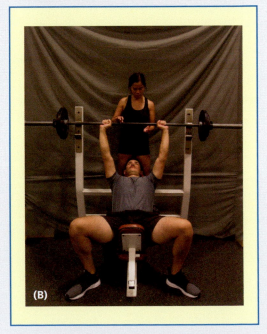

(B)

(C)

3   Stand at the head of the bench, behind the bar and grasp the bar with an alternated grip inside the lifter's hands. Assist the lifter with the bar off the rack.

4   When the lifter is ready, slowly transfer the weight of the bar to the lifter's hands.

5   Stand back out of the lifter's line of sight, ready to assist in case the movement cannot be completed at any point.

6   Once the desired number of repetitions has been completed, assist the lifter with returning the bar to the rack.

Dumbbell fly

Type of exercise

Upper-body/single-joint

Muscles used

Pectoralis major, pectoralis minor, deltoid (anterior), and serratus anterior

Starting position (A, B)

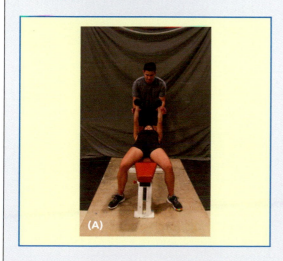

(A)

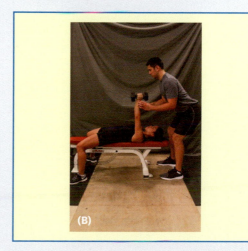

(B)

(continued)

(continued)

1   After selecting the appropriate dumbbells, sit on the edge of the bench with the dumbbells resting on thighs above the knee.
2   Firmly grasp the dumbbells with a closed grip and carefully lie back onto the bench, bringing the dumbbells into position near the shoulders.
3   While maintaining a five-point contact position, press the dumbbells into position above the chest with the palms facing each other and a slight bend in the elbows.

Action (C, D)

4   While maintaining a five-point contact position, lower the dumbbells in controlled manner out to the sides of the chest in a wide arc, while keeping a soft bend in the elbows.
5   While maintaining your position, raise the dumbbells back to the starting position, following the same path. Repeat for the desired number of repetitions.
6   Once the desired number of repetitions has been completed, lower the weight and place the face of the dumbbells on the thighs. Sit up with the help of a spotter if necessary.

Spotter

1   Clear the area in case the lifter needs to drop the weight.
2   Ask the lifter how many repetitions they intend to complete.

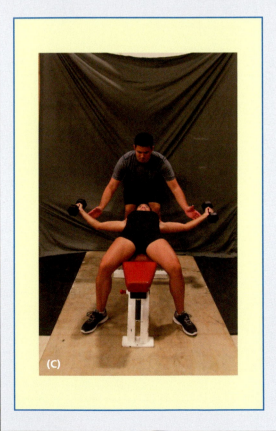

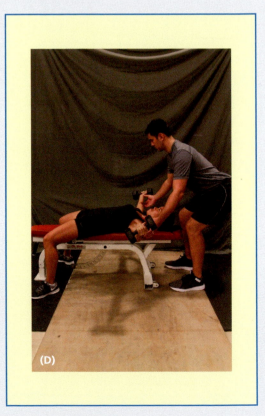

3   Stand at the head of the bench ready and prepared to assist the lifter.
4   Assist the lifter with getting the dumbbells into the starting position by lifting near the wrists.
5   Keep hands placed near the forearms throughout the lift.
6   Assist the lifter in sitting up and removing the dumbbells once the lift is completed.

Box 11.4   Upper back exercises

Dumbbell single-arm row

Type of exercise

Upper-body/multi-joint

Muscles used

Latissimus dorsi, middle trapezius, rhomboids, teres major, posterior deltoid, biceps brachii, brachialis, and brachioradialis

(A)   (B)

(continued)

(continued)

Starting position (A, B)

1   Place one hand and knee of the same side of the body on a bench with the torso parallel to the floor. Maintain a neutral spine and use a soft knee bend in the supporting leg.
2   With the opposing hand, grasp a dumbbell with a closed, neutral grip.

Action (C, D)

3   Simultaneously flex the elbow while pulling the dumbbell up to the torso while maintaining the starting position.
4   While maintaining position and under control, lower the dumbbell along the same path back to the starting position.

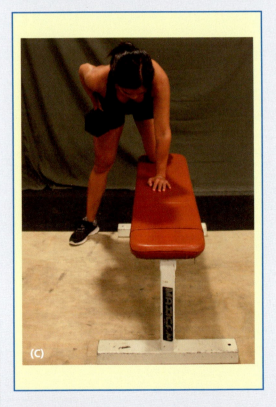

(C)

(D)

Lat pull-down

Type of exercise

Upper-body/multi-joint

Muscles used

Latissimus dorsi, trapezius, rhomboids, teres major, posterior deltoid, biceps brachii, brachialis, and brachioradialis

Machine setup (A, B)

1 Select your desired resistance on the weight stack.
2 Sit down and adjust the thigh pad so it sits securely on the thighs.
3 Stand up and grasp the bar firmly with a closed, pronated grip.
4 While maintaining this grip, return to the secure, seated position and slightly lean back.

Action (C, D)

5 While maintaining a neutral spine and stable posture, retract the shoulder blades and pull the bar down to the chest in a controlled manner. The elbows should move toward the body.
6 Maintain this position and return the bar up overhead in a controlled manner to complete the movement.
7 When the desired number of reps has been completed, maintain your grip on the bar, slowly stand up and return the bar to its original position while controlling the weight down to the stack.

(A)

(B)

(continued)

(continued)

(C)

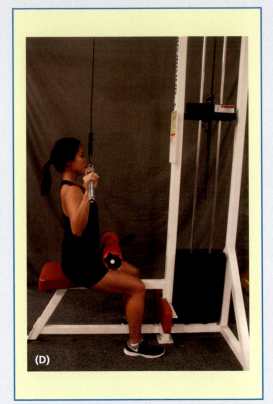

(D)

Seated cable row

Type of exercise

Upper-body/multi-joint

Muscles used

Latissimus dorsi, middle trapezius, rhomboids, teres major, posterior deltoid, biceps brachii, brachialis, and brachioradialis

Starting position (A)

1   Select your desired resistance on the weight stack.
2   Position yourself on a seated cable row machine with feet on the supporting platform with a soft bend in the knee.
3   Grasp the handle with a firm grip and position yourself with a neutral spine, upright posture, and retracted shoulder blades.

(A)   (B)

Action (B)

4   While maintaining this position, pull the handle towards the torso while flexing the elbows.

5   Slowly extend the elbows and return the handle to its starting position using a full range of motion.

6   When the desired number of reps has been completed, maintain your grip on the handle, slowly return the handle to its resting position while controlling the weight down to the stack.

Box 11.5   Shoulder exercises

Dumbbell seated shoulder press

Type of exercise

Upper-body/multi-joint

Muscles used

Deltoid (anterior and medial), trapezius (upper portion), serratus anterior, and triceps brachii

(continued)

(continued)

Starting position (A, B)

1   After selecting the appropriate dumbbells, sit on the edge of vertical shoulder press bench with the dumbbells resting on thighs above the knee.
2   While maintaining a five-point contact position, firmly grasp the dumbbells with closed grip and bring them into position just above the shoulder.

Action (C, D)

3   Press the dumbbells overhead until the elbows are fully extended, with spotter assistance if necessary.
4   Slowly bend the elbows to lower the dumbbells along the same path back to the starting position. Repeat for the desired number of repetitions.
5   Once the desired number of repetitions has been completed, carefully lower the weight so the face of the dumbbells rests on the thighs.

Spotter

1   Clear the area in case the lifter needs to drop the weight.
2   Ask the lifter how many repetitions they intend to complete.
3   Stand at the head of the bench ready and prepared to assist the lifter.
4   Assist the lifter with getting the dumbbells into the starting position by lifting near the wrists.
5   Keep hands placed near the forearms throughout the lift.

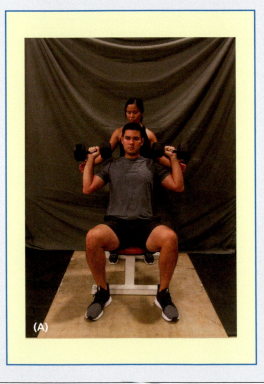

(A)

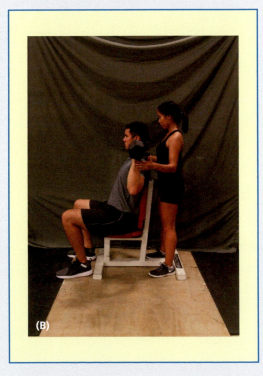

(B)

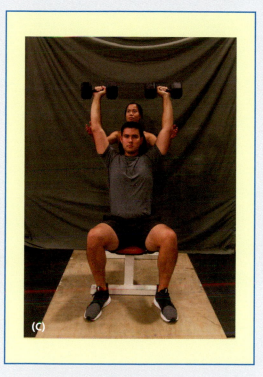

(C)   (D)

Machine shoulder press

Type of exercise

Upper-body/multi-joint

Muscles used

Deltoid, trapezius, serratus anterior, and triceps brachii

Machine setup

1   Adjust the seat so that the handles are aligned with the shoulders.
2   Select the appropriate resistance on the weight stack.
3   Position the body into a five-point contact position alignment and grip the handles.

Action

4   While maintaining the five-point contact position, press the handles upward in a controlled manner until the elbows are fully extended.
5   Return the handles down to the resting position. Repeat for the desired number of repetitions.

Barbell upright row

Type of exercise

Upper-body/multi-joint

Muscles used

Anterior, medial and posterior deltoid, trapezius, serratus anterior, brachialis, biceps brachii, and brachioradialis

Starting position (A, B)

1   Stand with feet shoulder-width apart with a soft bend in the knees.
2   Grasp the bar with a firm, closed, pronated grip. Hands should be slightly wider than shoulder-width apart.

(A)

(B)

Action (C, D)

(C)

(D)

(continued)

(continued)

3   Begin the lift by simultaneously flexing the elbows and elevating the shoulders, bringing the bar to about shoulder height.
4   Maintain a stable posture and avoid jerking or swinging the barbell.
5   After a brief pause, slowly lower the barbell along the same path back into the starting position. Repeat for the desired number of repetitions.

Box 11.6   Triceps exercises

Supine triceps extension

Type of exercise

Upper-body/single-joint

Muscles used

Triceps brachii

Starting position

1   Select an EZ bar with the desired weight and lie back on a bench maintaining a five-point contact position.
2   Press the bar over the chest with a firm, closed, pronated grip until the elbows are fully extended. Use spotter assistance if necessary.

Action

3   While maintaining the five-point contact position and keeping the elbows over the shoulders, slowly bend the elbows and lower the bar to the forehead. Avoid touching the forehead.
4   Press the bar back up to the starting position following the same path.

Spotter

1   Before the exercise begins, ensure the bar is evenly loaded and collars are in place.
2   Ask the lifter how many repetitions they intend to complete.
3   Stand at the head of the bench, behind the bar and grasp the bar with an alternated grip inside the lifter's hands. Assist the lifter with the bar.
4   Stand back out of the lifter's line of sight, ready to assist in case the movement cannot be completed at any point.
5   Once the desired number of repetitions has been completed, assist the lifter with the bar.

Triceps pushdown

Type of exercise

Upper-body/single-joint

Muscles used

Triceps brachii

Starting position (A)

1   Stand in front of the machine and grasp the handles with a firm, closed, pronated grip. Keep elbows tight to the body with a soft knee.
2   Keep the elbows in this position and upright posture throughout the movement.

Action (B)

3   While maintaining the starting position, push the handle down in a controlled manner until the elbows are fully extended.
4   Once completed, return to the starting position by flexing the elbows in controlled manner, following the same path that initiated the movement. Repeat for the desired number of repetitions.

Box 11.7   Biceps exercises

Barbell bicep curl

Type of exercise

Upper-body/single-joint

Muscles used

Biceps brachii, brachialis, and brachioradialis

Starting position (A, B)

1   Stand with feet shoulder-width apart and keep a soft knee.
2   Grasp the bar with a firm, closed, supinated grip with arms fully extended. Maintain a stable and upright posture throughout the movement.

(A)

Action (C, D)

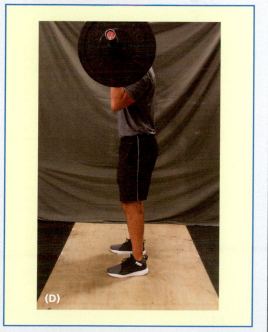

(continued)

(continued)

3   Raise the bar by flexing the elbows in a slow, controlled manner using a full range of motion. Avoid using momentum or "swinging" the bar, and avoid hyperextending the spine.

4   Lower the bar by extending the elbows, following the same path. Maintain control of the bar and a stable posture throughout the movement. Repeat for the desired number of repetitions.

Seated dumbbell bicep curl

Type of exercise

Upper-body/single-joint

Muscles used

Biceps brachii, brachialis, and brachioradialis

Starting position (A, B)

1   Sit on a vertical bench with feet shoulder-width apart. Maintain a five-point contact position.

2   Grasp the dumbbells with a firm, closed grip and keep them at the side of the body, with elbows fully extended.

Action (C, D)

(C)

(D)

(continued)

(continued)

3   Raise the dumbbells in a slow, controlled manner by flexing the elbows through a full range of motion. Maintain the five-point contact position and avoid using momentum or "swinging" the dumbbells.

4   Lower the dumbbells by extending the elbows along the same path as the upward movement. Repeat for the desired number of repetitions.

Box 11.8   Abdominal and lower back exercises

Abdominal crunch

Type of exercise

Trunk

Muscles used

Rectus abdominis, obliquus externus abdominis, tensor fascia latae, and rectus femoris

Starting position (A)

(A)

1   Lie supine (face up) on the floor with the feet on a bench to allow for a 90° bend at the knees and hips.
2   With the fingertips at each side of the head, lift the head off the floor.

Action (B)

(B)

3   Keeping the feet in position on the bench, curl the torso off the floor, moving the head and shoulders toward the thighs until the upper back is off the floor.
4   Return to the starting position following the same path used for the upward movement.

Curl all the way up until the upper back is off the floor.
    Keep the feet on the bench throughout the movement.
    Do not jerk the torso or arms to provide momentum to assist the movement.

Back extension

Type of exercise

Trunk

(continued)

(continued)

Muscles used

Longissimus thoracis, quadratus lumborum, iliocostalis lumborum, longissimus thoracis, iliocostalis thoracis, intertransversarii laterales lumborum, gluteus maximus, and hamstrings

Equipment setup (A)

(A)

1 Adjust the foot-position bar so that the upper pad rests on the hips and upper thighs.
2 Position yourself in the machine so that the legs are nearly straight and the torso is approximately 90° from the legs.
3 Cross the arms over the chest.

Avoid exaggerating the range of motion and rounding the back and shoulders during the movement.

Action (B)

4 Extend at the hips, raising the torso in a controlled and smooth motion until it forms a straight line with the legs.
5 Return to the starting position following the same path used for the upward movement.

Maintain a neutral spine throughout the movement.

(B)

Stability ball jack knife

Type of exercise

Trunk

Muscles used

Rectus abdominis

Starting position (A, B)

1   Lie in supine position (face up) and support the body in a plank/pushup position with the hands on the floor, slightly wider than shoulder-width.
2   Place one leg at a time on top of the stability ball until both upper shins are in contact with the ball.

Action (C, D)

3   Keeping the feet together, slowly pull the feet and knees in toward the torso until they are fully drawn in.
4   Slowly return to the starting position following the same path used for the inward movement.

(continued)

(continued)

(A)

(B)

(continued)

(continued)

Maintain a neutral spine position.
    Avoid letting the ball move to the side of the legs or letting the hips drop.
    Keep the abdominal muscles tight.

Stability ball roll-out

Type of exercise

Trunk

Muscles used

Rectus abdominis

Starting position (A, B)

(A)

(B)

1   Kneel on the floor and place the forearms on the stability ball.
2   Position the feet and knees slightly wider than shoulder-width.

Action (C, D)

3   Reach forward and roll out on the forearms until the movement becomes too difficult for you to go any farther forward, or until the body is fully extended.
4   Return to the starting position following the same path used for the outward movement.

Maintain a neutral spine position.
   Keep the abdominal muscles tight.

(continued)

(continued)

(C)

(D)

Prone plank

Type of exercise

Trunk

Muscles used

Rectus abdominis, internal obliques, and external obliques

Position (A, B)

1   Lie prone (face down) with the feet pointed straight behind hip-width apart.
2   Bend the elbows to about 90° directly under the shoulders and place the palms face down flat on the floor.
3   Keep the spine and head neutral and aligned with the torso so ankles, knees, hips, shoulders, and head are in a straight line.
4   Hold the position until failure or for the desired duration.

Keep the spine and head neutral by activating the abdominal muscles.
    Focus on the lower portion of the abdominal muscles.

(A)

(continued)

(continued)

(B)

Side plank

Type of exercise

Trunk

Muscles used

Internal obliques and external oblique

Position (A–D)

1   While lying on your side with the feet stacked on top of each other, bend one elbow to about 90° and place under the shoulder.
2   Keeping the spine and head neutral and in line with the torso, raise your hips off the floor until the bottom ankle, knee, hip, and shoulder are in a straight line.
3   Hold the position until failure or for the desired duration.
4   Switch and repeat for the other side.

Keep the spine and head neutral by activating the internal and external obliques.
    Focus on the lower side of the torso.

(A)

(B)

(continued)

(continued)

(C)

(D)

Paloff press

Type of exercise

Trunk

Muscles used

Rectus abdominis, erector spinae, internal obliques, external obliques, rhomboid major, and rhomboid minor

Starting position (A, B)

1   Start in a standing, half-kneeling, or kneeling position.
2   Hold a band or cable with both hands at the center of the chest and stand, half-kneel, or kneel perpendicular to the machine.
3   Keep a neutral neck, shoulder, low back, and hips at all times.

Action (C, D)

4   Slowly extend the elbows until they are fully extended, then return to the starting position.

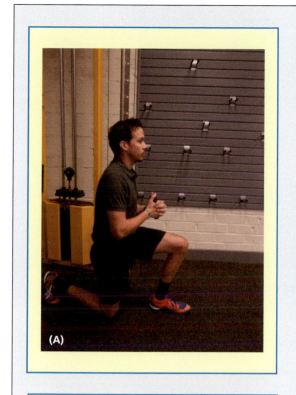

(A)

(B)

(C)

(D)

(continued)

Hollow position

Type of exercise

Trunk

Muscles used

Rectus abdominis, internal obliques, external obliques, and gluteals

Starting position

1   Lie on the ground in a supine position (face up), squeeze the gluteals and point the toes and extend the arms above the head.
2   Contract the abdominals to keep the lower back pressed to the floor in a neutral position.

Action (A–D)

3   While keeping the spine neutral, slightly elevate the feet, arms, neck, and upper back off the floor.
4   Hold the position for the desired time. Keeping the glutes squeezed pulling the belly button to the floor will help minimize any excessive arching of the lower back.

(A)

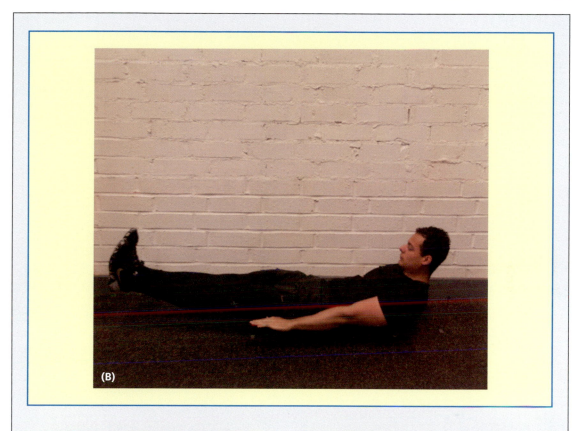

(B)

(C)

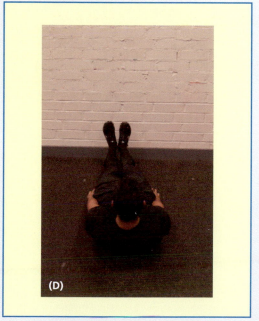

(D)

SUMMARY

Resistance training provides numerous benefits including increased muscular strength via neurological adaptations and increases in cross-sectional area (hypertrophy). Resistance training can also alleviate symptoms of age-related diseases such osteoporosis and osteopenia by increasing bone mineral density.

Prior to beginning a resistance-training program, an exerciser should be familiar with proper technique, attire, spotting techniques, and breathing techniques. If any of these principles is ignored, the exerciser increases his/her risk of injury. Prior to performing a specific exercise, the exerciser should know the proper movement of the exercise as described in this chapter.

MAXING OUT

1 An experienced strength-trained participant is performing a 3RM exercise in the back squat. How many spotters are required? Where should they be positioned? What are their responsibilities?

2 One of the roles of a spotter is to give verbal cues and verbal encouragement to the lifter. In this respect, a spotter should always be used. There are times when it is dangerous for a spotter to be near a rapidly moving bar. Can you describe a situation like this?

3 An inexperienced participant is deadlifting barefoot in a busy weight room. What action should the on-duty coach take? Why?

4 The Valsalva maneuver helps maintain a rigid torso and keep an upright posture. When is the best time to utilize this maneuver? At what point does its use become hazardous?

REFERENCES

1. Aaberg E. *Resistance Training Instruction*, 2nd ed. Champaign, IL: Human Kinetics. 2007.

2. Baechle TR, Groves BR. *Weight Training: Steps to Success*, 4th ed. Champaign, IL: Human Kinetics. 2012.

3. Bathgate KE, Galpin AJ. Lower-body exercises. In: *Strength Training*. LE Brown, ed. Champaign, IL: Human Kinetics. 2017.

4. Brooks GA, Fahey TD, Baldwin KM. *Exercise Physiology: Human Bioenergetics and Its Applications*, 4th ed. New York: McGraw Hill. 2005.

5. Haff GG, Triplett NT. eds. *Essentials of Strength Training and Conditioning*, 4th ed. Champaign, IL: Human Kinetics. 2016.

6. Fleck SR, Kraemer WJ. *Designing Resistance Training Programs*, 4th ed. Champaign, IL: Human Kinetics. 2014.

7. Galpin AJ, Bartolini JA. Explosive movements. In: *Strength Training*. LE Brown, ed. Champaign, IL: Human Kinetics. 2017.

8. Galpin AJ, Bagley JR. Torso exercises. In: *Strength Training*. LE Brown, ed. Champaign, IL: Human Kinetics. 2017.

9. Harman EA, Rosenstein RM, Frykman PN, Nigro GA. Effects of a belt on intra-abdominal pressure during weightlifting. *Med Sci Sports Exerc* 1989; 21(2):186–190.

10. Hoffman JR. ed. *NSCA's Guide to Program Design*. Champaign, IL: Human Kinetics. 2012.

11. Lander JE, Hundley JR, Simonton RL. The effectiveness of weight-belts during multiple repetitions of the squat exercise. *Med Sci Sports Exerc* 1990; 24(5):603–609.

12. Lander JE, Simonton RL, Giacobbe JKF. The effectiveness of weight-belts during the squat exercise. *Med Sci Sports Exerc* 1990; 22(1):117–126.

13. Nutter J. Physical activity increases bone density. *NSCA J* 1986; 8(3):67–69.

14. Salatto RJ, Rojo VM, Coburn JW. Upper-body exercises. In: *Strength Training*. LE Brown, ed. Champaign, IL: Human Kinetics. 2017.

15. Schoenfeld BJ. The mechanisms of muscle hypertrophy and their application to resistance training. *J Strength Cond Res* 2010; 24(10):2857–2872.

16. Zatsiorsky VM, Kraemer WJ. *The Science and Practice of Strength Training*, 2nd ed. Champaign, IL: Human Kinetics. 2006.

PART 3

EXERCISE PRESCRIPTION

Contents

CHAPTER 12

NEEDS ANALYSIS

Andy V. Khamoui, Michael C. Zourdos, and Lee E. Brown

OBJECTIVES

After reading this chapter, you will

- Understand the reasons for conducting a needs analysis.
- Be able to discuss the relationship between a needs analysis and the energy systems.
- Be able to discuss the relationship between a needs analysis and basic biomechanical factors.
- Understand the relationship between a needs analysis and injury risk.
- Understand the relationship between a needs analysis and exercise prescription.

KEY TERMS

Athlete testing and assessment
Basic movement analysis
Glycolytic
Injury risk

Metabolic and biomechanical requirements
Needs analysis
Oxidative
Phosphocreatine

Specific needs of the individual athlete
Sport injuries
Three major energy-producing systems

INTRODUCTION

Before a training program can be designed and implemented, a formal **needs analysis** must be conducted. A needs analysis is performed by the strength and conditioning professional to determine how an athlete might be best served by programmed training. It aims to identify the demands of the sport itself, as well as the **specific needs of the individual athlete**. In other words, a needs analysis comprises a major part of the initial planning and preparation (in addition to athlete testing and measurement, see Chapter 10) that is then used to inform and guide program design. Because adaptations are specific to the type of training performed, careful consideration must be given to the needs analysis – it is in effect, the foundation for an effective training program that prepares a given athlete for competition.

What does a needs analysis address? A needs analysis will typically address the metabolic and biomechanical requirements of the sport itself, and any unique requirements dictated by specific positions within that sport. Furthermore, a needs analysis may also seek to identify potential injuries encountered by an athlete, for the purpose of designing a training program that minimizes the risk of that injury (see Chapter 22, Injury prevention and rehabilitation).

In essence, the needs analysis aims to address the following major questions: 1) What are the metabolic (energy) requirements for an athlete based on their sport and position? 2) What are the biomechanical requirements demanded of an athlete during competition? 3) What are common injuries associated with an athlete's sport? By addressing these questions, the strength and conditioning professional is able to make informed decisions with respect to the acute program variables (i.e., exercise selection, order, load, sets, and repetitions) that comprise the day-to-day elements of a training program. Specifically, the training program can be designed to produce adaptations that at a minimum, meet the metabolic and biomechanical requirements for an individual athlete's sport and position (i.e., specificity of training).

METABOLIC ASPECTS OF SPORT

Energy systems overview

As described in Chapter 1, there are **three major energy-producing systems** or pathways: 1) **phosphocreatine**, 2) **glycolytic**, and 3) **oxidative**. These systems consist of enzyme-driven biochemical reactions of varying complexity that yield adenosine triphosphate (ATP). ATP is frequently referred to as a high-energy molecule because cleavage of the terminal phosphate bonds yield energy. The energy released is then used to power cellular events such as muscular contraction, and hence, movement and physical performance.

The three energy systems differ in both their rate of ATP provision, as well as their maximal capacity for generating ATP (1).

For instance, the phosphagen system consists of single-enzyme, oxygen independent (i.e., anaerobic) reactions that can be mobilized rapidly to provide a quick supply of ATP for muscular contraction. One of the principal reactions of this system is catalyzed by creatine kinase, which provides ATP from adenosine diphosphate (ADP) and phosphocreatine (PCr). Because the phosphagen system is mobilized quickly, it is also referred to as the immediate energy system. However, PCr stores in muscle are limited and this system has a low capacity for ATP provision, with maximal effort activity supported for less than 10 seconds. Beyond this duration (e.g., 1–2 minutes), muscular contraction is supported by the glycolytic system. Glycolysis yields ATP from the metabolism of glucose obtained from blood (i.e., circulating glucose) or from intramuscular glycogen. An example of an event that requires significant contribution from the glycolytic pathway of energy production is the 400 m sprint. For extended duration tasks (i.e., several minutes up to several hours), energy demands are met principally by oxidative pathways. The oxidative system metabolizes nutrient derived substrates such as glucose and fatty acids in a series of complex biochemical reactions requiring oxygen to generate ATP (e.g., TCA cycle, oxidative phosphorylation). These complex reactions are slower to activate and therefore have a lower rate of ATP provision; however, the oxidative system is high capacity because it has a greater overall ATP yield.

Metabolic demands of sport

Metabolic demands vary considerably between sports. For instance, endurance events such as marathon running or distance swimming will predominantly utilize oxidative pathways of energy production to sustain performance in that activity. At the other end of the spectrum, athletes that perform very brief, explosive movements such as short sprinters, shot putters, or weightlifters require significant contribution from the phosphagen system to execute their respective activities. Many team sports such as soccer, football, basketball, and hockey require contributions from both anaerobic and oxidative

TABLE 12.1 Approximate contribution of the three energy systems to sport

Sport	Phosphagen (%)	Glycolytic (%)	Oxidative (%)
Team-based			
American Football	70	25	5
Basketball	20	20	60
Baseball	95	5	—
Field hockey	20	25	55
Ice hockey	30	30	40
Lacrosse	20	25	55
Rugby	25	25	50
Soccer (football)	25	25	50
Volleyball	80	15	5
Water polo	20	25	55
Individual-based			
Boxing	30	45	25
Cycling	10	10	80
Fencing	85	10	5
Field events	100	—	—
Marathon	—	—	100
Skiing	35	25	40
Tennis	50	5	45
Track-distance	5	5	90
Track-mid distance	15	50	35
Track-short sprints	90	5	5
Wrestling	30	45	25
Mixed individual/team			
Rowing	10	40	50
Swimming-sprints	75	25	—
Swimming-distance	10	10	80

Adapted from: *NSCA's Guide to Program Design.* Hoffman JR (Ed.). Human Kinetics, Champaign, IL.

mechanisms of energy production. More often than not, a sport is likely to require some contribution from each of the energy systems, although one may predominate. There are only a few instances where a sport is reliant exclusively on one energy system (e.g., phosphagen system for field events and Olympic lifts, oxidative system for marathon). The approximate energy demands of various sports are listed in Table 12.1.

It is also important to note that even within the same sport, metabolic demands can change depending on an athlete's position. For example, a goalkeeper in soccer rarely ventures outside the 18-yard box. This position requires the goalkeeper to perform either quick short sprints in a linear direction to stop the opposing team's attack, vertical jumping under pressure to collect the ball mid-air, or explosive lateral movements (e.g., diving to stop a goal from being scored). With these unique positional requirements, the goalkeeper has metabolic demands that require energetic contribution primarily from the phosphagen system, and to a lesser extent the glycolytic system. Extended duration running of low to moderate intensity (i.e., long, slow, distance workout) that relies on oxidative pathways of energy production would not be a priority. After having identified these unique requirements in the needs analysis, training should prioritize tasks that make use of the requisite energy systems while incorporating competition-specific scenarios or tasks.

In contrast, the soccer midfielder covers all areas of the field to initiate a goal scoring opportunity, or disrupt the opposing team's attack. These duties require intermittent bouts of both short and longer distance sprints, interspersed with slower jogging for recovery. The overall distance covered by a soccer field player such as a midfielder during the course of a competitive match is substantial, reaching up to 11 km (~7 miles) (2). Interestingly, midfielders performed running or high-speed running (14.4–25.1 km·hr^{-1}) over a distance of roughly 2.5 km (~2 miles), in addition to maximal sprints accumulating 0.5 km (0.3 miles) (2). The remaining distance of approximately 8.3 km (~5 miles) is occupied by walking and jogging. Given these match requirements, the midfielder will require significant energetic contribution from both the oxidative and glycolytic systems; therefore, training should consist of activities that utilize those systems under comparable match conditions. Since maximal effort sprints were also performed during the match, albeit to a lesser degree, sprinting drills should also be included in the training program.

Based on the varied metabolic profiles encountered among sports, and for specific positions within a given sport, it is imperative to develop an individualized needs analysis for each athlete.

BIOMECHANICAL ASPECTS OF SPORT

Biomechanics overview

In addition to identifying metabolic demands, the needs analysis should also evaluate the basic biomechanical characteristics associated with an athlete's respective sport. Relevant features include the movement patterns performed during competition, muscles recruited and major joint actions, force requirements, movement velocity, acceleration, flexibility, and agility. Other factors to carefully consider include the desired training adaptations and their order of priority (i.e., strength, power, hypertrophy, muscular endurance). By having a basic understanding of these elements, the strength and conditioning professional can design a training program that approximates or exceeds the biomechanical demands that occur during competition, or which contain exercises that exhibit appropriate transfer to competition. From a practical standpoint, the strength and conditioning professional may find it useful to consult primary literature or obtain video of a given sport to accurately identify movement patterns and muscular recruitment. For a more complete discussion of biomechanics and resistance training, refer to Chapter 5.

Evaluating basic biomechanics

The basic biomechanical elements that can be described for a specific activity, and how this information guides program design, is illustrated in the following example. In the snatch, weightlifters are required to move a heavily loaded barbell seamlessly from the ground to an overhead position. A **basic movement analysis** of this lift would indicate that it is a whole body movement that begins with the athlete fully crouched, having significant flexion of the hips, knees, and ankles. The arms are also fully extended as the lifter grasps the bar.

The general sequence of events involves the first pull, in which the athlete lifts the barbell in a near linear path from the ground to approximately knee height, followed by transition of the bar around the knees. After this transition period, the athlete should be in a position where the knees, hips, and ankles are slightly flexed, with the barbell near mid-thigh level in preparation for the second pull of the lift. The second pull is characterized by explosive triple extension of the hips, knees, and ankles to propel the bar upwards while the lifter pulls him or herself underneath to "catch" the bar with arms fully extended overhead and the shoulder blades retracted. Based on the major joint actions, muscles heavily recruited to execute the first and second pull include the gluteus maximus, hamstrings, quadriceps, and triceps surae (i.e., hip, knee, and ankle extensors). In addition, the deltoids and trapezius muscles, as well as other scapular stabilizers comprise the upper body muscles that enable the pulling of the barbell and catch overhead. Therefore, leg strength and power, particularly of the hip and knee extensors, would be priorities for training as would shoulder strength and stability.

TABLE 12.2 Sample metabolic and biomechanical assessment by sport and position

Athlete 1 Field events-shot put	Athlete 2 Soccer midfielder	Athlete 3 Long-distance runner
Metabolic profile • Maximal effort explosive movement requiring the upper and lower body; very brief action, not exceeding a few seconds in duration. • Major energetic contribution provided by phosphagen system.	*Metabolic profile* • Intermittent short and long distance sprinting interspersed with jogging and walking over the course of a 90-min match. • Major contribution from glycolytic and oxidative systems; somewhat less contribution from phosphagen system.	*Metabolic profile* • Repeated, low tension muscle contractile activity performed for an extended duration (i.e., several minutes to hours). • Major contribution from oxidative mechanisms of energy production.
Biomechanical profile • Highly complex task requiring the generation of high limb velocities within a limited space. • Task requires proximal to distal sequence of muscular actions, which are initiated by the lower body and completed by the arms and hands; goal is to impart maximal velocity on the implement (i.e., release velocity). • Literature indicates several lower body biomechanical factors are related to shot put performance: peak rate of force development, peak force, and peak power output (16,17). These parameters may be modified by programmed training.	*Biomechanical profile* • Linear speed, agility, and fast footwork essential to execute goal-scoring opportunities, and thwart attacks by opposition. • Vertical jumping required to challenge opposition for ball in mid-air; also used for goal scoring (heading) • One-on-one defensive posture is executed by flexing the hips at initial contact with the opposing athlete; hip flexion lowers COM, and this in turn minimizes vertical COM displacement when performing defensive cutting movements (18). • Skilled performers of instep kick show greater trunk ROM and velocity; also positive relationship between peak hip flexion and ball velocity (19).	*Biomechanical profile* • Repetitive, low forces required of lower body muscles, trunk stabilizers, shoulders and arms (i.e., muscular endurance). • Running economy (RE), which refers to the energy demand when running submaximally at a given velocity, is recognized as a predictor of endurance performance – those with better RE use less energy (20). • Muscle-tendon complexes of the lower extremities (e.g., quadriceps, triceps surae) contribute to RE. Runners with high RE have greater compliance of the quadriceps tendon at low forces (<45% MVC), and greater muscular strength and tendon stiffness of the triceps surae (21).

COM, center of mass. ROM, range of motion. MVC, maximal voluntary contraction.

Other examples of how a basic movement analysis can inform program design is in American football. Linemen and receivers are two positions with widely different biomechanical requirements. Starting from a crouched position, linemen drive upward using the hip and knee extensors while concurrently performing pressing motions to block the opposing team (i.e., horizontal shoulder abduction/adduction, elbow extension, trunk stabilization). These motions are performed with maximal effort for only a few seconds in duration. Linear speed over long distances is not a major requirement for the position. Therefore, exercise selection that develops both upper and lower body strength and power would be beneficial for blocking, one of the principal tasks of a lineman. In contrast, receivers require both linear speed and change of direction ability to a significant extent, with vertical jump ability also being a necessity in order to outmaneuver the defense. Consequently, training for speed, agility, and quickness, and lower body power would be priorities for the receiving corps.

An example of basic assessment of both the metabolic and biomechanical demands of various sports and specific positions is shown in Table 12.2.

INJURY RISK

Sport injuries are often sustained by the musculoskeletal systems through contact that overloads a particular structure (e.g., impact between two opposing players causing acute injury), overload that occurs without contact (e.g., acute joint injury when performing rapid change of direction), or gradual overuse of tissue (i.e., muscle, tendon, bone, ligaments) from repeated microtrauma without appropriate recovery (3–5). Although injury is sometimes unavoidable, the needs analysis should give consideration to common injuries associated with a given sport. Specifically, the strength and conditioning professional should seek to identify any factors that predispose or increase risk for a particular injury. Are particular attributes predictive of **injury risk**? In addition, the injury history of the athlete should be noted, such as previous injuries sustained, elapsed time since the injury occurred, and any rehabilitative efforts. Specific measures may then be taken to prevent an injury from recurring, or training load can be adjusted accordingly. From a practical standpoint, these issues may be addressed to a better extent in consultation with the network of health professionals involved in the athlete's daily care, such as Certified Athletic Trainers (ATCs), physical therapists, and the sports physician.

As described in Chapter 10, **athlete testing and assessment** is also a key component of the needs analysis because performance on the test battery reveals the current physical status of the athlete. This information is then used to guide program design because identified deficiencies can be addressed when planning the training schedule (i.e., needs of the athlete). Data from these performance tests can also be helpful for identifying predisposition to injury.

Anterior cruciate ligament (ACL) rupture occurs at a greater frequency in female athletes compared to males participating in the same sport (6,7). Using isokinetic dynamometry to measure muscle function, it was reported that female athletes who sustained a non-contact ACL rupture had decreased hamstrings strength, but similar quadriceps strength compared to their male counterparts (8). Interestingly, female athletes who did not rupture their ACL showed similar hamstrings strength, but decreased quadriceps strength compared to the male athletes. Thus, this data suggests that knee extensor/flexor strength imbalance plays a role in susceptibility to non-contact ACL rupture in females, with decreased hamstring strength coupled to higher quadriceps strength increasing the risk for injury. By identifying a group with predisposition to ACL injury (i.e., females), and having an index of injury susceptibility (hamstrings and quadriceps strength), female athletes that show a deficit during pre-screening assessments can seek to improve hamstrings strength as a training goal.

The strength and conditioning professional should also document any previous or recurring injuries whenever possible, either from athlete self-reporting or based on feedback from the appropriate healthcare professional. Knowledge of previous or recurring injuries experienced by an athlete should be identified in the needs analysis so that program design can incorporate appropriate interventions. For example, ankle sprains occur with regularity in volleyball, soccer, and basketball. Since ankle sprains can arise from any load-bearing task, they are by far one of the most common injuries in sport (9). Evidence suggests that balance and proprioceptive training are effective for mitigating subsequent re-injury of the ankle (10–12). Technical instruction has also been reported to reduce the risk of ankle injury recurrence (e.g., take-off and landing technique when jumping in volleyball) (13). Thus, the athlete's needs (i.e., reducing ankle re-injury) can be addressed by allocating specific training that includes balance and proprioception development, and technical instruction if warranted. As mentioned previously, this aspect of athlete care (i.e., injury management) may be better managed in conjunction with the network of other professionals tasked with overseeing the health of the athlete.

Efforts to minimize injury risk should not be limited to the initial needs analysis. Managing injury risk requires regular surveillance of athlete well-being and monitoring of training load throughout the course of the competitive season. Improperly managed training loads in conjunction with insufficient recovery periods can lead to overuse injuries (e.g., tendinopathy, bone injuries, patellofemoral pain) (14). Furthermore, fatigue resulting from excessive training loads and insufficient recovery may compromise decision-making and coordination, which in turn may increase injury risk (14). Contractile function of skeletal muscle may also be impaired as a result of fatigue, thereby reducing joint stability and increasing risk of injury (15). Therefore, the strength and conditioning professional has a significant role in addressing injury risk during the needs analysis and initial program design, as well as throughout the competitive season.

SUMMARY

The major purposes of the needs analysis are to identify the demands of the sport and the needs of the athlete. When evaluating demands of the sport, the strength and conditioning professional should make note of the energetic requirements for a particular athlete, movement patterns associated with an athlete's sport and position, primary muscles recruited, and common sites of injury. Athlete testing and assessment is also an integral component of the needs analysis because this information reveals areas of deficiency that can then be addressed by programmed training. Since the initial planning and preparation for any training program begins with the needs analysis, this task is the cornerstone of program design. The strength and conditioning professional should make every effort to carefully consider the needs analysis, ensure that athletes are periodically re-evaluated to monitor ongoing progress, and implement appropriate adjustments when necessary.

REFERENCES

1. Egan B, Zierath JR. Exercise metabolism and the molecular regulation of skeletal muscle adaptation. *Cell Metab* 2013; 17(2):162–184.
2. Mallo J, Mena E, Nevado F, Paredes V. Physical demands of top-class soccer friendly matches in relation to a playing position using global positioning system technology. *J Hum Kinet* 2015; 47:179–188.
3. Roos KG, Marshall SW. Definition and usage of the term "overuse injury" in the US high school and collegiate sport epidemiology literature: a systematic review. *Sports Med* 2014; 44(3):405–421.
4. Yu B, Garrett WE. Mechanisms of non-contact ACL injuries. *Br J Sports Med* 2007; 41 Suppl 1:i47–51.
5. Bahr R, Krosshaug T. Understanding injury mechanisms: a key component of preventing injuries in sport. *Br J Sports Med* 2005; 39(6):324–329.
6. Sutton KM, Bullock JM. Anterior cruciate ligament rupture: differences between males and females. *J Am Acad Orthop Surg* 2013; 21(1):41–50.
7. Barber-Westin SD, Noyes FR, Smith ST, Campbell TM. Reducing the risk of noncontact anterior cruciate ligament injuries in the female athlete. *Phys Sportsmed* 2009; 37(3):49–61.
8. Myer GD, Ford KR, Barber Foss KD, Liu C, Nick TG, Hewett TE. The relationship

of hamstrings and quadriceps strength to anterior cruciate ligament injury in female athletes. *Clin J Sport Med* 2009; 19(1):3–8.

9. Hootman JM, Dick R, Agel J. Epidemiology of collegiate injuries for 15 sports: summary and recommendations for injury prevention initiatives. *J Athl Train* 2007; 42(2):311–319.

10. Mohammadi F. Comparison of 3 preventive methods to reduce the recurrence of ankle inversion sprains in male soccer players. *Am J Sports Med* 2007; 35(6):922–926.

11. McGuine TA, Keene JS. The effect of a balance training program on the risk of ankle sprains in high school athletes. *Am J Sports Med* 2006; 34(7):1103–1111.

12. McKeon PO, Hertel J. Systematic review of postural control and lateral ankle instability, part II: is balance training clinically effective? *J Athl Train* 2008; 43(3):305–315.

13. Stasinopoulos D. Comparison of three preventive methods in order to reduce the incidence of ankle inversion sprains among female volleyball players. *Br J Sports Med* 2004; 38(2):182–185.

14. Soligard T, Schwellnus M, Alonso JM, Bahr R, Clarsen B, Dijkstra HP, Gabbett T, Gleeson M, Hagglund M, Hutchinson MR et al. How much is too much? (Part 1) International Olympic Committee consensus statement on load in sport and risk of injury. *Br J Sports Med* 2016; 50(17):1030–1041.

15. Ortiz A, Olson SL, Etnyre B, Trudelle-Jackson EE, Bartlett W, Venegas-Rios HL. Fatigue effects on knee joint stability during two jump tasks in women. *J Strength Cond Res* 2010; 24(4):1019–1027.

16. Zaras ND, Stasinaki AN, Methenitis SK, Krase AA, Karampatsos GP, Georgiadis GV, Spengos KM, Terzis GD. Rate of force development, muscle architecture, and performance in young competitive track and field throwers. *J Strength Cond Res* 2016; 30(1):81–92.

17. Landolsi M, Bouhlel E, Zarrouk F, Lacouture P, and Tabka Z. The relationships between leg peak power and shot-put performance in national-level athletes. *Isokinetics and Exercise Science* 2014; 22(1):55–61.

18. Sasaki S, Koga H, Krosshaug T, Kaneko S, Fukubayashi T. Biomechanical analysis of defensive cutting actions during game situations: six cases in collegiate soccer competitions. *J Hum Kinet* 2015; 46:9–18.

19. Fullenkamp AM, Campbell BM, Laurent CM, Lane AP. The contribution of trunk axial kinematics to poststrike ball velocity during maximal instep soccer kicking. *J Appl Biomech* 2015; 31(5):370–376.

20. Saunders PU, Pyne DB, Telford RD, Hawley JA. Factors affecting running economy in trained distance runners. *Sports Med* 2004; 34(7):465–485.

21. Arampatzis A, De Monte G, Karamanidis K, Morey-Klapsing G, Stafilidis S, Bruggemann GP. Influence of the muscle-tendon unit's mechanical and morphological properties on running economy. *J Exp Biol* 2006; 209(Pt 17): 3345–3357.

Contents

CHAPTER 13

PROGRAM DESIGN

Nathan Serrano and Andrew J. Galpin

OBJECTIVES

After completing this chapter, you will be able to:

- Explain the basic training principles of overload, variation, and specificity for improving sport performance and general fitness.
- Explain and apply the modifiable variables to drive adaptation.
- Understand the difference between training and relative intensity.
- Know how and when to apply the rating of perceived exertion to an athlete's training.
- Understand and explain the basic idea of the SAID Principle, the common mistakes made implementing a program based on specificity.
- Plan programs for speed, power, strength, and endurance.
- Create a periodized program that meets the athlete's/coach's goals for the athlete.
- Understand the basics behind training for hypertrophy and fat loss.

KEY TERMS

Frequency

General Adaptation Syndrome (GAS)

Hypertrophy

Individualization

Maladaptation phase

Overload

Overreaching

Periodization

Post activation potentiation

Progression/ regression

Rating of perceived exertion (RPE)

Rebounding

Relative intensity

Rest interval

SAID Principle

Specificity

Training intensity

Variation

Volume

Volume load

INTRODUCTION

Designing a proper training program requires consideration of numerous variables as each adaptation (speed, strength, power, hypertrophy, conditioning, fat loss, etc.) presents unique challenges. A basic understanding of program design, combined with a foundational knowledge of human anatomy and physiology, allows coaches to efficiently and effectively create appropriate training programs that reduce injury risk while achieving athlete/client goals. This requires examination and discussion of the modifiable (choice, order, frequency, intensity, volume, rest, progression) and non-modifiable (i.e., gender, limb length, training age, etc.) variables. More importantly, while several of these key concepts hold extensive scientific backing, others have only recently received extensive study.

The purpose of this chapter is to briefly discuss the basic principles underlying the specific training adaptations that result from properly periodized and implemented resistance training programs. This requires exploring a mix of both i) traditional methodologies and ii) some of the more recent findings in the scientific studies regarding resistance training for athletic performance.

BASIC TRAINING PRINCIPLES

Nearly every successful training program includes a combination of the following three basic training principles: **overload**, **variation**, and **specificity**. The overload provides the challenge required for physiological adaptation. However, by definition, this creates some damage or otherwise overwhelming stress, increasing injury risk. Variation helps reduce this danger by dispersing the stress. It also enhances the robust nature of the adaptation, increasing the likelihood that the new physical abilities are expressible in multiple avenues. Specificity maximizes the transferability of the improved performance to the direct, intended target. Variation and specificity appear contradictory on the surface, yet a closer examination of their proper implementation reveals their true complimentary nature.

The human body is highly adaptable, but must undergo an abnormal stress, or **overload**, to induce physical change. Overload is the training stimulus that drives adaptation and can be achieved through any number of alterations to the seven modifiable variables (described later). When applied in appropriate doses, overload induces short-term fatigue, but eventually enhances performance (32).

The overload must exceed habitual training ability, making it a moving target as the athlete continually progresses. In other words, the stress must be constantly progressed and include **variation** via the manipulation of exercises that follow a progressive model. This can be achieved on a week to week or day to day basis by increasing exercise sets, repetitions, and load, or by altering rest intervals. Overloading over weeks to months is done by increasing training frequency.

Regardless of the specific overload strategy, the physiological responses to overload are generally the same. When a stressor is introduced to a system, an immediate response occurs, known as the *alarm phase*, where performance is decreased due to acute fatigue. Then a **rebounding** phase begins where the system begins to recover from the stressor. Ideally, this is followed by a *super compensation phase* where the performance is actually elevated above the starting point (5,10). This concept of alarm, rebound, and super compensation is collectively referred to as the **General Adaptation Syndrome (GAS)** and is presented in more detail in Chapter 14. The training program should be designed such that each time a new stimulus is introduced the athlete has sufficient time to rebound and compensate. However, poorly planned programs can invoke the final stage of GAS, which should be avoided because it can be detrimental to the athlete's health and performance. This phase is called the **maladaptation phase** and denotes a detraining effect due to over stimulating the system without proper recovery or rest periods (5,10).

The resulting adaptation will be specific to the overloading demand. This is known as the **SAID Principle** (specific adaptation to an imposed demand). The coach must strategically manipulate the seven modifiable variables to ensure the physical demand of exercise, and resulting adaptation, is reflective of the training goal (5,36,41). This is known as **specificity**, which is a process of creating a particular efficiency of movement and energy production in sport through progressive training (19,26,28,42,48). Some mistakenly interpret this concept to mean one should mimic sport movements in the weight room and/or add sport equipment exercises.

For example, a runner should not execute all strength training on one leg simply because running is an entirely single-leg support activity, and a lacrosse athlete does not need to hold a stick in his/her hand while doing all agility training to achieve specificity. Several factors such as muscle actions, range of motion, energy systems, speed of movement, primary joint angles and force vectors, muscle groups involved, and common injuries should be considered when determining specificity. An example would be performing jumping and landing mechanics that reduce the risk of injuries, teaching acceleration mechanics that will help the athlete become more efficient in their sprints, teaching deceleration mechanics for change of direction efficiency, basic movement patterns like squatting, hip hinging, and pulling and pushing with the upper body.

> Resistance training is meant to improve athleticism, not necessarily the specific athletic movements used in their sport.

The specificity mistakes explained earlier are problematic because they may not effectively target the athlete's weakness and they limit variation. Mindlessly increasing overload and specificity may yield short-term benefits, but in the long term is foolish, ineffective, and likely to cause injury by directing too much stress to a given area. The purpose of learning program design is to understand how to use variation to balance the need for continually increased overload and specificity.

The balance between specificity and variation is determined by the time of year, goals, chronological age, and training age. Well-designed training programs move from more variation to more specific as the athlete gets closer to season. The same trend occurs over chronological age as younger athletes should focus on variation, avoiding copious specificity until reaching advanced (post-collegiate) or professional levels. However, older athletes may stay more on one side of the continuum based on individual needs and goals. Imagine two hockey players (Corey and Rickey) are trying to earn more ice time. Corey may use more variation in his training as he is well-rounded, but needs a little improving in all

areas. Rickey may focus almost his entire off-season training on speed as he's the slowest player in the league.

Training age is independent of chronological age and represents the amount of time (in years) an athlete has spent physically training, preferably under the direction of a qualified strength and conditioning professional. Elite athleticism is not always indicative of being well-trained. A professional basketball player with less than two years' training ("beginner") is not physically prepared to handle the same training overload as a teammate with more than four years' training ("advanced"). The "beginner" should utilize more variation, while the "advanced" athlete may need more specificity. Thus, a large proportion of athletes, and nearly all non-athletes, should focus the majority of their training on general exercises and fundamental movement patterns, and not be over-reliant on specificity.

> Start simple and slowly progress athletes as they gain movement control.

Balancing overload, specificity, and variation is best achieved when coaches thoroughly understand the answers to a few basic questions before writing the program:

1 What are the physical demands of the sport?
2 What are the metabolic demands of the sport?
3 What are the biomechanical demands of the sport?
4 What are the common overuse injuries associated with the sport?
5 What performance variables (e.g., power, strength, etc.) are limiting the athlete's success in the sport?
6 What is the athlete's training history?
7 What is the athlete's injury history?

> Programs should be based on the demands of the sport and individual.

Modifiable variables

Rest can be described within an exercise (inter-set) as "rest interval", or from session to session as "frequency" (see later). The rest interval is the period of time that energy is being conserved in order to allow for ATP to be readily available for the next set and for the clearing of other metabolic substrates that can hinder performance (4). Proper rest intervals are vital and determined by the specific training goal. More rest is preferred for maximal strength, so more reps can be completed at heavier loads (9). Speed and power follow a similar concept as maximal neuromuscular function is mandated. This likely explains why more complicated intra-set rest strategies such as cluster sets are effective at conserving maximal strength and velocity over multiple sets (45).

Muscular endurance and fat loss require less rest because the goal is to induce metabolic stress, with less concern for maintaining relative intensity. **Hypertrophy,** or increases in muscular cross-sectional area, was also thought to require short rest intervals, yet recent research questions this assumption (35,37). More research is needed, but these initial findings suggest that while short intervals increase metabolic disturbance and tissue damage (both of which directly and independently stimulate growth), they limit the load and/or volume. This compromises mechanical tension (another independent stimulator of growth) and resultant strength gains. Conversely, longer rest intervals limit metabolic damage. Thus, a well-rounded hypertrophy program may necessitate inclusion of both rest strategies.

Frequency of training is the amount of sessions an athlete completes, per week. This is NOT synonymous with number of training days per week. It is common in high level mixed martial artists, swimmers, weightlifters, sprinters, and others to train multiple times a day. Two training sessions a day would total a weekly frequency of 14, not 7. This is done to accumulate large amounts of work but requires excess recover resources and/or abilities. The extreme frequencies would be for highly trained athletes since their habitual level is much higher than an untrained person or a recreational athlete (37).

> Even highly skilled athletes may not necessarily be highly physically trained, so progress their training volume and frequency slowly.

Intensity

Each training session must vary in intensity, which is the amount of work done in a session (**training intensity**) or within an exercise (**relative intensity**) (17,36,44). For example, lifting 90% of your one-repetition maximum (1RM) for two repetitions would equate to *relatively* large amounts of work, but lifting 65% of your 1RM for two repetitions would be much less intense. However, athletes typically do not lift 65% 1RM only two times (unless being performed explosively for the development of speed or power (5,13,23)). If more reps at 65% 1RM are completed, the amount of work would eventually match the previous example at 95% 1RM. In this example, the 95% lift would have a high relative intensity while the 65% for max repetitions would have a low relative, but high training intensity. Most athletes should be exposed to a combination of low and high relative and training intensities (47).

Some coaches use the **rating of perceived exertion** (RPE) as an indicator of intensity because it is easy to implement and track over months/years. RPE also provides additional useful feedback from the athlete, accounts for day to day fluctuations in physical ability, and can encourage athlete accountability. For example, if a coach tells an athlete that a given set should be done at an RPE of 8/10 (with 10 being the maximum exertion), the athlete knows it should be a challenging set. The athlete might then choose to slightly alter the prescribed repetitions or load to ensure the difficulty is not too low or too high. Keep in mind, the use of RPE as an intensity guide requires some calibration to what 1/10 and 10/10 feel like, so it may be too subjective for beginners (46).

Volume is the total number of reps performed (sets × reps), typically reported on a per exercise, per day, or per weekly basis. **Volume load** can also be calculated to show an overall amount of work performed by multiplying the volume by the load. For example, if John performed the back squat with 225 lbs for 5 sets of 5 repetitions, then his volume load was 5,625 lbs (25 reps × 225 lbs). This is an easy way of tracking and monitoring training on a given day or over a period of weeks, months, or years. This also highlights how volume and relative intensity are inversely related (30,31,37). As the intensity of an exercise goes up, the volume must go down. This is due to the effort demand of heavier load, reducing the energy remaining available to perform more repetitions. Both volume and intensity can remain high if a moderate to heavy load is used for many sets, in combination with proper rest intervals (9). This strategy has been shown to drive hypertrophy and strength adaptations (40–42). However, it should be done sparingly as the high training intensity is demanding, which increases risk of injury or overtraining.

Exercise **progression/regression** refers to increasing/decreasing the difficulty level of an exercise based on individual needs. This is often accomplished by reducing or adding dimensions of control, though many other methods exist. For example, a squat can be regressed to a leg press, or progressed to a single-leg squat. Mastering progression/regression enables coaches to quickly individualize workouts when training teams or groups of athletes.

> Individualization is the ability of a coach to create a program that fits the athlete's specific needs and uses exercises that fit his/her current abilities.

Exercise order

Exercise order refers to the progression from one exercise to the next in a given workout. Traditionally, order moves from the most complex/highest velocity movements to the least complex/lowest velocity because the former requires greater neurological input, which diminishes as fatigue occurs (5). Improper order compromises, or completely eliminates, the ability to develop speed, power, or strength.

Think about the demands of each exercise, and how that would influence the subsequent exercises. A fatigued neuromuscular system (caused by doing fatiguing exercises first) reduces the ability to generate maximum force and power. Thus, performing hang snatches after the highly fatiguing, high volume split squats would be a bad idea as it will hinder the athlete's ability to produce power, which is the major purpose of the exercise. In addition, it is generally best practice to place individuals

in the most dangerous situations (e.g., landing, implements over the head, complex movements, uncontrolled environments, etc.) first and progressing to safer settings (e.g., single joint exercises, machines, slower tempo, etc.) when fatigued.

Periodization

Periodization, presented in Chapter 14 is a phasic training path that leads to a future performance outcome. More plainly, it is the planned variation in training variables (mostly volume and intensity). Periodization is a combination of three distinct cycles presented in Chapter 14, microcycles, mesocycles, and macrocycles (5).

Organizing in this fashion allows for planned periods of **overreaching**, an overload micro or mesocycle known to temporarily compromise performance, but eventually inducing supercompensation when stress is reduced. Overreaching phases maintained for too long result in overtraining. The line between overreaching and overtraining is difficult to decipher and differs considerably from athlete to athlete. Proper monitoring of athlete fatigue, mood, nutrition, sleep, and attitude aid in avoiding overtraining.

> A good strength coach plans out the year's macrocycle and programs in one- to four-week intervals to create the best possible microcycles.

1 Sample program design for improving hypertrophy: increasing load from week to week

   a Monday: Hypertrophy (moderate volume)
   b Tues: Hypertrophy (high volume)
   c Wed: rest
   d Thurs: Hypertrophy (moderate volume)
   e Friday: Hypertrophy (high volume)
   f Saturday-Sunday: rest

2 Sample program design for improving power:

   a Monday: Hypertrophy (medium load, medium/high volume)
   b Tuesday: Strength (high load, low/medium volume)

c   Wednesday: Power (low load, low/medium volume)
d   Thursday: Hypertrophy (medium/high load, medium volume)
e   Friday: Strength (high/medium load, medium volume)
f   Saturday: Power (low load, low volume)
g   Sunday: rest

3   Sample program design for improving strength: goal-centered mesocycle with deload week

a   Week 1: Hypertrophy
b   Week 2: Hypertrophy
c   Week 3: Strength
d   Week 4: Recovery (deload)

A weightlifting athlete at the beginning of his/her training cycle might start with six training sessions a week with an average intensity at 68% of their main lifts. As the athlete enters the pre-competition phase of the cycle, the coach increases the frequency to nine sessions and sets the intensity at 75%, which slowly progresses to 95% over the next three months. Leading to the biggest competition of the year, the coach programs the athlete to have more practice with the competitive lifts and less accessory work. For example, the athlete might have a training session in the morning at the beginning of the pre-competition cycle that includes six sets of a snatch at 75% 1RM. The next exercise is back squats at 80% 1RM for five sets of five. The next training session in the afternoon calls for five sets of clean and jerks at 70% and a barbell shoulder press for four sets of eight at 65%. At the end of each training day the athlete also has split squats, bench press, core work, front, lateral and reverse shoulder raises. As the competition gets closer, the overall volume of training increases to ten sessions and the average intensity is 85–90% to elicit an overreaching effect. In the peaking phase of this cycle, the training is focused on recovery and maintaining the adaptations that were gained the previous four to six months. The coach might reduce training volumes down to six to seven sessions a week with the intensity holding at 85–95%, until the final week where the intensity drops back to ~70–80% to allow recovery.

A collegiate baseball shortstop, Jose, just came off his junior season and is starting his offseason training. The strength and conditioning coach has Jose training four days a week with little/no baseball specific activities. The first four to six weeks are focused on correcting any muscular or joint imbalances Jose developed over the season. In the next training phase (pre-season), the baseball team begins sport practice and only has weight training three days a week. The strength coach splits the training up in a lower body, upper body, and full body fashion. The lower body day Jose performs power cleans at 75–80% and squats at 80–85% 1RM. He is also still using some unilateral exercises like single-leg hamstring curls and glute bridges to maintain muscular balance as he heads into his season. The upper body day includes bench press, bent over rows, pull ups, and overhead stability drills to help strengthen his shoulder. The full body session has front squats for postural integrity, low volume plyometrics, and a mixture of lower body unilateral exercises, upper body presses, and horizontal pulling. Once the season starts, Jose is lifting twice a week with his practice and multiple games every week. This includes a push and pull day. The push session includes squats, bench, and shoulder stability work. During the pulling session, Jose is performing power clean pulls, deadlifts, pull ups, and bent over rows at 80–90% for only three or four sets of no more than three to five reps on most of these exercises to maintain strength, power, and speed with the limited time in the weight room. The strength and conditioning coach would also add specific exercises designed to reduce injury risk for baseball players.

Training for speed

Speed is arguably the most sought-after performance variable in athletic performance and is discussed in Chapter 17. Athletes improve speed when they increase i) the rate that a muscle contracts, ii) movement mechanics, or iii) strength. Untrained or beginner (young training age) athletes may benefit the most from improving strength (15,16,20,50,51). Speed involves three key concepts: acceleration, maximum velocity, and deceleration. During *acceleration*, generating force in the proper direction with magnitude decreases the number of strides necessary to move from point A to point B. This is termed stride length. Stride frequency requires speed within the muscle to decrease the time it takes for the foot to propel the body forward, drive the knee up, and cycle back down into the ground. This is best trained through maximum effort sprints with appropriate rest intervals or high power exercises (5). *Maximum velocity* deals with maintaining the built-up velocity during the acceleration phase. Most sports rarely reach maximum velocity due to the constant change of direction. Though there are many scientifically supported modes of training speed, *deceleration* is a forgotten tool. The ability to attenuate the forces (i.e., stop and control movement) is critical for rapid change of direction. A large amount of strength is required to overcome the eccentric loading during deceleration. Thus, a base of strength is required for speed development as both *acceleration* and *deceleration* rely upon force production.

Training for power

Speed multiplied by strength is power. In other words, power is the product of work and time. The more work done over a short period of time, the higher the power. This typically translates into a training prescription of lighter weights at high velocities (11,12). The optimal relative intensity (load) for peak power production differs from person to person and ranges from 30–85% 1RM. For instance, squat jumps appear to produce peak power around 30% 1RM, but weightlifting movements (8) (i.e., variations of the snatch or clean and jerk) exhibit peak power closer to 80–85% 1RM (21). Thus, athletes are encouraged to train across the entire power spectrum.

A great way to train power is through plyometric exercises, also addressed in Chapter 17. A plyometric by definition is cyclical and has a loading or (eccentric) phase, amortization (deceleration) phase, and an explosive force (concentric) phase (2,14–16). A common plyometric exercise is a depth to box jump, where an athlete steps off a box then rebounds off the ground up to another box. Low volumes are recommended for ballistic exercises such as this for two reasons. Firstly, fatigue

compromises performance, which reduces speed, force, or both, eliminating the purpose of the exercise (to produce maximal power). Secondly, the high demands increase injury risk, which only increases over time.

Training for strength

Muscular strength is defined as the ability of a muscle group to develop maximal contractile force against a resistance in a single contraction. The signal to contract comes from the nervous system and signals the muscle fibers to contract. However, the amount of force transmitted from the fiber, through the connective tissue, and to the tendon, determines how the bone is moved. Other biomechanical factors such as joint angle, pennation angle, and lever arms also influence limb movement. Thus, muscular strength is determined by a combination of neurological, muscular, connective tissue, and biomechanical factors. Connective tissue and biomechanical changes occur extremely slowly, if at all. Improvements in strength are therefore primarily a result of neurological and/or muscular adaptations. Increased motor unit recruitment, frequency of firing, and synchronization, as well as increased relaxation of antagonist muscle groups, or decreased Golgi tendon organ activation, result in greater force production. Changes in fiber type (48) or contraction kinetics (e.g., greater calcium affinity, faster sarcoplasmic reticulum recycling of acetylcholine, etc.) result in increased single fiber contractility (i.e., velocity of muscle fiber contraction), independent of size (hypertrophy) gains. However, muscle hypertrophy is usually associated with some strength gains as the increased size is mostly a result of thicker myosin and actin molecules, which increase the number of myosin and actin interactions, forming more cross-bridges. Together, it explains how individuals can get stronger without gaining excessive muscle mass, but gaining muscle will result in some strength gains, but will not optimize strength gains. The heavy neurological component leads many to describe physical strength as a "skill," meaning it requires much specific practice. It also explains that while exceptions exist, larger athletes will generally have greater *absolute strength* (total weight lifted), which is why sports like weightlifting, wrestling, and mixed martial arts require weight categories. However, the smaller athletes will often have greater *relative strength* (total weight lifted divided by body weight). The sport of weightlifting accounts for this by using a correction factor called the Sinclair score (which accounts for both absolute and relative strength) to determine overall champions.

Strength training should therefore include a range of repetitions and loads in order to stimulate neuromuscular, muscular, connective, and biomechanical adaptations. A strength phase for beginners should start with building a base through high volume and low/moderate intensity (to build hypertrophy, connective, and biomechanical factors) followed by a decrease in volume and increase of intensity (to challenge the muscle fiber and neuromuscular systems). More advanced athletes may be able to reduce the high-volume phase and spend more time developing the specific skill of strength.

> Lift heavy things often for best strength gains.

Training for hypertrophy

The three key ingredients to inducing skeletal muscle hypertrophy are tissue damage (soreness), mechanical stress (load), and metabolic stress (metabolites). Tissue damage can be accomplished through high reps of low to moderate loads, as well as eccentric loading of the muscle. This is not to say soreness is the number one goal of every training session, or that its relationship to growth is linear. Surely soreness is a general sign that adaptations may ensue; however, it should not be the goal of the strength and conditioning professional to induce muscle soreness as it is a poor indicator of resulting growth (29,38).

Mechanical stress relates to the magnitude of the load (i.e., how heavy it is). Mechanical stress and tissue damage are often associated together as high loads at moderate to high volumes tend to cause muscle damage. However, high intensity and low volume induces significantly less soreness. Research has also shown that metabolic stress increases muscle growth significantly through the collection of metabolic substances called metabolites (e.g., lactate, inorganic phosphate, and H+) which signal cellular growth (39). Metabolic stress is primarily a result of high volume in combination with low/no rest. When taken together, it is no surprise that recent research suggests that a continuum of rep ranges stimulates growth (32–35). Thus, a well-rounded program that emphasizes all three throughout a given week will likely produce the best results.

> Use a combination of heavy/low reps, moderate/moderate reps, and light/high reps to maximize hypertrophy.

Training for conditioning

Adaptations to conditioning occur both systemically (e.g., insulin sensitivity, lactate threshold, O_2 saturation, etc.) and on the cellular level (e.g., mitochondrial density, capillary density, metabolic enzymes, etc). Track sprinters often run multiple races in competition (e.g., qualifying, prelims, semifinals, and finals) and so they require a certain type of condition to adequately recover and repeat or improve their performance. Other sports like hockey, football, or basketball require movement bouts that last a little longer, but with intermittent bursts of intensity. These athletes require different types of conditioning than track sprinters, or even steady state endurance athletes like a triathlete. Thus, the athlete's conditioning should mimic the intensity and duration of their specific activities on the field. Primarily concentric-only exercises like cycling, sled pushing/towing, or rowing work well for conditioning, regardless of sport, since these exercises have relatively low skill requirements and their limited eccentric components moderate muscle soreness, allowing them to be performed at a high volume and frequency (24,29).

> Steady state endurance is not the only way to improve cardiovascular and muscular endurance.

Training for fat loss

There has been much debate as to what method of training is best for fat loss. That is, the loss of fat body mass and maintenance or gain of lean muscle mass. Fat loss requires a net caloric deficit, which is achievable with countless methods. Some individuals prefer continuous, steady-state endurance exercise (e.g., jogging, swimming, cycling, etc.) while others favor high intensity intervals (e.g., circuit weight training, repeated max effort cycling, etc.). The best answer probably lies in a combination of numerous conditioning and resistance training methods, all integrated in high variety.

> Training for fat loss has to be paired with a caloric deficit. Training alone will limit your success.

Q&A FROM THE FIELD

What is the best way to program for an adolescent beginning athlete?

It is a common misconception that training prepubescent athletes is detrimental to their growth and development. However, research has long shown that children and adolescent athletes can and should use a properly designed resistance-training program. This is not much different from training a beginner athlete, regardless of chronological age. The goal with any individual is to develop and eventually master good movement mechanics and postural integrity. The goal of training programs for beginner athletes should be to enhance long-term athletic development, not short-term improvements in any single performance goal (e.g., strength, power, hypertrophy, etc.). This typically means athletes should learn how to perform basic athletic movements like running, jumping, throwing, squatting, hip hinging, upper body pushing/pulling, rotating, and core stabilization. The focus should be placed on movement technique, efficiency, and quality rather than things like "amount of weight lifted" or speed. A generally good idea is to have the athlete perform a movement with a slow tempo and be able to maintain proper position, stabilization, and muscle sequencing (i.e., using the proper muscles in the proper order) throughout, for example a squat with a five second eccentric portion, five second hold in the bottom position, and five second concentric portion. If an athlete executes this for multiple reps while maintaining movement quality, then it may be appropriate to

progress the weight or increase the speed. If this is done properly, the short- and long-term injury risk are greatly reduced, allowing more training later in life, which ultimately leads to greater improvements in physical attributes and sport performance.

Q&A FROM THE FIELD

When is it appropriate to max out?

Maxing out or finding a maximum amount of weight an athlete can lift with proper form should be used sparingly because it is highly fatiguing for the athlete. This is not advisable for individuals that are still beginners in training age because they are still developing the movement patterns and can put the athlete at a high risk for injury.

Q&A FROM THE FIELD

What can you do if you're working with a sport coach who is adamant about testing the athletes' max lifts?

This is a common issue strength coaches must deal with, so you should work towards having a relationship with the sport coach that values your input. An alternative approach would be to perform the test where the "max" is considered as the maximum amount lifted until a breakdown in technique occurs. This can be thought of as the athlete's "technical 1RM." Skilled lifters may easily reach their true 1RM, while less experienced athletes may only achieve 70–80% of their true maximum. In both cases, the information is valuable and provides the appropriate details needed to assess your program quality and effectiveness. Exercise selection can also be modified to reduce some injury risk (however, even technically simple exercises can have a large risk if executed poorly). An example would be using an alternative exercise like a leg press as a crude measure of leg strength for an athlete with limited/no squatting experience. As the athlete develops, the back squat will eventually replace the leg press as the primary leg strength testing modality. Thus, while a leg press is indeed quite different from a squat, it may represent a reasonable mitigation of risk in this situation.

Q&A FROM THE FIELD

How do I know if I need to perform 1RM testing?

We recommend the strength coach ask the following questions prior to doing 1RM testing. Is the sport a maximal effort in nature (i.e., shotput, discus, weightlifting, or powerlifting)? If so, this merits more frequent 1RM testing. Does the athlete understand the safety hazards accompanied with 1RM testing? If not, use alternative testing strategies, or select exercises the athlete is highly skilled and competent in. Are there adequate strength and conditioning or other qualified personnel to act as spotters? If not, reconsider testing. Does the athlete have extensive experience in that movement at that high of a load? If so, then 1RM represents fairly low risk, so engage accordingly.

ADVANCED TRAINING METHODS

Post activation potentiation

Post activation potentiation (PAP) is a physiological phenomenon where a heavy lift (e.g., 80% 1RM deadlift) is used to activate the central nervous system immediately before performing a fast or explosive movement. PAP has received extensive study over recent years and appears highly effective for well-trained individuals (7,22,25,27,49), but may actually hinder performance in beginning athletes (1,8). This training style can also offer a great way to utilize traditional rest periods in large group training sessions for experienced high school (juniors and seniors with at least two years of properly instructed training) and college athletes. Some examples include performing a heavy squat immediately before a vertical jump, a heavy bench prior to a med ball chest press, or heavy deadlift before a short sprint.

Assisted and overspeed training

Studies have shown that assisted exercises, also known as *overspeed training*, improve movement velocity (6). The band or assisting device aids the athlete in their movement allowing an increased movement velocity and synchronous contractions of the involved muscles. Heavy elastic, or variable resistance bands (VRB), are effective tools for overspeed training (3,7). VRB also aid in reducing the eccentric loading of some movements allowing for an increased volume, without fatigue or resulting soreness. Other means of utilizing assisted or overspeed training include assisted jumping, towed sprinting (when the band is used to accelerate the athlete, not as added resistance), or speed bats for baseball/softball. Adding resistance in the form of sled towing and parachute running can improve acceleration, but not maximal velocity (43).

Dynamic variable resistance

Use of VRB has increased in popularity in recent years. This usually involves adding a VRB to already loaded exercises like the back squats, deadlifts, or bench press. This strategy has been shown to improve the time to peak power (time it takes to reach the highest power output during a given exercise), peak power (maximum power output during a given exercise), and time to peak velocity (time it takes to reach the highest velocity during a given movement) (18). This works by manipulating the human strength curve, which says the maximal strength of an exercise is determined by the maximal strength in the weakest part of the movement. In other words, a 1RM will be limited by the maximal strength at the weakest position, not the maximal strength at the strongest position. The band adds the least resistance at the weakest position, but increased resistance at the strongest position, meaning the muscles are progressively challenged throughout the exercise as the body simultaneously gains mechanical advantage.

SUMMARY

Adaptation is an important factor of training especially when performance is the primary goal. The athlete and coach must have a thorough understanding of the three basic training principles (overload, specificity, and variation) and theories to maximize the dose response of resistance exercise. All of the factors of training must be put into consideration (frequency, intensity, volume, rest, choice, order, and progression). Individuals should focus on constructing a plan that is progressive and varied, while also overloading the body. Plans are constructed in a periodized fashion and encompass a macrocycle, and several meso and microcycles. Proper manipulation of the basic training principles and modifiable variables produce the best, and most specific, adaptations and decrease the likelihood of injury.

REFERENCES

1. Arias JC, Coburn JW, Brown LE, Galpin AJ. The acute effects of heavy deadlifts on vertical jump performance in men. *Sports* 2016; 4(2):22.
2. Baker D. Comparison of upper-body strength and power between professional and college-aged rugby league players. *J Strength Cond Res* 2001; 15:30–35.
3. Bartolini JA, Brown LE, Coburn JW, Judelson DA, Spiering BA, Aguirre NW, Carney KR, Harris KB. Optimal elastic cord assistance for sprinting in collegiate women soccer players. *J Strength Cond Res* 2011; 25:1263–1270.
4. Bottaro M, Brown LE, Celes R, Martorelli S, Carregaro R, Vidal JCD. Effect of rest interval on neuromuscular and metabolic responses between children and adolescents. *Pediatric Exercise Science* 2011; 23: 311–321.
5. Brown LE, Greenwood M. Periodization essentials and innovations in resistance training protocols. *Strength Cond* 2005; 27: 80–85.
6. Cazas VL, Brown LE, Coburn JW, Galpin AJ, Tufano JJ, LaPorta JW, Du Bois AM. Influence of rest intervals after assisted jumping on bodyweight vertical jump performance. *J Strength Cond Res* 2013; 27:64–68.
7. Chiu L, Fry A, Weiss L, Schilling B, Brown L, Smith S. Postactivation potentiation response in athletic and recreationally trained individuals. *J Strength Cond Res* 2003; 17:671–677.
8. Chiu L, Schilling B. A primer on weightlifting: From sport to sports training. *Strength Cond* 2005; 27: 42–48.
9. Ciccone AB, Brown LE, Coburn JW, Galpin AJ. Effects of traditional vs. alternating whole-body strength training on squat performance. *J Strength Cond Res* 2014; 28: 2569–2577.
10. Coffey VG, Hawley JA. The molecular bases of training adaptation. *Sports Medicine* 2007; 37:737–763.
11. Cormie P, McBride JM, McCaulley GO. Power-time, force-time, and velocity-time curve analysis during the jump squat: Impact of load. *Journal of Applied Biomechanics* 2008; 24:112–120.
12. Cormie P, McCaulley GO, McBride JM. Power versus strength-power jump squat training: Influence on the load-power relationship. *Med Sci Sports Exerc* 2007; 39:996–1003.
13. Darmiento A, Galpin AJ, Brown LE. Vertical jump and power. *Strength Cond* 2012; 34:34–43.
14. de Villarreal ESS, Kellis E, Kraemer WJ, Izquierdo M. Determining variables of plyometric training for improving vertical jump height performance: a meta-analysis. *J Strength Cond Res* 2009; 23:495–506.
15. Ebben WP, Blackard DO. Strength and conditioning practices of National Football League strength and conditioning coaches. *J Strength Cond Res* 2001; 15:48–58.
16. Ebben WP, Carroll RM, Simenz CJ. Strength and conditioning practices of National Hockey League strength and conditioning coaches. *J Strength Cond Res* 2004; 18: 889–897.
17. Fry AC, Kraemer WJ, Ramsey LT. Pituitary-adrenal-gonadal responses to high-intensity resistance exercise overtraining. *J of Appl Physiol* 1998; 85:2352–2359.
18. Galpin AJ, Malyszek KK, Davis KA, Record SM, Brown LE, Coburn JW, Harmon RA, Steele JM, Manolovitz AD. Acute effects of elastic bands on kinetic characteristics during the deadlift at moderate and heavy loads. *J Strength Cond Res* 2015; 29:3271–3278.
19. Gehri DJ, Ricard MD, Kleiner DM, Kirkendall DT. A comparison of plyometric training techniques for improving vertical jump ability and energy production. *J Strength Cond Res* 1998; 12:85–89.
20. Harridge SDR, Bottinelli R, Canepari M, Pellegrino M, Reggiani C, Esbjornsson M, Balsom PD, Saltin B. Sprint training, in vitro and in vivo muscle function, and myosin heavy chain expression. *J of Appl Physiol* 1998; 84: 442–449.

21. Hori N, Newton RU, Andrews WA, Kawamori N, McGuigan MR, Nosaka K. Comparison of four different methods to measure power output during the hang power clean and the weighted jump squat. *J Strength Cond Res* 2007; 21:314–320.

22. Jo E, Judelson D, Brown L, Coburn J, Dabbs N. Influence of recovery duration after a potentiating stimulus on muscular power in recreationally trained individuals. *J Strength Cond Res* 2010; 24:343–347.

23. Kelly SB, Brown LE, Coburn JW, Zinder SM, Gardner LM, Nguyen D. The effect of single versus multiple sets on strength. *J Strength Cond Res* 2007; 21:1003–1006.

24. Kelly SB, Brown LE, Hooker SP, Swan PD, Buman MP, Alvar BA, Black LE. Comparison of concentric and eccentric bench press repetitions to failure. *J Strength Cond Res* 2015; 29: 1027–1032.

25. Khamoui A, Brown L, Coburn J, Judelson D, Uribe B, Nguyen D, Tran T, Eurich A, Noffal G. Effect of potentiating exercise volume on vertical jump parameters in recreationally trained men. *J Strength Cond Res* 2009; 23:1465–1469.

26. Kraemer WJ, Nindl BC, Ratamess NA, Gotshalk LA, Volek JS, Fleck SJ, Newton RU, Häkkinen K. Changes in muscle hypertrophy in women with periodized resistance training. *Med Sci Sports Exerc* 2004; 36:697–708.

27. Lowery RP, Duncan NM, Loenneke JP, Sikorski EM, Naimo MA, Brown LE, Wilson FG, Wilson JM. The effects of potentiating stimuli intensity under varying rest periods on vertical jump performance and power. *J Strength Cond Res* 2012; 26:3320–3325.

28. Murray DP, Brown LE, Zinder SM, Noffal GJ, Bera SG, Garrett NM. Effects of velocity-specific training on rate of velocity development, peak torque, and performance. *J Strength Cond Res* 2007; 21:870–874.

29. Nguyen D, Brown LE, Coburn JW, Judelson DA, Eurich AD, Khamoui AV, Uribe BP. Effect of delayed-onset muscle soreness on elbow flexion strength and rate of velocity development. *J Strength Cond Res* 2009; 23:1282–1286.

30. Ostrowski KJ, Wilson GJ, Weatherby R, Murphy PW, Lyttle AD. The effect of weight training volume on hormonal output and muscular size and function. *J Strength Cond Res* 1997; 11:148–154.

31. Peterson MD, Rhea MR, Alvar BA. Maximizing strength development in athletes: A meta-analysis to determine the dose-response relationship. *J Strength Cond Res* 2004; 18: 377–382, 204.

32. Ribeiro AS, Avelar A, Schoenfeld BJ, Fleck SJ, Souza MF, Padilha CS, Cyrino ES. Analysis of the training load during a hypertrophy-type resistance training programme in men and women. *Eur J Sports Sci* 2015; 15:256–264.

33. Ribeiro AS, Avelar A, Schoenfeld BJ, Trindade MCC, Ritti-Dias RM, Altimari LR, Cyrino ES. Effect of 16 weeks of resistance training on fatigue resistance in men and women. *J Hum Kinet* 2014; 42:165–174.

34. Schoenfeld B. Repetitions and muscle hypertrophy. *Strength Cond* 2000; 22:67–69.

35. Schoenfeld B. *Science and Development of Muscle Hypertrophy*. Champaign, IL: Human Kinetics, 2016.

36. Schoenfeld B and Dawes J. High-intensity interval training: applications for general fitness training. *Strength Cond* 2009; 31: 44–46.

37. Schoenfeld B, Ratamess N, Peterson M, Contreras B, Tiryaki-Sonmez G. Influence of resistance training frequency on muscular adaptations in well-trained men *J Strength Cond Res* 2015; 29:1821–1829.

38. Schoenfeld BJ, Contreras B. Is postexercise muscle soreness a valid indicator of muscular adaptations? *Strength Cond* 2013; 35:16–21.

39. Schoenfeld BJ, Contreras B. The muscle pump: potential mechanisms and applications for enhancing hypertrophic adaptations. *Strength Cond* 2014; 36:21–25.

40. Schoenfeld BJ, Contreras B, Ogborn D, Galpin A, Krieger J, Sonmez GT. Effects of varied versus constant loading zones on muscular adaptations in trained men. *Int J Sports Med* 2016; 37:442–447.

41. Schoenfeld BJ, Contreras B, Vigotsky AD, Ogborn D, Fontana F, Tiryaki-Sonmez G. Upper body muscle activation during low- versus high-load resistance exercise in the bench press. *Isokinetics and Exercise Science* 2016; 24:217–224.

42. Schoenfeld BJ, Ratamess NA, Peterson MD, Contreras B, Sonmez GT, Alvar BA. Effects of different volume-equated resistance training loading strategies on muscular adaptations in well-trained men. *J Strength Cond Res* 2014; 28:2909–2918.

43. Spinks CD, Murphy AJ, Spinks WL, Lockie RG. The effects of resisted sprint training on acceleration performance and kinematics in soccer, rugby union, and Australian football players. *J Strength Cond Res* 2007; 21:77–85.

44. Tufano JJ, Brown LE, Coburn JW, Tsang KKW, Cazas VL, LaPorta JW. Effect of aerobic recovery intensity on delayed-onset muscle soreness and strength. *J Strength Cond Res* 2012; 26:2777–2782.

45. Tufano JJ, Conlon JA, Nimphius S, Brown LE, Seitz LB, Williamson BD, Haff GG. Maintenance of velocity and power with cluster sets during high-volume back squats. *Int J Sports Physiol Perform* 2016; 11:885–892.

46. Wernbom M, Jarrebring R, Andreasson MA, and Augustsson J. Acute effects of blood flow restriction on muscle activity and endurance during fatiguing dynamic knee extensions at low load. *J Strength Cond Res* 2009; 23:2389–2395.

47. Willardson JM and Burkett LN. The effect of rest interval length on bench press performance with heavy vs. light loads. *J Strength Cond Res* 2006; 20:396–399.

48. Wilson J, Loenneke J, Jo E, Wilson G, Zourdos M, and Kim J. The effects of endurance, strength, and power training on muscle fiber type shifting. *J Strength Cond Res* 2012; 26:1724–1729.

49. Wilson JM, Duncan NM, Marin PJ, Brown LE, Loenneke JP, Wilson SMC, Jo E, Lowery RP, Ugrinowitsch C. Meta-analysis of postactivation potentiation and power: effects of conditioning activity, volume, gender, rest periods, and training status. *J Strength Cond Res* 2013; 27:854–859.

50. Yap CW and Brown LE. Development of speed, agility, and quickness for the female soccer athlete. *Strength Cond* 2000; 22:9–12.

51. Yetter M and Moir G. The acute effects of heavy back and front squats on speed during forty-meter sprint trials. *J Strength Cond Res* 2008; 22:159–165.

Contents

CHAPTER 14

PERIODIZATION OF RESISTANCE TRAINING: CONCEPTS AND PARADIGMS

William J. Kraemer and Matthew K. Beeler

OBJECTIVES

After completing this chapter, you will be able to:

- Apply the concepts of "evidence-based practice" to developing training and conditioning programs.
- Express an understanding of the "general adaptation syndrome" and how it fits into a periodized training model.
- Utilize the terminology related to periodized training programs.
- Develop an understanding and appreciation for the historical aspects of periodization.
- Understand and explain both "traditional" and "non-traditional" periodized models of training.
- Express an understanding of "flexible" non-linear programing.

KEY TERMS

Block periodization	Microcycle	Supercompensation
Competitive or realization block	Overtraining syndrome	Traditional or classic periodization
	Prioritization	
Conjugate periodization	Recovery	Training session
Evidence-based practice	Recovery block	Undulating non-linear periodization
General adaptation syndrome	Specific, transformation, or transmutation block	Variation
		Volume load
General block	Staleness	
Macrocycle	Step loading	
Mesocycle	Stress	

INTRODUCTION

What is **periodization** and how has it been transformed from a fundamental concept of training theory over the past century? The short answer is by evolving into many different periodized approaches to training athletes in all sports at all levels. First, one needs to understand that paradigms and frameworks provide ideas for program design and development (8).

Monitoring workouts and testing of athletes provides data as to the efficacy and success of a training model being used. Individualized testing and analysis is undertaken to directly determine effectiveness of the program design approach being used. If a training program is not meeting training goals, modifications should be made as needed. Thus, the training model is not static, but rather dynamic in its fundamental nature. Periodization of training allows for one very global theoretical paradigm arising out of the modern world of sports and exercise training theories. It can be configured in different sets, reps, intensity, volume, etc. to help mediate desired changes and meet the training goals. Finally, periodization is not one training model but consists of configurations of a program along with the short- and long-term sequencing used in exercise training progressions.

> A periodized training model is not static, but rather is dynamic in its fundamental nature.

Whether you are a strength coach, an athlete, or a dedicated fitness trainee, a resistance training program is only as successful as the understanding you have of the program being used and how it can be modified over time. While this chapter addresses periodization of resistance training, it is typically only one part of a total conditioning program (e.g., others include aerobic conditioning, anaerobic conditioning, flexibility, etc.). Ultimately, in such a chapter we can only provide "paradigms" to work with that have been successful both in anecdotal and/or research reports. However, it is important to understand that each individual will respond differently to each conditioning program or combinations thereof. This is due to the different genetic predispositions for inherent characteristics (e.g., muscle fiber type, connective tissue density, number of muscle fibers in various muscles) each individual has which mediate the physiological adaptations to a program. From a practical perspective, this means that training must be highly individualized. This challenge of individualization is not easily met when managing teams or large numbers of athletes in different sports. However, computerized software

systems for tracking workouts in real time and downloading and graphing workout results are becoming more and more affordable and accessible to more people each year.

> Individual athletes will respond differently to a specific conditioning program or combinations thereof.

In reading this chapter it is important to keep in mind that hundreds of articles, internet blogs, multitudes of book chapters, and many books have been written on this topic of training theory and more specifically about periodization of training. "Agreements and disagreements", "criticisms and claims of superiority", and "factual scientific findings", "disagreements between studies", and "mythology of training outcomes" abound in the literature and on the internet. Keep in mind each anecdotal idea arising from experiences or facts from scientific studies will have a different context for their interpretation and meaning (2). This means that one situational framework for findings that led to X effects may not be totally transferable or generalized to another situational framework (e.g., programs used for college athletes versus junior high school athletes). Care must be taken in your generalizations and appropriate accommodations made where necessary. Evaluating readings and struggling with what you want to do is just part of the professional art of being a strength and conditioning professional.

We acknowledge that a host of reference materials on this topic, especially since the 1990s, is available for further in-depth study to gain a more global understanding of the concepts related to periodization. We will try to point you in their direction as the chapter progresses as no one group or individual can really proclaim universal understanding on a topic. The hope is that you will use the concept of **evidence-based practice** in your view of any workout program or training model (2). This involves a systematic process in decision making with available knowledge on topics ranging from anecdotal to scientific findings in order to use an evidence-based process for best practices and decision making. Amonette et al. (2) have recently developed a new six-step evidence-based approach for such purposes. It is a cyclical process of the team looking at the question and then finding the best evidence and evaluating it with individual analyses and testing etc. The basic domains for this process are:

- Develop the question you are trying to answer for your program
- Search for evidence
- Evaluate the evidence
- Incorporate the evidence into practice
- Confirm the evidence to the individual
- Re-evaluate the evidence

This approach gives some valuable insights into decision making and evaluating various forms of knowledge in making exercise program design and progression decisions. Nevertheless, controversy is just part of the history and struggle for any training theory as it continues in its development with our empirical use and laboratory studies. As one coach said a long time ago about the field of strength and conditioning, "If you get into this field, the timid need not apply".

Keep in mind in the pursuit of program design that one starts with finding a basic "paradigm" or "framework" to work from in order to develop a resistance training program. The late University of Connecticut strength and conditioning coach, Jerry Martin, whom I (WJK) was honored to work with for so many years, used to tell me, "What do we know about the science of this particular approach to training for this sport?" Historically this is where "the rubber meets the road" and continues to do so as program ideas and theories along with training technology many times out-distance scientific facts. However, that is acceptable if one uses science as a compass to get started in a general direction and then moves on from there as that training data presents itself.

As training time goes forward, goals change as the body adapts to the exercise stimuli created by the conditioning programs, in this case resistance training. Resistance training program design is therefore a dynamic process of change in response to the achievement or lack thereof of training program goals. Concepts for progression have been put forth over the

years in general formats or paradigms for use by healthy individuals and athletes (1,30).

We often think of periodization in a singular training model or concept. However, again it is important to note that historically, periodization models in training theory are very diverse in nature, as are the sportsmen and women they are used for training. Thus, one might say there is no one periodized program, but rather a group of periodized training models that use some inherent concepts in the design of training programs to meet the diverse needs of many different athletes in different sports or individuals attempting to improve fitness, health, and performance. The purpose of this chapter is to provide a basic overview of periodization in resistance training as well as perspectives and insights for your consideration in program design.

> Periodization models are very diverse in nature as are the sportsmen and women they are used for training.

INCREASING INTEREST IN PERIODIZED TRAINING IN THE WESTERN WORLD

In the competitive worlds of weightlifting and track and field, it became apparent that training progression was one key to success. The thirst for such training information was driven by the success of the former Soviet Union and Eastern bloc countries in the Olympic Games from the 1960s forward. Dr. Tudor Bompa, formerly a Romanian Olympic crew athlete and a coach of multitudes of Olympic medal winners, and later a professor at York University in Canada, has been considered by many to be the individual who brought the concept of periodization to the Western world of sports training. He also has been one of the most prolific interpreters of periodized training theories with 14 books and a multitude of articles originating from the 1970s to today, including recent collaborations with current co-author Dr. Greg Haff from Edith Cowan University in Perth Australia (e.g., see (4–6,84). In 1975, Carl Miller, then the Head Coach of

USA Weightlifting, sent mimeographed (i.e., blue print) papers to all of its members overviewing the Bulgarian periodized training program used by their weightlifters. In many ways, this was big news to me (WJK) and many others who got the program approach in the mail from Coach Miller. This program was another version of classic periodization theories that had been developed in the former Soviet Union.

The exposure of the periodization concept in North America and its interpretation for American sport coaches was also driven by a few young scientists in the 1970s who were weightlifters themselves, most notably, Dr. Michael Stone and Dr. John Garhammer. Dr. Stone, formerly a physiologist at the National Strength Research Center at Auburn University, is now running an Olympic Center for Excellence in Sports Science and Coaching Education with an emphasis in weightlifting at East Tennessee State University. Dr. John Garhammer completed his doctoral degree in biomechanics at UCLA and later served as a professor at California State University, Long Beach. Their work in the area of periodized training continues today with presentations, books, and papers with special reference toward weightlifting and sports (see 11,13,14,69,71,73,74). Additionally, articles by Dr. Michael Yessis, a professor at the California State University at Fullerton, were also instrumental with his Russian translational sport training papers in his Yessis Review of Soviet Physical Education and Sports.

With the establishment of the National Strength and Conditioning Association (NSCA) in 1978 and the NSCA Journal, the stage was set to expose this concept to the world of strength and conditioning coaches working with other sports in the Western world, most notably the United States of America (see 12,70,72). By 1981 a long-awaited English translation from a German translation of the original Russian of a book by Professor Leonid Pavlovich Matveyev of the former Soviet Union became available. He overviewed many of the historical developments of periodized training for sports in the former Soviet Union (34). Additionally, the NSCA developed conference trips to the former Soviet Union in the early 1980s to allow coaches to interact with the sport training coaches at the time. The 1980s were a fertile time for prolific interest and desire to implement resistance training programs using periodization. From this, strength and conditioning professionals of all types were progressively exposed to periodization concepts and programs.

From this early exposure of the periodization model and concept, a plethora of different periodized training approaches would evolve over the years to address the needs of different sports and fitness training. As time went on the original concept of Professor Matveyev's model of periodization has not been without controversy. The concept of periodization originated in the early days of the Soviet Union's pursuit of athletic dominance. Professor Yuri V. Verchoshansky, another very notable Russian sport scientist and training theorist over the last 60 years, published a paper in 1998 in a German journal that was later translated into English in a number of publication outlets that criticized the original theory (78). The paper in English translation entitled "The end of periodization in the training of high performance sport" was a shocking title for many of us working in the area. Upon closer review, this Russian scientist who was considered the father of shock training and plyometric training in many people's opinion had some challenges to periodization concepts as originally developed.

First, his contention was the fact the Matveyev's early conceptualization of the training theory had not yet met rigorous scientific study due to the fact that achievements of the former Soviet Union's athletes in the World and Olympic competitions were so amazing. Furthermore, most of the original data arose for short-term training studies in only a few sports in the former Soviet Union's system early on in its development. Next, our understanding of many sports was limited or in its infancy. Finally, by the 1990s he postured that the original theory as proposed had its limitations in dealing with the modern competition calendars and sport demands, especially teams. Today, the NSCA continues to publish papers on periodization of resistance training concepts in professional journals and remains a valuable source of professional training and education.

WHY PERIODIZED TRAINING?

Without proper planning and design of an all-encompassing training program, results may not be optimal, and major training benefits may become stagnant or lost (75). Even in today's world of sports and fitness pursuits, not enough time is given to the importance of plain "rest" for physiological and psychological recovery. This is where periodization of training made a significant impact by formally planning for day(s) of rest. At its core, strength and conditioning periodization is simply a way to provide program variation in the training stimuli while using planned rest periods, ensuring proper restoration and recovery from each training session (16). Research studies, while ongoing in their pursuit of understanding different periodized training program approaches, clearly delineates that some form of periodization in a strength and conditioning program is superior to none (33,45,48,82). Again, the focus of any resistance training program must view training as it relates to the very specific needs of the individual's training goals.

> Periodization made a significant impact in the field by formally planning for day(s) of rest.

VARIATION AND REST ARE FUNDAMENTAL CONCEPTS TO ANY PERIODIZATION TRAINING MODEL

Planning training programs involves both progression and integration of all conditioning programs. In strength and conditioning, one of the key factors for optimal training outcomes is the "variation" provided in the exercise programs. Programs become even more challenging with athletes who address not only strength and power as performance outcomes but other performance capabilities as well (e.g., aerobic fitness, local muscular endurance). Training for both strength and power

in addition to maximal aerobic fitness is now often called a "compatibility issue" with concurrent or simultaneous training. It has been shown that aerobic endurance training can interfere and negatively impact strength and power development (18,19,28,35,49,54). This appears to be due to the effects of such concurrent training at the level of muscle fibers, especially the Type I (slow twitch fibers) found in motor units in the early recruitment order for force development (28). From this literature, proper frequency and intensity of each exercise needs to be considered so as not to push the individual into an acute "nonfunctional" overreaching condition (i.e., loss of performance with program mistakes that may be from an unknown source but recovered if stimuli are removed). If not addressed it could progress to an overtraining syndrome with long-term performance stagnation (53,67,68). Thus, how much aerobic training is needed by an athlete must be determined by the "needs analysis" of the sport, and many times for strength power sports it can be met with interval training (8).

Importantly, one can only address a few priorities in any one phase or cycle of training, thereby requiring coaches and athletes to understand that training "priorities" of each cycle have to be determined (8). Often failure in a training program is the result of trying to do too much with the limited amount of time available in any one specific training cycle. Thus, developing a resistance training program for many sports sits in a multidimensional environment of stressors and requires a lot of integrated prioritization and planning. Again, while outside of the scope of this chapter, we will try to point out some of the contexts that must be taken into consideration when designing a resistance-training program. Overall stresses that must be considered and understood for each athlete can be seen in Figure 14.1.

Optimal variation in the training stimulus is also augmented by strategic incorporation of rest days and weeks. In recent times, this reflects the concept of reliance and long-term successful participation in sport or other occupations (e.g., warfighters, firefighters, and police). The concept of "periodization" of training allows for planned variation in resistance

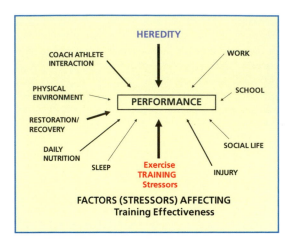

Figure 14.1 Factors (stressors) affecting training effectiveness.

program design while considering what other exercise or sport stressors must also be considered. No matter what the total demands are, "recovery" is the key factor for optimal conditioning progression as well as in sport competition. Recovery involves more than what is going on in the skeletal muscles; it spans to other organs and systems, including the brain. From studies on overtraining it appears that one or two complete days of rest in a week can reduce the potential for acute non-functional overreaching in strength or high force development (10).

While beyond the scope of this chapter, nutrition plays a huge role in the recovery process and was much more a part of periodization theory than what has been translated into the Western literature from its development in the former Soviet Union (80). Thus, only parts of the total concept of periodized training programs really came through, those being some of the strength training approaches or paradigms used with various sports (85,86). As noted before, other factors from nutrition to recovery therapies were also part of the overall programs. Today recovery techniques are a hot area of research and span a wide array of interventions from nutritional supplements to physical therapy type interventions (e.g., cryotherapy, compression) to neurological aspects (e.g., mindfulness, deprivation float therapy, and sleep therapies). But even with

different recovery interventions individual responses are highly variable, again pointing to the importance of keeping the concepts of "personalized medicine" or "individualized programing" front and center. In essence recovery is now a total body phenomenon, but periodization or the variation in conditioning programs plays a huge role as a modulator of conditioning stress.

Training periodization allows for the division of a training program into smaller periods, giving coaches and practitioners a structured and planned way to properly program exercise (23). Again, although there is considerable diversity in the exact strategies used to accomplish periodization, it is clear in all strategies that manipulating all, or some, of the core acute program variables (frequency, intensity, volume, rest periods, repetition velocity) in both short- and long-term programs is a key to success.

THEORETICAL BASIS FOR PERIODIZATION

Having worked as a professor with Dr. Vladimir Zatsiorsky, who came to Canada in 1989, to UCLA in 1990, and to the Pennsylvania State University in 1991, I (WJK) had the honor to work and teach with him for several years. Interestingly, together we taught a course on the theory of resistance training. Over the years it was interesting to hear of the evolution of training concepts in the former Soviet Union as overviewed in his seminal books, one edition of which I was honored to be a part of as a co-author (85,86). Our course integrated Eastern and Western thoughts of sports conditioning. Dr. Zatsiorsky was a physics and mathematical genius in biomechanics who has developed so many fundamental concepts in the biomechanics field. He has worked with some of the most legendary weightlifters of the Soviet Union (e.g., David Rigert, Vasily Alekseyev). His applications for training in sports, especially resistance training, grew out of this scientific base in the former Soviet Union. There he was Head of and the Chair of Biomechanics in the Central Institute of Physical Culture, Moscow; 1987–1989, Director of the All-Union Research Institute of

Physical Culture, Moscow; 1974–1987, Head and Professor of the Biomechanics and Chair in the Central Institute of Physical Culture, Moscow; 1960–1974, and Associate Professor and Full Professor at the Central Institute of Physical Culture, Moscow. From this experience I had with him, it was clear that math, physics, and computations of elite athletes' training progressions that led to successful outcomes were key to understanding periodization approaches developed over the decades in the former Soviet Union. This along with advanced technique training and individualization of programs made it work.

Special attention was also given to the bench-top research published in scientific journals related to stress. In particular, in the early years it was fascination with the work of a Canadian endocrinologist named Hans Selye, who was interested in stress. Dr. Selye was interested in the endocrine responses to external stressors and the response to the stress, which allowed for a biological meaning for an adaptive behavior to a pathogenic insult, and was the cornerstone of adaptive stress theory recently overviewed eloquently in a paper by Gorban et al. (15). In that proscess, Dr. Selye was interested in a variety of external stressors (e.g., chemical agents, disease, states, etc.) on endocrine function with a special focus on the adrenal cortex. Most of the time he utilized cellular or animal models (55–57,59–63,65). While he was never really an applied scientist, his findings were applied to training theory by other coaches, most notably Fred Wilt, a track coach at Purdue University, and Forbes Carlile, a swim coach from Australia, and other scientists including those from the former Soviet Union. From Dr. Selye's body of research it became apparent that a stress model existed. It showed that any new stressor had a type of tri-phasic response including an initial "alarm response" which could be generally tolerated for a period of time (e.g., six to eight weeks) before a turn for the worse or distress would occur, ultimately leading to the death of the organism. This resulted in a theory of stress conceptualized by Dr. Selye in a series of papers on stress adaptation syndrome that led to his later terming it **General Adaptation Syndrome** (58). As his research developed, he saw his work as having important influences

on health and wellbeing, which culminated in his 1956 book *The Stress of Life* (64).

From this General Adaptation Syndrome, it was then translated into a model for exercise or sports training over the years from the 1950s on. But this was essentially a general theory of stress. While it provided a framework of biological responses to pathogens, it could not address the multitude of highly integrated and very specific stressors arising from sport. Nevertheless, popularity for using this model as a basic starting point persisted and evolved. From a training perspective it essentially showed the need for rest in order to reset the body and allow recovery. Continued training with the same program was thought to lead to plateaus or training stagnation, which could then lead to a type of overtraining syndrome (9). Thus, there was a need to start over with the training process with a new program theoretically leading to a higher level of adaptive changes, later called "supercompensation" (see Figure 14.2).

Generally, periodization of training programs take advantage of the cyclical nature of response to stress in biological systems to force changes in programs preceded by rest periods. This augmented training effect by not pushing one into an overtraining syndrome was described by Russian scientist Nikolai N. Yakovlev as the supercompensation cycle as overviewed in a classic paper by Professor Atko Viru, who in his own right pioneered the field of exercise endocrinology and role of hormonal regulation as an underlying mechanism for energy and the plasticity of response to the stressors of exercise and exercise training (79). In response to stress, the body will initially attempt to adapt to meet the demands of the stressor. This was subsequently shown in research on the alarm reaction to different types of resistance training program progressions and methods to obviate the initial decreases (31,81). Interestingly, these studies showed that creatine supplementation and amino acids were shown to be effective in reducing this initial decrease seen with a new resistance exercise stressor. However, given proper rest, the individual becomes stronger and more resilient to further stressors as shown in many studies of the "repeated bout effect" first shown in 1987 by Dr. Pricilla Clarkson's

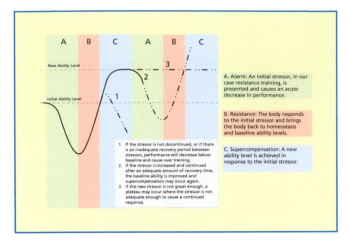

Figure 14.2 General adaptation syndrome (GAS).

group at the University of Massachusetts (38), and shown to be important even in such preparation for reducing muscle damage with a contact sport in the early practices of summer in American football (27).

Rest is a key factor in any periodization training program. A highly trained athlete or individual will require higher volumes and intensities to see progress in a training program (42). Thus, recovery is needed for repair of tissues and also psychological recovery from the training and the sport and this places a premium on quality rest phases. Here we see how the "practice and art" of the profession as a strength and conditioning coach comes into play. We will discuss this concept later in the chapter as the quality of the workout and the ability to recover become important for decisions as to the specific workout performed each day.

COMPLEXITY OF TRAINING CHANGES AND NEEDS IN A PERIODIZED PROGRAM

The complexity of training will increase as the athlete progresses in both their ability and experience with resistance training. Consequently, the rate of adaptation and the subsequent improvements from training decrease as the athlete becomes more experienced and

performance increases to genetic ceilings (51) (see Figure 14.3). However, while adaptations in one system may hit their genetic ceiling, other systems are not yet fully adapted and contribute to performance improvements. In a classic study of weightlifters over two years, Dr. Häkkinen and his colleagues at the University of Jyvaskyla in Finland showed that with long-term training in highly trained weightlifters only minor increases in muscle fiber size (i.e., little muscle hypertrophy) were observed (17). Thus, the improvements in performance were mediated by the nervous system, which also requires recovery in order to balance the sympathetic and parasympathetic systems, now often determined with heart rate variability analyses.

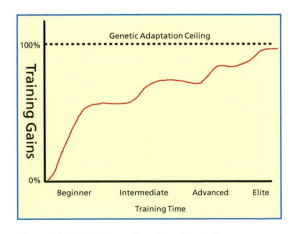

Figure 14.3 The genetic adaptation ceiling.

For example, training for power has many different adaptive windows for adaptation beyond the improvement of just force in the power equation. Attention to these other trainable characteristics (e.g., velocity) can help continue improvements in power when force may be hitting a ceiling for improvement (40). Often this is called **prioritization** of training. In one example during an in-season program, training NCAA Division I women volleyball players using the traditional periodized program with the focus on heavy loading for strength, approach jump power, and performance were decreased by about 5% by mid-season. Then with a shift in the focus of the primary variable now being power, and using more ballistic training emphasis, by the end of the season a 5% increase in power was observed but no different from the start of the season (39). Upon reflection of our study, while the change in the prioritization of the training shifted to recover lost power, a maintenance of maximal strength with a focus on ballistic power training and performance may have been a wiser choice. This study underscored that for a periodized training program to be effective, more frequent testing or monitoring of training logs is needed. There is a need to programmatically respond more quickly to changes in an athlete's workout performance or physical status in real time.

There is still very little empirical evidence showing one form of periodization as being superior to another in all cases or training situations for all athletes in different sports, but again some model of "variation" is superior to constant training approaches (7,8). Also, considerable variation can be found in the ways each individual practitioner describes and implements each type of periodization sequencing.

In this chapter we can only provide a basic overview to strength and conditioning professionals about periodization, but it is certainly not an exhaustive review of all known strategies of periodization, neither is it a pure scientific review of all known literature. It is, however, an overview of some of the primary concepts a strength and conditioning practitioner may consider and utilize to start his/her study of periodization. It will also allow you to employ some basic concepts in a resistance-training program to elicit a better training response than just using a constant programing approach.

PERIODIZATION TERMINOLOGY

As one becomes a student of periodization and training theory one can see that there is a multitude of terms used. This concern for a lack of universal understanding of such terminology has been a common issue historically for all of the exercise literature, and especially in training theory and periodization concepts (6,77,78,85,86). We will frame this chapter overview with some of the more common and accepted terms used in periodization program theory.

Common to most variations of periodization models, individual lengths of time during a periodization program can be described by certain terms from longest duration to smallest: multi- or single-year preparation, **macrocycle**, **mesocycle**, **microcycle**, and **training session**, which in some periodization approaches is a microcycle (see Figure 14.4). The many different periodization programs typically use some form of these common terms to describe their unique program structures.

The macrocycle is typically the longest-term planned phase and was originally meant to encompass an entire yearly season. In Olympic athletes, the quadrennial cycle is typically the longest duration planned phase, as it encompasses a four-year Olympic period. In modern times, sport has adapted to require several competitive seasons in a year and thus, the macrocycle can be represented by shorter, several month periods and repeated many times in a year as needed. The mesocycle is traditionally the culmination of several weeks of training, with the macrocycle normally comprised of multiple mesocycles. The microcycle may vary from a full week to several days in length, with the mesocycle consisting of multiple summed microcycles. The smallest training unit is the individual training session. Several training sessions can be summed to create a microcycle, yet as we will see in non-linear (also called undulating periodization) periodized training approaches, the single training session represents a microcycle.

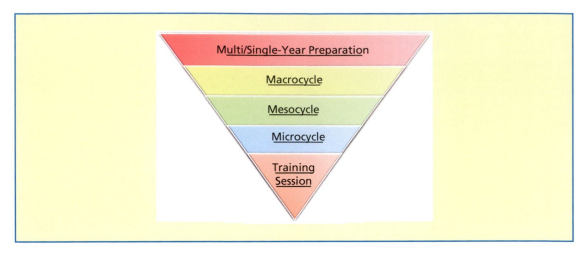

Figure 14.4 Progression from a single training session to a multi/single year preparation.

TRADITIONAL/LINEAR PERIODIZATION

The traditional model of periodization proposed from its original form used in the former Soviet Union has in recent times also been referred to as **linear periodization** due to an increasing intensity of resistance with each phasic cycle of training over time (8,10,66). At its core, **traditional or classic periodization** involves manipulating training volume and intensity in an opposing fashion over long periods of time, broken into separate training phases. This original phasic sequence approach has been criticized as not being able to address the needs of some elite athletes or sports with demanding schedules (78). Thus, one can use it as a paradigm and then alter training use and phase lengths etc. and in some cases integrate multiple periodization approaches in the same macrocycle (32,43). The terminology used to delineate these training phases and each phase's time-length varies greatly, depending on the specific sport and country of origin (see Figure 14.5). For example, traditional American sport specific terminology uses a pre-season to delineate the mesocycles done before the season starts whereas the American strength and power terminology breaks the pre-season up into a typical hypertrophy and subsequent strength

and power mesocycles. European terminology calls this pre-season mesocycle a preparatory and first transition phase. Following these general preparatory phases, a typical peaking, competitive, or in-season phase is used to allow the general preparation work to culminate in a maximum performance. Following these phases, some form of active rest is taken, with low volume and intensity work used to recover for the next macrocycle. In the recovery phase, training is generally not stopped, but instead sport specific training is generally ceased and all other forms of training are markedly decreased. The contents and length of the active recovery/off-season period depends on the level of the athlete, with high level athletes typically needing longer durations of rest than less experienced athletes. Also the drop off of volume of training is less dramatic in more highly trained strength/ power athletes (43).

Regardless of the terminology, the core setup of traditional periodization is similar between all variations. Classical traditional periodization typically uses a sequential method of programming exercise. This means that only one specific training goal (hypertrophy, max strength, power) is programmed for at one time. In the first mesocycle, volume is high, as a large amount of exercises is used with high volume in order to train many physical abilities at once with a large

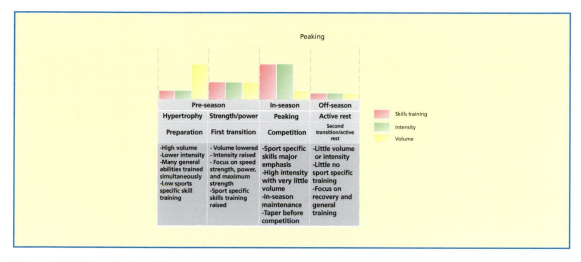

Figure 14.5 Periodized model to promote peaking during the in-season phase.

volume. Additionally, toleration of resistance exercise or a new program is developed in the first phase. Sports specific skills, as well as intensity, are kept low to account for this large general training phase. Typically, aerobic training, as well as muscular endurance, hypertrophy, and general movement technique work share the bulk of the **volume load** during the first mesocycles of traditional periodization. This initial mesocycle is meant to build the general abilities of the athlete. As the program progresses, the athlete begins the peaking/competitive/in-season phase. This period is marked by a decrease in volume, with subsequent increases in intensity and sports specific skills training. Typically, exercises meant to increase maximum strength as well as power are programmed along with higher volumes of sports specific practice in preparation for competition. The gains made in the previous general preparatory phases are culminated in a high intensity sport specific peaking phase that allows for maximum performance directly before a competition. The last period, active rest, allows the athlete to recover from the competitive phase using active rest techniques. Generally, the athletes do not completely abstain from programmed exercise, but all training is drastically reduced in volume and intensity. Sports specific training is normally ceased for this duration.

TRADITIONAL PERIODIZATION MODIFICATIONS

Minor modification may be made to the traditional linear model of periodization that may improve its efficacy for more advanced athletes (43). In particular, alterations in short-term programming of loading may help alleviate some of the shortcomings of traditional periodization.

Alterations in short-term programming of loading, particularly in advanced athletes, may improve the efficacy of a periodized program.

One major criticism of traditional periodization is the monotonous nature of the loading over a long-term program. Traditional periodization requires the athlete to train for a certain ability (hypertrophy, maximum strength, power) over the course of many weeks, possibly months with very similar loads and volumes. The practitioner may get around this limitation by programming short-term variations in the volume and intensity of training, termed **step loading**. Overall, the same discrete goals are trained in a similar fashion, but the short-term loading schemes allow for greater variation. For example, during the hypertrophy or pre-season phase a high volume of training is programmed for many different abilities such as hypertrophy, general aerobic conditioning, and muscular endurance. The practitioner may increase the total volume load for all exercise each week, typically for a total of two to four weeks, then program a rest week where the total volume load is significantly reduced for all exercises. This pattern resembles a staircase, where each step represents an increase in total volume load. The rest week is programmed to allow for restitution and recovery and prevent non-functional overreaching or overtraining. This pattern can be repeated as many times as needed for each mesocycle or phase of traditional periodization.

NON-TRADITIONAL PERIODIZATION

Since its mainstream adoption sometime in the middle of the twentieth century, periodization of sports training has seen a host of different variations come about to meet some of the original criticisms by Verhoshansky of being too phasic (77,78). Nevertheless, it was clear from the performances of the eastern Europeans and former Soviet Union in many international competitions that some form of periodization was essential for maximal performance in competition (16). However, modern research and techniques have made possible a deeper understanding of physiological and psychological adaptations to training that allow for a more well thought out approach to planning athletes' work. In many ways, the traditional model of periodization falls short, and the approach to training periodization is not optimal for athletes at high level or that have many competitions in a single season. The following programs have been developed to help alleviate these problems and may be more appropriate for higher level athletes competing multiple times in a competitive season.

Block periodization

One consequence of the rethinking of resistance training planning was a modified traditional periodization scheme known as **block periodization**. Vladimir Issurin defined it as "a training cycle of highly concentrated specialized workloads" (22,23). Essentially, each block is designed to focus on a discrete number of abilities with a large volume of different exercises focused on those few abilities. Unlike the thinking of traditional periodization, this non-traditional approach such as block periodization allows for great variation of volume and intensity within the daily and weekly programming (23). But much like traditional periodization, block periodization may still be considered a sequential method due to only one training goal being focused on within a one- to four-week period. In its essence, block periodization is a modified version of linear, or classical traditional, periodization. On a short-term scale, the training methods used as well as the volume and intensity programmed are where the differences exist. In its simplest form, each set of mesocycle blocks very much resembles the longer-term programming of traditional periodization. Block periodization progresses from a general training period with higher volumes and lower intensities towards a very specific block of high amounts of strength and power training with high intensity and low volume (41). This happens on a shorter time scale than traditional periodization, and many different microcycle schemes can be used to program short-term intensity and volume. Many of these mesocycles are summated to a macrocycle scheme. The total volume load when all mesocycles are summated follow a linear trend, where the absolute peak performance is completed after many individual mesocycles have been completed. Each mesocycle can be broken down into four blocks that vary in length but are typically described as lasting two to six weeks: general, specific, competitive, and recovery (Figure 14.6) (23).

General block

The **general block** focuses on accumulating training effects by implementing high volumes on the athlete's general abilities. Training focuses on the base abilities such as cardiorespiratory endurance, muscular hypertrophy, coordination, and general movement techniques (3,23).

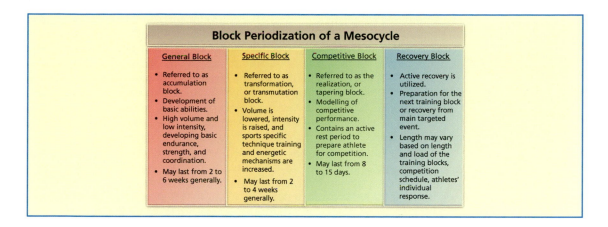

Figure 14.6 Block periodization of a mesocycle.

Adapted from Issurin (2010) (23)

Specific block

Also referred to as the **transformation block** or **transmutation block**, this period is character-ized by a lowering of volume, and an increase in intensity of the selected abilities. Typically, this block focuses on more sport specific tasks, allowing the delayed transmutation effects of the generalized training from the previous blocks to improve the more sport specific task.

Competitive block

The **competitive block** or **realization block** is typically used as a precompetitive phase. Generally, the training is focused on modeling the event or completing training that directly improves the event. Also included in this block typically is a tapering of training to allow for restitution before the event.

Recovery block

If directly following an event, a **recovery block** is typically used to allow for active rest. This block may be omitted if the mesocycle does not culminate in a specific event, and the beginning of the next block mesocycle can begin directly after the competitive block.

Block periodization's benefits

What makes block periodization different and unique from the traditional model is the flexibility in programming micro and meso-cycles to meet the needs of advanced athletes. The mesocycles in block periodization are typically much shorter and much more con-centrated than in traditional theory. Each block can consist of one to four microcycles concentrated on only a few specific abilities. The general block may focus on building large amounts of volume and workload on those few abilities. When transitioning to the spe-cific block, the large training residuals from the general block may lead to the performance of those abilities being at a higher level when competition or peaking comes. In the specific block, the targeted abilities are training with a higher intensity than in the general block, with lowered volume and an emphasis on training the energetic mechanisms and sport specific techniques needed in the individual athlete. The training residuals from this block are shorter than in the general block, but should still induce a training effect at the competitive or realization block. Finally, the realization or competitive block allows for the modeling of competitive performance. Typically, training load is markedly decreased and active recovery is achieved using volume load tapering. This block should allow the athlete to recover and prepare for competition. If no competition is imminent, this block may be used as a testing block, allowing the athlete to peak and test-ing the athlete's current ability. Many of these block mesocycles can be summated to create a macrocycle in which all of the training abilities are focused on and peaked many times with many different volume and intensity loads.

> Mesocycles in block periodization are typically shorter and more concentrated than in traditional periodization.

Block periodization attempts to address and rectify many of the weak points exposed in traditional periodization. To start, traditional methods emphasize the general training of many abilities at once, manipulating the volume and intensity in a counteractive fashion over a long period. As training intensity increases over time, the volume of the work goes down. Although appropriate for beginners needing improvements in many general abilities, this poses a problem for advanced athletes that may require large volumes and intensities in a single ability to achieve appropriate stimulus for adaptation (23). With the simultaneous training of many abilities, and no particular focus on any single ability, an advanced athlete may not receive the proper stimulus for ideal adaptation (24). Block periodization works to solve this problem by introducing concentrated blocks of work on a limited set of abilities. Volume load is concentrated on those specific skills, allowing for advanced athletes to experience a stimuli sufficient enough to improve in that ability.

Additionally, the simultaneous training of many different abilities, as in the traditional model, poses several other physiological problems (21). The physiological adaptations of many abilities are not compatible. For example, when resistance type training is done concurrently with aerobic type training, significant negative interactions occur, causing an inhibited response to hypertrophy and strength (83). Traditional models have the athlete training both abilities in a general preparatory stage, usually for a long period of time. Training blocks help alleviate this by focusing training on a discrete amount of abilities concentrated into shorter specific blocks of time that are physiologically congruent.

An additional physiological consideration is taken into account with block periodization. **Staleness** can present a problem with the traditional model. In the traditional model, typically long blocks of time are set aside for different phases of the training program, with only slight variation in volume and intensity. Also, this model uses many of the same exercises and modalities throughout that entire phase. Although an initial adaptation and improvement may be seen, stagnation may cause a plateau in performance (21). Blocks are designed to combat this staleness, using shorter duration periods that focus on discrete abilities, then a change is made in modalities and volume load to ensure staleness does not occur.

Arguably one of the most important elements of block periodization, and possibly why it was developed in the first place, is the consideration of multiple competitive events in a macrocycle (23). The traditional model is typically insufficient in planning a peaking phase for many events in a year, which may be typical in many high-level sports. Normally, there is a possibility for two to three peaks planned in the traditional model. For some sports, such as national level track and field, the need to peak for multiple competitive events throughout the year would not be considered under the traditional method. Therefore, in block periodization multiple macrocycles are developed to allow for many peaks in performance throughout a competitive year.

CONJUGATE PERIODIZATION

A key to success for advanced athletes may lie in ensuring they train with greater volume loads more frequently and with much more varied exercises than less advanced athletes. Block periodization is a step in the right direction for allowing great variation in workload and content of each workload at many different levels of periodization (43). One other advanced non-traditional periodization program may be employed to these ends. **Conjugate periodization** helps achieve this and is the work of Yuri Verhoshansky (76). In its essence, it is very similar to block periodization, but may offer more flexibility in inter- and intra-mesocycle variation. Conjugate periodization is an example of a concurrent method of periodization. In concurrent planning, more than one training goal may be focused on within the microcycle, with all abilities being focused on with the similar volume. Conjugate periodization may be used on the inter- or intra-microcycle scale.

The basic tenant of conjugate periodization lies in the use of concentrated periods of accumulation for a specific ability followed by a restitution period for that ability (66,76,77) (see Figure 14.7). Much like block periodization, this concentrated loading is specific to a discrete ability, like maximum strength, muscular endurance, or speed strength. Unlike block periodization, conjugate periodization uses many different concentrated loading periods for different abilities in close proximity to each other. For example, during the concentrated loading periods, that discrete ability is focused on for a series of microcycles, normally lasting only one week, but may also be a single day within the microcycle. Only minimal maintenance level work is done for all other abilities during this loading period. The large volume load concentrated on that ability causes the athlete to intentionally overreach, and performance of that ability declines (43). The

emphasis is then reversed, and a different discrete ability is trained that typically does not physiologically overlap with the first concentrated period. It is during this time that the first ability is allowed to recover using a restitution block. Again, only a minimal amount of maintenance work is done on the first ability while the second ability is trained with high volume. Theoretically, during the restitution period, **supercompensation** will occur in the first ability allowing for increased performance over the baseline when beginning the next concentrated loading period for that ability.

As stated before, practical programming with this method may vary. Some practitioners may choose to concentrate loading on a particular ability on the daily scale. This would allow hypertrophy, strength, and power loading to all be accomplished within the same week. This loading scheme does not vary significantly from week to week, so typically the lifts are varied frequently. In many cases, the lifts are changed each week to avoid overtraining, while achieving functional overreaching in each general skill area. The restitution periods would then possibly be programmed as its own separate week embedded within the mesocycle. Typically, even the most skilled lifters cannot continue at such high intensities indefinitely. Therefore, this restitution block may be applied once a month, or however frequently the practitioner chooses.

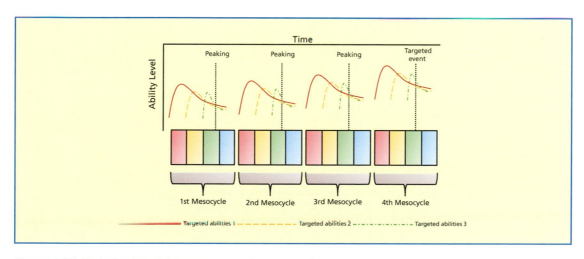

Figure 14.7 Periodized model to promote peaking at specific times in a competitive period.

NON-LINEAR (UNDULATING) PERIODIZATION

The evolution of "**undulating**" **periodization**, now called "**non-linear**" **periodization** arose from the need to achieve "quality workouts" within the construct of long sport seasons or when other demands on the athlete or individual impacted their ability to workout. The concept of using different workouts on each day of the week had been originally conceptualized, in part, by Charles Poliquin who started in Canada as a strength coach and became an entrepreneur founding strength fitness centers in Canada and the USA (44). To follow up on our prior discussion, at its core, conjugate periodization is a specific form of daily non-linear periodization. Each ability is concentrated on by a weekly basis in some forms of conjugate periodization. Unlike traditional or block periodization, a great variation in the volume and intensity of exercises is seen on a short-term scale.

Figure 14.8 shows a planned non-linear schedule for one week. It consists of different workouts each day with each workout being a microcycle. This comes from a planned mesocycle for 8–12 weeks with the priority of the training feature to be focused on noted (e.g., preparatory mesocycle). Each mesocycle may have a different frequency of different workouts yet they are mixed in with highly variable workouts. Then mesocycles are grouped together for the planned macrocycle. Typically in the research on non-linear periodization the planned method has been used with no real flexibility of the training sequence. Later this would evolve into another form of non-linear periodization where it is more flexible as to what is done day to day (i.e., called flexible non-linear periodization). This daily variation between hypertrophy, strength, and power abilities is the hallmark of daily non-linear periodization (36,37,46,47,50). Each performance variable gets adequate stimulation (i.e., high force or power intensities and volumes etc.) every week, whereas other methods may concentrate this exercise stimuli into longer periods or cycles and then the program's cycle moves to another set of workout protocols different from the one that proceeded it (e.g., going from four weeks of 8–12 reps at 65% of 1RM to 3–6 reps at 85–90% of 1RM for four weeks) (30,82).

While comparisons of different types of periodization plans are somewhat nonsensical due to the many factors and contexts that exist, popularity of this form of programing was spurred on with some early comparative research (48). Planned daily non-linear periodization was shown to be one way around the previous variation methods but also raises its

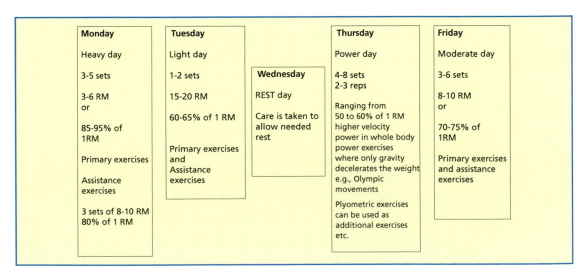

Figure 14.8 A planned non-linear periodized training schedule.

own concerns. Mainly, fatigue could be an issue. This fatigue could be due to many factors including sport practices, busy schedules, sleep loss, sickness, or just fatigue from the prior workout. Thus, the quality of the workout could be compromised. Ultimately just "going through the motions" in a workout would not really contribute to improvement in the training goal. As they say, "You cannot get faster by running slower" and thus quality of training is always an important factor along with recovery.

Evolution of flexible non-linear periodization

Working with the women's tennis players in one research program in the Center for Sports Medicine at Penn State University through the 1990s we (WJK) noticed how difficult it was to use typical linear periodization progressions. Continued sequence of the same loading etc. resulted in "good and bad" workouts where the athletes were unable to do the workouts at the prescribed intensity or volume. We were faced with an athlete with a long season and who really never stopped playing. Later we found this to be typical of so many other collegiate sports with fall and spring seasons. Many also had very long seasons (e.g., basketball, ice hockey, etc.). Thus, we took a cue from conjugate methods and Poliquin methods and created a planned non-linear program of different intensities and volumes on different days and later published some of these data (26,29). We also had the opportunity in the early 1990s to make comparisons with other programs or just playing tennis alone, which now would be considered a type of malpractice given what we now know about resistance training. We then sought out other methods of trying to improve this concept of non-linear programing. We started with planned non-linear periodization plans and then it morphed into a type of non-linear periodization approach I later called "flexible" non-linear periodization in which we had an overall planned mesocycle for 8 to 12 weeks but would make daily determinations if one could do the planned workout for that day, and if not we defaulted to another one or made it a rest day (25).

This concept would be put on hold until I (WJK) got back to the University of Connecticut (UCONN) in 2001 where basketball was the school's top sport. Working with strength and conditioning programs and the late Head Strength and Conditioning Coach Jerry Martin and his staff, most notably Coach Andrea Hudy who worked with the strength and conditioning for the basketball teams, I saw the same problem in this sport as I had noticed in tennis and other sports at Penn State. Now with a historic integration of sport and exercise science and athletics at UCONN, a unique opportunity existed and we proceeded to develop and implement a "flexible" non-linear periodized resistance training program. As Coach Martin said at the time, "We have the science but now we must see how we can implement it". The answer was **"flexible" non-linear programing** of workouts based on the ability of the athlete to do the workout. Coaches Jerry Martin, Andrea Hudy, and Chris West had developed some questions for this process. They were for pre-workout:

- What are we testing for?
- What affects the pre-workout test?
- What is the pre-workout test?
- How does the test decide the workout?
- What are the workouts?

Keeping in mind the stressors that impact the quality of workout, in those early times, we started to use training logs: could the athlete do the workout at or above the previous intensity, power output, and volume as the workout began? Could they perform a vertical jump to at least 90% of their best jump prior to a power workout? We had to convince some sport coaches that doing a workout after a practice may not yield many training benefits due to a lack of quality of the training stimuli. Were they sick or injured? Did they have a high fatigue rating on a fatigue scale? If there were negative implications, the workout was defaulted to another one they could do or they were told to take the day off and rest or go see the athletic trainer. Later we wrote about this and used flexible non-linear programs in almost all sports and many times in combination with linear programs when nothing could interfere with the workout cycle sequences (25,32). Coach Hudy would go on in 2004 to the University of Kansas and take flexible non-linear periodization programs to the next level with advanced pre-workout analyses (e.g., using force plate testing) as well as computer analyses of each workout repetition for force, velocity and power with advanced technologies on each power rack working with all of their Olympic sport teams, including basketball (20).

Key to any flexible non-linear periodized training program was the need for individualized monitoring and testing in order to determine the effectiveness of various training cycles or phases. While an early monitoring system was of the training logs themselves, this still remains an important aspect for observing program effectiveness. With on-line monitoring systems feeding computers the result of every set and repetition, a huge amount of training data is now available to strength coaches, but the challenges to keep up in real time use and its interpretation for the next workout has been daunting, especially with high numbers of athletes (52). As an example, in Figure 14.8, if one was not able to do the heavy day on Monday, as the workout started one would default to another workout, perhaps the light workout that had been scheduled for Tuesday and then do the heavy workout on Tuesday. It is always a give and take and evaluation of the ability of the individual to be able to do the workout and recover from prior day stressors. As the former strength coach of the Indianapolis Colts, Coach Jon Torine, who was the coach during their Super Bowl days once told me, "I come into the weight room and have a multitude of different programs going on with the players". From this they were able to optimize their own potential and have quality workouts and recovery (32).

SUMMARY

Periodization of resistance training has a long history and evolution as a training theory and one that continues to evolve today. Finding the model that best works for you in your situation is key to success. Understanding some of the fundamental principles and then doing more research and giving further thought to the context you are working within all play a role. We hope that this chapter will help provide a solid resource for the process you now have to undertake in your quest to help individuals or athletes be all they can be and reach their potential. No one source of information can give you all the answers but can create a process by which you find answers to your questions (2).

REAL-WORLD APPLICATION

Developing a question: similar to a needs analysis

Much like the needs analysis of a sport and its athletes, developing a research question requires taking a step back and looking at the bigger picture. For example, the sport of basketball requires the ability to jump; players also need to have long limbs. A researcher must look at his or her question with a similar mindset. For example, boxing requires chasing an opponent around the ring with rapid changes in direction. Because of this, it seems like chicken chasing may be beneficial to a boxer because it resembles chasing an opponent around the ring. Now that a background question has been developed, it is time to develop directed questions such as: How long will the subjects chase the chicken? What type of chickens will be used? Who will the subjects be so that the outcomes can be applied to boxing? What will foot speed be compared to? How many times will the boxer chase the chicken?

REAL-WORLD APPLICATION

Periodization for a young high school discus athlete

A high school freshman who is planning on throwing the discus this coming spring sits with her coach to determine how to prepare for the upcoming season. She is relatively untrained and has never participated in a resistance-training program, neither has she thrown the discus before. If you were to consult with her coach, how might you design the training program?

There are numerous ways in which the training program could be constructed. The best approach would be to consider this athlete's individual needs and mold the training program to her goals and objectives. Obviously, there are several strategies that could be considered based upon the concepts of periodization.

1 The first step is to consider this athlete's development as a long-term process in which a multiyear plan should be developed, specifically a quadrennial plan in which her highest levels of performance would be targeted for her senior year.
2 When constructing the annual training plan that will be used for her freshman year, the primary factors to consider are the development of a training base in which longer general preparatory phases would be considered. In this context, targeting strength development as well as performing conditioning activities to get this individual in shape are extremely important. Additionally, this athlete will need to learn how to throw the discus, so there will be substantial time working on remedial drill work at specific time points in the year.
3 To develop the annual training plan, a detailed list of competitions that this athlete will compete in should be generated. This will serve as the foundation for establishing the competitive phase of the annual training plan.
4 To monitor the athlete's progress, consider spacing performance assessments periodically throughout the training year which examine multiple factors such as muscular strength, muscular power, technical proficiency, and markers of throwing performance. These tests will help in the evaluation of this annual training plan's success.

It is obvious that his novice athlete will not require advanced training techniques. Consider some of the following:

1 Utilize a classic periodization model approach. This will allow the athlete to have longer periods of development, which will be the foundation for subsequent annual training plans.
2 Since she is a novice, she will require less training volume, intensity, and variation in order to get improvements. As she progresses, her program will need to be modified, specifically in subsequent annual training plans.
3 When implementing the training plan, it is important that the coach communicates with the athlete in order to garner feedback about how the athlete feels about the program as well as to educate the athlete about the training process and why things are being targeted at specific points.
4 Because this athlete has a low training base, be careful to only target a few complementary training factors at any given time point.

Q&A FROM THE FIELD

The strength and conditioning coaches on staff at the university are evaluating the use of chains and bands for power training phases. I cannot find a lot of evidence to support their use over traditional training methods. Should I implement this type of training?

Assistant Strength and Conditioning Coach

Training using bands or chains attached to the end of the barbell is a new and popular strength and power training method. It helps to overcome some limitations associated with traditional strength training (i.e., the mismatch between the constant force requirements of lifting a weight versus the variation in force-generating capacity through the range of motion). Chains and bands apply greater resistance at the top of the range of motion, potentially allowing for improved matching of force requirements to force-generating capacity.

There are few studies at this time evaluating this technique. It may be that following long-term training, there is no difference in power development during the bench press exercise in athletes using chains, bands, or traditional weight training methods. Given the lack of conclusive evidence, I would not replace traditional resistance training and plyometrics with chain or band training. However, it may be used sparingly to augment traditional training programs.

Q&A FROM THE FIELD

I recently visited with an elite weightlifting coach who coaches several Olympic weightlifters. She uses a conjugate periodization model with her athletes. Is that the type of program I should use with my youth weightlifting club?

Conjugate periodization is an advanced model of periodization for advanced athletes. For young athletes, consider a classic model of periodization. While the classic model may not be the best for intermediate and advanced athletes, it works well with novice or beginning athletes. It allows for a stabilization of training effects as well as technical mastery that is essential for the development of beginners.

MAXING OUT

1 Your little brother's high school football coach is telling the team to run until they puke during summer preseason training. Your brother and his friends complained to the coach, but he responded that they must do it because that is what his coach made them do 20 years ago when they won the state championship. Is this coach's rationale of training evidence-based? Based on what you learned in the chapter, explain how this conditioning program can become more evidence-based.

2 You are a practicing strength and conditioning coach. You attend a conference where researchers are suggesting that a new type of training is superior to all others and that coaches should immediately begin implementing it into their programs. As a coach, you know that this novel training strategy is not practical in the weight room. How would you go about asking the researcher to take the information presented to you and figure out a way to use it on a day-to-day basis?

3 The researcher from the scenario above tells you that if it can be done in the laboratory, it can be done in a weight room. Where can you look for additional information related to the topic so you can draw your own conclusions by combining the information you find with the novel training method?

4 You are working with a high school football player. What type of periodization model would most likely be the most effective for this athlete?

5 You are working with a soccer athlete in the general phase of training; how might you apply the block model of periodization?
6 You are talking with a fellow coach who wants to know how the classic model of periodization differs from the block model. How might you explain it?

CASE EXAMPLE

Designing a periodized training program for a recreational basketball player

Background

Lee is a recreational basketball player who has been resistance training for months. He reports that he is no longer getting stronger and feels as though he has hit a plateau. Following a consultation with you, you realize he has been doing the same workout for six months straight. Why have Lee's strength gains come to a halt, and what can be done to improve his situation?

Recommendations/considerations

Lee's strength gains have come to a halt likely because his program has lacked variability and his body has fully adapted to the stressors applied to his muscles. If Lee continues to do the same workouts, he will experience very few, if any, strength gains, hence his current situation. Lee should change his workout frequently. You should advise him to include hypertrophy workouts for four to six weeks, followed by strength workouts for four to six weeks with a focus on strength and power development. You should advise Lee to concentrate on strength and power because basketball relies heavily on the adenosine triphosphate-phosphocreatine (ATP-PCr) and glycolytic energy systems. In recreational basketball leagues, increased speed and jumping ability will most likely result in success.

REFERENCES

1. American College of Sports M. American College of Sports Medicine position stand. Progression models in resistance training for healthy adults. *Med Sci Sports Exerc* 2009; 41:687–708.
2. Amonette WE, English KL, Kraemer WJ. *Evidence-Based Practice in Exercise Science: The Six-Step Approach*. Champaign, IL Human Kinetics Publishers, 2016, p. 328.
3. Bartolomei S, Stout JR, Fukuda DH, Hoffman JR, Merni F. Block vs. weekly undulating periodized resistance training programs in women. *J Strength Cond Res* 2015; 29:2679–2687.
4. Bompa TO. *Power Training for Sport*. Oakville, ON: Mosaic Press, 1996.
5. Bompa TO. Variations of periodization of strength. *Strength Cond* 1996; 18(3):58–61.
6. Bompa TO, Haff G. *Periodization: Theory and Methodology of Training*. Champaign, IL: Human Kinetics, 2009.
7. Cissik J, Hedrick A, Barnes M. Challenges applying the research on periodization. *Strength Cond* 2008; 30:45–51.
8. Fleck SJ, Kraemer WJ. *Designing Resistance Training Programs*, 4th Ed. Champaign, IL: Human Kinetics, 2014, p. 520.
9. Fry AC, Kraemer WJ. Resistance exercise overtraining and overreaching. Neuroendocrine responses. *Sports Med* 1997; 23:106–129.
10. Fry AC, Kraemer WJ, Lynch MJ, Triplett NT, Koziris LP. Does short-term near-maximal intensity machine resistance training induce overtraining? *J Strength Cond Res* 1994; 8:188–191.
11. Garhammer J. Performance evaluation of Olympic weightlifters. *Med Sci Sports* 1979; 11:284–287.
12. Garhammer J. Periodization of strength training for athletes. *Track Technique* 1979; 79:2398–2399.
13. Garhammer J. Power production by Olympic weightlifters. *Med Sci Sports Exerc* 1980; 12:54–60.

14. Garhammer J. *Sports Illustrated Strength Training*. New York: Time Inc., 1986.

15. Gorban AN, Tyukina TA, Smirnova EV, Pokidysheva LI. Evolution of adaptation mechanisms: Adaptation energy, stress, and oscillating death. *J Theor Biol* 2016; 405:127–139.

16. Haff GG. Roundtable discussion: periodization of training – part 1. *Strength Cond* 2004; 26:50–69.

17. Häkkinen K, Pakarinen A, Alen M, Kauhanen H, Komi PV. Neuromuscular and hormonal adaptations in athletes to strength training in two years. *J Appl Physiol* 1988; 65:2406–2412.

18. Hickson RC. Interference of strength development by simultaneously training for strength and endurance. *Eur J Appl Physiol Occup Physiol* 1980; 45:255–263.

19. Hickson RC, Rosenkoetter MA, Brown MM. Strength training effects on aerobic power and short-term endurance. *Med Sci Sports Exerc* 1980; 12:336–339.

20. Hudy A. *Power Positions*. Kansas City, KS: Andrews McMeel Publishing. 2014.

21. Issurin V. Block periodization versus traditional training theory: a review. *J Sports Med Phys Fitness* 2008; 48:65–75.

22. Issurin V. *Principles and Basics of Advanced Athletic Training*. Muskegon Heights, MI: Ultimate Athlete Concepts, 2008.

23. Issurin VB. New horizons for the methodology and physiology of training periodization. *Sports Medicine (Auckland, NZ)* 2010; 40:189–206.

24. Kraemer WJ, Adams K, Cafarelli E, Dudley GA, Dooly C, Feigenbaum MS, Fleck SJ, Franklin B, Fry AC, Hoffman JR, Newton RU, Potteiger J, Stone MH, Ratamess NA, Triplett-McBride T, American College of Sports M. American College of Sports Medicine position stand. Progression models in resistance training for healthy adults. *Med Sci Sports Exerc* 2002; 34:364–380.

25. Kraemer WJ, and Fleck SJ. *Optimizing Strength Training: Designing Nonlinear Periodization Workouts*. Champaign, IL: Human Kinetics, 2007.

26. Kraemer WJ, Häkkinen K, Triplett-Mcbride NT, Fry AC, Koziris LP, Ratamess NA, Bauer JE, Volek JS, McConnell T, Newton RU, Gordon SE, Cummings D, Hauth J, Pullo F, Lynch JM, Fleck SJ, Mazzetti SA, Knuttgen HG. Physiological changes with periodized resistance training in women tennis players. *Med Sci Sports Exerc* 2003; 35:157–168.

27. Kraemer WJ, Looney DP, Martin GJ, Ratamess NA, Vingren JL, French DN, Hatfield DL, Fragala MS, Spiering BA, Howard RL, Cortis C, Szivak TK, Comstock BA, Dunn-Lewis C, Hooper DR, Flanagan SD, Volek JS, Anderson JM, Maresh CM, Fleck SJ. Changes in creatine kinase and cortisol in National Collegiate Athletic Association Division I American football players during a season. *J Strength Cond Res* 2013; 27:434–441.

28. Kraemer WJ, Patton JF, Gordon SE, Harman EA, Deschenes MR, Reynolds K, Newton RU, Triplett NT, Dziados JE. Compatibility of high-intensity strength and endurance training on hormonal and skeletal muscle adaptations. *J Appl Physiol* 1995; 78:976–989.

29. Kraemer WJ, Ratamess N, Fry AC, Triplett-McBride T, Koziris LP, Bauer JA, Lynch JM, Fleck SJ. Influence of resistance training volume and periodization on physiological and performance adaptations in collegiate women tennis players. *Am J Sports Med* 2000; 28:626–633.

30. Kraemer WJ, Ratamess NA. Fundamentals of resistance training: progression and exercise prescription. *Med Sci Sports Exerc* 2004; 36:674–688.

31. Kraemer WJ, Ratamess NA, Volek JS, Häkkinen K, Rubin MR, French DN, Gomez AL, McGuigan MR, Scheett TP, Newton RU, Spiering BA, Izquierdo M, Dioguardi FS. The effects of amino acid supplementation on hormonal responses to resistance training overreaching. *Metabolism* 2006; 55:282–291.

32. Kraemer WJ, Torine JC, Dudley J, Martin GJ. Nonlinear periodization: insights for use in collegiate and professional american football resistance training programs. *Strength Cond* 2015; 37:17–36.

33. Marx JO, Ratamess NA, Nindl BC, Gotshalk LA, Volek JS, Dohi K, Bush JA, Gomez AL, Mazzetti SA, Fleck SJ, Häkkinen K, Newton RU, Kraemer WJ. Low-volume circuit versus high-volume periodized resistance training in women. *Med Sci Sports Exerc* 2001; 33:635–643.

34. Matveev LP. *Fundamentals of Sports Training*. Moscow: Progress Publishers, 1981.

35. McCarthy JP, Agre JC, Graf BK, Pozniak MA, Vailas AC. Compatibility of adaptive responses with combining strength and endurance training. *Med Sci Sports Exerc* 1995; 27:429–436.

36. Miranda-Furtado CL, Ramos FK, Kogure GS, Santana-Lemos BA, Ferriani RA, Calado

RT, Dos Reis RM. A nonrandomized trial of progressive resistance training intervention in women with polycystic ovary syndrome and its implications in telomere content. *Reprod Sci* 2016; 23:644–654.

37. Miranda F, Simao R, Rhea M, Bunker D, Prestes J, Leite RD, Miranda H, de Salles BF, Novaes J. Effects of linear vs. daily undulatory periodized resistance training on maximal and submaximal strength gains. *J Strength Cond Res* 2011; 25:1824–1830.

38. Newham DJ, Jones DA, Clarkson PM. Repeated high-force eccentric exercise: effects on muscle pain and damage. *J Appl Physiol* 1987; 63:1381–1386.

39. Newton RU, Rogers RA, Volek JS, Häkkinen K, Kraemer WJ. Four weeks of optimal load ballistic resistance training at the end of season attenuates declining jump performance of women volleyball players. *J Strength Cond Res* 2006; 20:955–961.

40. Newton RU, Kraemer WJ. Developing explosive muscular power: Implications for a mixed methods training strategy. *Strength Cond* 1994; 16: 20–31.

41. Painter KB, Haff GG, Ramsey MW, McBride J, Triplett T, Sands WA, Lamont HS, Stone ME, Stone MH. Strength gains: block versus daily undulating periodization weight training among track and field athletes. *Int J Sports Physiol Perform* 2012; 7:161–169.

42. Peterson MD, Rhea MR, Alvar BA. Applications of the dose-response for muscular strength development: a review of meta-analytic efficacy and reliability for designing training prescription. *J Strength Cond Res* 2005; 19: 950–958.

43. Plisk SS, Stone MH. Periodization strategies. *Strength Cond* 2003; 25:19–37.

44. Poliquin C. Five steps to increasing the effectiveness of your strength training programs. *NSCA J* 1988; 10(3):34–39.

45. Rhea MR, Alderman BL. A meta-analysis of periodized versus nonperiodized strength and power training programs. *Res Q Exerc Sport* 2004; 75:413–422.

46. Rhea MR, Alvar BA, Ball SD, Burkett LN. Three sets of weight training superior to 1 set with equal intensity for eliciting strength. *J Strength Cond Res* 2002; 16:525–529.

47. Rhea MR, Ball SD, Phillips WT, Burkett LN. A comparison of linear and daily undulating periodized programs with equated volume and intensity for strength. *J Strength Cond Res* 2002; 16:250–255.

48. Rhea MR, Ball SD, Phillips WT, Burkett LN. A comparison of linear and daily undulating periodized programs with equated volume and intensity for strength. *J Strength Cond Res* 2002; 16:250–255.

49. Rhea MR, Oliverson JR, Marshall G, Peterson MD, Kenn JG, Ayllon FN. Noncompatibility of power and endurance training among college baseball players. *J Strength Cond Res* 2008; 22:230–234.

50. Rhea MR, Phillips WT, Burkett LN, Stone WJ, Ball SD, Alvar BA, Thomas AB. A comparison of linear and daily undulating periodized programs with equated volume and intensity for local muscular endurance. *J Strength Cond Res* 2003; 17:82–87.

51. Rippetoe M, Kilgore L, Pendlay G. *Practical Programming for Strength Training*. Wichita Falls, TX: The Aasgaard Company, 2007.

52. Sands WA, Kavanaugh AA, Murray SR, McNeal JR, Jemni M. Modern Techniques and Technologies Applied to Training and Performance Monitoring. *Int J Sports Physiol Perform* 2017; 12:S263–S272.

53. Schwellnus M, Soligard T, Alonso JM, Bahr R, Clarsen B, Dijkstra HP, Gabbett TJ, Gleeson M, Hagglund M, Hutchinson MR, Janse Van Rensburg C, Meeusen R, Orchard JW, Pluim BM, Raftery M, Budgett R, Engebretsen L. How much is too much? (Part 2) International Olympic Committee consensus statement on load in sport and risk of illness. *Br J Sports Med* 2016; 50:1043–1052.

54. Sedano S, Marin PJ, Cuadrado G, Redondo JC. Concurrent training in elite male runners: the influence of strength versus muscular endurance training on performance outcomes. *J Strength Cond Res* 2013; 27:2433–2443.

55. Selye H. The concept of stress as it appears in 1952. *Brux Med* 1952; 32:2383–2392.

56. Selye H. Dynamics of the general adaptation syndrome; the role of the adrenal and the anterior pituitary glands. *Lijec Vjesn* 1952; 74:137–143.

57. Selye H. The general-adaptation-syndrome and the diseases of adaptation. *Can Nurse* 1952; 48:14–16.

58. Selye H. The general adaptation syndrome (G-A-S) and gastroenterology. *Rev Gastroenterol* 1953; 20:185–190.

59. Selye H. General adaptation syndrome and diseases of adaptation. *Med Arh* 1952; 6:1–13.

60. Selye H. The general adaptation syndrome and the adaptation diseases. *Wien Klin Wochenschr* 1952; 64:781–783.

61. **Selye H.** The general adaptation syndrome as a basis for a unified theory of medicine. *Oral Surg Oral Med Oral Pathol* 1952; 5:408–413.

62. **Selye H.** Prevention of cortisone overdosage effects with the somatotrophic hormone (STH). *Am J Physiol* 1952; 171:381–384.

63. **Selye H.** Stress and disease. *Trans Am Laryngol Rhinol Otol Soc 312–326; discussion*, 326–319, 1955.

64. **Selye H.** *The Stress of Life.* New York: McGraw-Hill, 1956.

65. **Selye H.** Stress, hormones and inflammation. *Am J Proctol* 1955; 6:226–227.

66. **Siff MC, Verkhoshansky YV.** *Supertraining: Special Strength Training for Sporting Excellence – A Textbook on the Biomechanics and Physiology of Strength Conditioning for All Sport.* Denver, CO: Supertraining International, 1999.

67. **Soligard T, Schwellnus M, Alonso JM.** Infographic. International Olympic Committee consensus statement on load in sport and risk of injury: how much is too much? *Br J Sports Med* 2016; 50:1042.

68. **Soligard T, Schwellnus M, Alonso JM, Bahr R, Clarsen B, Dijkstra HP, Gabbett T, Gleeson M, Hagglund M, Hutchinson MR, Janse van Rensburg C, Khan KM, Meeusen R, Orchard JW, Pluim BM, Raftery M, Budgett R, Engebretsen L.** How much is too much? (Part 1) International Olympic Committee consensus statement on load in sport and risk of injury. *Br J Sports Med* 2016; 50:1030–1041.

69. **South MA, Layne AS, Stuart CA, Triplett NT, Ramsey M, Howell ME, Sands WA, Mizuguchi S, Hornsby WG, 3rd, Kavanaugh AA, Stone MH.** Effects of short-term free-weight and semiblock periodization resistance training on metabolic syndrome. *J Strength Cond Res* 2016; 30:2682–2696.

70. **Stone MH, O'Bryant H, Garhammer J.** A hypothetical model for strength training. *J Sports Med Phys Fitness* 1981; 21:342–351.

71. **Stone MH, O'Bryant H, Garhammer J, McMillian J, Ronsenek R.** A theoretical model of strength training. *NSCA J* 1982; 4: 36–39.

72. **Stone MH, O'Bryant H, Garmahmmer J, McMillian J, Rozenek R.** A theoretical model of strength training. *NSCA J* 1982; 4: 36–39.

73. **Stone MH, Stone M, Sands WA.** *Principles and Practice of Resistance Training* Champaign, IL: Human Kinetics 2007, p. 375.

74. **Stowers T, McMillan J, Scala D, Davis V, Wilson D, Stone M.** The short-term effects of three different strength-power training methods. *NSCA J* 1983; 5:24–27.

75. **Turner A.** The science and practice of periodization: a brief review. *Strength Cond* 2011; 33:35–46.

76. **Verkhoshansky Y.** *Fundamentals of Special Strength-Training in Sport.* Livonia, MI: Sportivny Press, 1986.

77. **Verkhoshansky Y.** Main features of a modern scientific sports training theory. *New Studies in Athletics* 1998; 13:9–20.

78. **Verkoshansky Y.** The end of "periodization" of training in top-class sport. *New Studies in Athletics* 1999; 14:47–55.

79. **Viru A.** Early contributions of Russian stress and exercise physiologists. *J Appl Physiol* 2002; 92:1378–1382.

80. **Volek JS.** Influence of nutrition on responses to resistance training. *Med Sci Sports Exerc* 2004; 36:689–696.

81. **Volek JS, Ratamess NA, Rubin MR, Gomez AL, French DN, McGuigan MM, Scheett TP, Sharman MJ, Häkkinen K, Kraemer WJ.** The effects of creatine supplementation on muscular performance and body composition responses to short-term resistance training overreaching. *Eur J Appl Physiol* 2004; 91:628–637.

82. **Willoughby DS.** The effects of mesocycle-length weight training programs involving periodization and partially equated volumes on upper and lower body strength. *J Strength Cond Res* 1993; 7:2–8.

83. **Wilson JM, Marin PJ, Rhea MR, Wilson SMC, Loenneke JP, Anderson JC.** Concurrent training: a meta-analysis examining interference of aerobic and resistance exercises. *J Strength Cond Res* 2012; 26:2293–2307.

84. **Wright GR, Bompa T, Shephard RJ.** Physiological evaluation of winter training programme for oarsmen. *J Sports Med Phys Fitness* 1976; 16:22–37.

85. **Zatsiorsky VM.** *Science and Practice of Strength Training.* Champaign, IL: Human Kinetics, 1995.

86. **Zatsiorsky VM, Kraemer WJ.** *Science and Practice of Strength Training.* Champaign, IL: Human Kinetics, 2006.

Contents

CHAPTER 15

AEROBIC EXERCISE PRESCRIPTION

Anthony B. Ciccone, Loree L. Weir, and Joseph P. Weir

OBJECTIVES

After completing this chapter, you will be able to:

- Understand what factors influence aerobic performance.
- Recognize the physiological changes that occur with positive aerobic adaptations.
- Know how to designate athlete-specific training intensities.
- Learn how to track athlete-specific positive and negative adaptations.
- Understand how to use absolute HR.
- Grasp how training can be programmed to enhance performance.

KEY TERMS

Absolute HR	General preparatory	Self-perceived exertion
$(a-v)O_2$ difference	period	Specific preparatory
Cardiovascular drift	Interval training	period
Competition period	Lactate threshold	Strategy
Continuous training	Maximal cardiac output	Training zones
Economy	Mechanical efficiency	VO_2 max
Fartlek training	Pacing	
Fractional utilization	Percentage of race pace	

INTRODUCTION

Endurance exercise performance is governed by the interplay of a variety of physiological, psychological, and mechanical factors. Here we define endurance performance as performance in exercise tasks that depend heavily on aerobic metabolism, as opposed to being primarily governed by muscle strength and/or power (e.g., throwing events in track and field, line play in American football) or anaerobic (phosphagen and glycolytic) metabolic systems (e.g., 400 meter sprint in track and field). Events such as 1500 meter and longer running events, cycling races, and most swimming events are primarily limited by factors amenable to aerobic exercise training. In addition, many popular team sports require various mixes of aerobic, anaerobic, and strength/power elements, and the strength and conditioning coach must design their programs accordingly.

While different sporting events and exercise tasks primarily are limited by specific factors, endurance performance is affected by the interplay of multiple metabolic, physiological, mechanical, and psychological/cognitive factors. The interplay of these factors is summarized in Figure 15.1. In general, maximal oxygen consumption (VO$_2$ max), mechanical efficiency (often called running economy when studying running physiology), and fractional utilization (percent of VO$_2$ max maintained during an event; reflects sustainable speed/power output) are considered the "Big 3" when focusing on aerobic exercise performance (1). The Big 3 are noted at the top of the figure and these factors will be discussed in more detail in subsequent sections. In general, aerobic training programs should be designed to increase VO$_2$ max, increase mechanical efficiency, and modify the fractional utilization.

ENDURANCE PERFORMANCE

At the bottom of Figure 15.1 we have noted three additional factors that can either directly or indirectly affect aerobic exercise performance. These are neuromuscular strength/power, **strategy/**

pacing, and anaerobic capacity. Because the emphasis of this chapter is on aerobic exercise prescription, we will only mention them briefly here. A large body of research has shown that strength and power training can improve mechanical efficiency, so aerobic exercise performance can be improved indirectly by the effect of strength/power training on mechanical efficiency. In addition, there may some direct effects of improved neuromuscular strength and explosiveness on endurance performance (2). We have combined strategy and pacing in the figure; however, a more detailed analysis, which is beyond the scope of this chapter, would reflect that strategy and pacing have cognitive, psychological, and physiological components. Indeed, the study of the physiology of pacing is a relatively new and exciting area of research in fatigue. Finally, anaerobic capacity is likely important in endurance events where a "kick" or sprint typically occurs at the end of the event. Information related to sprint training can be found in Chapter 17.

MAXIMAL OXYGEN CONSUMPTION

Maximal oxygen consumption, or VO$_2$ max, is one of the most common measurements taken in exercise physiology, and the research literature

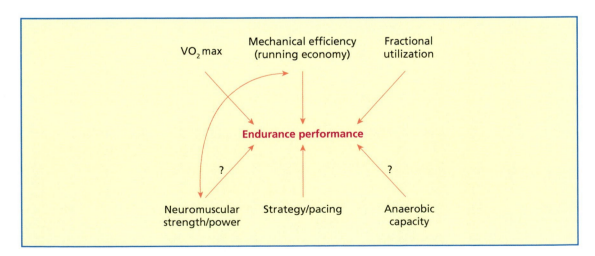

Figure 15.1 A theoretical representation of the major variables that influence endurance performance. Question marks indicate relationships that vary depending on performance task demands.

addressing VO_2 max is voluminous. The VO_2 max reflects the maximal amount of oxygen that can be extracted from the atmosphere and utilized for cellular respiration during exercise. Because the largest total energy yield, by far, comes from aerobic metabolism, getting oxygen to the mitochondria is critical for sustained exercise. The aerobic system requires the integration of pulmonary, cardiovascular, and skeletal muscle systems to engage in gas exchange, deliver oxygenated blood to the active tissues, and transfer oxygen from the blood (primarily bound to hemoglobin) to the mitochondria in the skeletal muscle. These same systems also serve to remove the products of exercise that accumulate (e.g., CO_2, H^+) during exercise and facilitate recovery between exercise bouts.

The units of oxygen consumption are typically expressed as either milliliters of oxygen per minute ($L \cdot min^{-1}$) or as milliliters of oxygen per kilogram of body weight per minute ($mL \cdot kg^{-1} \cdot min^{-1}$). The latter expression is a relative index, i.e., relative to body weight. There are statistical and theoretical concerns regarding the use of a simple ratio standard to create an index that is "independent" of body weight (see allometric scaling). However, ignoring that for a moment, it is apparent that one way to increase relative VO_2 max is to simply lose body mass. Even assuming no changes in pulmonary, cardiovascular, or skeletal muscle aerobic capacity, dividing maximal VO_2 by a smaller body mass will increase the relative VO_2 max. This may also have performance effects as it takes less energy in the form of ATP, and therefore a smaller oxygen consumption, to propel a less massive body.

Beyond changes in body mass, to develop training programs to increase VO_2 max, it is helpful to reflect on the basic equation that defines VO_2, known as the Fick equation. The Fick equation is as follows:

$$VO_2 = HR \; x \; SV \; x \; (a{-}v)O_2 \; diff$$

where HR = heart rate, SV = stroke volume, and $(a{-}v)O_2$ diff is the arteriovenous oxygen difference. Notice that the product of HR and SV equals the cardiac output (volume of blood pumped per minute), while the **$(a{-}v)O_2$ diff** is the difference in oxygen content between arterial and venous blood, which reflects the amount of oxygen that is extracted from blood as it passes through the capillary beds. For VO_2 max then, the Fick equation becomes

$$VO_2 \, max = HR_{max} \; x \; SV_{max} \; X \; x \; (a{-}v)O_2 \, diff \, max.$$

The primary ways to increase VO_2 max then are to increase maximal cardiac output and to increase the amount of oxygen that can be extracted from oxygenated blood by the active skeletal muscle.

Adaptations that can increase maximal cardiac output primarily occur with respect to changes in stroke volume (3). In general, exercise training does not increase maximal heart rate (4). The performance of the left ventricle, however, can be substantially improved. Typical long-term aerobic training programs can increase both the cavity size of the left ventricle (so that it can accept more blood) and the performance of the left ventricle during systole (5). In addition, expansion of blood volume and red blood cell volume (6) facilitate increased stroke volume (through the Frank-Starling mechanism) and total oxygen carrying capacity of the blood respectively. Collectively, these adaptations can increase the ability of the cardiovascular system to generate cardiac output.

Regarding the $(a{-}v)O_2$ diff, a variety of adaptations increase the ability to extract and utilize O_2 during endurance exercise (3). These include increases in capillary density in the trained muscle, increases in mitochondria and aerobic enzyme concentrations, and changes in muscle transport proteins on the muscle cell membrane (e.g., increases in MCT1 and MCT4 proteins that increase the ability to shuttle lactate between fast and slow twitch muscle fibers) (7).

> Aerobic endurance is affected by maximal oxygen consumption, lactate threshold, fuel utilization, muscle fiber type, and exercise economy.

MECHANICAL EFFICIENCY

Mechanical efficiency concerns the O_2 cost relative to the amount of work performed during an exercise task. In brief, a higher mechanical efficiency means that there will be a lower O_2 demand at a given speed/power output (PO), assuming all else is equal. Picture two individuals that have the same VO_2 max but different metabolic efficacies. The more efficient individual will use less O_2 than the competitor, and all else being equal this means that the exercise at a given speed/PO is "easier" and elicits a smaller fatigue response. Indeed, it has been hypothesized that much of the dominance in distance running by racers from East Africa is due, at least in part, to higher levels of running economy (8).

Mechanical efficiency does appear modifiable with training. Interestingly, a variety of strength and explosive power training protocols have been shown to improve mechanical efficiency in tasks such as running, cycling, and cross-country skiing (2). The training programs in the literature have run the gamut from high-load, low velocity tasks (e.g., squats at 4RM loads) to "reactive strength" training using tasks such as unweighted drop jumps and hops. The beneficial effects may be due, in part, to improvement in musculotendinous stiffness, which may translate to increases in the ability to store and release elastic energy (2). However, improvements in mechanical efficiency also occur with cycling (9), in which there is no appreciable eccentric component.

Improvements in efficiency following strength training may also be due to changes in motor unit activation. As motor units increase their force and power production capabilities, all else being equal fewer motor units would need to be recruited to generate a given speed/PO. As lower threshold motor units are generally populated by slow twitch muscle fibers, and slow twitch fibers are presumably more efficient (with respect to O_2 consumption) than fast twitch muscle fibers (10), this may translate a lower O_2 cost. In addition, improvements in rate of force development (RFD) with strength and power training may increase mechanical efficiency, perhaps by decreasing the contraction time during a repetition of the endurance task, which may improve transit time for blood flow through an active capillary bed (9). While the mechanism(s) linking strength training to improvements in mechanical efficiency are still largely speculative, the data are clear that strength/explosive power training can improve mechanical efficiency during predominantly aerobic tasks.

FRACTIONAL UTILIZATION AND TRAINING ZONES

The idea of **fractional utilization** is simply a way to quantify the intensity of aerobic

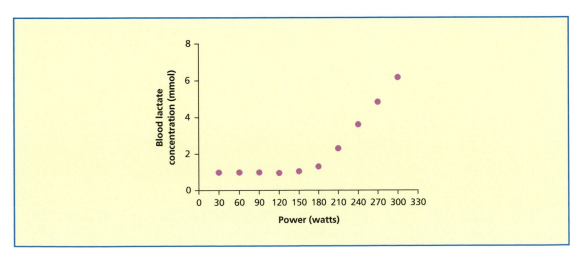

Figure 15.2 Example data from one subject showing the blood lactate (simulated) response during an incremental exercise test. Simulated data modified from table 2 of Morton (1989) (40).

exercise, but primarily from a metabolic perspective. The simplest way to quantify fractional utilization is based relative to VO_2 max. For example, assume two runners are running at the same speed. If one runner is running at 70% VO_2 max while the other runner is running at 80% VO_2 max, all else being equal, the second runner is at a disadvantage and will likely have a faster rate of fatigue development.

However, the picture becomes more complicated due to different physiological conditions that may be present at different levels of fractional utilization. The nomenclature can become confusing because different authors use different terms, and there is controversy over the physiological mechanisms that underpin different **training zones**. We will try to avoid getting mired in physiological controversies and focus on measurements that can be used to define metabolic training zones. However, in brief, we can use different techniques to define training zones/intensities, and these zones are referred to as moderate intensity (Zone 1), heavy intensity (Zone 2), and severe intensity (Zone 3).

Figure 15.2 shows the plot of measurements of blood lactate (simulated) taken during the performance of an incremental cycling exercise test to exhaustion in a hypothetical athlete; this type of test is typically used to quantify VO_2 max. Notice that lactate does not increase

in a linear manner with exercise intensity, but rather increases more abruptly after about 150 watts. The exercise intensity at this point has been called the anaerobic threshold or the lactate threshold; for clarity we will refer to this as the lactate threshold. Figure 15.3 shows a similar plot of gas exchange data. Notice the change in ventilation V_E and also the ratio of V_E to VO_2 around 150 watts; this discontinuity reflects an additional drive to ventilation beyond just the associated increase in VO_2. In general, the exercise intensity associated with changes in gas exchange and ventilation coincide in time with the lactate threshold, but the physiological links between the phenomena are controversial and the identification of the transition points is not always obvious. The changes in gas exchange and ventilation have been referred to as the ventilatory threshold or the gas exchange threshold. For purposes that will be discussed below, we will refer to this index as ventilatory threshold 1 (VT1).

In general, the transition in exercise intensity associated with the **lactate threshold** and/or VT1 defines the transition from moderate intensity (Zone 1) to heavy intensity (Zone 2) exercise. In theory, exercise intensities in Zone 1 are intensities that can be maintained somewhat indefinitely; for example, cycling at 90% of the power at VT1 resulted in task failure (inability to maintain the set power) in 180 to

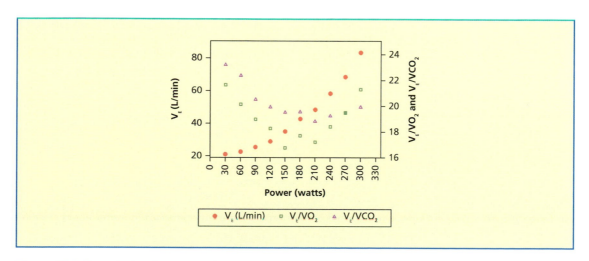

Figure 15.3 Example data from one subject showing the volume of expired air (VE), volume of oxygen (VO_2), and volume of carbon dioxide (VCO_2) at different cycling work rates (power) during an incremental exercise test. Data courtesy of H. Bergstom, University of Kentucky; data have been modified for clarity.

360 minutes depending on the exerciser (11). From a metabolic perspective, Zone 1 exercise does not result in an accumulation of blood lactate (11). In addition, the VO_2 response will level off (reach a steady state) such that VO_2 is elevated relative to resting values but does not drift upwards over time. Table 15.1 shows the exercise intensity, expressed as a percentage of the maximum heart rate, associated with VT1 from several different studies that reflect different populations.

In contrast, constant intensity exercise in the heavy intensity zone (Zone 2) does result in an increase in blood lactate levels; however, the blood lactate will reach a relative plateau – that is, blood lactate will reach a steady state. However, the VO_2 response will not reach a steady state and will drift upwards as the exercise bout continues; this is referred to as the VO_2 slow component. Maintaining exercise at a fixed power output in Zone 2 results in a faster rate of fatigue development than in Zone 1, and the rate of fatigue development will depend on the intensity of exercise within Zone 2 range. For example, a recent study reported that subjects cycling near the lower bound of Zone 2 reached task failure in 43.5 ± 16.2 minutes (11).

The third intensity zone is referred to as severe exercise (Zone 3). In Figure 15.3, notice the changes in gas exchange (specifically V_E/VCO_2) shown around the power outputs of 210–240 watts. At this point, the exercise intensity is such that ventilation accelerates at an even faster rate than that occurring at VT1. This second transition has been referred to as the respiratory compensation threshold, but we will refer to this as ventilatory threshold 2 (VT2). The demarcation between VT1 and VT2 defines the heavy (Zone 2) versus the severe (Zone 3) exercise intensity domains. As the name suggests, severe exercise is very high intensity exercise and maintaining a fixed exercise intensity in this domain would result in the exercise termination in about 2 to 14 minutes depending on the specific power output while in Zone 3 (11). In addition, exercise performed at power outputs in the severe intensity domain do not result in a steady state in either blood lactate or VO_2. Both will increase rapidly until the power cannot be maintained by the exerciser. Indeed, the VO_2 will drift up to VO_2 max at the point of task failure. Table 15.1 shows the exercise intensity, expressed as a percentage of the maximum heart rate, associated with VT2 from several different studies that reflect different populations.

There are other techniques used to identify the demarcation between heavy and severe exercise. Among these is the critical power (CP) test (see also critical speed (CS), critical torque) which is a test that allows for the quantification of the hyperbolic relationship between power output and the time to test failure and the respective powers. An example plot is shown in Figure 15.4. The asymptote of the relationship is called critical power and is a remarkably robust predictor of transition from heavy to severe exercise (12). In addition, CP/CS testing requires little equipment except an exercise modality (e.g., cycle ergometer, treadmill) and a stopwatch to record the time until task failure at each tested power/speed. While VT2 and CP/CS have both been used to define the transition

TABLE 15.1 A summary of mean ventilatory threshold (VT) data from different populations

Study	Mean age (yr)	Exercise status	VT1 mean (%HRmax)	VT2 mean (%HRmax)
Deruelle et al. 2006 (41)	63	trained cyclists	76.6	88.9
Neder and Stein 2006 (42)	31	nontrained	74.5	91.0
Ramos-Campo et al. 2016 (43)	23	professional basketball	74.9	93.6
Algrøy et al. 2011 (44)	24	professional soccer	78	87
Seiler et al. 2007 (45)	23	highly trained runners	77	86
Lucia et al. 2000 (46)	24	professional cyclists	78.2	90.4

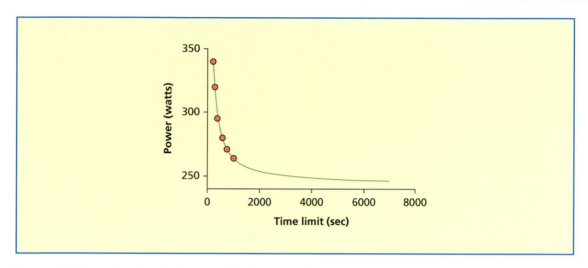

Figure 15.4 Example of a critical power (CP) plot for an illustrative subject. The subject performed five cycling bouts to task failure at fixed power outputs in the severe intensity domain. The time to task failure (Time Limit) at each power was used to derive the hyperbolic plot. The asymptote of the relationship (in this case ~ 250 watts) is termed critical power. Example data courtesy of H. Bergstrom, University of Kentucky; data have been modified for clarity.

from Zone 2 and Zone 3, and on average result in similar values, it should be noted that on an individual basis, the differences between estimates may not be trivial (13,14).

Collectively, identifying the power (or speed) that defines the moderate, heavy, and severe exercise domains provides a very useful tool to define training zones that can be used to design the aerobic training program. In practice, the heart rate values that occur at the transition from Zone 1 to Zone 2, and Zone 2 to Zone 3 are useful metrics to guide program design. That is, one can control training volume and intensity by assigning specific volumes of work in heart rate ranges that correspond to how much work is desired in each training zone. That is, advanced aerobic exercise prescriptions quantify the amount of training that is to be performed in each training zone, and modify these as individuals move through yearly periodization cycles. Furthermore, training can be modified to specifically target increasing the power output for a specific transition. For example, increasing CP would increase the bandwidth of the heavy exercise domain such that a power (or speed) that used to be in the severe domain is now in the heavy domain. This would increase endurance performance at that power (or speed) without necessarily increasing VO_2

max. Application of fractional utilization and training zones to exercise prescription is discussed in the Programming section below.

TYPES OF TRAINING

Continuous

Continuous training is planned exercise that is performed at a specific intensity for an extended period of time – typically lasting at least 20 minutes. However, one can argue that many athletes, such as team sports athletes, may benefit from continuous training sessions that require far less than 20 minutes of continuous exercise. Conversely, highly aerobic events such as marathons may require elite athletes to utilize greater than two-hour long continuous exercise sessions (15). It is important to note that the intensity of continuous training typically falls in the Zone 1 (moderate intensity) category. Conversely, higher intensity exercise, Zones 2 (heavy intensity) and 3 (severe intensity), are commonly prescribed using interval training. The need for continuous training is dictated by the length and intensity of each athlete's competition. For example, research has shown that

REAL-WORLD APPLICATION

Strength training and endurance athletes

Strength training, within reason, is important for endurance athletes. It can help to prevent injuries by targeting muscles and joints that are prone to injury. For example, it can help to improve strength imbalances in a runner's knee or a swimmer's shoulder. It can also help to improve an athlete's ability to apply force. Even though endurance athletes are taking many steps, strokes, or revolutions during a race, an athlete who can generate more force will still have the ability to get somewhere faster than the one who cannot.

There are a number of guidelines for strength training in endurance athletes:

1 Keep it in perspective. Endurance athletes are not strength and power athletes. They cannot tolerate high volumes and intensities of strength training combined with their endurance training; this can lead to overtraining or injury. Overly intense strength training can also be counterproductive in another way; putting on too much muscle will negatively affect an endurance athlete's exercise economy, thereby detracting from event performance.
2 Resistance training does not have to mean weight training. Since the focus is not on drastically increasing maximal strength or hypertrophy, resistance training can be done in a number of ways, including in the weight room, through calisthenics, and with medicine balls or other implements.
3 Keep the stresses of the athlete's endurance training in mind. If the athlete's endurance training stresses a given joint (e.g., the effect of pounding from running on the knee), then strength training should not further aggravate that.

Strength training is an ineffective tool for training maximal oxygen consumption; it does not effectively improve aerobic metabolism in trained athletes. However, it does an excellent job of improving one's anaerobic metabolism and one's tolerance to it. Adjusting the length of the sets and the recovery intervals can be a great way to further enhance these pathways.

elite cross-country running performance in the 10.13 km event is highly correlated to the amount of Zone 1 training time, but performance in the 4.175 km event is less correlated to the amount of Zone 1 training time (16). In practice, continuous exercise is typically prescribed by prompting athletes to cover a certain distance at a certain pace or cover a specific distance at a specific HR.

> Continuous training may lack specificity to many sports and activities and may expose athletes to overuse injuries. It does appear to improve maximal oxygen consumption and performance potential in endurance athletes.

Interval

Interval training is characterized by exercise that alternates between bouts of heavy or severe exercise intensities and bouts of rest or low to moderate exercise intensities. The advantage of interval training is that it allows athletes to achieve greater total exercise time above race pace and race HR, when compared to continuous training. Importantly, data suggests that performance enhancement in highly trained aerobic athletes comes from increases in high-intensity interval training (HIIT) volume and not from increases in moderate intensity exercise volume (17). Furthermore, the high intensity intermittent nature of interval training can more closely mimic the intermittent nature of many team sports, which should have the greatest transfer to competition (18). An undulating form of interval training is commonly known as **Fartlek training**, in which athletes perform bouts of aerobic exercise that vary in intensity and duration within the training session. This differs from traditional interval training where exercise and rest bouts are typically static throughout the training session. The benefit of Fartlek training is that athletes may mix moderate intensity exercise zone bouts with severe and heavy exercise bouts in an effort to benefit from both continuous and interval-type stressors in a single session.

The contribution of each energy system during an HIIT workout and the degree of adaptations that occur in response to training will vary as the differing training variables are manipulated. Manipulation of variables within a training program depends on the training goals, which in turn depend on the specific position/sport that the athlete is training for. The exact duration and intensity of the work and rest periods, and therefore the work:rest ratio, will vary according to the specific requirements of the sport. There is no single optimal work:rest ratio that will apply to all athletes because the individual characteristics, the metabolic demands of each sport, and the training goals for each athlete are unique. However, in general, intervals performed at higher intensities require lower work:rest ratios. In other words, rest intervals should be much longer than work intervals when exercise intensities are high.

> Interval training appears to be an effective way to target an athlete's deficiencies, but it is extremely demanding and requires a solid fitness base before this training activity is initiated.

PROGRAMMING

Adaptation tracking

Similar to resistance exercise prescription, both volume and intensity are of primary importance to aerobic exercise prescription. The prescription of nearly all aerobic exercise relies on prior knowledge of the aerobic capacity or some physiologic response to exercise. For aerobic exercise prescription, volume can be defined as distance or quantity of exercise duration. Although there are numerous metrics that have been used to prescribe continuous aerobic exercise intensity, the most practical metrics are: percentage of velocity or power at VO_2 max, percentage of maximum HR or **absolute HR**, **percentage of race pace**, and **self-perceived exertion**. All of these metrics can be obtained using a single exercise test or no exercise test. Although some of these metrics, such as percentage of velocity or power at VO_2 max, are most accurately measured via gas exchange measurements, power or velocity at VO_2 max can be estimated using an incremental exercise test without gas exchange measurements.

> Intensity and volume of training are inversely related. If the intensity of the exercise is high, the volume will be lower.

One major issue with the use of VO_2 max-derived metrics is that, as athletes improve their VO_2 max, they may have to periodically re-test their VO_2 max to ensure prescribed training intensities do not unintentionally decrease over time. It should also be noted that environmental factors such as temperature, wind resistance, and humidity will alter the metabolic stress of any given work rate such that aerobic training intensities based on a percentage of a work rate or specific pace may result in an inappropriate exercise intensity (19). For example, if a VO_2 max test was performed indoors in a comfortable environment and exercise is performed in a hot and humid environment (20), a cyclist who is told to cycle at a percentage of their wattage at VO_2 max will be exercising at an intensity that causes much more aerobic stress than is intended.

With the aforementioned drawbacks in mind, it is likely most convenient and appropriate to prescribe continuous aerobic exercise intensities using percentages of maximum HR or absolute HRs (15). The use of HR is appealing because maximum HR is very stable in the sense that it does not change much within a period of months, and is typically not affected by training. Furthermore, when an individual enhances their aerobic capacity, their heart rate will be lower at any fixed work rate (21). For example, if a cyclist has a maximum HR of 200 and they are told to exercise at 75% of their maximum HR, they may exercise at 200 watts on day one of their training program, but as the athlete undergoes positive aerobic adaptations, the wattage that elicits an HR response of 75% of their maximum should be higher on day 60 of the training program (Figure 15.4).

Percentage of maximum HR values may also be used to estimate approximate work rates that correspond to VT1 and VT2. This allows for the use of programming through the use of previously mentioned exercise zones. As seen in Table 15.1, VT1 and VT2 occur at approximately the same percentages of HR maximums across a wide variety of populations. Although these mean population sample values are similar, there is certainly variation within a population. Accordingly, without data from a graded exercise test with gas exchange analysis, it is difficult to determine HR values that correspond to VT1 and VT2. However, as previously discussed in this chapter, HR at critical power output may be used to determine the HR associated with VT2. When using HR to prescribe exercise intensities, the estimation of the athlete-specific VTs may be critical, as research suggests exercise prescribed based on person-specific thresholds can result in better aerobic adaptations when compared to general HR percentages (22).

More practically, athletes may use a talk test to estimate exercise zone transitions. Research suggests that the highest work rate at which an athlete can hold a conversation coincides with VT1, and the highest work rate at which an athlete can definitely not talk coincides with VT2 (23). Once the work rates are determined, HR responses at those work rates can be used to program future exercise prescription in desired intensity zones. However, prescribing continuous aerobic exercise using HR during periods of intensified training can result in unintentionally high exercise intensities. This is because periods of intensified training or overreaching can result in decreases in maximum HR (24). Although perceived effort is clearly a very convenient method of exercise prescription, without HR data, it may impair the practitioner's ability to detect positive and negative physiologic changes in athletes. Coaches should be aware of athletes who exhibit decreased performance, decreased maximal HRs, and increased submaximal perception of effort (24). Athletes who train in such a physiological state for a prolonged period of time (many weeks or months) may become overtrained. Thus, the collection of a variety of training data is necessary to analyze both positive and negative aerobic adaptations. A summary of the benefits and drawbacks of the previously mentioned exercise prescription metrics can be seen in Table 15.2.

The aerobic adaptations made by athletes are typically tracked by measuring HR responses to a known submaximal work rate. The periodic monitoring of such responses is critical in determining if athletes are positively or negatively adapting. For example,

TABLE 15.2 Benefits and drawbacks of different metrics that can be used for aerobic exercise prescription

	%VO$_2$ max work rate	Arbitrary distance	% Race pace	Perceived exertion	Absolute or % max HR
Does not require costly test(s)		X	X	X	X
Requires infrequent testing		X	X	X	X
Responds to environmental changes				X	X
Critical for detection of overtraining					X

a positively adapting cyclist should exhibit improvements in their 10 km time trial average wattage and decreases in their HR response (21) to a 150 watt work rate (Figure 15.5). A negatively adapting cyclist would exhibit decreases in 10 km time trial average wattage and increases in their HR response (25) to a 150 watt work rate (Figure 15.6). If the practitioner plans an overreaching microcycle (described in the Chapter 13, Program design), they should expect the cyclist to exhibit decreases in 10 km time trial average wattage and decreases in HR response to a 150 watt work rate. Similarly, positively adapting athletes should be able to exercise at higher work rates at specific HRs, whereas negatively adapting athletes will need to exercise at lower work rates to achieve a specific HR (Figure 15.4). It should also be noted that **cardiovascular drift** can make HR-based inferences difficult. Cardiovascular drift is the progressive increase in HR at a constant work rate that can occur at higher work rates and challenging environmental conditions such as training at altitude and in hot environments (15). To minimize the confounding effect of cardiovascular drift and the environment, workouts that are meant to be used for adaptation tracking should be performed in controlled environments at Zone 1 work rates.

Needs analysis

The first step that each strength and conditioning professional should take when developing a program for an athlete is to determine the needs of that athlete. Because all sports and athletes within each team do not require the same aerobic capacity, determining the aerobic demands of each athlete is of critical importance. For example, in soccer, elite mid-fielders typically have higher aerobic capacities than elite strikers and center-backs (26). Furthermore, the sport demands of each athlete may vary in the magnitude of benefit from enhancing aerobic capacity. Specifically, many sports are not continuous in nature and, instead, require athletes to perform intermittent bouts of high-intensity exercise separated by periods of rest, such as ice hockey, or periods of lower intensity exercise, such as soccer. These differences will be addressed in detail later in this section. Once the aerobic demands of the athlete are determined, the strength and conditioning professional must begin to consider the logistics of implementing an appropriate training program to obtain specific aerobic adaptations for the athlete(s). Arguably the most appropriate strategy is to begin by determining which in-season periods are most important. It is these periods from which the strength and

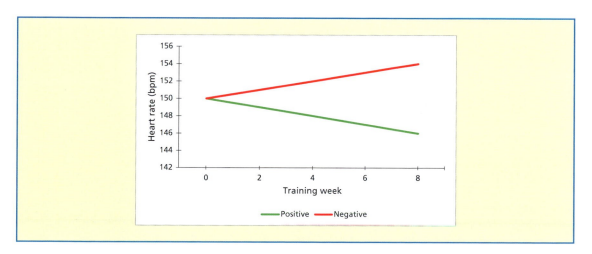

Figure 15.5 Theoretical heart rate responses to a 150 watt work rate throughout an eight-week training period. The green line indicates a response that is typical of an athlete who is improving aerobically, positively adapting. The red line indicates a response that is typical of an athlete who is detraining or regressing in performance, negatively adapting.

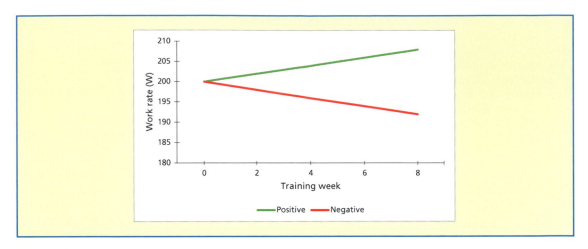

Figure 15.6 Theoretical work rates that correspond to a heart rate of 150 beats per minute throughout an eight-week training period. The green line indicates a response that is typical of an athlete who is improving aerobically, positively adapting. The red line indicates a response that is typical of an athlete who is detraining or regressing in performance, negatively adapting.

conditioning professional should work backwards to organize appropriate mesocycles and microcycles to attempt to maximize the athlete's performance or to increase the likelihood of team success. Finally, the intricacies of the program should be carefully determined with respect to training time availability, training resources, and any other logistical issues.

Aerobic training programs are underpinned by the same basic training principles as strength training: frequency, intensity, volume, rest, choice, order, and progression. These variables should be manipulated in an attempt to optimize performance around the periods that the strength and conditioning professional(s) and coaches have identified as being most crucial for success. When programming aerobic exercise, frequency refers to the spacing of aerobic training workout sessions. Intensity can be defined as relative work rate, and volume can be quantified as training distance or time. Rest can be defined as the non-exercising time between training bouts or training sessions. Exercise choice is the act of choosing the mode of exercise (i.e., cycling, running, rowing, etc.) for each workout. Exercise choice is important because some training movements are more similar to competition movements, which is related to how well training improvements may translate into competition improvements. This movement-related transfer of improvements

is known as specificity. For example, researchers have observed that progressive running training improves both running and cycling VO_2 max, whereas progressive cycling training improves cycling VO_2 max without improving running VO_2 max (27). Exercise order applies to workouts that contain different exercises. For example, an athlete may perform both resistance training and aerobic training within the same workout; in this situation, the strength and conditioning professional(s) would need to determine the order of these exercises. The training variable, progression, should be addressed by altering training in a way that progressively overloads the athlete in an attempt to achieve specific adaptations and enhanced performance. The seven training variables mentioned at the start of the paragraph should vary as athletes move from general preparatory to specific preparatory to competition periods of a macrocycle. It is important to note that the duration of these three periods can vary drastically between athletes, but the general training goals within each period should vary minimally.

Specific modes of exercise are selected to train specific energy systems. Once the mode of exercise is selected, intensity will be determined based on the specific exercise.

General preparatory period

During the **general preparatory period**, which is synonymous with offseason, athletes should have three primary training goals: recovery, conditioning, and general strength. Because the general preparatory period follows an athlete's competition period, if applicable, the athlete should ensure that they utilize this time to recover from any injuries that may have occurred in the course of the previous competition period. Seemingly healthy athletes also need to recover during the general preparatory period as it is generally thought that long periods of high volume and high intensity training increase the likelihood of injury or becoming overtrained. Although within a macrocycle, total training volume should be the lowest and rest should be highest during the general preparatory period, athletes still need to perform both aerobic and resistance exercise workouts during this time. The aerobic training sessions aim to create an aerobic "base" which is necessary to support the ensuing increase in training volume and intensity in the specific preparatory period (18).

Although strength training increases aerobic exercise economy (28), enhanced exercise economy is not necessary during non-competition periods. Actually, enhanced exercise economy during non-competition periods may force athletes to exercise at higher intensities or volumes to achieve a given increment in aerobic capacity. However, strength training has been shown to decrease the likelihood of hamstring injuries in soccer athletes (29). Thus, the general preparatory period can also be thought of as a pre-habilitation period. During this period, initial workout volumes, intensities, and frequencies should be conservatively estimated, as many athletes may begin the period in a severely detrained state. Furthermore, workouts should emphasize variety instead of specificity, because training variety has been shown to decrease the likelihood of overuse injury (30).

A variety of aerobic exercise modes, training zones, intensities, and volumes should be utilized along with a variety of strength training exercises and intensities. However, practitioners should tailor the distribution of aerobic and strength training workouts to each athlete with respect to the relative importance of aerobic capacity to their performance. Furthermore, for highly aerobic sports, this period should contain the highest relative distribution of Zone 1 training. For team sports, which are intermittent in nature, aerobic training may primarily consist of interval training. In this case, this period should contain the highest volume of longer duration intervals. For both continuous and interval training, it is crucial that athletes are progressively overloaded with both aerobic and strength stressors as to improve aerobic capacity and general strength before the specific preparatory period is reached.

When designing an aerobic exercise training program, keep the following factors in mind: warm up properly, balance the hard and easy days, establish a fitness base first, determine weak points and then train them, and don't neglect resistance training.

Q&A FROM THE FIELD

The university has had a successful cross-country team for the last several years. Recently I've been put in charge of designing their workouts. I understand how to incorporate the different types of endurance training, but I'm having trouble figuring out how to balance out the hard and easy days. How do I go about determining all that?
—Graduate assistant coach

This can be a confusing topic for any strength and conditioning professional. First, determine when the competitions are; this will dictate the training calendar. The period around the competitions will be your competition phase. This period will see the most intense training. The remaining time will be divided between preparation and precompetition. The precompetition phase usually lasts four weeks and consists of training of increasing intensity. Preparation should ideally make up the bulk of the training, with low to moderate intensity (intensity should increase over time).

Once the rough calendar has been determined, break each phase into four-week cycles. The easiest way to do this is to have a 3:1 approach (i.e., intensity increases for the first three weeks, then week four is a recovery week). This would mean that week two is more difficult than week one,

(continued)

(continued)

week three is more difficult that week two, and week four is less difficult than week two (though slightly more difficult than week one).

Within a 34-week cycle, decide on the intensity levels for each week. They may be high-intensity (i.e., three peaks), medium-intensity (i.e., two peaks), or low intensity (i.e., one peak) work. Remember that a race always counts as a peak. In general, the weeks in the competition phase will consist of high-intensity weeks; the rest of the training time (preparation and precompetition) will consist primarily of low- and medium-intensity weeks, with a few high-intensity weeks thrown in.

Once you've determined how many peaks a week will have, organize the training week around the peaks.

In summary, to help determine how to balance our hard and easy days, several steps may be taken:

1   Determine when the competitions are.
2   Divide up the calendar into competition, precompetition, and preparation phases.
3   Break each phase into four-week cycles.
4   Decide upon an intensity for each week within a four-week cycle.

Distribute the peaks according to the guidelines laid out in this chapter.

Specific preparatory period

As athletes leave the **specific preparatory period**, training volume will continue to increase, and athletes should have the strength and aerobic capacity to tolerate the high training volume required of the specific preparatory period. During this period, athletes should target technique, sport specific endurance, and maximal speed. Thus, the big difference between this stage and the general preparatory stage is that training volume increases for all training intensities (15,31). For highly aerobic sports, the volume in Zone 1 training is necessary to allow for athletes to train in Zones 2 and 3 for longer durations (18). Furthermore, intermittent maximal or near-maximal effort exercise bouts, such as interval sprints, should be periodically implemented. This will allow for athletes to develop neurological and anaerobic metabolism adaptations to facilitate

improvements in maximal work rates or speed. This implementation of the entire spectrum of exercise intensities ultimately allows for the highest quantity of heavy and severe exercise volume. This is important because research has shown that high intensity exercise volume is critical for performance enhancement of highly trained athletes (17,32). In other words, this period of time is said to improve the speed-endurance of aerobic athletes.

For highly aerobic athletes such as marathoners and cyclists, a distribution of approximately 20% of workouts in Zones 2 and 3 and 80% of workouts in Zone 1 has been shown to be highly effective in enhancing aerobic performance in a way that is typically superior to training programs that contain high volumes of Zone 2 training. The relative avoidance of Zone 2 and high volume of Zone 1 training is known as polarized training. A polarized training regimen has been successfully utilized by elite athletes of a wide variety of sports such as skiing, cycling, running, and rowing, to name a few (16,33,34). Practitioners may also utilize polarized training distributions within a workout where continuous moderate intensity exercise is performed before or in between higher-intensity exercise bouts. However, team sport athletes, such as soccer players, should not utilize the polarized training model, as repeated maximal or near maximal repeated sprint ability is desired. Thus, soccer players would benefit from a much larger percentage of Zone 3 volume than Zone 1 volume.

To facilitate this readiness, workouts should become increasingly sport specific throughout the training period. For example, a cyclist should transition to a lower percentage of running workouts and higher percentage of cycling workouts. Furthermore, a soccer player may want to perform drills or small-sided games that elicit the desired heart rate responses. To ensure that exercise economy is maximized, athletes should perform approximately two-weekly resistance training workouts using two to three sets of four to ten repetition-maximum loads performed with two to three minutes of rest between sets (28). These resistance exercises should primarily target the muscles that limit competition performance.

Although the absolute volumes of exercise performed in the three different intensity zones will differ between athletes, perspective is important. At an extreme end of the training volume spectrum, elite marathoners have been observed to run approximately 231 km per week when their volume peaked during their specific preparatory period (15). It is important to note that these elite marathoners also average approximately 13 aerobic training sessions per week. In one case study, a European 1500 meter men's champion performed a peak running volume of 156 km per week prior to their competition period (31). However, the 1500 meter athlete performed a much higher percentage of Zone 2 work (26.1%) than the marathoners (11%). This shows a clear volume distribution difference due to the specific intensity demands of the two events.

Throughout this period, practitioners should pay close attention to the training performance of each athlete and the HR responses each athlete has to know submaximal work rates, as previously detailed in the "Adaptation tracking" section of this chapter. HR responses to known submaximal work rates have been proposed as the best measurement to monitor fatigue due to its high signal to noise ratio (35). This information will allow for practitioners to most confidently determine if athletes are acquiring positive aerobic adaptations.

Competition period

By the end of the specific preparatory training period, athletes should be ready for the **competition period**. The competition period will contain the highest percentage of Zone 2 and 3 training and lowest total training volume (15,31), as the main goal of this phase is to maintain or increase each athlete's capacity for Zone 3 work rates: speed-endurance. However, part of the Zone 3 training volume will come from competitions. If competitions are separated by many days or weeks, any insufficiencies in high intensity volume must be accounted for through workouts. During this period, economy improvements gained in the specific preparatory period will likely be maintained by implementing a high intensity low volume strength training workout once a week (28). Resistance training should not be removed completely as research suggests that doing so can result in aerobic performance decrements (36).

Because competition readiness is highly dependent on athletes' recovery from workouts and competition, practitioners should have a general idea of how long each athlete takes to recover from a competition and variety of different workouts. For example, research has shown that elite soccer players exhibit impaired high intensity performance when matches are separated by three days, but performance is recovered with four days of rest between matches (37). This suggests that practitioners who train athletes with frequent competitions may need to concentrate on recovery and fatigue management rather than speed-endurance. Furthermore, data also suggest that athletes who have the capacity to perform a greater volume of high-intensity exercise in competition also recover from competition faster, in spite of their higher volume of in-competition exercise (38). This scenario also highlights why athletes should not rely on the competition period to increase their aerobic base or maximal work capacity.

However, it is possible, particularly in sports that spend a lot of practice time on tactics, for in-practice training intensities and volumes to inadequately stress the athletes in a way that results in negative aerobic adaptations. Thus, when training team sports athletes, practitioners should know the approximate relative distribution of time spent in each HR zone during competition. This information should be used as a general conditioning guide for determining workout intensity distributions to ensure that the maximal aerobic and anaerobic capacities of the athlete are maintained throughout the competition period. Athletes who have less frequent competitions will need to maintain their physiologic adaptations by maintaining a similar distribution of training intensities as in the specific preparatory period, except athletes should perform a higher percentage of Zone 3 training, a lower percentage of Zone 1 training, and a lower total training volume. Furthermore, if competitions are separated by weeks or months, athletes will likely benefit from a taper. Data gathered from a large quantity of swimming, running, and cycling studies suggest that the maintenance of exercise zone volume distribution while decreasing total exercise volume by 41–60% results in the greatest performance enhancements (39).

SUMMARY

Several factors influence aerobic performance including VO$_2$ max, running economy, fractional utilization, neuromuscular strength and power, anaerobic capacity, and strategy/pacing. With a sound aerobic training program, positive physiologic changes will occur over time that should be monitored periodically. Tracking aerobic fitness over time helps ensure that the training adaptations are sound, and also identifies any negative adaptations that should be monitored. Every athlete is different, and athlete-specific training intensities should be used. Absolute HR, or the percentage of maximum HR, is likely the most convenient and appropriate measure to use to prescribe continuous aerobic exercise intensities. Resistance training is effective in improving aerobic performance, and should be maintained through the general preparatory, specific preparatory, and competitive phases of training.

MAXING OUT

1 A track coach comes to you and wants to determine the distances for continuous training sessions for 800 meter runners. If you were to base those distances on the length of the race, how long should the continuous runs be?

2 A high school cross-country coach is trying to determine the duration, recovery time, and number of intervals for her high school athletes. What are the different ways presented in the chapter for determining this information? Which one would be the most appropriate for the coach's situation?

3 A recreational 5 km runner is having trouble with her warm-ups. She complains of feeling sluggish and has been having hamstring trouble during her runs. Her warm-ups currently consist of stretching for five minutes and then beginning her run, gradually increasing her pace over the first mile. List some things that can be modified in her warm-up to improve its effectiveness.

CASE EXAMPLE

Designing continuous, interval, and repetition training programs for a recreational cyclist

Background

You are employed as a personal trainer and hired by a recreational cyclist who wants to compete in a 20 mile race in 16 weeks. This individual has been cycling for three years recreationally and can easily complete the 20 miles; however, she would like to improve her speed and does not know how to go about doing so. Apply the guidelines presented in this chapter to design a 16-week-long workout program, training three times per week, to improve her performance in a 20 mile race.

Recommendations/considerations

We have 16 weeks. Starting backward from the competition, the four weeks prior (which we'll designate weeks one through four, week one being the week of competition) will be our competition phase and will consist of the most intense workouts (intervals and repetitions, some continuous work). Weeks five through eight will be a peaking phase and will see the gradual integration of high-intensity workouts (continuous work and intervals). Weeks 9 through 16 will be our preparation phase and will primarily consist of low- and medium-intensity workouts, mostly continuous work.

Implementation

Preparation phase

Our athlete will train three times per week: Tuesday, Thursday, and Saturday. Bowing to reality, the longest ride of the week will occur on Saturday (i.e., Saturdays will be the peak). On Tuesdays there will be a shorter ride at approximately 60% effort. On Thursdays there will be a moderate ride at 60% to 70% effort. On week 16 (i.e., the first week of training), the longest training session will be performed at the race distance (i.e., 20 miles); Tuesday's workout will be conducted at 50% of Saturday's distance (i.e., 10 miles); Thursday's workout will be conducted at 75% of Saturday's distance (i.e., 15 miles). Volume will be increased for the following weeks: 15, 14, 12, 11, and 10. Volume will be increased by 5% in each of these weeks. Weeks 13 and 9 will serve as recovery weeks; volume for these weeks will be equal to that for weeks 15 and 11. This means that by week 10, the distances for each day will be

Tuesday: 12.1 miles
Thursday: 18.15 miles
Saturday: 24.2 miles

Peaking phase

Our athlete will continue training three times per week. Beginning with this phase, Thursday will become the peak and will consist of interval training. Saturday will remain the longest day, with Tuesday as a recovery ride. Saturday's distances will never increase over 24.2 miles. Interval training will be designed initially to improve our athlete's ability to recover from lactic acid. As she is not an elite athlete, intensity will be 75%. Intervals will last three minutes. Since we are targeting recovery, she will achieve close to full recovery between intervals (i.e., two minutes of slow riding between each interval).

Week 8 will see long-ride volumes equal to that of week 12; this step back is being taken because of the addition of the intervals. In week eight, our athlete will perform only four intervals. The number of intervals, like the distance of the other rides, will increase over weeks seven and five, with week five being a recovery week. With this in mind, week six (the most difficult week) will look like this:

Tuesday: 12.1 miles
Thursday: six three-minute intervals (with two-minute recovery rides)
Saturday: 24.2 miles

Competition phase

With this phase, repetitions will be used on Tuesday's workout, Thursday will remain interval training, and Saturday will remain a continuous training session. Repetitions will consist of 90 seconds of near-maximal activity, followed by 450 seconds of recovery riding (i.e., 1:5 work: rest ratio). Intervals will now focus on training her to tolerate large levels of lactic acid; they will remain three minutes in length but recovery will be cut in half to one minute. Continuous training will continue to be capped at 24.2 miles.

Week four will see continuous training distances equivalent to those of week seven and the performance of only four intervals on Thursday's workout. This step back is being taken because of the addition of repetitions on Tuesday. Tuesday's workout will consist of four

(continued)

(continued)

repetitions during week four. Weeks 3 and 2 will see an increase in the number of repetitions, intervals, and continuous training distance (to 24.2 miles). Week one will be a recovery week, with the race being at the end of that week.

Week two (the most difficult week) will look like this:
Tuesday: six 90-second repetitions (450-second recovery rides)
Thursday: six three-minute intervals (one-minute recovery ride)
Saturday: 24.2 miles

REFERENCES

1. **Larsen HB.** Kenyan dominance in distance running. *Comparative Biochemistry and Physiology Part A: Molecular & Integrative Physiology* 2003; 136(1):161–170.

2. **Beattie K, Kenny IC, Lyons M, Carson BP.** The effect of strength training on performance in endurance athletes. *Sports Med* 2014; 44(6):845–865.

3. **Bassett DR, Howley ET.** Limiting factors for maximum oxygen uptake and determinants of endurance performance. *Med Sci Sports Exerc* 2000; 32(1):70–84.

4. **Ekblom B, Astrand P-O, Saltin B, Stenberg J, Wallström B.** Effect of training on circulatory response to exercise. *J Appl Physiol* 1968; 24(4):518–528.

5. **Pluim BM, Zwinderman AH, van der Laarse A, van der Wall EE.** The athlete's heart. *Circulation* 2000; 101(3):336–344.

6. **Sawka MN, Convertino VA, Eichner ER, Schnieder SM, Young AJ.** Blood volume: importance and adaptations to exercise training, environmental stresses and trauma sickness. *Med Sci Sports Exerc* 2000; 32:332–348.

7. **Dubouchaud H, Butterfield GE, Wolfel EE, Bergman BC, Brooks GA.** Endurance training, expression, and physiology of LDH, MCT1, and MCT4 in human skeletal muscle. *Am J Physiol Endocrinol Metab* 2000; 278(4):E571–E579.

8. **Foster C, Lucia A.** Running economy. *Sports Med* 2007; 37(4–5):316–319.

9. **Sunde A, Støren Ø, Bjerkaas M, Larsen MH, Hoff J, Helgerud J.** Maximal strength training improves cycling economy in competitive cyclists. *J Strength Cond Res* 2010; 24(8):2157–65.

10. **Jones A, Grassi B, Christensen P, Krustrup P, Bangsbo J, Poole D.** Slow component of VO_2 kinetics: mechanistic bases and practical applications. *Med Sci Sports Exerc* 2011; 43(11):2046–2062.

11. **Black MI, Jones AM, Blackwell JR, Bailey SJ, Wylie LJ, McDonagh ST, et al.** Muscle metabolic and neuromuscular determinants of fatigue during cycling in different exercise intensity domains. *J Appl Physiol* 2017; 122(3): 446–459.

12. **Poole DC, Burnley M, Vanhatalo A, Rossiter HB, Jones AM.** Critical power: an important fatigue threshold in exercise physiology. *Med Sci Sports Exerc* 2016; 48(11):2320–2334.

13. **Broxterman R, Ade C, Craig J, Wilcox S, Schlup S, Barstow T.** The relationship between critical speed and the respiratory compensation point: coincidence or equivalence? *Eur J Sport Sci* 2015; 15(7):631–639.

14. **Broxterman R, Ade C, Barker T, Barstow T.** Influence of pedal cadence on the respiratory compensation point and its relation to critical power. *Respiratory Physiology & Neurobiology* 2015; 208:1–7.

15. **Stellingwerff T.** Case study: nutrition and training periodization in three elite marathon runners. *Int J Sport Nutr Exe* 2012; 22(5):392–400.

16. **Esteve-Lanao J, San Juan AF, Earnest CP, Foster C, Lucia A.** How do endurance runners actually train? Relationship with competition performance. *Med Sci Sports Exerc* 2005; 37(3):496–504.

17. **Laursen PB, Jenkins DG.** The scientific basis for high-intensity interval training. *Sports Med* 2002; 32(1):53–73.

18. **Hedrick A.** Soccer-specific conditioning. *Strength Cond* 1999; 21(2):17.

19. **Jeukendrup A, Diemen AV.** Heart rate monitoring during training and competition in cyclists. *J Sports Sci* 1998; 16(sup1):91–99.

20. **Moyen NE, Ellis CL, Ciccone AB, Thurston TS, Cochrane KC, Brown LE, et al.** Increasing relative humidity impacts low-intensity exercise in the heat. *Aviation, Space, and Environmental Medicine* 2014; 85(2):112–119.

21. Henriksson J. Training induced adaptation of skeletal muscle and metabolism during submaximal exercise. *The Journal of Physiology* 1977; 270(3):661–675.

22. Wolpern AE, Burgos DJ, Janot JM, Dalleck LC. Is a threshold-based model a superior method to the relative percent concept for establishing individual exercise intensity? A randomized controlled trial. *BMC Sports Science, Medicine and Rehabilitation* 2015; 7(1):16.

23. Rodríguez-Marroyo JA, Villa JG, García-López J, Foster C. Relationship between the talk test and ventilatory thresholds in well-trained cyclists. *J Strength Cond Res* 2013; 27(7):1942–1949.

24. Halson SL, Bridge MW, Meeusen R, Busschaert B, Gleeson M, Jones DA, et al. Time course of performance changes and fatigue markers during intensified training in trained cyclists. *J Appl Physiol* 2002; 93(3):947–956.

25. Coyle EF, Martin W, Bloomfield SA, Lowry O, Holloszy J. Effects of detraining on responses to submaximal exercise. *J Appl Physiol* 1985; 59(3):853–859.

26. Boone J, Vaeyens R, Steyaert A, Bossche LV, Bourgois J. Physical fitness of elite Belgian soccer players by player position. *J Strength Cond Res* 2012; 26(8):2051–2057.

27. Roberts JA, Alspaugh JW. Specificity of training effects resulting from programs of treadmill running and bicycle ergometer riding. *Med Sci Sports* 1972; 4(1):6–10.

28. Rønnestad BR, Mujika I. Optimizing strength training for running and cycling endurance performance: A review. *Scand J Med Sci Sports* 2014; 24(4):603–612.

29. Askling C, Karlsson J, Thorstensson A. Hamstring injury occurrence in elite soccer players after preseason strength training with eccentric overload. *Scand J Med Sci Sports* 2003; 13(4):244–50.

30. Dufek JS. Exercise Variability: A Prescription for Overuse Injury Prevention. *ACSM's Health & Fitness Journal* 2002; 6(4):18–23.

31. Tjelta LI. A longitudinal case study of the training of the 2012 European 1500 m track champion. *Int J Appl Sports Sci* 2013; 25:11–8.

32. Castagna C, Impellizzeri FM, Chaouachi A, Bordon C, Manzi V. Effect of training intensity distribution on aerobic fitness variables in elite soccer players: a case study. *J Strength Cond Res* 2011; 25(1):66–71.

33. Fiskerstrand Å, Seiler K. Training and performance characteristics among Norwegian international rowers 1970–2001. *Scand J Med Sci Sports* 2004; 14(5):303–310.

34. Seiler KS, Kjerland GØ. Quantifying training intensity distribution in elite endurance athletes: is there evidence for an "optimal" distribution? *Scand J Med Sci Sports* 2006; 16(1):49–56.

35. Buchheit M. Monitoring training status with HR measures: do all roads lead to Rome? *Frontiers in Physiology* 2014; 5:73.

36. Karsten B, Stevens L, Colpus M, Larumbe-Zabala E, Naclerio F. The effects of sport-specific maximal strength and conditioning training on critical velocity, anaerobic running distance, and 5-km race performance. *Int J Sports Physiol Perform* 2016; 11(1):80–85.

37. Mohr M, Draganidis D, Chatzinikolaou A, Barbero-Álvarez JC, Castagna C, Douroudos I, et al. Muscle damage, inflammatory, immune and performance responses to three football games in 1 week in competitive male players. *Eur J Appl Physiol* 2016; 116(1):179–193.

38. Johnston RD, Gabbett TJ, Jenkins DG, Hulin BT. Influence of physical qualities on post-match fatigue in rugby league players. *J Sci Med Sport* 2015; 18(2):209–213.

39. Bosquet L, Montpetit J, Arvisais D, Mujika I. Effects of tapering on performance: a meta-analysis. *Med Sci Sports Exerc* 2007; 39(8):1358–1365.

40. Morton RH. Detection of a lactate threshold during incremental exercise? *J Appl Physiol* 1989; 67(2):885–888.

41. Deruelle F, Nourry C, Mucci P, Bart F, Grosbois J, Lensel G, et al. Optimal exercise intensity in trained elderly men and women. *Int J Sports Med* 2007; 28(07):612–616.

42. Neder JA, Stein R. A simplified strategy for the estimation of the exercise ventilatory thresholds. *Med Sci Sports Exerc* 2006; 38(5):1007–1013.

43. Ramos-Campo DJ, Rubio-Arias JA, Ávila-Gandía V, Marín-Pagán C, Luque A, Alcaraz PE. Heart rate variability to assess ventilatory thresholds in professional basketball players. *JSHS* 2016. doi:10.1016/j.jshs.2016.01.002.

44. Algrøy EA, Hetlelid KJ, Seiler S, Pedersen JIS. Quantifying training intensity distribution in a group of Norwegian professional soccer players. *Int J Sports Physiol Perform* 2011; 6(1):70–81.

45. Seiler S, Haugen O, Kuffel E. Autonomic recovery after exercise in trained athletes: intensity and duration effects. *Med Sci Sports Exerc* 2007; 39(8):1366–1373.

46. Lucía A, Hoyos J, Chicharro JL. Preferred pedalling cadence in professional cycling. *Med Sci Sports Exerc* 2001; 33(8):1361–1366.

Contents

CHAPTER 16

RESISTANCE TRAINING PRESCRIPTION

Michael C. Zourdos, Andy V. Khamoui, and Lee E. Brown

OBJECTIVES

After completing this chapter, you will be able to:

- Determine the critical variables related to resistance training prescription.
- Utilize a needs analysis to build a resistance training prescription.
- Understand how to manipulate the acute training variables for differing adaptations.
- Understand how a resistance training prescription fits within the structure of a periodized macrocycle.
- Appropriately progress critical variables at an individualized rate.

KEY TERMS

Assistance exercises	Frequency	Progressive overload
Autoregulation	Individualization	Repetition maximum
Closed kinetic chain exercise	Load (i.e., intensity)	(RM)
	Multi-joint exercises	Rest intervals
Exercise choice/ order	Open kinetic chain exercise	Single-joint exercises
		Volume

INTRODUCTION

Many factors must be considered when creating resistance training prescriptions including training variables such as volume, intensity, and frequency. The adaptations associated with each variable must be understood by the strength and conditioning professional to implement a successful prescription. Moreover, the individual needs of an athlete are paramount in determining the specifics of number of repetitions, sets, and training intensity. Importantly, data is available which demonstrates how to determine an athlete's needs and reveals systematic strategies to create a training prescription for long-term success of the athlete by manipulating these training variables.

Key tenets: progressive overload and specificity

Prior to discussing the intricate workings and configurations of exercise prescription it is essential to understand the basic principles of which all programs are based. These principles are **progressive overload** and specificity.

Progressive overload

Progressive overload is consistent and gradual increase of stress (i.e., volume or load) over time with resistance training (10). Consequently, skeletal muscle needs continual overload otherwise long-term adaptations will stall. Progressive overload can be achieved by: (i) increasing the load, or (ii) increasing total training volume (training volume = sets × repetitions × weight lifted) (47). Moreover, since training volume is the product of three variables, there are various ways in which volume can be increased. However, it must also be stated that caution should be used when achieving progressive overload, in that increasing load or volume should not occur at a magnitude which is unsustainable. Greater specifics will be discussed

later; however, as a rule, weekly progressions should stay with +2–5% of the previous training week's prescription, and rate of progression will slow over time (i.e., a beginner will progress at a faster rate than an experienced trainee).

Specificity stipulates that training adaptations occur specific to the muscle actions involved (37), speed of movement (9445), range of motion (46), muscle groups trained (55), energy systems involved (32,56), and intensity and volume of training (23,44,57). In other words, an athlete's body will adapt in a specific manner to how training is performed. Thus, to improve a specific skill, an athlete would practice that skill. One of the bases of resistance training exercise selection is specificity of the exercise to the performance task (i.e., weighted vertical jumps for a volleyball athlete). Ultimately, to determine exercise selection, a 'needs analysis' of the athlete must first be conducted to determine the most appropriate resistance training strategy to best prepare this athlete for competition.

Box 16.1 sets out some basic training principles, and Box 16.2 discusses how balancing overload, specificity, and variation may best be achieved.

Box 16.1   Basic training principles

Nearly every successful training program includes a combination of the following three basic training principles: **overload**, **variation**, and **specificity**. The overload provides the challenge required for physiological adaptation. However, by definition, this creates some damage or otherwise overwhelming stress, increasing injury risk. Variation helps reduce this danger by dispersing the stress. It also enhances the robust nature of the adaptation, increasing the likelihood that the new physical abilities are expressible in multiple avenues. Specificity maximizes the transferability of the improved performance to the direct, intended target. Variation and specificity appear contradictory on the surface, yet a closer examination of their proper implementation reveals their true complimentary nature.

Box 16.2   Balancing overload, specificity, and variation

Balancing overload, specificity, and variation is best achieved when coaches thoroughly understand the answers to a few basic questions before writing the program:

1   What are the physical demands of the sport?
2   What are the metabolic demands of the sport?
3   What are the biomechanical demands of the sport?
4   What are the common overuse injuries associated with the sport?
5   What performance variables (e.g., power, strength, etc.) are limiting the athlete's success in the sport?
6   What is the athlete's training history?
7   What is the athlete's injury history?

NEEDS ANALYSIS

Once the key tenants of progressive overload and specificity are understood, the practitioner next must perform a needs analysis of the individual in question when designing a resistance training prescription. Chapter 12 discusses a needs analysis for the resistance trained athlete. This ensures that the key tenants are being met; however, it will also increase the likelihood of overall adherence to training and minimizing unnecessary training.

When designing a needs analysis, questions can be posed in two categories: (i) sport needs and (ii) athlete availability to most effectively determine the needs analysis.

> Performing a needs analysis assists the strength and conditioning professional in designing a specific and individualized resistance exercise program.

GENERAL PRESCRIPTION

Once a needs analysis is determined of the specific sport and athlete the practitioner can begin to implement the general prescription of the program. For resistance training the components of this general prescription are: modality (i.e., free weight- vs. machine-based training), exercise selection, exercise order, and contraction type (i.e., eccentric vs. concentric). Therefore, this section will examine the variants of general exercise prescription and explain how to program those variants based upon the pre-determined needs analysis.

Exercise selection

For an athlete, the overarching aim of exercise selection is implementing exercises which will transfer to sport-specific performance; thus, chosen exercises should coincide with the aforementioned principles of specificity. Three classifications which should be considered when selecting a specific exercise are: (i) single- or multi-joint, (ii) large or small muscle group, or (iii) open or closed kinetic chain. **Single-joint exercises** stress one joint (or muscle group). For example, the biceps curl stresses elbow flexion (biceps muscle group). While skill required to complete a single-joint exercise is minimal and injury risk is low (1),

the sport-specific transfer and overall muscle recruitment is lower in single vs. multi-joint exercises. Contrastingly, **multi-joint exercises** stress two or more joints (or muscle groups). For example, the back squat stresses hip and knee extension, which includes gluteus, hamstrings, and quadriceps muscle groups. These exercises require more complex neural activation and coordination; thus multi-joint exercises are likely more effective than single-joint for enhancing muscle strength and power (1).

Indeed, when multi-joint exercises are included in resistance training prescription there is a transfer of the increased strength to sprint performance (59). Therefore, both multi- and single-joint exercises can be utilized; however, coaches should consider that greater musculature is recruited with multi-joint exercises and there is greater transfer to sport-specific performance; yet single-joint exercises should still be utilized to target weak muscle groups in individual athletes. Thus, a practitioner should consider the results of the needs analysis to implement exercises for individual athlete weak points.

> Multi-joint exercises that stress large muscle groups invoke a greater metabolic and hormonal stimulus than single-joint exercises that stress small muscle groups.

Free weights and machines

Once a decision regarding single- or multi-joint and specific exercise selection has been made, coaches and athletes must decide if these exercises should be performed with free weights (barbells and dumbbells) or weight machines (plate loaded or weight stack). Weight machines (e.g., leg extensions, leg curls, pull downs) are largely safe because of the minimal skill required to utilize this modality (10,58). However, free weights often require a movement pattern, which is more performance task-specific; thus free weights are more likely to improve sport performance than weight machines (10). Ultimately, like single-joint exercises, free weights can be used to target a weak muscle group. Additionally, while beginners should utilize multi-joint exercises (i.e., squats, bench presses, and deadlifts) with very low loads to practice a movement pattern and elicit neural adaptations, machine-based training can also be utilized to achieve progressive overload in the early stages of training. Importantly, the use of free weights in novices is important to build skill and appropriate motor patterns early on as free weights will become the predominant modality as an athlete becomes more experienced (10).

Modalities of resistance training

When using free weights, barbells and dumbbells will be the primary modes of resistance training. In addition to large multi-joint exercises (i.e., back squat and deadlift) recruiting greater musculature than eccentric exercise, it is often noted that another benefit is the enhanced acute hormone response (i.e., greater acute testosterone and growth hormone) with multi-joint exercises; however, it is now known that this acute response is not particularly important (60). Furthermore, an additional consideration with free weights is to choose an **open kinetic chain** or **closed kinetic chain** exercise. An open kinetic chain exercise necessitates that the distal end of the moving segment is not in contact with the ground or a fixed surface (i.e., biceps curl or bench press). Conversely, the distal end of the moving segment is indeed in contact with a fixed surface (i.e., back squat). Often closed kinetic chain exercises coincide with being multi-joint exercises such as the back squat; thus large musculature is recruited, whereas in an open chain movement there is lower muscle activation of an antagonist muscle group (4,5).

Furthermore, it is necessary to consider the agonist–antagonize relationship when prescribing training. Essentially, if an antagonist becomes too strong compared to the agonist such that an imbalance occurs, the risk of injury increases in the antagonist muscle. For example, if bench presses are regularly performed, yet there is minimal to no back training (i.e., rowing movements), then the back musculature will be more susceptible to injury. Essentially, upper-body pulling motions should be utilized to balance out upper-body pushing motions. Specifically, a row can be used to balance out a bench press (horizontal motions) and a pull-up could be utilized to balance out an overhead press (vertical motions).

In accordance with specificity, triple extension exercises (i.e., extension of the hip, knee, and ankle) can be utilized to coincide with the principle of specificity in preparation for sports in which triple extension is utilized (i.e., explosive running and jumping).

It must be noted that alternative forms to barbells and dumbbells of free weight resistance training do exist. These alternative forms include: medicine balls, plyometrics, elastic tubing, and body-weight exercises. While these variants are not the overall base of a resistance training prescription, they can be performed at a high velocity since little resistance is utilized, thus increasing specificity within explosive sports. Therefore, these explosive modalities should be used in more experienced athletes once a strong base of training has been established.

> All major muscle groups should be trained during a resistance exercise program to avoid muscular imbalances.

Exercise order

After training modalities are established the order in which resistance training exercises are performed must be determined. The **exercise order** (the sequencing of specific exercises within a session) significantly affects force production, fatigue rate, and muscle recruitment patterns during a session (6–8). Consequently, training volume (sets × repetitions × weight lifted) or intensity may be compromised on exercise performed later in a training session due to fatigue accumulation; thus progress on those exercises over the long term is attenuated due to the lower volume (9). Therefore, to maximize progress, the most important exercises, usually the multi-joint exercises, should be performed first in a session due to their abilities to recruit a high amount of musculature and transfer to sport-specific performance. Moreover, when choosing order within multi-joint exercises which require spinal loading preference should be given to those which do not increase fatigue (e.g., back squat before leg press). It is also important to consider that full-body training might not take place every session (i.e., a split-type training program might be used); however, when training all major muscle groups in one session, here is a point-by-point guide to determining exercise order (10):

- Perform large muscle group before small muscle group exercises
- Perform multi- before single-joint exercises
- Rotate upper and lower body exercises (i.e., upper first on Monday, lower first on Wednesday, upper first on Friday, etc.)
- Utilize 'power' or explosive barbell exercises which require triple extension first, i.e., power cleans before back squats (11).
- Rotate between pushing and pulling upper body exercises

Overall example
- Power clean
- Back squat
- Dumbbell bench press
- Barbell row
- Barbell curl

Muscle action

Most resistance exercises include concentric (CON) and eccentric (ECC) muscle actions. CON means that the muscle shortens as it produces force; ECC indicates that the muscle lengthens as it produces force. For example, during the arm curl exercise the biceps perform a CON action as the weight is lifted and an ECC action as the weight is lowered. Although ECC actions result in more delayed onset muscle soreness due to greater muscle damage (35,36) than CON actions, improvements in dynamic muscular strength are greatest when ECC actions are included in the repetition movement (as opposed to CON-only movements) (37). Considering that exercises typically used within resistance training exercise prescriptions include CON and ECC muscle actions, that excluding ECC movements reduces gains in strength, and that there is not much potential for variation in this acute program variable, it is recommended that CON and ECC muscle actions are included in all resistance training programs. Additionally, most exercises begin with the eccentric portion of the lift (i.e., squats and bench presses),

so the benefit of the stretch reflex aids the concentric portion. However, a few exercises (i.e., deadlifts) begin with the ECC. Thus, if doing multiple repetitions on the deadlift and minimal time occurs (< four seconds) between repetitions, an athlete may find the second repetition to be easier than the first repetition. Therefore, it is recommended to take at least four seconds between repetitions on a deadlift to allow the benefit of the stretch reflex to dissipate, so that each repetition is a true deadlift.

> Resistance training exercises should include CON and ECC muscle actions.

Repetition velocity

Force is equal to mass times acceleration; therefore, performing an exercise slowly reduces the associated muscular forces. Data has indicated that force production is significantly lower for an intentionally slow velocity (five seconds CON; five seconds ECC) compared to a voluntary velocity (38). Furthermore, over the course of ten weeks, the use of a very slow velocity (ten seconds CON; five seconds ECC) compared to a slow velocity (two seconds CON; four seconds ECC) led to significantly less strength gains (39). Furthermore, moderate and fast velocities have been shown to be more effective for increasing the number of repetitions performed, work and power output, and volume (40–42) and for increasing the rate of performance gains (41). Therefore, intentionally slow concentric velocities are not recommended.

It is important to note that unintentionally slow velocities will occur as there are strong and very strong inverse correlations between barbell velocity and percentage of 1RM (61) in that as percentage of 1RM increases velocity decreases. However, this is a natural consequence of a heavier load and should not be confused with intentionally slow movement velocity.

> Athletes should intend to perform exercises with a fast lifting velocity, as intentionally slow velocities diminish gains.

ACUTE TRAINING VARIABLES

A fundamental component of resistance training prescription is prescribing the acute training variables (volume, intensity, frequency, and rest intervals). These components are highly dependent upon time of year (in-season vs. off-season) where an athlete is within a periodized macrocycle. Periodization will be discussed later; however, we will establish the basics of the acute training variables in the present section.

Training volume

Total training **volume** can be defined as: volume = sets (number) × repetitions (number) x weight lifted. For example, if three sets of eight repetitions were performed at 100 kg, the equation would be as follows: volume = 3 × 8 × 100 kg, which would result in 2400 kg. However, absolute volume is often misleading when examining different athletes due to different strength levels. Thus, relative volume can be calculated in this case using percentage of one-repetition maximum (1RM) in place of load. In the previous example, if 100 kg represents 70% of 1RM, the relative volume equation would be: relative volume = 3 × 8 × .70, which would equal 16.8. Thus, alteration of any of the three components will alter total or relative training volume. While determination of how much volume to prescribe will come later, for now it is important to understand that training volume will be dependent upon time of year (more training volume in the off-season vs. in-season) and training status (greater training volume in experienced vs. inexperienced). Moreover, training volume influences neural (24), metabolic (3025,26), and hormonal (15–17,27–31) and enhances the magnitude of muscle damage; thus the appropriate amount of volume should be prescribed to achieve adaptations, yet not be so excessive as to prevent recovery in time for the next training session. Table 16.1 shows an example of weekly training volumes with varying frequencies.

> Increased metabolic and hormonal responses are associated with high training volume.

Exercise intensity

Intensity can be defined as the absolute load being lifted, the percentage of 1RM being utilized, or the amount of stress at the end of a set which can be determined by rating of perceived exertion (RPE) (61). Importantly, intensity will be somewhat dependent upon volume, in that with more volume, typically a lighter absolute load is utilized (12). Specifically, there is an inverse relationship between the load and the maximal number of repetitions performed in that as the load increases the number of repetitions that can be performed decreases (14). In terms of intensity as a percentage of 1RM often a repetition prescription will be made utilizing percentage-based training.

For example, four sets of six at 75% of 1RM (expressed as: 4 × 6 @ 75%). Another way to prescribe repetitions could be with RM zones such as four sets at 10–12RM where a specific load would be estimated by the athlete and/or coach that would lead to muscular failure between 10 and 12 repetitions. In this example of muscular failure, the athlete can also determine intensity by the resistance training-specific – one to ten repetitions in reserve (RIR)-based RPE scale (Table 16.2), in which an RPE value corresponds to a number of RIR (61). Specifically, if failure

TABLE 16.1 Demonstration of weekly training volumes with varying frequencies

	Monday	Wednesday	Friday	Total volume
Example A	10 × 10 @100 kg	No training	No training	10,000 kg
Example B	4 × 10 @ 100 kg	5 × 8 @ 110 kg	6 × 4 @ 120 kg	11,280 kg

This table demonstrates that excessive volume in one day may result in diminished training frequency due to inability to recovery vs. lower daily training volume, which facilitates better recovery and thus more frequency and volume over time.

TABLE 16.2 Resistance training-specific rating of perceived exertion scale

Rating	Description of perceived exertion
10	Maximum effort
9.5	No further repetitions but could increase load
9	1 repetition remaining
8.5	1–2 repetitions remaining
8	2 repetitions remaining
7.5	2–3 repetitions remaining
7	3 repetitions remaining
5–6	4–6 repetitions remaining
3–4	Light effort
1–2	Little to no effort

Adapted from (61)

is reached that means the set was completed, maximum effort was achieved, and no additional repetitions could be performed, which would be an RPE of 10 (zero RIR). However, stopping one repetition short of failure would correspond to a 9RPE (one RIR) and an 8RPE would be an RIR of two.

The RIR-based RPE scale is a practical way for coaches and athletes to assess the intensity of a specific set, and as discussed later to individualize progression and daily loading. It also must be noted that altering training load affects hormonal (3,15–18), neural (19,20), and metabolic (21,22) responses and adaptations to resistance training. Further, the amount of repetitions which can be performed at a specific intensity is individualized, which makes the RIR-based RPE scale especially useful to keep intensity similar when coaching in a team setting yet allowing for different percentages of 1RM; nonetheless, Table 16.3 provides general guidelines for repetitions allowed at specific intensities of 1RM.

If using percentage of 1RM to prescribe training load, it is paramount that an accurate 1RM is established. Thus, below is a protocol and feedback tools which can be used to accurately determine a 1RM.

Frequency and session structure

Training **frequency** can be used to note the total number of sessions within a week (i.e.,

TABLE 16.3 Relationship between percentage of 1RM, repetitions performed, and RIR-based RPE

RPE	Repetitions performed							
	1	2	3	4	5	6	7	8
10	100%	95%	91%	87%	85%	83%	81%	79%
9.5	97%	83%	89%	86%	84%	82%	80%	77.5%
9	95%	91%	87%	85%	83%	81%	79%	76%
8.5	93%	89%	86%	84%	82%	80%	77.5%	74.5%
8	91%	87%	85%	83%	81%	79%	76%	73%
7.5	89%	86%	84%	82%	80%	77.5%	74.5%	71.5%
7	87%	85%	83%	81%	79%	76%	73%	70%

1RM = one-repetition maximum
RPE = rating of perceived exertion
RIR = repetitions in reserve

Adapted from (62).

three total sessions) or the total number of times within a week a specific exercise or muscle group was trained. For the latter, an example would be that total training days were six (Monday–Saturday); however, back squats were performed three times a week (i.e., Monday, Wednesday, and Friday) and bench presses were performed three times a week (i.e., Tuesday, Thursday, and Saturday). Frequency will be dependent upon training status and of course the initial needs analysis; for example, if an athlete is well-trained and the sport requires a significant hypertrophy and power then training blocks of higher volume may be needed; thus, increased frequency. Consequently, training volume will also dictate frequency; if required volume is high then a frequency of two to three times per week per muscle group will be needed to achieve higher volumes. Indeed, a recent meta-analysis suggests two to three times per week on a muscle group is superior to once a week for adaptations (63), and this is in part due to the ability to perform greater total volume across more weekly sessions.

It is also imperative to understand how total volume or contraction type affects muscle damage and subsequent recovery. Greater training volume in one session will incur more myofiber damage, thus causing increased recovery time. Furthermore, a focus on eccentric contractions will also enhance the damage response (64) and elongate recovery. Therefore, when high session volume or an eccentric focus is implemented, more than 48 hours of recovery is warranted, whereas 48 hours may be sufficient following more standard training sessions. Moreover, untrained athletes or beginners may require more recovery than trained lifters. Consequently, introductory cycles should be structured for beginners which are aimed to protect against excessive muscle damage or elicit the repeated bout effect (RBE), in that repeated training of the same exercise or muscle group will attenuate the muscle damage response (65). Once the RBE has occurred to a magnitude which produces low muscle damage to training like the initial bout, then frequency can be increased, which will in turn cause greater training volume. The periodization section includes details regarding setting up training cycles. For now

it is important to remember the basic guidelines of a frequency per muscle group of two to three times per week and to manage the muscle damage/fatigue and recovery balance so as to not induce too much fatigue in one day such that it prevents recovery for the next scheduled training session.

Training frequency in the competitive season

In brief, greater general preparation (i.e., hypertrophy and base strength) is built in the off-season for an athlete. Building base hypertrophy and strength will require greater levels of training volume as volume is closely associated with both hypertrophy (66) and strength (67); however, in-season an athlete is aiming to maintain strength and power output. Therefore, training volume will be lower in-season as increased training volume in-season may decrease power output due to excessive volume. Ultimately, in-season there is a greater increase on skill practice (i.e., specificity), and high training volume may be unsustainable due to the demands of on-field practice and game/match play.

Rest intervals

Rest intervals, the time between sets, can significantly influence acute and chronic responses to resistance training. For years, it was recommended that short rest intervals (i.e., 30–90 seconds) be used to maximize muscle growth due to increased lactate (32), which facilitates a greater acute growth hormone release than longer rest intervals (15–17). However, it is now known that acute anabolic hormone elevation is not a causative factor in long-term skeletal muscle growth (60). Rather, total training volume is the variable which is most closely associated with muscle growth; thus rest intervals which are too short may be detrimental to hypertrophy as performance on subsequent sets may be diminished (13). Indeed, over four weeks, short (30–40 seconds) rest intervals attenuated strength increases compared to long (2–3 minutes) rest intervals (33,34). Thus, to maximize strength and training volume it is recommended that rest intervals that are at least two minutes are optimal for strength gains; however, if an individual athlete needs greater recovery to ensure successful completion of a subsequent set, that is also recommended. Thus, rest intervals from two to five minutes are sufficient.

> Short rest periods are associated with greater metabolic and hormonal responses; however, very short rest periods might attenuate strength gains.

Exercise selection across session-type

Overall, multi-joint compound exercises are superior to single-joint exercises for hypertrophy, strength, and power adaptations. However, single-joint exercises are certainly useful to balance out a weak muscle group, which can be determined in an individual needs analysis or target a muscle group that is especially beneficial in a sport. Moreover, a single-joint exercise may be able to prevent injury (i.e., neck flexion and extension in football).

Ultimately, multi-joint exercises are most effective for increasing overall hypertrophy and strength because they enable a greater amount of weight to be lifted (43), which will in turn lead to greater training volume. Multijoint compound exercises also stress multiple muscle groups within a single exercise and are specific to the movement demands of most sports.

For power training not only are multi-joint exercises recommended, but also total-body and closed kinetic chain exercises (e.g., power clean, deadlift) due to the requirement of rapid force production (107) in sport-specific movement patterns. Importantly, exercises which require a slow deceleration phase are not typically used for power training; thus jump squats would be recommended over regular back squats. Indeed, data examining the bench press indicates that deceleration occurs during 24 to 40% of the concentric movement (48,49), the deceleration phase increases to 52% when performing the lift with a lower percentage (81%) of 1RM (48), and the deceleration phase increases when attempting to move the bar rapidly to train at a high movement velocity (49). This is in contrast to ballistic resistance exercises (explosive movements that enable acceleration throughout the full range of motion) which limit the deceleration associated with traditional resistance exercises (50–52). For instance, loaded jump squats with 30% 1RM loads have been shown to increase vertical jump performance to a greater extent than traditional back squats (52). Therefore, it is recommended that strength and conditioning coaches choose exercises that allow acceleration throughout the range of motion (e.g., power clean, power snatch, jump squats, plyometrics) to maximize transfer to athletic performance during power training phases.

Muscular endurance training exercises stressing multiple or large muscle groups are associated with the greatest acute metabolic responses (2,53,54). This is important because high metabolic demand is a stimulus for adaptations leading to improved local muscular endurance (e.g., increased mitochondrial density and capillary number, fiber type transitions, buffering capacity). Therefore, it is recommended that multiple or large muscle group exercises are emphasized in programs aimed at improving local muscular endurance.

Rest intervals

As previously stated, even though short rest intervals do not allow lactate to clear and elicit large acute hormone responses, it is now known that the acute hormone release is not causative in long-term hypertrophy, rather total training volume is more indicative of hypertrophy. Additionally, longitudinal studies (33,34) have shown greater strength increases with long rest intervals, where at least two to three minutes is recommended for strength on primary exercises (e.g., back squat, bench press, deadlift). Moreover, two to three minutes is also recommended for hypertrophy so as not to sacrifice total training volume. For **assistance exercises** or single joint exercises (e.g., biceps curls, leg curls), one to two minutes of rest might suffice (10). Two to three minutes are also recommended to rest between sets for power training so as to fully recover and not compromise repetition velocity to coincide with the goal of power-type training.

PROGRESSION

How to alter training variables over time will be addressed in this section by discussing the various ways to progress training load from week to week using the exercise prescription based on a periodized model.

Periodization

Periodization strategies are discussed in Chapter 14. Briefly, a year of training can be referred to as a **macrocycle**, which contains **mesocycles** (i.e., four to six weeks, commonly referred to as 'training blocks'), and **microcycles** which are usually one to two weeks of training. Within a periodized macrocycle volume will decrease over time and intensity will increase as competitions approach. Thus, there will be greater hypertrophy-type or high-volume training in the off-season and the beginning of macrocycle while strength- and power-type training will occur as volume decreases later in the macrocycle.

Progression

Even though information has been presented on how to lay out a training program, progression has not yet been examined. In general, **progression** is the act of moving forward toward a specific goal (10), more specifically in the resistance training context, it is the ability to progress training load over time or from week to week. Importantly, even though human physiology is similar across individuals, the individual rate of adaptation to resistance training is different as there are high, low, and moderate responders to training (68). There are three main ways to progress weekly training load that will be discussed: (i) arbitrary progression, (ii) autoregulatory progressive resistance exercise (APRE), and (iii) autoregulation based upon RPE. Each of these progression strategies has positives and negatives, and there is not necessarily a right or wrong strategy, rather progression strategy determination should occur based upon the needs analysis.

Arbitrary progression

An arbitrary weekly progression is simply adding load from one week to the next on the same exercise by a pre-determined amount (i.e., 2.5 or 5 kg.). The drawbacks to this progression model are obvious: (i) an athlete may not be progressing at a rate fast enough to meet the load progression and thus might fail on the following week's training, or (ii) an athlete might progress faster than the rate of progression; thus, the pre-planned training might not provide a great enough stressor to achieve the desired adaptation. However, this model might be beneficial to keep novices from progressing too quickly. Since novices can make progress on minimal volume and load is a component of total volume, progressing at a minimal 2.5 kg per week may be advisable so as to not risk injury by progressing too quickly in novice individuals.

Autoregulatory progressive resistance exercise (APRE)

The APRE progression strategy adds load based on the previous week's performance (69). For example, if in week one of a mesocycle an athlete is prescribed five sets of four repetitions on the back squat with a plus set (plus set means the last set is performed for as many repetitions as possible), then the amount of repetitions on the plus set is used to determine the following week's training load. Specifically, if nine to ten repetitions are performed then a larger increase of +7.5 kg could be taken, while a +5 kg change could be taken for a seven to eight repetition performance, and five to six repetitions would result in a +2.5 kg increase in load. Additionally, it may be advisable to use percentage increases in load across different individuals as a 7.5 kg increase is a 3.75% change for an individual with a starting squat 1RM of 200 kg, yet a 7.5% change for an individual with a 100 kg starting 1RM. A positive aspect of APRE is individualized load progression, which is consistent with the principle that adaptations rates are highly variable among individuals. However, one drawback is that this method is basing progression solely on one set during a given week; thus the athlete may have atypical excitability or performance during that one set leading to a higher than advisable progression for the following week.

Autoregulation based upon RPE

The third and final progression strategy laid out is to progress load based upon the previous week's RPE values. To accomplish this the athlete needs to record an RIR-based RPE (61) following each set or the last set of each main compound lift during the previous week. Then, there is an inverse relationship between RPE and load progression. For example, if the predicted RPE or goal RPE for the previous week was 8 (i.e., 2 RIR) yet the actual average RPE for that day or last set RPE was 5 (i.e., 5 RIR), then a large load increase (i.e., +7.5 kg) could be taken for the following week. However, if actual RPE was 7, a small load increase (i.e., +2.5 kg) could be administered or no change could be made if the predicted or goal RPE of 8 was met. Like APRE, the advantage of progressing with RPE is that this progression is individualized. An advantage of RPE progression vs. APRE is that APRE is basing weekly progression solely on one training session, whereas in an RPE progression model load could be progressed differently on each specific day. The individual day progression might

be especially useful within a daily undulating periodization model (i.e., Monday-hypertrophy training; Wednesday-power training; and Friday-strength training) as some athletes might be better at muscular endurance and thus might have low RPEs on Monday; however, they might have high RPEs on the strength day; thus each day can be progressed accordingly. On the other hand, a drawback of this progression model is that data has indicated that RPE ratings are improved with training status, in that trained individuals record RPE more accurately than untrained (61). Additionally, experience with the RIR-based RPE scale itself improves the quality of RPE ratings; therefore, a limitation of this model is the individual's ability to accurately gauge how many RIR they have after each set.

SUMMARY

The two main tenants of any resistance training exercise prescription are the principles of specificity and progressive overload. Once a needs analysis is performed, i.e., the specific needs of an athlete are determined, a program can be laid out which implements the appropriate general

TABLE 16.4 Basic implementation guidelines for an exercise prescription

Exercise selection:	Multi-joint, large muscle mass exercises including power exercises should be emphasized
Exercise order:	(i) power exercises; (ii) multi-joint, large muscle mass exercises; (iii) single-joint, small muscle mass exercises
Loading:	Power exercises: 30–50% 1RM Strength exercises: > 80% 1RM
Volume:	Multiple-sets, one to six repetitions per set
Rest intervals:	Fundamental exercises: two to three minutes Assistance exercises: one to two minutes
Frequency:	Four sessions per week
Workout structure:	Split routine
Muscle actions:	Concentric and eccentric
Repetition velocity:	Power exercises: intent to perform the repetitions as quickly as possible Strength exercises: volitional speed

prescription (i.e., free weights vs. machines), training volume and intensity between hypertrophy-, strength-, and power-type training, and periodizing and progressing these training variables over the course of a macrocycle to peak performance for the competitive season. Practically, to appropriately accomplish these goals it is strongly recommended that the athlete and/or coach methodically track all training variables to ensure accurate data is accumulated. A spreadsheet can be especially effective to track each training session. If data is tracked then coaches and athletes can appropriately implement progression not only throughout a macrocycle, but data can be reviewed in subsequent training years to improve program design/exercise prescription and enhance performance. Table 16.4 sets out some basic implementation guidelines for an exercise prescription, and Boxes 16.3 and 16.4 set out suggested cluster sets and rest intervals, and volume load, respectively.

Box 16.3   Cluster sets and rest intervals

Rest can be described within an exercise (inter-set) as a **rest interval**. The rest interval is the period that energy is being conserved to allow for ATP to be readily available for the next set and for the clearing of other metabolic substrates that can affect performance. Proper rest intervals are vital and determined by the specific training goal. This may explain why more complicated intra-set rest strategies such as cluster sets are effective at conserving maximal strength and velocity over multiple sets. Cluster sets require the athlete to rest for 20–30 seconds between each repetition (36). This could be done two to three times before taking a full rest (two to five minutes) between sets. For example, 5×3 would be executed in the following fashion: 1 rep (30 second rest), 1 rep (30 second rest), 1 rep (30 second rest), two to five minute rest; repeat entire cycle five times. This obviously extends total workout time considerably, but yields impressive results.

Box 16.4   Volume load

Volume load can also be calculated to show an overall amount of work performed by multiplying the volume of training by the load. For example, if John performed the back squat with 102.5 kgs for five sets of five repetitions, then his volume load was 2,562.5 kgs (25 reps x 102.5 kgs). This is a way of tracking and monitoring training on a given day or over a period of weeks, months, or years. This also highlights how volume and relative intensity are inversely related (27,28,34). As the intensity of an exercise goes up, the volume must go down. This is due to the effort demand of heavier load, reducing the energy remaining available to perform more repetitions. Both volume and intensity can remain high if a moderate to heavy load is used for many sets, in combination with proper rest intervals. This strategy has been shown to drive hypertrophy and strength adaptations. However, it should be done sparingly as the high training intensity is demanding, which increases risk of injury or overtraining.

REFERENCES

1. **Ratamess NA, Alvar BA, Evetoch TK, et al.** Progression Models in Resistance Training for Healthy Adults. *Med Sci Sports Exerc* 2009; 41:687–708.

2. **Ballor DL, Becque MD, Katch VL.** Metabolic responses during hydraulic resistance exercise. *Med Sci Sports Exerc* 1987; 19:363–367.

3. **Kraemer WJ, Ratamess NA.** Endocrine responses and adaptations to strength and power training. In: Komi PV, eds. *Strength*

and Power in Sport. Oxford, UK: Blackwell Science, 2003.

4. Wilk KE, Escamilla RF, Fleisig GS, et al. A comparison of tibiofemoral joint forces and electromyographic activity during open and closed kinetic chain exercises. *Am J Sports Med* 1996; 24:518–527.

5. Escamilla RF, Fleisig GS, Zheng N, et al. Biomechanics of the knee during closed kinetic chain and open kinetic chain exercises. *Med Sci Sports Exerc* 1998; 30:556–569.

6. Häkkinen K, Komi PV Alen M. Effect of explosive type strength training on isometric force- and relaxation-time, electromyographic and muscle fibre characteristics of leg extensor muscles. *Acta Physiol Scand* 1985; 125:587–600.

7. Brennecke A, Guimaraes TM, Leone R, et al. Neuromuscular activity during bench press exercise performed with and without the preexhaustion method. *J Strength Cond Res* 2009; 23:1933–1940.

8. Simao R, Farinatti PDTV, Polito MD, et al. Influence of exercise order on the number of repetitions performed and perceived exertion during resistance exercise in women. *J Strength Cond Res* 2007; 21:23–28.

9. Dias I, de Salles BF, Novaes J, et al. Influence of exercise order on maximum strength in untrained young men. *J Sci Med Sport* 13:65–69.

10. Kraemer WJ, Adams K, Cafarelli E, et al. American College of Sports Medicine position stand. Progression models in resistance training for healthy adults. *Med Sci Sports Exerc* 2002; 34:364–380.

11. Kraemer WJ Ratamess NA. Fundamentals of resistance training: progression and exercise prescription. *Med Sci Sports Exerc* 2004; 36:674–688.

12. Sforzo FA Touey PR. Manipulating exercise order affects muscular performance during a resistance exercise training session. *J Strength Cond Res* 1996; 10:20–24.

13. Kraemer WJ. A series of studies: the physiological basis for strength training in American football: fact over philosophy. *J Strength Cond Res* 1997; 11:131–142.

14. Willardson JM, Kattenbraker MS, Khairallah M, et al. Research note: effect of load reductions over consecutive sets on repetition performance. *J Strength Cond Res* 2010; 24:879–884.

15. Kraemer WJ, Fleck SJ, Dziados JE, et al. Changes in hormonal concentrations after different heavy-resistance exercise protocols in women. *J Appl Physiol* 1993; 75:594–604.

16. Kraemer WJ, Gordon SE, Fleck SJ, et al. Endogenous anabolic hormonal and growth factor responses to heavy resistance exercise in males and females. *Int J Sports Med* 1991; 12:228–235.

17. Kraemer WJ, Marchitelli L, Gordon SE, et al. Hormonal and growth factor responses to heavy resistance exercise protocols. *J Appl Physiol* 1990; 69:1442–1450.

18. Raastad T, Bjoro T, Hallen J. Hormonal responses to high- and moderate-intensity strength exercise. *Eur J Appl Physiol* 2000; 82:121–128.

19. Komi PV, Vitasalo JH. Signal characteristics of EMG at different levels of muscle tension. *Acta Physiol Scand* 1976; 96:267–276.

20. Sale DG. Neural adaptations to strength training. In: Komi PV, eds. *Strength and Power in Sport*. Oxford, UK: Blackwell Scientific, 1992.

21. Fleck SJ. Cardiovascular adaptations to resistance training. *Med Sci Sports Exerc* 1988; 20:S146–151.

22. Stone MH, Wilson GD, Blessing D, et al. Cardiovascular responses to short-term olympic style weight-training in young men. *Can J Appl Sport Sci* 1983; 8:134–139.

23. Campos GE, Luecke TJ, Wendeln HK, et al. Muscular adaptations in response to three different resistance-training regimens: specificity of repetition maximum training zones. *Eur J Appl Physiol* 2002; 88:50–60.

24. Häkkinen K, Pakarinen A, Alen M, et al. Relationships between training volume, physical performance capacity, and serum hormone concentrations during prolonged training in elite weight lifters. *Int J Sports Med* 1987; 8 Suppl 1:61–65.

25. Willoughby DS, Chilek DR, Schiller DA, et al. The metabolic effects of three different free weight parallel squatting intensities. *J Hum Mov Stud* 1991; 21:53–67.

26. Benton MJ, Swan PD. Influence of resistance exercise volume on recovery energy expenditure in women. *Eur J Sport Sci* 2009; 9:213–218.

27. Craig BW, Kang H. Growth hormone release following single versus multiple sets of back squats: total work versus power. *J Strength Cond Res* 1994; 8:270–275.

28. Gotshalk LA, Loebel CC, Nindl BC, et al. Hormonal responses of multiset versus single-set heavy-resistance exercise protocols. *Can J Appl Physiol* 1997; 22:244–255.

29. Kraemer WJ. Endocrine responses to resistance exercise. *Med Sci Sports Exerc* 1988; 20:S152–157.

30. **Mulligan SE, Fleck SJ, Gordon SE, et al.** Influence of resistance exercise volume on serum growth hormone and cortisol concentrations in women. *J Strength Cond Res* 1996; 10:256–262.

31. **Vanhelder WP, Radomski MW, Goode RC.** Growth hormone responses during intermittent weight lifting exercise in men. *Eur J Appl Physiol Occup Physiol* 1984; 53:31–34.

32. **Kraemer WJ, Noble BJ, Clark MJ, et al.** Physiologic responses to heavy-resistance exercise with very short rest periods. *Int J Sports Med* 1987; 8:247–252.

33. **Pincivero DM, Lephart SM Karunakara RG.** Effects of rest interval on isokinetic strength and functional performance after short-term high intensity training. *Br J Sports Med* 1997; 31:229–234.

34. **Robinson JM, Stone MH, Johnson RL, et al.** Effects of different weight training exercise/rest intervals on strength, power, and high intensity exercise endurance. *J Strength Cond Res* 1995; 9:216–221.

35. **Vissing K, Overgaard K, Nedergaard A, et al.** Effects of concentric and repeated eccentric exercise on muscle damage and calpain-calpastatin gene expression in human skeletal muscle. *Eur J Appl Physiol* 2008; 103:323–332.

36. **Ebbeling CB Clarkson PM.** Exercise-induced muscle damage and adaptation. *Sports Med* 1989; 7:207–234.

37. **Dudley GA, Tesch PA, Miller BJ, et al.** Importance of eccentric actions in performance adaptations to resistance training. *Aviat Space Environ Med* 1991; 62:543–550.

38. **Keogh JWL, Wilson GJ Weatherby RP.** A cross-sectional comparison of different resistance training techniques in the bench press. *J Strength Cond Res* 1999; 13:247–258.

39. **Keeler LK, Finkelstein LH, Miller W, et al.** Early-phase adaptations of traditional-speed vs. superslow resistance training on strength and aerobic capacity in sedentary individuals. *J Strength Cond Res* 2001; 15:309–314.

40. **Lachance PF Hortobagyi T.** Influence of cadence on muscular performance during push-up and pull-up exercises. *J Strength Cond Res* 1994; 8:76–79.

41. **Morrissey MC, Harman EA, Frykman PN, et al.** Early phase differential effects of slow and fast barbell squat training. *Am J Sports Med* 1998; 26:221–230.

42. **Hay JG, Andrews JG, Vaughan CL.** Effects of lifting rate on elbow torques exerted during arm curl exercises. *Med Sci Sports Exerc* 1983; 15:63–71.

43. **Stone MH, Plisk SS, Stone ME, et al.** Athletic performance development: v-1 set vs. multiple sets, training velocity and training variation. *NSCA J* 1998; 20:22–31.

44. **Schlumberger A, Stec J, Schmidtbleicher D.** Single- vs. multiple-set strength training in women. *J Strength Cond Res* 2001; 15:284–289.

45. **Kanehisa H, Miyashita M.** Specificity of velocity in strength training. *Eur J Appl Physiol Occup Physiol* 1983; 52:104–106.

46. **Knapik JJ, Mawdsley RH, Ramos MU.** Angular specificity and test mode speificity of isometric and isokinetic strength training. *J Orthop Sports Phys Ther* 1983; 5:58–65.

47. **Fleck SJ, Kraemer WJ.** *Designing Resistance Training Programs.* Champaign, IL: Human Kinetics, 1997.

48. **Elliott BC, Wilson GJ, Kerr GK.** A biomechanical analysis of the sticking region in the bench press. *Med Sci Sports Exerc* 1989; 21:450–462.

49. **Newton RU, Kraemer WJ, Häkkinen K, et al.** Kinematics, kinetics, and muscle activation during explosive upper body movements. *J Appl Biomech* 1996; 12:31–43.

50. **Newton RU, Kraemer WJ.** Developing explosive muscular power: implications for a mixed methods training strategy. *Strength Cond* 1994; 16:20–31.

51. **Newton RU, Kraemer WJ, Häkkinen K.** Effects of ballistic training on preseason preparation of elite volleyball players. *Med Sci Sports Exerc* 1999; 31:323–330.

52. **Wilson GJ, Newton RU, Murphy AJ, et al.** The optimal training load for the development of dynamic athletic performance. *Med Sci Sports Exerc* 1993; 25:1279–1286.

53. **Scala D, McMillan J, Blessing D, et al.** Metabolic cost of a preparatory phase of training in weight lifting: a practical observation. *J Appl Sport Sci Res* 1987; 1:48–52.

54. **Tesch PA.** Short- and long-term histochemical and biochemical adaptations in muscle. In: Komi PV, eds. *Strength and Power in Sport.* Boston, MA: Blackwell Scientific Publications, 1992.

55. **Kraemer WJ, Nindl BC, Ratamess NA, et al.** Changes in muscle hypertrophy in women with periodized resistance training. *Med Sci Sports Exerc* 2004; 36:697–708.

56. Schuenke MD, Mikat RP, McBride JM. Effect of an acute period of resistance exercise on excess post-exercise oxygen consumption: implications for body mass management. *Eur J Appl Physiol* 2002; 86:411–417.

57. Rhea MR, Alvar BA, Ball SD, et al. Three sets of weight training superior to 1 set with equal intensity for eliciting strength. *J Strength Cond Res* 2002; 16:525–529.

58. Foran B. Advantages and disadvantages of isokinetics, variable resistance and free weights. *NSCA J* 1985; 7:24–25.

59. Seitz LB, Reyes A, Tran TT, de Villarreal ES, Haff GG. Increases in lower-body strength transfer positively to sprint performance: a systematic review with meta-analysis. *Sports Medicine* 2014 Dec 1; 44(12):1693–1702.

60. Mitchell CJ, Churchward-Venne TA, Bellamy L, Parise G, Baker SK, Phillips SM. Muscular and systemic correlates of resistance training-induced muscle hypertrophy. *PloS One.* 2013 Oct 9; 8(10):e78636.

61. Zourdos MC, Klemp A, Dolan C, Quiles JM, Schau KA, Jo E, Helms E, Esgro B, Duncan S, Merino SG, Blanco R. Novel Resistance Training–Specific Rating of Perceived Exertion Scale Measuring Repetitions in Reserve. *J Strength Cond Res* 2016 Jan 1; 30(1):267–275.

62. Helms ER, Cronin J, Storey A, Zourdos MC. Application of the repetitions in reserve-based rating of perceived exertion scale for resistance training. *Strength Cond* 2016 Aug; 38(4):42–49.

63. Schoenfeld BJ, Ogborn D, Krieger JW. Effects of resistance training frequency on measures of muscle hypertrophy: a systematic review and meta-analysis. *Sports Medicine* 2016 Nov 1; 46(11):1689–1697.

64. Nosaka K, Newton M. Concentric or eccentric training effect on eccentric exercise-induced muscle damage. *Med Sci Sports Exerc* 2002 Jan 1; 34(1):63–69.

65. Zourdos MC, Henning PC, Jo E, Khamoui AV, Lee SR, Park YM, Naimo M, Panton LB, Nosaka K, Kim JS. Repeated bout effect in muscle-specific exercise variations. *J Strength Cond Res* 2015 Aug 1; 29(8):2270–2276.

66. Flann KL, LaStayo PC, McClain DA, Hazel M, Lindstedt SL. Muscle damage and muscle remodeling: no pain, no gain? *J Exp Biol* 2011 Feb 15; 214(4):674–679.

67. Zourdos MC, Jo E, Khamoui AV, Lee SR, Park BS, Ormsbee MJ, Panton LB, Contreras RJ, Kim JS. Modified daily undulating periodization model produces greater performance than a traditional configuration in powerlifters. *J Strength Cond Res* 2016 Mar 1; 30(3):784–791.

68. Petrella JK, Kim JS, Mayhew DL, Cross JM, Bamman MM. Potent myofiber hypertrophy during resistance training in humans is associated with satellite cell-mediated myonuclear addition: a cluster analysis. *J Appl Physiol* 2008 Jun 1; 104(6):1736–1742.

69. Mann JB, Thyfault JP, Ivey PA, Sayers SP. The effect of autoregulatory progressive resistance exercise vs. linear periodization on strength improvement in college athletes. *J Strength Cond Res* 2010 Jul 1; 24(7):1718–1723.

Contents

CHAPTER 17

PLYOMETRIC, SPEED, AGILITY, AND QUICKNESS EXERCISE PRESCRIPTION

Casey M. Watkins, Saldiam R. Barillas, Megan A. Wong, and Lee E. Brown

OBJECTIVES

After completing this chapter, you will be able to:

- Understand exercise prescription for speed, quickness, agility, and plyometrics.
- Understand and appreciate both mechanical and neuromuscular aspects of training for speed, quickness, agility, and plyometrics.
- Be able to integrate the components of a sprint training program with the phases of linear sprinting.
- Be able to prescribe different progressions and variations of speed, quickness, agility, and plyometric exercises.

KEY TERMS

Acceleration phase
Agility
Assisted sprinting
Attainment phase
Contractile elements
Eccentric overload
Galloping
Hop
Jump
Leap
Maintenance phase

Mechanical model
Neural feed-forward
　mechanism
Neuromuscular model
Noncontractile elements
Overspeed
Plyometric exercises
Reaction time (RT)
Reciprocal innervation
Resisted sprinting
Shuffling

Skipping
Stretch shortening cycle
　(SSC)
Stride frequency
Stride length
Support phase
Swing phase
Throwing
Toss

INTRODUCTION

In most sports, athletes perform short (5–20 m) or long (20–40 m) sprints, change direction rapidly, or jump for height and/or distance. Therefore, linear acceleration and multidirectional speed, agility, along with vertical, horizontal, and lateral jumping movements are essential elements of successful athletic performance. These locomotor skills are learned at young ages as children participate in unstructured playful activities. Maturation and experience will help refine the movement patterns associated with these skills; however, instruction on the mechanical aspects of locomotion is typically required to improve efficiency, performance, and to limit the likelihood of injury. Once the global and segmental mechanical aspects of a skill have been mastered, training can focus on improving and ultimately maximizing performance. The types of exercises or drills prescribed to an athlete will be based on identified mechanical flaws or muscular weaknesses. To date the manipulation of acute training variables for speed, agility, quickness, and plyometric training is unclear but will certainly depend on their athletic goals' (short and long term) developmental stage, as well as chronological and training age.

To design a training regimen for an athlete, sport performance professionals need to consider aspects from several domains. First, a clear understanding of the sequence of motor development from childhood to adulthood for running, jumping, and changing direction is important. This will help guide the selection of appropriate drills or exercises for inexperienced, mature, and advanced athletes. Second, sports performance professionals should clearly recognize mature movement patterns associated with global and segmental mechanics and understand the specific muscular actions involved. This will help them to identify movement flaws, instruct athletes on appropriate changes, and assist skill improvement during childhood and through adolescence. Finally, understanding how to manipulate acute training program variables (e.g., sets, reps, frequency, volume) will prove to be the most challenging aspect of improving and maximizing performance, since research is scarce regarding sprint, agility, quickness, and plyometric training. Nevertheless, appropriate training principles are applied to ensure sufficient stimulation to improve performance while minimizing excessive overload.

This chapter begins with an overview of the **stretch shortening cycle (SSC)** and briefly describes factors that impact SSC efficiency. Next, the developmental sequence of sprinting, jumping, and changing direction is illustrated, which includes characteristics for mature motor skill performance. Then a brief list of exercises and drills is provided to help develop and improve sprinting, jumping, and agility skills. Finally, general guidelines for program design are recommended.

THE SSC

All explosive movements, whether sprinting, jumping, and/or changing direction, have one major component in common: the SSC. The SSC can be described simply as the coupling of an eccentric action with a concentric action. In other words, when a muscle or muscle group is eccentrically loaded (i.e., stretched) and is immediately followed by a shortening action, then an SSC has occurred. Think of a rubber band's ability to snap back with more force the further it is stretched. Although SSC motions are common in everyday tasks (e.g., walking), their use in athletics is often intended to enhance performance. By rapidly coupling eccentric-concentric actions, the muscular force and power output during the concentric phase are enhanced (1). This, in turn, allows athletes to run faster, jump higher, and change direction quicker.

Although the SSC has been studied in great detail, the mechanisms responsible for

REAL-WORLD APPLICATION

Muscle elasticity

Releasing a rubber band from a stretched position will allow it to snap back into its original shape. Similarly, stored elastic energy will provide additional force when muscle shortening is preceded immediately by a stretch. During the stretch, energy is stored in the muscle, just as it is stored in the stretched rubber band. The stored elastic energy of muscle is one reason plyometric exercises increase power output.

greater power production are still debated (1–5). Two models may contribute to a complex mechanism, which results in enhanced power production during the concentric portion of the SSC. The first is the **mechanical model**, first illustrated by A. V. Hill (6), which describes contractile and non-contractile elements (discussed in Chapter 3). The second is the **neuromuscular model**, which outlines the fine interplay of nervous and muscular systems. **Contractile elements** are contained within the sarcomere of a muscle and consist of actin and myosin. **Noncontractile elements** consist of the series elastic component (SEC), also known as the muscle-tendon unit (5), and the parallel elastic component (PEC), which consists of the connective tissues surrounding individual fibers, muscle bundles, and the entire muscle (i.e., endomysium, perimysium, and epimysium). The mechanical model states that muscle force is increased due to the reutilization of elastic energy by the SEC (5). In other words, when a muscle is eccentrically loaded (i.e., stretched) and immediately followed by a concentric action at high velocities and forces, elastic energy (EE) will be produced, stored (as potential energy), and ultimately released (kinetic energy) from the muscle-tendon unit and increase force and power output. On the other hand, the neuromuscular model suggests that preactivation of a muscle or muscle group is partially responsible for the force and power potentiation during the concentric phase of n SSC (1,3). A comparison of jumps initiated from either a static squat position or by beginning with a countermovement shows that there is a greater amount of time to develop force and muscular activation prior to shortening by the contractile element during the countermovement jump (3). Both the elastic properties and the activation by the central nervous system work together to produce increased force during the concentric portion. In addition, sprinting and agility skills have shown pre-activation of a majority of the leg muscles prior to the support phase (7–9), suggesting that movement speed would be dramatically reduced otherwise. In all likelihood, both models contribute to the enhancement of force and mechanical power output during SSC. In fact, during the early extension phase of a static squat jump, it has been shown that the SEC is stretched only slightly (10). This is most likely due to the large amount of shortening of the contractile element. Just prior to toe-off during a running gait (about 100 milliseconds), there is a reversal in roles where the contractile element does not change in length and the SEC rapidly shortens and releases stored energy (48). Therefore, each model may provide a stimulus during different portions of a given SSC.

Practically speaking, the mechanical model illustrates that non-contractile units store EE alleviating mechanical strain on contractile units producing force, and thus increase energy turnover/efficiency (11). The SEC does not change length but can be stretched rapidly by an eccentric muscle action, stored EE, and will rapidly return back to normal length, releasing EE, normally at the start of a concentric muscle action of high velocity movements (11). Therefore, according to the mechanical model, the force from a maximal concentric muscle action (100% maximal effort) will be able to utilize EE stored by the preceding eccentric muscle action (20% maximal effort) resulting in a net gain in force (120% maximal effort) (11,12).

> The SSC is an important physiological reflex that enhances muscular power output. Both mechanical and neural factors contribute to power potentiation.

> Neural control and reflexes of skeletal muscle are governed by two receptors: muscle spindles and Golgi tendon organ.

> Muscle spindles and GTOs are responsible for the enhancement or inhibition of muscular actions by monitoring the rate of stretch and detecting tension in muscle.

Impacting factors

In performing exercises that involve SSC, there are several factors that can impact the enhancement of force or power output of the movement. Another factor affecting SSC, especially during jumping, is the use of the upper extremities. Swinging the arms while performing a countermovement jump creates more downward vertical ground reaction force; consequently, a greater amount of upward vertical force is generated (Newton's law of action-reaction), propelling the body higher or further during flight (13). Arm swing also contributes to takeoff velocity during vertical and horizontal jumping actions (13,14). Swinging the arms during sprinting increases velocity compared to sprinting without arm actions (9). Choosing whether or not to swing the arms can significantly contribute to the execution of SSC drills and consequently affect athletic performance.

Studies have reported gender differences in SSC ability by using indirect measurements such as countermovement jump height or sprinting ability. Typically, boys and men exhibit greater absolute power than girls or women. In addition, larger increases are observed in maximal power for boys compared to girls during adolescence (15). Greater amounts of lean body tissue (i.e., muscle mass) are believed to be responsible for these differences; however, when normalized for body weight, the differences between boys and girls are often minimized (16,17). Reports have shown higher peak velocity during countermovement jumps for men as compared to women (18,19). In fact, one study concluded that the difference in peak power between men and women was solely due to movement velocity (18). Other factors such as fiber-type composition, anaerobic metabolism, and neuromuscular aspects may also contribute to gender differences (15). Although these differences exist, there is no evidence to suggest that men and women respond to SSC training differently; therefore, program design should reflect developmental stage, training experience, and the particular sport rather than gender.

Sprinting, jumping, and changing direction require complex multi-joint movements, which must have specific coordination between agonists and antagonists to ensure movement efficiency. There are reflexes that stimulate agonists while simultaneously inhibiting antagonists. This is termed **reciprocal innervation** (20,21). Alterations in this relationship can be impacted by increased strength or fatigue (22–24). For example, strengthening agonists will increase acceleration of the movement, while strengthening antagonists will allow deceleration to occur over a shorter time (44). The overall effect would be a heightened capacity to perform explosive SSC actions.

Fatigue, on the other hand, reduces the effectiveness of the SSC through a host of mechanisms. The mechanisms responsible for altered SSC function may be influenced by whether the fatigue was generated during submaximal or maximal exercise (25,26). Therefore, the duration of recovery from previous training sessions may be heavily dependent on the type and intensity of SSC drills performed.

This brief overview of SSC identifies several aspects that must be considered in designing a training regimen or exercise session. First, the use of arm swing is an integral component of locomotion and should be considered in selecting drills or exercises. For example, proper arm actions should always be implemented for younger, inexperienced athletes who are still learning the fundamental locomotor skills. Second, improving overall strength should be regarded as a priority for improving locomotor skills that require SSC. Children will become stronger through growth and development, but they may still benefit from playful activities or body-weight exercises that can increase strength. Athletes can include resistance training to enhance force capacity, depending on training age. Training age can be quantified as fundamental movement quality. Fundamental movement skills development has been shown to ensure safe and effective performance of more complex sports movements (27). Although gender will play a role in the difference of force and power production following puberty, variations between boys and girls at younger ages are minimal. Therefore, children should be taught proper movement mechanics regardless of gender; however, beyond puberty, training regimens should target performance limitations of the individual athlete and may be designed toward particular gender differences. Finally, unless there are specific needs that require an athlete to perform sprints, jumps, or changes in direction in a fatigued state, SSC exercises should be performed early within a training session and appropriate rest given between subsequent training sessions.

> Many factors can contribute to SSC function, such as fiber-type distribution, gender, age, muscle activation patterns, fatigue, and arm actions.

I work with many youth soccer teams (12- to 14-year-olds) and continually find the need to work on fundamental movement skills, such as sprinting and agility. What are appropriate drills and progressions to use with this age group?
—high school strength and conditioning coach

The ability to perform stopping and starting tasks in sports such as soccer is important. Coupling deceleration with reacceleration, however, may be one of the most challenging motor skills to teach younger athletes, since other things like balance, orientation, rhythm, and anticipation will set the foundation for more advanced skills. Nevertheless, an appropriate progression is an important consideration in selecting drills for your athletes.

First, teach your athletes how to accelerate properly. Next, develop their ability to stop or decelerate. Then begin to combine these skills in a linear acceleration, deceleration, and reacceleration sequence. Finally, couple linear stopping with reacceleration in different directions. Each of these steps must start at slow speeds and progress to faster movements, ultimately producing athletes who can start, stop, and restart in a variety of directions at maximal speed. Below are two drills to include in your training plan.

Seated to marching arm swing. Before athletes begin in locomotion they need to find the rhythm with their arm swing. Start with the athletes seated on the ground with either legs straight or bent knees and get their elbows to 90°. Cueing can vary here, but the goal is to have one arm swing forward as the other swings back while maintaining 90° at the elbow. Having the athlete focus on the elbow to move will keep the athlete from chopping the forearm down. Once the athlete has the rhythm seated, have them stand up and perform the same arm swing while marching. Here the athlete should have the opposite knee raised to the arm forward, e.g., left knee should be up if the right elbow is forward.

Linear walk to stride. Instruct the athletes to transition from walking to a jog and then slow back down again over short distances (5–10 yd). Once slower speeds are perfected, have your athletes increase the speed of acceleration. Be sure they use a multiple-step stopping technique when slowing down and avoid using one large step. You can also specify a distance for your athletes to stop within (e.g., 2–4 yd) and thereby heighten the intensity.

Jog-stop-turn-jog. Once your athletes can perform linear stopping and starting drills at higher speeds, you can introduce slight changes in direction by having the athletes move between cones. Initially instruct your athletes to completely stop when they reach a cone, plant their outside foot, simultaneously rotate their torso toward the new direction, and finally resume jogging. You should begin with shallow angles (130–160°) and progressively make them more challenging (90, 60, and 45°). When your athletes can perform changes in direction at slower speeds with minimal flaws, gradually increase the speed.

Be sure to progress slowly; it may take several months or longer to develop appropriate movement skills. Provide ample practice time when athletes are fresh (at the beginning of practice) and continually give feedback.

PLYOMETRICS

Plyometric exercises are specifically designed to utilize the SSC. Many upper- and lower-body exercises exist; it is beyond the scope of this chapter to include an all-inclusive list, but several examples are provided at the end of the chapter. This section provides a discussion on intended uses, the importance of instructions, complex training outcomes, and proper exercise terminology for plyometric training.

Terminology

There are three main movement skills; a few of their derivatives are listed below. First, a **jump** involves a takeoff from one or both feet and a landing on both feet simultaneously. Second, a **leap** (sometimes called a bound) occurs from taking off on one foot and landing on the other. Finally, a **hop** is when the takeoff and landing occur on the same single foot. Other common fundamental skills are the gallop, shuffle, and skip. **Galloping** and **shuffling** are a combination of a step and leap, whereas **skipping** requires combining a step with a hop. It becomes somewhat more difficult to distinguish types of upper-body actions. One distinction that can be used is throwing and tossing. **Throwing** actions

REAL-WORLD APPLICATION

Angular motion and human movement

The human body is designed for angular motion around joints, which causes linear motion of the center of gravity of the body. Think about rowing a boat: the blade of an oar enters the water, the oar itself is relatively inflexible, and there is an oarlock providing a pivot point. This lever system works to provide the propulsion that moves the boat forward. Foot contact during the support phase, muscle activation providing stiffness, and motion around the hip joint all ultimately allow horizontal motion.

REAL-WORLD APPLICATION

Absorption of energy

An egg that has been thrown at you will break when you catch it unless you "give" with it and catch it softly. Similarly, in landing from a jump, or similar movement, the athlete can learn to land softly. Instead of all of the energy dissipating on impact, it is spread out over a larger period. Landing softly decreases the chance of impact-related injuries. The transition from eccentric to concentric muscle action, however, must occur rapidly to utilize the stored elastic energy in the muscle.

will be considered when an overhand movement is used to propel an object, whereas a **toss** occurs when an underhand action is employed. Plyometric exercises also exist for the core. Core exercises can be classified as stability, anterior-posterior flexion and extension, rotation, and lateral flexion and extension.

Developmental sequence

Moving from the ground to the air and back down to the ground can be accomplished by three major movement patterns – jumping, leaping, and hopping. All individuals will develop these skills based on experiences throughout childhood, and some will perfect them later in life due to coaching from more knowledgeable instructors. It is important to understand some of the key movement characteristics as well as to be able to identify the developmental difficulties associated with these motor skills. With that said, it is beyond the scope of this chapter to provide all of the criteria to evaluate the

different stages of all jumping skills; therefore, a brief overview follows for vertical jumping and horizontal leaping. More detailed information can be found in the references (28,29).

Vertical jumping is common to many sports, and its initiation can begin as early as two years of age (29). Many steps are involved in the developmental transition from inefficient jumping actions to proficient movement skills. In younger or inexperienced jumpers, there is only a small preparatory counter-movement action. In addition, full extension of the hips, knees, and ankles does not occur. Often the legs are tucked (knee flexion) under during the flight phase, so the center of mass is not elevated. Another characteristic is that there is difficulty jumping and landing on both feet. A small step can usually be observed when a one-footed takeoff and landing occurs. Arm action is also asymmetrical and is not necessarily coordinated with the body or legs. Mature jumping patterns differ dramatically, and changes will occur quickly. For example, there is an appropriate preparatory counter-movement action of the legs that is followed by a more forceful extension of the hips, knees, and ankles (29). The movement patterns of the legs are now also coordinated with those of the arms, so that there is an increase in ground reaction forces (preparatory countermovement phase) as well as an improvement in peak vertical velocity (extension phase). During the flight phase, the trunk remains upright; and upon landing, there is appropriate flexion of the hips, knees, and ankles to reduce the forces on impact.

Horizontal leaping (or bounding) is another common jumping skill that is similar to running in that there is an air phase when body weight is transferred from one leg to the other. Unlike running, leaping requires a prolonged air phase with greater vertical height and more horizontal distance covered. Early attempts at leaping typically resemble modestly exaggerated running movements. There is an inability to propel the body upward or for greater horizontal distances (29). There is a high degree of conscious effort to perform this movement; therefore, the entire motion is ineffective and often appears stiff. The arms are not used for generating force but rather for maintaining balance. Mature leaping includes forceful extension of the support leg to maximize horizontal and vertical distances, and the arms are now coordinated and assist in force development.

Interestingly, chronological age does not guarantee mature jumping or leaping patterns, as adolescents and adults have been found to display immature or ineffective mechanical characteristics. These can range from preparatory, takeoff, and landing inefficiencies. Therefore, sports performance professionals should not assume that movement skills have been mastered simply due to chronological age. A critical examination of these motor skills is important to identify performance deficiencies. Only when proper takeoff and landing characteristics are evident should a training program focus on improving and maximizing performance.

Intended purpose

Plyometric exercises are used in a variety of settings (e.g., athletic training, strength and conditioning, physical therapy); although no formal classification system has been developed, it is important to understand the purpose and expected outcomes of any plyometric exercises chosen for a training program. For simplicity, the following section describes the instructions used for two very distinct areas of motor development: injury prevention and performance enhancement, both of which are important for any athlete.

Injury prevention

Some approaches to injury prevention have used plyometric exercises in an attempt to improve neuromuscular control, alter biomechanical risk factors, and provide instructions on general proprioceptive and stability development (30–33). This requires specific instructions that typically focus on reducing landing forces to minimize risk potential. These types of instructions can be effective in a short time (e.g., one to three sessions) (34,35), but they must be used regularly, because adaptations appear temporary.

A common mechanism of injury occurs on landing from a jump. This is often due to improper mechanics, where landing forces are not appropriately dissipated because the hips, knees, or ankles are extended and/or rotated. As an example, these mechanical flaws are associated with noncontact injuries to the anterior cruciate ligament (ACL). By instructing athletes to land with greater hip, knee, and ankle flexion, the landing forces can be significantly reduced (32,36). Although programs using these types of instructions have shown success in reducing landing forces and noncontact ACL injury rates, the effect on performance enhancement is extremely questionable, because no attention is given to maximizing concentric movement velocity. Therefore, these types of instructions for plyometric exercises may be reserved for younger athletes who require proprioceptive and motor development or kept within the context of clinical rehabilitation. Healthy or more advanced athletes might also benefit from this type of work if fundamental motor skills are not fully developed; however, if performance improvement is the intended outcome, other instructions may be necessary.

Improving power

Plyometric drills are most often incorporated into a strength and conditioning program with the intention of improving SSC capability, power, and ultimately performance (e.g., vertical jump, linear sprint speed). Because power is related to both force and velocity, the question regarding which is more responsible for power improvements is often asked.

It has been reported that the use of plyometric exercises alone can improve jumping ability (37–40). Peak velocity during the concentric phase, however, appears to be the key component for countermovement jump performance (13,14,41). Research has shown that improvements of 12.7% in takeoff velocity accounted for 71% of the observed improvement in jumping performance (14). In addition, the use of light (30% of 1RM) compared to heavy (80% of 1RM) squat jump loads has been shown to provide greater velocity specificity and improvements in jumping and acceleration (42). Maximizing power production varies across component exercises of jumping. Light (< 30%), Moderate (30–70%), and Heavier (70%) loads relative to 1RM have been shown to maximize power production in the jump squat, squat, and clean, respectively (43). This underscores the importance of instruction for takeoff technique and the ability to take off with maximal velocity. Therefore, landing and jumping mechanics should be viewed as separate motor skills and trained independently.

> Plyometric drills used for injury prevention, rehabilitation, or motor skill development should focus on proper jumping and landing mechanics. Training with the intention to improve performance (maximal takeoff velocity) should be the focus.

The performance of SSC drills in isolation during training is not common, and the combination of resistance training and plyometric exercises is often integrated into training regimens. One classic study demonstrated that the combination of resistance and plyometric training caused greater improvements in vertical jump ability than either training modality alone (44). Other research has provided indirect support for this notion by reporting that neither resistance training nor plyometric exercises alone can provide a stimulus any greater than the other when targeting performance enhancement (40). It therefore appears that one cannot

increase power simply by becoming stronger and that utilizing any increase in strength at appropriate speeds is the key factor for performance enhancement (45).

The implementation of plyometric exercises at appropriate times to maximize performance for a particular competition requires careful program design. The duration for a given mesocycle may be as short as several weeks and as long as several months. Shorter-duration programs (six weeks) do not provide adequate stimulation or enough time for major adaptation to occur in adults (46), but interventions implemented over 8 to 12 weeks can improve vertical jump height and power production (38,47). Youth athletes with an adequate training age of proper fundamental movement skill have seen increased rebound jump height (48), reactive strength index (49), agility and power (50) vertical jump performance (51), and running velocity (52), with plyometric training interventions ranging from 4–12 weeks.

> The combination of resistance and plyometric training provides a significant stimulus for improving performance. The use of high-intensity drills for a minimum of eight weeks seems necessary.

ACUTE TRAINING VARIABLES

The acute training variables – volume, frequency, and intensity – must be planned on a daily basis and are key components of the exercise, which relate strongly to the potential effectiveness of the training program.

Volume

Foot contacts or distance covered are the most common methods for determining plyometric volume. Often volume is prescribed based on classifying the individual as a beginner, intermediate, or advanced athlete (53); however, there is no scientific support for this approach. In fact, studies examining the effects of plyometrics on performance have used between 30 and 200 jumps per day (37,40,44,46,47,54–56). The volume of work should be based on the intent of the session (i.e., performance versus learning), the intensity of the drills (i.e., high versus low), the training age of the athlete (i.e., inexperienced versus advanced), and other variables, such as the sport itself and the particular goals of the training cycle. Volume is inversely related to intensity. Two leg plyometrics are less intense than single-leg plyometrics. If intensity is increased, then volume should be decreased in order to reduce risk of injury. Additionally, if a coach is working with an athlete for the first time who was predominantly sedentary, their capacity to handle high eccentric loads is probably low. These athletes would be given less volume of plyometrics compared to elite athletes of the same age.

Frequency

The number of plyometric training sessions performed weekly will be governed by many factors. In general, one or two sessions during the season and three to four sessions during the off season may be sufficient; however, available evidence suggests that two to three days per week may be optimal for improving performance (37,40,44,46,47,54–56). The frequency of plyometric sessions will be dictated by the need for recovery from other training or practice sessions. It may also be affected by the demands of the sport. For example, volleyball and basketball require a large volume of jumps to be performed on a daily basis. Therefore, it may be unreasonable to include in-season plyometric sessions. If plyometric exercises are implemented with the intent to teach proper motor skill development and the demands are small, then more frequent (four to five days per week) sessions could be prescribed.

Intensity

The intensity of plyometric drills is often qualified with terms such as *high, moderate,* or *low intensity*. Overcoming eccentric muscle force of the hamstring, specifically bicep femoris, have been shown to quantify jumping plyometric intensity (57). A coach may use basic biomechanic and gravity principles to gauge plyometric intensity. For example, an athlete with a heavy body mass will have large landing forces. The same heavy athlete may land with greater hip, knee, and ankle flexion, resulting in lower landing forces than a lighter athlete who lands with less flexion in those joints. Therefore, muscle-tendon stiffness, gravity, and fatigue affect the intensity of plyometric drills. Adding complexity to a drill will alter the intensity. For example, a single-leg hop will be more intense than a two-leg countermovement jump. Unilateral plyometrics increase strain on the working leg due to the nature of one leg dissipating ground reaction forces instead of two. When comparing a leap to a two-leg jump, there is increased strain on the concentric portion of the takeoff leg and on the eccentric portion of the landing leg.

The intensity of the exercises used may impact the outcome in targeting performance enhancement. For example, one study compared depth jump training to countermovement jump training; even though both groups significantly improved jump height, the range of improvement was larger for the individuals performing depth jumps (47). On the other hand, if injury prevention is the primary focus, it will be helpful to implement a variety of less challenging exercises. Much more research is necessary in this area prior to drawing any definitive conclusions regarding an intensity classification system for plyometrics.

LINEAR SPRINTING

Linear sprint speed is a key component for successful athletic performance in most sports. Sprinting is made up primarily of two key elements: **stride length** and **stride frequency** (58). Increasing performance depends on increasing one of these variables, while maintaining the other. Linear sprinting can typically be divided into three distinct phases: **acceleration** (0–20 m), **attainment** (20–35 m), and **maintenance** (above 35 m). These distances will certainly differ between individuals and should be used only as a temporal guide to the various phases. When breaking down the 100 meter race, these terms are commonly used for the phases of the race: initial acceleration (0–20 m), acceleration or extended pick up (20–40 m), maximum velocity (40–70 m) and maintenance/deceleration

TABLE 17.1 Changes during linear sprint running as athletes increase their velocity (Adapted from Kovacs M. *Understanding Speed: The Science Behind The 100 Meter Sprint.* Birmingham, AL: Metis Publishing; 2005)

STRIDE LENGTH short→medium/long and maintain 1.30m→1.47m→2.35m (maximum velocity)	Initially, short strides increase to moderate to longer strides throughout the acceleration stage. Once maximum velocity is reached (50–70 meters), stride length should be maintained (and not increased).
TOTAL STRIDE TIME relatively constant throughout the race range from 0.21 seconds to 0.26 seconds	Total stride time is the combination of ground contact time and flight time (time in air). Total stride time is relatively constant; however, the percentage of time spent during ground contact and flight time is vastly different during the different stages of the race.
GROUND CONTACT TIME long→short→shorter and maintain 0.22 seconds→0.11 seconds→0.09 seconds	The amount of time the foot is in contact with the ground. Ground contact time moves from long ground contacts at the beginning of acceleration (as a mechanism to generate force into the ground) to very short ground contacts as maximum velocity is reached.
FLIGHT TIME short→longer→longest 0.03 seconds→0.08 seconds→0.119 seconds	The time during each stride spent in the air. Flight time is short during the first few strides of acceleration but becomes longer as velocity increases.
SHIN ANGLE TO GROUND Small→medium→medium and maintain	The angle between the anterior shaft of the tibia and the ground starts at a very small angle. As stride length increases and body position changes (more upright) as velocity increases, the shin angle to the ground increases to between 70–85°.
VELOCITY slow→fast→fastest→fast (0 m/s→7 m/s →10 m/s→12 m/s→10 m/s)	Slow at the onset of the race and increases rapidly over the first 20 meters. Velocity increases more gradually for the next 30–40 meters until maximum velocity is reached, between 50–70 meters. Once maximum velocity is reached it can only be maintained for approximately 10–20 meters.
STRIDE FREQUENCY	Slow stride frequency at the beginning of the race increases rapidly as velocity increases.
HEEL HEIGHT FROM THE GROUND	This is directly related to the height of knee lift throughout each stride. At the beginning of acceleration, the heel height and knee height are rather low. As the athlete increases their velocity the heel and knee height increase throughout the acceleration period.

(70–100 m). A forward body lean and exponential increases in both stride length and frequency occur during the initial eight to ten strides. Increased stride frequency contributes primarily during the acceleration phases of sprinting and plateaus around 10–15 meters for novice, and around 25 meters for elite sprinters. Stride length, on the other hand, continues to increase up to 25–30 m for novice, and up to 45 m for elite sprinters. (59). These factors are only beneficial if the athlete can simultaneously maintain or decrease ground contact time. Research has shown starting position trunk angle is around 42°–45° in elite sprinters and decreases to about 5° during maximal velocity (60). Acceleration is useful not only for linear sprinting, but a whole myriad of sports where athletes are required to overcome inertia and need to quickly pick up speed (i.e., football, rugby, basketball). The ability to produce a powerful downward force, gain momentum and quickly generate high velocities is of the utmost importance during the acceleration phase (61).

Untrained sprinters, and adolescents, generally reach maximal velocity around 20–30 m. On the other hand, world-class sprinters can continue to accelerate as much as 50–70 m before reaching maximum velocity, suggesting they are better able to gradually increase their speed, may have better limb coordination strategies, and allowing them to increasingly generate forces (58,60,61). An understanding of the movements involved and specific muscular actions responsible for creating movement will allow sports performance professionals to design drills and develop training regimens that are appropriate for improving linear sprinting performance during all phases (Table 17.1). Bounding and other plyometrics are commonly used to increase speed during acceleration and maximal velocity running phases. Several key sprint mechanics drills are displayed at the end of this chapter.

Reaction time

Reaction time is defined as the time from the stimulus (gun signal, ball, opponent movement, etc.) until the production of force by the athlete. Reaction time has been broken into two separate parts: "premotor" and "motor" time. Premotor time is the time from the stimulus until the first sign of EMG electrical activity in the muscles. Motor time has been defined as the time from the first electrical activity in the muscles until the production of visible force (limb movement) by the muscles (62). To perform the sprint start effectively, the important muscles (gluteals, quadriceps, gastroc-soleus complex) should be activated before any force can be detected against the blocks (63). Reaction time has been recorded to respond quicker in a sprinter's front leg than their back leg (63).

After the gun signal, leg extensor muscles, as the producers of the greatest amount of force, must contribute maximally to the production of optimal force. For improving the starting action, it is advisable to recruit all

extensor muscles in the lower limbs before any force can be detected against the blocks.

For more than 100 years the accepted figures for simple reaction times for college-age individuals has been about 190 ms (0.19 sec) for light stimuli and about 160 ms (0.16 sec) for sound stimuli (64,65). However, the fastest athletes in the world consistently have reaction times less than 0.15 seconds (63,66). In identical events women have been shown to have longer reaction times than men (67). However, reaction time does not correlate well with

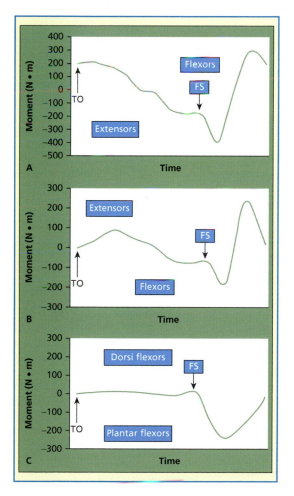

Figure 17.1 Muscle dominance during sprinting around the A. hip, B. knee, and C. ankle. TO = toe off; FS = foot strike. (Adapted from Mann RV. A kinetic analysis of sprinting. *Med Sci Sports Exerc* 1981;13:325–328.)

> **Box 17.1   Sprinting gait (69)**
>
> 1   Early flight: From toe-off to maximal hip extension. Gluteal muscles decelerate backward motion of the thigh eccentrically.
> 2   Midflight: Forward leg swing, the foot is in mid-air and not in contact with the ground. Concentric hip flexion accelerates the thigh forward. Quick transition from eccentric knee extension to eccentric knee flexion.
> 3   Late flight: Eccentric knee flexion to decelerate leg swinging forward, stabilization of knee joint, and concentric hip extension to absorb ground impact forces.
> 4   Early support phase: Continued hip extension minimizes braking forces and ground contact shock absorption, slight knee flexion also preventing knee joint hyperextension.
> 5   Late support: Triple extension and forward body propulsion, backwards thigh deceleration.

sprints lasting longer than a few seconds (63). The fastest reaction times do not influence a race over a long distance, and any distance more than 20 meters is not typically influenced by an individual's reaction time in elite athletes. It is important to understand, in sports that cover shorter distances (i.e., racket sports or field sports), an improved reaction time can make a valuable difference.

Developmental sequence

The main difference between walking and running is the absence of a double support phase and the presence of a flight phase, respectively. The earliest attempts to run occur around 2–3 years of age or approximately 6–7 months after a child learns how to walk (28,29). By observing these movements in young children, one often notes a brief flight phase with a limited range of motion in the legs. This will result in shortened stride length. In addition, the thighs and arms swing away from the body, most likely acting to help stabilize and balance the body during the flight and support phases (28). Their stance is often wider to aid in balance as well. As children mature, they develop movement patterns that are more efficient and powerful. For example, maturity will bring about an increase in muscle mass and strength, which will provide more ground force and increase stride length, which are

strongly related to sprint speed (61,68). Other changes in sprint mechanics include full leg extension, keeping the actions of the extremities in the anterior-posterior plane, and maintaining bent elbows (28). The development of motor skill patterns will impact coordination strategies, energy expenditure, fatigue rates, injury risk, and ultimately linear sprint performance.

Sprinting gait

Sprinting is a complex motor skill for which specific kinetic and kinematic patterns emerge. Box 17.1 shows a basic breakdown of leg actions for sprinting. In addition, Figure 17.1 shows the average moments around the hip, knee, and ankle joints during a complete stride. The following discussion briefly outlines the two phases of a sprint: the **flight phase** and **support phase**. The flight phase can be broken down into early flight, mid-flight, and late-flight, important recovery and ground contact preparation. The support phase can be broken up into early and late support and is composed primarily of eccentric braking (deceleration) and forward propulsion. This overview describes factors associated with movement patterns and forces applied both concentrically and eccentrically. It should provide a context from which to design drills and develop a training program targeted at improving or maximizing sprinting speed in advanced athletes.

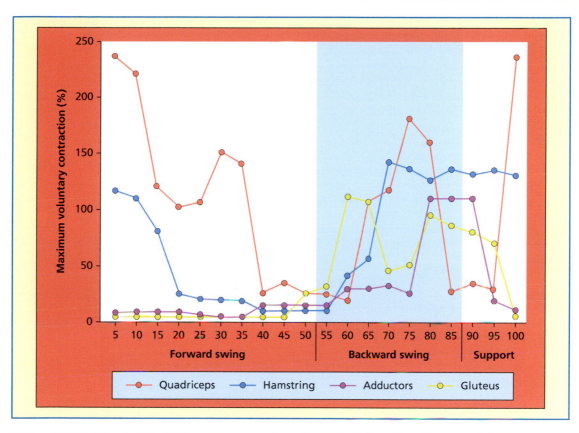

Figure 17.2 Relative muscle activation patterns during a sprint stride. (Adapted from Wiemann K, Tidow GN. Relative activity of hip and knee extensors in sprinting: implications for training. *New Studies Athletics* 1995;10(1):29–49.)

Swing phase

At toe-off, maximum extension (about 185°) of the hip occurs (70), while knee extension is approximately 145° (71). During early flight, both hip flexor and knee extensor muscle activity greatly increases, as they are eccentrically loaded, meaning muscles are forcibly lengthened rather than shortened. This acts to decelerate leg rotation (72) and helps with quick leg recovery (Figure 17.2). The transition from early-flight to mid-flight is the first SSC observed in the sprint cycle. The quick eccentric extension of the hip flexors stores potential energy, which is released during the resulting concentric action and contributes to overall force of the upper leg. The quicker the amortization phase, or time between eccentric and concentric phases, the more potential force there is for the athlete to use during

their forward swing. This is caused by concentric hip flexor action, which actively rotates the upper leg anteriorly (73). Maximum hip flexion occurs two-thirds of the way through the swing phase and corresponds with contralateral toe-off. About this time there is a switch from knee flexion to knee extension. Figure 17.2 shows relatively little muscle activation of the quadriceps during this time in the swing cycle (9), indicating that knee extension is mainly brought about by momentum from hip flexion, which provides a whip-like action of the lower leg during the swing phase. The hamstrings now act eccentrically, halting knee extension, to prevent over-stepping, while simultaneously beginning hip extension during late-flight (74). Practically speaking, greater forward swing forces of the knee contribute to greater downward hip forces and ground contact, acting to propel the athlete forward faster. This is the second SSC observed during the swing phase of the sprinting cycle.

The adductors are active during early flight (just after toe-off) and late flight stabilizing the knee by counterbalancing the external rotation and abduction action of the gluteus group (9) (see Figure 17.2). Tibialis activity begins at toe-off and remains throughout the entire swing phase, whereas gastrocnemius activity is minimal during most of this phase and does not increase until immediately prior to foot contact (75). This pre-activity is thought to help prepare the joint, assisting in decreasing the vertical forces during ground contact as well as creating a more efficient SSC of the gastrocnemius.

Support phase

Once the foot has made contact with the ground, hip extensor muscles (e.g., hamstrings and gluteus) act concentrically (8). The gluteus maximus is continuously active (76), extending the hip but also stabilizing it (see Figure 17.2). The hamstrings are responsible for providing the necessary force to propel the body forward and are the key contributors to linear sprint speed (9). Higher-level sprinters have shown the ability to decrease horizontal braking by creating larger forces and generating more power in the hip extensors and knee flexors during early support (72). This extremely brief sub-phase should be recognized as the most important time of the sprinting cycle, realizing that hip extension is the main action responsible for linear sprint speed. Therefore, to maximize speed, gluteal muscles power generation is critical in the support phase as early as possible.

A transition of muscle action occurs during late support when the hip flexors begin to act eccentrically and decelerate leg rotation (72). It appears the main function of the knee joint during the support phase is to transfer power in a proximal-to-distal direction (i.e., hip to ankle). There is a large amount of knee extensor muscle activity to stabilize the knee, transfer forces from the hip to the ankle, and keep the height of the center of mass constant, preparing the trunk for forward propulsion. Lending support to this notion, one study reported negligible power from the knee during late support (77). Therefore, during the attainment and

maintenance phases of a sprint, the knee extensors should not be considered a muscle group that produces forward propulsion. In fact, if the knee extensors activated maximally during support, it would produce a disproportionate upward force rather than forward propulsion. This would lead to a higher and subsequently longer flight phase (9), in turn reducing linear sprinting performance. The primary role of the muscles surrounding the ankle joint is to assist in maintaining the height of the center of mass at foot contact and to provide some thrust, albeit minimal, of the body in the anterior-posterior plane (74,75).

> Sprinting requires horizontal power production from the hip extensors and knee flexors to propel the body forward during the early portion of the support phase. Maintaining a stable center of gravity occurs through eccentric actions of the gluteus, quadriceps, and gastrocnemius muscle groups.

Acute training variables

The acute training variables are the specific variables that are manipulated to produce intended variation in volume, frequency, and intensity of training. They must be planned accordingly and strongly relate to the potential effectiveness of the training program.

Volume

The volume of linear sprint work will be characterized by the total distance covered during a given training session. It might be beneficial to consider sprint drills (e.g., A-skips, B-skips) and sprint capacity exercises separately, or quantify volume load, characterized by distance multiplied by the intensity of the exercise, either characterized by effort or percentage of their maximum velocity. Sprint drills may be included daily during the warm-up routine with a focus on perfecting mechanical technique, or as dedicated drills during the workout. Regardless, mastery of sprint mechanics is vital before increases in volume or intensity should occur. The volume of work dedicated to improving sprint capacity will be governed by the characteristics of a given sport and possibly by requirements of a specific position. A sprinter will spend the majority of his or her training time dedicated to linear sprinting, whereas a basketball player will divide up his or her program, including other variables including vertical jump ability, lateral agility, and upper body power. Other program variables that contribute to the amount of time dedicated to sprint speed improvements include the metabolic and linear sprint characteristics (i.e., average frequency and distance). A football lineman will spend almost no time, or energy, running distances greater than 10 m, whereas a receiver can sprint up to multiple hundred meters in a game, and will have a different resulting stress. Creating a needs analysis for the athlete based on the linear speed requirements and metabolic demands will help tailor the program specifically. There is a great deal of variability in program design, so definitive guidelines on linear sprint volume are limited. The most important critical variables are adaptability and attentiveness to how the athlete is responding to the program. No program will be optimal for every athlete; individualization is key based on their specific needs.

Frequency

Performing high-intensity sprint training is physically demanding, therefore the number of weekly sessions will depend on recovery from other training and practice sessions. Untrained athletes will need more rest, compared to athletes that are accustomed to the type of training and intensity. Whenever programming high-intensity training, it is advised to incorporate drills slowly and allow the athlete to gradually increase intensity, or volume to prevent injury. It may be sufficient to schedule two to three sessions per week, depending on additional demands placed on the athlete.

Intensity

Training to improve sprint capacity will typically involve maximal efforts; however, submaximal bouts of work can be used with inexperienced athletes to develop technique. It is important to practice good movement patterns slowly until they create a new motor program and the desired movement becomes natural to the athlete. Always emphasize quality repetitions over quantity, or the likelihood of injury will increase especially during states of fatigue. With that in mind, younger athletes should focus on

drills that will enhance mechanics, while more advanced athletes can be prescribed maximal-effort bouts of work, targeting specific linear sprint distances.

Two additional methods shown to increase running velocity are assisted and resisted sprints (78). Both **resisted** and **assisted sprinting** use implements to add additional intensity compared to body weight sprints. These methods should not be prescribed to any athlete who has not mastered linear sprint mechanics. Extreme caution is warranted even for those athletes who have mature movement patterns, since resisted and assisted sprints can have negative consequences which may result in negative movement mechanics and increased injury potential. Assisted and resisted sprinting should be incorporated into an athlete's program at a very low volume and frequency until the athlete understands the increased demands of the exercises and feels comfortable under the new conditions.

Assisted running (e.g., high-speed treadmill exercises, towing, or downhill running) will permit an athlete to run faster than his or her natural pace and is typically prescribed to help increase stride frequency (i.e., improve turnover rate). In congruence, four-week assisted sprinting training (14.7% assistance) have shown significantly increased values for both mean velocity and mean acceleration during the first 25 yards of a 40 yd maximal sprint test in collegiate women's soccer players, compared to resisted and traditional sprint training. The greatest increases in velocity and acceleration with assisted sprinting were seen in the first 5 yd which is especially important for field athletes who are required to make repeated 5 yd and 10 yd cutbacks (78). Another study found similar results looking at the acute effect of rest intervals; assisted sprinting resulted in decreased sprint times compared to body weight sprinting during the first 5 m of a 20 m sprint after two minutes' rest following intervention (79; measurements in metric).

However, when used improperly, running at supramaximal speeds could increase stride length and decrease stride frequency compared with maximal running (80–82). These alterations could potentially cause an increase in the horizontal distance from the foot to the center of mass at ground contact, resulting in greater braking forces during the support phase, greater stabilization stress on the joints, and increasing the likelihood of injury (81). Running too far above an athlete's maximal velocity, an athlete will start to mechanically slow themselves down as a protective mechanism, and training benefits will be negated (71). Therefore, this type of training should be limited to experienced athletes.

Resisted running includes dragging a weighted sled or running uphill, often prescribed to increase stride length during body weight sprinting. Resisted sprinting is thought to increase stride length by increasing the force production of the hip and knee extensors (78). When used correctly, resisted sprinting programs (12.6% body mass) have been shown to increase running velocity and acceleration during the later portion of a 40 yd sprint, with the greatest increases occurring during the 15–25 yd portion of the 40 yd sprint (83). Several mechanical alterations occur with resisted sprints. Improper use of resistance can cause alterations in overall posture even when running up slight grades (3°) or pulling minimal weight (12% of body mass) (82,84). These changes in sprint mechanics may be detrimental to linear speed if too much resistance is added; therefore, caution is warranted in prescribing resisted sprint drills. One error many coaches make is to increase the incline before an athlete is ready (inappropriate training and strength levels) or increase the angle of incline by an extreme level that causes reduced effectiveness and increases chance of injury and/or inappropriate mechanics. Movement mechanics change considerably as the incline is increased disproportionately to skill level. It is advisable to limit inclines to below 6° even with highly developed adult athletes.

AGILITY

Changes in direction occur often during many athletic activities and include deceleration followed immediately by reacceleration of the entire body or individual body segment(s). This ability, termed **agility**, has been described as an efficient, coordinated movement in multiple planes performed at multiple velocities (85,86). However, recent research has started to differentiate between planned and unplanned bouts of agility. Young adds to the traditional definition by acknowledging agility as "a rapid whole-body movement with a change in velocity or direction in response to a stimulus" (87,88). Planned or closed agility drills are when an athlete is instructed prior to the beginning of the test to complete a 5–10–5 test (measurements in metric) by sprinting 5 m to the right, stop changing direction, sprinting 10 m to the left, stop changing direction again and sprinting back through the start. A ballroom dancer performing the mambo or salsa, or a slalom skier are examples of planned agility, where the athlete knows the movement routine prior to the competition. A fighter dodging a punch or kick, a rugby player tackling their opponent, a tennis player hitting a volley are all examples of unplanned agility. Individuals involved in the development and improvement of sport performance, however, often regard agility as a locomotor skill where an athlete simply changes direction by decelerating the body and reaccelerating in a new direction (85,86). However, reactive agility is a much more complex, multi-faceted skill comprised of not only an athlete's physical and motor control abilities, but their cognitive and perceptual abilities as well. Reactive agility is an independent attribute and needs to be practiced in the context specific to competition (85,89). Additional qualities are considered important and contribute to agility performance, including dynamic balance, spatial awareness, rhythm, and visual processing (90). A high degree of complexity is present within this fundamental athletic motor skill.

Quickness

Quickness is often grouped together with speed and plyometrics but is also a facet of agility. All of these skills will involve some carry-over, but should be addressed as individual skills and trained as thus. Quickness is defined as explosive power or maximal power in the shortest amount of time (91). Explosive power is extremely important to most sports, where there is often not enough time to reach maximal strength. Baseball players at the bat, or volleyball players jumping to spike the ball have less than 0.5 seconds to recruit power (60). Plyometrics have been used to increase quickness by increasing firing rate and neural loop synchronization (91).

Developmental sequence

Learning to become agile requires the development of appropriate movement patterns and, more importantly, the ability to integrate locomotor skills efficiently (e.g., running, jumping) with proprioceptive awareness and often decision-making. As children learn to walk fast and run (at 1.5–3 years of age), they make attempts to be elusive and change direction when being chased. Their movement efficiency is often poor, however, and associated with awkward arm motion, overall unbalanced posture, and a general lack of timing and coordination. These are all characteristics described earlier in the section on the developmental sequence of sprinting. Because a variety of aspects are included in the ability to change direction, it is difficult to precisely identify a specific developmental sequence, as found in other locomotor skills.

Nevertheless, at planned intervals, either general or specific drills can be implemented to develop agility appropriately. For instance, children aged 5–8 years should perform a large variety of general movement patterns to develop a foundation of motor skills. This could include arm and leg movements in a stationary position, rhythmic jumps in place, or locomotor drills that incorporate spatial orientation. Learning the temporal characteristics of general movements is extremely beneficial, especially prior to initiating more specific drills or activities. Closed agility drills, where the initiation, execution, and termination of a drill are clearly established, should dominate during this period. Children involved with athletics should be able to perform general drills with minimal flaws prior to advancing to more demanding exercises.

Young athletes will be able to move more quickly as they mature and finish puberty. For reasons of safety and injury prevention, however, any athlete new to agility training should initially perform drills at submaximal speeds. Weaving within a set of linear cones, running a figure-eight pattern, or learning how to integrate several locomotor skills into one exercise are all beneficial for athletes learning kinesthetic awareness of their body, acceleration, deceleration, and change of direction. Drills that include sharp changes in direction performed at high running speeds are unlikely to benefit agility development, especially when mastery has not yet been achieved (92,93). Closed drills should still predominate in this window of time; however, some open drills can be included sparingly to add a reactive component with visual or audio stimuli.

Alterations in body size, structure, and body mass will influence a young athlete's coordination and proprioception. During this stage, take the time to perfect locomotor skills that are already developed, allowing the athlete to become more comfortable with his or her new body (85). Greater difficulty and more challenging drills can certainly be added to the training regimen, but throughout this stage general agility and a variety of movement patterns should still be emphasized as they encourage overall athletic development.

More complexity and specificity are the focus of agility training during later teenage years (post-puberty) and can now be regularly implemented within the training plan (85). The same drill can be made more difficult simply by using different field conditions, decision-making elements, including a partner, or implementing an area or time restriction. These are all acceptable methods to increasingly challenge an athlete's ability to change direction effectively (85). Athletes should perform nearly all of the drills at high speeds, as slower movements have been shown to alter muscle activation patterns (94). However, if muscle mechanics are compromised due to muscle imbalances or technique issues, then these areas should be improved in ancillary movements and exercises, not as part of an agility training session. An example would be an athlete who struggles to change direction effectively and has weak gluteus medius strength; he or she should focus on developing gluteus medius strength in the gym, while still working on agility movements close to (or at) game speed.

Impacting factors

The ability to coordinate a smooth and rapid transition between stopping and starting is a distinct advantage for athletes performing changes in direction. Body awareness, and the ability to keep center of mass over one's base of support helps in quick transitions, and cutting movements, and keeping the body stabilized to prevent injury (95). Inefficient transitions caused by poor deceleration mechanics or an elongated support phase might allow a defender to maintain close proximity, not allowing an offensive player to become open to receive a pass (e.g., football, soccer, lacrosse). Enhanced agility must be developed in concert with many other proprioceptive and kinesthetic skills, such as balance, orientation, reactiveness, rhythm, visual processing, timing, and anticipation (90). With that in mind, several variables will impact how drills and exercises are performed, namely movement velocity, the angle of direction change, and whether a movement is planned (closed skill) or unplanned (open skill).

Effects of movement velocity
Agility drills can be performed at slow or fast running speeds. Slower running speeds are associated with greater ground-contact time during the deceleration phase compared to faster running speeds (300 vs 170 ms, respectively) (93,94,96). As in linear sprinting, pre-activation of knee flexors and extensors occurs immediately prior to ground contact, which serves to prepare the joints for eccentric loading during deceleration. An increase in muscle pre-activation at higher running speeds has led some to suggest that a neural feed-forward mechanism exists to protect the hip and knee joints from the increased eccentric and rotational loads. A **neural feed-forward mechanism** indicates that the protective musculature would pre-activate as a protective mechanism to decrease the chance of injury through neural control. It may also stimulate an increase in SSC ability and enhance the transition from eccentric to concentric muscle actions.

During the support phase, the adductors and gluteus medius are constantly active and are primarily responsible for stabilizing the hip. A highly integrated agonist-antagonist relationship between the quadriceps and hamstrings provides the ability to change direction (94). More specifically, the knee extensors work to decelerate the body upon ground contact, while hip extensor activity predominates during the late support phase. An unequal distribution of strength between these muscles could cause excessive stress on the ligaments, and tendons surrounding the joint, emphasizing the importance of strength symmetries between opposing

muscles (97). Hip extension provides the necessary horizontal propulsion of the body in the new direction. Recall from the section on linear sprinting that hip extension is important during the early portion of the support phase. This apparent difference from linear sprinting should be considered in developing drills or exercises focused on improving agility performance.

Effects of angles
Changes in direction can be considered shallow (less than 45°) or sharp (more than 45°). When athletes are observed in the laboratory and asked to perform sharp changes in direction, there is a large reduction in approaching velocity. Often there is an inability to appropriately execute the drill even with the reduction in approaching velocity (92,93). The fact that these movements are preplanned further highlights the difficulty of performing such maneuvers. It also indicates the need for incorporating drills into training regimens for elite athletes with mature movement skills. Drills that focus on the ability to make drastic changes in movement, requiring a decision-based component while maintaining speed, will provide the necessary stimulus for adaptation and transfer to competition. On the other hand, inexperienced athletes should focus on more rounded patterns performed at slightly slower speeds and avoid demanding drills.

Changes in direction can be performed with an open or a crossover step. During the early stages of development, it might be beneficial to teach young athletes both movement skills. These steps should be performed at slow speeds, with specific attention given to proper mechanics. An analysis of open-step changes in direction shows internal rotation, whereas crossover steps produce external rotation on the knee. These loads can be up to five times greater than in linear running (92). In addition, crossover steps produce varus loads, while open steps show a mixture of varus and valgus loading at the knee (92). Changes in direction using an open step increase the activity of the vastus medialis and gluteus medius (93,98). This acts to (a) create stability around the hip joint during stance and (b) counter the valgus loads associated with this movement. Closely observe your athletes as they perform agility drills to ensure proper mechanics and include resistance training exercises that target the quadriceps and gluteus muscles, which will help stabilize the knee.

Effects of anticipation

Whether a skill is preplanned (closed) or unplanned (open) will also impact movement patterns and joint loads. For example, an offensive soccer player may attempt several preplanned cutting maneuvers to elude a defensive player. On the other hand, the defensive player must continually adjust to the visual stimulus and anticipate the movements of the offensive player, making changes of direction reactive, or unplanned. Both positions will use planned, and unplanned bouts of agility throughout the course of the game to initiate and react to changes of stimulus. The difference between preplanned and unplanned changes in direction has effects on external varus/valgus and internal/external rotational loading (92,98), muscle activation patterns (98), and body preparation (93).

Compared to an unplanned change in direction, a preplanned open step change in direction shows a slight crossover with the step prior to the pivot foot being planted, an earlier rotation of the pivot foot in the new direction, and a greater body lean (93). Flexion/extension loads are similar in planned and unplanned cutting actions, but there is greater knee flexion when movements are unplanned (92). In addition, a reduction in the whole movement angle occurs during an unplanned change of direction (92). These are all protective mechanisms that provide additional time for appropriate muscle activation, proper joint stabilization, and decreased internal joint forces.

Performing an unplanned cutting maneuver increases the valgus and internal rotation loads by 70% and 90%, respectively. Interestingly, muscle activation only increases by 10–20% (92,98). Furthermore, general muscle activation patterns emerge during unplanned changes in direction, indicating nonspecific coordination between anterior/posterior and medial/lateral synergistic muscle pairs (92). On the other hand, preplanned actions produce specific activation patterns of the vastus medialis and biceps femoris to counter the external valgus and internal rotation loads, respectively (92). The inability of the neuromuscular system to initiate the appropriate adjustments

during unplanned changes in direction reduces the efficiency and velocity of the movement. Therefore, to enhance the ability to decelerate, include exercises that increase the eccentric ability of muscles (e.g., resistance training) as well as drills that focus on improving reactive ability (e.g., plyometrics).

> Factors such as velocity of movement, angle of change, or anticipation will impact muscular activation patterns, kinematics, and joint forces. Exercises that develop muscular stability, eccentric muscle strength, and reactive ability should be included for maximal athletic development.

Acute training variables

Limited information exists on how to improve agility; however, training for linear speed will not improve the ability to change direction and vice versa (88,99). In fact, linear sprint speed, power, and agility are independent performance characteristics, where ability in one variable is not associated with the others (100). Programming of these skills should be based on the requirements of the competition. Specificity of training demands attention to each skill individually to see performance increases. This means that agility training should be an integral component of an athlete's training regimen.

Volume

Specific training sessions dedicated to the development or improvement of agility can utilize guidelines similar to those of linear sprint training, where volume is the total distance covered. Volume load (distance x intensity) should still be considered as some intense drills will impart a greater degree of stress on the athlete compared to lesser intense drills and should be accounted for. Inexperienced athletes may require more time to learn proper mechanics and perform general movement patterns. Advanced athletes can perform a greater volume of work. Understanding the relative contribution of changing direction to the sport or position will help to guide the sports performance professional in determining the appropriate volume appropriate for high-level athletes.

There are numerous agility drills; the conditioning specialist is limited only by the imagination when designing these drills. Agility drills should focus on changing direction quickly and using multiple footwork patterns. These drills should also be sport-specific in terms of movement patterns, footwork patterns, distances, work intervals, rest intervals, and intensities. Although it would be impossible to make a comprehensive list of agility drills, sample drills are described in Figures 17.3 to 17.21 in Box 17.2. These drills can be easily changed from one workout to the next for variety.

Frequency

Inexperienced athletes can include agility daily as a part of a warm-up routine. Regular attention to proper mechanics is vital for the development of appropriate movement skills. Program design for advanced athletes will depend on the time of the year, sport specific requirements, and other training demands. The intent or focus of exercises can be adjusted to incorporate them more or less frequently.

Intensity

The intensity of agility drills will depend on factors such as running velocity, preplanned (closed) versus unplanned (open) drills, and sharpness of the angles. Young, inexperienced athletes need to perfect general, preplanned motor patterns before performing sport-specific drills. Body weight resistance exercises and less demanding plyometric drills will also benefit the ability to change direction. As an athlete becomes more advanced, specific movement patterns can be included. The drills can be increasingly reactive and may include a wide variety of angles.

INTEGRATION OF SPEED AND AGILITY DRILLS

Depending on the sport and the time of the training cycle, the focus may be on either speed or agility or possibly both. If the focus is on maximizing forward running speed, three to four training sessions per week may be devoted to speed. Agility training may be performed occasionally for variety. The opposite will be true if the focus is on agility.

Most sports – soccer, for example – require both speed and agility. If speed and agility are both training goals, one to two sessions per week can be devoted to speed, and one to two to agility. Well-conditioned athletes may be able to benefit from combined sessions, using both speed and agility exercises. These exercises should be performed early in a training session so that the athlete is fresh. Performing speed and agility exercises while the athlete is fatigued on a regular basis may not be as effective in improving performance.

Box 17.2   Speed and agility exercises

Plyometric exercises

Countermovement jump

Starting position
The athlete stands with feet shoulder width apart, the body in an upright posture and looking straight ahead (Figure 17.3A).

Movement sequence
Begin with a preparatory countermovement by flexing the hips and knees. Maintain an upright body posture (Figure 17.3B). Once at the bottom position, immediately jump vertically (Figure 17.3C). Land in same spot from where the jump was initiated and flex the hips and knees to reduce landing forces.

Figure 17.3 Countermovement jump. (A) starting position; (B) countermovement; (C) jump.

Variations

Manipulate the depth of the preparatory counter-movement. Keep the hands placed on the hips to eliminate arm swing. Add degrees of rotation so that the athlete will land facing a different direction.

Scissor jump

Starting position

The athlete stands with the feet a shoulder width apart, the body in an upright posture, looking straight ahead. Take a half step forward with the right foot and a half step backward with the left.

Movement sequence

Begin with a preparatory countermovement by flexing the hips and knees. Maintain an upright body posture (Figure 17.4A). Once at the bottom position, immediately jump vertically (Figure 17.4B). While in the air, switch the positions of the legs so that the landing will occur with the left leg forward and the right leg behind. Be sure that the knees remain pointed forward and avoid caving inward (Figure 17.4C).

(continued)

(continued)

(A)

(B)

Variations
Keep the hands placed on the hips to eliminate arm swing. Attempt to perform a double switch of the legs while in the air, so that landing occurs in the same position as the takeoff.

Broad jump

Starting position
The athlete stands with the feet a shoulder width apart, the body in an upright posture, looking straight ahead.

Movement sequence
Begin with a preparatory countermovement by flexing the hips and knees. During the downward movement, the body will lean slightly forward and the arms should be coordinated with a posterior swing (Figure 17.5A). At the bottom of the countermovement, jump horizontally in the anterior direction (Figure 17.5B). Land with an upright body posture and head looking forward. Flex the hips and knees to reduce landing forces and be sure the knees are pointing forward and not caving inward (Figure 17.5C).

(C)

Figure 17.4 Scissor jump. (A) countermovement; (B) jump, with right leg forward; (C) landing, with left leg forward.

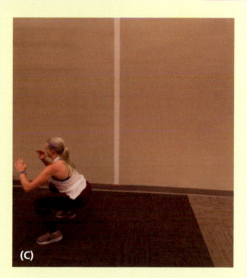

Figure 17.5 Broad jump. (A) countermovement; (B) jump; (C) landing.

Variations
Eliminate arm swing. Take off from two feet and land on one foot.

Linear bounds

Starting position
Although starting from a stationary position is possible, it may be more comfortable by beginning with several lead-in steps.

(continued)

(continued)

(A)

(B)

Figure 17.6 Linear bound. (A) starting position; (B) bound.

Figure 17.7 Lateral cone jump. (A) countermovement; (B) lateral jump; (C) landing.

Movement sequence

This drill can be compared to an exaggerated run. Forcefully drive off the rear leg (Figure 17.6A) with the intent to gain as much vertical height and horizontal distance possible (Figure 17.6B). On landing with the contralateral leg, immediately generate maximal force to propel the body again.

Lateral cone jump

Starting position

The athlete stands with the feet a shoulder width apart, the body in an upright posture, looking straight ahead, with a cone placed directly to the side.

Movement sequence

Begin with a preparatory countermovement by flexing the hips and knees (Figure 17.7A). Maintain an upright body posture. Once at the bottom position, immediately jump, propelling the body vertically as well as laterally (Figure 17.7B). Land on the opposite side of the cone and flex the hips and knees to reduce landing forces (Figure 17.7C).

(continued)

(continued)

Variations
Keep the hands placed on the hips to eliminate arm swing. Add degrees of rotation so as to land facing in a different direction.

Lateral bounds

Starting position
The athlete stands with the feet a shoulder width apart, the body in an upright posture, looking straight ahead.

Movement sequence
Begin with a preparatory countermovement by flexing the hips and knees. Maintain an upright body posture. During the downward phase, begin to shift the body weight to the left leg (Figure 17.8A).

(A)

(B)

Figure 17.8 Lateral bound. (A) countermovement; (B) lateral movement; (C) downward movement; (D) landing.

Once at the bottom position, propel the body laterally with the left leg (Figure 17.8B) and land on the right (Figure 17.8C). Be sure to flex the hips and knees on landing while also keeping the body inside the vertical plane of the knee (Figure 17.8D).

Variation
Add anterior movement to this drill where the athlete will follow a zig-zag or diagonal pattern with each bound.

(continued)

(continued)

Chest throw

Starting position

The athlete stands with the feet a shoulder width apart, holding a medicine ball in the center of the chest.

(A)

(B)

Figure 17.9 Chest throw. (A) countermovement; (B) release.

Movement sequence

Begin with a preparatory countermovement by flexing the hips and knees. Maintain an upright body posture (Figure 17.9A). During the upward phase, begin to simultaneously extend the arms with the legs. As the legs reach peak extension, the medicine ball is released with the intent of obtaining maximal horizontal distance (Figure 17.9B).

Variation

Perform this exercise from your knees or with a partner.

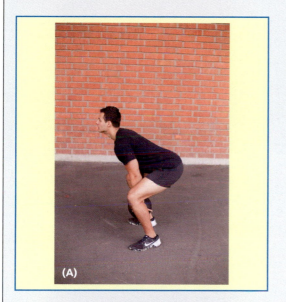

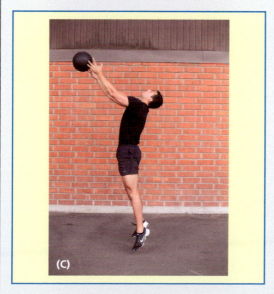

Figure 17.10 Scoop toss. (A) countermovement; (B) upward phase; (C) full leg extension; (D) release.

(continued)

(continued)

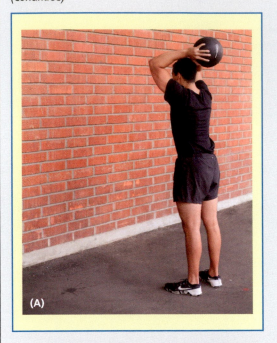

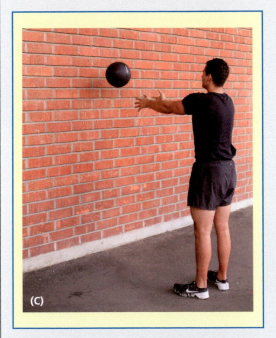

Figure 17.11 Overhead throw. (A) starting position with elbows flexed; (B) extension of elbows; (C) release.

Scoop toss

Starting position
The athlete stands with the feet a shoulder width apart, holding a medicine ball by the hips with the arms fully extended.

Movement sequence
Begin with a preparatory countermovement by flexing the hips and knees. Maintain an upright body posture and extended arm position (Figure 17.10A). During the upward phase, while the legs are extending, begin to flex at the shoulders, keeping the elbows extended (Figure 17.10B). As full leg extension is reached (Figure 17.10C), release the medicine ball with the intent of obtaining maximal vertical height (Figure 17.10D).

Variation
Perform this drill with a partner.

Overhead throw

Starting position
The athlete stands in a staggered stance, with an upright posture, holding a medicine ball directly overhead with the elbows extended.

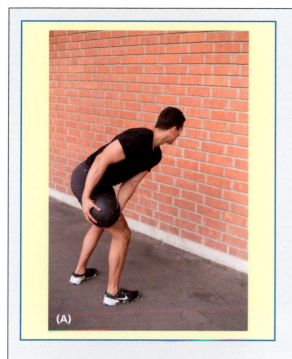

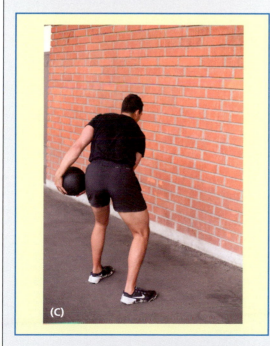

Figure 17.12 Lateral toss. (A) starting position with rotated torso; (B) release; (C) catch.

Movement sequence

Begin with a preparatory flexion of the elbows so that the medicine ball is behind the head (Figure 17.11A). Immediately extend the elbows (Figure 17.11B) and release the ball toward the wall (Figure 17.11C). Attempt to hit the wall so that the ball rebounds directly into your hands with your elbows still extended.

Variation

Perform this drill by maintaining extended elbows, moving only from the shoulder.

Lateral toss

Starting position

The athlete stands with the feet a shoulder width apart and holding a medicine ball by the hips with the arms fully extended.

Movement sequence

The athlete rotates the torso to the left while simultaneously slightly flexing the hips and knees (Figure 17.12A). During the return, the hips and knees are extended and

(continued)

(continued)

Figure 17.13 Two-handed put throw. (A) starting position with rotated torso; two-handed put throw; (B) with full extension and release.

the ball is released toward the wall at a slight angle (Figure 17.12B). As the ball rebounds off the wall, the athlete catches and performs the same action to the opposite side of the body (Figure 17.12C).

Variations
Perform this drill with a partner. Maintain the rotation to the same side of the body.

Two-handed put throw

Starting position
The athlete stands with the feet a shoulder width apart, holding a medicine ball in the center of the chest.

Movement sequence
Begin by rotating the torso to the right (Figure 17.13A) and flexing the hips and knees into a deep squat position. Once at the bottom, immediately extend the hips and knees while simultaneously rotating toward the starting position. The medicine ball will be thrown with the right hand (guide with the left). Fully extend the hips, knees, and right elbow, attempting to maximize the vertical height of the ball (Figure 17.13B). Follow through completely by rotating to the left.

Variation
Perform this drill with a partner.

Figure 17.14 Wood chop throw. (A) starting position; (B) semisquat position; (C) arc movement; (D) release.

(continued)

(continued)

Wood chop throw

Starting position
The athlete stands with the feet a shoulder width apart, holding a medicine ball at the center of the chest (Figure 17.14A).

Movement sequence
Begin by rotating the torso to the right and flexing the hips and knees into a semi-squat position (Figure 17.14B). Move the ball in an arc from knee height to slightly above the head (Figure 17.14C). Rotate the torso toward the start position, throwing the ball toward the ground (Figure 17.14D).

Variation
Attempt to move and position yourself to catch the ball to initiate the next repetition.

Sprint mechanic drills

Quick step

Starting position
This drill begins with the athlete jogging/running in place (Figure 17.15A).

Figure 17.15 Quick step. (A) starting position; (B) step movement.

Movement sequence

Swing the hands rapidly, being sure to initiate the movement from the shoulder joint. The feet should contact the ground with the ball of the foot during every support phase. Shoulders should remain relaxed. Maintain a visual focal point directed straight ahead (Figure 17.15B).

The purpose of this drill is to enable the athlete to establish proper movement patterns (e.g., body alignment, support foot position, arm swing) without the mechanical or metabolic loads associated with high-speed horizontal movement.

Variation

Start at slower movement speeds and increase gradually from a jog into a run and finally a sprint.

B-march

Starting position

The athlete should begin this drill in a "marching" posture facing straight ahead (Figure 17.16A).

Movement sequence

Lift the knee (Figure 17.16B) and pull the knee back to the ground. Although the knee is lifted and pulled back, it must be understood that the motion originates and is designed to accentuate the action about the hip. Keep the lower leg relaxed (do not kick; the lower leg will naturally have a whip-like motion when relaxed). Contact the ground with the ball of the foot and concentrate on "pulling" the body horizontally. Maintain visual focal point directed straight ahead. Keep shoulders relaxed. Proper arm swing should be maintained throughout.

The purpose of this drill is to create the appropriate muscle activation patterns during late swing through mid-support.

Figure 17.16 B-march. (A) starting position; (B) knee extension.

(continued)

(continued)

Variation

Start with a marching action and advance into skipping and finally skipping with a transition to a short sprint.

Stride cycles

Starting position

The athlete begins this drill by jogging or running forward (Figure 17.17A).

Movement sequence

Jog or run on the balls of the feet over a predetermined distance (e.g., 20–30 yd) (Figure 17.17B). At a prescribed number of steps, perform a complete sprint cycle with one leg. Complete this repetition at a higher speed, contacting the ground on the ball of the foot and again "pulling" the body horizontally with hip extension (Figure 17.17C). Allow the athlete to transition into maximum effort linear sprinting by integrating single-leg full sprint cycles (swing and support phase) at pre-scribed intervals. All cycles should be performed near or at maximum speed.

Variation

Start with a high number of jogging/running steps (five to seven) between cycles, gradually reducing this (to one to three), and finally coupling into a double cycle (both the left and the right foot complete a cycle without jogging/running steps in between).

(A)

(B)

Figure 17.17 Stride cycle. (A) starting position; (B) jogging movement; stride cycle; (C) hip extension.

Five-point agility run

Starting position

The athlete should start in an athletic "ready" position facing the direction of the first sprint.

Movement sequence

Start at position X and run to position 1 as quickly as possible, returning to position X. Continue running to positions two to five, always returning to position X after each one (Figure 17.18). The purpose of this drill is to improve agility by requiring quick stops, quick starts, rapid accelerations, and changes of direction.

Focus on an explosive start and accelerate to maximum speed as rapidly as possible, keeping the center of gravity low to stop quickly, and keeping the center of gravity on the back edge of the base of support.

Variation

This drill can be performed with various movements including sprinting, shuffling, and backpedaling. It can also be performed both clockwise and counterclockwise, and the distance of each sprint can be varied.

T-drill for combining lateral and forward/backward movement

Starting position

The athlete should start in an athletic "ready" position facing the direction of the first sprint.

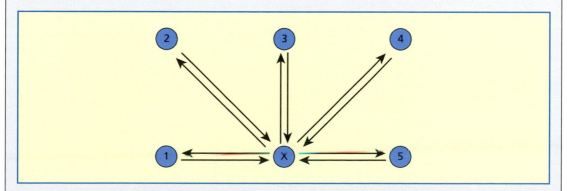

Figure 17.18 Five-point agility run.

(continued)

(continued)

Movement sequence

Start at cone 1 and sprint to the left side of cone 2. Move around cone 2 and shuffle to the right to and around cone 3. Then shuffle to the left all the way back across to and around cone 4. Then shuffle to the right back to cone 2, then backpedal backward to cone 1 (Figure 17.19). The purpose of the T-drill is to train the athlete to rapidly and effectively transition from forward/backward, forward/lateral, and backward/lateral movement patterns.

The focus of this drill is not only forward/backward/lateral movements but also the ability to transition from one to the other. The center of gravity should be kept low, and on the back edge of the base of support when changing direction.

Variation

The footwork patterns and the distance between cones can be altered.

Five dot drill

Starting position
The athlete should start in an athletic "ready" position facing forward.

Movement sequence
There are various movement patterns for this drill. One common pattern is for the athlete to start with one foot on each of the two nearest dots, approximately 2 ft apart. She then jumps in a hopscotch pattern to the two farthest dots, approximately 3 ft away. The athlete then jumps backward in the same manner to the starting position (Figure 17.20). This movement is repeated as many times as desired.

The athlete should maintain her center of gravity as close as possible to the center dot to facilitate rapid movement and maintaining balance. The athlete should maintain an athletic position during the drill with the center of gravity low. Encourage the athlete to move her feet as rapidly as possible. The purpose of the five-dot drill is to develop the ability to move the feet quickly while

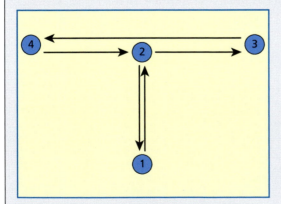

Figure 17.19 T-drill for combining lateral and forward/backward movement.

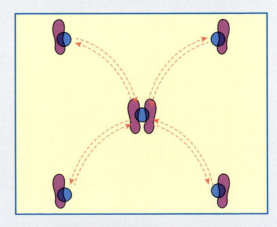

Figure 17.20 Five-dot drill.

maintaining an athletic balanced position, using both single and double leg movements in forward/backward patterns.

Variation

Other movement patterns can be used for this drill, such as jumping with both feet together and jumping to each dot individually. The spacing of the dots can also be increased or decreased. Any variation or combination of movements can be used in one specific drill. The length of time the athlete performs the drill can be modified, or the number of single or double leg foot contacts can be used as an estimate of workload.

Hexagon drill

Starting position

The athlete should start in an athletic "ready" position facing forward in the middle of a hexagon.

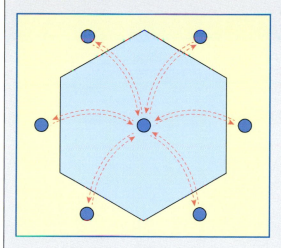

Figure 17.21 Hexagon drill.

Movement sequence

Jump over one side of the hexagon and return back to the middle. Then jump over each of the six sides of the hexagon in order, always returning to the inside of the hexagon following each jump (Figure 17.21). The purpose of the hexagon drill is to develop the ability to move the feet quickly while maintaining an athletic balanced position using both single and double leg movement patterns.

Variation

The pattern can be performed clockwise or counterclockwise. The size of the hexagon can also be varied.

SUMMARY

Explosive movements such as sprinting, jumping, and changing direction are vital to success in nearly all sports. The effective utilization of the SSC (coupling eccentric and concentric muscle actions) to increase power output and ultimately enhance performance is the major purpose of all explosive training techniques, drills, and exercises. Scientific evidence indicates that both mechanical and neural factors regulate SSC ability. In addition, fiber-type distribution, the use of the upper extremities, gender, age, agonist and antagonist strength, and fatigue can either attenuate or augment the SSC. More importantly, program design and drill selection should weigh heavily on the experience of the athlete(s), with a focus on general motor development (agility, balance, and coordination) for younger athletes and greater sport specificity with relative increases in loads and difficulty for advanced athletes. Training programs utilizing plyometric, sprint, and agility drills should address all these factors in a controlled, technique-focused training program to improve performance and limit the likelihood of injury.

MAXING OUT

1   A high school baseball coach asks the new strength and conditioning coach if she will watch his athletes perform their plyometric routine, which includes depth jumps. When they perform the depth jumps, she notices that many of them have poor landing mechanics (e.g., little flexion of the hips and knees, the knees buckling inward). What would be an appropriate suggestion she could make to the coach regarding how the drills should be performed?

2   A varsity track sprinter wants to start lifting weights in an attempt to become faster. He has never been involved in resistance training before. Initially, what muscle groups and what types of exercises would be most beneficial?

3   An elite-level tennis player wants your suggestions for new ways to improve the team's ability to change directions. Which program variables should be the focus of their training and how can they be manipulated to stimulate performance improvements?

CASE EXAMPLE

Designing a plyometric training program for a women's college volleyball player (outside hitter)

Background

You are employed as a strength and conditioning coach at a Division I university. One of your responsibilities is to train the women's volleyball team year-round. The coach has asked specific attention to be given to improving the vertical jump performance of the three outside hitters. They have all played volleyball for more than seven years and have a minimum of three years' experience with resistance training. Their landing and jumping mechanics are sound and they have the three highest 1RM squat scores on the team. Using a needs analysis, identify the jumping characteristics of collegiate women's outside hitters and develop an eight-week plyometric cycle leading into the preseason.

Recommendations/considerations

Begin with a needs analysis of jumping volume for the group of players. Watching several videos from the previous season should provide you with a very reasonable understanding of the types and volumes of jumps performed. You find the maximal number of spikes and blocks performed per game is approximately 34 and 27, respectively. If it is necessary to play four games to determine the outcome of a match, then an outside hitter could expect to perform nearly 250 jumps per match (136 spikes and 108 blocks). A movement analysis indicates that to perform a spike, the athlete must first generate horizontal velocity and transfer it to vertical motion. On the other hand, a block begins from a quasi-static squat position and has only vertical motion.

Implementation

Select exercises that are closely associated with the motor skills. For example, power skips performed for linear distance or maximal height would both provide a suitable stimulus for this group of athletes. Depth jumps could also be used sparingly to develop the ability to decelerate and change directions rapidly, as is found during the spike. Any type of vertical jumping drill would be appropriate to focus on blocking ability. More specifically, the block is started from a quasi-static position; therefore, a drill such as box jumps would fit into the training program. The athletes should be instructed to perform all exercises with maximal takeoff velocity throughout the entire training cycle. An attempt is made to equate the actual volume observed during competition to what is prescribed during training. This should occur over several weeks and only be implemented during select training sessions. Progressive overload and a periodized schedule will allow for proper recovery between training schedules.

Results

Using appropriate progressions for volume and intensity and providing adequate rest should provide the necessary stimulus for improved performance and greater jumping ability. Regular assessment (approximately every two to three weeks) of performance using volleyball-specific vertical jump tests will provide the necessary feedback to monitor your program.

REFERENCES

1. Walshe AD, Wilson GJ, Ettema GJ. Stretch-shorten cycle compared with isometric preload: contributions to enhanced muscular performance. *J Appl Physiol* 1998; 84:97–106.

2. Bobbert MF. Dependence of human squat jump performance on the series elastic compliance of the triceps surae: a simulation study. *J Exp Biol* 2001; 204:533–542.

3. Bobbert MF, Gerristen KG, Litjens MC, et al. Why is countermovement jump height greater than the squat jump height? *Med Sci Sports Exerc* 1996; 28:1402–1412.

4. Ettema GJ. Muscle efficiency: the controversial role of elasticity and mechanical energy conversion in stretch-shortening cycles. *Eur J Appl Physiol* 2001; 85:457–465.

5. Finni T, Ikegawa S, Lepola V, et al. Comparison of force-velocity relationships of vastus lateralis muscle in isokinetic and in stretch-shortening cycle exercises. *Acta Physiol Scand* 2003; 177:483–491.

6. Hill AV. Mechanics of the contractile element of muscle. *Nature.* 1950; 166:415–419.

7. Belli A, Kyröläinen H, Komi PV. Moment and power of lower limb joints in running. *Int J Sports Med* 2002; 23:136–141.

8. Kyröläinen H, Komi PV, Belli A. Changes in muscle activity patterns and kinetics with increasing running speed. *J Strength Cond Res* 1999; 13(4):400–406.

9. Wiemann K, Tidow GN. Relative activity of hip and knee extensors in sprinting: implications for training. *New Studies Athletics* 1995; 10(1):29–49.

10. Kurokawa S, Fukunaga T, Fukashiro S. Behavior of fascicles and tendinous structures of human gastrocnemius during vertical jumping. *J Appl Physiol* 2001; 90:1349–1358.

11. Lichtwark GA, Wilson AM. Is Achilles tendon compliance optimised for maximum muscle efficiency during locomotion? *J Biomech* 2007; 40(8):1768–1775.

12. Turner A, Jeffreys I. The Stretch-Shortening Cycle: Proposed Mechanisms and Methods for Enhancement. *Strength Cond* 2010; 32(4):87–99.

13. Harman EA, Rosenstein MT, Frykman PN, et al. The effects of arms and countermovement on vertical jumping. *Med Sci Sports Exerc* 1990; 22:825–833.

14. Ashby BM, Heegaard JH. Role of arm motion in the standing long jump. *J Biomech* 2002; 35:1631–1637.

15. Martin RJ, Dore E, Twisk J, van Praagh E, Hautier CA, Bedu M. Longitudinal changes of maximal short-term peak power in girls and boys during growth. *Med Sci Sports Exerc* 2004; 36(3):498–503.

16. Kearney JT, Rundell KW, Wilber RL. Measurement of work and power in sport. In: Kirkendall DT, ed. *Exercise and Sport Science.* Philadelphia, PA: Lippincott Williams & Wilkins; 2000.

17. van Praagh E. Development of anaerobic function during childhood and adolescence. *Pediatric Exercise Science* 2000; 12:150–173.

18. Caserotti P, Aagaard P, Simonsen EB, et al. Contraction-specific differences in maximal muscle power during stretch-shortening cycle movements in elderly males and females. *Eur J Appl Physiol* 2001; 84:206–212.

19. Harrison AJ, Gaffney S. Motor development and gender effects of stretch-shortening cycle performance. *J Sci Med Sport* 2001; 4:406–415.

20. Fox SI. *Human Physiology.* 8th ed. New York: McGraw-Hill; 2004.

21. **Moritani T.** Motor unit and motorneuron excitability during explosive movements. In: Komi PV, ed. *Strength and Power in Sport.* Oxford, UK: Blackwell; 2003.

22. **Jaric S, Ropret R, Kukolj M, et al.** Role of agonist and antagonist muscle strength in performance of rapid movements. *Eur J Appl Physiol Occup Physiol.* 1995; 71:464–468.

23. **Jaric S.** Changes in movement symmetry associated with strengthening and fatigue of agonist and antagonist muscles. *J Motor Behav* 2000; 32:9–15.

24. **Avela J, Komi PV.** Interaction between muscle stiffness and stretch reflex sensitivity after long-term stretch-shortening cycle exercise. *Muscle and Nerve* 1998; 21:1224–1227.

25. **Strojnik V, Komi PV.** Fatigue after submaximal intensive stretch-shortening cycle exercise. *Med Sci Sports Exerc* 2000; 32:1314–1319.

26. **Strojnik V, Komi PV.** Neuromuscular fatigue after maximal stretch-shortening cycle exercise. *J Appl Physiol* 1998; 84:344–350.

27. **Oliver JL, Lloyd RS, Meyers RW.** Training Elite Child Athletes: Promoting Welfare and Well-Being. *Strength Cond* 2011;3 3(4):73–79.

28. **Haywood KM, Getchell N.** *Life Span Motor Development.* 3rd ed. Champaign, IL: Human Kinetics; 2001.

29. **Gallahue DL, John CO.** *Understanding Motor Development.* 6th ed. New York: McGraw-Hill; 2006.

30. **Caraffa A, Cerulli G, Projetti M, et al.** Prevention of anterior cruciate ligament injuries in soccer. A prospective controlled study of proprioceptive training. *Knee Surg Sports Traumatol Arthrosc* 1996; 4:19–21.

31. **Griffin LY.** The Henning program. In: Griffin LY, ed. *Prevention of Noncontact ACL Injuries.* Rosemont, IL: American Academy of Orthopaedic Surgeons; 2001.

32. **Hewett TE, Stroupe AI, Nance TA, Noyes FR.** Plyometric training in female athletes: decreased impact forces and increased hamstring torques. *Am J Sports Med* 1996; 24:765–773.

33. **Silvers HJ, Mandelbaum BR.** Preseason conditioning to prevent soccer injuries in young women. *Clin J Sport Med* 2001; 11:206.

34. **McNair PJ, Prapavessis H, Callender K.** Decreasing landing forces: effect of instruction. *Br J Sports Med* 2000; 34:293–296.

35. **Onate JA, Guskiewicz KM, Sullivan RJ.** Augmented feedback reduces jump landing forces. *J Orthop Sports Phys Ther* 2001; 31:511–517.

36. **Mandelbaum BR, Silvers HJ, Watanabe DS, et al.** Effectiveness of a neuromuscular and proprioceptive training program in preventing anterior cruciate ligament injuries in female athletes: 2-year follow-up. *Am J Sports Med* 2005; 33:1003–1010.

37. **Brown ME, Mayhew JL, Boleach LW.** Effect of plyometric training on vertical jump performance in high school basketball players. *J Sports Med Phys Fit* 1986; 26:1–4.

38. **Fatouros IG, Jamurtas AZ, Leontsini D, et al.** Evaluation of plyometric exercise training, weight training, and their combination on vertical jumping performance and leg strength. *J Strength Cond Res* 2000; 14:470–476.

39. **Luebbers PE, Potteiger JA, Hulver MW, et al.** Effects of plyometric training and recovery on vertical jump performance and anaerobic power. *J Strength Cond Res* 2003; 17:704–709.

40. **Wilson GJ, Murphy AJ, Giorgi A.** Weight and plyometric training: effects on eccentric and concentric force production. *Can J Appl Physiol* 1996; 21:301–315.

41. **Lees A, Rojas J, Ceperos M, et al.** How the free limbs are used by elite high jumpers in generating vertical velocity. *Ergonomics* 2000; 43:1622–1636.

42. **McBride JM, Triplett McBride T, Davie A, et al.** The effect of heavy- vs light-load jump squats on the development of strength, power, and speed. *J Strength Cond Res* 2002; 16:75–82.

43. **Soriano MA, Jimenez-Reyes P, Rhea MR, Marin PJ.** The optimal load for maximal power production during lower-body resistance exercises: a meta-analysis. *Sports Med* 2015; 45(8):1191–1205.

44. **Adams K, O'Shea J, O'Shea K, et al.** The effect of six weeks of squat, plyometric, and squat-plyometric training on power production. *J Appl Sports Sci Res* 1992; 6:36–41.

45. **Bobbert MF, Van Soest AJ.** Effects of muscle strengthening on vertical jump height: a simulation study. *Med Sci Sports Exerc* 1994; 26:1012–1020.

46. **Young WB, Wilson GJ, Byrne C.** A comparison of drop jump training methods: effects on leg extensor strength qualities and jumping performance. *Int J Sports Med* 1999; 20:295–303.

47. **Gehri DJ, Ricard MD, Kleiner DM, et al.** A comparison of plyometric training techniques for improving vertical jump ability and

energy production. *J Strength Cond Res* 1998; 12:85–89.

48. Meylan C, Malatesta D. Effects of in-season plyometric training within soccer practice on explosive actions of young players. *J Strength Cond Res* 2009; 23(9):2605–2613.

49. Lloyd RS, Oliver JL, Hughes MG, Williams CA. The effects of 4 weeks of plyometric training on ractive strength index and leg stiffness in male youths. *J Strength Cond Res* 2012; 26(10):2812–2819.

50. Faigenbaum AD, McFarland JE, Keiper FB, et al. Effects of a short-term plyometric and resistance training program on fitness performance in boys age 12 to 15 years. *J Sci Med Sport* 2007; 6:519–525.

51. Kotzamanidis C. Effect of plyometric training on running performance and vertical jumping in prepupertal boys. *J Strength Cond Res* 2006; 20(2):441–445.

52. Matavulj D, Kukolj M, Ugarkovic D, Tihanyi J, Jaric S. Effects of plyometric training on jumping performance in junior basketball players. *J Sports Med Phys Fit* 2001; 41:159–164.

53. Radcliffe JC, Farentinos RC. *High-Powered Plyometrics*. Champaign, IL: Human Kinetics; 1999.

54. Clutch M, Wilton M. The effect of depth jumps and weight training on leg strength and vertical jump. *Res Q Exerc Sport* 1983; 54:5–10.

55. Diallo O, Dore E, Duche P, et al. Effects of plyometric training followed by a reduced training programme on physical performance in prepubescent soccer players. *J Sports Med Phys Fit* 2001; 41:342–348.

56. Potteiger J, Lockwood R, Daub M, et al. Muscle power and fiber characteristics following 8 weeks of plyometric training. *J Strength Cond Res* 1999; 13:275–279.

57. Jarvis MM, Graham-Smith PG, Comfort P. A methodological approach to quantifying plyometric intensity. *J Strength Cond Res* 2014; 30(9):2522–2532.

58. Manzer S, Mattes K, Holländer K. Kinematic analysis of sprinting, max vs acceleration. *Biology of Exercise*. 2016; 12(2). www.biologyofexercise.com/images/issues/1225.pdf.

59. Schmolinsky G. *Track and Field: The East German Textbook of Athletics*. London: Sport Book Pub; 2000.

60. Baechle TR, Earle RW. *Essentials of Strength Training and Conditioning*. 3rd ed., 2008.

61. Mackala K, Fostiak M, Kowalski K. Selected determinants of acceleration in the 100m sprint. *J Hum Kinet* 2015; 45:135–148.

62. Schmidt RA, Lee TD. *Motor Control and Learning*. 3rd ed. Champaign, IL: Human Kinetics; 1999.

63. Mero A, Komi PV. Reaction time and electromyographic activity during a sprint start. *Eur J Appl Physiol* 1990; 61:73–80.

64. Galton F. On instruments for (1) testing perception of differences of tint and for (2) determining reaction time. *Journal of the Anthropological Institute* 1899; 19:27–29.

65. Brebner JT, Welford AT. Introduction and historical background sketch. In: Welford AT, ed. *Reaction Times*. New York: Academic Press; 1980:1–23.

66. Gambetta V, Winckler G. *Sport Specific Speed: The 3S System*. Sarasota, FL: Gambetta Sports Training Systems; 2001.

67. Mero A, Komi PV, Gregor RJ. Biomechanics of sprint running. *Sports Medicine* 1992; 13(6):376–392.

68. Bissas AI, Havenetidis K. The use of various strength-power tests as predictors of sprint running performance. *J Sports Med Physical Fit* 2008; 48(1):49–54.

69. Putnam CA, Kozey JW. *Substantive Issues in Running*. Boca Raton, FL: CRC Press Inc., 1989.

70. Sinning WE, Forsyth HL. Lower-limb actions while running at different velocities. *Med Sci Sports* 1970; 2:28–34.

71. Kivi DM, Maraj BK, Gervais P. A kinematic analysis of high-speed treadmill sprinting over a range of velocities. *Med Sci Sports Exerc* 2002; 34:662–666.

72. Mann RV. A kinetic analysis of sprinting. *Med Sci Sports Exerc* 1981; 13:325–328.

73. Mann RA, Moran GT, Dougherty SE. Comparative electromyography of the lower extremity in jogging, running, and sprinting. *Am J Sports Med* 1986; 14:501–510.

74. Mann R, Sprague P. A kinetic analysis of the ground leg during sprint running. *Res Q Exerc Sport* 1980; 51:334–348.

75. Dietz V, Schmidtbleicher D, Noth J. Neuronal mechanisms of human locomotion. *J Neurophysiol* 1979; 42:1212–1222.

76. Jacobs R, van Ingen Schenau GJ. Intermuscular coordination in a sprint push-off. *J Biomech* 1992; 25:953–965.

77. Johnson MD, Buckley JG. Muscle power patterns in the mid-acceleration phase of sprinting. *J Sports Sci* 2001; 19:263–272.

78. Upton DE. The effect of assisted and resisted sprint training on acceleration and velocity in Division IA female soccer athletes. *J Strength Cond Res* 2011; 25(10):2645–2652.

79. Nealer AD, Malyszek K, Wong M, Costa P, Coburn J, Brown L. Influence of rest intervals after assisted sprinting on bodyweight sprint times in female collegiate soccer players. *J Strength Cond Res* 2016; 31(1):88–94.

80. Bosco C, Vittori C. Biomechanical characteristics of sprint running during maximal and supra-maximal speed. *NSCA J* 1986; 1:39–45.

81. Corn RJ, Knudson D. Effect of elastic-cord towing on the kinematics of the acceleration phase of sprinting. *J Strength Cond Res* 2003; 17:72–75.

82. Paradisis GP, Cooke CB. Kinematic and postural characteristics of sprint running on sloping surfaces. *J Sports Sci* 2001; 19:149–159.

83. Upton DE. The effect of assisted and resisted sprint training on acceleration and velocity in Division 1A female soccer athletes. *J Strength Cond Res* 2011; 25(10):2645–2652.

84. Lockie RG, Murphy AJ, Spinks CD. Effects of resisted sled towing on sprint kinematics in field-sport athletes. *J Strength Cond Res* 2003; 17:760–767.

85. Drabik J. *Children & Sports Training: How Your Future Champions Should Exercise to Be Healthy, Fit, and Happy.* Island Pond, VT: Stadion; 1996.

86. Verstegen M, Marcello B. Agility and coordination. In: Foran B, ed. *High Performance Sports Conditioning.* Champaign, IL: Human Kinetics; 2001.

87. Sheppard JM, Young WB, Doyle TL, Sheppard TA, Newton RU. An evaluation of a new test of reactive agility and its relationship to sprint speed and change of direction speed. *J Sci Med Sport* 2006;9(4):342–349.

88. Young WB, McDowell MH, Scarlett BJ. Specificity of sprint and agility training methods. *J Strength Cond Res* 2001; 15(3):315–319.

89. Little T, Williams AG. Specificity of acceleration, maximal speed and agility in professional soccer players. *J Strength Cond Res* 2005; 19(1):76–78.

90. Ellis L, Gastin P, Lawrence S, et al. Protocols for the physiological assessment of team sports players. In: Gore CJ, ed. *Physiological Tests for Elite Athletes.* Champaign, IL: Human Kinetics; 2000.

91. Herodek K, Joksimovic A, Nejic D, Rakovic A, Markovic K, Stankovic D. Plyometric training and its effects on quickness. *Research in Kinesiology* 2011; 39(2):171–176.

92. Besier TF, Lloyd DG, Cochrane JL, et al. External loading of the knee joint during running and cutting maneuvers. *Med Sci Sports Exerc* 2001; 33:1168–1175.

93. Rand MK, Ohtsuki T. EMG analysis of lower limb muscles in humans during quick change in running directions. *Gait Posture* 2000; 12:169–183.

94. Neptune RR, Wright IC, van der Bogert AJ. Muscle coordination and function during cutting movements. *Med Sci Sports Exerc* 1999; 31:294–302.

95. Zazulak BT, Hewett TE, Reeves NP, Goldberg B, Cholewicki J. Deficits in neuromuscular control of the trunk predict knee injury risk: a prospective biomechanical-epidemiologic study. *Am J Sports Med* 2007; 35(7):1123–1130.

96. Bencke J, Naesborg H, Simonsen EB, et al. Motor pattern of the knee joint muscles during side-step cutting in European team handball. *Scand J Med Sci Sports* 2000; 10:68–77.

97. Boling MC, Padua DA, Marshall SW, Guskiewicz K, Pyne S, Beutler A. A prospective investigation of biomechanical risk factors for patellofemoral pain syndrome: the Joint Undertaking to Monitor and Prevent ACL Injury (JUMP-ACL) cohort. *Am J Sports Med* 2009; 37(11):2108–2116.

98. Besier TF, Lloyd DG, Ackland TR. Muscle activation strategies at the knee during running and cutting maneuvers. *Med Sci Sports Exerc* 2003; 35:119–127.

99. Wroble RR, Moxley DP. The effect of winter sports participation on high school football players: strength, power, agility, and body composition. *J Strength Cond Res* 2001; 15:132–135.

100. Mayhew JL, Piper FC, Schwegler TM, et al. Contributions of speed, agility, and body composition to aerobic power measurement in college football players. *J Appl Sports Sci Res* 1989; 3:101–106.

Contents

CHAPTER 18

IMPLEMENT TRAINING

Allen Hedrick

INTRODUCTION

In competitive athletics, today, more than ever, a tremendous emphasis is placed on strength and conditioning as a method to improve athletic performance. More and more frequently financial resources are directed toward building bigger and better strength and conditioning facilities. In addition, through educational and professional organizations, the knowledge base of strength and conditioning coaches continues to improve.

> Resistance training is recognized as a necessary component of training programs designed to improve athletic performance.

SIMILARITY IN TRAINING PROGRAMS

Though there are exceptions, the majority of strength and conditioning programs meant to improve athletic performance emphasize free weight training as the preferred method of training (8,21,25,28). Further, many of those programs emphasizing free weight training place a priority on performing the Olympic-style exercises (1,10,11,23). In addition, most strength and conditioning coaches design their training programs based on the concept of periodization, organizing their training programs into specific cycles. Each of these cycles has a specific physiological goal, with the ultimate goal to bring athletes to a peak at the appropriate point in the competitive season (2,7,15,16,27). There are variations in the periodization model used from program to program. However, if you reviewed the training programs used in strength and conditioning facilities across the country you would likely find many similarities in the programs designed from location to location.

As a result, there are a significant number of athletes training in high quality facilities being directed by well-educated strength and conditioning professionals employing programs that have similarities in design. Thus, it becomes difficult to provide your athletes with a significant competitive edge through their strength and conditioning programs. The challenge for the strength and conditioning coach is to find ways to design training programs based on scientific principles and guidelines while at the same time manipulating the strength and conditioning programs they design to provide their athletes with a competitive advantage.

> The majority of strength and conditioning coaches accentuate free weight training and performance of the Olympic-style exercises following a periodized training program. As a result, it is difficult to design training programs that provide your athletes with a competitive advantage.

RELYING ON SCIENCE

The amount of research in the field of sports science has dramatically increased, evaluating a broad spectrum of topics. Because of this, it is important that the strength and conditioning coach takes advantage of the available information and applies it appropriately. The majority of any training program should be based on what sports science has determined to be the best approach to achieving the desired goal.

(a)

Figure 18.1 Heavy medicine ball.

(b)

Figure 18.1 *(continued)*

Because of the wide spectrum of research occurring in the area of sports science, the majority of any training program should be based on science.

Lack of implement training research

However, there are still methods of training used to improve athletic performance that have little or no scientific evidence to support or refute. One such area that is lacking scientific research is the value of training with **implements** (non-standard resistance training modes, such as **kegs**, **tires**, or sandbags) as compared to the more traditional barbell, dumbbell, or strength training machine. Based on a review of the literature, limited research has been conducted evaluating the effectiveness of training with non-standard equipment, such as tires, **logs**, kegs, **stones** (or heavy medicine ball, Figure 18.1a and b) and

similar, for lack of a better term, strongman type implements (4,22,30,31,32). This is surprising given that most strength and conditioning professionals are diligent in exploring alternative training strategies as a means to gaining an advantage (4).

One area that is lacking research is the value of performing strength training activities with non-traditional resistance training implements.

TRAINING PRINCIPLES

Despite this lack of research, the same principles that apply to traditional training methods can be used to guide the use of implement training. Perhaps most important is the concept of training movements, not muscle groups (14,18,24,26,27). That is, increases in strength and/or power will occur primarily in the movement used during training. This concept suggests the more similar a training exercise is to the sport or activity, the greater the probability of transfer. Advocates of strongman training have suggested that this type of training is more specific than other forms of strength training and may help bridge the gap between training in the weight room and improving athletic performance.

Further, as will be discussed, certain implements and activities, such as flipping a tire or performing a fireman's carry, provide the opportunity for training in horizontal movement patterns. Horizontal training movement patterns are not the norm in most traditional strength training exercises, such as cleans, squats, and bench press.

Transferability of implement training to sports performance

As suggested by Zemke et al. (32), some non-traditional training methods transfer very effectively to athletic performance, and their inclusion in an athletic strength and conditioning program can be of value. Those strongman movements that most closely replicate movements in sports will have the greatest transfer, especially in contact sports such as football, wrestling, hockey, and rugby (32). This occurs because the movement pattern used in training can be similar to the movement pattern seen during competition (for example, as just mentioned, the movement of "flipping a tire" transfers well to blocking, tackling, wrestling, and so on). One reason for this is that the sequential extension of the hip, knee, and ankle, known as triple extension, that occurs when flipping a tire, vertical jumping, or performing the weightlifting movements is an important explosive movement in many sports (32).

> Although there is a lack of research evaluating implement training, the same principles that are applicable to conventional training modes can be applied to implement training.

A second aspect that can make implement training of value is that this type of training increases variation in the training program. This variation has the effect of reducing the physiological and psychological staleness that can occur when performing the same strength training movements repetitively over weeks and months. As suggested by Zemke et al. (32), strongman implements can provide a novel training stimulus when integrated into a strength and conditioning program and provide the benefits of increased muscular hypertrophy, strength, endurance, while at the same time providing possible increases of sport specific strength and increased enjoyment of training.

In support of this, a recent study of 220 strength and conditioning coaches found that 81% of those coaches responding believe that they had achieved good to excellent results from strongman training with their athletes (31). Advocates of strongman training have suggested that this type of training may help bridge the gap between traditional weight room training and best and functional strength (31).

To investigate this belief, Winwood et al. (31) performed a study comparing traditional modes of training and strongman type training and their effects on body composition, muscular function, and performance measures. The principal finding in this study was non-significant between group differences and body composition and functional performance measures after seven weeks of resistance training.

> Some non-traditional training methods can be used to effectively train sport specific movements and provide variation in the training program.

Water-filled implements

One implement training method that theoretically seems as if it could be of value in the training programs of certain types of athletes (i.e., football, hockey, wrestling) is the use of water-filled implements (water-filled implements are objects such as kegs or specially designed training logs or water-filled dumbbells where the majority of the resistance is provided by water contained within the implement). It has been suggested that significant levels of strength and muscular development can be achieved by combining traditional weight training exercises such as the squat and deadlift with the lifting of heavy and awkward hard to manage objects such as water-filled kegs (30).

Water as a form of resistance provides a unique training stimulus because water provides an **active fluid resistance** (the water contained within the object is constantly moving during performance of the exercise, providing an active resistance) rather than a static resistance (12,13,30). Contrast that to a typical exercise where the resistance (in the form of a weight stack, barbell, or dumbbell) is relatively static, that is, there is very little if any extraneous movement occurring. Further, consider that most training programs emphasize exercises from the sports of powerlifting (i.e., bench press, squats) and/or weightlifting (i.e., cleans, jerks). When the proper technique is mastered in these movements, the body and bar travel through specific movement patterns. As a result, variation in movement patterns during this type of training are severely limited (32).

Strongman training provides unbalanced training

While there have been a number of studies evaluating unstable surface training (22) there has been very little research evaluating the value of training with an active fluid resistance. But, applying the concept of specificity, it makes sense that training with an active fluid resistance could provide a sport-specific supplemental method of training (for certain types of athletes) as compared to lifting exclusively with a static resistance. This is because in many situations, athletes encounter dynamic resistance (in the form of an opponent) as compared to a static resistance. To achieve the greatest muscular response during unstable training the load should be as unstable as safety allows (22).

Further, because the active fluid resistance enhances the need for stability and control, this type of training may reduce the opportunity for injury because of improved joint stability (32).

> Water-filled implements provide the athlete with the opportunity to train against an active fluid resistance rather than the static resistance that most traditional training methods provide.

Implement training should supplement traditional methods

It is not being suggested that implement training should become the primary form of resistance training for athletes. Barbells and dumbbells are proven tools that have been shown to be very effective at developing increases in strength and power. However, if the goal of training is to gain a competitive edge, then supplementing traditional training with implement training may be a viable option.

> Implement training should be used to supplement traditional exercises (i.e., exercise machine, barbell, and dumbbell exercises) that make up the typical athletic resistance training program.

PROGRAM DESIGN

Examples of supplementing traditional training methods with implement training are provided in Tables 18.1 through 18.3. The following list gives explanations of the abbreviations used in the workouts presented in the tables.

- TB: Total body exercise; this is one of the Olympic-style lifts or related training exercises
- CL: Core lift; this is a multi-joint exercise such as a squat
- AL: Auxiliary lift; this is a single joint exercise such as a biceps curl
- DB: Dumbbell; the exercise is performed with a dumbbell
- WT: Weighted; the exercise is performed with an external resistance to provide added intensity
- MR: Manual resistance; the exercise uses a partner as the form of resistance
- MB: Medicine ball; the exercise is performed with a medicine ball
- Alt: Alternating; the exercise is performed alternating legs or alternating arms (depending on the exercise being performed)
- DB/tire squat clean: On the days our athletes perform dumbbell hang cleans we provide them with the opportunity to perform a tire flip. This tire flip is performed with a movement similar to the pull sequence seen when performing a clean.

TABLE 18.1 Hockey: Strength Cycle 1

DATES: April 28–May 25

CYCLE: Strength 1

GOAL: To increase muscle strength, because of the positive relationship between strength and power

LENGTH: 4 weeks

INTENSITY: Complete the full number of required repetitions on the first set only prior to increasing resistance

PACE: *Total* body lifts performed as explosively as possible. All other exercises lift explosively, lower under control

REST: 2:30 between total body lifts, 2:00 between all other exercises

SETS/REPS:

April 28–May 4: TB=4 × 5, CL=4 × 7, AL=3 × 8

May 5–May 11: TB=4 × 2, CL=4 × 4, AL=3 × 8

May 12–May 18: TB=4 × 5, CL=4 × 7, AL=3 × 8

May 19–May 25: TB=4 × 2, CL=4 × 4, AL=3 × 8

MONDAY	WEDNESDAY	FRIDAY
TOTAL BODY	TOTAL BODY	TOTAL BODY
Clean TB	DB hang clean/tire flip TB	Hang alt foot snatch TB
LOWER BODY	LOWER BODY	CHEST
Squat CL	DB/keg/log 1-leg squat CL	Bench press CL
Keg/log lateral squat CL	DB/keg/log hockey lunge CL	
60-second stabilization		TRUNK
	TRUNK	WT Russian twist 3 × 15
	MB trunk twist 3 × 15	WT toe touchers 3 × 15
TRUNK	DB/keg/log SLDL 3 × 12	
Band twits 3 × 15		SHOULDERS
WT reverse back ext 3 × 12		Keg/log shoulder press CL
	CHEST	MR front raise 2 × 8
UPPER BACK	DB/keg/log bench press CL	
MR row 2 × 8		NECK
	UPPER BACK	MR flex/ext 2 × 8
NECK	DB/keg/log row CL	
MR lat flexion 2 × 8		

TABLE 18.2 Running backs/wide receivers: Strength Cycle 2

DATES: March 29–May 2

CYCLE: Strength 2

GOAL: Increase muscle strength, because of the positive relationship between strength and power

LENGTH: 5 weeks

INTENSITY: Select a resistance that allows completion of the full number of required repetitions on the *first* set only prior to increasing resistance

PACE: Total body lifts performed explosively. All other exercises lift explosively, lower under control

REST: 2:30 between total body exercises, 2:00 between all other sets and exercises

SETS/REPS:

March 29–April 4: TB=4 × 5, CL=4 × 6, AL=3 × 6

April 5–April 11: TB=4 × 3, CL=4 × 4, AL=3 × 6

April 12–April 18: TB=4 × 5, CL=4 × 6, AL=3 × 6

April 19–April 25: TB=4 × 3, CL=4 × 4, AL=3 × 6

April 26–May 2: TB=4 × 5, CL=4 × 6, AL=3 × 6

MONDAY	WEDNESDAY	FRIDAY
TOTAL BODY	TOTAL BODY	TOTAL BODY
Clean TB	DB hang clean/tire flip TB	Split alter ft snatch balance TB
UPPER BODY	LOWER BODY	LOWER BODY
Bench press CL	DB/keg/log 1-leg squat CL	Squats CL
	DB/keg/log lateral squat CL	Keg/log walking lunges CL
TRUNK		1 × 60-sec stabilization
MB decline 1-arm throws 3 × 15	TRUNK	
WT reverse back ext 3 × 12	DB press crunch 3 × 15	TRUNK
	DB/keg/log SLDL 3 × 12	WT alter V-ups/with MB 3 × 15
SHOULDERS		DB back ext 3 × 12
MR front raise 2 × 8	CHEST	
	DB/keg/log incline press CL	UPPER BACK
UPPER BACK		Bent row CL
MR up-right row 2 × 8	ARMS	
	MR stand triceps 2 × 8	NECK
NECK	MR stand biceps 2 × 8	MR flex/ext 2 × 8
MR lateral flexion 2 × 8		

TABLE 18.3 Volleyball: Power Cycle 2

DATES: May 31–June 27

CYCLE: Power 2

GOAL: Increases in muscle power because of the positive relationship between muscle power and performance

LENGTH: 4 weeks

INTENSITY: Complete the full number of repetitions in good form on the first set only prior to increasing resistance

PACE: Total body lifts performed as explosively as possible. Timed lifts performed at a pace that allows completion of the required number of repetitions in the specified time period

REST: 3:00 between total body sets and exercises, 2:30 between all other sets and exercises

SETS/REPS:

May 31–June 6: TB=5 × 2, TL=4 × 4@5 sec (1.3)

June 7–June 13: TB=5 × 3, TL=4 × 6@9 sec (1.5)

June 14–June 20: TB=5 × 2, TL=4 × 4@5 sec (1.3)

June 21–June 27: TB=5 × 3, TL=4 × 6@9 sec (1.5)

MONDAY	WEDNESDAY	FRIDAY
TOTAL BODY	**TOTAL BODY**	**TOTAL BODY**
Hang clean TB	DB split alt ft alt snatch balance TB	Split alt ft snatch TB
DB hang split alt ft alt snatch TB	DB hang split alt ft alt snatch TB	Split alt ft jerks TB
LOWER BODY	**LOWER BODY**	**CHEST**
Squats (2 sets) TL	DB/keg/log 1-leg front squat CL	Bench press (2 sets) TL
Keg/log squats (2 sets) TL	DB/keg/log lateral squat CL	Keg/log bench press (2 sets) TL
		1 × 60-sec stabilization
TRUNK	**TRUNK**	
2-hand bar twist 3 × 10	MB ankle chop/twist 3 × 10 MB	**TRUNK**
WT back ext 3 × 8	DB/keg/log SLDL 3 × 12	MB decline throw 3 × 10
UPPER BACK	**CHEST/SHOULDER**	**SHOULDERS**
Bar/keg/log bent row TL	DB alt bench press TL	Keg/log shoulder press TL
ROTATOR CUFF	**ROTATOR CUFF**	**ROTATOR CUFF**
Internal rotation 2 × 12	Full cans 2 × 12	Functional rotation 2 × 12

DESCRIPTION OF SUGGESTED TRAINING IMPLEMENTS

Kegs

The number of kegs needed in the training program, and the range of weights from the lightest to the heaviest keg, will depend on the number of athletes training with kegs at one time and the types of keg exercises placed into the training program. You can think of each keg as a training station; ideally you will want no more than three athletes per keg. Certain exercises, such as a keg front raise, require a fairly light weight (e.g., 20 lb) while some athletes may be able to go as heavy as 300 lbs on a keg squat.

Be aware that because of the additional balance and stability requirements athletes will not be able to use the same amount of weight in a keg exercise that they will performing the same exercise with a barbell. Though initially this may seem to compromise potential increases in strength; consider that the athletes may be building a higher level of transferable strength; that is strength that can be used effectively during competition.

The kegs can be filled to the desired weight by removing the cap, placing the keg on a scale, and using a hose to fill the keg with water until the desired weight is reached. Another technique that can be used to fill the keg is to cut off the spout of the keg, pour the desired amount of water and sand into the keg, and weld the spout back on; a full-size keg, filled with water, will weigh about 160 lb. To further increase the weight of the keg, sand can be mixed in with water. Sand is advantageous because it is inexpensive and, because it stays wet inside the keg, it maintains its dynamic characteristics, moving inside the keg as the exercise is performed.

Keg stands can be built to make it easier to perform exercises such as squats, lunges, or shoulder press. The purpose of these stands is to securely hold the keg in place at shoulder height to make it easier to place the keg in the correct position to perform the selected exercise. You can think of the keg stands as being similar to a squat rack where the bar is held in place at about shoulder height so that the athlete can place it on the back to perform a squat.

Most kegs are built with a handle on the top end. The bottom end is typically built with a lip that allows the user to more effectively grip that end of the keg. By gripping the handle at the top end and using the lip at the bottom end a secure grip can be achieved when handling the keg. However, caution must still be taken when using the kegs to perform resistance training exercises. The ability to grip the keg is not as secure as when using a barbell or dumbbell. Further, the water movement within the keg creates a difficult resistance to control. The spotter must take great care when a keg exercise is being performed, and the lifter must remember to use a lighter resistance than would be used when performing the same exercise with a barbell or dumbbell.

> The number of kegs needed to supplement the strength training program, and the range of poundage needed in the kegs, will depend on the number of athletes training and the types of keg exercises being performed. It is important to remember that exercises performed with the kegs are more difficult than the same exercise performed with a barbell or dumbbell. Because of this the athlete will have to reduce the training weight when performing a keg exercise as compared to the same exercise performed with a barbell or dumbbell.

Logs

The (6 ft long "tubes" with a 12 in circumference) are filled with water. Extending out from each tube is piping the size of a standard barbell so that additional weight plates can be attached to the log. The ability to rapidly change the weight of the log limits the need to have a large number of logs available at various weights.

The logs are designed with handles to make it easier to hold onto the implement. Because of the length of the logs the water has the opportunity to travel a significant distance as compared to the kegs, increasing the dynamic nature of the movement.

Similar to the kegs, because of the instability of the implement athletes will not be able to perform exercises performed with the log with the same weight that they would perform the identical exercise with a barbell. Err on the side of caution and slowly increase the weight lifted with this type of training as the athlete demonstrates the ability to control the implement during exercise.

> Because the logs are 6 ft long, the water contained within the log can move a significant distance, increasing the dynamic characteristics of the exercise and thus the degree of difficulty of the movement.

Water-filled dumbbells

Water-filled dumbbells (smaller versions of the water-filled logs) are used as a typical dumbbell. Water displacement is less than what occurs when using the logs because the length of the dumbbells is much shorter than the logs. However, the movement of the water still provides an additional challenge to the athlete as compared to a typical dumbbell. Water-filled dumbbells provide a unique training stimulus and thus have the potential to provide the athlete with a competitive advantage.

> Although less dynamic resistance occurs using water-filled dumbbells as compared to the kegs or logs (because the dumbbells are shorter than the kegs or logs and thus provide less opportunity for dynamic movement of the water), water-filled dumbbells still provide a unique training stimulus for the athlete.

Tires

The tires (used truck and heavy equipment tires) can be modified so that the athlete can attach additional weight in the center of the tire to adjust the resistance to their specific strength levels. Unlike the kegs, logs, and water-filled dumbbells where a variety of exercises can be performed, the tires are only flipped. The tire flip requires a heavy tire to be flipped end-over-end as quickly as possible (17).

To perform the movement the athlete crouches down in front of the tire, grabs the underside of the tire with a supinated grip approximately shoulder-width apart; and forcefully extends the ankle, knee, hip to flip the tire over.

One common technique used to flip the tire that could increase the likelihood of injury is the use of a single-leg support position when repositioning the hands to push the tire over. This technique places a high degree of stress on the supporting leg and should be avoided (29).

However, done correctly, using the tires does provide some advantages. First, flipping the tire provides athletes with greater variety in their training program, which is a positive (29). Further, while most gym-based strength training exercises involve vertical movement patterns (i.e., cleans, squats, deadlifts, bench press) with two feet side by side (31), most human-based movements consist primarily of horizontal motion occurring as a result of unilateral ground reaction force production (14). Flipping a tire primarily involves horizontal movement and, using the principle of training specificity, is an example of the type of non-traditional strength training exercises that should be considered (31,32).

An additional advantage of including tire flips in the workout is that athletes who have an injury (typically wrist, elbow, shoulder, or back) that prevent them from performing the Olympic-style exercises safely and pain free, may still be able to perform a tire flip without aggravating the injury. Finally, because there is no catch phase in flipping a tire, the athlete sometimes feels better able to concentrate on the explosion phase of the movement.

> The tires provide a unique and challenging variation for athletes who regularly perform cleans or high pulls as part of their workout.

Chains

One mode of training that has become increasingly popular is adding lengths of chain to the end of the barbell (3,5,6,9,19,20,23). The rationale for the use of **chains** is that the chain provides a variable resistance. When performing a typical barbell exercise the weight remains constant throughout the performance of the exercise (11). Theoretically,

Figure 18.2 Use of chains.

chain training provides a variable resistance throughout the range of motion of the exercise (5,6,9,20,22). For example, when performing a squat or clean, the chains collect on the floor at the bottom of the movement, adding the least amount of additional resistance at this point of the exercise (which is the point where the muscle is able to generate the least amount of force). As the bar is lifted out of this low position, the bar gets progressively heavier as more and more links of chain are lifted off the floor until the bar gets to its heaviest point, which is where the muscles generate the greatest amount of force (9). (Figure 18.2a and b)

However, despite the increasing popularity of using chains, and the widespread belief that the use of chains provides an advantage, these claims remain mostly anecdotal (5,6,9,20). While it has been suggested that the use of chains promotes power, acceleration, motor control, stabilization, and enhanced neurological adaptation (20), these claims are primarily anecdotal because only a limited number of studies have been conducted evaluating what effect, if any, chains provide during training, and these studies have provided mixed results in terms of the effectiveness of using chains (5,20).

Despite these mixed study results and primarily anecdotal claims, athletes who make use of chains during training believe that chains positively affect their training, increase performance, and require greater effort (5). If an athlete believes chain training is more difficult and requires greater effort during training, this may lead to increased performance over time.

DESCRIPTION OF IMPLEMENT EXERCISES PROVIDED IN EXAMPLE WORKOUTS

The list of exercise descriptions provided later is not an inclusive list of the exercises that can be performed with the implements discussed in this chapter. Rather, this list is a description of the implement exercises included in the example workouts provided earlier. Most of the implement exercises are performed very

similarly to the same exercises performed with traditional strength training equipment.

It is important to note that the Olympic-style exercises are not performed with either kegs or logs. Because of the technical difficulty of performing these types of exercises, and the awkwardness of using these implements, the chance of injury performing these types of exercises with these implements is too great. However, all of the Olympic-style exercises can be safely performed with the water-filled dumbbells by those athletes who have good technique when performing these exercises with standard dumbbells.

Remember that in all of the exercises performed with implements, the training weight must be reduced in comparison to what an athlete would use with a traditional barbell or dumbbell.

Exercise descriptions for the water-filled dumbbells are not included in this list. Movements using the water-filled dumbbells are identical to movements using standard dumbbells and are therefore not described.

Exercise descriptions

Keg/log lateral squat: (Figure 18.3a, b, c). Place the keg or log on the back, as when performing barbell squats. Place the feet as wide as comfortable while maintaining the ability to perform the movement with correct technique. Keeping the left knee straight and the left foot planted, flex the right knee while sitting back at the hips and moving the hips laterally to the right. Return to the starting position and alternate the movement to the opposite side until the required number of repetitions has been performed.

Tire flip: (Figure 18.4a, b, c). Place the feet about shoulder width apart. Keeping the back arched sit back at the hips (not allowing the knees to drift forward of the toes) and assume an underhand grip on the tire. The hands should be slightly wider than shoulder width apart. Use the legs to lift the tire so that the hands are raised to a mid-shin position. The arms should be fully extended, the back arched, and the feet flat on the floor. Using a jumping action explode up through the legs and flip the tire onto its side, remembering to keep the back arched through the entire movement. Once the tire has been flipped onto its side step forward and aggressively push the tire onto its opposite side.

Figure 18.3 Keg/log lateral squat.

Figure 18.3 *(continued)*

Figure 18.4 Tire flip.

Figure 18.4 *(continued)*

Keg/log 1-leg squat: (Figure 18.5a, b, c, d). Place the keg or log on the back, as when performing barbell squats. Stand about a stride's length away from a utility bench. Reach back with one leg and place the foot on the bench. Keeping the back arched initiate the movement by sitting back at the hips, not allowing the knee to drift forward of the toes on the forward foot. Continue to sit back until the mid-thigh has achieved a parallel position. Maintaining an arched back position return to the starting position. Repeat with the opposite leg.

Keg/log hockey lunge: (Figure 18.6a, b, c, d, e, f). Place the keg or log on the back, as when performing barbell squats. Take an exaggerated stride with the right leg, stepping forward so that the right foot is 14–16 ins wider than the right shoulder and then lower the body so that the right knee is behind the toes on the right foot and the left leg is bent with the left knee just off the floor. From that bottom position stride forward in one continuous movement with the left leg and take an exaggerated stride with the left leg as described above; the right leg is bent and the right knee is just off the floor. It is important to keep the back arched during the entire performance of this exercise.

Keg/log straight leg dead lift: (Figure 18.7a, b, c, d). Stand on a pair of plyometric boxes or utility benches, 18–20 ins high. The keg should be sitting on the end between the two boxes. Squat down and, keeping the back arched, pick up the keg. Holding the keg at arms-length in front of the body, bend the knees slightly. Maintaining that slight knee bend and the arch in the back, rotate forward at the hips and lower the keg to a point just short of touching the floor directly underneath the feet, then return to the starting position.

Keg/log bench press: (Figure 18.8a, b, c, d). Assume a lying position on a flat utility bench, feet on the floor and butt on the bench. Place the keg or log on the chest as when performing a barbell bench press and grip the implement. Fully extend the arms, keeping the butt on the

(a)

Figure 18.5 Keg/log 1-leg squat.

Figure 18.5 *(continued)*

Figure 18.5 *(continued)*

Figure 18.6 Keg/log hockey lunge.

Figure 18.6 *(continued)*

(d)

(e)

Figure 18.6 *(continued)*

Figure 18.6 *(continued)*

Figure 18.7 Keg/log straight leg dead lift.

Figure 18.7 *(continued)*

Figure 18.7 *(continued)*

Figure 18.8 Keg/log bench press.

Figure 18.8 *(continued)*

(d)

Figure 18.8 *(continued)*

bench and the feet flat on the floor. Lower under control. The spotter(s) must be diligent in assisting the lifter during performance of this exercise.

Keg/log shoulder press (Figure 18.9a, b, c, d): Grip the keg or log high on the chest. Using a shoulder width split stance with the feet press the keg or log directly overhead until the arms are fully extended, then lower under control. It is important to not lean back while performing the exercise, the back should remain straight. Lower through the full comfortable range of motion.

Keg/log incline press (Figure 18.10a, b, c, d): Assume a lying position on an incline bench, feet on the floor and butt on the bench. Place the keg or log on the chest as when performing a barbell incline press and grip the implement. Fully extend the arms, keeping the butt on the bench and the feet flat on the floor. Lower under control. The spotter(s) must be diligent in assisting the lifter during performance of this exercise.

Keg/log walking lunges (Figure 18.11a, b, c, d, e, f, g, h): Place the keg or log on the back, as when performing barbell squats. Take an exaggerated stride with the right leg and then lower the body so that the right knee is behind the toes on the right foot and the left leg is bent with the left knee just off the floor. From that bottom position stride forward in one continuous movement with the left leg and take an exaggerated stride with the left leg, the right leg is bent, and the right knee is just off the floor. It is important to keep the back arched during the entire performance of this exercise.

Keg/log squats (Figure 18.12a, b, c, d): Place the keg or log on the back, as when performing barbell squats. Place the feet about shoulder width apart. Keeping the back arched, initiate the movement by sitting back at the hips, not allowing the knees to drip forward of the toes. Continue to sit back until the mid-thigh has achieved a parallel position. Maintaining an arched back position, return to the starting position.

Figure 18.9 Keg/log shoulder press.

Figure 18.9 *(continued)*

Figure 18.10 Keg/log incline press.

Figure 18.10 *(continued)*

Figure 18.11 Keg/log walking lunges.

(c)

(d)

Figure 18.11 *(continued)*

(e)

(f)

Figure 18.11 *(continued)*

Figure 18.11 *(continued)*

Figure 18.12 Keg/log squats.

Figure 18.12 *(continued)*

Figure 18.13 Keg/log side lunge.

Figure 18.13 *(continued)*

(e)

(f)

Figure 18.13 *(continued)*

Keg/log side lunge (Figure 18.13a, b, c, d, e, f): Place the keg or log on the back, as when performing barbell squats. Place the feet about shoulder width apart. Step directly laterally with the right foot through a comfortable range of motion. Keeping the left knee straight and the left foot planted, flex the right knee while sitting back at the hips and moving the hips laterally to the right. Return to the starting position and alternate the movement to the opposite side until the required number of repetitions has been completed.

Keg/log bent row (Figure 18.14a, b, c, d): Place a keg on its side in front of the body or stand behind a log, depending upon which implement is to be used. Bend the knees slightly and rotate at the hips to lower the upper body so the shoulders are parallel with the hips. The shoulders should be directly over the implement. Keeping the back arched, reach down and grasp the implement. Pull the arms back so that each elbow slides along the rib cage and lift the implement to the chest, then return to the starting position.

Keg arch lunge (Figure 18.15a, b, c, d, e, f, g): Place the keg or log on the back, as when performing barbell squats. Place the feet about shoulder width apart. Imagine an arch on the floor in front of where you are standing, starting a stride length away directly lateral of the right foot and ending a stride length away directly lateral of the left foot. Initiate the movement by lunging directly laterally with the right foot to the right edge of the arch while keeping the right knee behind the toes on the right foot and the left leg straight. Return to the starting position. Alternate lunging with each leg, gradually working from one corner of the arch to the opposite corner of the arch with each step. The number of steps and the placement of the foot on each step will depend on the number of required repetitions.

(a)

Figure 18.14 Keg/log bent row.

Figure 18.14 *(continued)*

(d)

Figure 18.14 *(continued)*

(a)

Figure 18.15 Keg arch lunge.

Figure 18.15 *(continued)*

Figure 18.15 *(continued)*

Figure 18.15 *(continued)*

REAL-WORLD APPLICATION

Unstable resistance or unstable surface?

This chapter discusses several forms of implements used in training programs that provide an unstable resistance: kegs, sandbags, etc. Implements are available that provide an unstable surface or an unstable base from which the athlete is required to produce force. One question then becomes: which modality is more appropriate, an unstable resistance or an unstable surface?

The answer to this question is most certainly sport-specific. One point of consideration will be the degree to which a supporting surface is "unstable" while performing sport-specific activities.

A stability ball is a common piece of equipment used in training athletes today. A "balance disk" or "wobble board" is used in some cases to provide an unstable surface underneath a planted foot. As a strength and conditioning professional, you must be able to evaluate these exercise modalities and determine whether they are specific to the sport for which the athlete is training.

In many sports, the ground is the primary surface the athlete uses to generate ground reaction force. In some cases, the ground is slippery (wet grass) or allows sliding (a clay tennis court). Is a slippery surface the same as an unstable surface? Probably not.

Although this does not mean that an unstable surface should never be used, you as a strength and conditioning professional should have a reason for using any piece of equipment. These modalities may be very useful in the rehabilitation of specific injuries. Since conditioning programs should progress from general to specific, it may be that unstable surfaces are useful in the general conditioning phase but not applicable to the sport-specific phase. It is important to be aware that most studies that have evaluated training on unstable surfaces have found that the ability to generate peak force is compromised on these types of surfaces (22).

Before using an unstable surface in a sport-specific conditioning phase, evaluate the sport and have a specific rationale for using the modality.

Q&A FROM THE FIELD

Differences of opinion exist in the field about training modalities and the use of various implements. Many of the implements lack a solid foundation in the research literature in terms of effectiveness. As pointed out by Winwood et al. (30), training with non-traditional implements is speculative given that no research has examined the chronic effects of strongman training. Further, while several strength and conditioning practitioners have made some suggestions on what strongman implements could be incorporated in strength and conditioning programs for strong male athletes, very little research has examined how strongman training techniques are actually used (30).

Should we, as professionals, be concerned about that fact? How should we deal with questions about the lack of research when speaking with administrators, coaches, and parents?

Admittedly, there is a lack of research on many of the implements discussed in this chapter. Does that mean that we must wait for that research to be done before using these implements? Not really. As long as we apply safe and effective principles of training, implement training can be safely added to any training program. According to Zemke et al. (32), by following general weight training safety recommendations, including lifting with good lifting mechanics and correct loading using the principle of progressive overload, implement training can be performed successfully with low risk with athletes of all ages and strength and skill levels. Further, as suggested by Zemke et al. (32), the use of strongman implements also plays a role in injury prevention. Traditional

(continued)

(continued)

training with an emphasis on perfectly executed movements and avoiding dangerous situations may actually lessen an athlete's preparedness for potentially harmful situations encountered in the field of play and place the athlete at an increased risk of injury.

To justify the exercise as related to a specific sport, the concepts of specificity and transferability can be used. Future research will provide additional evidence related to the effectiveness of the various implements discussed in this chapter. As professionals, even though we do not need to wait on that research to utilize these innovative methods of training, we must keep up with new research and be willing to adjust our training programs accordingly. We must also consider the entire body of research on a specific topic. A single study is unlikely to "prove" or "disprove" the effectiveness of a single training implement.

SUMMARY

There is a tremendous emphasis placed on strength and conditioning to improve athletic performance. Training facilities keep getting bigger and better, and the knowledge base of strength and conditioning coaches continues to increase. While there are subtle differences in program design, most strength and conditioning coaches emphasize free weight training and performance of the Olympic-style exercises in a program based on periodization. Because of these similarities it becomes difficult to provide your athletes with a competitive advantage.

With the amount of information available today the vast majority of any strength and conditioning program should be based on what science tells us is the best approach. Unfortunately, as of now, there has been little research evaluating the value of training with various types of implements such as kegs or tires. Despite this lack of research, the same principles that apply to traditional training methods should be used to guide the use of implement training, including the concept of selecting exercises that mimic the movements found in the sport the athlete is training for. That is, those non-traditional movements that best replicate movements seen in the sport the athlete is training for will have the greatest transfer. This occurs because the movement pattern used in training is similar to the movement pattern seen during competition.

An additional aspect that makes implement training valuable is that this type of training increases variation in the training program. This added variation can reduce the physiological and psychological staleness that can occur when performing the same exercises repetitively over weeks and months. Thus, such non-traditional training methods such as water-filled implements, tires, and chains can all be used to effectively enhance the training program.

MAXING OUT

1. You are introducing a new implement in your conditioning program for baseball players. Name the implement, briefly discuss how you will introduce it into the conditioning program over the next four weeks, briefly describe the exercises you will use with the implement and explain how you expect this form of training to benefit your athletes.

2. In evaluating the athletic ability of a high school basketball player, his coach tells you he needs better balance and stability. He is already performing resistance training using a standard free weight resistance. Would you consider using a training modality that incorporates an active fluid resistance? Why or why not?

3. Some of the athletes in your program are complaining of lower back pain. The only significant change in the program is an increase in the volume and intensity of power cleans over the past two weeks. Would you consider tire flipping as an alternative to power cleans? Why or why not?

CASE EXAMPLE

Brian

Background

Bryan is a 6 ft, 215 lb sophomore division I running back. His test results are as follows:

a   bench press: 370 lb
b   squat: 500 lb
c   clean: 330 lb
d   40 yd dash: 4.5
e   Vertical jump: 38 in

He is very committed to his strength and conditioning program, and rarely misses a training session. Despite his impressive testing results he is looking for ways to improve his athletic performance and his position coach feels he needs to develop more functional strength to reach his potential as a football player. What are some training techniques that could be used to help this athlete achieve his goals?

Recommendations/considerations

With his superior strength levels, it is doubtful that further enhancing his strength levels will have a positive effect on performance. For example, he could focus on increasing his squat from 500 lb to 525 lb, but it is questionable whether this would have the effect of improving on-the-field performance.

What might be more effective at improving performance is to integrate water-filled implement exercises into his training program, giving him the opportunity to train using an active fluid resistance. For example, exercises such as keg bench press (to help pass blocking and straight arm capabilities) and log lunges (to help him maintain balance during contact) could be worked into his training program to help improve his athletic performance, converting his "weight room strength" to "functional strength".

Tyrone

Tyrone is a 6 ft 11 ins 230 lb sophomore who is the starting center for his division I college basketball team. During the last game Tyrone landed awkwardly after coming down with a rebound and strained his lower back. Tyrone is able to complete the majority of his resistance training program without aggravating his back condition. However, he has found that the catch phase when performing a clean does cause him some pain. He is concerned because he has found that performing cleans does help his vertical jump ability and makes him feel more explosive on the court. What is a possible alternative exercise that he could perform that would mimic the triple extension jumping action that occurs when performing a clean without aggravating his strained lower back?

To mimic the jumping action that occurs when performing a clean and to eliminate the pain that occurs during the catch phase, Tyrone could be instructed on how to properly flip a tire (#3 Triple Extension). Once he has learned the correct movement pattern he could attempt the movement on a light weight unloaded tire to make sure the exercise did not cause any pain in his strained lower back. From there a gradual increase in training intensity could occur, making sure that he maintained good technique and that he continued to be able to perform the movement pain free.

REFERENCES

1. **Allerheiligen B.** In-season strength training for power athletes. *Strength Cond* 2003; 25(3):23–28.

2. **Baker D.** Applying the in-season periodization of strength and power training for football. *Strength Cond* 1998; 20(2):18–24.

3. **Baker DG, Newton RU.** Effect of kinetically altering a repetition via the use of chain resistance on velocity during the bench press. *J Strength Cond Res* 2009; 23(7):1941–1946.

4. **Berning JM, Adams KJ, Climstein M, Stamford BA.** Metabolic demands of "junkyard" training: pushing and pulling a motor vehicle. *J Strength Cond Res* 2007; 21(3):853–856.

5. **Berning JM, Coker CA, Briggs D.** The biomechanical and perceptual influence of chain resistance on the performance of the Olympic clean. *J Strength Cond Res* 2008; 22(2); 390–395.

6. **Berning JM, Adams KJ.** Using chain for strength and conditioning, *Strength Cond* 2004; 26(5):80–84.

7. **Brooks TJ.** Women's collegiate gymnastics: a multifactorial approach to training and conditioning. *Strength Cond* 2003; 25(2):23–37.

8. **Coker CA, Berning JM, Briggs DL.** A preliminary investigation of the biomechanical and perceptual influence of chain resistance on the performance of the snatch. *J Strength Cond Res* 2006; 20(4):887–891.

9. **DeGarmo R.** University of Nebraska in-season resistance training for horizontal jumper. *Strength Cond* 2000; 22(3):23–26.

10. **Gadeken SB.** Off-season strength, power, and plyometric training for Kansas State volleyball. *Strength Cond* 1999; 21(5):49–55.

11. **Hedrick A.** Using uncommon implements in the training programs of athletes. *Strength Cond* 2003; 25(4):18–22.

12. **Hedrick A.** Athlete strongman. *Pure Power* 2003; 3(5):66–74.

13. **Keogh J.** Lower body resistance training: increasing functional performance with lunges. *Strength Cond* 1999; 21(1):67–72.

14. **Krough JWL, Payne AL, Anderson BB, Atkins P.** A brief description of the biomechanics and physiology of a strongman event: the tire flip. *J Strength Cond Res* 2010; 24(5):1223–1228.

15. **Kirksey B, Stone MH.** Periodizing a college sprint program: theory and practice. *Strength Cond* 1998; 20(3):42–47. 1998.

16. **Kraemer WJ, Vescovi JD, Dixon P.** The physiological basis of wrestling: implications for conditioning programs. *Strength Cond* 2004; 26(2):10–15.

17. **Krough JWL, Payne AL, Anderson BB, Atkins P.** A brief description of the biomechanics and physiology of a strongman event: the tire flip. *J Strength Cond Res* 2010; 24(5):1223–1228.

18. **McGill SM, McDermott A, Fenwick CMJ.** Comparison of different strongman events: trunk muscle activation and lumbar spine motion, load, and stiffness. *J Strength Cond Res* 2009; 23(4):1148–1161.

19. **McMaster DT, Cronin J, McGuigan M.** Forms of variable resistance training. *Strength Cond* 2009; 31(1):50–64.

20. **Murlasits Z, Langley J.** In-season resistance training for high school football. *Strength Cond* 2002; 24(4):65–68.

21. **Neelly KR, Terry JG, Morris MJ.** A mechanical comparison of linear and double-looped hung supplemental heavy chain resistance to the back squat: a case study. *J Strength Cond Res* 2010; 24(1):278–281.

22. **Ostrowski SJ, Carlson LA, Lawrence MA.** Effect of an unstable load on primary and stabilizing muscles during the bench press. *J Strength Cond Res* 2017; 31(2):430–434.

23. **Parakh AA, Domowitz FR.** Strength training for men's and women's ice hockey. *Strength Cond* 2000; 22(6):42–45.

24. **Pollitt D.** Sled dragging for hockey training. *Strength Cond* 2003; 25(5):7–16.

25. **Rosene JM.** In-season, off-ice conditioning for minor league professional ice hockey players. *Strength Cond* 2002; 24(1): 22–28.

26. **Siff MC.** Functional training revisited. *Strength Cond* 2002; 24(5):42–46.

27. **Szymanski DJ, Fredrick GA.** College baseball/softball periodized torso program. *Strength Cond* 1999; 21(4):42–47.

28. **Young W, Pryor J.** Resistance training for short sprints and maximum-speed sprints. *Strength Cond* 2001; 23(2):7–13.

29. **Waller W, Piper T, Townsend R.** Strongman events and strength and conditioning programs. *Strength Cond* 2003; 25(5):44–52.

30. **Winwood PW, Cronin JB, Keough WL, Dudson MK, Gill ND.** How coaches use strongman implements in strength and conditioning practice. *Int J Sports Sci Cond* 2014; 9(5):1107–1125.

31. **Winwood PW, Cronin JB, Posthumus LR, Finlayson SJ, Gill ND, Keough WL.** Strongman vs. traditional resistance training effects on muscular function and performance. *J Strength Cond Res* 2015; 29(2):429–439.

32. **Zemke B, Wright G.** The use of strongman type implements and training to increase sport performance in collegiate athletes. *Strength Cond* 2011; 33(4):1–7.

PART 4

SPECIAL TOPICS

Contents

CHAPTER ⑲

APPLIED SPORT PSYCHOLOGY

Traci A. Statler

OBJECTIVES

After completing this chapter, you will be able to:

- Understand the term mental toughness and recognize the components of this concept in athlete populations.
- Understand that the strength and conditioning coach cannot directly motivate athletes.
- Realize that the weight room is an appropriate place for athletes to set goals.
- Help athletes control their arousal levels.
- Explain what some differences may be between a confident athlete and an athlete who is not.
- Notice that most aspects of sports psychology are athlete-driven.

KEY TERMS

Achievement motivation	Instructional self-talk	Positive self-talk
Broad external focus	Intensity of effort	Process-based goals
Broad internal focus	Interactional view	Product-based goals
Concentration	Inverted-U hypothesis	Routine
Confidence	Mental toughness	Self-talk
Direction of effort	Motivation	Shifting
Emotions	Narrow external focus	Situation-centered
Goal ladder	Narrow internal focus	view
Individual zone of optimal	Negative self-talk	SMART goals
functioning (IZOF)	Participant-centered view	Superstition

INTRODUCTION

The primary goal of any strength and conditioning coach or personal trainer is to effectively improve athletic performance and fitness using proper strength and conditioning techniques, drawing from the scientific fields of anatomy, exercise physiology, biomechanics and nutrition. Effective practitioners will be skilled in program design, be adept in the teaching, reinforcement and monitoring of exercise technique, be familiar and comfortable with physical testing and evaluation, and have a variety of organizational and administrative skills (1). The addition of a working understanding of concepts from the field of sport and performance psychology may assist the coach or trainer in the attainment of this primary goal.

It has been argued that the role of sport psychology is to "help athletes achieve more consistent levels of performance at or near their physical potential by carefully managing their physical resources through appropriate psychological strategies and techniques" (2). A basic understanding of these strategies and techniques may help the strength and conditioning coach encourage more consistent effort in the weight room, generate better composure and ability to deal with distractions during workouts and foster more motivated and confident athletes.

The scientific discipline of sport psychology generally has three major goals: (i) observing and measuring psychological phenomena; (ii) investigating the relationship between psychological variables and performance; and (iii) applying this theoretical knowledge in performance settings to improve overall athletic performance (2). Therefore, the purpose of this chapter is to focus on the last of these goals, with the aim of helping you – the strength and conditioning coach – effectively integrate some critical sport psychology skills and situational cues into your training programs with the aim of improving your athlete's overall training and performance.

MENTAL TOUGHNESS

Turn on any televised sporting event or read any sport-related website and you will see and hear contributors talking about the **mental toughness** of the competitors. Oftentimes, sport analysts will use this term in reference to a number of different characteristics or when describing a host of different behaviors. Mental toughness is an umbrella term that many coaches, athletes, media outlets and others have used when referring to the "constellation of psychological factors that appear to discriminate between good and great athletes" (10). It is a multifaceted construct, with key components encompassing values, attitudes, thoughts and emotions, and often centering on sport psychology concepts like confidence, attentional control, motivation, positive attitude, resilience, thriving in pressure situations, and contextual sport intelligence (10).

Mental toughness can be effectively defined as:

[a] collection of experientially developed and inherent sport-specific and sport-general values, attitude, emotions and cognitions that influence the way in which an individual approaches, responds to, and appraises both negatively and positively construed pressure, challenge and adversity to consistently achieve his or her goals.

(11)

It encapsulates an athlete's ability to deal effectively with, and thrive through pressure, challenge and adversity when things are going well, in addition to when things are challenging (11). Clearly, as described in this definition, mental toughness is a desirable characteristic for any athlete.

With regard to the strength and conditioning coach, mental toughness is both something you may see evidenced in the behaviors of the athletes you supervise, as well as something that you can have an active part in developing. The weight room is an ideal location to train the enhancement of mental toughness, resilience and positive attitude specifically because of the inherent focus on hard work, patience and sacrifice within this environment. Every day in the weight room, or during conditioning drills, is an opportunity to effectively manage pressure, train appropriate focus and attention, build confidence and motivation, and generally foster beneficial behaviors. Each of these is a component piece of this multifaceted idea of mental toughness.

Recognize, however, that while a certain level of mental toughness is clearly a desirable thing, there can be some potential downsides.

For example, highly mentally tough athletes will often push themselves beyond their limits in exercises and drills. While this can be a beneficial characteristic in some settings (like over-speed training), in others it can be disastrous. An athlete rehabbing from injury who evidences high levels of mental toughness may push themselves past their limits in hopes of speeding up the process, but in reality, that determination may impede their progress. Further, a strong desire to achieve success combined with the high work ethic seen in mentally tough athletes can sometimes increase the likelihood of overtraining or over-reaching. An awareness and recognition of the components of mental toughness evidenced in your athletes is key, as the strength and conditioning coach is often in an ideal position to see these characteristics put to the test. Each of these component skills of mental toughness will be discussed in further detail in the rest of this chapter, because as the strength and conditioning coach, you are in the perfect position to help lead these athletes in the right direction.

MOTIVATION

As a strength and conditioning coach you may often find yourself wondering why some athletes you work with seem highly motivated and constantly strive for success in the weight room and on the field of play, whereas others seem to lack this motivation, appearing to simply "go through the motions" during workouts, practices and performance situations. Understanding motivation will probably be the most important psychological construct you will need as a strength coach, but it is also one you have little direct control over. You cannot motivate your athletes, but you can help them to better motivate themselves.

Motivation can be defined simply as the intensity and direction of one's effort (3). It is an inner condition that initiates, directs and sustains a person's behaviors. **Direction of effort** refers to whether an individual will seek out, approach or be attracted to certain situations (4). For example, an athlete might be attracted to the weight room because they

understand the relationship between training and sport performance. Along the same lines, an athlete might avoid the weight room because they do not enjoy the feeling of fatigue that often results from a hard workout. Both of these examples refer to the direction or one's effort – either toward the weight room or away from it. **Intensity of effort** refers to how much effort a person puts forth in a particular situation (4). For example, an athlete may attend daily workout sessions, but not put forth very much effort during that workout. On the other hand, an athlete may only have a short period of access to the training facility, yet make the most of every minute. This intensity is an indicator of motivation. Direction and intensity of effort are generally very closely related as those who are drawn to an activity (direction) will often put forth effort in that activity (intensity), and conversely, those who seem lackadaisical about their workouts, often do not have much attraction to the activity in the first place.

> Because motivation is "an inner condition," it is not something that you as the coach can give to your athletes. You cannot motivate someone else. However, you may be able to influence them in such a way that they can better motivate themselves.

Approaches to understanding motivation

Although motivation is something that works differently for everyone, most people can conceptualize how their own motivated behavior comes from a combination of three different orientations. These are the participant-centered view, the situation-centered view and the interactional view. The **participant-centered view** (sometimes called the trait-centered view) contends that motivated behavior is predominantly a function of individual characteristics, like a person's personality, their goals or their needs. Individual characteristics are what determine how motivated a person will be in any given situation. This could, for example, describe those who seem to excel in all areas of their lives, no matter the circumstances or environment. The **situation-centered view** (sometimes called the state-centered view), however, is in direct contrast to this. This view argues that a person's motivation is primarily determined by the situations in which they find themselves. You can likely think of situations where you would describe yourself as highly motivated, but others where your motivation is lacking. You are still the same person, but now the situation is different. The reality though is that while there may be some personality characteristics that influence your motivation, and you find yourself motivated in some situations but not others, most of us would generally argue that our motivated behaviors are a function of both our traits (who we are) and our states (how we feel at the moment, in the environment in which we find ourselves). Therefore, the view of motivation most widely accepted is the **interactional view**. The interactional view of motivation contends that "motivation results neither solely from participant factors nor solely from situational factors" (4). Rather, the best way to understand motivation is to consider both the person and the situation and how these two interact.

> The best way to understand motivated behavior is to consider both the person and the situation and examine how these two factors interact with each other.

Achievement motivation

As a strength coach, understanding that your athletes all participate in their respective sports for different reasons, approach the training expectations for their sports in different ways and experience motivation for these activities differently, will be critical in enhancing the level of service you can provide. To best tailor your services to the motivations of each athlete, an understanding of what specifically motivates them to act or behave in certain ways is needed. One construct that has emerged from the sport psychology literature to help with this is **achievement motivation**.

Achievement motivation refers to a person's orientation to strive for task success, persist in the face of failure and experience pride in accomplishments (5). It is an understanding

of this motivation that gives the coach insight into an athlete's desire and willingness to strive for excellence and under what circumstances they are willing to do so. As strength coaches, knowing if an athlete is motivated to achieve success, even if there is a likelihood of failing, tells us a lot about that athlete. It tells us that this athlete will challenge himself or herself. They will put in the extra effort to be sure they are getting the most out of every workout, even if they are not seeing immediate results. They will experience a sense of pride when they accomplish goals they have set for themselves, and they will not overly berate themselves when they fail, because they recognize that they have given their all.

Similarly, being able to recognize an athlete who is motivated to avoid failure is also beneficial for the strength coach. While these concepts may sound the same, from a motivational perspective, achieving success and avoiding failure are very different. Based on outward behaviors, the athlete motivated to avoid failure may look very similar to the one motivated to achieve success; however, an athlete motivated to avoid failure generally pushes themselves for very different reasons. This is a person who strives to avoid situations where failure can be internally attributed. This means that their prime motivation is to avoid blame or responsibility for failure. They will push themselves in the weight room if they perceive that they have the ability to be successful – not because they want to experience the success, but because they do not want to be held accountable for failing. If they perceive a training goal as highly challenging, they will not even make the attempt, because they do not want to take the risk of failing. For this athlete, motivation comes not from a desire to be successful, but more from a desire to protect the ego. They will appear motivated in environments where they can be successful because if they are successful, then the ego is safe. However, they may just as likely take on tasks with a very low probability of success, because if they then fail, the ego is still protected – the attitude being that there was little expectation of success in the first place, so why not give it a shot? This athlete will embrace simple tasks and impossible tasks, but shy away from anything truly challenging.

> Motive to avoid failure is not about avoiding failure – it is about avoiding situations where failure can be attributed internally. It is about protecting one's ego.

> Goal setting can provide direction, enhance motivation, give feedback on progress and foster a sense of support when used effectively.

Athletes with a motive to succeed will generally focus on the pride and confidence they experience when they are successful. They will often say that things within their control, like high effort and skill, account for their success. When they do fail, they often feel a sense of guilt, because they believe that they have it within their power to do better. On the other hand, athletes with a motive to avoid failure will more often focus on the sense of shame or worry that they experience when they are unsuccessful. They often attribute their failure to things outside of their control, like luck, bad officiating or the skill of the other team. When they are successful, they will generally feel a sense of relief and feel grateful because they have managed to protect their ego. Paying attention to how your athletes explain or attribute their success and failure, and observing their emotional reactions to these situations, can therefore tell you a lot about their achievement motivation.

GOAL SETTING

One effective tool for enhancing motivation is through setting and hopefully achieving the goals we set for ourselves. Additionally, setting goals can provide direction, give feedback and foster a sense of support as one works toward the attainment of a task. Effective goal setting produces a number of beneficial behavioral changes including more productive training and practice sessions, which generally result in more focused competition behavior.

The weight room is a great place to encourage goal setting. This is one location where the athlete has the most control over their own performance and is a place they spend concentrated amounts of time. Potential areas in strength and conditioning where goal setting might prove effective include learning appropriate lifting technique and skill refinement, improving overall strength and/or endurance, targeting specific performance markers (i.e., 1RMs, jump heights, sprint times), developing "quality practice" behaviors and dealing with distractions.

Process versus product goals

There is much discussion within the field of sport psychology about the most effective way to structure or create goal statements. Many have argued that performers should focus more on creating and reinforcing **process-based goals**, or goals that are centered in the present rather than **product-based goals**, or those that focus more on an outcome. The idea behind this supposition is that if one effectively works toward attaining process-based goals, the probability of achieving the desired outcomes or results correspondingly increases. The outcomes will take care of themselves. Others have stated, however, that in sport settings, the outcome is what really matters, so should the goal statement not then reflect this?

The reality is that every athlete is different. Some are highly motivated by the outcome or product-focused goal, using that to drive their daily behaviors – the proverbial carrot before the horse. Others may be distracted by the product goal, as it is something outside of the present. It is something "out there" and not what I need to be thinking about right now. Some find that outcome-focused goals elevate anxiety, as the athlete is fixating on something not entirely within their control. As the coach, understanding how your athletes respond to different types of goal structures and how those varying goal statements help or hinder overall performance can assist you in better structuring your program designs to coincide with that athlete's tendencies.

> Both process and product goals can be effective at providing direction and motivating an athlete; however, process goals raise the probability that the desired outcomes will occur.

Effective structure

As the strength coach, you are contributing to, if not fully creating, the daily, weekly, monthly, seasonal and yearly fitness goals for every athlete on the teams with which you work. As you design the training programs for these athletes, you may choose to discuss with them the rationales behind the plans you generate. Your training plans are in essence a description of the goals you have for these athletes. They fill one main purpose of goal setting: providing direction. Your training programs give the athlete the direction they need, every day, week or month, to attain the long-term strength, fitness, power or endurance plans you have for them. When the athlete then takes these training programs and begins to implement them, they may wish to create additional goal statements that correspond to the training plan. These goal statements may serve a variety of purposes, including the development of motivation, the enhancement of confidence, and the satisfaction and sense of pride that comes from success.

Goal ladders

A Chinese proverb states, "A journey of a thousand miles begins with a single step." This idea applies well to the creation of effective goals. Many of us can clearly list a number of long-term goals we have for ourselves – win the championship, get that great job, get an "A" in that class, etc. An understanding of the long-term goal likely also applies to the athletes in your weight room as well (bench x-number of pounds, jump this high, get my Vo_2 max to here, etc.). The long-term goal is often easy to conceptualize. It is the understanding of where to go from there – the single steps – that can be challenging. This is where "goal ladders" can be helpful.

Goal ladders are simply conceptual diagrams that outline the steps needed to attain the desired long-term goal. If, for example, the long-term goal for one of your athletes is to improve their front squat 1RM, you will likely have a plan in your head for how you will progressively train that athlete to attain this outcome goal. It is unlikely that you would expect to see improvement in this skill without creating a strategic, periodized training plan that progressively outlines what the athlete will do today, this week, this month and this season to attain this goal. Goal ladders are specific to the goal for which they are created, but generally follow a structure that includes a series of short-term, medium-range and long-term

goals that all lead to the final outcome goal. Therefore, if the long-term goal is to improve one's 1RM by 5% by the end of this microcycle, an evaluation of several medium-range and short-term goals must occur. What needs to happen in order for me to improve by 5%? What can I do this week to improve the likelihood of that? What can I do today to take a step toward this? What can I do in this set? The purpose of each goal ladder is to give the performer something they can do right now that will take them one step closer to that long-term goal.

> Goal ladders are conceptual diagrams that show the progression of goal development along the path toward achieving the long-term goal.

SMART goals

The acronym **SMART** has often been used to guide people in the effective formation of their goal statements. The letters stand for the following:

- S – Specific – Goals need to be written or conceptualized behaviorally, in that they must provide specific guidelines on what to do or think or feel right now. The goal, "I will train with intensity" may sound good, but what does it really mean? What does "with intensity" look like? Rather, "I will focus on proper body alignment in every squat repetition I perform in practice today" is a more effective and specific goal statement.
- M – Measurable – How will you know if you have attained a desired goal if there is no way to determine its attainment? Effective goals should have some way of establishing success or failure built into their wording. At the end of your workout, you should be able to look at your goals' statements and definitively determine if you have met them.
- A – Attainable – Goals should be challenging, but attainable. If goals are set "too easy," there is no sense of accomplishment generated when success is attained. If the goal for today's practice is simply, "Complete every repetition indicated in my

training plan for today's workout," and this is an athlete who regularly completes training sessions in full, there is no motivation, reward or feedback to be garnered from this goal statement.

- R – Realistic – Though goals must be challenging, they cannot be unreachable. If I am an athlete just coming off a lower back injury, and my goal for today's practice is to complete a set of dead-lifts at my pre-injury weight, I am clearly not going to attain my goal. If goals are set "too hard," the likelihood of failure is high and will thus have a tendency to be demotivating.
- T – Time-Framed – Give yourself a time frame to accomplish your goals. Having a specific window for completion of your goals gives you motivation and structure that may be lacking otherwise. This guideline also corresponds to the "Attainable" and "Realistic" descriptors as well.

Q&A FROM THE FIELD

I coach a lot of different athletes and don't really have time to sit down with each one more than once a season to discuss their training goals. How can I effectively monitor how they are progressing?

– DI College Strength and Conditioning Coach

Providing feedback to your athletes need not be an overly time-consuming process. If you meet with your athletes individually at the start of the season, you can have a discussion about the various fitness and performance goals that athlete will have. If you can periodically review these goals, perhaps just a few each week, you can focus on providing encouragement and support to those athletes at that time. You may also encourage your athletes to share their goals with other members of the team so they may continually encourage each other and hold each other accountable. Lastly, if you are able to publicly reward or acknowledge athletes who are making respectable progress toward their goals, you will likely find that your athletes' motivation improves thereby reinforcing the process without you having to do much.

ENERGY AND AROUSAL MANAGEMENT

As explained earlier in this book, an understanding of how the human body creates energy to fuel various processes is critical for any effective strength and conditioning coach. As stated in Chapter 1 (Bioenergetics), "human movement requires energy, and energy is vital for athletic performance." Though they were talking specifically about bioenergetics from a physiological perspective, the reality is that in order for an athlete to perform effectively, they also need to effectively manage their mental energy.

Mental energy is generated, maintained, depleted and refreshed via our emotions. **Emotions** are strong feelings, having both physical and psychological manifestations that serve to energize behaviors. These energy-impacting emotions can have both beneficial and detrimental effects on human performance, often depending on how a person interprets them. Emotions are beneficial to performance when they get us excited, cause us to feel motivated, elevate confidence in ourselves and push us to challenge ourselves in performance. Emotion can be detrimental, however, when there is too much or too little (a performer being too "amped up" or "too flat") or when we lose control of our emotions and cease to function effectively in a performance environment (i.e., an athlete who cannot control their anger or frustration).

> Emotions are generators of mental energy and can be beneficial or detrimental to performance depending upon how a person interprets them.

Factors affecting mental energy

Athletes often pay the most attention to their mental energy levels when it comes time for competition; however, it is also important to recognize how these energy levels affect performance in practice and training conditions as well. Helping your athletes understand what things "drain their battery" prior to beginning their training sessions can help mitigate potential injury. Helping them understand what things "charge their battery" can generate more motivated, focused workouts. This "charging and draining" of one's proverbial battery is simply a way of understanding how arousal levels impact performance. Athletes who are unable to effectively regulate their arousal levels may find themselves experiencing decreases in performance, as well as increased stress and worry. In order to perform at one's best, athletes need to recognize what factors contribute to the most ideal arousal levels for their performances.

A simple tool for evaluating what factors impact your athletes' arousal levels is to have them reflect on what their best performance felt like. Ask them to describe the circumstances of that day, including things like their nutrition, rest and other physical and mental demands they may have been facing. Then have them compare that to their worst performance (or any day where they felt particularly "off"). What factors were different? What were the same? Ask them which of these factors are things they can control. Once the controllable factors are identified, then encourage them to manipulate these factors to help generate an ideal arousal level for performance. If they identify factors outside of their control, remind them that these are things outside of their control, and focusing on those will only "drain their batteries." Instead, ask if there are any tools they can use to compensate for these interfering factors.

"Ain't no use worrying about things beyond your control, because if they're beyond your control, ain't no use worrying … Ain't no use worrying about things within your control, because if they are within your control, ain't no use worrying." – Mickey Rivers

Identifying effective arousal levels

Before you can help your athletes get to the "right" level of arousal or mental energy for performance, they first need to determine what that right level is for them. Optimum arousal is different for every person, and often differs within that person depending on the situation. For example, think about how much arousal or energy you need to perform a Fartlek workout. Is this the same level you would need for a plyometric test?

What about for cardiovascular endurance training? Clearly each of these activities will require a different level of mental energy (as well as physical energy) to perform effectively. It is important for every athlete to know what arousal levels work best for them in different situations. Too much arousal can lead to nervousness, anxiety, muscle tension and/or over-aggressiveness. Too little arousal can lead to distraction, apathy and concentration problems.

Optimal arousal levels will differ from person to person, and from situation to situation. Performers need to identify what arousal levels work best for them in a variety of circumstances.

In an effort to better understand the relationship between energy/arousal levels and performance, many sport psychology professionals turn to the **inverted-U hypothesis** for a basic explanation. The inverted-U hypothesis states that performance will improve as arousal levels increase up to some optimal point. Beyond that point, however, further increases in arousal will cause performance to suffer (Figure 19.1).

When the performer is experiencing low arousal or energy levels, they will feel "flat," sluggish or tired until the energy level rises to a more optimum point. Their attention

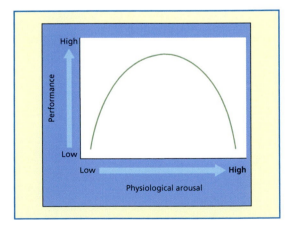

Figure 19.1 The inverted-U hypothesis. Performance will improve with increases in arousal levels up to some optimum point, whereupon further increases in arousal will cause a performance decrement.

will wander, they experience a sense of apathy regarding the performance and their body will feel physically heavy. Then as arousal increases, the performer will begin to feel more energetic, motivated and confident. This ideal performance state will begin to deteriorate, however, if the person cannot keep that mental energy level at the appropriate point. If arousal continues to increase past this ideal state, performance will start to decline, with the performer now feeling too "amped up," intense or frantic. They will feel high levels of muscle tension, have difficulty focusing, may have difficulty breathing and may feel hyperactive. As the strength coach, you will often be able to see behavioral examples of all of these levels in your athletes. Helping them recognize their arousal levels may help them better manage these variations, thus improving their overall performance during workouts.

It is important to recognize though that not all athletes performing the same tasks will need the same level of mental energy. Every athlete will have their own **individual zone of optimal functioning (IZOF)** or state at which their best performance occurs. The inverted-U and IZOF constructs can help you better explain this energy-performance relationship to your athletes. Furthermore, having high or low levels of arousal is not always necessarily detrimental. Some athletes report needing to feel really excited in order to perform effectively (i.e., certain extreme sport athletes) and if they are feeling low or even moderate arousal levels, they have difficulty performing well. The practical reality is that how an athlete handles their arousal level is far more important than how much arousal they may have. The weight room is an ideal environment for helping your athletes learn to manage arousal levels more effectively, as you can manipulate arousal in this controlled environment to illustrate how the differences correspond to their perceptions of feeling ready to perform.

Maintaining appropriate arousal levels

The reality is that every athlete or performer will experience pressure at some point in their career – it is a defining characteristic of competition – but it is the mentally skilled performer who can stay composed enough to perform despite that pressure. When your athletes recognize that they have too much arousal to perform effectively, can they calm themselves down? If they notice that they are too "flat," can they increase their arousal enough to get the job done? These are skills your athletes need on the competitive fields and courts, but having these abilities will also serve them well in the weight room and during training.

When you notice an athlete who seems to be overly pumped, is having difficulty focusing and seems to be acting in a hyperactive way, you can suggest some very basic relaxation techniques to bring them back to that ideal performance zone. These are also effective tools for maximizing training effectiveness. Encouraging the athlete to slow down, close their eyes and take a few deep breaths is a quick method to decrease arousal levels. Another is having them take their pulse and try to actively slow it down. Sometimes the immediate physical feedback from measuring heart rate can help them recognize what over-arousal feels like. If the athlete can learn to control him/herself, "then they have an opportunity to control the situation, instead of letting the situation control them. The athlete must find a relaxation technique that works for them; practice it; master it; and then reap the benefits in … their performance" (6).

> Slow, controlled, deep breathing is an effective tool for managing the sensation of too much arousal, and is highly effective at bringing energy levels back to an ideal state.

More than likely, however, you will be confronted with athletes on the opposite side of this spectrum: those who have too little arousal to perform effectively during their workouts. These athletes will look sluggish, will be easily distracted, will be moving slowly and will lack enthusiasm. When you see this is your weight room, you can suggest some simple activation techniques. First, research shows that mood is often impacted by music (7). If the athlete is too "flat," suggest a more up-beat play list on their iPod. Even if you do not allow headphones in your weight room, you likely have some sort of stereo system – crank it up! Respiration rate also impacts arousal level, but rather than using it to calm down, in this instance encourage the athlete to use it to pump up. Increasing one's respiration rate elevates heart rate and increases arousal levels. The use of energizing cue words, self-talk and creating images of successful attempts can also be useful here. These will be discussed in more depth later in this chapter, but are also typical sport psychology "tools" or skills often described in detail in many sport psychology textbooks.

CONCENTRATION (FOCUS)

"Every athlete quickly recognizes that without appropriate concentration their performances will be inconsistent, error prone, and less than optimal. Concentration therefore is a skill and must be learned" (6). **Concentration** can be defined as the ability to focus on appropriate cues in a given situation and control your responses to these cues for the execution of a particular skill (4). Concentration (or focus) therefore, is a skill athletes will need to perform effectively in competition, but it is also one critical for effective performance in practice and conditioning sessions. Unfortunately, it is a skill that often gets overlooked until it is notably absent – that is, it is one of the psychological skill areas that may only become visible when an athlete's behavior reveals a lack of appropriate sport focus (8).

Attention styles

One useful framework for understanding how focus and concentration works in performance settings has been Robert Nideffer's model of attention styles (Figure 19.2). This model suggests that an athlete's focus continually shifts between four quadrants, varying along two intersecting continuums from broad to narrow and from internal to external (9). This then implies that there is not just one type of concentration or attention style; rather there are several different types that can affect performance at different times and in different ways throughout performance. Furthermore, like

the previous discussion of arousal levels, there is no one attention style that is best for every person in every situation. Each type of athletic performance may demand one or several attention styles throughout a performance. Each athletic situation requires a variety of specific attention styles to perform adequately. Even within the same athletic team, the concentration demands on individual athletes may be quite different. It is therefore imperative for an athlete to learn to shift his/her focus in an appropriate manner as the situation requires. In order to do this effectively, athletes must master the ability to focus in each of the four quadrants as well as be able to shift between each as necessary (9).

The first attention style is a **broad external focus**, where the performer will rapidly assess a situation, taking in a variety of information from the external environment. In a strength and conditioning context, this would be the necessary focus needed at the beginning of a workout where the athlete would look around the room and identify things like how many others are present, where the water containers are located and the volume of the music. The next style is a **broad internal focus**, where the athlete will begin to analyze and plan their reaction to the information assessed, in essence, creating a game plan or strategy. Carrying the same example forward, this would be when the athlete contemplates the fact that there

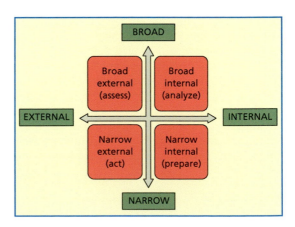

Figure 19.2 Nideffer's theory of attentional style. Performers need to master the ability to effectively shift their attention between each of these four quadrants.

are several other athletes waiting to use the Olympic platforms, so he or she decides to rearrange their workout to take advantage of the available cardiovascular equipment. The next category of focus is **narrow internal**. This is where the athlete must now be able to center their concentration on mentally rehearsing a performance skill or regulating an emotional state. This stage of concentration is where an athlete internally prepares to act. In our weight room example, this could be the athlete creating a mental image of themselves setting the speed and incline of the treadmill and creating the necessary energy level for a good cardio session. The fourth category of concentration is **narrow external**, where the athlete will focus entirely on one or two external cues to actually perform the action necessary. This is where the athlete will pay attention to the treadmill's display, noting items like miles per hour and METs. The final requirement of attentional style needed for an athlete to perform effectively is referred to as **shifting**. While this is not a separate attentional style in and of itself, it is a critical ability for effective performance. It is absolutely necessary for an athlete to have a certain amount of attentional flexibility within any given situation. In essence, they need to be adept at "bouncing" back and forth between the four categories to assure that they are picking up all relevant cues and filtering out all irrelevant ones. For example, if our athlete on the treadmill were only focused on the display's readout (narrow external), they might miss the cue of their coach who just came into the weight room looking for them (broad external). Clearly, effective concentration requires that you be adept at shifting your focus to the appropriate cues at the appropriate times.

> Effective concentration requires a performer to be adept at shifting between a broad external, broad internal, narrow internal and narrow external focus of attention as needed to perform in any given situation.

Distractions

The ability to maintain concentration while immersed in competition or practice drills is critical to effective performance. However, the human brain is not capable of maintaining effective focus for the full duration of an athletic event or workout session. Therefore, we must be able to identify the factors that generate distractions and learn how to effectively deal with them so as not to interfere with performance.

Once you can recognize potential distractions, you can then create a plan for dealing with them. Athletes often report that their distractions come simply from thinking about the wrong things at the wrong times – that they have an inappropriate attentional style. Athletes often come into the weight room still focused on the things that happened earlier in their day, either at practice, or during school, or with relationships they have outside of the sporting arena. Letting go of those thoughts so that you can focus on the appropriate cues will be critical to the attainment of a good workout. Athletes tend to lose their focus when they choose instead to pay attention to events and experiences that occurred in the past, start thinking about those that will occur in the future, focus on things outside of their control or on things irrelevant to the task at hand. Furthermore, experiencing excessive anxiety or being overly tired can also cause distraction, as the athlete is then focused on inappropriate cues. As the coach, you can contribute to the creation of an effective performance environment by encouraging your athletes to get enough rest prior to their workouts, creating a non-threatening environment for your athletes and encouraging them to practice their concentration skills while training.

Refocusing strategies

There are several tools or strategies one can use to practice concentration. The weight room is often an ideal environment for this as well because it is usually a location where a multitude of things are going on at the same time, with several people doing different things, and loads of potential distractions present. If an athlete can effectively tune their ability to shift between all the needed attentional styles throughout the duration of a workout, chances are high that they will be able to transition those skills out onto the playing fields and courts. The following are some suggestions for practicing concentration skills:

- "Distraction inoculations" – Create tools that simulate the typical distractions your athletes report. Things like taped recordings of crowd noise, confederate observers watching a practice session as if they were spectators, judges or other coaches on-site evaluating the athlete as they work out, or negative words or phrases scattered around the facility to invoke negative thoughts will all work. Have the athletes practice maintaining the effective focus despite these distractions, in essence "inoculating" them to their existence.

- Cue words and positive self-talk – Cue words or phrases are things that can be said out loud or in one's head that remind the athlete to focus on specific things. For example, an athlete just learning the proper form for a power clean might choose to say the instructional cue words "Scoop!" or "Catch!" to remind themselves to focus on these elements of technique. Another might choose to use more motivational cue words (like "Come on! You've got this!") to get their energy level up and focus themselves on the feeling needed to perform well. The key to cue words is to keep them simple. More on self-talk will be provided later in this chapter.

- Routines – Pre-performance routines improve focus by helping the athlete transfer their attention from task-irrelevant concepts that might distract them from their preparation to those task-relevant thoughts they need to get ready to perform (4). These can be used before the training session begins (to prepare for your workout), during your workout in preparation for a challenging lift or set, and even after your workout to transition your focus away from the activities in the weight room back to whatever activity is next. Recognize, however, that routines are not the same things as superstitions. A **routine** is a conscious decision to perform an action or series of actions with the express purpose of benefitting performance in some way. A **superstition** is an action taken for fear of what might happen if the action is not taken. Routines direct focus to appropriate cues needed for effective performance. Superstitions draw focus away from these relevant cues, instead focusing on the irrelevant cue of fear of outcomes.

- Two-minute drill – The two-minute drill is one many coaches use in a variety of settings to get their athletes to focus on what they will do in a particular situation. Concerning concentration training, the two-minute drill is simply telling yourself to focus on whatever action you are performing for the next two minutes. At the end of that two-minute period, you are giving yourself permission to let your attention wander. When the two minutes start, you are committing to fully directing your focus to the task-relevant cues needed to perform. You may become aware of internal or external distractions, but as soon as you recognize them, you make a conscious effort to bring your focus back to the task at hand. You are fully committed and fully invested in this thing right here, right now, because you know you only have to focus for two little minutes. This is a great exercise for practicing concentration skills because it echoes the realities of many sports. Most sporting events are composed of short bursts of plays, downs, attempts, sets or heats, followed by some sort of brief "rest" period. This occurs in resistance and interval training as well, and presents a great opportunity to challenge the athlete to focus for "just this next ten-rep set" or "just this next interval" as this will get them adept at shifting in and out of intense focus.

The skills of concentration are probably the most relevant of all the psychological skills for actual performance but they can only be mastered if the athlete has learned to control their arousal levels first. Concentration, anxiety, arousal and self-confidence are all intricately interwoven, with each of these factors greatly dependent upon effective concentration skills.

A gymnast is faced with maintaining concentration during competition

During a gymnastics competition, there are many distractions that occur. There are external variables that may affect an athlete's concentration and may detract from her optimal performance. The gymnast's first event of the meet is the floor exercise. While on the floor, the gymnast has many variables on which to focus. This event involves the playing of music and synchronization of movements to the music. She will have to be able to concentrate on specific cues in the music to stay on point. In addition, competitions tend to have large crowds. Thus, there may be an excess amount of noise. She will have to be able to concentrate on the task at hand and cancel out the noise from the crowd. If she is able to focus, she will most likely perform near or at optimal level.

CONFIDENCE AND SELF-TALK

All other things being equal, a confident athlete will perform better than one without confidence (8). **Confidence** is the belief that one's abilities are greater than or equal to the demands placed upon them. It is the belief that you can successfully perform a desired behavior or generate a desired outcome. Confidence is most often situation-specific, though some athletes seem to exhibit confidence across a variety of different domains. More often, however, people are confident in some elements of their lives and less confident in others, or in one skill but not others. Confidence is a critical component for effective sport participation. A confident athlete will:

- Set challenging goals for themselves
- Recover from set-backs, losses or disappointments fairly quickly
- Persist when faced with adversity
- Focus on success and the relevant cues necessary to attain it
- Stay cool under pressure situations
- Trust themselves, their perceptions and their decisions
- Push themselves past their perceived limits

An observant strength and conditioning coach will generally be able to spot an athlete lacking in confidence. They will give up easily when situations get challenging, they are generally

unwilling to take risks, they will struggle maintaining focus, they will appear tentative and they will protect themselves, both physically and mentally. The good news though is that confidence is a "teachable" skill. Like many of the other sport psychology skills described in this chapter, confidence can be developed through practice, thereby improving overall performance.

> All other things being equal, a confident athlete will generally outperform one with low confidence because they challenge themselves more, trust in their abilities and stay focused on the task-relevant cues needed to perform well.

Building, enhancing and maintaining confidence

As a coach, you are in a position to assist athletes in developing, enhancing and maintaining their confidence levels, both as they relate to their sports as well as in more general aspects of their lives. Although research shows that a large part of a person's confidence is generated from success in past performances, the reality is that several other experiences and sources can contribute to this characteristic as well. Training hard and effectively can contribute to effective performance, which can enhance confidence levels. Breaking down complex skills or tasks into manageable parts and succeeding at these steps can also enhance confidence levels. Recognizing and taking control over the things you can control, and letting go of those that you cannot, can further enhance confidence. It is important to recognize that it is not just the "big" things that contribute to building confidence – each "little" accomplishment does too. When viewed from this perspective, every successful day in the weight room or hard workout completed can contribute to the development of confidence.

As their strength coach, the ways in which you interact with your athletes can contribute to or deteriorate their confidence in themselves. Be aware of how you communicate with your athletes, both verbally and nonverbally, during your interactions with them. You spend a great deal of time communicating expectations, teaching new skills and behaviors, providing feedback and correcting errors, and encouraging and rewarding achievement. In each of these areas, you have an opportunity to develop and reinforce confidence by acknowledging success (even the small ones) and focusing on the constructive element of criticism, rather than just the critical. Try to "catch" your athletes being successful, rather than just catching their errors.

TYPES OF SELF-TALK

The internal language athletes use with themselves has the ability to impact everything described thus far in this chapter – the setting of challenging but realistic goals, the initiation and sustaining of motivation, the trust in self to manage arousal levels, and the ability to direct and redirect focus. This internal language – self-talk – is essentially the process of thinking and cognition. It is the running dialogue you have going on in your head all the time. Self-talk is closely related to confidence in that a person's self-talk is generally representative of what they believe.

There are essentially three types of performance-influencing self-talk – instructional, negative and positive. Instructional self-talk was alluded to earlier in this chapter in the discussion of using cue words to direct focus. Instructional self-talk helps the performer focus on technical, tactical or task-related elements of performance with the goal of improving execution (4). Encouraging your athletes to use instructional self-talk can be beneficial in the development and reinforcement of confidence because each instance can be viewed

as a mini attempt at being successful. When an athlete gives themselves that instructional cue and then is able to follow through on that action, they have just experienced success. Knowing their instructional self-talk and reinforcing it is a great way to help your athletes develop their confidence.

The next category, negative self-talk, is the most damaging to athletic performance but is difficult to completely avoid or control. It is generally critical and self-demeaning, interfering with a performer's appropriate focus. Any time negative emotions (distress, anxiety, fear or frustration) occur, chances are the vast majority of athletes will respond by talking to themselves negatively. Effective physical performance can therefore be destroyed by negative self-talk. Negative self-talk and negative thinking are virtually the same thing, and are generally caused by fear of failure, fear of success, comparison to others, insecurity, poor confidence and unrealistic expectations (6). Negative self-talk lessens the control athletes have over themselves, as it inhibits constructive and reinforcing thought patterns, thus eroding confidence and impairing performance.

Positive self-talk, on the other hand, is the type of talk that programs our minds with ideas that enable us to manage situations more effectively. Positive self-talk consists of reinforcing statements we say to ourselves generally increasing energy, effort and positive attitude, but that do not carry any task-specific cues (4). It is solution directed, not problem focused. Positive self-talk focuses on the process, stays in the present moment and is designed to be uplifting. It is essential for athletes to learn to talk to themselves from a positive perspective, thus enhancing the probability of consistent and optimal performance. Like any skill though, positive self-talk must be practiced to acquire positive, solution-focused inner dialogue. Habits of positive thinking can become integrated and automated by an athlete if they consciously practice developing it.

SUMMARY

It can be argued that the weight room, in and of itself, is a performance environment. The activities contained therein are like sporting events, and the strength and conditioning coach is in the role of the team leader. As such, all the tools of sport psychology that a sport coach can implement with their athletes on the field of play and in performance practices can be replicated and reinforced in the weight room by the strength and conditioning coach.

The full complement of sport psychology skills and tools that might benefit an athlete during their workouts is beyond the scope of this one chapter; however, several of the most relevant constructs have been presented here. The concepts of goal setting, motivation, energy and arousal management, concentration, self-talk and confidence development are all elements of sport psychology training that every athlete can use to better not only their performance, but their experience of that performance as well. Athletes who have practiced with these mental skills are better able to perform more consistently across competitions, recover their composure more quickly after a mistake or distraction, and perform at their best when the pressure is on. As the strength and conditioning coach, you are in a prime position to assist your athletes with these critical constructs.

MAXING OUT

1 A head coach indicates that he is concerned about the motivation levels of his athletes for their training sessions. The coach asks the strength and conditioning coach to help "pump up" the athletes to get them more motivated for workouts. What does the strength and conditioning coach need to understand about motivation? How might they be able to better understand the existing motivation levels of the athletes? What might they be able to do to impact that motivation?

2 A football player tells the strength and conditioning coach that his main training goal for the season is simply "to get stronger." How can the coach work with this athlete to improve the structure and phrasing of this goal statement? How might they work together through this process to develop effective short-term and long-term goals to attain this season-long mission?

3 Why is it important for an athlete to understand the ideal arousal level needed for them in the weight room? If they find that they are "too low," what might they do to elevate this energy level? If they find they are "too high," how might they get more "pumped up"?

4 Strength and conditioning requires different types of attention and focus at different times. When might an athlete need to have a "broad external" focus? A "broad internal" one? When would they need a more internal focus?

5 What kinds of self-talk might be beneficial for an athlete during conditioning training? How does an athlete's self-talk relate to their confidence?

CASE EXAMPLE

A change in playing stats

Background

Mike has been playing soccer for the past five years. He is currently a junior and playing for his college team. He had been starting each match; however, he has recently lost his starting position. Mike is not putting as much effort into each practice, being antisocial toward teammates. As well, he has been nonresponsive during practices. What could Mike be suffering from and what might be done to help him?

(continued)

(continued)

Recommendations/considerations

The behaviors exhibited by Mike could illustrate that he is suffering from decreased motivation. The strength and conditioning coach or sport psychology consultant could communicate with Mike to establish his main motivators and possibly reevaluate what he wants from the sport.

Implementations

A sport psychology consultant could work in unison with the strength and conditioning coaches and athletes to develop different strategies or techniques to better help athletes find motivation in their sport. Possible ways of accomplishing this would be by setting goals, as well as finding meaning within themselves and their sport. Over time, Mike will hopefully find new motivation with himself to perform at his optimal level, in turn possibly regaining his status within the team.

REFERENCES

1. Triplett NT, Williams C, McHenry P, Doscher M. *Strength & Conditioning Professional Standards & Guidelines* (online). Available: www.nsca-lift.org/publications/SCStandards.pdf. 2009.

2. Hatfield BD, Brody EB. Psychology of athletic preparation and performance. In: Baechle TR, Earle RW, eds. *Essentials of Strength Training and Conditioning*, 3rd ed. Champaign, IL: Human Kinetics, 2008; 187–207.

3. Sage G. *Introduction to Motor Behavior: A Neuropsychological Approach*, 2nd ed. Boston, MA: Addison-Wesley, 1977.

4. Weinberg RS, Gould D. *Foundations of Sport and Exercise Psychology*, 4th ed. Champaign, IL: Human Kinetics, 2007.

5. Gill D. *Psychological Dynamics of Sport and Exercise*. Champaign, IL: Human Kinetics, 2000.

6. Henschen KP, Statler TA, Lidor R. Psychological factors of tactical preparation. In: Blumenstein B, Lidor R & Tenenbaum G, eds. *Psychology of Sport Training*. Oxford, UK: Meyer & Meyer, 2007, 104–114.

7. Karageorghis C, Terry P. The psychophysical effects of music in sport and exercise: A review. *Journal of Sport Behavior* 1997; 20:54–68.

8. *Sport Psychology Mental Training Manual: Coaches' Guide*. United States Olympic Committee, 2006.

9. Nideffer RM, Segal M. Concentration and attention control training. In Williams JM ed. *Applied Sport Psychology: Personal Growth to Peak Performance*, 4th ed. Mountain View, CA: Mayfield, 2001, 312–332.

10. Gucciardi DF, Mallett CJ. Mental toughness. In Hanrahan SJ and Andersen MB eds. *Routledge Handbook of Applied Sport Psychology*. London: Routledge, 2013. 547–556.

11. Gucciardi DF, Gordon S, Dimmock JA. Advancing mental toughness research and theory using personal construct psychology. *Int Rev Sport Exerc Psychol* 2009; 2:45–72.

Contents

CHAPTER 20

STRENGTH TRAINING FOR SPECIAL POPULATIONS

Marie E. Pepin, Joseph A. Roche, and Moh H. Malek

OBJECTIVES

After reading this chapter, you will be able to:

- Identify various populations that will benefit from specific exercise programs.
- Demonstrate an understanding of the roles of strength training in different special populations.
- Discuss the role of strength training in various musculoskeletal diseases and the role of strength training in attenuating the progressive nature of these diseases.
- Implement an appropriate exercise prescription for various special populations.

KEY TERMS

Activity of daily living (ADL)	Down syndrome	Osteopenia
Adolescents	Epiphyseal plates	Osteoporosis
Aging	Muscular dystrophy	Resistance training
Cerebral palsy (CP)	Myopathies	Sarcopenia
Children	Neuropathies	Spinal cord injury (SCI)

INTRODUCTION

People are living longer, often with one or more chronic diseases. Athletes with disabilities are shattering stereotypes. Physicians are prescribing exercise for their patients to manage medical conditions such as cardiovascular disease and diabetes. Limited insurance coverage may lead a person with hemiplegia out of the physical therapy clinic and into the gym. These are just some of the reasons why

exercise management for special populations has become so important.

Venues such as hospital-based wellness centers, fitness centers, and assisted living facilities have a wide mix of clients with special needs. In 2002, Malek et al. (78) found that the majority of health fitness instructors surveyed in the Southern California area lacked the level of knowledge needed to safely train special populations. Therefore, the purpose of this chapter is to introduce the reader to a variety of special populations and the current findings related to exercise as a form of intervention. This chapter should be used as a reference by the health fitness instructor rather than a strict guideline.

As in the case of any training regimen, the health fitness instructor needs to design an individualized program in close consultation with the client. For example, one client with a spinal cord injury may desire the strength and endurance to enter athletic competition; another may desire the strength and endurance to be able to get out of bed independently. In any case, it is imperative to work in close communication with the physician, physical therapist, or other primary care personnel to ensure the safety of the special population client. The health fitness instructor must understand the client's needs and precautions, where to get more information, and most importantly, be alert to problems and know when to take action or call for medical help. Though caution is essential, it is equally important not to deny those with special needs the opportunity to reap the benefits of exercise.

This chapter touches upon cardiovascular exercise and flexibility, but the focus is on resistance training. **Resistance training** has become a critical component of exercise programs for athletes, in marked contrast to previous generations who were instructed to avoid resistance training for fear of becoming "muscle bound". More importantly, resistance training is now recognized as an important component of overall health and fitness in the general population (46). There are, however, groups of individuals whose participation in resistance training requires special scrutiny. In this chapter, resistance training for several populations with special needs is discussed, and unique aspects and possible contraindications for resistance training are considered. For those populations where resistance training is appropriate, the general principles of program design are the same as for the general population. That is, factors such as proper warm up, periodization, and specificity need to be incorporated in all programs. Caution needs to be employed to avoid injury and overwork, but it should be noted that the benefits of resistance training only occur through the application of progressive overload, and

high intensity training (in terms of % 1RM) is often necessary for optimal benefits even in special populations.

GERIATRICS

In 2014, there were over 46.2 million people aged 65 and older living in the United States, accounting for just more than 14.5% of the total population or about one in every seven (17). This number will continue to grow over the next two decades as the Baby Boomers age and the population of people 65 and older in 2060 is projected to be over 98 million (17). Among community-resident Medicare beneficiaries age 65 and older, 28% have difficulties with at least one **activity of daily living (ADLs)** which is attributable to the decrease in physical activity associated with aging. Indeed, only 42% of persons aged 65 to 74 and 29% of persons 75 and older report that they engage in regular leisure-time physical activity (109). Only 16.1% reported meeting strength training guidelines and this number decreases to 10.1% for those with difficulty walking a quarter of a mile (66). Due to the size of this demographic and the need for physical activity in the geriatric clients, health fitness professionals will increasingly interact with this population. The wellness professionals' primary goal will be to maintain or improve the elderly person's ability to perform daily activities through exercise training.

Published systematic reviews (15,18) support the beneficial effect of exercise interventions on frail and pre-frail older adults. Some of the beneficial effects of exercise training reported include improved performance of ADL, physical functioning, balance performance, gait, strength, and quality of life as well as decreased fall incidence. Findings for recent studies also suggest that older adults who exercise following recommended published strength guidelines have 46% lower odds of all causes of mortality than those who do not (67).

While the benefit of exercising is evident, the optimal program type remains to be determined. A multimodal program that includes resistance training seems the best strategy to

TABLE 20.1 The parameters leading to the greatest strength improvements

Parameter	Demonstrated the most improvement in strength
Mode of muscle action	No difference between isometric, concentric, and eccentric actions
Duration	50–53 weeks
Frequency	2–3x/ week
Sets	2–3 sets
Repetitions	7–9 repetitions
Intensity	70–79% of 1RM
Total time under tension per repetition (duration of contraction)	6 seconds 2 seconds for isometric exercises, 2.5 for concentric portion and 3 seconds for eccentric portion
Rest time between sets	60 seconds
Rest time between repetitions	4 seconds

improve strength and function in the physically frail elderly (18). A systematic review by Borde et al. (15) reports that the best predictors of improved muscle strength were exercise intensity, exercise duration, and duration of muscle contraction during each repetition. The parameters leading to the greatest strength improvements are summarized in Table 20.1.

Many types of resistance training equipment are available to choose from. Martins et al. (80) investigated the effects of elastic band training in the healthy elderly and in elderly persons with co-morbidities. They found that elastic band training was effective at improving strength especially in the healthy elderly and those with functional limitations. Despite causing difficulty in objectively monitoring and prescribing a specific intensity, elastic bands can be a good choice of equipment because they are portable, easy to use, and inexpensive. In clients with limited resources, exercises using own body weight can improve strength in the elderly (122).

In summary, a multimodal exercise program that includes resistance training, balance training, flexibility, and aerobic conditioning should be implemented. Exercises that are functional, that use large muscle groups, and that combine low and high intensity training at various speeds seem indicated. When working with older adults, the exercise professional should get a doctor's clearance before implementing an exercise program, must consider the client's pathologies and co-morbidities, monitor vitals closely, start at a lower intensity, and advance the exercises progressively both in terms of intensity and complexity.

Aging and sarcopenia

The typical **aging** process has deleterious effects on human skeletal muscles and is associated with loss of muscle mass, muscle strength and power, and eventually difficulty with ADL. Isokinetic strength declines at a rate of about 1.4 to 2.5% per year after age 65, depending on muscle group and contraction velocity (44). From ages 20 to 80, there is a roughly 40% loss of muscle fiber number accompanied by a general reduction in muscle fiber size (71). Some studies have found that between the ages of 20 and 80 years, skeletal muscle mass decreases by 35 to 40% (30,31). A progressive and generalized loss of muscle mass and strength with advanced age is referred to as **sarcopenia** (23,32). Sarcopenia is common, happening in 5% of the community-dwelling individuals and in as much as 33% in frail elderly individuals in nursing homes. The impact of sarcopenia is profound. Sarcopenia can not only impact an older person's quality of life but is also an independent risk factor for difficulties with ADLs, longer hospital stays, higher rates of hospital re-admission, osteoporosis, falls, and even death (23,30,31,43,45,71). Sarcopenia likely contributes to the decline in basal metabolic rate and the progressive increase in the percentage of body fat observed with age. (56,59) Consequently, interventions geared at decreasing sarcopenia are of utmost importance.

Exercise training has been proposed as the best intervention to improve sarcopenia and much of the focus has been on the benefits of resistance training. (68,120,128). Moritani and deVries (89) were the first to show that resistive exercises could result in significant increases in muscle strength in the elderly. Since then, numerous studies have investigated the effect of resistance training on muscle strength, muscle mass, and function in older persons. In 2014, Cruz-Jentoft et al. (23) published a systematic review on the effect of exercise training on sarcopenia. The authors found that two out of four studies reviewed reported increased muscle mass with resistance training compared to standard rehab or low intensity home exercise program (HEP). Similarly, three out of four studies reported increased strength and three out of three reported increased function when compared to control. Multimodal exercise programs (combination of resistance, aerobic, flexibility, and balance training) generally improved muscle strength but not muscle mass. The authors concluded that exercise training in older adults is safe and can improve muscle strength and physical performance (1,31,39,69,118,129). While evidence supports resistance training for strength and physical performance improvements in the elderly, it is less clear which exercise mode or parameters are optimal for this purpose.

Osteoporosis

Osteoporosis is a systemic process of diminishing bone mass and deterioration of internal bone structure that results in increased risks of fracture. Approximately 9.9 million Americans are affected by osteoporosis (50) and the prevalence is even higher in older adults. Almost half of Caucasian women aged 50 and older will experience an osteoporotic fracture in their lifetime (50) and the worldwide incidence of hip fracture is projected to increase by 240% in women and 310% in men by the year 2050 (42). Osteoporotic-related fractures affect more than 2 million Americans annually and involve the wrist, hip, and vertebrae most commonly (50). Hip fractures often carry severe consequences; 60% of patients who suffered a hip fracture will be unable to regain their previous level of functional independence (50) and about 20% of hip fracture patients aged 50 and older will die in the year after their fracture (42).

Although diagnosing osteoporosis is improving with the advent of bone mineral density (BMD), osteoporosis is still known as a "silent disease" because the first sign of the disease is often a fracture. For this reason, awareness of risk factors and prevention is crucial (Box 20.1).

Box 20.1   Risk factors for osteoporosis

Female sex
Thin and/or small frame
Advanced age
Family history of osteoporosis
Postmenopausal (including surgically induced)
Amenorrhea (abnormal absence of menstrual periods)
Anorexia nervosa
Low lifetime calcium intake
Vitamin D deficiency
Medications (corticosteroids, chemotherapy, and others)
Inactive lifestyle
Cigarette smoking
Excessive use of alcohol
Low testosterone levels in men

Exercise has become a primary treatment recommendation for osteoporosis. To understand how exercise might affect osteoporosis, consider the process of bone remodeling. Bone is a dynamic tissue in which old, weakened tissue is resorbed and then replaced by new, stronger material. Peak bone mass is reached during young adult life, then gradually diminishes as more bone is resorbed than created. **Osteopenia** is defined as low bone mass, or BMD between 1.0 and 2.5 standard deviations below the mean of young normal adults. Osteoporosis is defined according to the National Institute of Health (NIH) as BMD greater than 2.5 standard deviations below the norm. Since bone responds to physical forces by increasing bone formation, it would be logical to assume that the stresses created during exercise could lead to increased bone density. A systematic review of 43 randomized controlled trials on postmenopausal women shows that exercise improves bone mineral density slightly compared to the control (55). In this same meta-analysis, the most effective type of exercise for increasing BMD to the neck of the femur was non-weight bearing high intensity progressive resistance exercises to the lower limbs (55). The most effective intervention for BMD at the spine were combination exercise programs (variety of static and dynamic weight and non-weight bearing exercises). Fractures and falls were reported as adverse events during exercise programs in some studies, emphasizing that precautions must be taken and fall prevention strategies implemented when working with clients with or at risk of osteoporosis.

While the ideal training program to improve BMD has yet to be defined, there are practical guidelines that can be incorporated into a structured fitness regime. The Delphi consensus has these recommendations for health professionals working with clients with osteoporosis (47):

1 Work on fall prevention through strength, mobility, balance, and postural training
2 Teach safe movements such as keeping good posture and using good body mechanics
3 Prevent or slow rate of bone loss through exercise (weight bearing and resistance training)
4 Strength training should focus on functional exercises and target major muscle groups with the exception of spinal flexors, extensors, and rotators. Proper alignment of the spine is crucial and careful, slow progression recommended.
5 Aim for meeting or exceeding national physical activity recommendations.

Certain precautions must be taken when exercising a client with osteoporosis. Avoid spinal flexion or rotation during exercises and teach the client to maintain a straight spine with erect posture during exercises. This will minimize increased loads on the vertebral bodies that might cause compression fractures. Overhead compressive loads and other high loading exercises should be avoided. Flexibility exercises that improve posture and balance are indicated but ballistic movements should be avoided. Reduce fall hazards through safe exercise choice, close supervision, and guarding.

In summary, bone mass attained early in life and maintained through exercise, diet, and healthy lifestyle choices is the best route to prevent osteoporosis, but once present, a comprehensive program including resistance training is likely of some benefit (53).

> Evidence suggests that resistance training and weight bearing exercise are essential for the client with osteoporosis.

PEDIATRICS

Many children are active in competitive sports, but there is a growing number who are sedentary and overweight. The obesity prevalence in adolescents has more than doubled since the late 1980s. According to the Center for Disease Control and Prevention, approximately 18% of children aged 6–11 and 21% of adolescents aged 12–19 are obese. With this trend comes an increased risk for diseases such as asthma, diabetes, and hypertension which can follow a child into adulthood, potentially resulting in disability and early mortality.

Some children are born with a disability such as **cerebral palsy** or **Down syndrome**.

While these conditions are also found in adults, they are included in this section as they first significantly affect physical functioning during childhood. Families and schools may turn to fitness centers as exercise outlets for these children as an adjunct to physical therapy, or when insurance funds are depleted. Health fitness professionals can play a key role in getting the pediatric population started on a life-long path of physical fitness.

Healthy children and adolescents

The process of growth and development in **children** (before puberty) and **adolescents** (after puberty) results in increases in muscle size and muscle strength (33–37). Much of the strength increase seen during childhood is simply due to increases in muscle size. However, the maturation of the musculoskeletal and nervous systems lead to increases in muscle strength that are larger than can be completely accounted for simply by increased muscle mass (33–37). That is, there is an "age effect" that results in older children and adolescents being stronger, pound for pound, than younger individuals (123).

Of interest have been the effects of resistance training in the context of growth and development. Specifically, can resistance training enhance strength development beyond what would be expected to be seen as a normal consequence of growth and development? Numerous studies and reviews have shown that resistance training in children and adolescents is effective in increasing muscle strength (12,35,37,70,95). The benefits appear to transfer to performance on other motor skills such as the vertical jump performance, running, or throwing (12,35,70). Prior to puberty, anabolic hormone concentrations are quite low, which limits the potential for resistance training to cause significant hypertrophy. Despite this, resistance training does increase muscle strength in this population. This suggests that the dominant effect is via neurological adaptations (13,35). After puberty, both male and female children are capable of gaining substantive changes in both muscle size and muscle strength with properly implemented resistance training programs.

Other known benefits of resistance exercise training include: it enhances bone mineral density, improves body composition, reduces body fat, improves insulin-sensitivity in overweight adolescents, enhances cardiac function in obese children, and possibly reduces risks of sport-related injuries (74). Despite the potential benefits of resistance training, many misinformed coaches, parents, and health professionals recommend against resistance training for fear of injuries and delayed growth. Specifically, there is fear that resistance training will cause damage to the **epiphyseal plates** (growth plates at the ends of long bones) (34) which could interfere with growth. In addition, resistance training could cause strains and sprains, especially of the low back, and other accidental injuries. However, several studies have found that resistance training in youth is quite safe and has comparable (13,34,35) or lower injury risks as when compared to resistance training in adults (74). The World Health Organization (WHO), the National Strength and Conditioning Association (NSCA), the American Academy of Pediatrics (AAP) and many other reputed national and international organizations recommend that children and adolescents participate in properly designed and supervised resistance training programs (74). Several recommendations (74) have been put forward to maximize safety of resistance training in youth. The athlete engaging in resistance training should be intellectually mature in order to follow directions and abide to safety rules. He/she needs to have sufficient coordination, balance, and control to complete the tasks safely. The program should be supervised by a qualified professional with knowledge of strength and conditioning principles and of the unique needs of children. The training load should be increased progressively and be adapted to the child's physical and emotional maturity as well as training experience rather than pure chronological age. The proper technique and proper biomechanics must be emphasized at all times. While training at or near 1RM was previously not recommended (13), new evidence shows that high intensity training is safe in trained and technically competent children (34,74) and may lead to greater improvements in strength and physical performance than lower intensity training (70).

The optimal resistance exercise dosage for physical performance in youth has been investigated in a systematic review by Lesinski et al. (70). The authors reported improved strength performance with fewer repetitions at a higher intensity. Nonetheless, the authors advise that the training be adapted to the needs of the child/adolescent and that the intensity be increased only after proper technical skills are acquired. Also of interest was the finding that the improvements with resistance training were found in all athletes studied (age 6–18 years), irrespective of chronological or biological age. Table 20.2 summarizes the parameters that lead to the strongest gains in Lesinski's review (70).

General knowledge supports a properly designed and supervised resistance training program that incorporates periodization principles to vary volume and intensity throughout the year. Each session should include a comprehensive warm up period and a cool down. Training programs should target all the major muscle groups and liberally include compound, multi-joint, and functional exercises (35). A variety of different training modalities are appropriate, including free weights, body weight, resisted calisthenics, and machines. Weight machines have the advantage of not requiring as much balance and coordination free weights and often do not require a spotter. However, they may pose other challenges in youth such as large incremental increases in resistance (5–10 lbs per plate) and poor sizing of machines and levers for small children (26). These should be considered when choosing the proper equipment. Progression should initially emphasize increases in repetitions before increases in resistance, and light loads should be employed when learning new movements so that proper technique is learned. Indeed, the use of a broomstick in lieu of a weight bar may be appropriate when initially learning proper technique for complex free weight exercises. The reader is recommended these resources for additional information on training guidelines in youth (70,74).

In closing, considering the evidence available of the effects of resistance training in youth, it appears as though the benefits of resistance training significantly outweigh the risks, and resistance training is therefore recommended as part of a comprehensive exercise program to gain and maintain health in children and adolescents (70,74).

INTELLECTUAL DISABILITIES AND DOWN SYNDROME

An intellectual disability (ID) (formerly called mental retardation) is defined by the American Association on Intellectual and

TABLE 20.2 Suggested resistance training dosage in youth by Lesinski (70)

Parameter	Dosage that had the strongest effect
Type of training	Free weights strongest effect on muscle strength while complex training had most effect on sport-specific performance
Training period	>23 weeks for strength 9–12 weeks for optimal vertical jump height
Frequency	1, 2 or 3x/week had similar effects
Intensity	80–89% of 1RM for strength gains
Number of sets	5 sets for optimal strength improvements 3 sets for vertical jump performance
Repetitions	6–8 reps for strength gains 3–5 or 9–12 for plyometric training
Rest	3–4 min between sets for strength gains

Developmental Disabilities (AAIDD) as "a disability characterized by significant limitations in both **intellectual functioning** and in **adaptive behavior**, which covers many everyday social and practical skills. This disability originates **before the age of 18"** (57,82). ID are relatively common, affecting just over 1% of the population (82). One of the major causes of ID is Down syndrome (DS), which is a genetic disorder that is characterized by cognitive delay, distinct facial features such as epicanthal folds of the eyelids, relatively flat occiput and nasal bridge, and short limbs (51). Among its manifestations are low muscle tone (hypotonia) and joint laxity (38,51). These latter factors can lead to increased risk of musculoskeletal and orthopedic problems (51).

Several studies have shown that persons with IS and/or DS are significantly less active (11), have less muscle strength and endurance (9,19), and have functional declines occurring at a younger age (11) than healthy aged matched adults. Individuals with DS have been shown to be significantly weaker than age and sex matched individuals with mental retardation other than DS (9,19). This weakness is correlated with low bone mineral density, and risk for osteoporosis is elevated in those individuals affected by DS (9). Finally, individuals with DS are also at increased risk of obesity, diabetes, and cardiovascular disease (38) compared to healthy controls. Increasing physical activity and fitness seems therefore an important goal in the management of DS and has the potential to improve health, premature loss in function, and quality of life.

To date, a few studies have examined the effects of resistance training in persons with mental retardation generally, or in DS specifically. Shields and Taylor (111) found that a ten-week machine-based resistance training program resulted in a significant increase in lower limb muscle strength (~42%) in adolescents with DS but no improvement in upper body strength. The magnitude of improvement in muscle strength was similar to those reported in other populations. The participants in Shield and Taylor's study performed six exercises targeting major muscle groups for 3 sets of 12 repetitions (or until fatigue) and resistance was increased when 3 sets of 12 could be completed. Similarly, Shields et al. (112) reported

significant increase in lower extremity muscle strength from a resistance program (ten weeks of a machine-based weight training program twice a week, 3 × 12 reps for 7 different exercises at 60–80% 1RM) compared to a program of social activities (ten weeks of supervised social activities) in participants with DS aged 14–22 years. A systematic review by Li et al. (72) reported on the effect of various exercise interventions on four different fitness outcomes. In this study, strength and balance were significantly improved with programs consisting of mixed training (resistance training with balance training or aerobic conditioning) but not when resistance training was implemented on its own. One study only had studied progressive resistance programs on upper body endurance and found endurance to be significantly improved after intervention (72). In addition, Li et al. reported no serious adverse effects from exercising in this population and the only minor side effect reported was sore hands from holding the weight equipment (72). Though the data is still limited, studies suggest that persons with ID and DS can receive substantial benefits from physical activity (11,72,93). The importance and effects of resistance training in isolation are not well known. More studies need to be undertaken to study the impact of resistance training on strength, function, and quality of life and to determine optimal parameters in persons with ID.

The exercise professional should be creative in the ways to explain the exercises to ensure proper understanding in this population. Simple and short descriptions may be helpful. Modifications may be needed to adapt for tone issues in clients with DS. Care should be taken to maintain good joint alignment and good quality of movement to avoid further laxity in the joints. Exercises in extremes of joint ROM and causing excessive loading on loose joints should be avoided. When in doubt, consulting a physical therapist for guidance may be helpful.

MUSCULAR DYSTROPHIES

Muscular dystrophies (MD) are a group of about 30 inherited muscular diseases that are associated with progressive muscle weakness and loss of muscle tissue (a.k.a. muscle wasting) (76,91). In MD, the primary pathology lies within muscle cells (better known as muscle fibers or myofibers) and not in the motor nerve supply to the muscle. This distinction from other neuromuscular diseases is important while planning exercise interventions for patients with MD, because the very nature of the myofibers are altered in MD, leading to myofibers being highly susceptible to contraction-induced damage or aberrant recovery from injurious muscular contractions (4,5,63,92,96,100,101). As a result, the principles that guide exercise prescription for healthy individuals or individuals with muscle wasting secondary to neurological disorders, might not be suitable for patients with MD. Moreover, since each type of MD has a distinct pathological basis, and since different patients with the same type of MD might show varied rates of disease progression, the idea of personalized exercise prescription is highly relevant for patients with MD. For more information on the different types of MD, the reader is directed to reviews by Emery et al. and the Muscular Dystrophy Association website (28,76,85,103).

For this section, it would suffice to state that, in all types of MD, skeletal muscle undergoes repeated cycles of degeneration and regeneration. When muscle regeneration is unable to keep up with the rate of degeneration, myofibers are permanently lost, resulting in muscle wasting. When exposed to injurious eccentric contractions, muscles that lack dystrophin (implicated in Duchenne MD (DMD) and Becker MD (BMD) respectively) and muscles that lack dysferlin (implicated in limb-girdle **muscular dystrophy** (LGMD) type 2B and Miyoshi myopathy (MM)) undergo extensive myofiber damage, inflammation, and regeneration compared to healthy muscles (101). This data suggests that muscle loading can lead to greater damage in muscles affected by some forms of MD, than seen in healthy muscle (100–102). Repeated exposure to injurious muscle loading during ambulation, ADL, and in some cases, aggressive exercise, may possibly be depleting the regenerative capacity of affected muscles over time (65,77,88). Since patients with certain types of MD experience accelerated muscle weakness and wasting with increased muscular activity, the type of wasting that is seen, at least in some forms of MD, could be compared to an overuse syndrome (8,126). Moreover, MD, by definition, is progressive in nature, so the benefits of exercise are likely to be palliative and not curative. As a palliative intervention, one of the goals of resistance exercise could be to maintain sufficient muscle strength in order to preserve independent mobility and participation in ADL for as long as possible.

In an exercise-based interventional study by Sveen and colleagues (114), the authors studied patients with LGMD2A (linked to calpain), LGMD2I (linked to FKRP) and BMD to examine if strength training increased muscle strength without causing additional muscle damage (114). The investigators found that, after 24 weeks of low-intensity resistance training (LOIT), which involved performing 3 sets of 12–15 repetitions (40–80% of 1RM), at a frequency of 3 days per week, subjects with MD (N = 8) showed approximately 60% and 40% improvement in strength in the biceps brachii and quadriceps femoris, respectively. Interestingly, healthy control subjects who also participated in the same study only showed approximately 20% and 30% improvement in strength in the biceps brachii and quadriceps femoris, respectively, which suggests that muscles of patients with certain types of MD might actually be hyperresponsive to exercise. In a separate arm of these exercise studies, Sveen and colleagues (114) also evaluated the effect of a high intensity resistance training protocol (HIT) performed over 12 weeks. In the HIT study, subjects trained at increasing levels of intensity during weeks 0–4 (12–8 repetitions, 70–80% 1RM), 4–8 (10–6 repetitions, 75–86% 1RM), and 8–12 (8–4 repetitions, 80–92% 1RM), at a frequency of 3 times per week. In addition to the biceps brachii and quadriceps femoris, the wrist flexors and extensors and the ankle plantarflexors were also exposed to resistance training. Out of the six subjects with MD who participated in the study, one patient dropped out due to muscle soreness and CK elevation, and another patient dropped out due to time constraints. Based on data from the 4 subjects who completed the study, it was found that only the wrist flexors and extensors significantly increased in strength after 12 weeks. Further, even though there was no significant increase in CK levels in the four subjects that completed the study, the subjects did report pain in tendons and joints, indicative of excessive loading. The studies by Sveen et al. (114) thus suggest that low intensity resistance training might be safe and effective for patients with certain types of MD. However, similar to the position taken by the authors of this book chapter, Sveen and colleagues (114) advise careful supervision and monitoring of patients with MD participating in a resistance training program, in order to ensure that the exercises are indeed beneficial and not doing further harm to the muscles.

A study by Alemdaroglu et al. (3) on children with DMD (8–12 years), compared the effects of arm ergometry performed under expert supervision in the laboratory (N = 12) to ROM-strengthening exercises performed as part of a home program (N = 12). The children in the ergometry group exercised for 40 minutes, 3 times per week for 8 weeks, at 50% maximal resistance. The ROM-strengthening group performed ROM exercises for various upper extremity muscle groups (active resisted, active assisted, or passive, depending on the subject's ability), five times per week for eight weeks. On completion of the study, subjects in the ergometry group showed increased strength in only two of the upper extremity muscles or muscle groups that were tested, whereas the ROM-strengthening group showed increased strength in seven of the muscles or muscle groups. Both groups showed improvements in functional outcome. This study did not measure exercise-induced muscle damage (for example, CK or MRI). Nonetheless, as with the Sveen et al. (114) study, this study demonstrates that dystrophic skeletal muscles might have the potential to respond positively to strengthening exercise.

In summary, individuals with MD may benefit from an exercise program. Since MD is progressive in nature, muscle wasting and weakness will continue to occur irrespective of whether or not patients exercise. However, since maintenance of muscle mass and strength, and prolongation of ambulatory capacity are priorities in the rehabilitative management of MD, incorporating a program of strengthening

exercises that is customized to the patient may be beneficial, especially early in the disease process (114). It is important to remember that dystrophic muscles might be highly susceptible to exercise-induced muscle damage and that they respond to exercise in unique ways depending on the genetic mutations that cause the dystrophy (101). Depending on the extent of progression, dystrophic muscles might also be deficient in their ability to regenerate from injurious muscle activity. Due to these reasons, it is critical that exercise sessions and post-exercise recovery are carefully monitored, and that exercise dosages are carefully adjusted to derive the benefits of exercise without further aggravating the dystrophic process in affected muscles. Since eccentric contractions, and to a lesser extent isometric contractions, are known to induce muscle injury, it might be advisable to focus on exercises that involve predominantly concentric muscle contractions. As with other disease conditions, it is imperative that patients with any type of MD obtain clearance from a physician before starting or changing an exercise program. Finally, it is worth noting that several promising experimental therapies are likely to become available to patients in the coming years (21,75,86,90,99,115,130). It is therefore all the more important that patients do the best they can to preserve functional muscle mass and stay as active as possible, so that they may be good candidates for newer gene- and/or cell-based therapies as they become available.

NEUROMUSCULAR DISEASE

Neuromuscular diseases can be due to damage or dysfunction in the CNS, the peripheral nerves (**neuropathies**), or the muscle tissue itself (**myopathies**). Common symptoms of neuromuscular diseases include spasticity (which is a velocity dependent resistance to stretch), rigidity, weakness, and sensory loss. These symptoms can further lead to inactivity and deconditioning, which can then exacerbate motor dysfunction. Historically, activities like resistance exercise have been discouraged for neuromuscular diseases due to concerns about overstrain and possible exacerbation of spasticity. However, it is now becoming clear that in many cases that risk of overwork is much less than previously feared, and concerns regarding spasticity exacerbation are unfounded (24,41). Indeed exercise, and in particular resistance exercise, can be a useful tool in the rehabilitation and subsequent management of many neuromuscular conditions, especially for those conditions where weakness is a primary contributor to loss of function.

STROKE

It is typically reported that approximately 795,000 people experience a stroke each year in the United States (125). Strokes are the fifth leading cause of death in the United States and the leading cause of serious long-term disability in adults (83). Stroke reduces mobility in more than half of stroke survivors age 65 and over. The combined direct and indirect costs of stroke are estimated at an annual $34 billion.

There are two general categories of stroke. An ischemic stroke is conceptually similar to a myocardial infarction in that occlusion of a cerebral artery occurs as a consequence of plaque formation. In contrast, a hemorrhagic stroke results from the loss of structural integrity of a cerebral blood vessel and subsequent bleeding. Both types of stroke can lead to significant changes in muscle function including weakness and spasticity. The motor symptoms are typically most severe on one side of the body (contralateral to the side of the lesion in the brain) so hemiplegia is common, although even the "good" side frequently shows motor deficits. It was previously thought that motor deficits that had not normalized within the first six months following a stroke were permanent, and that neural plasticity was limited. It is now clear, however, that the extent of neural plasticity is greater than previously thought and significant improvements can occur well after the acute stage of stroke recovery.

Intensive rehabilitation following rehabilitation is standard and works toward improving gait, balance, and function, decreasing tone, and increasing quality of movement and independence with home exercise programs (HEP). After a stroke, individuals demonstrate

lower levels of physical activity, cardiorespiratory fitness, strength, and power compared to age matched healthy controls (107). These deficits and the physical inactivity that occurs post stroke often remains beyond the discharge timeframes from rehab. A properly designed exercise program seems therefore crucial in this population and has the potential to improve function, quality of life, and reduce future cardio-vascular complications (106). A recent systematic review of the literature by Saunders et al. (107) found sufficient data to ascertain the benefit of cardiovascular and mixed programs (resistance and cardiovascular) on walking performance, independence with walking, mobility, and balance.

Historically, resistance training was discouraged for people following a stroke, often on the argument that resistance training might lead to increased spasticity or cause other adverse effects. However, it appears that participation in fitness programs does not lead to adverse effects in stroke survivors (107) and that spasticity is not exacerbated by resistance training specifically (10,110). Resistance training has also been shown in some studies to have positive impact on measures of strength (10,29,110,116) and function (29). As with other populations, the improvement in strength has been mainly attributed to adaptations in neural control. Engardt et al. (29) showed increases in agonist EMG following eccentric and concentric-only training from 24 to 33%. The hypertrophic potential of paretic muscle due to stroke has not yet been examined. However, it seems likely that significant adaptations at the muscle level occur, especially given that paretic muscle is significantly deconditioned and would be highly responsive to increased loading.

Two recent systematic reviews have attempted to summarize the evidence on resistance training and elucidate the questions regarding its benefit (104,107). Saunders et al. (107) report some studies that showed benefits from resistance training on the ability to weight-bear, on walking speed during a Time Up and Go test, and some measures of balance. Sometimes, the effect of resistance training was small, and no effect was found for time to ascend one flight of stairs, walking ability, or quality of life. Resistance training combined with cardiovascular training clearly improved balance, had positive effects on mobility (as measured by the Time Up and Go), and improved walking speed and walking capacity. Caution in interpretation of results is warranted as the trials showing benefits were confounded by additional training time in the study group compared to the control group, affecting the strength of the conclusion. The authors conclude that there is insufficient data to reliably determine the effects of resistance training post stroke. Resistance training combined with cardiovascular training seems beneficial for walking performance and balance. The authors recommend, when implementing a fitness program, to choose exercises specific to the goal targeted and be "task-related". In this fashion, if weakness is the major deficit contributing to difficulty getting up from a chair, resistance training should be implemented; if walking is the difficulty, a treadmill program is advisable; and if the patient is at risk for falls, a balance program might be most appropriate.

A similar systematic review performed by Salter et al. (104) looked at resistance training specifically in the first three months after a stroke. The authors report no significant adverse effects from resistance training but little to no effect on strength, upper limb function, or mobility. The authors conclude that there is insufficient data to recommend resistance training in the first three months after a stroke. The authors state, however, that the intensity of training was below ACSM recommended parameters for older adults and that this insufficient load might have contributed to the lack of improvement. Finally, the authors propose that the repetitive nature of resistance training and the lack of task specificity might not be ideal to promote cortical reorganization and improve functional activities early after a stroke.

To date, most studies have employed relatively short training periods (≤ 10 weeks) and longer-term effects are unknown (107). Further, studies often had methodological shortcomings such as small sample sizes, inconsistent contact time across groups or poorly defined resistance training protocols (104,107). More research needs to be performed to further define the effects of resistance training on motor function post stroke, and to improve understanding of the different resistance training parameters (e.g., optimal intensity range, appropriate frequency and volume of training, unilateral vs. bilateral training) on outcomes. In the meantime, an individualized program focusing on functional activities appears to be a viable option. Particular attention should be afforded to safety and fall prevention. Exercise modification may be necessary to accommodate hypotonic joints (by providing greater joint support) and hypertonic joints (by modifying body and joint position to optimize movement quality). Clients who have had a stroke often suffer from cardio-vascular diseases, so vitals should be monitored closely and Valsalva avoided during training.

SPINAL CORD INJURY

Spinal cord injury (SCI) most often results from motor vehicle accidents (38%) and falls (30.5%), followed by violence (13.5%) and sports injuries (9%)(20). According to the National Spinal Cord Injury Statistical Center, there are approximately 282,000 persons living with an SCI in the United States today. There are 17,000 new cases per year with 80% of those being of the male gender (20). The estimated lifetime cost for a 25-year-old who survives an SCI ranges from $1.58 million to $4.72 million (20).

Categorization of SCI is complex and depends not only on the level of the injury but also whether the injury is complete or incomplete. For a detailed explanation on classification, the reader is advised to consult the *International Standards for Classification of Spinal Cord Injury* updated in 2011 (64). Briefly, C1-T1 injuries result in tetraplegia (formerly quadriplegia) and causes impairments (decreased sensation and motor ability) of the arms, trunk, legs, and pelvic organs; T2 and below injuries result in paraplegia and cause impairments of the trunk, legs, and pelvic organs below the level of the injury. A complete SCI will lead to complete loss of sensation and paralysis below the level of the lesion.

The lack of neural drive in individuals with SCI results in often pronounced weakness and secondary muscle atrophy; exercise is usually the recommended intervention to improve upon those deficits. Volitional exercise is used to exercise non-paralyzed or partially paralyzed muscles, and functional electrical stimulation enhanced activities are often prescribed for limbs without volitional movements (14,54). In addition to the primary motor and neurological deficits discussed earlier, those with SCI are at high risk for secondary problems like cardiovascular diseases, circulatory insufficiencies, osteoporosis, skin breakdown, musculoskeletal dysfunctions, pain, and early mortality (27,58). It has been suggested that much of this morbidity and early mortality in persons with SCI is due to inactivity related illnesses (27). Research has indicated that some of these problems may be mitigated with a structured exercise program incorporating appropriate precautions. For example, exercise interventions have been shown to decrease paralysis related bone loss (52), improve blood lipid profiles and platelet aggregation, reduce stress and depression, and improve glucose tolerance and insulin sensitivity (27). Also, a strength training program is often helpful for shoulder girdle pain, a common complaint among those with paraplegia (apparently due to the stresses of wheelchair propulsion and transfers) (58). Indeed, improvement in shoulder strength and pain was noted in a study that employed shoulder resistance exercises using elastic bands (25). Circuit resistance training, which incorporates periods of low-intensity/high repetition movements (such as a free-wheel arm ergometry) interspersed with a series of resistance training exercises (such as free weights, weight machines, or elastic bands), has also been shown to be effective at improving strength and decreasing shoulder girdle pain (52,58).

A systematic review by Hicks et al. (54) looked at the effects of exercise interventions on strength, body composition, and functional performance in persons with SCI. The authors included 82 studies in their review and concluded that although the study quality was generally low, there was consistent and good evidence that exercise, performed two to three times per week at moderate-to-vigorous intensity, increases physical capacity and muscular strength in the chronic SCI population. The evidence of the positive effects of exercise

training on body composition and functional performance was low and there was insufficient evidence on the effectiveness of exercising in the acute phase of SCI. Furthermore, Hicks et al. looked specifically of the effects of voluntary resistance training on non-paralyzed muscles of SCI subjects and found that the muscles responded in a fashion similar to those of healthy subjects. Various modes of training were used (circuit resistance training, body weight-supported treadmill training (BWSTT), arm ergometry, and kayak ergometry), and improvements in strength were seen with as little as five weeks of training. Parameters that led to clear benefits included training three times per week and performing two to three sets at 70–80% of 1RM. Results also showed that nine low quality studies reported improvements in wheelchair skills and propulsion following an exercise program of either arm, wheelchair, or rowing ergometry. Most participants trained three times per week at a moderate to high intensity. A more recent RCT by Torhaug et al. (117) showed similar benefits from resistance training. The authors reported that bench press strength training at 85–95% 1RM for six weeks was effective at improving arm strength and wheelchair propulsion work economy in individuals with paraplegia (117). Bochkezanian et al. (14) systematically reviewed the effect of combined strength and aerobic training on various outcomes. The authors reported that two out of seven studies reported improvements in aerobic fitness, four out of five showed improvements in at least one strength outcome, and one out of two demonstrated improvements in quality of life. The authors stated that muscle strength training had most benefits when initiated at 50–80% 1RM and progressed as tolerated. The authors concluded that more studies need to be performed to determine the benefits of combined aerobic and strength training in order to better guide prescription.

There seems to be benefits from exercise training in SCI; however, the effects of exercise conditioning are inversely proportional to the severity of the primary injury (58). For example, those with tetraplegia may require electrical stimulation or passive movements to use an upper body ergometer resulting in a markedly reduced aerobic training effect

---

Box 20.2   Signs and symptoms of autonomic dysreflexia

- Pounding headache
- Blurred vision
- Nasal congestion
- Piloerection (goose bumps)
- Profuse sweating above level of injury
- Anxiety
- Sudden increase in systolic blood pressure
- Cardiac dysrhythmias

---

(40). In addition, training is not without risks, and reports of adverse effects have been documented. To address this concern, Warms et al. (121) reviewed the literature on adverse effects and reported that no serious effects of volitional exercise and functional electrical stimulation (FES)-enhanced exercises had been documented in the studies reviewed (25,117).

In general, the recommendations for resistance and aerobic training for individuals with SCI are not significantly different from recommendations for the general population, and should take into consideration specificity, overload, progression, and regularity (40). The reader is recommended to read the article by Tweedy et al. that describes the Australian position on exercise guidelines in spinal cord injury subjects (119). The exercise specialist must be aware of the precautions that must be heeded when working with SCI clients. For example, when working with persons with a T6 or higher SCI, one must be aware of the potential life-threatening condition known as autonomic dysreflexia (Box 20.2). Symptoms include an excessive rise in blood pressure, slow heart rate, headache, blurred vision, and congestion. It can be set off by a noxious stimulus below the level of the injury, such as pressure to a limb or a full bladder. Immediate intervention consists of identifying and removing the noxious stimuli, monitoring blood pressure, and seeking medical help (40). Other precautions include risk of fractures due to osteoporosis, overuse pain due to muscle imbalances, hypotension, and difficulty maintaining thermal stability (58).

Knowledge of the type of injury and related precautions can minimize the risks and enhance the outcome of exercise programming for persons with SCI.

CARDIOVASCULAR DISEASE

Cardiovascular disease (CVD), which includes coronary heart disease and stroke, remains the leading cause of death among Americans and is estimated to have an economic cost of over $207 billion each year (22,98). The major risk factors for cardiovascular disease include hypertension, elevated serum total cholesterol, cigarette smoking, and diabetes mellitus (6). In order to reduce the mortality and morbidity associated with cardiovascular diseases, researchers have examined the effects of exercise (1,61). Recently, Sattelmair et al. (105) conducted a meta-analysis examining the dose-response relationship of physical activity on the risks for coronary heart disease. The investigators systematically reviewed studies published from 1995 to 2009 in which the effect of exercise was evaluated on cardiovascular risk factors. They found that exercise reduced cardiovascular risk factors in a dose-response manner. That is, higher levels of physical activity were associated with a lower risk of developing cardiovascular disease. Indeed, individuals who engaged in 150 minutes per week of moderate-intensity physical activity had a 14% lower coronary heart disease risk compared with those reporting no physical activity, while those engaging in 300 minutes per week of moderate-intensity physical activity had a 20% lower risk. A systematic review performed in 2012 (73) found similar benefits from physical activity and concluded that:

[a] high level of leisure time PA [physical activity] and moderate level of occupational PA have a beneficial effect on cardiovascular health by reducing the overall risk of incidence of coronary heart disease and stroke . . . by 20 to 30 percent and 10 to 20 percent, respectively.

The effects of resistance exercise may also reduce cardiovascular risk factors (16,97,124). Kelley and Kelley (60) found that resting systolic and diastolic blood pressure decreased by 2 to 4% following dynamic resistance training exercise in adults. Similar results were found for reductions in resting blood pressure for children and adolescents (62). In addition, resistance training improves insulin sensitivity and glucose tolerance, and the improved muscle strength likely decreases the physiological stress of activities of daily living (49,84,97). The comprehensive review by Braith and Stewart (16) describes the evidence for the effect of resistance training for prevention of CVD (see Table 20.3). The authors conclude that resistance training appears to contribute to CVD reduction and that the evidence supports the guidelines of including moderate intensity resistance training for CV health. Table 20.3 summarizes resistance training prescription as per Braith and Stewart (16).

In addition to reducing cardiovascular disease risk factors, resistance training is increasingly incorporated into cardiac rehabilitation programs in individuals already diagnosed with coronary artery disease. For example, Ades et al. (2) examined the effects of resistance training on functional capacity in older women with coronary heart disease (CHD). A total of 42 CHD subjects were divided into two groups which either performed two sets of eight exercises for the major muscle groups or met three times a week for 40 minutes with a cardiac rehabilitation specialist. The investigators found that the

women in the weight training group improved their functional capacity and therefore were able to perform ADL without adverse effects (2). Marzolini et al. (81) published a meta-analysis on the effect of combined aerobic and resistance training versus aerobic training alone in individuals with coronary artery disease. The authors concluded that combined aerobic and resistance training was more effective than aerobic training alone in improving body composition, strength, and some indicators of cardiovascular fitness, and did not compromise participant safety. Yamamoto et al. (127) reviewed the effect of resistance training on its own in middle-aged and elderly patients with CAD. A total of 22 trials with a total of 1,095 participants were included. The authors concluded that resistance training was effective at improving upper and lower extremity strength, exercise capacity, VO$_2$ max in both middle-aged and elderly, and improved mobility in the elderly participants. The optimal exercise intensity was not described, and intensity varied from 40–80% 1RM in the included studies for a duration of 6–29 weeks.

Gielen et al. (48) reviewed and described the benefits of exercise training in patients with a variety of heart diseases and made clinical recommendations. The authors report benefits of exercise training in patients with stable CHD, post myocardial infarction, stable diseases of heart valves, pulmonary arterial hypertension, and chronic heart failure. Gielen et al. (48) included resistance training in the treatment recommendation for all of these diseases. The reader is advised to read this review for more detailed information regarding contraindications and specific recommendations for each disease entity. The exercise specialist is recommended to gain sufficient knowledge of the heart condition prior to intervention and having the client exercise under proper medical supervision.

Resistance training is also part of most treatment interventions for chronic stable heart failure (CHF). Individuals with CHF have significant fatigue and shortness of breath with physical activity, and much of the effects seem to be due to changes in skeletal muscle tissue including type I muscle fiber atrophy. In a systematic review by Smart el al. (113), resistance training in combination with intermittent

TABLE 20.3 Summary results from Braith and Stewart (16) regarding the role of resistance training (RT) in CVD prevention

Action	Specifics
Decreases glycosylated hemoglobin (HbA1c) indicating improved glycemic control	Intensity-dependent: benefits maximized when training performed at 70 to 90% 1RM and training > 2 months.
Reduction in blood pressure (BP)	Reductions of approximately 3 mm Hg for both systolic and diastolic BP in people with normal BP. Effect of RT only on BP in hypertensive individuals is not known.
Increase central arterial stiffness	During high-intensity and high-volume training (up to 6 sets) regimens. Central stiffness was not seen with other RT regimens and was not associated with increases in BP.
Reduces total body fat	Good evidence. Increased muscle mass by at least 1–2 kg and 40% reduction in visceral fat with RT combined with a healthy diet.
Improves lipid profiles	Little evidence but participants tested had cholesterol within normal values at the start of the studies.
Resistance training exercise prescription per Braith and Stewart (16).	
Exercise mode	Machines are preferred for safety and ease of use; hand-held weights, barbells, and elastic bands can also be used.
No. of exercises	8 to 10 exercises for the major muscle groups: chest, shoulders, arms, back, abdomen, thigh, lower legs.
Intensity	30 to 40% of 1RM for upper body and 50% to 60% for lower body exercises. If 1RM testing is not possible or advisable, use a weight that can be lifted for 8 to 10 repetitions; increase weight when 15 repetitions can be done easily.
Duration	Session including a single set of 8 to 10 exercises should take about 20 minutes.
Frequency	At least twice per week.
Precautions	Risk/benefit ratio of resistance exercise is very favorable. Contraindications to RT are the same as those for aerobic exercise. Treatment for systolic BP >160 mm Hg or diastolic BP >100 mm Hg should be initiated before starting any type of exercise program. Avoid extended breath-holding to minimize exaggerated BP response.

aerobic training led to larger improvements in peak VO$_2$ compared to intermittent aerobic exercise alone in patients with heart failure. This improvement in peak VO$_2$ is of great importance as it is likely to improve the dyspnea and quality of life of individuals with CHF and is a strong predictor of improved prognosis in this population. Exercise training 3–5 days per week for 20 to 60 minutes is usually recommended, but in patients with poor activity tolerance, 3–5 minutes duration 3–4 times a day may be used. Several authors reviewed the effect of resistance training specifically in patients with SHF and all recommend it to be included in the overall patient management (79,87,94,108). Readers are directed to Mandic et al. (79) for more information on physiological effects of resistance training in CHF patients and to Selig et al. (108) for specific exercise guidelines recommendations/ contraindications. Table 20.4 summarizes the current resistance training guidelines for heart failure patients who have slight to no limitations in physical activity; in general, low resistance/high repetition is usually recommended at the initiation of the program and is progressed slowly as tolerated.

Current resistance training guidelines for heart failure patients with no limitations or only slight limitation to physical activity (79,108) are shown in Table 20.4.

In conclusion, the principles of resistance training do not differ in those with heart diseases than in those without, but particular attention must be paid to minimize risks of cardiovascular events during training, and increased supervision and monitoring is recommended. Contraindications to resistance training include unstable angina, uncontrolled hypertension (systolic $\geq$ 160 mm Hg, diastolic $\geq$ 100 mm Hg), uncontrolled dysrhythmias, severe valvular disease, hypertrophic cardiomyopathy, left ventricular outflow obstruction, and untreated congestive heart failure (7,97). Patients need physician approval prior to training, initial intensity should be low, and progression should be relatively slow. After surgery, up to three months may be required before starting resistance training (97) and particular caution is needed when initiating exercises with patients who had open heart surgery due to the incision they received through the sternum.

> A combination of aerobic exercise and circuit resistance training improves skeletal muscle function, vasculature to skeletal muscle, as well as functional capacity in patients with cardiovascular disease.

SUMMARY

Resistance exercise in concert with cardiovascular and flexibility exercise is an important component of exercise programs in the general population. It is increasingly apparent that resistance exercise provides significant benefits to children, adolescents, and the well elderly. Furthermore, resistance exercise appears to provide significant benefits to individuals with a variety of conditions such as COPD, AIDS, diabetes, and neuromuscular diseases. With few exceptions (Duchenne muscular dystrophy), the benefits of resistance exercise far outweigh the potential risks, especially when properly designed and supervised. Nonetheless, caution should be applied when introducing progression into a program. Using a team approach with appropriate health care providers can enhance the safety and effectiveness of the program. Future research needs to further delineate the program design variables (intensity, frequency, volume, etc.) that maximize benefits (including functional outcomes) while minimizing deleterious effects for different diseases and syndromes. In addition, longer-term studies need to be performed to assess the benefits and risks of prolonged resistance exercise for these special populations.

TABLE 20.4 Current resistance training guidelines for heart failure patients with no limitations or only slight limitations to physical activity

Sets	1 set progressed to up to 3 sets
Repetitions	6 to 15
Number of exercises	4 to 8 for the major muscle groups
Intensity	RPE range of 11 to 15 (6 to 20 point Borg Scale) or 40–50% 1RM initially and progressed to 50–60% 1RM later on
Muscles targeted	Small muscle groups/few muscles at a time
Length	Short work phases
Work to rest ratio	1:2

MAXING OUT

1 A 30-year-old man wants assistance in designing an exercise program. He is 100 pounds overweight, smokes one pack of cigarettes per day, and complains of knee pain when climbing stairs. What parameters should his program have? Are there any special considerations?

2 An 85-year-old male had a stroke five years ago and has some residual right-sided weakness with mild spasticity, although he is able to walk independently and live alone. His daughter has brought him to the gym and wants him to start an exercise program. His goal is to stay as independent as possible. Is it safe to start him on a resistance training program? What types of exercise would be most appropriate for him?

3 A 44-year-old male volunteer coach for the high school football team wants to start working out with his son who is on the team. He had a heart attack six months ago, and has completed cardiac rehabilitation phases 1, 2, and 3. Now he wants to stay fit and asks for some advice. What are some guidelines and precautions for an exercise program?

CASE EXAMPLE

Background

Mr. Jackson, a 76-year-old avid golfer, complains that he is having increasing difficulty with bending, walking on hills and uneven ground, and getting in and out of the golf cart. He has a history of bilateral knee osteoarthritis controlled with NSAIDs, and hypertension controlled with medication. He admits not adhering to exercise programs in the past but is now motivated because he wants to continue golfing.

Intervention

After having Mr. Jackson complete a health screen questionnaire and getting clearance from his physician, exercise testing is performed as outlined in another chapter in this volume. The components of the fitness program should focus on strength and flexibility of the lower extremities targeting major muscle groups used in daily activities and golf, aerobic conditioning, and balance and coordination activities. Review sections on sarcopenia, osteoarthritis, and cardiovascular disease for more information.

For resistance training, a five- to ten-minute warm-up should be followed by strength training for major muscle groups, focusing on lower extremities, but including upper extremities and trunk as all are important for golf and other activities of daily living. Begin with 65 to 75% of 1RM, and progress to 85 to 100% of 1RM as tolerated, 2 to 3 sessions per week, 8 to 12 repetitions. Knee pain should be monitored, and activities modified if increased pain and inflammation are reported. For example, open chain knee extensions could be replaced with closed chain leg presses, load could be reduced, or arc of motion modified to a pain-free range. The session would end with stretching to the major muscle groups.

For aerobic conditioning, a combination of activities could be used including treadmill walking, stationary bicycling, and water activities. Treadmill walking is functional, and inclines can be gradually introduced to simulate hill walking. Stationary bicycling has the advantage of providing knee range of motion, which can be increased by lowering the seat height. Water aerobics can provide cardiovascular conditioning while minimizing joint stresses. Mr. Jackson should be taught perceived level of exertion, age-related target heart rate, and advised to monitor his blood pressure. He could be encouraged to join an exercise group to enhance adherence.

Supervised but simple balance and coordination activities such as grapevine walking, single-leg balance, and walking on an exercise mat to simulate uneven ground can become independent once safety is established. Mr. Jackson should be educated on the importance of an ongoing program, warning signs for cardiovascular disease, and osteoarthritis precautions.

REFERENCES

1. **ACSM.** American College of Sports Medicine Position Stand. The recommended quantity and quality of exercise for developing and maintaining cardiorespiratory and muscular fitness, and flexibility in healthy adults. *Med Sci Sports Exerc* 1998; 30: 975–991.

2. **Ades PA, Savage PD, Cress ME, et al.** Resistance training on physical performance in disabled older female cardiac patients. *Med Sci Sports Exerc* 2003; 35:1265–1270.

3. **Alemdaroglu I, Karaduman A, Yilmaz OT, et al.** Different types of upper extremity exercise training in Duchenne muscular dystrophy: effects on functional performance, strength, endurance, and ambulation. *Muscle Nerve* 2015; 51:697–705.

4. **Allen DG, Gervasio OL, Yeung EW, et al.** Calcium and the damage pathways in muscular dystrophy. *Can J Physiol Pharmacol* 2010; 88:83–91.

5. **Allen DG, Whitehead NP, Yeung EW.** Mechanisms of stretch-induced muscle damage in normal and dystrophic muscle: role of ionic changes. *J Physiol* 2005; 567:723–735.

6. **American College of Sports Medicine., Franklin BA, Whaley MH, et al.** In: ACSM's *Guidelines for Exercise Testing and Prescription*, 6th ed. Philadelphia, PA: Lippincott Williams & Wilkins; 2000:33–130.

7. **American College of Sports Medicine., Whaley MH, Brubaker PH, et al.** ACSM's *Guidelines for Exercise Testing and Prescription*, 7th ed., 30th anniversary ed. Philadelphia, PA: Lippincott Williams & Wilkins; 2006.

8. **Angelini C, Peterle E, Gaiani A, et al.** Dysferlinopathy course and sportive activity: clues for possible treatment. *Acta Myologica: Myopathies and Cardiomyopathies: Official Journal of the Mediterranean Society of Myology* / edited by the Gaetano Conte Academy for the study of striated muscle diseases 2011; 30:127–132.

9. **Angelopoulou N, Matziari C, Tsimaris V, Sakadamis A, Souftas V, Mandroukas K.** Bone mineral density and muscle strength in young men with mental retardation (with and without Down syndrome). *Calcified Tissue International* 2000; 66:176–180.

10. **Badics E, Wittman A, Rupp M, Stabauer B, Zifko UA.** Systematic muscle building exercises in the rehabilitation of stroke patients. *Neurorehabilitation* 2002; 17:211–214.

11. **Bartlo P, Klein PJ.** Physical activity benefits and needs in adults with intellectual disabilities: systematic review of the literature. *Am J Intellect Dev Disabil* 2011; 116:220–232.

12. **Behringer M, Vom Heede A, Matthews M, et al.** Effects of strength training on motor performance skills in children and adolescents: a meta-analysis. *Pediatr Exerc Sci* 2011; 23:186–206.

13. **Bernhardt DT, Gomez J, Johnson, MD, Martin TJ, Rowland TW, Small E, LeBlanc C, Malina R, Krein C, Young JC, Reed FE, Anderson SJ, Griesemer BA, Bar-Or O.** Strength training by children and adolescents. *Pediatrics* 2001; 107:1470–1472.

14. **Bochkezanian V, Raymond J, de Oliveira CQ, et al.** Can combined aerobic and muscle strength training improve aerobic fitness, muscle strength, function and quality of life in people with spinal cord injury? A systematic review. *Spinal Cord* 2015; 53:418–431.

15. **Borde R, Hortobagyi T, Granacher U.** Dose-response relationships of resistance

training in healthy old adults: a systematic review and meta-analysis. *Sports Med* 2015; 45:1693–1720.

16. Braith RW, Stewart KJ. Resistance exercise training: its role in the prevention of cardiovascular disease. *Circulation* 2006; 113:2642–2650.

17. Bureau USC. U.S. Census Bureau Facts for Features: Older Americans Month – May 2016.

18. Cadore EL, Rodriguez-Manas L, Sinclair A, et al. Effects of different exercise interventions on risk of falls, gait ability, and balance in physically frail older adults: a systematic review. *Rejuvenation Res* 2013; 16:105–114.

19. Carmeli E, Ayalon M, Barchad S, Sheklow SL, Reznick AZ. Isokinetic leg strength of institutionalized older adults with mental retardation with and without Down's Syndrome. *J Strength Cond Res* 2002; 16:316–320.

20. Center NSCIS. *Spinal Cord Injury (SCI) Facts and Figures at a Glance.*

21. Chicoine LG, Rodino-Klapac LR, Shao G, et al. Vascular delivery of rAAVrh74.MCK. GALGT2 to the gastrocnemius muscle of the rhesus macaque stimulates the expression of dystrophin and laminin alpha2 surrogates. *Mol Ther* 2014; 22:713–724.

22. Chobanian AV, Bakris GL, Black HR, et al. Seventh report of the Joint National Committee on prevention, detection, evaluation, and treatment of high blood pressure. *Hypertension* 2003; 42:1206–1252.

23. Cruz-Jentoft AJ, Landi F, Schneider SM, et al. Prevalence of and interventions for sarcopenia in ageing adults: a systematic review. Report of the International Sarcopenia Initiative (EWGSOP and IWGS). *Age Ageing* 2014; 43:748–759.

24. Curtis CL, Weir JP. Overview of exercise responses in healthy and impaired states. *Neurology Report* 1996; 20:13–19.

25. Curtis KA, Tyner TM, Zachery L. Effect of a standard exercise protocol on shoulder pain in long-term wheelchair users. *Spinal Cord* 1999; 37:421–429.

26. Dahab KS, McCambridge TM. Strength training in children and adolescents: raising the bar for young athletes? *Sports Health* 2009; 1:223–226.

27. Ditor DS, Hicks AL. Exercise therapy after spinal cord injury: the effects on heath and function. *Crit Rev Biomed Eng* 2009; 37:165–191.

28. Emery AE. The muscular dystrophies. *Lancet* 2002; 359:687–695.

29. Engardt M, Knutsson E, Jonsson M, Sternhag M. Dynamic muscle strength training in stroke patients: effects on knee extension torque, electromyographic activity, and motor function. *Archives of Physical Medicine and Rehabilitation* 1995; 76:419–425.

30. Evans WJ. Effects of exercise on body composition and functional capacity of the elderly. *J Gerontol* 1995; 50A:147–150.

31. Evans WJ. Exercise training guidelines for the elderly. *Med Sci Sports Exerc* 1999; 31:12–17.

32. Evans WJ. Effects of exercise on senescent muscle. *Clinical Orthopaedics and Related Research* 2002; 403S:S211–S220.

33. Faigenbaum AD, Milliken LA, LaRosa Loud R, Burak BT, Doherty CL, Westcott WL. Comparison of 1 and 2 days per week of strength training in children. *Research Quarterly for Exercise and Sport* 2002; 73:416–424.

34. Faigenbaum AD, Milliken LA, Westcott WL. Maximal strength testing in healthy children. *J Strength Cond Res* 2003; 17:162–166.

35. Faigenbaum AD, Kraemer WJ, Cahill B, Chandler J, Dziados J, Elfrink LD, Forman E, Gaudiose M, Micheli LJ, Nitka LM, Roberts S. Youth resistance training: position statement paper and literature review. *Strength Cond* 1996; 18:62–75.

36. Faigenbaum AD, Westcott WL, Long C, LaRosa R, Loud M, Delmonico M, Micheli L. Relationship between repetitions and selected percentages of the one-repetition maximum in healthy children. *Pediatric Physical Therapy* 1998; 10:110–113.

37. Falk B, Tenenbaum G. The effectiveness of resistance training in children. *Sports Med* 1996; 22:176–186.

38. Fernhall B. Physical fitness and exercise training of individuals with mental retardation. *Med Sci Sports Exerc* 1993; 25:442–450.

39. Fiatarone MA, Marks EC, Ryan ND, Meredith CN, Lipsitz LA, Evans WJ. High-intensity strength training in nonagenarians: effects on skeletal muscle. *Journal of the American Medical Association* 1990; 263:3029–3034.

40. Figoni SF. Spinal cord disabilities: paraplegia and tetraplegia. In: Durstine JL, Moore GE eds, *ACSM's Exercise Management for Persons with Chronic Diseases and Disabilities.* 2nd ed. Champaign, IL: Human Kinetics; 2003:247–253.

41. Forrest G, Qian X. Exercise in neuromuscular disease. *Neurorehabilitation* 1999; 13:135–139.
42. Foundation IO. *Facts and Statistics*. 2015.
43. Frontera WR, Suh D, Krivickas LS, Hughes VA, Goldstein R, Roubenoff R. Skeletal muscle fiber quality in older men and women. *Am J Physiol* 2000; 279:C611–C618.
44. Frontera WR, Hughes VA, Fielding RA, et al. Aging of skeletal muscle: a 12-yr longitudinal study. *J Appl Physiol* 2000; 88:1321–1326.
45. Frontera WR, Hughes VA, Fielding RA, Fiatarone MA, Evans WJ, Roubenoff R. Aging of skeletal muscle: a 12-yr longitudinal study. *J Appl Physiol* 2000; 88:1321–1326.
46. Garber CE, Blissmer B, Deschenes MR, et al. American College of Sports Medicine position stand. Quantity and quality of exercise for developing and maintaining cardiorespiratory, musculoskeletal, and neuromotor fitness in apparently healthy adults: guidance for prescribing exercise. *Med Sci Sports Exerc* 2011; 43:1334–1359.
47. Giangregorio LM, McGill S, Wark JD, et al. Too fit to fracture: outcomes of a Delphi consensus process on physical activity and exercise recommendations for adults with osteoporosis with or without vertebral fractures. *Osteoporos Int* 2015; 26:891–910.
48. Gielen S, Laughlin MH, O'Conner C, et al. Exercise training in patients with heart disease: review of beneficial effects and clinical recommendations. *Progress in Cardiovascular Diseases* 2015; 57:347–355.
49. Goldberg L, Elliot DL, Keuhl KS. Cardiovascular changes at rest and during mixed static and dynamic exercises after weight training. *J Appl Sport Sci Res* 1988; 2:42–45.
50. Golob AL, Laya MB. Osteoporosis: screening, prevention, and management. *Med Clin North Am* 2015; 99:587–606.
51. Goodman CC, Glanzman A. Genetic and developmental disorders. In: Goodman CC, Boissonnault WG, Fuller KS. ed, *Pathology Implications for the Physical Therapist*, 2nd ed. Philadelphia, PA: Saunders; 2003:829–870.
52. Hammond ER, Metcalf HM, McDonald JW, et al. Bone mass in individuals with chronic spinal cord injury: associations with activity-based therapy, neurologic and functional

status, a retrospective study. *Arch Phys Med Rehabil* 2014; 95:2342–2349.
53. Helleckson KL. NIH releases statement on osteoporosis prevention, diagnosis, and therapy. *Am Fam Physician* 2002; 66:161–162.
54. Hicks AL, Martin Ginis KA, Pelletier CA, et al. The effects of exercise training on physical capacity, strength, body composition and functional performance among adults with spinal cord injury: a systematic review. *Spinal Cord* 2011; 49:1103–1127.
55. Howe TE, Shea B, Dawson LJ, et al. Exercise for preventing and treating osteoporosis in postmenopausal women. *Cochrane Database Syst Rev* 2011, DOI: 10.1002/14651858. CD000333.pub2: CD000333.
56. Hughes VA, Frontera WR, Wood M, Evans WJ, Dalla GE, Roubenoff R, Fiatarone Singh MA. Longitudinal muscle strength changes in older adults: influence of muscle mass, physical activity, and health. *J Gerontol A Biol Sci Med Sci* 2001; 56A:B209–B217.
57. Intellectual AAo, (AAIDD) aDD. *Definition of Intellectual Disability*. 2013. AAIDD.
58. Jacob PL, Nash MS. Exercise recommendations for individuals with spinal cord injury. *Sports Med* 2004; 34:727–751.
59. Jette AM, Branch LG. The Framington disability study: II-. The Framingham Disability Study: II. physical disability among the aging. *AJPH* 1981; 71:1211–1216.
60. Kelley GA, Kelley KS. Progressive resistance exercise and resting blood pressure: a meta-analysis of randomized controlled trials. *Hypertension* 2000; 35:838–843.
61. Kelley GA, Kelley KS, Tran ZV. Walking and resting blood pressure in adults: a meta-analysis. *Prev Med* 2001; 33:120–127.
62. Kelley GA, Kelley KS, Tran ZV. The effects of exercise on resting blood pressure in children and adolescents: a meta-analysis of randomized controlled trials. *Prev Cardiol* 2003; 6:8–16.
63. Khairallah RJ, Shi G, Sbrana F, et al. Microtubules underlie dysfunction in Duchenne Muscular Dystrophy. *Sci Signal* 2012; 5:ra56.
64. Kirshblum SC, Burns SP, Biering-Sorensen F, et al. International standards for neurological classification of spinal cord injury (revised 2011). *J Spinal Cord Med* 2011; 34:535–546.
65. Krag TO, Hauerslev S, Sveen ML, et al. Level of muscle regeneration in limb-girdle

muscular dystrophy type 2I relates to genotype and clinical severity. *Skelet Muscle* 2011; 1:31.

66. Kraschnewski JL, Sciamanna CN, Ciccolo JT, et al. Is exercise used as medicine? Association of meeting strength training guidelines and functional limitations among older US adults. *Prev Med* 2014; 66:1–5.

67. Kraschnewski JL, Sciamanna CN, Poger JM, et al. Is strength training associated with mortality benefits? A 15 year cohort study of US older adults. *Prev Med* 2016; 87:121–127.

68. Latham NK, Bennett DA, Stretton CM, et al. Systematic review of progressive resistance strength training in older adults. *J Gerontol A Biol Sci Med Sci* 2004; 59A:48–61.

69. Latham NK, Bennett DA, Stretton CM, et al. Systematic review of progressive resistance strength training in older adults. *J Gerontol A Biol Sci Med Sci* 2004; 59A:48–61.

70. Lesinski M, Prieske O, Granacher U. Effects and dose-response relationships of resistance training on physical performance in youth athletes: a systematic review and meta-analysis. *Br J Sports Med* 2016, DOI: 10.1136/bjsports-2015-095497.

71. Lexell J, Taylor CC, Sjostrom M. What is the cause of the ageing atrophy? Total number, size and proportion of different fiber types studied in whole vastus lateralis muscle from 15- to 83-year-old men. *Journal of the Neurological Sciences* 1988; 84:275–294.

72. Li C, Chen S, Meng How Y, et al. Benefits of physical exercise intervention on fitness of individuals with Down syndrome: a systematic review of randomized-controlled trials. *Int J Rehabil Res* 2013; 36:187–195.

73. Li J, Siegrist J. Physical activity and risk of cardiovascular disease: a meta-analysis of prospective cohort studies. *International Journal of Environmental Research and Public Health* 2012; 9:391–407.

74. Lloyd RS, Faigenbaum AD, Stone MH, et al. Position statement on youth resistance training: the 2014 International Consensus. *Br J Sports Med* 2014; 48:498–505.

75. Long C, McAnally JR, Shelton JM, et al. Prevention of muscular dystrophy in mice by CRISPR/Cas9-mediated editing of germline DNA. *Science* 2014; 345:1184–1188.

76. Lovering RM, Porter NC, Bloch RJ. The muscular dystrophies: from genes to therapies. *Phys Ther* 2005; 85:1372–1388.

77. Luz MA, Marques MJ, Santo Neto H. Impaired regeneration of dystrophin-deficient muscle fibers is caused by exhaustion of myogenic cells. *Brazilian Journal of Medical and Biological Research = Revista brasileira de pesquisas medicas e biologicas* 2002; 35:691–695.

78. Malek MH, Nalbone DP, Berger DE, et al. Importance of health science education for personal fitness trainers. *J Strength Cond Res* 2002; 16:19–24.

79. Mandic S, Myers J, Selig SE, et al. Resistance versus aerobic exercise training in chronic heart failure. *Curr Heart Fail Rep* 2012; 9:57–64.

80. Martins WR, de Oliveira RJ, Carvalho RS, et al. Elastic resistance training to increase muscle strength in elderly: a systematic review with meta-analysis. *Arch Gerontol Geriatr* 2013; 57:8–15.

81. Marzolini S, Oh PI, Brooks D. Effect of combined aerobic and resistance training versus aerobic training alone in individuals with coronary artery disease: a meta-analysis. *EJPC* 2012; 19:81–94.

82. Maulik PK, Mascarenhas MN, Mathers CD, et al. Prevalence of intellectual disability: a meta-analysis of population-based studies. *Res Dev Disabil* 2011; 32:419–436.

83. Mayo NE. Stroke. 1. Epidemiology and recovery. *Physical Medicine and Rehabilitation State of the Art Reviews* 1993; 7:1–25.

84. McCartney N, McKelvie RS, Martin J, et al. Weight training induced attenuation of the circulatory response of older males to weight lifting. *J Appl Physiol* 1993; 74:1056–1060.

85. MDA. *List of Neuromuscular Diseases.* 2016.

86. Mendell JR, Rodino-Klapac L, Sahenk Z, et al. Gene therapy for muscular dystrophy: lessons learned and path forward. *Neurosci Lett* 2012; 527:90–99.

87. Meyer K. Resistance exercise in chronic heart failure: landmark studies and implications for practice. *Clin Invest Med* 2006; 29:166–169.

88. Morgan JE, Zammit PS. Direct effects of the pathogenic mutation on satellite cell function in muscular dystrophy. *Experimental Cell Research* 2010; 316:3100–3108.

89. Moritani T, deVries HA. Potential for gross muscle hypertrophy in older men. *Am J Physical Med* 1980; 35:672–682.

90. Nelson CE, Hakim CH, Ousterout DG, et al. In vivo genome editing improves muscle function in a mouse model of Duchenne muscular dystrophy. *Science* 2016; 351:403–407.

91. NLMS. *Muscular Dystrophy.* 2016.

92. Oak SA, Zhou YW, Jarrett HW. Skeletal muscle signaling pathway through the dystrophin glycoprotein complex and Rac1. *J Biol Chem* 2003; 278:39287–39295.

93. Oviedo GR, Guerra-Balic M, Baynard T, et al. Effects of aerobic, resistance and balance training in adults with intellectual disabilities. *Res Dev Disabil* 2014; 35:2624–2634.

94. Palevo G, Keteyian SJ, Kang M, et al. Resistance exercise training improves heart function and physical fitness in stable patients with heart failure. *J Cardiopulm Rehabil Prev* 2009; 29:294–298.

95. Payne VG, Morrow Jr JR, Johnson L, Dalton SN. Resistance training in children and youth: a meta-analysis. *Res Q Exerc Sport* 1997; 68:80–88.

96. Petrof BJ, Shrager JB, Stedman HH, et al. Dystrophin protects the sarcolemma from stresses developed during muscle contraction. *Proc Natl Acad Sci USA* 1993; 90:3710–3714.

97. Pollock ML, Franklin BA, Balady GJ, et al. AHA Science Advisory. *Resistance Exercise in Individuals With and Without Cardiovascular Disease: Benefits, Rationale, Safety, and Prescription – An Advisory from the Committee on Exercise, Rehabilitation, and Prevention, Council on Clinical Cardiology, American Heart Association.* Position paper endorsed by the American College of Sports Medicine. Circulation 2000; 101:828–833.

98. Prevention CfDCa. *Heart Disease Fact Sheet.* 2016.

99. Robinson-Hamm JN, Gersbach CA. Gene therapies that restore dystrophin expression for the treatment of Duchenne muscular dystrophy. *Hum Genet* 2016; 135:1029–1040.

100. Roche JA, Lovering RM, Roche R, et al. Extensive mononuclear infiltration and myogenesis characterize recovery of dysferlin-null skeletal muscle from contraction-induced injuries. *Am J Physiol Cell Physiol* 2010; 298:C298–C312.

101. Roche JA, Ru LW, Bloch RJ. Distinct effects of contraction-induced injury in vivo on four different murine models of dysferlinopathy. *J Biomed Biotechnol* 2012; 2012:134031.

102. Roche JA, Tulapurkar ME, Mueller AL, et al. Myofiber damage precedes macrophage infiltration after in vivo injury in dysferlin-deficient A/J mouse skeletal muscle. *Am J Pathol* 2015; 185:1686–1698.

103. Sahenk Z, Mendell JR. The muscular dystrophies: distinct pathogenic mechanisms invite novel therapeutic approaches. *Curr Rheumatol Rep* 2011; 13:199–207.

104. Salter K, Musovic A, Taylor NF. In the first 3 months after stroke is progressive resistance training safe and does it improve activity? A systematic review. *Top Stroke Rehabil* 2016, DOI: 10.1080/10749357.2016.1160656: 1–10.

105. Sattelmair J, Pertman J, Ding EL, et al. Dose response between physical activity and risk of coronary heart disease: a meta-analysis. *Circulation* 2011; 124:789–795.

106. Saunders DH, Greig CA, Mead GE. Physical activity and exercise after stroke: review of multiple meaningful benefits. *Stroke* 2014; 45:3742–3747.

107. Saunders DH, Sanderson M, Hayes S, et al. Physical fitness training for stroke patients. *Cochrane Database Syst Rev* 2016; 3:CD003316.

108. Selig SE, Levinger I, Williams AD, et al. Exercise & Sports Science Australia Position Statement on exercise training and chronic heart failure. *Journal of Science and Medicine in Sport / Sports Medicine Australia* 2010; 13:288–294.

109. Services AoAAfCLUSDoHaH. A profile of older Americans: 2013. DOI: www.aoa.acl.gov/Aging_Statistics/Profile/2013/Index.aspx.

110. Sharp SA, Brouwer BJ. Isokinetic strength training of the hemiparetic knee: effects on function and spasticity. *Archives of Physical Medicine and Rehabilitation* 1997; 78:1231–1236.

111. Shields N, Taylor NF. A student-led progressive resistance training program increases lower limb muscle strength in adolescents with Down syndrome: a randomised controlled trial. *J Physiother* 2010; 56:187–193.

112. Shields N, Taylor NF, Wee E, et al. A community-based strength training programme increases muscle strength and physical activity in young people with Down syndrome: a randomised controlled trial. *Res Dev Disabil* 2013; 34:4385–4394.

113. Smart NA, Dieberg G, Giallauria F. Intermittent versus continuous exercise training in chronic heart failure: a meta-analysis. *Int J Cardiol* 2013; 166:352–358.

114. Sveen ML, Andersen SP, Ingelsrud LH, et al. Resistance training in patients with limb-girdle and Becker muscular dystrophies. *Muscle Nerve* 2013; 47:163–169.

115. Tabebordbar M, Zhu K, Cheng JK, et al. In vivo gene editing in dystrophic mouse muscle and muscle stem cells. *Science* 2016; 351:407–411.

116. **Teixeira-Salmela LF, Olney SJ, Nadeau S, Brouwer B.** Muscle strengthening and physical conditioning to reduce impairment and disability in chronic stroke survivors. *Archives of Physical Medicine and Rehabilitation* 1999; 80:1211–1218.

117. **Torhaug T, Brurok B, Hoff J, et al.** The effect from maximal bench press strength training on work economy during wheelchair propulsion in men with spinal cord injury. *Spinal Cord* 2016, DOI: 10.1038/sc.2016.27.

118. **Trappe S, Williamson D, Godard M.** Maintenance of whole muscle strength and size following resistance training in older men. *J Gerontol A Biol Sci Med Sci* 2002; 57:B138–B143.

119. **Tweedy SM, Beckman EM, Geraghty TJ, et al.** Exercise and sports science Australia (ESSA) position statement on exercise and spinal cord injury. *Journal of Science and Medicine in Sport / Sports Medicine Australia* 2016, DOI: 10.1016/j.jsams.2016.02.001.

120. **Villareal DT, Steger-May K, Schechtman KB, et al.** Effects of exercise training on bone mineral density in frail older women and men: a randomised controlled trial. *Age Aging* 2004; 33:309–312.

121. **Warms CA, Backus D, Rajan S, et al.** Adverse events in cardiovascular-related training programs in people with spinal cord injury: a systematic review. *J Spinal Cord Med* 2014; 37:672–692.

122. **Watanabe Y, Tanimoto M, Oba N, et al.** Effect of resistance training using bodyweight in the elderly: comparison of resistance exercise movement between slow and normal speed movement. *Geriatr Gerontol Int* 2015; 15:1270–1277.

123. **Weir JP, Housh TJ, Johnson GO, Housh DJ, Ebersole KT.** Allometric scaling of isokinetic peak torque: the Nebraska Wrestling Study. *Eur J Appl Physiol* 1999; 80:240–248.

124. **Williams MA, Haskell WL, Ades PA, et al.** Resistance exercise in individuals with and without cardiovascular disease: 2007 update – a scientific statement from the American Heart Association Council on Clinical Cardiology and Council on Nutrition, Physical Activity, and Metabolism. *Circulation* 2007; 116:572–584.

125. **Williams WGR, Jiang JG, Matcher DB, Samsa GP.** Incidence and occurrence of total (first-ever and recurrent) stroke. *Stroke* 1999; 30:2523–2528.

126. www.jain-foundation.org. *Patient Stories*. 2016.

127. **Yamamoto S, Hotta K, Ota E, et al.** Effects of resistance training on muscle strength, exercise capacity, and mobility in middle-aged and elderly patients with coronary artery disease: a meta-analysis. *Journal of Cardiology* 2016; 68:125–134.

128. **Yarasheski KE.** Exercise, aging, and muscle protein metabolism. *J Gerontol A Biol Sci Med Sci* 2003; 58:M918–922.

129. **Yarasheski KE, Pak-Loduca J, Hasten DL, et al.** Resistance exercise training increases mixed muscle protein synthesis rate in frail women and men >/=76 yr old. *Am J Physiol* 1999; 277:E118–125.

130. **Zhao C, Farruggio AP, Bjornson CR, et al.** Recombinase-mediated reprogramming and dystrophin gene addition in mdx mouse induced pluripotent stem cells. *PLoS One* 2014; 9:e96279.

Contents

CHAPTER 21

AGE AND GENDER TRAINING CONSIDERATIONS

Tammy K. Evetovich and Joan M. Eckerson

OBJECTIVES

After completing this chapter, you will be able to:

- Identify the gender-specific physiological and anatomical considerations that a coach or strength and conditioning professional should consider before designing a training program.
- Understand nutritional considerations specific to women.
- Appreciate the effect of the menstrual cycle on athletic performance and physical activity.
- Understand the factors that affect an exercising pregnant woman.
- Understand strength and power relationships as a function of gender and age.
- Understand the effect of strength training on bone mineral density in women and older adults.

KEY TERMS

Amenorrhea	Glycogen	Micronutrient
Anemia	Hemoglobin	Oral contraceptive
Basal metabolic rate (BMR)	Hemolysis	Osteoporosis
Corpus luteum	Macronutrient	Progesterone
Disordered eating	Menarche	Radiation
Electrolyte	Menstrual cycle	Recommended dietary allowance (RDA)
	Menstruation	

INTRODUCTION

Age and gender refer to special populations that will be focused on in greater detail in this chapter. Both are discussed in Chapter 20, Special populations. Based upon the research that has been undertaken and the endorsement of several respected organizations, it is clear that women and older adults can and should participate in strength and conditioning activities so that they may enjoy the health and athletic benefits that can lead to better quality of life and performance. This chapter will attempt to address some of the many physiological, anatomical, sociological, and psychological considerations that come to the forefront when considering women and older adults and how they should be trained for fitness, competition, and health.

TRAINING CONSIDERATIONS FOR FEMALES

In 1970, only 1 out of every 27 high school girls played varsity sports. Today, that ratio is 1 in 2.5, which is similar to the participation rate of high school boys (1 in 2). To gain a better appreciation of the overall change, the number of females participating in high school sports increased from 294,015 in 1971 to 2,472,043 in 1997 to over 3,000,000 today, and women participating in college sports has more than tripled, from 31,000 to 250,000.

The increase in athletic participation among women has been largely attributed to Title IX legislation, which states that: "No person in the United States shall, on the basis of sex, be excluded from participation in, be denied the benefits of, or be subjected to discrimination under any education program or activity receiving Federal financial assistance." Although athletic participation was not directly mentioned in the law, because Title IX prohibits sex discrimination in any educational program or activity at any educational institution that is a recipient of federal funds, it includes high school, college, and university athletes. Other organizations have long recognized that women should be afforded the opportunity to compete athletically and participate in all forms of physical and training activities:

> National Collegiate Athletic Association (NCAA) "An athletics program can be considered gender equitable when the participants in both the men's and women's sports programs would accept as fair and equitable the overall program of the other gender. No individual should be discriminated against on the basis of gender, institutionally or nationally, in intercollegiate athletics." (NCAA Gender-Equity Task Force – www.ncaa.org)

> The Women's Sports Foundation "we want equal opportunity for our daughters to play sports so they too can derive the psychological, physiological and sociological benefits of sports participation. Sport has been one of the most important socio-cultural learning experiences for boys and men for many years. Those same benefits should be afforded our daughters." (www.womenssportsfoundation.org)

> American Association of University Professors (AAUP) "Enhancing athletic opportunity for young women and girls is of vital importance because of the significant physical, psychological, and sociological benefits those opportunities provide. A number of studies have recognized the role that athletic opportunities for women provide in promoting greater academic success, responsible social behaviors, and increased personal skills." (2)

The increase in the number of females participating in athletics over the last 50 years has resulted in growing interest in research for this population. The consensus is that the benefits of physical activity on health and social behaviors is similar to that observed in men, and also provides benefits specific only to women including a decreased risk of breast cancer and osteoporosis; decreased incidence of smoking and depression; decreased teenage pregnancy rates; better performance in the classroom; prevention of heart disease; and a healthier body weight.

There has also been considerable research to help answer the question, of whether men and women should be considered separately and uniquely when designing strength and conditioning programs, optimizing nutritional status, and encouraging a healthy psychological profile given their anatomical, physiological, and psychological differences.

> National Strength and Conditioning Association (NSCA) (32) regarding strength training for female athletes: "It appears that proper strength and conditioning exercise programs may increase athletic performance, improve physiological function and reduce risk of injuries. These effects are as beneficial to female athletes as they are to men. The question that has to be addressed is whether female athletes require different training modalities, programs or personnel than those required by male athletes.

Due to similar physiological responses, it seems that men and women should train for strength in the same basic way, employing similar methodologies, programs and types of exercises. Coaches should assess the needs of each athlete, male or female, individually, and train that athlete accordingly. Coaches should keep in mind that there are many more differences between individuals of the same gender than between men and women. Still, there are many psychological and/or physiological considerations that should be taken into account in training female athletes."

Gender differences

There are substantial differences between men and women when considering anatomical and physiological variables that may impact training and performance. Table 21.1 provides a gender comparison for many of these variables. For example, from an anatomical perspective, on average, women are shorter than men, have higher percent body fat, and have smaller bone mass. Physiologically, women have higher resting heart rates, lower lung volumes, unique hormone profiles, and similar muscle fiber type distribution patterns. In addition, women tend to be weaker than men in absolute terms, but when strength is expressed per unit of muscle mass the differences begin to disappear.

In general, men and women respond similarly when examining strength, hypertrophic, and metabolic responses to training. Both sexes have specific training needs and their programs should be based upon their objectives, activities that they will participate in, and their individual genetic predispositions. However, there are some training considerations that come to light in that many of the anatomical and physiological gender-related differences noted in Table 21.1 could potentially translate into variations in training methods and athletic performance. For example, with regard to resistance training, given that some research has

TABLE 21.1 Gender comparisons of men to women

Physiological and anatomical variables	Gender comparison
Height	Women are shorter than men
Weight	Women weigh less than men Women have more fat weight than men Women have less fat free weight than men
Circumferences	Women generally have smaller circumferences
Diameters	Women generally have smaller diameters with narrower shoulders, smaller chest diameters, but a wider pelvis relative to their body size
% body fat	Women have higher body fat (average for 20- to 34-year-old men and women is 12% and 28%, respectively)
Bones	Women have smaller bones than men, with peak bone mass occurring around age 25
Ligaments	Women have smaller ligaments and may have differences in ligament laxity due to differences in steroidal hormones
Joints	Women have greater joint laxity
Absolute strength	Women are 35–80% as strong as men (35–50% for upper body and 60–80% for lower body)
Muscle fiber cross-sectional area	Women less than men

(continued)

TABLE 21.1 (continued)

Physiological and anatomical variables	Gender comparison
Fast-twitch to slow-twitch muscle fiber area	Women less than men
Intramuscular fat and connective tissue	Women greater than men
Strength per unit of muscle cross-sectional area	Women are equal to men for the most part, although this is debatable for the upper body whereby women may be less than men
Resting testosterone levels	Women lower than men
Muscle hypertrophy	The degree to which female muscle hypertrophies is smaller in absolute terms, but the relative degree of hypertrophy is equal to that of men
Resting growth hormone levels	Women greater than men
Rate of muscle force development	Women slower than men in absolute terms but relatively the same (based on a percent of maximal force)
Fiber type	Muscle fiber type (slow vs. fast twitch) distribution patterns are similar for men and women
Posture	Women have greater anterior pelvic tilt, femoral internal rotation, knee hyperextension, and knee valgus
Q angle	Quadriceps (Q angle) = 8–15 in men and 12–19 in women
Flexibility	Women are more flexible than men at all ages and throughout the lifespan
Lung volume	Women have lower tidal and ventilatory lung volumes
Heart rate	Adult women have average 5–10 beats/minute faster resting heart rates than adult men
VO_2 max	Women less than men
Cardiac output	Women less than men
Hemoglobin	Women less than men
Reaction time	Women same as men
Running economy and endurance	At the same submaximal velocity elite male runners are more economical then female runners
Limb length	Women have shorter limb length relative to body length
Pelvis width	Women wider than men
Shoulder width	Women narrower than men
Intercondylar notch	Women narrower notch
Posterior tibial slope	Women greater slope
Surface area to body mass ratio	Women larger than men
Sweat rate	Women lower rate than men

found that women may have less upper-body strength, even when taking into consideration strength relative to lean body mass and cross-sectional area, it may be beneficial for the female client/athlete that participates in sports and activities that require strong upper body strength (swimming, power lifting, softball, volleyball) to spend a greater amount of time during training on their upper body strength (10). In addition, it has been suggested (10) that women should devote more time, particularly during the off-season, to resistance training that causes a high metabolic demand, with high volume and multiple sets with short rest periods (hypertrophic training), given that this may increase the acute hormone response to exercise, stimulate lean body mass, and then further stimulate an acute hormonal response. The increased acute hormonal response during the hypertrophic phase would then result in greater development in the strength and power phases of a training program.

Also, coaches and personal trainers may want to consider altering lifting technique for some women. It is thought that narrow shoulder width observed in women may be cause for concern when performing overhead lifts. Thus, coaches and personal trainers should pay close attention to hand spacing in women. Also, because of differences between the sexes in the Q angle and greater pelvic width, some have suggested that women may want to perform squats with a toe forward stance; however, others have not deemed this change necessary. Therefore, the strength and conditioning professional should make their best judgment on what technique and stance is appropriate for each athlete.

Other gender-related anatomical variations that may lead to altered training and measurement methods include the following:

- Women have smaller bones and, therefore, lower bone mass. Strength training and weight bearing exercises may be particularly important to incorporate into their strength and conditioning routine so that they are not as likely to develop **osteoporosis** later in life.
- Women have smaller ligaments and there is some thought that this may be responsible for the higher incidence of ligament injury, particularly at the knee. In addition, greater joint laxity, possibly due to gender differences in hormone profiles, may increase the risk for injury in women.
- Body fat and body weight recommendations should be based upon % body fat not body weight. Optimal levels of % body fat are sport specific, and coaches/athletes should be aware that accurate assessment of body fat can be difficult and is dependent upon the type of technique used and the competence of the person performing the measurements. Before any weight loss or weight gain program is undertaken, coaches and personal trainers need to be aware of the societal signals that may be pressuring women and affecting their assessment of their own body image. **Eating disorders** are observed at a higher rate in women and team weigh-ins or other public measurements of weight should be discouraged to avoid making them self-conscious of their body weight. For athletes, it is recommended that body fat gain and loss programs should be undertaken in the off-season under the guidance of a nutritionist or other professional educated on the recommended nutrition levels for **macronutrients** and **micronutrients**, so that body fat goals can be met in a healthy manner (3).

Social and psychological considerations for resistance training

Progress has been made to encourage women to participate in strength and power training activities. However, cultural and sociological pressure is an issue that needs to be considered when expecting the female client to adhere to a strength training program. There are still concerns about feminine appearance, appropriateness of behavior, self-esteem, and self-consciousness both inside and outside the weight room. In addition, there continues to be misinformation about the importance of strength training for maximizing female athletic performance. A survey by Poiss et al. (37) indicated that male student-athletes were more likely to consider weight training an essential part of every training program regardless of sport and were more likely to weight train more days per week with more minutes per training session.

Not only are women struggling to decide whether to incorporate resistance training into their training routine, but some coaches of female athletes do not consider it a principal component of an overall conditioning program (37). This same survey indicated that weight training was more frequently required by coaches of male student-athletes than by coaches of female student-athletes. The authors went on to say that this difference was an "indication that coaches of women athletes may not consider weight training an important element as part of an athlete's regular training program," and it is clear that we must teach that weight training is important for female and male student-athletes.

There are many points to reflect upon when attempting to understand the social stigmas that women encounter when considering whether to begin and adhere to a strength training program. The following are some general considerations and recommendations when attempting to create an environment that is more socially acceptable and inviting to female resistance trainers:

- Help women realize that it is not physiologically possible (due to their hormonal profile) to amass large amounts of muscle. Women who avoid heavy resistance training should know that body circumferences do not tend to change dramatically with the increase in muscle mass that accompanies resistance training. In fact, circumferences may decrease due to a loss of fat with training.
- Having a female role model in the weight room is important for social acceptance, particularly for young girls. Therefore, both male and female strength and conditioning coaches need to be available in all facilities.
- Make sure men and women have equal access to weight room equipment so that they will be more likely to adhere to a program.
- Create a weight room environment and culture that is not intimidating to women.
- Make sure that separate men's and women's weight rooms have equitable types of equipment and machines.
- When setting up fitness room equipment, consideration should be given to the layout of the facility and the ability of a woman to maintain her modesty while lifting. This may mean that certain pieces of equipment should be turned or faced toward a wall or be placed in a more private area so that the woman feels comfortable in the weight room environment.
- Consider not having mirrors on some walls in a fitness facility so that individuals can participate in floor work and face away from the middle of the facility and not be concerned about how their reflection may be viewed by others in the facility.
- Make sure that there is a wide array of weights and machines that can accommodate all levels of weight training and are the proper dimensions for many different types of body weights, statures, and sizes.
- Remove all magazines and reading materials that may have sexist images or portray women in an unhealthy manner from the weight room and other training facilities.
- Do not allow language in the weight room that someone may find offensive.
- Do not play music or television programs in the weight room that are offensive or sexist.

Improving resistance training adherence

In an article (19) that outlined strategies for improving resistance training adherence in female athletes, the primary approaches included:

- Develop a positive relationship with the athlete.
- Learn about the athlete's history and confidence related to resistance training.
- Learn about the athlete's perceptions, expectations, and goals.
- Educate the athlete.
- Identify constraints and possible reasons for lapses in adherence.
- Develop appropriate goals.
- Start and progress the athlete appropriately.
- Create a program that is conducive to the constraints of the athlete.
- Create alternatives to weight room strength training.
- Create group exercise sessions to provide peer modeling of resistance training.

- Retest strength and functional abilities, reward progress.
- Provide a planned and unplanned feedback system.
- Create an exercise environment conducive to resistance training adherence.

Although great progress has been made in convincing women that weight training is safe, socially acceptable, and beneficial for maximizing fitness and performance, there is still much work that needs to be done. It can be challenging for educators, personal trainers, and coaches to facilitate adherence to a resistance training program in women. Raising social awareness, erasing myths, confronting negative attitudes, and challenging stereotypes are all important tasks that must be undertaken to bolster support so that women can be viewed as athletes and competitors in the weight room without having to sacrifice their femininity.

Menstrual cycle

Many times, coaches, strength and conditioning professionals, athletes, and other active women ask the question, "Does the menstrual cycle affect athletic performance and adherence to physical activity programs in women?" In short, they are asking whether the steroid hormone fluctuations that occur during the **menstrual cycle** can maximize or hinder performance depending upon the phase of the cycle. Before we can examine this question, however, a basic understanding of the menstrual cycle is necessary.

Follicular phase

The menstrual cycle can be divided into three phases: the follicular phase, ovulation, and the luteal phase. The follicular phase begins with the onset of **menstruation** (day 1) and lasts through about day 13. During this phase, immature eggs called primordial follicles begin to develop into primary follicles, in response to an increase in **follicle-stimulating hormone** (FSH), which starts to produce very low levels of **estrogen**. Although about 20 follicles begin developing during a cycle, only one attains maturity and is released and continues to produce estrogen. The estrogen level continues to

increase and peaks about 24–48 hours before ovulation. The rising level of estrogen stimulates the hypothalamus to secrete **luteinizing hormone** (LH) so that there is an LH "surge" during the late follicular phase. It is this surge that triggers ovulation. Thus, in summary, FSH is needed to make the follicles mature, the growing follicles release estrogen which ultimately results in the LH surge. As LH surges, estrogen levels begin to decrease and another hormone, **progesterone**, begins to increase.

Ovulation

The LH surge causes the primary follicle to burst and release its egg (ovulate). This release usually occurs around day 14 of a 28-day cycle.

Luteal phase

After ovulation, the luteal phase begins and continues until the first day of menstruation (beginning of the follicular phase). During this phase, the empty follicle is now called the **corpus luteum**, or yellow body, which is secreting primarily progesterone. Progesterone levels will reach a peak about seven days after ovulation. The hormones secreted during this phase prevent new follicles from developing and any further release of eggs so that multiple ovulations do not occur during a cycle. In addition, progesterone is important in supporting a pregnancy should the egg be fertilized and the corpus luteum will continue to support the egg until the placenta can take over. If fertilization does not occur, the corpus luteum will quickly begin to stop functioning as the luteal phase progresses and progesterone levels begin to decrease. It is this decrease in hormone levels that triggers menstruation and allows a new cycle to begin. The menstrual cycle will begin anew and FSH will begin to stimulate the maturation of primordial follicles.

Given our brief discussion on the phases of the menstrual cycle, it is apparent why those working with female athletes wonder whether the menstrual cycle and the associated fluctuations in steroid hormones (estrogen and progesterone in particular) that occur over the cycle, could affect performance. As discussed, estrogen starts to increase in the follicular phase, peaking around ovulation, and during the luteal phase both estrogen and progesterone are elevated. It is hypothesized that these fluctuations in hormones could have many physiological ramifications that could adversely affect performance including changes in thermoregulation, respiration, and strength of muscular contraction. Several review papers (29,30,31,45) have been published over the years examining the effect of menstrual cycle phase on performance.

Although this topic has been examined quite extensively, there is still much research that needs to be conducted to fully understand the effect of the menstrual cycle on exercise performance. Small sample sizes and case studies, the type of subjects used in the studies (trained vs. untrained; sport specific athletes), different types of exercise testing in the research, study eligibility criteria, method for verification of menstrual cycle phase, examining maximal neural activation versus voluntary muscle actions, **oral contraceptive** usage and dosage, menstrual history, menstrual disturbances, all need to be considered when examining the research. Nevertheless, a recent report (45) attempted to provide the most recent findings in the research on this matter for muscle strength and fatigability, maximal oxygen consumption (VO$_2$ max), and prolonged aerobic activities.

> It is possible that the hormone fluctuations that occur across the menstrual cycle can affect performance.

Effect of the menstrual cycle on muscular strength and endurance

Steroid hormones like estrogen and progesterone may improve strength and delay muscle fatigue at certain phases of the menstrual cycle. Many studies have been conducted on women yet it is difficult to compare studies when hormone concentrations and menstrual cycle phase were not verified, the maximum force-generating capacity of the muscle was not reached (superimposed electrical stimulation was not applied to the muscle), and/or

the subjects were taking some type of oral contraceptive ("the pill"). When limiting this discussion to studies whereby maximal electrical stimulation was applied, hormone level verification was conducted accurately, and subjects were non-pill users, it was concluded (45) that menstrual cycle phase does not affect muscle strength and fatigability. There was a more recent study (5), however, that satisfied all the methodological considerations above and did find a significant increase in strength (isokinetic knee extension and flexion and isometric knee flexion) around ovulation. Thus, although much research has been conducted in this area, the effects of the menstrual cycle on muscular strength are still unclear.

Effect of the menstrual cycle on endurance performance

Although there are potentially many factors that could theoretically affect aerobic endurance performance across the menstrual cycle, two issues have come to the forefront and have received the most interest: fluid and body temperature changes.

Effect of the menstrual cycle on body fluids and body weight

Changes in body weight due to fluctuations in fluid retention across the cycle could affect VO$_2$ max. Fluid fluctuations may also affect plasma volume, which could ultimately affect the ability to transport oxygen (**hemoglobin** concentration) to the working tissues. In addition, blood loss that occurs during menstruation could affect performance. Studies examining this topic have not done a good job verifying menstrual cycle phase with hormone measurements and/or did not conduct measurements often enough during the cycle to provide an answer as to whether athletes should be concerned about whether their performance may be affected. However, after examining the literature, there may be two potential factors that the coach and athlete may want to consider. First, if daily measurements of body weight are conducted, there may be some indication that a slight increase in body weight may be present during the late luteal and early follicular (during menstruation) phases. In those sports where body weight plays a crucial role, performance may be affected. Second, women who lose significant amounts of blood (more than 80 mL) during menstruation have been shown to have a significantly lower hemoglobin concentration (45), which may affect endurance performance.

Changes in body temperature

Body temperature (BT) increases during ovulation and remains elevated during the luteal phase (40) because of an increase in progesterone levels. An increase in BT could affect female athletes in many ways such as increasing heart rate and/or creating greater cardiovascular strain (particularly in the heat). It has been determined that for every 1° increase in BT, the resultant increase in HR may be as much as seven beats per minute. The increase in BT observed in the luteal phase is only about 0.5°. Thus, most studies report no change in exercising heart rate over the menstrual cycle.

Heat illness in females

During exercise, heat is produced with muscular activity, and if the heat production is compounded by a decreased ability to dissipate the heat (via conduction or **radiation**), as in the case of a hot or humid environment, there is an increased risk of developing a heat illness. The threshold for the onset of sweating may be higher during the luteal phase, and as stated earlier, there is also a slight increase in core temperature during this phase (25,31), which, one might speculate, may put them at a greater risk for heat illness. However, women have been shown to be very tolerant to heat while exercising, across all phases of the menstrual cycle. In fact, a review by Marsh and Jenkins (31) suggests that the surge in estrogen observed before ovulation may lower the hormonally increased set point, which could prove to be a beneficial adaptation for women exercising in the heat at this point in the menstrual cycle. To avoid heat illness for all athletes, it is important that they understand the symptoms of heat illness and adjust their training and competition schedule whenever possible so that they are not exercising during the hottest part of the day.

Menstrual cycle and hormonal training considerations

There are not many indications that there are physiological variables that affect exercise performance across the menstrual cycle for regularly menstruating women participating in strength-specific or anaerobic/aerobic sports and activities. The only potential physiological factor that may be of concern to the coach of a female is that there is possibly a detrimental effect on performance for those women that participate in prolonged exercise in the heat during the luteal phase. In these instances, athletes and coaches may want to adjust their training and competition schedule to the woman's menstrual cycle, so that the time spent in training is used most efficiently.

To control extraneous variables and verify menstrual cycle phases, most studies examining the effect of the menstrual cycle on performance only use **eumenorrheic** (regularly menstruating) subjects. With that in mind, most findings suggest that eumenorrheic female athletes should not be affected by menstrual cycle phase; however, we do not know if this statement holds true for those women who have menstrual disturbances. There is much inter- and intra-individual variation with regard to the effect that the menstrual cycle can have on each specific woman and recognition of this individuality should be considered.

Although there are not many physiological indicators that have been shown to affect performance with regard to the menstrual cycle, can we definitively conclude that, for the most part, a woman's menstrual cycle does not affect her performance? Just ask any woman and she will tell you that the effect of the menstrual cycle should not be discounted. Why? Many women report that changes in energy, mood, pain, etc., are apparent during certain phases of their cycle (usually before or during menstruation) and that their performance is affected due to discomfort, lack of motivation, and/or changes in mental status and mood. Thus, coaches and strength and conditioning professionals may want to consider whether there are methods to make the active and competitive woman more comfortable whether it be the use of ibuprofen to help with pain and discomfort, medications to help regulate the cycle, stress management techniques to help with mood fluctuations, and/or methods to motivate the athlete or recreationally active woman so that she can perform at peak levels. Women usually understand their bodies very well and should experiment with all kinds of methods and techniques and find what works best for them.

Using oral contraceptives to manipulate the cycle

One method that some women utilize if they are concerned about the effect the menstrual cycle may have on their performance, or if they wish to control symptoms that accompany their menstrual cycle (mood changes, discomfort, etc.), is to use oral contraceptives (OCs). A review (38) nicely outlined the prevalence of use of OCs in female athletes. It was reported through published and anecdotal data that use of OCs has increased from 5 to 12% in the early 1980s to 83% of elite athletes in 2008 (38).

OCs are small pills that are taken by mouth daily and are a combination of synthetic estrogen and progesterone. OCs usually come in a package of 28 pills that contain 21 active pills with hormones and 7 placebo pills; however, there are many other formulations. In addition, there are other methods of absorbing these small amounts of hormones into the body (vaginal rings, injection, vaginal inserts) but most research that has been reviewed for this topic involved OC ingestion. Nevertheless, all serve to prevent pregnancy primarily by preventing ovulation. How? Going back to our discussion of the phases of the menstrual cycle, oral contraceptives "fool" the body so that it produces less FSH and LH so that the follicle is not developed and released.

Due to the consistent consumption of these small amounts of hormones on a daily basis it is thought that women are considered to be in a more "stable" hormonal environment (even though there is a placebo week where hormones are withdrawn) and that performance, therefore, will be less affected by hormonal fluctuations. Some have also hypothesized that the small amounts of steroid hormones found in these pills could help build strength. OCs are often prescribed for a variety of reasons

including: prevention of pregnancy, to regulate the cycle particularly with **amenorrhea**, to prevent cramping/pain, to regulate heavy flow, to aid in performance, to prevent injury (7), and possibly as a means to prevent menstruation for convenience and psychological reasons. For the most part, however, most users of OCs are taking these synthetic hormones to prevent pregnancy and to alleviate the discomfort associated with menstruation.

However, what if the pill actually affected performance based upon physiological factors? The review by Rechichi et al. (38) indicated that there is the potential for aerobic capacity, anaerobic capacity, anaerobic power, and reactive strength to vary between users of oral contraceptives when compared to non-OC users. However, it was noted that due to variations in methodological procedures in studies examining this issue (again, small sample sizes in the research studies, the type of subjects used in the studies, and different types of formulations of OCs), it is difficult to discern whether OCs affect performance. However, the review did provide the following conclusions:

> Anaerobic activity – it is unclear whether anaerobic performance is affected by OC consumption. There have been some studies that have shown that anaerobic capacity and reactive strength (important in sprinting and jumping performance) (39) could be affected at certain times in the OC cycle.

> Muscular strength – it is generally accepted that the hormones found in OCs do not have enough of an androgenic effect to influence muscular strength over an OC cycle (34).

> Aerobic performance – there is very little evidence to suggest that aerobic performance is affected by OC use.

Advantages and disadvantages of OC usage

There are many factors that need to be considered by an athlete and her coach while reviewing the research so that an informed decision can be made as to whether taking an OC would be beneficial. Before deciding a woman should consider the potential advantages and disadvantages of using OCs.

Potential advantages

- For women who do not want to become pregnant, the pill may be an acceptable form of contraception.
- For women who are amenorrheic and have the potential for developing **osteoporosis**, OC usage may be beneficial. However, it should be noted that there are conflicting reports as to whether OCs can actually help prevent bone loss in amenorrheic individuals.
- For women who want to manipulate their cycle (delaying or initiating menstruation) for training and competition purposes, the pill may be helpful. It should be noted that this is a controversial use for the pill and some physicians do not condone this method since not menstruating can mask health problems that manifest themselves through changes in the amount of bleeding that is observed.
- For women who would like to experience the convenience of not menstruating there are some OC formulations that limit the number of times per year that menstruation will occur.
- For women who have significant cramping and pain before and during menstruation OCs may alleviate the discomfort.
- For women who think the menstrual cycle could affect their performance from a physiological standpoint (affecting strength, aerobic capacity, anaerobic performance) and want to have a more stable hormone profile across the cycle, OC use may be for them.
- For endurance athletes who experience severe blood loss during menstruation, OCs may reduce blood loss and decrease the potential for impaired oxygen carrying capacity.
- For women who think that the more stable hormone environment provided by OCs will help prevent injury (7), perhaps they will choose to take the pill, although athletes should not be advised that OCs will definitely reduce the risk of injury.

Potential disadvantages

Some women who take OCs experience side effects such as fluid retention, breast tenderness, and nausea. In addition, there is the possibility of **hypertension**, cardiovascular disease, and increased risk of breast cancer for some women. Of particular concern for athletes may be the weight gain that for some (not all), can accompany pill usage since that can directly affect performance. In addition, it actually can be a controversial decision when a woman is deciding whether or not to take the pill. For example, some think that taking a synthetic hormone is considered unethical. These individuals may not think any exogenous hormones should be put into the body.

Regardless of the reason, an athlete needs to make an informed and individualized decision, in consultation with her strength and conditioning professional and physician as to whether taking the pill is a good decision. Daily consumption of an OC can affect each woman in a different manner. This decision can be affected by an athlete's moral values, type of sport in which she competes, individual physiological response to the pill, level of menstrual discomfort, health profile, etc., and the right of a woman to make this decision on an individualized basis should be respected and not dictated.

Female athlete triad

As discussed in Chapter 4, the Skeletal System, the menstrual cycle does not, for the most part, affect performance. However, does exercising and participating in athletics affect the menstrual cycle? Women involved in intense exercise can experience disturbances in the menstrual cycle including delayed **menarche**, cessation of menstruation, and infertility. In fact, when these disturbances in the menstrual cycle are accompanied by other risk factors (**disordered eating**, low bone mineral density, inadequate caloric intake), it is referred to as a syndrome known as the female athlete triad.

The female athlete triad is a term used to refer to the relationship between low energy intake, menstrual disturbances, and low bone mineral density. The estimated prevalence rate has been reported to be as high as 62% in female athletes (although men can be diagnosed with this syndrome as well) (8). At particular risk are those women that compete in sports and activities where leanness, low body weight, and body image are considered important. It should be noted that it is not just competitive athletes that are at risk, but those women and young girls who regularly engage in intense physical activity should also be considered at high risk.

The syndrome begins with inadequate dietary intake. This can be a result of severe restriction of calories (due to an intentional reduction in food intake, **disordered eating**, or intense physical training without a concomitant increase in calories). If low caloric intake continues, the athlete can then experience a disrupted menstrual cycle. In addition, the low caloric intake results in the inadequate intake of certain vitamins and minerals (such as vitamin D and calcium) and lower hormone levels (estrogen) that are essential for normal bone growth and building. The inability to reach peak bone mass during the early years of a woman's life may not be reversible and may ultimately result in a diagnosis of osteoporosis. The low bone mineral density observed in these women may also put them at greater risk (when compared to eumenorrheic women) for stress fractures (4).

Coaches and trainers can be instrumental in recognizing the signs and symptoms of this syndrome. Early detection and diagnosis are critical to prevent compromised health in the long term. There are many published guidelines for the recognition, diagnosis, and treatment of the triad (4,6,8,9). It is recommended that screening occurs during the pre-participation exam or annual health screening. Treatment of this disorder requires a multi-discipline approach among the coach, strength and conditioning professional, physician, a dietitian, and family. Treatment may involve a combination of nutritional counseling (these women should be carefully monitored for adequate caloric intake and proper nutrition), psychological counseling, family involvement, and pharmacological therapy.

Although most coaches and strength and conditioning professionals may not be clinically trained to treat someone with an eating disorder, they should be acquainted with some of the signs and symptoms (8):

- Changes in eating habits (unnecessary dieting, not eating, secretive or ritualistic eating habits)
- Changes in exercise behaviors (excessive or unnecessary exercising)
- Exercising while injured despite medically prescribed activity restrictions
- Depression
- Restlessness
- Distorted body image and exhibiting self-criticism
- Intense fear of gaining weight and excessive frequency of weight measurements
- Social withdrawal
- Irritability
- Insomnia
- Concerns about eating in public or frequently eating secretively
- Inflexible thinking and limited spontaneity
- Cold intolerance
- Constipation or other bowel irregularities
- Stress fractures
- Amenorrhea or menstrual dysfunction
- Dry skin
- Brittle hair and nails
- Dizziness
- Low blood pressure
- Irregular heartbeat
- Sores in the mouth or throat
- Damaged teeth or gums
- Use of diet pills, laxatives, or diuretics
- Going to the bathroom immediately after a meal or snack
- Hair loss
- Low heart rate (bradycardia)
- Low blood sugar (hypoglycemia)
- Muscle cramping
- Callus or abrasion on back of hand (from inducing vomiting)
- Fine downy body hair (lanugo)
- Lethargy and fatigue
- Eating until the point of pain or discomfort (binge eating)
- Substance abuse (legal, illegal, prescription, or over-the-counter)

Nutritional considerations in females

Caloric intake for an inactive woman should be between 1600 to 2000 calories per day. However, when women exercise, there is a need for increased caloric intake to 2200 to 2400 calories per day or more and up to 3000 calories per day may be necessary for extremely active competitive athletes. Further, a more specific recommendation of 39 to 44 kcal/kg body weight/day may be necessary for strength training female athletes (43). It has also been recognized that women may need to consume slightly more kcals during the follicular phase of their menstrual cycle to maintain body weight given that the resting energy expenditure rate is higher during the luteal phase compared to the follicular phase. For an excellent description of a more detailed method for calculating energy requirements in young woman athletes, see the review by Volek et al. (43).

As active women age, their calorie requirements decrease primarily as a result of a progressive loss of muscle mass, commonly referred to as sarcopenia. It has been estimated that roughly 20–30% of lean mass is lost between the third and eighth decade of life (15), which results in a decrease in the **basal metabolic rate (BMR)**. Older, active individuals have an advantage over their sedentary peers, since exercise helps maintain muscle mass and, thus, keeps their BMR higher; however, a decrease in energy requirements is a natural function of aging. For example, the energy requirement for an 80-year-old woman is approximately 400 kilocalories less per day compared to a 20-year-old woman of the same height, weight, and physical activity level (41).

Unfortunately, women are at a greater risk than men for micro- and macro-nutrient deficiencies, since it is more common for women to resist increasing their calorie intake, participate in disordered eating (ten times more prevalent in women than men), eliminate a particular food item from their diet, focus on consuming only a few certain food items, or participate in severe weight loss practices because of fears of gaining weight and changing their appearance. In addition, there are many sports that are "weight dependent" whereby because the athlete's performance is affected by their weight they try to cut their caloric intake to keep their body weight low. Further, for many athletic competitions there are contour-revealing uniforms or the body appearance is important for scoring. These sports include gymnastics, long distance running, ballet, diving, and skating,

to name a few. Women in these sports in particular may be struggling to balance their food intake with concerns about their performance and body image. For these reasons, the female athlete may be deficient in many vitamins and minerals because they just are not eating enough food and/or are not getting enough variety of foods. This ultimately can affect the female athlete's health, performance, and body image. The following is a discussion of nutritional considerations that are specific to the female athlete. For a thorough discussion of nutritional consideration for all athletes, see Chapter 7, Nutrition, in this book.

Minerals that are particularly important for female athletes include iron, calcium, zinc, and magnesium. Iron is important for transporting oxygen to working muscles and for production of metabolic enzymes. The **recommended dietary allowance (RDA)** is 15 mg for teenage women, 18 mg for adult women, and 8 mg for older women, since iron needs decrease with the onset of menopause. Iron intake in women is often inadequate due to low calorie intake, excessive sweat loss, foot-strike **hemolysis** (particularly for endurance runners), and women may lose a significant amount of iron each month with blood loss due to menstruation. Thus, most women are not aware that they have **anemia** (low iron levels) and that their performance may be suffering due to lack of iron. Some 40 to 50% of women have a certain degree of iron depletion even though they may not have overt anemia (26). Although their iron needs are lower, older women can experience iron depletion and anemia, particularly if their energy intake is low. Runners tend to have a greater risk of having anemia and black adolescent female runners have twice the incidence of anemia when compared to white female runners (26). Further, recent reports have indicated that all types of athletes (not just runners) may exhibit a decline in their iron status during training and that iron supplementation may be beneficial for both endurance and team sport female athletes (22).

Calcium is important for building bones and teeth, muscle contraction, nerve impulse conduction, and fluid regulation. Women may find themselves deficient in calcium consumption due to disordered eating, elimination of certain food items from their diet, dieting, low calorie intake, and menstrual dysfunction. The RDA for calcium for women between the ages of 19 and 50 years is 1000 mg. However, women at risk of calcium deficiency for the above-mentioned reasons may require as much as 2000 mg to help prevent stress fractures (16). Calcium requirements increase to 1200 mg per day for women over the age of 50, primarily as a result of the decrease in estrogen that occurs at menopause. It is not uncommon for the calcium status in older women to be low due to a decreased intake of dairy products, as well as a decrease in intestinal absorption, which may lead to lower bone density and osteoporosis. Vitamin D is necessary for calcium absorption, so a vitamin D deficiency can also contribute to osteoporosis. The RDA for vitamin D for women between the ages of 19 and 70 is 600 IU; however, because it is difficult to meet RDA in the diet, vitamin D supplementation is recommended.

Zinc is important for several body processes including wound healing and immunity, tissue growth and repair, and gene expression. Zinc is also a component of several enzymes necessary for carbohydrate, protein, and fat metabolism and is involved in protein synthesis. Therefore, adequate zinc intake is important for athletic performance and recovery from exercise (3). The RDA for zinc is 8 mg per day for women, and supplementation is not usually necessary if athletes are consuming zinc-rich foods in the diet such as beef and other dark meats, fish, eggs, whole grains, legumes, and dairy products. Because it has been suggested that zinc may help prevent upper respiratory infections and relieve cold symptoms, zinc supplementation is practiced by some athletes. Whether or not zinc is effective for preventing colds is still under debate; however, it should be noted that high levels of zinc can interfere with the absorption of iron and copper. In addition, it does not appear that zinc deficiency impairs performance, since the body can compensate by increasing intestinal absorption (18). The RDA for zinc does not increase with age, however, because it is important for wound healing, immunity, and protein synthesis, and it is important that older women receive adequate intakes.

Magnesium is important for bone health, protein synthesis, and blood clotting, and acts as a co-factor for hundreds of enzymatic reactions. Magnesium may also play a role in blood pressure regulation and help prevent muscle cramps. The RDA is 310 mg for women aged between 19 and 30 and 320 mg for women over 30 years old. Magnesium is not normally considered when discussing nutritional considerations for women who consume a balanced diet, but a recent position statement by the American College of Sports Medicine (3) reported that women who participate in "body-conscious sports" (such as gymnastics and dance) may have inadequate intakes, which could impair carbohydrate metabolism, and hormone and cardiovascular function. Athletes who ingest rich sources of magnesium including green leafy vegetables, whole grains, legumes, nuts, and seafood will likely not benefit from supplementation; however, symptoms such as muscle weakness, cramping, and irritability could indicate a magnesium deficiency.

Deficiency in one or more of the B vitamins is common among female athletes. Although research that has examined the impact of B-vitamin deficiency on athletic performance is limited, it is recommended that women consume vitamin B rich foods such as whole grains, green leafy vegetables, fortified cereals, as well as animal and dairy products or consider a B-complex supplement. Vitamin B12 is a special concern to vegetarians and vegan athletes, since it is only found naturally in animal products and their by-products.

Macronutrients

Macronutrients include carbohydrates, protein, fat, and water that are needed by the body in large amounts and are critical for optimal training and performance. The RDA for protein for healthy adults is 0.8 g/kg body weight; however, physically active women need higher intakes. The recommendation for strength athletes is 1.4–2.0 g/kg; endurance athletes 1.2–2.0 g/kg; and team sports 1.2–1.6 g/kg. For athletes interested in losing or gaining weight, the recommended range is 1.6–2.0 grams/kg. Expressed as a percentage of energy intake, the recommended range is 12–20% of total calories. Because muscle mass declines with age, it is recommended that older adults consume protein in the range of 1.0–1.3 g/kg (3).

Carbohydrates are considered the "master fuel" and the amount needed on a daily basis by athletes is dependent upon several factors including body weight, total calorie needs, the metabolic demands of their sport, and their stage of training or competition. The recommended proportion of energy from carbohydrate is 45–65%; however, when expressed relative to body weight, the general recommendation for athletes is 5–10 g/kg body weight (3). These recommended ranges do not change with age, but the amount of carbohydrate needed is typically lower for older athletes due to lower total energy needs. Because of their rich nutrient content, athletes are encouraged to consume carbohydrates in the form of whole grains, fruits, vegetables, and dairy products and limit their intake of foods high in sugar.

Calories from fat should account for at least 20% of an athlete's total energy intake and the recommended range is 20–35%. However, many women avoid fat because of their misconception that consuming fat will result in weight gain. While the consumption of high amounts of saturated fat may not be healthy, fat is energy dense and is an essential source of energy, and is necessary for transporting fat-soluble vitamins, and for synthesizing hormones. Some studies have indicated that women metabolize fat more efficiently and rely less upon glycogen during resistance exercise and moderate intensity aerobic exercise (65–75% of VO_2 max) compared to men. Therefore, it has been suggested that a higher percentage of calories from fat in the diet may be advantageous for women to enhance energy production from intramuscular fat stores and spare glycogen (40).

Women who avoid eating fat and have a low amount of total body fat have an increased risk for menstrual disturbances and may also be at risk for developing the female athlete triad. Fat digestion and absorption is not significantly altered with age; therefore, although fat intake may decrease due to lower total energy needs, the recommended proportion of fat as a percentage of total calories does not change. Foods that contain essential fatty acids (nuts, seeds, vegetable oils, fatty-fish, avocados) should be emphasized, while foods higher in saturated fat should be consumed in moderation.

Water is the most essential of all the nutrients, second only to oxygen for maintaining life, and accounts for approximately 55–65% of total body weight. Body water is lost through the kidneys (urine), skin (sweat), lungs, and feces and it is imperative that daily water intake is equal to water loss to maintain hydration. The goals of hydration during exercise are to maintain electrolyte balance and plasma volume, since a water loss of only 2–3% of body weight can lead to a decrease in muscle function and strength performance (27). The general recommended intake for women is 2.7 liters per day, which represents intake from drinking water, watery foods, and other water-containing beverages. However, hydration needs will vary depending upon body weight, environmental factors, and exercise intensity and duration. The following represents general recommendations for proper hydration:

- Adjust fluid intake for environmental temperature and humidity rates.
- Drink when thirsty – with age, individuals do not perceive thirst as effectively.
- Drink enough so that the urine is slightly yellow.
- Monitor body weight changes pre and post workout to approximately match fluid intake with sweat rate – for most individuals, 7–10 ounces every 10–20 minutes during exercise will help maintain body weight and prevent dehydration. Plain water is typically adequate for training sessions lasting < 1 hour; however, a sports drink containing electrolytes is recommended for longer exercise sessions.

Table 21.2 provides specific recommendations for nutrients that are important or commonly deficient in women.

TRAINING CONSIDERATIONS FOR OLDER ADULTS

Another population that may benefit from strength training, but who also must be considered separately and uniquely when designing training programs, are older adults.

The number of older adults has grown, and will continue to grow over the next few decades. For example:

TABLE 21.2 Recommended intakes for nutrients of concern for women

	Good sources	AI or RDA for women 19–50 years	AI or RDA for women 51–70 years
Iron	Beans, spinach, dried fruits, meat, liver	18 mg/day	8 mg/day
Calcium	Milk, yogurt, cheese, salmon, sardines, broccoli, spinach, kale	1000 mg/day	1200 mg/day
Zinc	Meat, milk, seafood	8 mg/day	8 mg/day
Magnesium	Nuts, seafood, green leafy vegetables, whole-grains	310–320 mg/day	320 mg/day
Vitamin C	Citrus, green leafy vegetables	75 mg/day	75 mg/day
B Vitamins	Lean meats, dairy products, whole grains, eggs	Thiamin 1.1 mg/day Riboflavin 1.1 mg/day B6 – 1.3 mg B12 – 2.4 mg Folate – 400 DFE (dietary folate equivalents)	Thiamin 1.1 mg/day Riboflavin 1.1 mg/day B6 – 1.5 mg B12 – 2.4 mg Folate – 400 DFE
Vitamin D	Milk, egg yolk, salmon, sardines with bones, fish oils, beef liver, fortified cereal	600 IU/day	800–1000 IU/day*
Protein	Lean meats, eggs, milk, yogurt, beans, nuts, soy	0.8 g/kg	0.8 g/kg
Carbohydrates	Fruits, vegetables, brown rice, whole grain bread and cereals, potatoes	130 g	130 g
Fats	Oils, nuts, seeds, avocados, lean meat, low-fat dairy	20–35% of daily intake	20–35% of daily intake
Water	Drinking water and other beverages; watery fruits and vegetables	2.7 L/day	2.7 L/day

RDA = Recommended dietary allowance; AI = Adequate intake.

*Recommendation from Capatina et al. (12).

- Between 2015 and 2050, the proportion of the world's population over 60 years will nearly double from 12% to 22%.
- By 2020, the number of people aged 60 years and older will outnumber children younger than 5 years.

The increase in population for this age-specific segment of the population has led the World Health Organization to issue a caution that "All countries face major challenges to ensure that their health and social systems are ready to make the most of this demographic shift."

Similar to the physical activity participation barrier that women have faced in the past, older adults have on occasion faced a stigma that they are physically limited in their abilities to participate in strength and conditioning activities. However, there is considerable research that indicates that as we age strength and conditioning has many health benefits for both genders. This statement is supported by many notable organizations.

American College of Sports Medicine: "muscle-strengthening activity is particularly important in older adults, given its role in preventing age-related loss in muscle mass, bone, and its beneficial effects on functional limitations."

American Heart Association (AHA): "strengthening muscles provides the ability to perform everyday activities and helps protect the body from injury."

Tufts University and Centers for Disease Control: "For older adults, strength training requires little time and minimal equipment and that it's safe, even for people with health problems."

Strength and power training with age

There are significant changes that occur with age when considering anatomical and physiological variables that may impact training and performance. Table 21.3 provides a list of many of these variables. For example, from an anatomical perspective, on average, older individuals are shorter, have higher percent body fat, and have less bone mass. Physiologically, older adults have higher resting but lower maximal heart rates, lower lung volumes, unique hormone profiles, and decreased brain and cognitive function. As a result of these changes, the functional changes in an older adult may include decreased strength and power, an increase in the likelihood of falling, a decreased ability to thermo-regulate, more bone fractures, slower gait speed, slower reaction times, and reduced exercise tolerance.

Aging is also associated with the onset of chronic diseases including hypertension, arthritis, heart disease, diabetes, and lung disease. In some cases, the decrease in functional capacity may make it hard for older adults to remain independent and perform normal functions associated with daily living, including opening a jar, reaching into a cupboard, cleaning their home, preparing food, bathing, and other types of common activities that occur throughout the day. Given these changes in functional capacity, older individuals may not be encouraged to engage in strength and conditioning activities due to safety concerns and a belief that they may not be capable. However, research has made it clear that not only can older individuals participate in all forms of physical activity, but they must if they want to remain independent, improve their quality of life, prevent disease, combat disease, and participate in their communities.

TABLE 21.3 Anatomical and physiological variables

Physiological and anatomical variables	Change with increasing age	Functional change
Muscle weight and body fat	Increases • More fat weight • Less fat free weight – lose 3/kg muscle mass per decade	Increased obesity which leads to chronic disease
Bones	Decline in bone mass	• Osteoporosis • Increased fractures • Increased falls
Epidermis of skin	• Atrophies with age • Loses tone and elasticity	Sweating and body temperature regulation may be affected

(continued)

TABLE 21.3 *(continued)*

Physiological and anatomical variables	Change with increasing age	Functional change
Joints	Reduced hyaline cartilage	Osteoarthritis and stiffer/painful joints
Muscle	• Higher % slow twitch fibers compared to younger counterparts • Lower number of motor units • Decreased contractility • Sarcopenia • Decrease in pH in muscle cell • Rate of muscle force development decreases • Decreased flexibility	• Reduced muscle strength and power
Lung volume	• Decreased vital capacity • Slower expiratory rate volumes • Chest deformities • Narrowing of small airways • Decreased surface area of lung • Loss of lung elasticity • Lower residual volume	• Increased COPD (shortness of breath, excess mucous, poor exercise tolerance) • Decreased exercise capacity • Reduced oxygen delivery
Cardiovascular	• Slower myocardium conductivity • Increased thickness of ventricular wall • Chamber volume changes	• Maximum heart rate decreases • Cardiac output decreases • Blood pressure increases • Reduced blood flow to muscles and organs • Longer heart rate recovery
Hormones	• Growth hormone decreases • Increased insulin levels • Reduced testosterone and estrogen • Decreased sensitivity of beta receptors • Decreased insulin response at the cellular level	• Decreased muscle mass • Decreased regulation of homeostasis • Increased levels of blood glucose
Thermoregulation	• Decreased sweating rate • Decreased skin blood flow	• More instances of thermal distress
Brain, nerve, and cognitive function	• Brain tissue loss • Increased demyelinization • Increased postural hypotension • Slower reflexes • Poor depth perception • Loss of peripheral vision • Decreased ability to detect spatial information	• Reduced coordination • Decreased reaction time • Increased falls and loss of balance

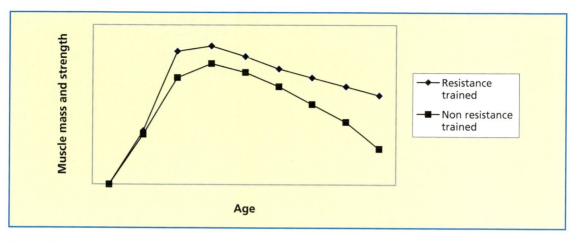

Figure 21.1 A comparison of resistance trained and nonresistance trained individuals with age. Resistance training may prevent sarcopenia as well as prevent the decline in strength over the lifespan.

A notable study by Fiatarone et al. (19) indicated that in ten previously sedentary subjects, 86–96 years of age and presenting with diseases associated with old age (coronary artery disease, hypertension, osteoporosis, arthritis), eight weeks of resistance training three times per week of just the knee extensors increased strength by 174% and improved gait speed by 48%. Two subjects eliminated the use of their canes, and one subject who could not rise from a chair was able to do so by the end of the study, all from training only one muscle group. To prevent the debilitating effects of sarcopenia (age-related loss of muscle), evidence is emerging indicating that resistance training and conditioning can prevent the decline in strength over the lifespan (Figure 21.1).

In addition, physical activity, including strength and conditioning activities, can also reduce the signs and symptoms of many diseases and chronic conditions in the following ways:

Arthritis – Reduces pain and stiffness and increases strength and flexibility.

Diabetes – Improves glycemic control.

Osteoporosis – Builds bone density and reduces risk for falls.

Heart disease – Reduces cardiovascular risk by improving overall fitness.

Obesity – Increases metabolism, which helps burn more calories and helps with long-term weight control.

Back pain – Strengthens back and abdominal muscles to reduce pain.

Better sleep – sleep more deeply and awaken less often.

Mental state – reduce depression and boost self-confidence and self-esteem, along with improved cognition and delaying or slowing the progression of dementia.

Strength – Increased strength of bones, muscles, and connective tissues (tendons and ligaments).

Injury – Lower risk of injury, bone fractures, and falls.

Training considerations for anatomical and physiological age differences

Coaches, trainers, and fitness professionals can help older adults realize real fitness gains, improve their quality of life, and increase their functional capacity with appropriate training and prescription principles. This holds true for even the frailest individuals who have lost their ability to live independently. In general, an older adult will respond similarly to their younger counterpart when examining strength, hypertrophic, and metabolic responses to training. However, an older adult may have specific training needs, and their programs should be based upon their objectives, baseline characteristics, and individual health profile. Because of the anatomical and physiological changes that occur with aging, as outlined in Table 21.3, variations in training and physical activity levels may need to be considered:

- Given the potential for many chronic diseases, aerobic, muscle-strengthening, and flexibility activities need to be evaluated individually with types and amounts prescribed that meet preventive, therapeutic, and health recommendations.
- Take a gradual and stepwise approach when prescribing activity to minimize the risk for injury or some other type of negative health event.
- Because bone mass decreases with age, strength training and weight bearing exercises may be particularly important to incorporate into an older adult's strength and conditioning routine so that osteoporosis may be prevented or delayed.
- Exercises that target balance and core stability are of particular importance to this age group given the brain and muscle changes that occur with age. Any activities that maintain or increase flexibility using sustained stretches are good for not only increasing functionality but for improving joint stiffness.
- For those with balance and joint difficulties, aquatic resistance training has distinct advantages over traditional types of resistance training in the weight room and is an excellent alternative environment for older adults.
- For resistance training, use Theraband, weight machines, or free weights depending upon the goals and capabilities of the individual.
- An exercise program for someone with arthritis will differ considerably from a healthy individual (14). Given the fact that joints may be eroding and can be further

damaged with activity, the following should be considered in exercise programming:

- o It may be difficult to grasp dumbbells or bars.
- o Individuals with arthritis tend to be more deconditioned and less used to vigorous types of activity when compared to their healthy counterparts.
- o Using proper body mechanics is particularly important for the person with arthritis.
- o Water activities may be preferred by an arthritic client, particularly with warmer water. These activities could include water aerobics, underwater treadmill walking, and water resistance activities for improving strength.
- o Yoga or Tai Chi may be a good alternative type of activity.
- o The ability to perform through a full range of motions may be an issue for someone with arthritis.
- o Arthritic individuals may be more likely to exhibit symptoms of depression and have poor sleep quality.
- o There may be more fear of new activities in an arthritic client.
- o If an activity causes joint pain during or after exercise, it should not be undertaken.

- The chronic health conditions of older adults increase the risk of injuries related to physical activity. However, "there is insufficient research on effective strategies to prevent injuries" (36) in older adults. Many risk management practices are based upon decreasing liability, expert opinion, and long-term standard practices. However, it is noted that most popular and accepted risk management practices can be effective as evidenced by the rarity of serious injury in most studies using older adults. Accepted risk management practices for an older adult include:

- o Use moderate activity versus high intensity activity.
- o Take a more gradual stepwise approach when progressing in an exercise program.
- o Good supervision is important to not only prevent injury but also improve the

confidence of the older adult as they perform physical activity.
- ○ Avoid reaching absolute fatigue during an acute workout session.

Specific exercise prescription recommendations for older adults

Training programs for older adults should include resistance training, flexibility, and cardiorespiratory endurance (20). It should be noted, however, that exercise prescription in older adults can vary considerably. This is not surprising given the wide range of fitness levels within this population. Thus, specific recommendations for varying levels of fitness are provided below.

Resistance exercise

- Low level – at least one set of 1–15 reps at moderate intensity of 8–10 exercises using all major muscle groups, at least two days per week.
- Moderate level – 2–4 sets of 8–15 reps at 60–80% of 1RM, two to three days per week.
- High level – many studies have shown that the overload principle with progressive adjustments in load are effective in older adults.

Balance training

Depending upon the capabilities and confidence of the individual, the following describes a progression program for balance training in older adults:

- Sitting and standing exercises with external support.
- Sitting exercises without external support.
- Standing exercises including double leg stance and no external support.
- Standing exercises including single leg stance, gait, and no external support.
- Perturbation exercises, reactive and proactive.

Cardiorespiratory endurance

- Low level – Multiple bouts of activity lasting 10 minutes or more in duration (or whatever the individual is capable of doing).

- Moderate level – moderate intensity activity 30 minutes, 5 days per week or 20 minutes of vigorous intensity activity 3 days per week or a combination of both.
- High level – Moderate intensity activity for up to 60 minutes per day in bouts of at least 10 minutes to total 150–300 minutes per week or more vigorous intensity activity to total 75–100 minutes per week.

> It is important for older individuals to participate in all forms of physical activity if they want to remain independent, improve their quality of life, prevent disease, combat disease, and participate in their communities.

Exercise adherence in older adults

Given the range of health benefits that older adults experience with increased physical activity, it is important to consider those factors that affect their ability to adhere to an exercise program. A recent review (36) focused on what elements of an older person's situation increase adherence and pointed out some interesting factors. For example, there is increased adherence for older adults who live alone, come from a higher socioeconomic status, have attained a higher educational degree, report a better initial health status, have recently been diagnosed with a heart condition, are not showing signs of depression or loneliness, and are not at high risk for falling. Some strategies to increase adherence for older adults include:

- Offering social support.
- Offering a supervised program.
- Keeping instruction simple and less demanding.
- Providing reminders.
- Using a peer-mentoring model.
- Planning appropriate activities.
- Stressing the importance and value of participation (optimal physical function, wellness, quality of life, independence).
- Paying attention to signs of depression and psychological well-being.

Understanding what factors influence adherence in older adults is important for exercise professionals so that their clients can obtain optimal health benefits for any type of physical activity program or prescription.

Physical activity and cognition in older adults

Physical activity has been shown to provide beneficial effects on the mental state and brain function of older adults. Studies have reported reduced depression and boosts in self-confidence and self-esteem, delaying or slowing the progression of dementia, improved ability to cope with stress, and help in the management of Alzheimer's (1). Of particular interest given the purpose of this chapter are recent reports which suggest that resistance training can improve both chronic and acute cognition. Cognition is broadly defined as factors that affect memory, reasoning, comparison, perception, spatial awareness, comprehension, and learning. Long-term strength training programs in older adults have been shown to improve cognitive performance tests, spatial awareness, and reaction time. Acute resistance training has been shown to improve cognitive performance by "affecting anticipation, motor planning, and orienting" possibly due to increased heart rate and blood flow to the brain (1). Altug (1) summarized the potential mechanisms for increased cognition with resistance exercises as follows:

- Increased blood flow with the concomitant improvement in transportation of nutrients and oxygen to the brain.
- Reduced blood viscosity and better blood flow to the brain.
- Increases in IGF-1 serum concentrations to promote neural growth, survival, and differentiation.
- Increased activity of antioxidant enzymes and therefore reduced oxidative damage in the brain.
- Anatomical changes in the brain (i.e., reduced beta-amyloid [Alzheimer's-related protein] load).
- Greater physiological arousal with increased heart rate.
- Increased neurotransmitters in the brain.

Age related changes in muscle metabolism and strength performance in males and females

The natural decline in sex hormones that occurs with aging leads to changes in skeletal muscle structure, function, and metabolism. In men, testosterone decreases approximately 2–3% every year after age 30 and, for women, estrogen levels decrease during menopause (21). With age, the skeletal muscle atrophies and is displaced by adipose and fibrous tissue, particularly in type II muscle fibers. In addition, glucose, fat, and protein metabolism are reduced in skeletal muscle, which also contributes to muscle deterioration. Other changes in muscle quality including a reduced capillary-to-myofiber ratio, decreased mitochondrial density, and an increase in pro-inflammatory cytokines resulting in chronic low-grade inflammation also contribute to a deterioration in muscle mass. This involuntary, age-related loss of muscle tissue is referred to as sarcopenia and is highly correlated with decreases in muscular strength, as well as an increased risk of frailty and disability. Interestingly, the rate of change in muscle quality and atrophy is different between men and women. For example, although men typically have a greater percentage of muscle mass compared to women, they lose muscle at a faster rate than women and also experience greater losses in strength. Further, in men, body mass index (BMI), mean strength and power, and testosterone concentrations are strong predictors of appendicular muscle mass; however, in women, only BMI predicts muscle mass and suggests that there are different mechanisms driving sarcopenia in men and women (21).

The decrease in muscle mass that occurs with aging, as well as physical inactivity, results in decreases in maximal isometric, concentric, and eccentric force, as well as the rate of force development and power (24). A study by Petrella et al. (35) that examined age-related differences in 1RM strength of the knee extensors reported that older men and women (60–75 years) had significantly lower strength (men 41%; women 29%) compared to young adults (20–35 years) and that strength declines were more rapid in men versus women. When comparing strength values in an older cohort, Lamoureux et al. (28) reported significant differences between "old" (mean age 63) and "older" (mean age 76) healthy adults for 1RM strength of the leg extensors (46%), hip flexors (42%), hip adductors (56%) and abductors (59%), and plantar flexors (65%). Therefore, the greatest losses in strength occur in adults > 75 years. Other cross-sectional studies using subjects between the ages of 65–89 report that maximal strength declines at an annual rate of approximately 1.5% and that power declines by 3.5%, and that after the age of 90, muscle power is markedly reduced (24).

In addition to age-related loss in muscle mass, women also experience decreases in bone mineral density (BMD) and, consequently, have an increased risk of osteoporosis as a result of the decline in estrogen following menopause. In fact, it has been estimated that BMD declines approximately 0.5% per year starting around age 40 (11), and that they may lose up to 5% of bone mass per year in the first few years of menopause (23). Resistance training is a powerful stimulus for bone formation and maintenance, and also improves muscular strength in older adults. A systematic review by Gomez-Cabello et al. (23) suggests that resistance training is most effective for increasing strength and BMD in older adults using high-loading intensities (75–80% 1RM) at 2–3 sets of 8–12 repetitions, 3 times per week for at least 4 to 6 months (23,46). Multi-component programs that incorporate strength, aerobic, high impact, and/or weight bearing exercises have also been shown to improve strength and BMD, particularly in post-menopausal women (23). Examples of specific exercises shown to be most effective include: squats, leg press, hip adduction/abduction, knee extension, hamstring curls, latissimus pull down, seated row, military press, bench press, bicep curls, regular and reverse wrist curls, power cleans, and jumping and stair climbing with weighted vests (46). Whole body vibration training, which uses high-frequency mechanical stimuli applied by a vibrating platform, is a relatively new exercise intervention that has been investigated for its potential to stimulate bone formation and strength in older women (44). The results of studies are equivocal with regard to its effects on strength and muscle mass, but it may result in modest increases in BMD at the hip and femur (42).

SUMMARY

Although men and women have similar responses to training, there may be some modifications in training regimens that can be made, such as focusing upon upper-body strength or altering lifting technique, to optimize health, fitness, and athletic performance. There are specific differences that must be considered when working with an older population. Changes in cardiovascular health, bone changes, impaired cognition, and an ever-changing health status are just a few variables that are altered as we age that the strength and conditioning professional must deliberately factor into an exercise program.

There are specific differences that may need to be addressed when designing and implementing a strength and conditioning regimen for women. Many women are participating in strength training programs, but there still remains a social stigma that must be overcome so that she feels comfortable and accepted in a weight room. Although a woman's menstrual cycle does not, for the most part, affect her performance, each woman should be treated as an individual and adjustments to the training and competition schedule may be warranted. When disturbances in the menstrual cycle are observed, it may be prudent to screen a woman for the female athlete triad and respond appropriately to treat or prevent this serious condition. Part of that treatment may involve nutritional and psychological counseling and involvement of many supporting individuals.

Aging leads to changes in skeletal muscle mass, structure, and metabolism, which results in declines in strength and power, functional disability, and reduced quality of life. Older adults who participate in regular physical exercise have been shown to preserve a greater amount of their strength, power, and BMD compared to their low-active peers (30). Resistance training and other types of weight-bearing exercises (stair climbing, jumping) are superior to lower intensity exercises, such as walking, for improving muscle strength and BMD. Therefore, it is recommended that healthy, older adults perform heavy resistance training that uses the major muscle groups, as well as other types of weight-bearing exercise at least two to three times per week to preserve bone mass and muscle mass and strength.

Q&A FROM THE FIELD

There are many forms of calcium supplements on the market. If I determine that my diet is calcium deficient and therefore should take a supplement, which formulation is best?

There are many forms such as calcium citrate, calcium carbonate, calcium lactate, calcium gluconate, oyster shells, and bone meal. Calcium citrate is the best absorbed form of calcium although calcium carbonate also absorbs very well in a more acidic environment. Examine labels and look for the elemental calcium content (expressed in mg), not the total content. Some pills may have less elemental calcium, which would require you to take more pills to meet the daily requirement. On the label. you may also see the United States Pharmacopeia (USP) or Consumer Lab (CL) abbreviation, which would indicate that the supplement has voluntarily met the industry standards for quality and purity. Finally, try to take your supplement along with a meal as this increases gastric acidity and slows transit time which promotes calcium absorption.

MAXING OUT

You are working with a group of female long distance runners who want a more specific recommendation with regard to how much fluid they should consume in order to remain hydrated during training and competition. The following protocol may be used to calculate the amount of fluid needed (13):

1 Make sure you are properly hydrated before the workout – your urine should be pale yellow.
2 Do a warm-up run until you begin to sweat, then stop. Urinate if necessary.
3 Weigh yourself naked with a floor scale (accurate to 0.1 kg).
4 Run for one hour at an intensity similar to your targeted race or training run.
5 Drink a measured amount of a beverage during the run, if you are thirsty. It is important that you measure exactly how much fluid you consume during the run.
6 Do not urinate until post-body weight is recorded.
7 Weigh yourself naked again on the same scale you used in step 3.
8 You may now urinate and drink fluids as needed.

CASE EXAMPLE

Background

A personal training client has informed you that she is pregnant. Her exercise routine included biking, lifting weights, body weight exercises, and step aerobics. What are some adaptations that you should incorporate into her routine?

Recommendations/considerations

Some simple adaptations can be made. Beginning in the second trimester, you should avoid lifting weights while standing still to resist pooling of blood in the legs. Thus, instruct her to sit down when performing lifts whenever possible. Machine leg curls and leg extensions are good substitutes for lunges and squats to avoid falls with the shift in the center of gravity. Some doctors say step aerobics workouts are acceptable if you can lower the height of your step as pregnancy progresses, but caution should be taken as the risk of falls increases. Exercise during cooler parts of the day. Choose stationary biking over land biking. Consider incorporating swimming into her routine. It is a great alternative for staying active. She may want to transition from weight-bearing activities to non-weight bearing activities (stationary biking, swimming, yoga, weights in an upright or seated position, walking) as the pregnancy progresses.

REFERENCES

1. Altug Z. Resistance exercise to improve cognitive function. *Strength Cond* 2014; 36(6):46–50.
2. American Association of University Professors. Position Paper. *Title IX: Gender Equity in College Sports*, 2003.
3. American College of Sports Medicine, Academy of Nutrition and Dietetic, and Dietitians of Canada Joint Position Statement. *Nutrition and Athletic Performance. Med Sci Sports Exerc* 2016;48(3):548–568.
4. American College of Sports Medicine. Position Statement. *The female athlete triad. Med Sci Sports Exerc* 2007; 39(10):1867–1882.
5. Bambaeichi E, Reilly T, Cable NT, et al. The isolated and combined effects of menstrual cycle phase and time-of-day on muscle strength of eumenorrheic females. *Chronobiol Intl* 2004; 21:645–660.
6. Beals KA. *Disordered Eating Among Athletes: A Comprehensive Guide for Health Professionals*. Champaign, IL: Human Kinetics, 2004.
7. Bennell K, White S, Crossley K. The oral contraceptive pill: a revolution for sportswomen? *Br J Sports Med* 1999; 33:231–238.
8. Bonci CM, Bonci LJ, Granger LR, et al. National Athletic Trainers' Association Position Statement. Preventing, detecting, and managing disordered eating in athletes. *Journal of Athletic Training* 2008; 43:80–108.
9. Brunet M. *Unique Considerations of the Female Athlete*. Florence, KY: Delmar Cengage, 2010.
10. Burger ME, Burger TA. Neuromuscular and hormonal adaptations to resistance training: implications for strength development in female athletes. *Strength Cond* 2002; 24:51–59.
11. Calatayud J, S Borreani, D Moya, JC Colado, and NT Triplett. Exercise to improve bone mineral density. *Strength Cond* 2013, 35(5):70–74.
12. Capatina C, Carsote M, Poiana C, Berteanu M. Vitamin D deficiency and musculoskeletal function in the elderly. *Strength Cond* 2015, 37(1):25–29.
13. Casa DJ. Proper hydration for distance running: identifying individual fluid needs. *Track Coach* 2004; 167:5321–5328.
14. Cheatham SW, Cain M. Rheumatoid arthritis: exercise programming for the strength and conditioning professional. *Strength Cond* 2015; 37(1):30–39.
15. Dalbo VJ, Roberts MD, Lockwood CM, Tucker PS, Kreider RB, Kerksick CM. The effects of age on skeletal muscle and the phosphocreatine energy system: can creatine supplementation help older adults. *Dyn Med* 2009, 8:6 doi:10.1186/1476-5918-8-6.
16. Escalante G. Nutritional considerations for female athletes. *Strength Cond* 2016; 38:57–63.
17. Fiatarone MA, Marks EC, Ryan ND, Meredith CN, Lipsitz LA, Evans WJ. High-intensity strength training in nonagenarians. Effects on skeletal muscle. *JAMA* 1990; 263:3029–3034.
18. Fink HH and Mikesky AE. *Practical Applications in Sports Nutrition*, 5th ed. Burlington, VA: Jones and Bartlett, 2018.
19. Fischer DV. Strategies for improving resistance training adherence in female athletes. *Strength Cond* 2005; 27:62–67.
20. Geithner CA and McKenney DR. Strategies for aging well. *J Strength Cond Res* 2010; 32(5):36–52.
21. Gheller BJF, Riddle ES, Lem MR, Thalacker-Mercer A. (2016). Understanding age-related changes in skeletal muscle metabolism:

differences between females and males. *Ann Rev Nutr*, 2016; 129–156.

22. **Goldstein ER.** Exercise-associated iron deficiency: a review and recommendations for practice. *Strength Cond* 2016; 38(2):24–34.

23. **Gomez-Cabello A, Ara I, Gonzalez-Aguero A, Casajus JA, Vicente-Rodrıguez G.** Effects of training on bone mass in older adults: a systematic review. *Sports Med* 2012; 42:301–325.

24. **Granacher U, Muehlbauer T, Gruber M.** A qualitative review of balance and strength performance in healthy older adults: impact for testing and training. *J Aging Res* 2012: 708905, 2012.

25. **Hazelhurst LT, Claassen N.** Gender differences in the sweat response during spinning exercise. *J Strength Cond Res* 2006; 20:723–724.

26. **Ireland ML, Ott SM.** Special concerns of the female athlete. *Clin Sports Med* 2004; 23:281–298.

27. **Judelson DA, Maresh CM, Anderson JM, Armstrong LE, Casa DJ, Kraemer WF, Volek JS.** Hydration and muscular performance: does fluid balance affect strength, power and high-intensity endurance? *Sports Med* 2007; 37(10):907–921.

28. **Lamoureux EL, Sparrow WA, Murphy A, Newton RU.** Differences in the neuromuscular capacity and lean muscle tissue in old and older community-dwelling adults. *J Gerontol Biol Sci Med Sci A* 2001; 56(6):M381–M385.

29. **Lebrun C.** Effect of the different phases of the menstrual cycle and oral contraceptives on athletic performance. *Sports Med* 1993; 16:400–430.

30. **Lebrun C.** The effect of the phase of the menstrual cycle and the birth control pill on athletic performance. *The Athletic Woman* 1994; 13:419–441.

31. **Marsh SA, Jenkins DG.** Physiological responses to the menstrual cycle. *Sports Med* 2002; 32:601–614.

32. **National Strength and Conditioning Association.** *Position Paper on Strength Training for Female Athletes.* Lincoln, NE NSCA, 1990.

33. **Nelson ME, Rejeski WJ, Blair SN, Duncan PW, Judge JO, King AC, Macera CA, Castanedasceppa C.** Physical activity and public health in older adults: recommendation from the American College of Sports Medicine and the American Heart Association. *Med Sci Sports Exerc* 2007; 39(8):1435–1445.

34. **Nichols AW, Hetzler RK, Villanueva RJ, et al.** Effects of combination oral contraceptives on strength development in women athletes. *J Strength Cond Res* 2008; 22:1625–1632.

35. **Petrella JK, Kim JS, Tuggle SC, Hall SR, Bamman MM.** Age differences in knee extension power, contractile velocity, and fatigability. *J Appl Physiol* 2005; 98(1):211–220.

36. **Picorelli AM, Pereira LS, Pereira DS, Felício D, Sherrington C.** Adherence to exercise programs for older people is influenced by program characteristics and personal factors: a systematic review. *Journal of Physiotherapy* 2014; 60:151–156.

37. **Poiss CC, Sullivan PA, Paup DC, et al.** Perceived importance of weight training to selected NCAA Division III men and women student-athletes. *J Strength Cond Res* 2004; 18:108–114.

38. **Rechichi C, Dawson B, Goodman C.** Athletic performance and the oral contraceptive. *Int J Sports Physiol Perform* 2009; 4:151–162.

39. **Rechichi C, Dawson B.** Effect of oral contraceptive cycle phase on performance in team sports players. *J Sci Med Sport* 2009; 12:190–195.

40. **Stephenson LA, Kolka MA.** Thermoregulation in women. *Exerc Sport Sci Rev* 1993; 21:231–262.

41. **Smolin LA, Grosvenor MB.** *Nutrition: Science and Applications.* Hoboken, NJ: John Wiley, 2008.

42. **Verschueren S, Bogaerts A, Delecluse C, Claessens AL, Haentjens P, Vanderschueren D, Boonen S.** The effects of whole-body vibration training and vitamin d supplementation on muscle strength, muscle mass, and bone density in institutionalized elderly women: a 6-month randomized, control trial. *J of Bone Min Res* 2011; 26(1):42–49.

43. **Volek JS, Forsythe CE, Kraemer WJ.** Nutritional aspects of women strength athletes. *Br J Sports Medicine* 2006; 40:742–748.

44. **Von Stengel S, Kemmler W, Bebenek M, Engelke K, Kalender WA.** Effects of whole-body vibration training on different devices on bone mineral density. *Med Sci Sports Exerc* 2011; 43(6):1071–1079.

45. **Xanne AK, de Jonge J.** Effects of the menstrual cycle on exercise performance. *Sports Med* 2003; 33:833–851.

46. **Zehnacker CH, Bemis-Dougherty A.** Effect of weighted exercises on bone mineral density in post menopausal women. A systematic review. *J Geriatr Phys Ther* 2007; 30:79–88.

Contents

CHAPTER 22

INJURY PREVENTION AND REHABILITATION

Todd S. Ellenbecker, Jake Bleacher, Tad Pieczynski, and Anna Thatcher

OBJECTIVES

After completing this chapter, you will be able to:

- Understand the role and personnel responsible for the comprehensive care of injured athletes.
- Understand the biomechanics of the knee, spine, and shoulder.
- Understand the role of resistive exercise in injury prevention.
- Understand the stages of injury recovery and characteristics of inflammation in the human body.

KEY TERMS

Articular cartilage	PRICE method	Strain
Contusion	SHARP	Tendonitis
Macrotrauma	Sprain	Tendonosis
Microtrauma		

INTRODUCTION

The purpose of this chapter will be to overview the role of strength and conditioning in the prevention of injuries. Included in this chapter will be an overview of the sports medicine professionals responsible for providing care for the athlete, as well as the stages of recovery and healing from a musculoskeletal injury. Basic definitions of musculoskeletal injuries will also be included along with more detailed descriptions of shoulder, knee, and spinal anatomy, and biomechanics, along with common injury patterns, and exercise implications applicable for strength and conditioning professionals working with athletes with a history of musculoskeletal injury, and especially with those athletes hoping to prevent them.

Some of the most basic principles of injury prevention have the most profound influence for strength and conditioning professionals as well as other clinicians in sports medicine. These include adequate pre-activity development of muscular strength, endurance, balance, and proper flexibility, and often most importantly, proper sport biomechanics or technique (1). As will be covered later in this chapter, many injuries in athletes occur from overtraining and overuse (2). Improper levels of muscular strength and endurance are often cited as critical factors in the development of injuries such as rotator cuff **tendonitis** (3), humeral epicondylitis (4), as well as patellofemoral pain and shin splints (5).

Additionally, sports medicine research profiling various populations of athletes has also identified characteristic patterns of muscular development that create muscular imbalances and can lead to injury (6). One example of a muscular imbalance identified with isokinetic testing of the glenohumeral joint of overhead athletes was reported by Ellenbecker (7) whereby significant increases in the strength of the internal rotators were measured on the dominant arm of professional baseball pitchers without concomitant increases in strength of the external rotator musculature creating a muscular imbalance. Similar studies in elite level tennis players (8,9) have identified similar imbalances between the internal and external rotators. Byram et al. (11) has shown how alterations in the muscular balance in the shoulder of professional baseball pitchers (external/internal rotation ratio) increase the risk of shoulder injury. Their study highlights the importance to the strength and conditioning professional, physical therapist and athletic trainer of ensuring that proper exercise prescription is followed to allow for balanced strength development for both injury prevention and performance enhancement. The external/internal rotation ratio is a great example of a very important parameter to measure and track in throwing athletes to decrease injury risk and guide proper exercise prescription and muscle group emphasis in both conditioning and rehabilitation programs (11).

Careful evaluation and application of stretching programs are other important factors in injury prevention. While studies directly linking flexibility training and injury prevention are not clear-cut, the consensus among sports medicine professionals is that muscular inflexibility can inhibit optimal performance, and lead to joint and muscle tendon injury in the repetitive environment athletic individuals train and compete in (1). Despite recent changes in the application of static and dynamic stretching programs, sport scientists still believe specific types of flexibility training to be important in both performance enhancement and injury prevention.

Finally, the use of proper sport technique and biomechanics is a critical factor in the prevention of injury. The link between improper use of the kinetic chain in throwing and racquet sports and arm injury has been outlined by Kibler (11). The use of sport technique that optimizes power generation from the lower extremity and trunk and allows for the transfer of force from the ground reaction forces up through the lower extremities and trunk to the upper extremity is recommended. While in many cases the strength and conditioning professional cannot directly evaluate this facet of the injury prevention program, referral of athletes to qualified individuals such as high level sport specific coaches and sport biomechanists is highly recommended.

PRE-PARTICIPATION PHYSICALS

Although it is beyond the scope of this chapter to completely outline all facets of the pre-participation physical, the basic premise of the physical as well as key components should be discussed. Several complete references on pre-participation physicals can serve as excellent resources when designing or developing a pre-participation physical (11,12). In general, the pre-participation physical is an integral part of the injury prevention process. The actual physical is designed to evaluate the athlete's body using a specific series of evaluation methods or tests that screen or identify key factors that could lead to an injury if the athlete were to participate in that sport without rehabilitation or other preparative measures.

> Pre-participation physicals are an important part of the comprehensive care of the athlete. Using a structured evaluation process, key structural deficits, and strength and flexibility deficiencies can be identified that can decrease the risk of injury or reinjury.

Though some of the basic tests are provided in nearly all physicals (measurement of height, weight, heart rate, blood pressure, etc.), most physicals are made specific to the sport or activity that the athlete or group of athletes is participating in. One example would be the careful evaluation of rotator cuff strength and shoulder flexibility in baseball and tennis players as well as swimmers. This area would not be emphasized as heavily for soccer players or other primarily lower body athletes. Careful development of the actual components of the pre-participation physical with the entire sports medicine team is necessary since many specialists and types of clinicians are needed to ensure that the most thorough evaluation is made. Additionally, the important role follow-up, tracking, and ultimately, re-testing plays cannot be overlooked.

ROLES OF HEALTH CARE PROFESSIONALS INVOLVED IN INJURY PREVENTION AND REHABILITATION

Numerous health care professions are involved in sports injury management. Depending on the sports program (e.g., high school, college, professional team, community recreation), professionals in medicine, chiropractors, psychology, biomechanics, exercise physiology, nutrition, physical therapy, athletic training, and strength and conditioning, may be involved in injury management. The diversity of health professionals involved in injury management allows the athlete to recover not only physically, but also emotionally and socially.

The areas of injury prevention, recognition, and rehabilitation are common interests to professions including: physicians, physical therapists, athletic trainers, and strength and conditioning professionals. These four professions commonly have extensive involvement throughout the rehabilitation process and will be further discussed.

- *Physicians*: The physician is responsible for the health care of an injured athlete, including diagnosing and treating injuries. When an injury occurs, the physician makes the ultimate decision on when it is safe to return to sport activities. The physician guides other members of the team throughout the rehabilitation process.
- *Physical therapists*: According to the American Physical Therapy Association, the scope of practice for a physical therapist includes: providing services to patients who have impairments, functional limitations, disabilities, or changes in physical function and health status resulting from injury, disease, or other causes; interaction and practicing in collaboration with a variety of professionals; addressing risk factors and behavior that may impede optimal functioning; providing prevention and promoting health, wellness, and fitness; consulting, educating, engaging in critical inquiry, and administration; and directing and supervising support personnel (13). Physical therapists practice in a wide variety of settings including: hospitals, outpatient clinics, research centers, fitness centers, and sports training facilities. Physical therapists can receive specialist certifications in seven different areas including both orthopedics and sports through the American Board of Physical Therapy Specialties.
- *Athletic trainers*: Performance domains of the certified athletic trainer as defined by the National Athletic Trainers' Association Board of Certification include: prevention of athletic injuries; recognition, evaluation, and immediate care of injuries; rehabilitation and reconditioning of athletic injuries; health care administration; and professional development and responsibility (2). School districts, colleges and universities, sports medicine clinics, professional teams, and industrial settings may employ athletic trainers. The athletic trainer is often present at sport practices and games, and therefore likely to be the first person to evaluate an injury and provide acute treatment. Their daily presence at sport practices also allows athletic trainers extensive involvement throughout the entire rehabilitation process.
- *Strength and conditioning professionals*: Strength and conditioning professionals have the knowledge of appropriate exercise techniques to work in conjunction with other members of the health care team to develop and supervise reconditioning programs. It is important that strength and conditioning professionals are informed of injuries and any precautions to exercise as they may be the only person involved with the athlete once return to sport has occurred. Strength and conditioning professionals play an important role in the transition from a controlled, supervised rehabilitation program to a lifelong, independent exercise program.

The strength and conditioning professional plays a key role in injury prevention by developing a sports-specific exercise plan that may decrease the risk of injuries common in a specific sport. The strength and conditioning profession, by working closely with the sports medicine team, also plays an important role in the transition from a rehabilitation program to full participation in the sport.

Because sports injury management involves a multidisciplinary team, it is essential to have good communication to allow a safe return to athletic activity as soon as possible. Within each individual sports medicine team, there should be agreement on the specific roles for each member. The roles of sports medicine professionals are increasingly overlapping as practitioners extend from the "traditional" work settings, complete continuing education, and attain specialist certifications. However, each professional brings his or her unique expertise to the sports medicine team that will enhance injury prevention, recognition, and rehabilitation. Despite research evidence, sports medicine (including injury management and return to play criteria) is not an exact science. The sports medicine team must discuss varying philosophies and theories to provide consistent, up to date care. Communication must also occur with the athlete, coach, team members, and family members when appropriate. To allow optimal injury recovery, responsibilities of all professionals involved in injury management include: communication, continuing education, promoting athlete safety, and understanding the mental and physical demands of sport.

Working in the field of sports medicine requires teamwork, optimal knowledge, and understanding of the roles of all of the members of the sports medicine team. This team is required to best serve the athlete.

INJURY CLASSIFICATION

Injuries occur on a regular basis in sporting activities. In successfully treating athletic injuries in a rehabilitation setting, the health professional needs to understand the mechanism and type of injury which has occurred. When classifying an injury, we use various definitions to outline the extent and severity of the injury in order to adopt the appropriate methods of treatment at the appropriate stages of healing.

Overuse injuries are often a result of **microtrauma**, where the involved tissue becomes inflamed and painful over an indeterminate amount of time, secondary to forces which exceed the strength and healing rate of the tendon or involved structure. **Tendonitis** refers to inflammation of the tendon and associated sheath, whereas **tendonosis** involves degeneration of the tendon (14).

An injury which occurs at a single point in time, with an identifiable source, is termed a **macrotrauma**. There are varying degrees of macrotraumatic events, and they can be categorized as intrinsic or extrinsic. Intrinsic injuries are the result of forces (mechanical, environmental, or situational) which supersede the ability of the athlete to respond and avoid injury (1,2,15). A shot-putter who ruptures his pectoralis tendon while attempting to best his opponent's distance is an example of an intrinsic injury. Extrinsic injuries occur when an identifiable source outside of the athlete's control is the primary cause of trauma. A running back tackled directly at his knee by an opponent's helmet causing rupture of the knee ligaments is an example of an extrinsic injury.

There exists a continuum when classifying injury severity. A **strain** occurs when the involved tissue(s) is subject to forces invoking a graded local inflammatory response, without disrupting the structural integrity of the tissue. A baseball pitcher who throws 100 pitches in a game at high velocities experiences local soreness in the shoulder girdle secondary to placing a strain on the contractile tissue around the shoulder. The healing rate with a strain is usually several days to a week, if further immediate stressors are avoided.

A **sprain** occurs when contractile or non-contractile tissue are subject to forces exceeding the inherent strength of the tissue, causing pain, local or diffuse inflammation, and varying degrees of functional and structural tissue loss. Different classification systems for sprains exist. Typically classified with a numerical scale (1,14,16), the lower numbers indicate the least amount of tissue damage, and the high numbers usually indicate a complete rupture or functional loss of the structure. For example, a grade I ankle sprain involves microscopic tearing of the ligament without loss of function, and may take weeks to heal, and a grade III ankle sprain involves a complete tearing of the ligament with complete loss of function and will likely require surgical intervention (16). Treatment of the athlete then varies based on the degree of severity of their injury.

Contusions can occur to muscle, bone, and cartilage, and are typically the result of a collision with an outside force such as an opponent, the ground, or a foreign object. Contusions to muscle tissue can also be classified by severity based on the amount of hemorrhage, pain, ROM limitations, and the extent of tissue involvement. The grading system is similar to ligamentous injuries with grade 1 injuries involving mild pain and limitations, and grade 3 injuries being the most severe, with herniation of the muscle through the fascial envelope along with possible bruising of the underlying bone. Severe contusions may require surgery or evacuation of the hematoma. Care must be taken with moderate to severe muscle contusions to avoid further complications, such as functional loss of the muscle or myositis ossificans, which is a condition involving calcification within the muscle tissue resulting from additional inflammation or trauma (2). **Articular cartilage** is a thin layer of specialized tissue covering joint surfaces in synovial joints such as the knee or hip. The cartilage promotes normal movement between joint surfaces and reduces potentially harmful forces such as shear or compression between the joint surfaces. Articular cartilage receives nutrition through components within the synovial fluid that bathe the joint during normal movement. Injuries to articular cartilage pose a challenge, due to the lack of a direct blood supply, and limited ability to self-repair. When injuries to articular cartilage or synovial joints do occur, the goals should be to promote healing by decreasing joint effusion, maintaining ROM and movement between joint surfaces, while preventing overloading to the joint surfaces (15).

PHASES OF TISSUE HEALING: CLINICAL TREATMENT AND EXERCISE CONSIDERATIONS

After an acute musculoskeletal injury, there are three phases of tissue healing: inflammation, proliferation/repair, and maturation/remodeling. Health professionals need to identify the healing phase to determine appropriate treatment and exercise. Although each phase is defined by certain characteristics, healing occurs along a continuum and phases overlap. Phase durations are given as guidelines only and vary based on factors including type of tissue and injury severity. Clinical judgment must be used to determine appropriate treatment as healing progresses. Signs and symptoms should be continually monitored throughout the healing phases and treatment adjusted as necessary. The physiology, signs and symptoms, treatment, and exercise considerations will be described for each phase.

Inflammation phase

Inflammation is the body's first response to injury and is necessary to begin the healing process. The inflammation phase begins immediately after injury and can last up to approximately six days (17). The purposes of inflammation are to protect the body against foreign material, destroy and remove foreign materials (e.g., bacteria, damaged cells, dead tissue), localize the injury, and ultimately promote tissue healing and regeneration (17,18). Although inflammation is necessary to recognize an injury has occurred and to begin the healing process, it can become undesirable as it is a nonspecific response that can occur in an excessive amount. For example, the same inflammatory response occurs whether there is foreign material present (e.g., infection) or if no foreign material is present (e.g., ankle sprain). Another example involves the inflammatory response of scar tissue formation. This response is useful when damage such as a muscle tear occurs but can be detrimental to the tissue and decrease function in chronic inflammatory conditions. Prompt recognition and treatment of an injury will help control the inflammatory response, optimize the healing environment, and allow earlier return to activity.

Physiology

After tissue damage and cell death from an injury, chemicals are released that cause several vascular and cellular changes. Immediately following trauma, the first cells to arrive at the injured site are platelets (2). Platelets release serotonin, responsible for immediate vasoconstriction at the injured site. Following the brief period of vasoconstriction, histamine is released from mast cells (connective tissue cells). Histamine increases vascular permeability and causes vasodilation, resulting in increased swelling. Bradykinin is another chemical released by injured tissue that increases permeability. Increased vascular permeability increases swelling by allowing fluids and proteins out of the capillaries and into the tissues. An osmotic pressure imbalance is created as blood and plasma proteins enter the interstitial space. Swelling results as more fluid moves into the area to return pressure to normal. Prostaglandins and leukotrienes are two other chemicals causing increased permeability and vasodilation, resulting in swelling and pain. Prostaglandins are produced in nearly all tissues and released in response to damaged cells. Many pain and anti-inflammatory medications work by affecting prostaglandin synthesis.

The cellular response consists of increased leukocytes (white blood cells) in the injured area due to increased permeability. Neutrophils and macrophages are two kinds of leukocytes found at the injury site. They are responsible for phagocytosis and removal of debris. Neutrophils destroy bacteria when present (18).

To control the amount of fluid in the tissue area and localize injury, blood coagulation must occur. This process begins with damaged cells releasing thromboplastin, which causes prothrombin to be converted into thrombin. Next, fibrinogen is converted into a fibrin clot that shuts off blood supply to the injured area. This prevents the spread of infection by blocking off the area, keeps foreign agents at the site with greatest white blood cell activity, forms a clot to stop bleeding, and gives a framework for tissue repair (19).

Signs and symptoms

Signs and symptoms used to identify the physiologic changes of inflammation phase are remembered by using the acronym **SHARP**: **S**welling, **H**eat, **A**ltered function, **R**edness, and **P**ain. Swelling is assessed visually, through palpation, and with anthropometric measurements (measurement taken circumferentially around an extremity). Intensity of the inflammatory response and swelling is usually proportional to the amount of tissue damage; however, amount of swelling is not always an accurate predictor of injury severity. Skin that is warm to the touch is another sign of the inflammation process. Altered function is a consequence of damaged tissue, swelling, heat, and pain. Redness is assessed visually with bilateral comparison. Pain is a subjective measure. Quantitative pain rating scales (e.g., visual analog scale – rating pain on a scale from 0 to 10) can be used to monitor pain levels throughout the rehabilitation process.

Treatment

Goals of clinical treatment and exercise during the inflammation phase include:

- Prevent further injury
- Decrease swelling and pain
- Establish baseline measurements of signs and symptoms (pain level, swelling, ROM, strength, functional ability)
- Maintain overall fitness level

Many of these goals are accomplished by following the **PRICE method** of **P**rotection, **R**est, **I**ce, **C**ompression, and **E**levation.

- *Protection*: Based on injury location and severity, protection of the injured area can be accomplished using a splint, sling, brace, or assistive device such as crutches. Splinting assists in decreasing muscle guarding and breaking the pain-spasm-pain cycle.

- *Rest*: Rest is often applied as "relative rest" or "restricted function". Based on injury severity, clinical judgment is used to determine the balance between protection and safe, early mobilization. Although injured tissue needs to be protected and immobilized, prolonged rest can lead to tissue contractures and loss of range of motion. Even if the injured area needs to be immobilized, appropriate exercise can be performed with uninjured areas to minimize losses in overall fitness level (see Exercise considerations below).

- *Ice/cryotherapy*: The primary goal of cryotherapy is to decrease tissue temperature (18). The decreased temperature subsequently results in other physiological changes to promote healing. Decreased metabolism is one of the main benefits of cryotherapy used for acute injuries. Decreased metabolism minimizes secondary hypoxic injury by decreasing the oxygen need of the cell. Secondary hypoxic injury is tissue death that occurs after the initial injury due to lack of oxygen supply. Tissues near the injured site die because the inflammatory process decreases blood flow. With decreased blood flow, cells that survived the initial injury die because they cannot get enough oxygen or get rid of waste products. Other benefits of cryotherapy are decreased vascular permeability and vasoconstriction. Cryotherapy should be applied as soon as possible after evaluation of an acute injury. However, it is important to do an adequate evaluation before muscle spasm, pain, and stiffness increase. Prompt application of cryotherapy cannot reverse the initial trauma, but decreasing secondary hypoxic injury will decrease the overall amount of injured tissue. Cryotherapy should be applied with a cooling to rewarming ratio of 1:2; initially ice may be applied for approximately 30 minutes every 1½ to 2 hours (18).

- *Compression*: Compression can be applied via an intermittent compression pump or elastic bandage. Compression controls edema formation and decreases swelling by promoting reabsorption of fluid.

- *Elevation*: Elevation decreases capillary hydrostatic pressure, which forces fluid out of the capillary in an uninjured state.

> The strength and conditioning professional should be aware of the PRICE method of treating injuries. Some of these treatment methods may also be utilized during the post-injury transition from rehabilitation to full participation in the sport.

In addition to the treatments already discussed, health care professionals may use a variety of other modalities to promote healing and control the inflammatory process. A common form of electrical stimulation used for control of acute pain is sensory level stimulation. TENS (transcutaneous electrical nerve stimulation) units are devices that provide sensory level stimulation. One disadvantage of this modality is that symptom relief occurs only while the TENS device is being used (20) (Figure 22.1).

Ultrasound is another modality that may be used to promote healing. During the inflammatory phase, pulsed ultrasound should be used for its non-thermal effects including altered membrane permeability to promote tissue healing (17). The use of continuous ultrasound produces heat in the tissues and is contraindicated during the inflammatory phase. Various applications of electrical stimulation and ultrasound may be used to facilitate delivery of a topical drug into the tissues, known as iontophoresis and phonophoresis, respectively. Use of any of the above modalities is decided upon by an appropriately trained health care professional.

Exercise considerations

Based on injury severity, gentle range of motion of exercises may be indicated near the end of the inflammatory phase. Performing early range of motion will decrease the negative effects of immobilization. Each type of tissue responds differently to immobilization and remobilization. Negative effects of immobilization on muscle include: decreased muscle fiber size, decrease in size and number of mitochondria, decrease in muscle tension produced, increase in lactate concentration with exercise, and a decrease in total muscle weight (15). Early controlled passive or active motion may be used postoperatively to retard muscle atrophy and tissue contracture. It also allows for diffusion of synovial fluid to nourish articular

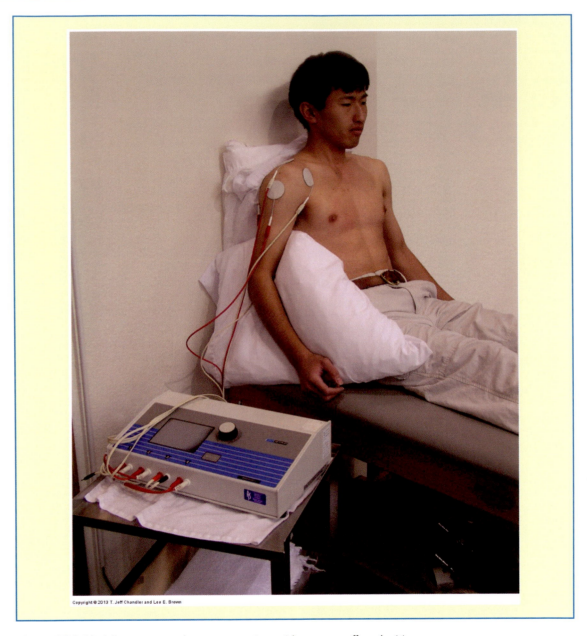

Copyright © 2013 T. Jeff Chandler and Lee E. Brown

Figure 22.1 Modality set-up used to treat a patient with rotator cuff tendonitis.

cartilage, meniscus, and ligaments. In postoperative cases, the physician protocol must be followed when progressing range of motion and strengthening exercises.

Strengthening of the injured tissue is generally not indicated during this phase. However, maintenance of overall fitness including strength, flexibility, and endurance is important for both the physical and psychological return to sport (1). An athlete with a lower extremity injury may use an upper body ergometer to minimize loss of cardiovascular endurance. Aquatic physical therapy may be an alternative if lower extremity weight bearing restrictions are present.

Strength exercises of noninvolved areas may be performed if they do not risk reinjury. A balance between strengthening for overall fitness and rest must be maintained to allow the body to heal and prevent fatigue.

Repair phase

The repair phase begins once inflammatory debris has been removed, approximately 3 to 20 days after injury (17). According to some sources, the repair phase may last up to six weeks (2). Events during the repair phase include scar formation, tissue regeneration, and tissue repair, which increase strength at the injured site.

Physiology

A lack of oxygen at the injured site stimulates neovascularization, the formation of new capillaries. The formation of new capillaries increases blood flow, oxygen, and nutrients at the injured site. Collagen synthesis occurs as fibroblastic cells begin producing collagen fibers. During this phase, the collagen is laid down randomly and is weak in structure.

The formation of scar tissue after injury is a normal response; however, excessive collagen deposition and scar formation can hinder the healing process. As scar tissue matures, it becomes inelastic, firm, and lacks blood flow. This type of tissue forms adhesions, which decrease range of motion and function. Therefore, it is important to promote proper healing and decrease the amount of scar tissue formation.

Signs and symptoms

During the repair phase, the signs and symptoms of the inflammation response subside. The amount of swelling remains constant or begins to subside. Skin temperature and color approaches that of the contralateral side. Although pain decreases overall, palpable tenderness or pain with specific movements may still be present. Skin color is similar to the contralateral extremity; however, ecchymosis may be present. Function slowly improves throughout the repair phase.

Treatment

Goals of treatment during the repair phase include:

- Continue to decrease inflammation
- Maintain ROM by minimizing contracture and adhesion formation
- Regain strength and function

Modalities should be used as needed to increase exercise tolerance and continue to promote healing. In addition to controlling pain, modalities are used to increase circulation prior to exercise and decrease circulation (and swelling) afterward. Thermotherapy, which was contraindicated in the inflammation phase, is safe to use once there is no active swelling. Monitoring the signs and symptoms of the inflammatory response will help determine when swelling is no longer active and begins to decrease. Thermotherapy promotes healing by increasing circulation, decreasing pain, and increasing collagen extensibility. Common forms of thermotherapy include moist hot packs, warm whirlpools, and continuous ultrasound. After exercise, many of the same treatment interventions used during the inflammation phase should be continued. Cryotherapy, electrical stimulation, compression, and elevation will control pain and swelling that may result from exercise.

In addition to modalities, manual therapy techniques including passive range of motion, and joint mobilizations may be used to further decrease pain and increase range of motion. Joint mobilizations will help restore normal joint motion when range of motion is limited due to joint capsule tightness (15).

Exercise considerations

Active-assisted and active range of motion exercises should be initiated if not already included in treatment at the end of the inflammation phase. Range of motion is performed under controlled, supervised conditions, as the collagen is still weak during this phase. As soon as pain and swelling are controlled, strengthening exercises for the injured area can be initiated. Proper exercise progression will aid healing by increasing circulation, increasing oxygen and optimizing collagen realignment.

Range of motion and strengthening exercises promote optimal healing of soft tissue and collagen by causing realignment along lines of stress in a similar manner as bone responds to stress according to Wolff's law (Chapter 4).

Exercise should place progressively increasing amounts of stress on the healing tissues. Davies (22) described an exercise progression continuum to be used during rehabilitation. Although all stages are listed here, the later stages are not appropriate until the repair phase due to increased stress placed on the tissue. The exercise progression is as follows: submaximal multiple angle isometrics, maximal multiple angle isometrics, submaximal short arc exercises, maximal short arc exercises, submaximal full ROM exercises, maximal full ROM exercises.

Multiple angle and short arc exercises are performed to allow exercise throughout pain-free range of motion. In addition to strengthening muscles at the range of motion where the exercise is performed, strengthening also occurs up to 10° (isometric) or 15° (isokinetic) on either side of the range of motion at which the exercise is performed (21). Therefore, performing exercises in a safe, pain-free range of motion will increase strength into the affected areas (Figure 22.2). While isometric exercises are often the least functional and sport specific, they can be included in the early exercise progression following a joint injury as joint motion is not present during isometric exercise. This often minimizes joint stress and allows for early strengthening following an injury or surgery.

Figure 22.2 Cybex isokinetic knee extension exercise using a short arc of range of motion between 90° and 60°.

In addition to strengthening, proprioceptive exercises should be included. The term proprioception describes the sensation of joint movement (kinesthesia) and joint position (joint position sense) (22). Proprioception is decreased after trauma to tissues containing mechanoreceptors, such as muscles, ligaments, and joints. A joint with decreased proprioceptive feedback and joint position sense is at greater risk for reinjury. Examples of injuries where joint proprioception is decreased include ankle sprains and shoulder (glenohumeral joint) dislocations (23). By incorporating proprioceptive exercises into a rehabilitation program, the neuromuscular control and dynamic joint stabilization needed for athletic activities are improved (22). Examples of basic proprioceptive exercises include single leg balance and balance board activities for the lower extremity as well as applications like rhythmic stabilization (also known as perturbation) and weight bearing exercises like planks for the upper extremity (Figure 22.3).

Tissue response to exercise should be constantly monitored. Increased pain and swelling implies too much stress has been placed on the tissue. When signs and symptoms of inflammation reoccur or increase, exercise should be decreased and treatment discussed during the inflammation phase as indicated.

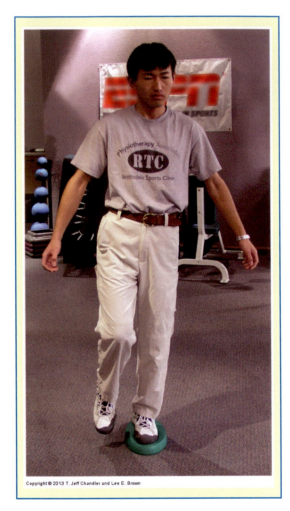

Copyright © 2013 T. Jeff Chandler and Lee E. Brown

Figure 22.3 Unilateral lower extremity proprioception exercise using a Thera-band stability trainer.

Remodeling phase

The last stage in the healing process is the remodeling phase. Even though a person may have returned to prior level of function, the remodeling phase can continue more than a year after the initial injury (19).

Physiology

Near the end of the repair phase, the tensile strength of the collagen increases and the number of fibroblasts diminishes, signaling the start of the maturation phase. According to Davis' law (21), realignment and remodeling of the collagen fibers results from tensile forces. As stress to the collagen is increased, the fibers realign in a position of maximum efficiency, parallel to the lines of tension. Collagen becomes more organized and its strength increases.

Signs and symptoms

Signs and symptoms present since the inflammation phase will continue to decrease and eventually disappear by the end of the remodeling phase. There will be minimal to no swelling, pain with motion, and pain with palpation. Function continues to approach pre-injury levels. Initial measurements including swelling, ROM, and strength should be reevaluated.

Treatment

The primary goal of treatment during the remodeling phase is to regain the prior level of function of the injured tissue. Modalities will be continued as needed, as in the repair phase, to maintain optimal healing environments and assist in regaining full range of motion. However, modality use is decreased as exercise tolerance increases. Manual therapy and joint mobilizations should be continued until full range of motion is achieved. Collagen will continue to realign along the lines of stress applied by range of motion and strengthening activities.

Exercise considerations

Regaining full strength is an emphasis during the remodeling phase. Exercises are progressed as discussed in the repair phase. Signs and symptoms are monitored to prevent placing too much stress on the tissue and risking reinjury. Proprioceptive exercise should also be progressed. As strength and proprioception are increased, functional activities simulating work or sport requirements should be included. Speed of movement, type of muscle contraction, and length of activity are important factors to consider when developing functional activities. Functional and sport specific exercises are incorporated into the Return to activity phase discussed in the next section.

Phases of healing must be kept in mind as health professionals continue to push earlier return to sport. Clinical judgment will determine appropriate exercise and treatment progression through the healing phases to allow optimal return to sport. Since return to competitive sport activities often occurs before the healing phases are complete, continued strengthening and bracing should be incorporated as necessary to prevent further injury. A strength and conditioning professional assists the transition from the controlled, supervised environment of a rehabilitation clinic to a lifelong independent exercise program for injury prevention. It is imperative during this phase that the strength and conditioning specialist work closely with the rehabilitation professional (physical therapist and athletic trainer) to ensure that essential levels of strength, muscular balance, endurance, proprioception, and range of motion have been returned to the injured athlete prior to entering a return to play state. The return to activity phase is a critical phase in the rehabilitation of an injured athlete, and recent consensus documents and studies have been published and summarized to emphasize the important steps rehabilitation professionals must follow to optimize the patient's success during this portion of the rehabilitation (24). The use of objective testing is imperative during this phase of rehabilitation following injury. Examples included instrumented manual muscle testing (10), isokinetic testing, and range of motion measurement (21,25,26) with each measure providing critically important information to allow clinical decision making required for returning an athlete to their sport or activity.

RETURN TO ACTIVITY PHASE: THE ROLE OF THE INTERVAL PROGRAM

Of all the stages in the rehabilitation process, the return to sport or full activity is easily the most anticipated by all persons in the sports medicine team and clearly the most anticipated both physically and mentally by the patient. Despite the popularity of this stage of the recovery process, this phase is probably the least well defined, and is filled with guidelines and ambiguous rules that often are not predicated on research, functional outcomes,

or evidence-based practice themes. Many methods can be used to define or determine whether the athlete is ready for a return to full activity. Most clinicians and sports scientists recommend the inclusion of as much objectively based testing as possible. Use of clinical testing comes in two primary categories. These categories are subjective and objective. Subjective tests are designed to be completed by the patient themselves and typically involve questions geared at obtaining the patient's perceived level of function.

> The return to activity phase is an extremely critical part of the rehabilitation process that should be based on function rather than time or symptoms. The strength and conditioning professional should have a defined role in this phase of the recovery process.

Objective testing is performed in several areas to determine the appropriateness of a return to sport. Determination of a return of range of motion of the injured joint or joints is carefully performed with a goniometer, or additional flexibility testing can be done using standardized tests like the sit and reach maneuver which measures low back and hamstring flexibility. Typically, a return of range of motion equal to the contralateral or uninjured extremity is striven for. Exceptions to matching range of motion or strength to the opposite side must include injury to the opposite side, or presence or either exceptional range of motion or strength on one side from playing a unilateral sport such as tennis or baseball. In most patients, however, using a goal of achieving at least the range of motion or strength levels of the uninjured side is an appropriate goal.

A determination of strength must also be made before the patient can be returned to sport or aggressive activities without injury. Typical strength comparisons again use the opposite side as a baseline and employ either manual muscle testing techniques or more sophisticated equipment like isokinetic or hand-held dynamometers that further objectify strength levels and are capable of reliably testing strength at multiple velocities that more appropriately match the speeds that the muscles and joints function during ADLs or some sport activities. Initiation of return to sport programs such as running and throwing are not recommended when deficits in muscular strength are 20% or more (21). Therefore, while these isolated types of muscle performance tests cannot simulate all functional demands, they provide the clinician with a valid and reliable measure or indicator of muscular performance around an injured joint.

In addition to the objective tests for strength and range of motion, testing specifically designed to assess the function of the limb or the whole individual are recommended. These are typically called functional tests. Examples of functional tests are hop and jump tests and the vertical jump test. One particularly popular test is the one leg hop test. In patients with an injured knee, this test can be performed simply in a clinic using a tape measure and piece of tape to delineate starting position. The patient takes off and lands on the same limb with comparison of one limb to the other performed. Failure to reach the distance generated on the contralateral side indicates often an inability to generate gross lower extremity power in the lower extremity, as well as very often a hesitancy in landing and having the eccentric control necessary to absorb the load following the jump. In addition to the actual distance, quantitative assessment of these patients often provides valuable insight as to the patient's readiness to absorb the impact load on landing, and ability to land on one leg. Often patients will land on both legs to shield the injured extremity from the stress and eccentric overload inherent in landing. Information gleaned during functional testing is imperative for the clinical decision making process that must be undertaken when considering a patient for a full return to activity. The reader is referred to the following sources for more extensive information on functional tests for the upper and lower extremities and trunk (27, 28).

THE INTERVAL SPORT PROGRAM

Several key components are inherent in an interval sport return program. These are warm-up, alternate day performance scheduling, integration with conditioning, progressive stages of intensity, proper biomechanics and evaluation of mechanics, and cool-down or after care. Each of these important components form the currently used interval sport return programs and can easily be adapted into nearly any sport or activity.

Warm-up

Despite the understandable anticipation that a patient has upon returning to a sport following the hiatus required following injury or during rehabilitation, a proper warm-up must precede actual performance in the interval program. Despite recent evidence that the acute effects of stretching may diminish jump and power performance for a period of up to 20 minutes (29,30), the potential injury prevention or reinjury benefits of stretching and warm-up make this an important initial stage in the interval program. Typically, the warm-up consists of a light cardiovascular workout to elevate local tissue temperature and increase blood flow to the peripheral aspects of the limbs (31). This warm-up is then followed by static stretches with isolated positioning of the muscle's origin and insertion such that controlled and static elongation occurs. Hold times of 15 to 30 seconds have been reported to produce plastic deformation of the tissue and enhance the flexibility and range of motion of the hamstrings and other muscles (31).

Alternate-day performance schedule

Interval sport performance programs typically have an alternate day performance schedule. This is designed to allow the musculature and static restraint mechanisms surrounding the injured joint or joints a period of recovery before sport activity is again administered. Additionally, the day off following performance allows the patient and clinician time to determine the tolerance of the body to the previous day's level of performance. Close monitoring of all subjective symptoms and objective signs is an important part of determining when the next stage or intensity or activity is initiated. Therefore, alternate day performance of the interval program is recommended.

Integration with other conditioning

This is perhaps one of the most difficult aspects of returning a patient to their sport. The importance of continuing with strength and range of motion exercises during the interval program is widely recognized. Restoration of final muscular balance and obtaining the last few degrees of flexibility and motion around a formally restricted joint are all aspects that require continued rehabilitative exercise and conditioning during this phase. Though there is limited work published in this area, several clinical suggestions or guidelines are typically followed. Performance of sport specific activity is recommended before or prior to any strength or power training. This is to ensure that the body's musculature, which provides the dynamic stability for the joints, is properly functioning and not fatigued during the functional performance. Additionally, exercises to segments even far away from the injured segment may complicate functional performance.

Progressive stages of intensity

For a program to truly be interval in nature, it must contain progressive stages of gradually increasing intensity. These progressive stages allow patients and clinicians to responsibly progress the stresses applied to the postoperative or post-injury tissue. One example is an interval throwing program. The interval throwing program contains gradually progressive stages or steps of both increasing distance and volume (number of throws). Careful monitoring of the patient through this program finds them increasing distance from as little as 30 to 45 feet initially, to as much as 120 to 150 feet based on the type of position they play in baseball. Within each distance is a progression in the number of throws as well. This allows for independent increases in the intensity of the throwing (longer distance) as

well as an increase in the number of repetitions, which challenges the patient's ability to withstand repeated stresses and builds endurance. For a complete description of an interval throwing program used in shoulder rehabilitation, see Wilk and Arrigo (7). Interval tennis programs follow similar guidelines and can be found in Ellenbecker (3) and Ellenbecker and Wilk (32).

Proper biomechanics and evaluation of mechanics

Another critical part of the interval return process is the emphasis on proper biomechanics. Many times, returning from an injury or surgery leaves the athlete with deficits in muscle balance, range of motion, and proprioception or kinesthetic awareness in the limb or affected joint and hence sets the athlete up for compensatory movement patterns. Often these movement patterns can lead to injury in the segment being rehabilitated or in adjoining segments. A perfect example of this is when someone is returning to tennis play after a knee arthroscopy and they develop tennis elbow because of problems with lower body movement and an increase in the contribution and loading on the arm. Another example would be illustrated in the athlete returning to throwing after a shoulder injury and due to a loss in external rotation range of motion "short-arms" the ball resulting in greater loading on the inside (medial aspect) of the elbow joint (33).

Therefore, careful monitoring of the athlete's mechanics is indicated during the return to activity phase. This can be accomplished by having the health care clinician observing the interval process, as well as having the interval process performed in the presence of a coach or even sports biomechanist. Rehabilitation professionals can utilize readily available two-dimensional filming on cell phones and tablets with commercially available software available at little or no cost to provide visual feedback to facilitate the identification of injury producing mechanics and enhance methods used to improve mechanics. Davis et al. (34) has demonstrated critical time points and variables to focus on in throwing athletes during two-dimensional filming that can be used to perform a throwing analysis. These factors include premature opening of the lead shoulder, improper front foot placement, and elbow and forearm positioning (34).

Aftercare

Equally important as the warm-up, the cool-down or after care after the interval return program is an essential part of this process. In the earlier phases of the interval program, where oftentimes a physical therapist or athletic trainer is supervising the program being executed in the clinical setting, the remainder of a rehabilitation program is typically completed on the same day as the interval sport return program. So, following the throwing or running or whatever the sport activity is, rehabilitation exercises geared at restoring optimal muscle balance and fatigue resistance, joint range of motion, as well as proprioception and balance are commenced. This allows the athlete to continue perfecting the injured areas during the interval return process and ensures that a day of nearly complete recovery can be followed on the day following the interval program and rehabilitative exercise session. After care in this situation is guided by the rehab professional.

During the later stages of the interval program, athletes are typically performing these activities independently off-site. Therefore, strict instruction regarding the amount, intensity, and duration of maintenance exercises must be shared with the athlete as well as the specific instructions for post-session stretching and icing. The use of ice to create vasoconstriction in the affected area is widely accepted in clinical medicine and sports medicine arenas. The amount of time that ice is used after an injury or following a return to full activity varies and has not been formally studied. Current recommendations are typically for application of ice following post-workout stretching. Following an organized and consistent program of after care will ensure that off-site interval program execution mirrors the program initially designed in the clinical setting and is thought to minimize the risk of reinjury and facilitate the return to activity.

OVERVIEW OF KNEE MECHANICS AND EXERCISE APPLICATIONS

Knee anatomy and biomechanics

The knee joint is commonly injured during athletic activities. Knowledge of knee anatomy and biomechanics should be considered when designing exercise programs to prevent and rehabilitate lower extremity injuries. The knee joint is classified as a synovial joint and consists of the tibiofemoral and patellofemoral articulations. Motion at the tibiofemoral joint occurs in flexion, extension, and internal and external rotation. The screw home mechanism occurs at terminal knee extension and involves the tibia externally rotating on a fixed femur in open kinetic chain activity. Movement at the patellofemoral joint consists of three translations: medial/lateral, superior/inferior, and anterior/posterior. The patella also can rotate in three directions: medial/lateral rotation in frontal plane, medial/lateral tilt in transverse plane, and flexion/extension in sagittal plane.

There are four main ligaments providing stability to the knee joint: anterior cruciate ligament, posterior cruciate ligament, medial collateral ligament, and the lateral collateral ligament. Another commonly injured structure in the knee is the meniscus. The knee has a lateral and medial meniscus, with the medial meniscus having a higher incidence of injury. The meniscus functions to absorb shock by dissipating forces over a larger surface area, aiding in joint lubrication, and increasing joint congruency and stability (35).

Common knee injuries and exercise considerations

Traditionally, rehabilitation for knee injuries often focuses on strengthening exercises for the quadriceps and hamstring muscles; however, total leg strengthening of those muscles both proximal and distal to the joint is important, as well as exercises to restore balance and proprioception. Restoring the normative strength ratio between knee flexion and extension strength is an important rehabilitation goal. A 2:3 ratio of knee flexion to extension strength is desirable and supported in the literature (25). Total leg strengthening, especially of the hip and core muscles, is key as proximal muscle weakness is often associated with knee and other distal lower extremity injuries. Proprioceptive and balance exercises are also indicated after a lower extremity injury, as trauma to tissues containing mechanoreceptors will often result in decreased proprioception. These rehabilitation principles are further discussed below in relation to two common knee injuries, patellofemoral pain syndrome and anterior cruciate ligament (ACL) injury.

Patellofemoral pain syndrome

Related knee anatomy and biomechanics

The patella is a sesamoid bone imbedded in the quadriceps tendon that functions to optimize the extensor mechanism by increasing the leverage and thus the force capability of the quadriceps muscles (35). It articulates with the trochlear groove of the femur via a large, primary weight-bearing lateral patellar facet and a much smaller medial patellar facet. This articulation of the patella within the trochlear groove is commonly referred to as patellar tracking and often plays a vital role in patellofemoral pain. The trochlear groove is bordered by the lateral and medial femoral condyles with the lateral condyle typically being much larger, which serves as a bony block to lateral patella translation. Depth of the trochlear groove changes as it is much shallower superiorly and gets deeper as it goes inferiorly. Patellar articulation is also complicated by Q-angle, or normal knee valgus position of the femur against the tibia, which produces a natural tendency for the patella to translate laterally. The quadriceps muscles are the prime movers of the patella and provide dynamic stability. Contraction of these muscles cause the patella to translate superiorly, laterally, and posteriorly. When the quads contract, this produces a compressive force at the patellofemoral joint. Static restraints such as the retinaculum further stabilize the patella and impact patella tracking. As the knee moves through a full range of motion in either a weight-bearing and non-weight-bearing position, the patella is exposed to an ever-changing degree of quadriceps compression forces and changes in patella contact surface area all depending on where it lies in the trochlear groove.

Etiology of injury

Patellofemoral pain syndrome is the most common knee disorder seen in orthopaedic practice (36). The term generally encompasses any type of anterior knee pain located in or around the patella. Specific diagnoses that may be included under this general term include: chondromalacia patella, patellar tendonitis, patellofemoral malalignment, plica syndrome, and Osgood Schlatter disease (37).

Success in treating this syndrome is dependent on determining the cause of the pain, which can often be multifactorial. Only after identifying the cause(s) of patellofemoral pain can appropriate treatment be determined. A classification system of patellofemoral disorders has been developed by Wilk et al. (38) to serve as a foundation for clinical interventions. Categories within this classification system include: patellar compression syndromes, patellar instability, biomechanical dysfunction, direct patellar trauma, soft tissue lesions, overuse syndromes, osteochondritis diseases, and neurologic disorders. Pathological findings that may need to be addressed when treating patellofemoral pain syndrome include: abnormal patellar alignment, patellar hypo- or hypermobility, gluteus and quadriceps weakness, muscle strength/flexibility imbalances, and soft tissue restrictions. Rehabilitation for patellofemoral pain syndrome commonly includes the following: quad strengthening, addressing muscle strength and flexibility imbalances throughout the entire lower extremity, orthotic devices, soft tissue mobilization and stretching of lateral structures (retinaculum and IT band), aerobic conditioning, and taping and bracing (5). Patellofemoral pain often occurs as a secondary injury. Therefore, it is necessary to consider the patellofemoral joint during all knee joint rehabilitation programs to prevent causing additional injuries.

Exercise considerations

Exercises for patellofemoral pain syndrome should be related to the specific pathological findings of the evaluation. The following are general exercise suggestions that apply to developing strength programs to treat and prevent patellofemoral pain syndrome.

- *Perform exercises through pain-free ranges of motion that minimize patellofemoral joint stress.* Relatively safe ranges of motion in which to perform patellofemoral rehabilitation have been recommended. Due to the different effects of quad compressive force and patella contact surface area in the open and closed kinetic chain positions, it has been recommended to perform open kinetic chain exercise between the angles of 90° and 45° of knee flexion and between 50° and 0° of knee flexion for closed kinetic chain activities (15). Wallace et al. (39) found an increase in patellofemoral joint reaction forces as flexion angle increased during squat exercise. It is thus recommended to avoid knee flexion angles greater than 60° in an attempt to reduce patellofemoral stress during closed kinetic chain activities. Avoiding deep knee flexion exercise in the closed kinetic chain as well as terminal knee extension in the open kinetic chain is ideal for minimizing stress and ultimately pain in these patients.
- *Focus on general quad strengthening.* A common analogy regarding the patella is that of "a train that sits on a track". As the primary mover of the patella or "train", the quadriceps also provide dynamic stability through compressive forces that work to maintain congruency on "the track" or trochlear groove. For those who demonstrate weak quadriceps, strengthening exercises have been shown to be very effective in reducing pain, increasing function, and increasing patella contact area in those with patellofemoral pain (40). A systemic review of the literature by Bolgla and Boling (41) further supports the use of quadriceps strengthening in patellofemoral pain patients. The idea that exercise can specifically target the medial quads and especially the vastus medialis oblique (VMO) muscle has been proven to be rather ineffective. The VMO has been shown to have no separate innervation or fascial plane separation between the proximal and distal fibers of the vastus medialis thus making it impossible to isolate. Activation of these muscles is thus an "all or none" response. A systematic

review of EMG studies by Smith et al. (42) concluded that some of the more common exercise modifications or methods that traditionally have been used to preferentially enhance VMO activity over the other quad muscles does not actually do so. Focus should thus be placed on choosing quadriceps exercises in appropriate ranges of motion that minimize patellofemoral stress and can be completed pain free.
- *Focus on proximal hip strengthening.* Back to the "train on a track" analogy, another approach to decreasing patellofemoral pain is to control the "track" underneath the "train". Excessive hip internal rotation and hip adduction are often associated with patellofemoral pain patients, especially in females (43,44,45,46). These motions increase laterally directed forces along the joint and are comparable to pulling the "track out from underneath the train". Strengthening of the hip extensors, hip abductors, and external rotators are of key importance in rehabilitation of patellofemoral patients. Performing closed kinetic chain exercises utilizing more of a hip strategy (butt back, knees behind toes, forward trunk position) allows for greater hip muscle activation than a quad dominant strategy (upright trunk, knees past toes). Promoting a forward trunk position with squatting and running has been shown to increase hip extensor activation while reducing use of quads and decreasing patellofemoral stress (47,48). A thorough evaluation of the hip and lower extremity kinetic chain will allow deficiencies at the hip to be determined and allow for corrective exercise and should be completed for all patellofemoral pain patients.

Anterior cruciate ligament injury

Related knee anatomy/biomechanics

One of the most common injuries to the knee during athletic injuries is rupture of the ACL. The ACL is the primary restraint to anterior translation of the tibia on the femur in the open kinetic chain. In the closed kinetic chain, the ACL functions to prevent posterior displacement of the femur on the tibia. Depending on the direction and amount of force, injury to the medial collateral, lateral collateral, and posterior cruciate ligaments or menisci may also occur with an ACL injury. Depending on the severity of injury and activity level of an individual, operative or nonoperative treatment may be chosen. For active individuals with a torn ACL, surgical reconstruction is usually the treatment of choice.

After reconstructive surgery, the emphasis of rehabilitation progresses from range of motion to strength and proprioception. Regaining full knee extension is important for normal knee biomechanics during gait and to prevent secondary complications. Once strengthening exercises are initiated, it is important to consider force on the ACL during lower extremity strength exercises. The greatest amount of force is placed on the ACL between 0° and 30° of knee flexion in the open kinetic chain. Guidelines for strengthening exercises are discussed below.

Rehabilitation after ACL injury

Goals of ACL reconstruction and rehabilitation include: restoration of knee stability, preservation of knee cartilage, expedient return to daily activities including sport participation, and early recognition of complications (49). Exercise progression will be based on the orthopedic surgeon's protocol. Factors that may influence healing rate and exercise progression are: preoperative condition of the knee, type of graft used, and concomitant injuries. General exercise guidelines after ACL reconstruction are as follows:

- *Regain knee flexion and extension strength.* The hamstring muscles are the dynamic restraint to anterior translation of the tibia on the femur. Increasing the strength and control of the hamstring muscles will increase dynamic stability of the knee joint and decrease ACL strain. The quadriceps must also be strengthened as atrophy occurs due to pain and swelling. Regaining strength of the quadriceps muscles is needed for control of the knee joint. As mentioned earlier, the ratio of knee flexion to extension strengthening should be at least 2:3 (25).
- *Incorporate proprioceptive exercises.* Lower extremity proprioceptive exercises are indicated since decreased proprioception occurs after ACL injury. Mechanoreceptors providing proprioceptive input regarding positional

stability from the knee are impaired after a torn ACL resulting in decreased input from the knee joint to the central nervous system (50). The resulting decreased neuromuscular control and proprioception increase risk of reinjury. There are numerous exercises to improve proprioception including single leg balance activities on surfaces such as foam and balance boards.

- *Include unilateral exercises.* A study by Neitzel et al. (51) found subjects that had undergone ACL reconstruction significantly unloaded the involved extremity when performing a parallel squat 6 to 7 months postoperatively. Not until 12 to 15 months postoperatively did bilateral weight bearing normalize. Therefore, unilateral strength exercises should be performed to achieve maximal strength gains in the involved extremity.
- *Strengthen muscles in both the closed and open kinetic chain.* Strengthening exercises should simulate functional activities. Both regular daily activities such as gait and sport activities require muscles to function in the open and closed kinetic chains. Closed kinetic chain exercises involve co-contraction of the muscles surrounding a joint and are characterized by a linear stress pattern and fixture of the distal segment of the extremity to the ground of supportive surface (26). Closed kinetic chain exercises utilize multiple joints and joint axes. One prime example of a closed kinetic chain exercise is the squat or lunge. Closed kinetic chain exercise in a lower extremity involves co-contraction of the quadriceps and hamstring muscles. Anterior translation of the tibia on the femur is minimized by hamstring contraction, decreasing strain on the ACL. Open kinetic chain exercise is characterized by a rotator stress pattern, and isolated joint and muscle function. The distal aspect is technically allowed to swing freely in space. One example of an open kinetic chain exercise is the knee extension exercise. Open kinetic chain exercises are recommended when trying to isolate quadriceps when strengthening. Due to increased strain on the ACL from approximately 0° to 30° of knee extension in the open kinetic chain, exercises must be performed with appropriate modifications (limit last 30° of knee extension) (Figure 22.4).

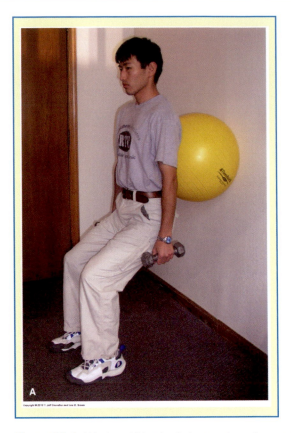

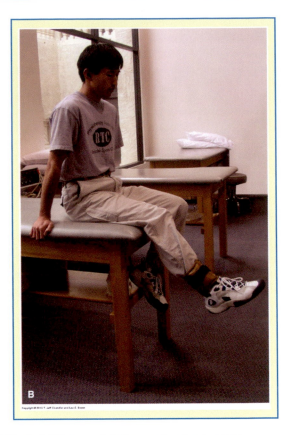

Figure 22.4 (A) closed kinetic chain exercise using a stability ball; (B) open-chain knee extension exercise.

Nonoperative treatment

Nonoperative treatment is usually only chosen by less active individuals. The laxity from a torn ACL increases the risk of future meniscal and **articular cartilage** damage. Cartilage damage will continue to increase knee pain and limit function over time. Similar to the postoperative rehabilitation goals, nonoperative goals include regaining hamstring and quadriceps muscle strength and lower extremity proprioception. The same exercise principles discussed earlier for postoperative strengthening can be applied.

Anatomy and biomechanics of the shoulder

The shoulder or glenohumeral joint is the most mobile joint in the human body. The shoulder complex is comprised of several

joints; however, the discussion here will be primarily focused on the glenohumeral and scapulothoracic joints. Codman (52) identified the delicate balance during upper extremity elevation between the glenohumeral and scapulothoracic joints. He termed this the scapulohumeral rhythm. According to Codman (52), for every 2° of glenohumeral joint motion, 1° of scapulothoracic motion occurs. This relationship points out the important role the scapulothoracic joint plays in shoulder function and how important proper strength and endurance of the muscles that stabilize the scapula are for normal function. The muscles that stabilize the scapula include the serratus anterior, trapezius, rhomboids, and levator scapulae. The important upward rotation of the scapula that the serratus anterior and trapezius perform is required to optimize the length tension relationship of the rotator cuff muscle tendon units as well as move the acromion from the path of the elevating humerus (11).

The stability of the glenohumeral joints "ball and socket" articulation is provided by both static and dynamic elements. The static elements include the glenoid labrum, articular capsule, as well as negative intra-articular pressure (7). The dynamic stabilizers of the glenohumeral joint include the four rotator cuff muscle tendon units and the biceps long head (53).

One of the most important biomechanical principles in shoulder function is the deltoid rotator cuff force couple. This phenomenon known as a force couple explains how the rotator cuff and deltoid muscles work together to provide arm movements (54). The deltoid provides force primarily in a superior direction when contracting unopposed during arm elevation. The rotator cuff must provide both compressive force as well as an inferiorly directed force to prevent impingement of the rotator cuff tendons against the overlying acromion. Failure of the rotator cuff to maintain humeral congruency leads to glenohumeral joint instability, rotator cuff tendon pathology, and labral injury (7). Imbalances in the deltoid rotator cuff force couple, which primarily occur during inappropriate training and development of the deltoid without strengthening of the rotator cuff, exacerbate the superior migration of the humeral head provided by the deltoid and lead to impingement. The exercises listed below can be applied to ensure that a balanced training program for the shoulder and upper extremity is followed and is particularly important for overhead athletes such as baseball players, tennis players, and swimmers.

Common injuries of the shoulder

In the early 1970s, Neer (55) introduced the concept of shoulder impingement. Impingement refers to the mechanical impingement or compression of the rotator cuff tendons between the humeral head and the acromion. The subacromial space is only reported at 6 to 14 mm in normal subjects (56), and with muscular imbalance and/or fatigue, capsular range of motion restriction, and repeated overuse in overhead positions, rotator cuff impingement occurs producing a progression of disability.

This progression, according to Neer (55), starts with edema and hemorrhage initially and, with continued overuse, could result in partial and full thickness tears from the mechanical stresses of compression and impingement. Impingement typically responds to nonoperative rehabilitation, which consists of modalities to decrease inflammation and pain, as well as proper exercises which activate and strengthen the rotator cuff muscles using positions that do not place the rotator cuff in a compressed or impinged position to allow for healing.

More recently, medical professionals and scientists have understood the important role glenohumeral joint instability plays in rotator cuff disease. Impingement of the rotator cuff against the acromion may occur secondary to glenohumeral joint instability from attenuation of the static stabilizers such as capsular laxity, labral pathology, and abnormal work or sport biomechanics (57,58,59). Excessive translation or subluxation of the humeral head relative to the glenoid can occur in athletes and individuals with capsular laxity, often developed from repetitive overuse in the overhead movement patterns used in throwing or serving (57). Additionally, shoulder instability can occur from a traumatic event such as a fall on an outstretched arm or the combined movement of abduction and external rotation in contact sports. This can result in a full dislocation of the humeral head from the glenoid. Careful application of rotator cuff and scapular exercises are again indicated in these patients to improve dynamic stabilization.

Application of resistive exercise for the glenohumeral joint

The anatomical and biomechanical concepts outlined earlier in this chapter provide a framework for the clinician to choose exercise positions and movement patterns to increase both strength and muscular endurance in patients and individuals with shoulder injury or weakness. In addition to the concepts such as the scapular plane position, avoidance of impingement positions, and the important role force couples play in producing controlled glenohumeral joint motion, are electromyographic (EMG) studies that specifically measure individual muscular activity patterns with traditionally utilized exercise patterns.

Blackburn et al. (60) used electromyography to measure muscular activity in the posterior rotator cuff during traditional shoulder exercise using isotonic weights. The authors identified a position that has been referred to as the "Blackburn position", which consists of prone horizontal abduction with 100° of abduction and an externally rotated humeral position. This position was reported to involve high levels of muscular activity in the supraspinatus muscle, infraspinatus, teres minor, and scapular stabilizers (60,61,62). This prone position has become a classic exercise in many rehabilitation programs for both glenohumeral joint impingement and instability (60). Modification of this exercise using only 90° of abduction to decrease potential subacromial contact and compression has been recommended (3,63).

In addition to the Blackburn et al. study (60), Townsend et al. (61) provided the most comprehensive analysis of shoulder muscle activity during traditional exercises used during rehabilitation programs. Examples of exercises used during rotator cuff rehabilitation are pictured in Figure 22.5. These exercises utilize positions outlined in this chapter and have confirmed high levels of muscle activation of the rotator cuff while placing the shoulder in a comfortable "non-impingement position". Exercises to improve strength and muscular endurance are also recommended for the scapular stabilizers. Moseley et al. (64) outlined the muscular activation patterns of the scapular muscles during rehabilitation exercises. Application of seated rows, push-up with a "plus", which involves accentuating scapular protractions, are considered "core scapular" exercises based on this research.

The use of exercises with 90° of abduction are indicated to provide sport specific conditioning of the rotator cuff (3). Figure 22.6 shows how external rotation can be performed with the shoulder elevated 90° in the scapular plane. The scapular plane position is the plane 30° anterior to the coronal or frontal plane of the body and is a position that is characterized by high levels of bony congruity between the humeral head and glenoid as well as neutral tension in the glenohumeral capsule (65). The use of the scapular plane position is highly recommended during rehabilitation.

A

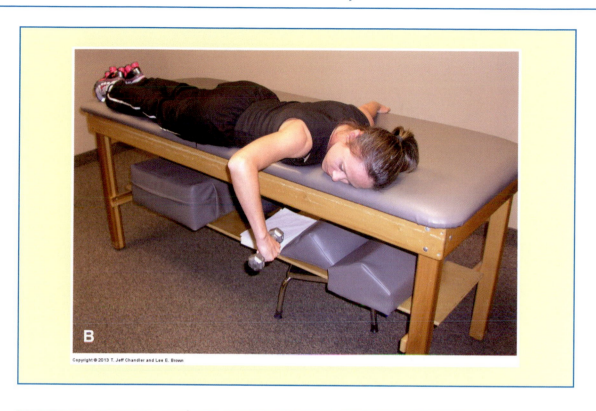

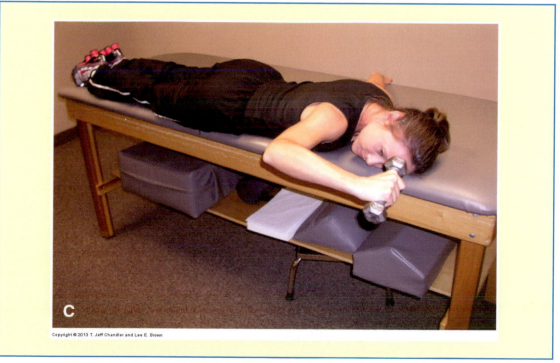

Figure 22.5 *(continued)*

(continued)

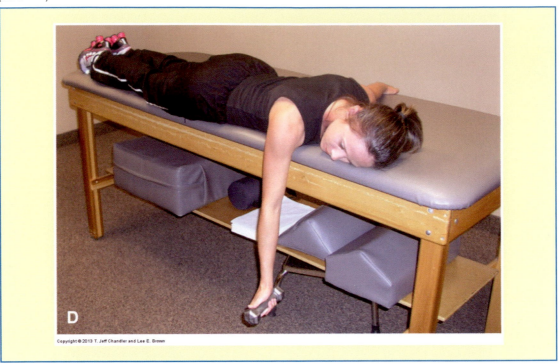

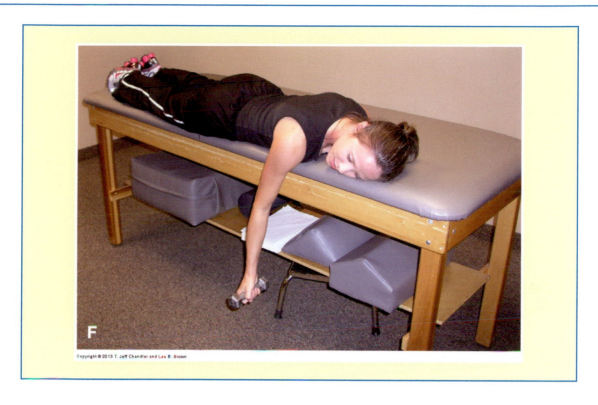

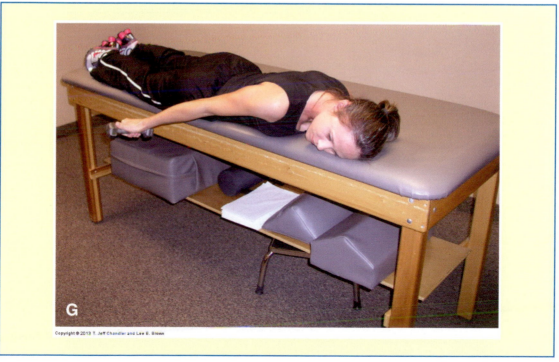

Figure 22.5 *(continued)*

(continued)

Figure 22.5 Rotator cuff exercises used to strengthen the rotator cuff and scapular stabilizers based on EMG research.

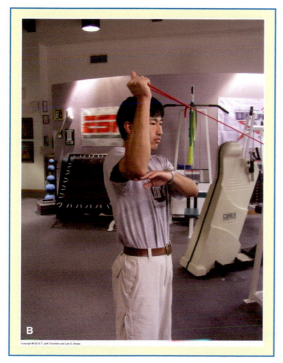

Figure 22.6 External rotation exercise with Theraband using 90° of elevation in the scapular plane (A) start position; (B) end position.

Finally, modification of traditional exercises performed by many athletes and active individuals in the gym is followed and recommended. Limiting shoulder forward and lateral raises to only 90° is highly recommended along with performing lat pull downs in front of the head rather than behind (66). Limiting the range of motion during bench presses and pec deck exercises to positions in front of the scapular plane to decrease stress on the front of the shoulder is also widely recommended (66).

With specific reference to individuals who perform extensive amounts of weight training as one of their primary forms of exercise or in training for their sport, recent research has demonstrated the importance of muscular balance and the consequences of unbalanced weight training. An additional example of adaptation of the human shoulder's deltoid rotator cuff force couple can be demonstrated in a recent study by Kolber et al. (67). They studied 55 subjects who were recreational weightlifters, 24 of which had subacromial impingement. The subjects with subacromial impingement had significantly decreased body weight adjusted external rotation and lower trapezius strength compared to the weightlifters without shoulder pain. Body weight adjusted strength ratios of the abductors, internal rotators, and upper trapezius (prime movers) were comparable between both groups of weightlifters showing comparable and expected neuromuscular adaptation to resistance exercise training. These findings, however, coupled with the significant decrease in external rotation and lower trapezius strength ratios in the injured weightlifters, highlight the importance of muscular balance between the rotator cuff and deltoid musculature and its potential role in shoulder injuries such as subacromial impingement (67). Proper balance between the rotator cuff, scapular musculature, and prime movers (deltoid, pectoralis, upper trapezius, etc.) is of key importance for shoulder injury prevention.

The spine

Anatomy

The spine consists of 33 segments divided into 5 regions (cervical, thoracic, lumbar, sacral, and

coccygeal), with the first 24 or pre-sacral vertebrae having the most clinical relevance. The
S- shape curve of the spine allows increased
shock absorption and overall flexibility and is
due to the cervical and lumbar lordosis combined with the thoracic and sacral kyphosis.
The spine has several key functions from an
anatomical and biomechanical standpoint. It
serves to house and protect the spinal cord and
vital organs. It functions to dissipate weight-
bearing forces of the head and trunk to the
pelvis and allows controlled movement of the
spine against gravity. The spine can be divided
into individual blocks or units called spinal
segments. The spinal segment is considered the
functional (Figure 22.7) unit within the spinal
column, and consists of the disc-vertebral body
interface, the facets or zygapophyseal joints,
and the ligaments, muscles, and vessels which
innervate the segment. Together, the individual
functional units or spinal segments function to
allow for coordinated movement (68).

The size and mass of the spinal segment
increases from the cervical to the lumbar
spine to allow for increased weightbearing on
the lower segments. In addition, regional differences in the structure of the spine exist to
accommodate for the functional demands and
movement patterns that are unique to an area
of the spine. In the cervical spine, for example,
the orientation and shape of the joint surfaces allows for greater freedom of movement
allowing for positioning of the head in space.
In contrast, the thoracic spine has significantly
less total ROM, due to the articulation of the
ribs and the shape of the spinal motion segment, and this is due to the primary role being
protection of vital organs and increasing respiratory efficiency. In the lumbar spine the size
and shape of the disks are larger to allow for
increased weightbearing, and the orientation
of the facet joints are primarily in the sagittal
plane, allowing for greater flexion and extension movements with minimal rotation (68).

In a normal upright standing posture, 84%
of the weightbearing forces are transmitted
through the vertebral body and disc-vertebral
body interface, with the remaining 16%
being borne by the articular facet joints. The
intervertebral disc-interface consists of the cartilaginous vertebral end plates on the superior
and inferior surfaces of the vertebral body, and
the interposed disc. The disc consists of the
nucleus pulposus at the center, comprised of a
mucoid material with a water binding capacity giving it a gelatinous composition. The
nucleus is surrounded by the annulus fibrosis
comprised of concentric layers of collagen and
fibrocartilage designed to resist tensile, tor-
sion, and compressive loads imparted to the
disc (69) (Figure 22.8). The oblique orientation
of the annular fibers reinforces the strength of
the disc, allowing resistance to the directional
forces and movements exerted by the nucleus.
Based on the design of the disc, it is thought
to have characteristics of a hydraulic system,
where the self-contained nucleus cannot be
compressed, and therefore exerts pressure

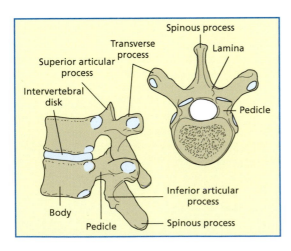

Figure 22.7 Anatomy of the vertebrae.

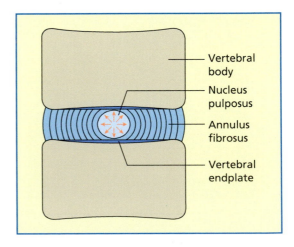

Figure 22.8 Structure of the intervertebral disc.

outwards toward the vertebral end-plates and annular rings (70). Due to the relative avascularity of the disc, most disc nutrition occurs through diffusion via the vertebral end plate during cycles of loading and unloading, allowing for adequate exchange of nutrients and waste products. With age, the composition of the nucleus becomes less distinct from the annular fibers due to changes in the chemical composition in the nucleus.

Biomechanics of the spine

Movement in the spine occurs in a three-dimensional model where the individual segments have 6° of freedom or motion components. On a basic level, movements at the spinal segments have varying degrees of translation and rotation that occur when movement is produced in cardinal movements such as flexion, extension, sidebending, and rotation. The term coupling patterns is used to describe the accompanying movements between the vertebrae as primary movements are produced. The coupling patterns are the result of the geometry of the individual vertebrae, connecting ligaments, and discs. For example, when the spine is flexed, there is accompanying superior and inferior translation or gliding of the individual segments accounting for the coupling movements. Another example of coupling occurs when the cervical spine is sidebent or laterally flexed. The vertebral segments will rotate in the same direction as the sidebending motion (71). Coupling patterns need to occur for normal spinal movement, and the degree and types of patterns vary based on the region of the spine and spinal posture when the movement is produced (71).

Clinical manifestation of coupling patterns becomes relevant when dysfunction occurs either due to degeneration or mechanical locking of the joint. This frequently happens when one attempts to perform a combined movement such as retrieving an object by bending forward and rotating causing mechanical locking of the facet joint. This biomechanical alteration causes pain and restriction with movement.

Muscles of the spine

Humans rely heavily on the muscles of the spinal column for movement, postural control, and stability of the individual segments as we perform activities from a very basic level to highly advanced movements like sports. The role of the various vertebral muscles is based on their size, attachments, and location. The complex interaction of muscle activity to concurrently produce movement while affording stability is the foundation of efficient spinal motion.

The anterior muscles in the abdominal wall consist of the rectus abdominus, external and internal obliques, and transverse abdominus. Collectively, the primary movements produced by these muscles are flexion and rotation of the trunk, with minimal muscle activity during normal erect standing (72). These muscles also act to regulate pelvic position by counterbalancing the pull of the back extensors. The transverse abdominus plays a key role in achieving spinal stabilization by forming a rigid cylinder, increasing intra-abdominal pressure when contracted. The horizontal orientation of the fibers and the attachment into the thoraco-lumbar fascia provide this stabilizing role (Figure 22.9).

The erector spinae muscles are posteriorly situated to the spine, and run the entire length of the spine, and consist of the superficial and deep divisions. Together, the erector spinae muscles act to extend the spine while lifting, and consequently are intermittently active to counteract the gravitational flexion line of pull on the body (72).

The stabilizing role of the deep erector spinae is evident when considering the line of pull of the deep erector spinae and the opposing iliopsoas (69). The contralateral antero-posterior line of pull in these muscles acts as a guy wire check system for stability of the lumbar spine in the sagittal plane. The multifidus is an important segmental stabilizer in the lumbar spine. It is present throughout the entire spine but is thickest in the lumbar region. With the segmental attachment, along with their orientation of pull, the multifidus muscles are thought to act as important stabilizers in the lumbar spine during lifting and rotational movements of the trunk (16).

Back injuries from and functional implications of lifting

Injuries in the spine occur frequently, with an estimated 80% of the general population

Figure 22.9 Role of intra-abdominal pressure in protecting the spine during lifting.

experiencing low back pain at some point in their life (16). The etiology of back pain is not clearly understood, and oftentimes, identifying the source or cause of back pain is difficult. However, in many cases, mechanical back pain is a result of faulty body mechanics, postural habits, and repetitive stresses which may be avoided.

The **neutral spine** is a posture which reduces the stress to the static structures of the spine, and minimizes muscular effort by optimally aligning the segments in their most natural resting position. The neutral spine is achieved through finding the neutral position of the pelvis. This is done by flexing and extending the pelvis to end ranges, appreciating the sense of the extremes, and finding the middle range, where there is the least amount of strain to the spine. Maintaining this neutral spine position provides the optimal position of the spinal curves for muscle length, joint position sense, and equally distributes the forces along the spinal segment(s).

When lifting weights or performing functional lifting, several concepts should be followed to avoid risk of injury. Minimizing the distance of the object to be lifted by keeping it close to the body reduces the joint reaction forces and intradiscal pressure within the spine. By holding a weighted object away from the body, the lever arm is dramatically increased, requiring higher muscle forces to maintain equilibrium, while significantly increasing intradiscal pressure (15) (Figure 22.10). For example, while performing front raises with dumbbells with the elbows extended, the intradiscal pressure is exceedingly high. By simply flexing the elbows and keeping the dumbbells closer to the body, the lever arm is reduced, thereby lessening the forces acting on the spine. The role of obesity and the development of lower back problems are also related to having a larger lever arm acting on the lower back when the abdomen protrudes anteriorly.

Studies have demonstrated the importance of generating large intra-abdominal pressures within the spine through the contraction of the stabilizing muscles of the paraspinals and abdominals when lifting heavy weights, and when performing pushing movements against heavy resistance (5). The amount of weight, as well as the speed at which the lift is performed, correlates with

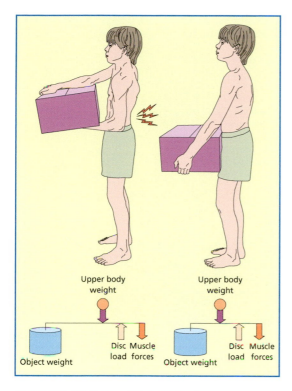

Figure 22.10 Proper lifting mechanics.

the increase in intra-abdominal pressures to support the spine, reinforcing the importance of the role of the stabilizing muscles of the trunk when lifting or pushing (see Figure 22.9). Some of the more common lifts requiring adequate stabilization to reduce the risk of injury are the weighted squat and deadlift. While performing a weighted squat or deadlift, it is important to maintain the spine in a neutral position, avoiding excess lumbar flexion or extension throughout the movement, by increasing intra-abdominal pressure through contraction of the abdominal and paraspinal stabilization muscles. This concept of back stabilization through muscular contraction should be utilized with any type of resistance training where the spine lacks adequate stabilization and is at the forefront of core-stabilization training.

> Core stabilization is an important concept for the strength and conditioning professional in terms of both performance and injury prevention. A number of appropriate methods can be utilized to train the core.

Core stabilization training has reached new levels of popularity within athletic and exercise training circles because it has been shown that this type of training not only reduces the risk of injury through focusing on the important role of the stabilization muscles but enhances muscular control and efficiency. Traditional lifting methods have been supplemented with exercises utilizing core training to improve performance. Supplemental core exercises should be included with traditional lifting exercises during daily workouts to engage these very important trunk muscles. Some of the more common exercises include:

1 Push-ups with feet or hands on a ball (Figure 22.11)
2 Bench press with back on ball, unsupported at the hips (Figure 22.12)
3 Reverse sit-up with feet on ball
4 Trunk rotation in standing or sitting on a ball
5 Opposite arm and leg in quadruped
6 Prone isometric abdominals
7 *Bridging with feet on a ball* (Figure 22.13)
8 Lunges with trunk rotation
9 Thera-band sidestepping
10 Side-lying plank with unilateral row (Figure 22.14)

Maintaining adequate flexibility in the muscles of the low back and lower extremities is also very important due to the influence they have with pelvic alignment and control. Tight hamstrings, paraspinals, or hip flexors can adversely position the pelvis in too much flexion or extension predisposing one to injury or degenerative changes over longer periods. An example of this need for adequate flexibility can be demonstrated in what is termed lumbar-pelvic rhythm, which is a sequential sharing of motion between the paraspinals and hip extensors in the act of bending forward to touch your toes. During the initial bending movement, the pelvis is locked by the hip extensors for approximately the first 60° of motion with movement primarily coming from the lumbar segments. This is followed by approximately 25° of hip motion when the paraspinal muscles become more active to allow for the additional motion to achieve full forward bending. The reverse sequence occurs with return from full flexion, with lumbar extension, followed by pelvic extension. The implications are with inadequate range of motion or muscle

Figure 22.11 Push-up over a stability ball.

Figure 22.12 Bench press exercise performed using a stability ball to increase the muscle activity of the core.

Figure 22.13 Knee to chest exercise using a stability ball.

Figure 22.14 Plank with unilateral row using elastic resistance. (A) start position and (B) end position of the row.

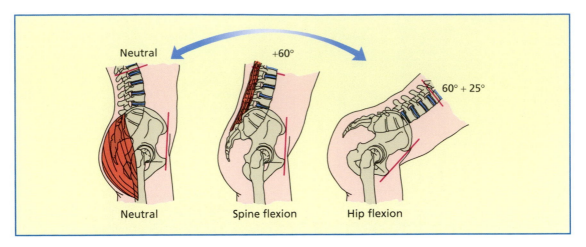

Figure 22.15 Muscle activity in forward bending. Bending forward is a two-part movement involving both the spine and the pelvis. Part 1 involves the first 60° of movement, and part 2 involves an additional 25° of forward trunk flexion.

activation in either area, injury may result from motion compensations due to an abnormal lumbar-pelvic rhythm (Figure 22.15).

SUMMARY

Injury prevention and rehabilitation involve a coordinated effort from various health care professionals. Strength and conditioning professionals must be aware of the stress placed on body tissues during strengthening exercises to minimize injury risk. When pain or injury does occur, activity needs to be modified, and referral to an appropriate health care professional should be made as needed. Communication between sports medicine professionals is vital in transitioning an athlete from a supervised rehabilitation program to a return to sport interval program, and ultimately an independent conditioning program. Conducting pre-participation physicals, identifying muscular strength and endurance deficits, awareness of joint and body mechanics during strengthening exercises, and appropriate activity progression after injury are all ways to minimize injury risk and maximize sport performance.

MAXING OUT

1 A basketball player at a rural high school sustains an ankle sprain. There is no health care professional present at the time of the injury. What actions should be taken?
2 What muscles should be addressed by exercises in a core stabilization program?

CASE EXAMPLE

Designing a return to sport conditioning program for a personal training client

Background

You are a personal trainer at a sport performance training facility. One of your clients is an 18-year-old male, competitive tennis player who has just completed two months of rehabilitation for shoulder impingement. He has been cleared by his doctor to return to play. He presents to you for assistance with a conditioning program to help him prevent future injuries.

He has not been playing tennis during his rehabilitation but has been riding a stationary bike to maintain cardiovascular endurance. His shoulder pain has dissipated, and he is eager to return to the court. You perform an assessment of his musculoskeletal durability to assist with the development of a conditioning program for the client and offer advice on a return to sport program.

Considerations

Your musculoskeletal durability assessment includes testing for the core, lower extremities, and upper extremities. You make note of the client's core and strength deficits as well as his lower extremity flexibility limitations and include exercise appropriate to address these areas. You also take into consideration the client's history of shoulder impingement and ensure that modifications are made to traditional upper extremity exercise to avoid reaggravation of his shoulder. While the client reports maintaining cardiovascular endurance by cycling for the past two months, you feel that a more sport-specific agility program would be ideal for preparing him for a return to the dynamic movement pattern performed on the court.

Implementation

You take into consideration the key components of an interval return to sport program and prescribe the following for this client:

- *Warm-up*: Prior to stepping onto the court, perform five minutes of jumping rope, followed by a stretching program I have designed to target your lower extremities.
- *Alternate day performance scheduling*: Schedule your return to tennis session for every other day. Your days off from tennis will allow you to determine your tolerance to the previous day's level of performance and will allow you a period of recovery between sessions.
- *Integration with conditioning*: Your conditioning program should be performed on your days off from tennis. The conditioning program will include agility training to prepare you for the dynamic movements on the court and further improve your endurance. The strengthening portion of your program will include total body strengthening but will place emphasis on your core and hips, where you demonstrate deficits. Though your shoulder pain has diminished, it will be important to continue rotator cuff strengthening during your return to tennis to ensure that the strength you developed while in rehabilitation is not lost.
- *Progressive stages of intensity*: Your return to tennis should follow a schedule of gradually progressed intensity. You should follow the progression as listed in the return to tennis protocol given to you by your physician or therapist and closely monitor your tolerance to each stage of progression.
- *Proper biomechanics*: Performing your return to tennis program with your coach is essential to ensure that proper mechanics are maintained.
- *Cool-down*: Following your interval tennis program performance, you should again perform the stretching program targeting your lower extremities and commence with ice to your shoulder as you have been doing in rehabilitation.

Results

Because of your advice, your client was compliant with the interval return to tennis program supervised by his coach and maintained an alternate-day schedule that allowed him to closely monitor his response to each stage of progression. He was able to demonstrate steady improvements in core strength, lower extremity flexibility, and agility. Two months following his return to tennis, he was able to return to competitive tennis without pain. He was performing at a higher level than prior to his shoulder injury, likely secondary to his improved agility and increased power with his serves.

REFERENCES

1. Taylor J, Stone R, Mullin MJ, et al. Comprehensive Sports Injury Management: From Examination of Injury to Return to Sport, 2nd ed. Austin, TX: PRO-ED, Inc, 2003.

2. Arnheim DA, Prentice WE. *Principles of Athletic Training*. 9th ed. St Louis MO: McGraw-Hill Companies, 1997.

3. Ellenbecker TS. Rehabilitation of shoulder and elbow injuries in tennis players. *Clin Sports Med* 1995; 14(1):87–109.

4. Nirschl RP, Sobel J. Conservative treatment of tennis elbow. *The Physician and Sports Medicine* 1981; 9:43–54.

5. Fulkerson JP. Diagnosis and treatment of patients with patellofemoral pain. *Am J Sports Med* 2002; 30(3):447–456.

6. Chandler TJ, Kibler WB, Stracener EC, et al. Shoulder strength, power, and endurance in college tennis players. *Am J Sports Med* 1992; 20:455–458.

7. Ellenbecker TS, Mattalino AJ. Concentric isokinetic shoulder internal and external rotation strength in professional baseball pitchers. *J Orthop Sports Phys Ther* 1997; 25(5):323–328.

8. Wilk KE, Arrigo CA. Interval sport programs for the shoulder. In Andrews JR, Wilk KE eds, *The Athlete's Shoulder*. New York: Churchill Livingstone, 1994.

9. Ellenbecker TS. Shoulder internal and external rotation strength and range of motion in highly skilled tennis players. *Isok Exercise Science* 2:1–8, 1992.

10. Ellenbecker TS, Roetert EP. Age specific isokinetic glenohumeral internal and external rotation strength in elite junior tennis players. *J Sci Med Sport* 2003; 6(1):63–70.

11. Byram IR, Bushnell BD, Dugger K, Charron K, Harrell FE, Noonan TJ. Preseason shoulder strength measurements in professional baseball pitchers: Identifying players at risk for injury. *Am J Sports Med* 2010; 38(7):1375–1382

12. Kibler WB. The role of the scapula in athletic shoulder function. *Am J Sports Med* 1998; 26(2):325–337.

13. American College of Sports Medicine. *Position Statement on Pre-participation Physicals*. Indianapolis, IN: ACSM.

14. American Physical Therapy Association. *Guide to Physical Therapist Practice*, 2nd ed. Alexandria, VA: American Physical Therapy Association, 2001.

15. Kraushaar BS, Nirschl RP. Tendonosis of the elbow (tennis elbow): clinical features and findings of histological, immunohistochemical, and electron microscopy studies. *J Bone Joint Surgery* 1999; 81–A(2):259–278.

16. Andrews JR, Harrelson GL, Wilk KE, eds. *Physical Rehabilitation of the Injured Athlete*, 3rd ed. Philadelphia, PA: W.B. Saunders Co, 2004.

17. Richardson JK, Iglarsh A. *Clinical Orthopaedic Physical Therapy*. Philadelphia, PA: W.B. Saunders Co, 1994.

18. Cameron MH, ed. *Physical Agents in Rehabilitation: From Research to Practice*. Philadelphia, PA: W.B. Saunders Company, 1999.

19. Knight KL. *Cryotherapy in Sports Injury Management*. Champaign, IL: Human Kinetics, 1995.

20. Prentice WE. The healing process and the pathophysiology of musculoskeletal injuries. In Prentice WE, *Rehabilitation Techniques in Sports Medicine*, 2nd ed. St Louis, MO: Mosby-Yearbook, 1994.

21. Davis HG. Conservative Surgery, As Exhibited in Remedying Some of the Mechanical Causes That Operate Injuriously Both in Health and Disease. New York: D. Appleton & Company. 443 and 445 Broadway. 1867. https://books.google.com/books?id=5gycXSqzr7oC&printsec=frontcover&dq=inauthor:%22Henry+Gassett+Davis%22&hl=en&sa=X&ved=0ahUKEwiz1vOc-LLaAhVh8IMKHeOnDW4Q6AEILjAB#v=onepage&q&f=false.

22. Robinson AJ, Snyder-Mackler L. *Clinical Electrophysiology: Electrotherapy and Electrophysiologic Testing*, 2nd ed. Philadelphia, PA: Lippincott Williams and Wilkins, 1995.

23. Davies GJ. A Compendium of Isokinetics in Clinical Usage and Rehabilitation Techniques. 4th ed. Onalaska, WI: S and S Publishers, 1992.

24. Lephart SM, Pincivero DM, Giraldo JL, et al. The role of proprioception in the management and rehabilitation of athletic injuries. *Am J Sports Med* 1997; 25:130–137.

25. Smith RL, Brunouli J. Shoulder kinesthesia after anterior glenohumeral joint dislocation. *Phys Ther* 1989; 69(2):106–112.

26. Ardern CL, Glasgow P, Schneiders AG, Witvrouw E, Clarsen B, Cools AM, Gojanovic B, Griffin S, Khan K, Moksnes H, Mutch S, Phillips N, Reurink G, Sadler R, Gravare Silbernagel K, Thorborg K, Wangensteen A, Wilk K, Bizzini M. Consensus statement on return to sport from the First World Congress in Sports Physical Therapy. *Bern Br J Sports Med* 2017 Jul; 51(13):995.

27. Davies GJ, Heidersceit BC, Clark M. Open kinetic chain assessment and rehabilitation. *Athletic Training Sports Health Care Perspective* 1995; 1(4):347–370.

28. Ellenbecker TS, Davies GJ. The application of isokinetics in testing and rehabilitation of the shoulder complex. *J Athl Train* 2000; 35(3):338–350.

29. Reiman MP, Manske RC. *Functional Testing in Human Performance*. Champaign, IL: Human Kinetics 2009.

30. Ellenbecker TS, Davies GJ. *Closed Kinetic Chain Exercise. A Comprehensive Guide to Multiple Joint Exercises*. Champaign, IL: Human Kinetics, 2001.

31. Avela J, Kyrolainen J, Komi P. Altered reflex sensitivity after repeated and prolonged passive muscle stretching. *Am J Phys Med* 1999; 86:1283–1291.

32. Kokkonen J, Nelson A, Cornwell A. Acute muscle stretching inhibits maximal strength performance. *Res Q Exerc Sport* 1998; 69(4):411–415.

33. Zachazewski JE, Reischl S. Flexibility for the runner: specific program considerations. *Topics in Acute Care and Trauma Rehabilitation* 1986; 1:9–27.

34. Ellenbecker TS, Wilk KE. *Sport Therapy for the Shoulder*. www.humankinetics.com/products/all-products/Sport-Therapy-for-the-Shoulder-With-Online-Video. 2017.

35. Marshall RN, Elliott BC. Long-axis rotation: the missing link in proximal to distal sequencing. *J Sports Science* 2000; 18:247–254.

36. Davis JT, Limpisvasti O, Fluhme D, Mohr KJ, Yocum LA, Elattrache NS, Jobe FW. The effect of pitching biomechanics on the upper extremity in youth and adolescent baseball pitchers. *Am J Sports Med* 2009; 37(8):1484–1491.

37. Magee DJ. *Orthopedic Physical Assessment*, 3rd ed. Philadelphia, PA: W.B. Saunders Co, 1997.

38. Wood L, Muller S, Peat G. The epidemiology of patellofemoral disorders in adulthood: a review of routine general practice morbidity recording. *Prim Health Care Res Dev* 2011; 12(2):157–164.

39. Davies GJ, Manske RC, Slamma K, et al. Selective activation of the vastus medialis oblique: what does the literature really tell us? *Physiotherapy Canada* 2001; 53:100–115.

40. Wilk KE, Davies GJ, Mangine RE, et al. Patellofemoral disorders: a classification system and clinical guidelines for nonoperative rehabilitation. *J Orthop Sports Phys Ther* 1998; 28(5):307–322.

41. Wallace DA, Salem GJ, Salinas R, et al. Patellofemoral joint kinetics while squatting with and without an external load. *J Orthop Sports Phys Ther* 2002;32(4):141–148.

42. Chiu JK, Wong YM, Yung PS, Ng GY. The effects of quadriceps strengthening on pain, function, and patellofemoral joint contact area in persons with patellofemoral pain. *Am J Phys Med Rehabil* 2012; 91(2):98–106.

43. Bolgla LA, Boling MC. An update for the conservative management of patellofemoral pain syndrome: a systematic review of the literature from 2000 to 2010. *Int J Sports Phys Ther* 2011; 6(2):112–125.

44. Smith TO, Bowyer D, Dixon J, et al. Can vastus medialis oblique be preferentially activated? A systematic review of electromyographic studies. *Physiother Theory Pract Feb* 2009; 25(2):69–98.

45. Noehren B, Pohl MB, Sanchez Z, et al. Proximal and distal kinematics in female runners with patellofemoral pain. *Clin Biomech* 2012; 27(4):366–371.

46. Wirtz AD, Willson JD, Kernozek TW, et al. Patellofemoral joint stress during running in females with and without patellofemoral pain. *Knee* 2012; 19(5):703–708.

47. Willson JD, Davis IS. Lower extremity mechanics of females with and without patellofemoral pain across activities with progressively greater task demands. *Clin Biomech* 2008; 23(2):203–211.

48. Boling MC, Padua DA, Alexander Creighton R. Concentric and eccentric torque of the hip musculature in individuals with and without patellofemoral pain. *J Athl Train* 2009; 44(1):7–13.

49. Farrokhi S, Pollard CD, Souza RB, et al. Trunk position influences the kinematics, kinetics, and muscle activity of the lead lower extremity during the forward lunge exercise. *J Orthop Sports Phys Ther* 2008; 38(7):403–409.

50. Teng HL, Powers CM. Sagittal plane trunk posture influences patellofemoral joint stress during running. *J Orthop Sports Phys Ther* 2014; 44(10):785–792.

51. DeCarlo M, Klootwyk T, Oneacre K. Anterior cruciate ligament. In Ellenbecker TS ed., *Knee Ligament Rehabilitation*. Philadelphia, PA: Churchill Livingstone, 2000.

52. Beynnon BD, Ryder SH, Konradsen L, et al. Effect of anterior cruciate ligament trauma and bracing on knee proprioception. *Am J Sports Med* 1999; 27(2):150–155.

53. Neitzel JA, Kernozek TW, Davies GJ. Loading response following anterior cruciate ligament reconstruction during the parallel squat exercise. *Clin Biomech* 2002; 7(7):551–554.

54. Codman EA. *The Shoulder*. Privately printed, Boston, MA, 1934.

55. Rodosky MW, Harner CD, Fu F. The role of the long head of the biceps muscle and superior glenoid labrum in anterior stability of the shoulder. *Am J Sports Med* 1994; 22:121–130.

56. Inman VT, Saunders JB, Abbott LC. Observations on the function of the shoulder joint. *J Bone Joint Surgery* 1944; 26(1):1–30.

57. Neer CS. Anterior acromioplasty for the chronic impingement syndrome in the shoulder. *J Bone Joint Surgery* 1972; 54A:41–50.

58. Cotton RE, Rideout DF. Tears of the humeral rotator cuff: a radiological and pathological necropsy survey. *J Bone Joint Surg* 1964; 46B:314–328.

59. Jobe FW, Kivitne RS. Shoulder pain in the overhand or throwing athlete. *Orthop Rev* 1989; 18:963–975.

60. Walch G, Boileau P, Noel E, Donell ST. Impingement of the deep surface of the supraspinatus tendon on the posterosuperior glenoid rim: an arthroscopic study. *J Shoulder Elbow Surgery* 1992; 1:238–245.

61. Burkhart SS, Morgan CD, Kibler WB. The disabled throwing shoulder: spectrum of pathology Part I: Pathoanatomy and biomechanics. *Arthroscopy* 2003; 19(4):404–420.

62. Blackburn TA, McLeod WD, White B, et al. EMG analysis of posterior rotator cuff exercises. *J Athl Train* 1990; 25:40–45.

63. Townsend H, Jobe FW, Pink M, et al. Electomyographic analysis of the gelnohumeral muscles during a baseball rehabilitation program. *Am J Sports Med* 1991; 19:264–272.

64. Ballantyne BT, O'Hare SJ, Paschall JL, et al. Electromyographic activity of selected shoulder muscles in commonly used

therapeutic exercises. *Phys Ther* 1993; 73:668–682.

65. Ellenbecker TS. *Clinical Examination of the Shoulder*. Philadelphia, PA: Elsevier Saunders, 2004.

66. Moseley JB, Jobe FW, Pink M. EMG analysis of the scapular muscles during a shoulder rehabilitation program. *Am J Sports Med* 1992; 20:128–134.

67. Saha AK. Mechanism of shoulder movements and a plea for the recognition of "zero position" of glenohumeral joint. *Clin Orthop* 1983; 173:3–10.

68. Gross ML, Brenner Sl, Esformes I, Sonzogni, JJ. Anterior shoulder instability in weight lifters. *Am J Sports Med* 1993; 21(4):599–603.

69. Kolber MJ, Hanney WJ, Cheatham SW, Salamh PA, Masaracchio M, Liu X. Shoulder joint and muscle characteristics among weight-training participants with and without impingement syndrome. *J Strength Cond Res* 2017; 31(4):1024–1032.

70. Hertling D. The spine: general structure and biomechanical considerations. In: Hertling D, ed., *Management of Common Musculoskeletal Disorders*. Philadelphia, PA: Lippincott Williams & Wilkins, 2005.

71. Porterfield JA, DeRosa C. *Mechanical Low Back Pain: Perspectives in Functional Anatomy*. Philadelphia, PA: W.B. Saunders Co, 1991.

72. Cailliet R. *Low Back Pain Syndrome*, 2nd ed. Philadelphia, PA: F.A. Davis, 1981.

73. White AA, Panjabi MM. *Clinical Biomechanics of the Spine*. 2nd ed. Philadelphia, PA: J.B. Lippincott, 1990.

74. Norkin CC, Levangie PK. *Joint Structure and Function*. 2nd ed. Philadelphia, PA: F.A. Davis, 1992.

Contents

CHAPTER 23

ERGOGENIC AIDS

Colin D. Wilborn, Lem Taylor, and Jaci N. Davis

OBJECTIVES

After completing this chapter, you will be able to:

- Define and explain the role of ergogenic aids in sports.
- Demonstrate an understanding of the role of anabolic-androgenic steroids (AASs) in sports.
- Discuss and advise athletes on the role of fluid replacement beverages before, during, and after exercise.
- Discuss and advise athletes on the role of caffeine, creatine, and other potential ergogenic aids for specific events.

KEY TERMS

Adenosine triphosphate (ATP)
Anabolic
Anticatabolic agent
Arginine, ornithine and lysine
Aspartic acid
Beta-alanine
Beta-hydroxy-beta-methylbutyrate (HMB)
Boron
Branched-chain amino acids (BCAAs)
Caffeine
Carnitine
Chromium
Coenzyme Q_{10}

Colostrum
Conjugated linoleic acid (CLA)
Creatine
Creatinine
Dehydration
DHEA and androstenedione
Epigallocatechin gallate (EGCG)
Ergogenic aids
Essential amino acids (EAAs)
Glucosamine
Glutamine
Glycerol
Glycogenolysis
Glucose-alanine cycle

Green tea extract
Hydration
Hypohydration
Inosine
Isocaloric
Isoflavones
Ketoisocproate
Loading cycle
Lipolysis
Medium chain triglycerides
Osteoarthritis (OA)
Ribose
Sports drinks
Sulfo-polysaccharides
Thermogenic
Vanadium
Zinc/magnesium aspartate

INTRODUCTION

Ergogenic aids are substances (including nutrients, nutritional supplements, and drugs) that improve athletic performance. *Nutritional ergogenic aids* include substances that contain fats, carbohydrates, proteins, vitamins, and/or minerals. Fats, carbohydrates, and proteins provide energy (calories) to produce **adenosine triphosphate (ATP)**. Vitamins and minerals regulate energy-producing metabolic pathways. *Nutritional supplements* are nutrients in a concentrated form. Drugs can have an effect on cellular function that can directly or indirectly improve performance.

Numerous substances have been studied in the quest for improved athletic performance in multiple sports and athletic events. The conditions under which a substance might have a positive effect vary depending on metabolic requirements of the exercise, as well as the environmental conditions. The list of nutritional supplements that do not work would be endless.

Q&A FROM THE FIELD

I am concerned about my boyfriend. He wants to lift weights every day. He is always looking in the mirror and flexing his muscles. He spends a lot of time lifting weights and his muscles are extremely well developed. He is taking lots of different supplements. What is muscle dysmorphia, and what can we do for him if he has it?

Let me offer an example. Joe, a man 5 ft 10 in tall with extremely hypertrophied muscles, walks over to the squat rack, his eyes focused and his concentration fierce. He is a regular at the gym and is admired for his well-developed pecs, lats so large that his arms appear uncomfortably pushed inches away from his body, and powerful quads. Yet at 230 lb, Joe feels scrawny. He is embarrassed by what he perceives to be an underdeveloped body and tormented by the fear of losing the muscle he has if he doesn't work out for hours daily and follow a strict muscle-building diet. His kitchen is filled with large canisters of protein powder, a cupboard full of supplements touted to build muscles, and a scale to measure everything, but Joe is still displeased with his body.

Joe suffers from **muscle dysmorphia**, a preoccupation with his body image and the feeling that his body is not muscular enough. Like many other men who suffer from this disorder, Joe actually has a well-defined, muscular physique. Because of its striking similarity to other body-image distortions, muscle dysmorphia has been referred to as reverse anorexia or bigorexia and is considered to be a type of body dysmorphic disorder seen primarily in men. It is not surprising that an individual with body dysmorphia would take a lot of supplements to help him reach his goal.

Men suffering from muscle dysmorphia often lift weights for hours, pay meticulous attention to their diet, use various ergogenic aids, frequently check their bodies out in mirrors, and may spend more than five hours daily obsessing about their musculature. Like those who suffer from anorexia or other body-image disorders, these individuals are often depressed and may also experience anxiety, especially at the thought of anything disrupting their workout or diet regimen.

It isn't known how many men suffer from muscle dysmorphia, since large-scale studies have not been conducted. In addition, the etiology of muscle dysmorphia is unclear, though many theories have been presented; researchers believe that it may follow a psychosocial model with an underlying biological or genetic predisposition combined with social influences. The sociocultural theory is also believed to be a significant contributing factor. This view describes the societal pressures placed on men to fit media images of masculinity that include a fit, muscular physique. For years, women have been subjected to images of how a desirable female "should" look. Similarly unrealistic expectations for men, however, have become popular only in recent years.

Those who suffer from muscle dysmorphia rarely seek help for many reasons, including embarrassment over their preoccupation, the anxiety they feel at the thought of having to reduce their gym time during treatment, and the fear of a potential decrease in muscle mass once they start treatment. Proposed treatment options include cognitive behavioral therapy and the use of antidepressant medication.

—*Marie Spano, MS, RD*

TYPES OF ERGOGENIC AIDS/SUPPLEMENTS

This chapter focuses on several supplements that have been shown to have a positive effect and have been supported by research in a variety of settings to be ergogenic.

β-alanine

β-**alanine** is a naturally occurring non-essential amino acid that is found in many common food sources, such as chicken and turkey. β-alanine is thought to be a rate-limiting precursor to intramuscular carnosine synthesis. Carnosine, a natural buffer, is synthesized within the muscle but is dependent upon the levels of histidine and more specifically, β-alanine. Because of this fact, the utilization of β-alanine supplementation has become prevalent. β-alanine supplementation does in fact result in an increase in muscle carnosine levels and has been shown to potentially decrease fatigue and improved performance in high-intensity exercise settings by buffering hydrogen ions (H+). Thus supplementation of β-alanine leads to increased levels of intracellular muscular carnosine, which can have a buffering effect and potentially delay the onset of muscular fatigue and enhance performance (1).

The research around supplementation of β-alanine has been developed quite extensively since the early 2010s. A more detailed review of this research can be seen in a review article by Sales and associates (36). Overall, β-alanine supplementation has been reported to increase muscular strength and power, increase training volume, and delay fatigue, and thus improve performance in both aerobic and anaerobic settings. Specifically, a recent study by Smith and colleagues (40) found that β-alanine supplementation (6 g/day for days 1–21; 3 g/day days 22–42) for six weeks resulted in increases in VO$_2$ peak, time to exhaustion, training volume, and lean body mass when combined with high-intensity interval training. It should be noted that the increases in performance that occurred with the β-alanine supplementation occurred in the last three weeks of the training period, in which no further increases were observed in the placebo group on the same performance markers. Despite the fact that more research is needed on different aspects and issues of β-alanine supplementation, it is safe to say that there is sound evidence to support the use of β-alanine as an ergogenic aid.

> β-alanine may provide an indirect ergogenic effect by increasing carnosine levels in skeletal muscle, thus increasing the buffering capacity which can enhance performance and training volume.

Arginine, ornithine, and lysine

Lysine is an essential amino acid and **arginine** is considered semi-essential because it may become essential during periods of growth. **Ornithine** is a nonessential amino acid not found in proteins but important for efficient nitrogen removal in the urea cycle. Ornithine α-ketoglutarate (OKG) is ornithine bound with α-ketoglutarate (a Krebs cycle intermediate), which is supposed to enhance the efficiency of absorption.

Supplementation with arginine, lysine, and/or ornithine (or OKG) has been proposed to enhance growth hormone levels in circulation, leading to greater muscle mass development (51).

Researchers attempted to determine if oral supplementation of these amino acids could raise growth hormone levels. In one study the combined daily supplementation of arginine and lysine (1.2 g each) increased the level of growth hormone, but the individual supplements did not (52). In a related study, daily supplementation with both arginine and lysine (2.4 g) or ornithine and tyrosine (1.85 g) failed to increase circulating growth hormone levels in male bodybuilders (53).

The research involving supplementation of arginine, lysine, and ornithine is somewhat contradictory. An important consideration regarding the efficacy of these supplements is that even in the studies that noted an increase in growth hormone, the research protocols did not extend to assessing changes in lean body mass, measures of strength, or insulin-like growth factor-1 (IGF-1). IGF-1 was noted to be unchanged in one study that failed to demonstrate a rise in growth hormone (54). At this time supplementation of arginine, lysine, and ornithine to raise growth hormone levels is not supported.

Aspartic acid

Aspartic acid is a nonessential amino acid found in proteins and has also been suggested as a possible means of slowing muscle glycogen depletion during endurance efforts. The idea is that aspartic acid could serve as a source of oxaloacetate (OAA). OAA is a key intermediate of the Krebs cycle and combines with acetyl CoA derived from fatty acids and other fuel sources to form citrate. This would reduce the need for OAA derived from glycolysis, and thus the need for glycogen, during strenuous exercise. The result would be an enhancement in endurance performance by extending the time to fatigue associated with glycogen depletion.

In general, researchers have failed to demonstrate that aspartic acid supplementation is beneficial to endurance or strength training performance (55). For instance, when 6 g of potassium-magnesium aspartate was provided to young males for a day prior to cycling at 75% VO_2 max, there was not a positive change in the participants' time until exhaustion (56). Aspartic acid supplementation also did not positively influence plasma ammonia concentrations or other factors related to energy metabolism, namely glucose, lactate, and FFA levels.

Boron

Boron is an essential mineral involved in bone mineral metabolism, and it has been speculated that at least some of its influence on bone is related to steroid hormone metabolism. One study demonstrated that boron supplements were able to raise testosterone levels (57). On this basis, boron supplementation was thought to be a means of increasing testosterone production, which would lead to gains in muscle mass and strength. However, what is often overlooked is that the participants of that study were postmenopausal women who received 3 mg of boron daily after following a low-boron diet (57). Serum estrogen levels were also raised by the boron supplements.

In studies involving athletic populations, boron supplementation has not been proven to increase testosterone levels. For instance, male bodybuilders who took 7.5 mg of boron daily for seven weeks had no changes in measures of testosterone, lean body mass, and strength versus training alone (58,59).

Branched-chain amino acids

Amino acids are the building blocks of proteins. The amino acids leucine, isoleucine, and valine are collectively known as the **branched-chain amino acids (BCAAs)**. Supplementation with BCAAs does not seem to improve short-term exercise performance, but may reduce muscle breakdown during clinical conditions of wasting (e.g., starvation, postsurgery, burns) and periods of prolonged exercise. According to the "central fatigue hypothesis," during prolonged exercise, the plasma levels of BCAAs decrease and levels of fatty acids increase. The increase in fatty acids causes an increase in the levels of free tryptophan, which is a precursor to serotonin, a neurotransmitter that causes feelings of sleepiness and depression. In other words, decreases in BCAAs during prolonged exercise can, in theory, increase the mental effort necessary to perform. Use of BCAAs as an ergogenic aid may attenuate the increase in serotonin, thus reducing perceived exertion and mental fatigue during prolonged exercise. Although there is some support for these effects during prolonged cycling, marathon running, and time trials, an equal number of studies have shown no beneficial effect from BCAA supplementation. Since the side effects from BCAAs appear to be minimal, individuals competing in events lasting two or more hours, especially events in the heat, may wish to experiment with repeated liquid doses of BCAAs. One approach that has yielded positive effects is to ingest a total of 5 to 10 g of BCAAs dissolved in 1 L of fluid (i.e., drinking 150 mL of the solution every 10 to 20 minutes) (6).

Another interesting aspect of BCAAs, that has only recently been explored, is their potential effect on weight loss. During a moderate-protein (1.5 g/kg of body weight per day), lower-carbohydrate (100 to 200 g/day) diet, the increased intake of BCAAs (especially leucine) is thought to have positive effects on muscle protein synthesis, insulin signaling, and sparing of glucose use by stimulation of the **glucose-alanine cycle**. This leads to more fat loss and a greater sparing of lean tissue compared to an isoenergetic, higher-carbohydrate diet (20). Additional research regarding the effects of BCAAs on changes in body composition is warranted, but this notion is supported in the fact that **isocaloric** replacement of carbohydrates with lean protein sources does elicit benefits on improving body composition.

> BCAAs may have positive ergogenic effects related to their anticatabolic effect; however, fairly large doses must be consumed.

Caffeine

Caffeine is a bitter white alkaloid ($C_8H_{10}N_4O_2$) often derived from tea or coffee. Perhaps the most commonly consumed drug in the United States, caffeine is an effective ergogenic aid. Research on caffeine is easily accessible and is typically focused on caffeine's role in promoting lipolysis and energy expenditure (1), stimulating the central nervous system, and acting as a performance-enhancing aid for many types of athletic activity (3,4). Both older (65 to 80 years of age) and younger (19 to 26 years of age) men show a similar **thermogenic** response to caffeine ingestion, but the increase does seem to be blunted as age increases. Caffeine ingestion has been shown to stimulate both **lipolysis** and energy expenditure (1). It is not clear whether the lipolytic effect of caffeine is associated with increased lipid oxidation or futile cycling between triglycerides and free fatty acids (FFAs). Also, it is not known whether the effects of caffeine are mediated via the sympathetic nervous system.

Caffeine can also act as a potent ergogenic aid in multiple settings. Caffeine has been

removed from the World Anti-Doping Agency's (WADA) banned list update. Ingesting caffeine (5 mg/kg body weight) can significantly increase exercise time to exhaustion and moderate intensities (4). Caffeine ingestion can also improve maximal anaerobic power and sprint-swimming performance in trained swimmers among various other things. For a complete review of the effects that caffeine has on performance, see the position stand from the International Society of Sports Nutrition (13). Table 23.1 lists the caffeine content of various beverages.

> A large volume of data supports the ergogenic effects of caffeine as well as its thermogenic properties.

TABLE 23.1 Caffeine content of various products (23)

Product	Serving	Milligrams of caffeine
Starbucks coffee (tall)	12 oz	375
Red Bull	12 oz	120
Mountain Dew	12 oz	55
Diet coke	12 oz	45
Dr. Pepper	12 oz	41
Sunkist orange	12 oz	41
Starbucks espresso	1 oz	35
Coca-Cola classic	12 oz	34
Nestea sweetened iced tea	12 oz	26
Barqs root beer	12 oz	22
Hot chocolate	12 oz	8

Carnitine

Carnitine is β-hydroxy-γ-trimethylammonium butyrate, which is found in a variety of tissues and is concentrated in muscle. Two amino acids, lysine and methionine, are used to make carnitine, and synthesis occurs in the liver and kidneys. Carnitine transport mechanisms are necessary for movement of long chain fatty acids (LCFAs) into the mitochondrial matrix, the site of β-oxidation. Shorter chain fatty acids are able to diffuse into the mitochondrial matrix without assistance (60).

With regard to athletic performance, carnitine supplementation has been thought to potentially increase fat utilization, which could reduce the rate of glycogen loss and extend performance in endurance sports. Also, for sports with aesthetic considerations such as figure skating, gymnastics, and bodybuilding, enhanced fat utilization at rest and during exercise could enhance muscular appearance.

However, the results of nearly all of the experimental trials have not revealed a positive influence on either fatty acid utilization or glycogen sparing, neither does carnitine supplementation postpone the onset of fatigue. Furthermore, the overwhelming conclusion of research done on L-Carnitine suggests that the supplement does not enhance muscle carnitine content, fat metabolism and/or weight loss in trained individuals (61). Studies have also negated carnitine's effects on anaerobic- and aerobic performance (61).

Chromium

Chromium is an essential mineral and as a component of glucose tolerance factor (GTF), it is believed to be vital in the appropriate metabolism of energy nutrients. Chromium supplements are marketed largely as chromium picolinate as well as chromium nicotinate and chromium chloride.

Chromium supplementation is touted to increase metabolic rate and aid in weight reduction and increases in lean body mass. Chromium would accomplish these feats by enhancing the effects of insulin on muscle tissue. Insulin is considered to be generally anabolic by inhibiting protein breakdown and supporting protein synthesis. Such enhancement of muscle tissue could then lead to increased strength and power and increased energy expenditure and fat utilization at rest. Several well-designed research studies have been unable to demonstrate that chromium supplementation influences weight loss, LBM, or muscular strength (62,63).

Coenzyme Q_{10} (ubiquinone)

Coenzyme Q_{10} is often referred to as CoQ_{10} or ubiquinone. Ubiquinone may be found in all cells and is more concentrated within mitochondria. It is believed to exist attached to proteins of the electron transport chain as well as unattached and mobile. The free ubiquinone appears to function more as an antioxidant whereas the bound ubiquinone functions more as a component of the electron transport chain. Ubiquinone might enhance aerobic energy metabolism in muscle or help limit free radical stress during and perhaps after endurance exercise (64).

Research supporting ubiquinone supplementation as a way to improve athletic performance is limited. In one study, Finnish top-level cross-country skiers who received 90 mg/day of supplemental ubiquinone had improved indices of physical performance including VO_2 max (65). Other research efforts have also failed to show that ubiquinone supplementation had a positive impact on aerobic performance or a desirable influence on indicators of energy metabolism in the plasma (such as lactate) (66).

Studies involving ubiquinone supplementation and antioxidant capacity have shown some positive results. For instance, when endurance athletes were provided with 60 mg/day of ubiquinone in combination with vitamin E and vitamin C, the researchers reported improvements in their serum and LDL antioxidant potential (67). Ubiquinone has also been tested to potentially have a synergistic effect when paired with exercise training resulting in a decrease in hypertension and congestive heart failure (68).

Colostrum

Colostrum is a component of human breast milk or cow's milk, found at its highest concentration two to three days after a female gives birth. It is a rich source of protein, antibodies, and growth factors. Several compelling studies demonstrate an ergogenic effect of colostrum supplementation (2,9). Such supplementation (20 g/per day for eight weeks) combined with aerobic and heavy resistance training significantly increased bone-free lean body mass (mean increase of 1.49 kg) compared to whey protein (2).

Another investigation demonstrated the potential ergogenic effects of colostrum supplementation by comparing the effects of bovine colostrums to whey protein powder. Using a randomized, double-blind, placebo-controlled parallel design, 51 men completed 8 weeks of resistance and plyometric training while consuming 60 g/day of bovine colostrum or concentrated whey protein powder. By week eight, peak vertical jump power and peak cycle power were significantly greater in the colostrum group as opposed to the whey protein group. Interestingly, there were no differences between groups with regard to anaerobic work capacity, 1RM or plasma IGF-1 (9).

> Data for colostrum supplementation support daily doses ranging from 20 to 60 g to enhance performance as well as to promote gains in lean body mass.

Conjugated linoleic acids (CLA)

Conjugated linoleic acids are a group of at least 28 isomers of linoleic acid that is found in the diet through meat and dairy sources. CLAs are made up of double bonds that are conjugated together with only a single bond between them thus giving them their name.

It has been debated whether or not CLAs could be used in exercise supplements to promote muscle growth. CLAs may have an effect of lean tissue accretion, but only a few current studies have been done on this topic and have not proven there to be a large benefit (69,70). More so than with other supplements, there is a promise that CLAs can be used to help promote general health and reduce fat mass over time (71). This use of CLAs needs to be further researched before any certain benefit can be stated.

Creatine

Creatine is a naturally occurring nitrogenous compound made in the liver, kidneys, and pancreas from the amino acids arginine, glycine, and methionine. Creatine is found in relatively high amounts in meat, fish, and poultry. In fact, adults and teenagers who regularly consume these foods typically eat 1 to 2 g of creatine per day, an amount equal to its natural rate of excretion by the kidneys, where creatine is converted to **creatinine**. Vegetarians who do not consume meat or fish have reduced body stores of creatine. Interestingly, when these individuals are fed creatine, they retain more of it in their bodies (in comparison to nonvegetarians), suggesting that creatine might actually be "essential" to a normal diet. In a 154 lb adult man, about 120 g of creatine is found in the body, 95% of which is in skeletal muscle (42).

A large body of literature demonstrates the ergogenic properties of creatine (17,19,45). This literature is summarized in a recent position stand on creatine (10). The following discussion is by no means a comprehensive discussion of creatine; however, it does give the reader an insight into this effective ergogenic aid.

On ingestion, creatine is absorbed into the bloodstream through the small intestine and reaches peak levels 60 to 90 minutes later (42). Creatine is thought to serve at least four vital functions:

1 It stores energy that can be used to regenerate ATP.
2 It enhances energy transfer between the mitochondria and muscle fibers.
3 It serves as a buffer against intracellular acidosis during exercise.
4 It stimulates **glycogenolysis** (glycogen breakdown) during exercise.

Collectively, these effects underscore creatine's central role in energy metabolism and explain why this substance has been the subject of intensive study (17,45).

A common analogy used by exercise scientists is that creatine is to the weightlifter/sprinter what carbohydrate is to the distance runner. Of the well-controlled human trials on creatine, about two-thirds have shown benefits from its use. Depending on the initial fitness level of the subjects, these have included the following:

- Increased dynamic strength and power (approximately 5% to 15%)
- Increased body weight and lean body mass (approximately 2% to 5%)
- Increased sprint performance (approximately 1% to 5%)

As little as three days of creatine supplementation (0.35 g/kg of fat-free mass) can increase thigh muscle volume and may enhance cycle sprint performance in elite power athletes, with the effect being greater in females as sprints are repeated (50). Creatine supplementation in conjunction with heavy resistance training increased total body mass, fat-free mass, thigh volume, muscle strength, and myofibrillar protein (48).

Creatine is considered beneficial to weightlifters and athletes involved in sports requiring short, repeated bursts of high power (e.g., wrestling, rowing, sprint running/swimming/cycling, football, rugby, volleyball, soccer, hockey, lacrosse). Additionally, a growing body of evidence points to the health/medical benefits of oral administration of creatine monohydrate. For instance, creatine supplementation may protect against neuronal degeneration in amyotrophic lateral sclerosis and Huntington's disease and in chemically mediated neurotoxicity (41). Creatine may protect the immature brain from hypoxic-ischemic injury. Also, creatine supplementation has a "significant positive effect on working memory (backward digit span) and intelligence (Raven's Advanced

Progressive Matrices), both tasks that require speed of processing" (29). Creatine supplementation has applications that extend beyond the athletic realm. The health benefits of creatine may indeed be a positive area of research in the future.

What are the potential risks (side effects) of using creatine? The only consistently reported "side effect" in humans has been weight gain. Despite inflammatory reports in the media of a link between creatine use and muscle cramps/pulls, dehydration/heat exhaustion, and kidney/liver disorders, these effects have not been documented by independent research. To the contrary, studies have either reported no effect (on kidney/liver function or musculotendinous stiffness) or an improved response from creatine use (a lower incidence of muscle cramps/pulls) (46). In one study of 98 athletes, long-term supplementation with creatine (up to 21 months) did not adversely affect a 69-item panel of serum, whole blood, or urinary markers of clinical health status (19). A long-standing myth holds that creatine supplementation is harmful to the kidneys. This is clearly not the case. Neither short-, medium-, nor long-term oral creatine supplementation causes detrimental effects on the kidneys of healthy individuals (28).

In a lay article published on the internet, a comparison of 28 creatine distributors revealed that over half were selling products containing contaminants. The overall purity of each product averaged about 90%, but there were dramatic differences in the amount of several potentially toxic impurities. Athletes considering creatine use should exercise the following precautions:

1   A **loading cycle** is not needed. Rather than ingesting 20 to 30 g for the first 5 to 7 days and then 5 g/day thereafter, take only about 3 to 5 g daily.
2   Cycle periods of use (four to eight weeks) with periods of nonuse (four weeks).
3   Purchase the product from a reputable manufacturer who is able to provide a "certificate of analysis," including all of the following information:

- Appearance (should be white to pale cream)
- Assay (should be at least 95% creatine)
- Moisture content (should be less than or equal to 12.5%)
- Residue on ignition (should be less than or equal to 1%)
- Microbial/pathogenic contamination (should be negative for *Escherichia coli*, *Staphylococcus aureus*, and *Salmonella*)
- Yeasts and molds (should be less than 50 g)
- Poisons/heavy metals (should be less than 10 ppm for lead and mercury)
- Other contaminants (should be less than 3 ppm for arsenic, 30 ppm for dicyandiamide, and nondetectable for dyhydrotriazine)

> Creatine is the most widely studied ergogenic aid since the late 1990s. Creatine used for regular supplementation has been shown to increase skeletal muscle mass and muscle fiber size and improve anaerobic exercise performance. No evidence is available that regular creatine supplementation is harmful to otherwise healthy individuals.

DHEA and androstenedione

Dehydroepiandrosterone (DHEA) is a steroid hormone produced and released from the adrenal glands. DHEA is derived from cholesterol and can be converted to androstenedione, which in turn can be converted to testosterone. DHEA circulates both independently and loosely bound to albumin and sex hormone-binding globulin (SHBG), whereas DHEAS circulates strongly bound to albumin. The ability of tissue to convert DHEA and androstenedione to testosterone and/or estrogens relies on the presence of steroidogenic and metabolizing enzyme systems. Both androstenedione and testosterone can be converted to estrogens via *aromatase*. Many tissues produce these converting enzymes including the gonads (testes and ovaries), liver, kidneys, and adipose and endometrial tissue. This allows the conversion of DHEA and androstenedione to the androgens and estrogens to be regulated at the tissue level. Skeletal muscle lacks the ability to convert androstenedione to testosterone.

Supplementation of DHEA and/or androstenedione has been marketed as a means of increasing testosterone levels, which in turn could promote greater LBM, strength, and power. Although many studies have not resulted in increased testosterone levels after 100 mg of DHEA supplementation, Ostojic and associates measured significant increases in testosterone after 28 days of 100 mg of DHEA per day in young male athletes (91). While testosterone levels were increased, overall body composition was not affected by the supplement. After 28 days of 1600 mg/day DHEA supplementation, untrained males reduced body fat percentage by 31% suggesting that higher dosages result in LBM benefits (72). The International Olympic Committee (IOC) and the National Collegiate Athletic Association (NCAA) currently ban DHEA and androstenedione from use in sports. Also, supplementation of these substances may influence the ratio of testosterone to epitestosterone (T/E), which is used to screen for steroid doping by organizations such as the IOC and NCAA.

Essential amino acids

Of the 20 amino acids used to form proteins, nine are considered **essential amino acids (EAAs)** because your body does not produce them and you need to consume them in your daily diet. A growing body of literature demonstrates the efficacy of EAA supplementation in enhancing physical performance (7,43,44). The **anabolic** response to the consumption of an oral cocktail containing EAAs plus carbohydrate (EAC) before versus after heavy resistance exercise was studied (44). Six healthy subjects (three men and three women; average age 30.2 years, height 1.71 m, weight 66 kg) consumed the EAC (6 g of EAAs plus 35 g of sucrose in 500 mL water) either immediately before or after exercise (in a randomized order). The exercise bout consisted of ten sets of eight reps of the leg press (80% of 1RM), and eight sets of eight reps of the leg extension (80% of 1RM). The rest interval was about 2 minutes, with the total exercise time roughly 45 minutes. The investigators then examined phenylalanine uptake across the leg as a measure of muscle protein accretion. Over a three-hour period, taking the EAC before exercise resulted in a net phenylalanine uptake that was about 160% greater than that noted when the EAC was taken after exercise. Furthermore, work from the same

laboratory found that the nonessential amino acids are not required to stimulate protein synthesis. Finally, there is a dose-dependent effect of EAA ingestion on muscle protein synthesis (7). Thus, a relatively small dose (6 g) of EAA may confer a significant anabolic response.

> The essential amino acids play a critical role in promoting skeletal muscle anabolism and should be a component of most meals and snacks throughout the day.

Glucosamine

Glucosamine is a combination of glutamine and glucose (amino polysaccharide). Following ingestion and absorption of glucosamine, it is incorporated into molecules called proteoglycans, which are part of the joint cartilage. This process is thought to help maintain the integrity of the joint as well as repair damaged cartilage. Glucosamine may also stimulate chondrocytes, or cartilage-producing cells, to make new cartilage. The regular consumption of glucosamine may alleviate the signs and symptoms of **osteoarthritis (OA)**. Glucosamine supplementation may provide some degree of pain relief and improved function in persons experiencing regular knee pain, which may be caused by prior cartilage injury and/or OA. At a dosage of 2000 mg/day, most of the noted improvement occurs within eight weeks (8). A meta-analysis examined clinical trials of glucosamine from January 1980 to March 2002. This study demonstrated that glucosamine (alone or in combination with chondroitin sulfate) reduced pain and damage to the knee joint. No differences were found in adverse events between placebo and glucosamine, indicating that the supplement appears to be safe (33).

> Regular supplementation of glucosamine may decrease the symptoms associated with OA.

Glutamine

Glutamine is the most plentiful nonessential amino acid in the human body, particularly in the plasma and skeletal muscle, and has numerous physiological functions. Although the body can synthesize glutamine, it does become a "conditionally" EAA in cases of major trauma such as surgery, illness, and over-training. Even an intense workout or multiple intense workouts that lead to over-training are a cause for decreased glutamine levels. Among other things, glutamine acts as a cell-volume regulator (32) and has **anti-catabolic properties**. It may stimulate muscle protein synthesis (31) and support immune function. Although more research is necessary, there are limited data to support its ability to increase cellular hydration and stimulate protein synthesis, and most show that glutamine supplementation does not lead to increases in muscle mass, improvements in body composition, strength, and/or improvements in exercise performance (11).

Clinical evidence for the exogenous use of glutamine supplementation in critically ill patients for the maintenance of muscle mass and immune function is well supported. Glutamine's role as an ergogenic aid as it relates to immune function may be of greater significance to athletes than its ability to increase muscle mass. Glutamine use may modify the apparent immunosuppression that is observed after prolonged, exhausting exercise. After such strenuous exercise, the concentration of glutamine in the blood is severely decreased. Supplementation of glutamine in this situation may decrease the incidence of illness in these athletes. The influence of glutamine on time to exhaustion and power before and after a prolonged bout of exercise has been examined (27). One group ingested a carbohydrate-plus-glutamine (Glu) beverage and a placebo group ingested a carbohydrate-only beverage (Pl). The Glu group significantly increased time to exhaustion compared to Pl. Peak power in the Glu group was similar in both trials, whereas the Pl group was still significantly lower after the second trial six days later. Therefore, glutamine supplementation seemed to help the Glu group exercise longer and recover quicker than the Pl group.

There is a sound physiological rationale and some evidence that glutamine supplementation can have a positive impact on muscle mass and strength gains in athletes. More convincing, though, is evidence that supports exogenous glutamine supplementation for immune system function, especially with prolonged, exhausting exercise.

> Glutamine is an amino acid that may be needed in greater quantities during times of severe stress. Despite the various important roles of glutamine, current evidence does not support that glutamine supplementation can increase muscle mass or body composition.

Glycerol

Glycerol is a small, simple molecule consisting of three carbons and three hydroxyl (OH) groups. Glycerol serves as the backbone for fat molecules and can be an energy resource during exercise and fasting. The use of glycerol for energy occurs largely through its conversion to glucose (via gluconeogenesis) by the liver. Glycerol has been touted as a possible ergogenic aid for two reasons. First, it is a substrate for gluconeogenesis and thus may become an important resource for glucose production during endurance bouts. Second, supplemented glycerol distributes evenly throughout body fluid and may provide an osmotic influence that could help an athlete hyperhydrate prior to exercise in a warmer environment. This would have special application to sports in which water intake typically fails to match water losses in sweat.

Researchers reported that glycerol-induced hyperhydration just before moderate exercise was more effective than water-induced hyperhydration in reducing the thermal stress associated with exercise in the heat (73). The study provided 1 g of glycerol + 21.4 mL of H_2O per kilogram of body weight. In another study, researchers provided 1.2 g of glycerol + 26 mL of H_2O per kilogram of body weight to trained runners (74). They noted that the glycerol supplementation had no advantageous effect over water hyperhydration in terms of heart rate, rate of perceived exertion, fluid retention, or running performance in an environment mimicking an athletic race. Knight and colleagues concluded from another study that glycerol ingestion resulted in decreased performance in endurance sports (75).

Based on the available research, it seems that the ergogenic potential of glycerol-aided hyperhydration is still under scrutiny and more research is needed.

Green tea extract

Green tea extract has a high content of caffeine and catechin polyphenols, which could increase 24-hour energy expenditure and fat oxidation in humans. **Epigallocatechin gallate (EGCG)** is a purified catechin derived from green tea and is the main active component of the biological activity of tea polyphenols. For instance, one study compared three treatments: green tea extract (50 mg caffeine and 90 mg EGCG), caffeine (50 mg), and placebo, which were ingested at breakfast, lunch, and dinner. Green tea extract resulted in a significant increase in 24-hour energy expenditure as well as a decrease in respiratory quotient, indicating a greater reliance on fatty acid oxidation. Green tea has thermogenic properties and promotes fat oxidation beyond that explained by its caffeine content. Green tea extract may play a role in the control of body composition by thermogenesis, fat oxidation, or both, but the results to date are mixed at best.

> EGCG is one of the primary active components of green tea. To date, it seems that EGCG supplementation does not have a clear cut ergogenic effect directly related to performance. However, research supports its use as an agent to increase energy expenditure and fat oxidation.

Beta-hydroxy-beta-methylbutyrate

Beta-hydroxy-beta-methylbutyrate (HMB) is a natural component of fish and milk. As a breakdown product of the essential amino acid leucine, HMB is thought to increase strength and lean body mass by acting as an anticatabolic agent in muscle (i.e., decreasing muscle protein breakdown) (26). Studies have verified these beneficial effects, particularly in untrained men and women who consume 1.5 to 3.0 g of HMB per day, divided into two doses, for at least four weeks. One study suggested that its effects on strength and lean body mass can be further enhanced by coingesting creatine (Cr dose: 20 g/day for seven days followed by 10 g/day thereafter) (15). Although the exact mechanism(s) behind its effects are unclear, the research suggests that the effects on body composition are not significant and there

tends to be a more substantial effect on lower-body strength than upper body strength, and these responses do not seem to occur in previously resistance trained men (35). Ingestion of HMB appears to be safe and may even have beneficial effects on cardiovascular health (e.g., decreasing total cholesterol, LDL cholesterol, and blood pressure) when doses of at least 3 g/day are ingested for up to eight weeks (26).

> HMB supplementation may have an anticatabolic effect and increase strength, but the effects seem to be limited to untrained individuals.

Hydration

Dehydration has negative effects on performance (37). Inadequate hydration can refer to either **hypohydration** (being dehydrated prior to exercise) or exercise-induced dehydration, which occurs during exercise. Either state of dehydration can negatively impact muscle metabolism, body temperature regulation, and cardiovascular function, with performance decrements occurring with as little as a 1% to 2% reduction in body weight.

Water and commercial **sports drinks** can be very effective in maintaining performance or delaying the inevitable decrease in performance, especially in endurance or team sports that last longer than one hour. It is recommended that individuals consume a nutritionally balanced diet and drink adequate fluids in the 24-hour period prior to training or competition. The American College of Sports Medicine Position Stand on Exercise and Fluid Replacement (92) recommends that prehydration, if needed, should be initiated several hours before exercise to allow for excretion of excess fluid. Maintaining proper hydration prior to exercise is simple and generally should not be an issue if prudent measures are followed.

Fluid replacement during exercise is extremely critical not only to exercise performance but also to health. Without proper fluid replacement during prolonged exercise or exercise in a hot and humid environment, heat-related illness and cardiovascular issues can become life-threatening. To minimize these conditions, it is recommended that water losses via sweating be replaced at a rate equal to the sweat rate. Athletes should replace the weight lost during exercise by drinking fluid. Unfortunately, individuals generally do not sufficiently replace lost fluid at a rate equal to water loss. This is referred to as "voluntary dehydration." Water alone is not always sufficient to replace the fluid deficit incurred due to exercise, especially long-duration exercise with high sweat rates. Complete restoration of fluid lost during exercise cannot occur without replacement of electrolytes, primarily sodium.

Along with sodium, the addition of carbohydrates to fluid-replacement solutions can enhance the intestinal absorption of water (38). More importantly, though, ingestion of a carbohydrate-containing beverage during exercise will help maintain blood glucose concentration and thus delay reliance on muscle glycogen stores as well as ultimately delaying fatigue (12). This is especially true in sessions lasting longer than one hour. An optimal carbohydrate solution of 4% to 8% helps maintain blood glucose concentrations and replace fluid lost via sweating. The inclusion of carbohydrates in rehydration solutions is necessary to maintain blood glucose concentrations for optimal performance in exercise lasting longer than one hour. It is also important to note that fructose should not be the predominant carbohydrate in a fluid-replacement solution due to its low glycemic index and the associated relatively slow increase in blood glucose. Frequent ingestion of water and commercial sports drinks (containing electrolytes and carbohydrates) during exercise is certainly one of the simplest and most beneficial ergogenic aids available.

> Hydration is a critical factor governing exercise performance in the heat. Both water and sports drinks are effective tools to help prevent, maintain, and replenish hydration status in athletic populations.

Inosine

Inosine in the form of nucleotide inosine monophosphate (IMP) is used to make AMP and GMP, which in turn can be phosphorylated to the high-energy phosphate molecules ATP and GTP. IMP is made in many cells using ribose-5-phosphate via the pentose phosphate pathway and the amino acids aspartic acid, glutamine, and glycine with the assistance of folate.

Because ATP is derived from IMP, it seems logical that inosine supplementation might be able to enhance ATP levels in muscle cells. This would enhance maximal contractile activities, such as during weight training and sprinting, and increase performance and adaptation to exercise.

In general, researchers have reported that inosine supplementation does not improve athletic performance (71). In a different study, male cyclists were provided with 5 g of inosine (or placebo) for 5 days before performing a 30-minute self-paced cycling bout at a constant load followed by a supramaximal sprint to fatigue (77). The inosine supplementation failed to alter metabolic and performance parameters during the self-paced cycling bout, and the supramaximal cycling sprint time to fatigue was actually shorter than the placebo trial, suggestive of an ergolytic effect. Other research has also failed to determine a metabolic or performance benefit of inosine supplementation (76).

Studies have also failed to demonstrate that inosine supplementation increases unloading of O_2 in muscle tissue by increasing 2,3-DPG in RBCs (76,77). Furthermore, blood analysis revealed that uric acid levels may be increased due to inosine supplementation (76,77), which raises concerns about the effect of chronic supplementation on health.

Thus it seems that inosine supplementation may not improve measures of aerobic performance and short-term power production and may actually have an ergolytic effect under some conditions.

Isoflavones

Isoflavones are proteins that are derived from soy food. They have a similar chemical structure to that of mammalian estrogen. Because of their comparable structure, isoflavones have the ability to either increase estrogen activity or compete with estrogen for receptor sites and decrease health risks that are involved with excess estrogen. Alongside this health benefit, it has also been thought that isoflavones contain anti-cancer characteristics, can ease menopausal symptoms, fight against osteoporosis, as well as aid against cardiovascular disease.

In conclusion there may be some health benefits, but that is debatable and may require further research before a conclusive decision is made.

Ketoisocproate

Alpha-**ketoisocproate** is a branched chain keto acid that is a metabolite of leucine metabolism. Ketoisocproate (KIC) is widely known to inhibit the enzymatic activity of the branch-chain alpha-keto dehydrogenase complex and therefore is thought to have anticatabolic properties in the muscle. If proven to be effective, the supplementation of this BCAA would help minimize protein degradation during resistance training, ergo resulting in greater gains in muscle mass from training.

Research on BCAAs and its effects on exercise has only recently started and even less is available on KIC individually. One group of researchers tested the effects of a glycine-arginine-a-ketoiscoparoic (GAKIC) acid blend on its ability to reduce fatigue during high intensity performance. The participants for this study were well-trained male cyclists who in a double blind randomized trail either consumed a placebo drink or the GAKIC blend and then were put through a series of exhaustive exercise trials and then their rate to fatigue measured. At the conclusion of the study there was no difference between the placebo group and the GAKIC group on rate of fatigue, therefore it was said that the supplement had no ergogenic effect (78).

There is still potential for KIC to be proven effective for resisting against protein catabolism during exercise, but at this moment it is still too early to tell.

Medium chain triglycerides

Medium chain triglycerides (MCTs) contain medium chain (length) fatty acids (MCFAs), which have 6 to 12 carbon atoms. Fat digestion releases these fatty acids, which can be absorbed directly into the portal vein, as they are water soluble. Thus MCFAs are available sooner after ingestion than long chain fatty acids because MCFAs bypass chylomicron formation. In addition, medium chain fatty acids may not require the carnitine transport system to cross the mitochondrial inner membrane like long chain fatty acids.

Because MCFAs can be absorbed and circulate dissolved in the plasma, they can be rapidly available to muscle. Furthermore, if transport into the mitochondria is a rate-limiting step in longer chain fatty acid oxidation, then MCFAs may enhance fat utilization by skipping this step. Increased fatty acid oxidation during endurance activity could in theory decrease the need for carbohydrate and thus slow glycogen depletion.

The results of some studies do indeed suggest that MCFAs derived from MCT supplementation prior to an endurance bout may serve as an energy source during endurance exercise, especially when consumed with carbohydrate (79,80). Yet the contribution of pre-exercise MCT supplements to fuel used during exercise is still small.

A few research efforts have attempted to determine whether MCT supplementation can influence performance. For instance, researchers provided a placebo, carbohydrate, or carbohydrate and MCTs to cyclists during a 100-km time trial ride (81). The researchers reported that the carbohydrate enhanced performance in comparison to the placebo, but that the addition of MCT did not make a difference. In a related study, athletes cycled for two hours at 63% VO_2 max and then performed a simulated 40 km time trial while consuming carbohydrate or carbohydrate plus MCT (82). Here again the carbohydrate supplementation improved measures of performance, but the MCT did not provide an additive effect. Another study failed to elicit performance improvements with MCT supplementation during sprinting in trained cyclists and the authors mentioned that MCT might actually have caused negative performance effects (83). One review of the literature also concluded that there was very little convincing scientific evidence to recommend MCT use to improve exercise performance (71).

At this time the use of MCT as an ergogenic aid is very questionable. Clearly, ingested MCT can be used for fuel during exercise, but whether that affects the oxidation of carbohydrate, more specifically muscle glycogen, is in doubt. One of the largest concerns for MCT supplementation is the potential for gastrointestinal discomfort, including diarrhea (79). Also, its theoretical use would seem to be limited to ultra-endurance athlete populations.

Ribose

Ribose is a five-carbon carbohydrate. Ribose as ribose-5-phosphate is made in many cells via the pentose phosphate pathway. Ribose-5-phosphate can then serve as a building block for adenosine, which itself is a building block for ATP. It has been speculated that ribose supplementation could lead to increased ATP levels in skeletal muscle and thus greater power production during very high intensity activities. This enhanced overload could in turn lead to greater muscular adaptations (hypertrophy).

Although research addressing the potential application of ribose supplementation to physical performance is limited, a couple of human studies and a few studies performed on rats provide some insight. One study compared ribose and dextrose supplementation (10 g) in female rowers over an eight-week period (84). The participants on the dextrose supplement had greater performance increases than the ribose supplement group leading researchers to believe that ribose was ineffective. In another study, five days of ribose supplementation (10 g/day) resulted in no effect on anaerobic capacity in 19 trained males completing a Wingate test (85). A similar study with moderately trained cyclists (all men) also did not find any differences or increases in anaerobic exercise capacity with a ribose supplementation of 3 g (86). Based on the research it appears that ribose is ineffective at promoting ergogenic effects during aerobic or anaerobic exercise.

Sulfo-polysaccharides

Sulfo-polysaccharides are dietary supplements that have been said to increase strength and muscle mass during resistance training. The research on this ergogenic aid is scarce and inconclusive. One study done in 2006 tested its effects on resistance trained males, who either ingested 800 mg/day or 1000 mg/day during an eight-week training period. At the outset, fourth, and eighth weeks of the study, subjects provided a fasting blood sample, and completed a series of muscular strength and endurance tests. After the statistics were run on the data it was determined that there was no significant training adaptation due to the supplementation (87).

At this time, more research needs to be done to determine if the benefits of sulfo-polysaccharides actually exist.

Vanadium

Vanadium is a minor mineral and is believed to be nutritionally essential. It is believed to be involved in insulin metabolism and/or to function in some capacity that mimics the activity of insulin. Vanadium is typically marketed in the form of vanadyl sulfate. Like chromium picolinate, the positively charged vanadium is bound to the negatively charged sulfate molecule. Vanadium as a sport supplement was popularized in the 1990s as diabetic rats became more glucose tolerant when they were provided with vanadium. Because vanadium seemed to somehow mimic the actions of insulin, it was speculated that vanadium supplements might prove anabolic in weight trainers and bodybuilders. Like chromium, vanadium was touted to enhance lean body mass by increasing amino acid uptake by muscle in conjunction with enhanced protein synthesis and inhibition of protein breakdown.

The little research done so far does not support the notion that vanadium supplements enhance LBM and strength in well-nourished people and athletes. Researchers provided individuals in a 12-week weight training study with vanadyl sulfate (or placebo) at a level of 0.5 mg/kg of body weight daily (88). They measured changes in 1RM and 10RM for the leg extension and bench press and assessed body composition using DXA scans. Vanadyl sulfate supplementation failed to improve strength gains or change body composition relative to the placebo group. In addition, two of the participants receiving the vanadyl sulfate supplements dropped out of the study due to side effects.

Zinc/magnesium aspartate (ZMA)

Zinc/magnesium aspartate's main ingredients include zinc monomethionine aspartate, vitamin B6 and magnesium aspartate. Zinc is an essential mineral found in animal and plant sources, is associated with amino acids, and is involved in almost all human operations. Skeletal muscle on average contains 60% of zinc stores, and absorption of zinc could possibly be enhanced in the presence of certain amino acids. Protein production is an important function of zinc, therefore it is plausible that zinc supplementation would increase LBM and strength gains. Magnesium, also an essential mineral, is found in food sources such as wholegrain cereals, nuts, seafood, and spices. Some 60% of magnesium in the body is stored in the bones and it is required for 300+ reaction systems, including amino acid linking. Similar to zinc, a supplement of magnesium is thought to positively affect muscle mass development and strength. It is also thought that a deficiency in zinc and/or magnesium may reduce testosterone and IGF-1 in the body (71).

A study conducted in 2000 supplemented college football players during spring training with ZMA daily for eight weeks (89). Posttesting revealed an increase in testosterone and IGF-1 in the supplement group as well as greater strength increases than the placebo group. It was concluded that ZMA supplementation is beneficial for trained athletes.

Another study concluded the opposite – that ZMA supplementation did not increase training adaptations in resistance trained males (90). Wilborn and associates measured body composition, 1RM and endurance in leg and bench press, anaerobic power, and hormone levels. No significant differences were seen between the ZMA supplement group and the placebo group.

Based on the research, it appears that the effects of ZMA supplementation need to be further examined and studied to determine whether or not trained and untrained individuals will experience an ergonomic or ergolytic effect.

While support for magnesium supplementation is conflicting, it does appear that zinc has a positive effect on immune function in trained individuals (71). Gleeson and Bishop discuss zinc supplementation and its positive effects on immunity while warning individuals of the risk of toxicity, which would lead to other negative health effects (93). One study demonstrated that zinc supplementation reduced the negative effects of exercise in an acute exercise session (94). It was not known whether the same benefits would be seen in individuals participating in chronic physical activity.

NUTRITION BEFORE AND AFTER WORKOUTS

Strenuous exercise, whether aerobic or anaerobic, can reduce various energy substrates (glycogen, protein, stored phosphagens [ATP, phosphocreatine], intracellular triglycerides), increase muscle protein breakdown, damage cell membranes, cause fluid loss, and temporarily impair immune function. The manner in which these physiological changes occur and how they respond to different interventions has provided clues to researchers as to what and when to eat with regard to optimizing performance.

REAL-WORLD APPLICATION

Supplements versus foods

1 Eat about six meals each day. Healthy foods are the basis of sound nutrition. Frequent small meals increase metabolism.
2 Supplements should be treated only as an additional "tool" for achieving your goals. They are not magic potions that will cure the adverse effects of poor training and diet. When combined with sound nutrition, supplements could help athletes make substantial improvements in performance, recovery, and immunity.
3 Creatine is clearly a safe and effective supplement that can enhance LBM, muscle strength, and power with little to no side effects.
4 Always consume a postworkout carbohydrate-protein shake within 30 minutes of completing exercise (strength and endurance) to expedite recovery and promote gains in LBM.
5 Supplements should never take the place of real food.

Assuming that body hydration and muscle glycogen levels are adequate, a successful pre-exercise strategy is to provide a small amount of carbohydrate (25 to 50 g) along with 6 g of EAA (or 40 g of complete protein) approximately 15 minutes prior to resistance training (43,44). This specific combination of carbohydrates and EAA has been shown to increase muscle protein synthesis 160% more than ingesting the same cocktail post-exercise (45). In this case, the exercise bout was for the lower body only (i.e., ten sets of eight reps of leg press at 80% of 1RM and eight sets of eight reps of leg extension at 80% of 1RM). Interestingly, research from the same lab found that adding nonessential amino acids to the mix does not increase protein synthesis. In other words, only the essential amino acids are needed to promote anabolic processes in muscle (7).

Nutrition during the post-exercise period accomplishes three goals: (a) it puts the brakes on protein degradation, (b) it increases muscle protein synthesis, and (c) it rapidly initiates the process of muscle glycogen regeneration. An "optimal" food/beverage has yet to be identified. Based on research conducted over the past few years (6), however, a carbohydrate-to-protein ratio that ranges from 4:1 to approximately 1:1 may expedite recovery as well as enhance muscle glycogen synthesis *and* net protein status (14,43,44). Athletes should use a lower ratio of carbohydrates to protein when the volume of work (sets times reps) being performed is low, and a higher ratio when the volume of work being performed is high. Practically, this means that athletes interested in increasing LBM as well as muscular strength and power should consume a post-workout beverage containing at least 100 cal and as much as 500 cal (and a combination of protein and carbohydrate) within 30 minutes of exercise. It is critical to consume this immediately after training or competition.

Anecdotally, many athletes find that adding 3 to 5 g of creatine and 5 to 10 g of BCAAs to their pre- and/or postworkout beverages provides an enormous benefit.

> Consuming a combination of carbohydrate and protein immediately after exercise will expedite recovery and perhaps improve subsequent performance.

ANABOLIC-ANDROGENIC STEROIDS IN SPORTS

Anabolic-androgenic steroids are synthetic forms of testosterone, the primary male hormone. Testosterone is responsible for both anabolic (muscle growth) and androgenic (secondary sex characteristics) effects that begin at puberty in males. The anabolic and androgenic characteristics of the drug go hand in hand, thus the name anabolic-androgenic steroids (AASs). The androgenic properties of the drug are responsible for many of the negative side effects reported.

AASs are generally effective in promoting muscle growth. Although some forms of AASs can be obtained as a legal prescription drug for certain medical conditions, they are illegal for possession without a prescription. AASs can be prescribed for males with delayed puberty, inadequate endogenous testosterone production, and individuals with muscle-wasting diseases. AASs are against the rules of most sport governing bodies. Because of their pronounced effect on muscle size and strength, these drugs are widely used and abused by athletes, particularly in strength and power sports.

Abuse of AASs, however, can lead to potentially serious health problems, some irreversible. In addition to using AASs to improve athletic performance, many individuals are using AASs simply to improve physical appearance. Anabolic steroids come in both oral and injectable forms. Athletes, in an attempt to maximize the benefits of AAS use, will cycle the drugs rather than use them continuously. Cycling means taking multiple doses of steroids over a period of time and then going off them for a period of time before starting again. One concern is that athletes often combine several different types of steroids in an effort to maximize their effectiveness and minimize negative effects (referred to as "stacking"). Many of the studies looking at the negative effects of AAS use are looking at the effects of a prescription dose, not a dose that is stacked and/or cycled. It is quite possible that the larger doses used by athletes would cause the side effects to be even more pronounced.

The side effects from abusing AASs may include liver tumors (usually benign), negative blood lipid changes (increases in low-density-lipoprotein (LDL) (bad) cholesterol, and decreases in high-density-lipoprotein (HDL) (good) cholesterol), fluid retention, high blood pressure, and severe acne. Since AASs are male hormones, they produce different side effects in males, females, and adolescents. In males, common side effects are shrinking testicles, reduced sperm count, infertility, baldness, gynecomastia (breast development), and an increased risk of prostate cancer. In females, anabolic steroids can cause male hair growth patterns on the face and body, male-pattern baldness, enlargement of the clitoris, and a deepened voice. Adolescents may experience premature closure of epiphyseal discs, causing stunted growth. Negative side effects are likely a result of the type of AAS used, the dose, frequency, and duration of use. Notice that males tend to develop feminine side effects and females tend to develop masculine side effects. In males, excess androgens (excess testosterone) are converted to estrogen, a primary female hormone. It is the estrogen production in males that is related to the feminine side effects. Many, but not all, of the side effects are irreversible when the athlete stops taking AAS.

What does all this mean to the strength and conditioning professional? First of all, we should be aware that the athletes we work with may be using AASs to enhance performance or appearance. Second, we must be able to provide sound advice to athletes and parents based on the legality of using AASs. Third, competition and sports should be based on the concept of fair play. The use of AASs by athletes to enhance performance crosses this line and jeopardizes the athlete's safety.

Q&A FROM THE FIELD

I've been hearing a lot of talk about using myostatin blockers. I am not familiar with these. What are they, and how effective are they? Do they pose any dangers?

I have seen these supplements in health food stores; they have been marketed with claims that they bind to serum myostatin and inhibit it. Myostatin causes muscle atrophy and wasting. Therefore, myostatin blockers could basically remove the inhibition of muscle growth and allow unlimited potential in muscle mass. One study has recently shown that Cystoseira canariensis, a brown sea algae that is the active ingredient in

myostatin blockers, does exhibit binding specificity for serum myostatin (30). We have recently shown that C. canariensis binds myostatin; however, when combined with heavy weight training, 1200 mg × d-1 of C. canariensis had no effect in reducing the level of serum myostatin or in preferentially increasing muscle strength and mass and decreasing fat mass (47). Therefore, the results from this study suggest that there is no apparent anabolic benefit from ingesting myostatin-blocking supplements.

Myostatin appears to negatively regulate skeletal muscle growth. In the blood, myostatin appears to work in part by slowing down and inhibiting the growth of muscle.

Recent studies with adult rodents showed that antibodies were created against myostatin, increasing total body mass, muscle mass, muscle size, and absolute muscle strength. The implication is that a myostatin blocker could conceivably provide benefits as an ergogenic aid or in the treatment of patients with muscle wasting diseases.

—**Darryn Willoughby, PhD, CSCS, FISSN, Baylor University**

Q&A FROM THE FIELD

A friend in my class says he is taking a supplement containing nitric oxide (NO). He says he has gained 10 lb of muscle in a month. What does research say about NO stimulators (arginine and argine alpha-ketoglutarate)? Is there any evidence that they might help athletes gain muscle mass?

The problem here is that you have some fairly complex physiology being thrown around about NO without any substantive human data showing an effect on exercise performance or body composition. For instance, we know that arginine is an amino acid that participates in the maintenance of muscle and lean tissue throughout the body. It can be converted into ornithine, another amino acid. Its presence can stimulate the release of certain endogenous anabolic hormones, such a growth hormone and IGF-1. There is supposedly a better-absorbed form of arginine on the market called arginine alpha-ketoglutarate. This supplement is marketed under various names with claims that it accelerates the body's natural production of

(continued)

(continued)

NO, vastly augmenting blood flow to muscles. It is also claimed that this product adds new muscle fibers, not muscle water, and that this addition of lean muscle combined with ingestion of the supplement will decrease body fat and enhance recovery. Unfortunately, there appear to be no scientific studies to validate any of these claims. Future research will reveal the effectiveness of this supplement.

Based on the current research, pure arginine may be better and more effective than arginine alpha-ketoglutarate. Arginine has been well researched and has many beneficial effects, especially in terms of cardiovascular health. Its main mechanism of action lies in boosting NO. NO is a signaling molecule within muscle cells that may have many anabolic effects, including increased nutrient transport and vasodilatation. Arginine boosts NO by stimulating NO synthase, the enzyme that makes NO. Research suggests it may help improve exercise performance, support

protein synthesis, boost growth hormone levels at higher doses, and even help replenish postworkout glycogen stores.

OKG (ornithine ketoglutarate) (a salt formed from one molecule of alpha-ketoglutarate and two molecules of ornithing) is a metabolic regulator and precursor for glutamine and arninine. Glutamine promotes protein synthesis in skeletal muscle. OKG is also a precursor for other amino acids and ketoacids, which are important for protein synthesis in skeletal muscle. OKG is also a precursor for other amino acids and ketoacids, which are important for protein synthesis. OKG stimulates the secretion of hormones such as insulin and human growth hormone and has an anabolic effect on muscles. It can also help with ammonia detoxification. This could be of significance, since high levels of ammonia are prevalent among body builders and other athletes. Therefore, OKG has been marketed as a sports supplement for helping to build muscle.

—**Darryn Willoughby, PhD, CSCS, FISSN, Baylor University**

SUMMARY

TABLE 23.2 Summary of ergogenic aids

Nutrient/ supplement	Actions	Dosage	Comments	References
Aromatase inhibitors	Block the aromatase activity thus increasing endogenous levels of serum testosterone.	~75 mg/day (hydroxyandrost-4-ene-6,17-dioxo-3-THP ether and 3,17-diketo-androst-1,4,6-triene)	Research has confirmed that aromatase inhibitors can increase serum testosterone levels with supplementation. One trial also found a significant decrease in fat mass during supplementation.	49
BCAA	May increase fat-free mass; anticatabolic effect; may ameliorate performance decrement.	BCAA (12–14 g/day; 50% L-leucine, 25% L-isoleucine, 25% L-valine)	High dose BCAA supplementation may be ergogenic.	25
Caffeine	Lipolytic agent; increases mental alertness; increases thermogenesis; may enhance performance.	200–400 mg (acute dose)	No longer a banned substance; most commonly consumed drug.	1,13

Colostrum	May increase LBM; may enhance performance.	20–60 g/day for several weeks	Compared to whey protein, may be more anabolic.	2,9
Creatine	May increase LBM; may enhance performance (i.e., sprints, 1RM, repeated anaerobic exercise bouts, etc.).	3–5 g/day; for loading phase (if chosen), 20–25 g/day for about a week	Enormous scientific support for ergogenic effect.	5,10,45,50
EAA	May increase muscle protein accretion.	6 g (acute dose increases net muscle protein balance)	Has greater anabolic effects when taken preworkout versus postworkout.	7,43
EGCG	A component of green tea; may increase thermogenesis beyond the normal effects of caffeine.	270 mg/day	May have antioxidant and anti-carcinogenic effects; data show enhanced thermogenesis.	34
Glucosamine	May treat symptoms of osteoarthritis.	1500 mg of glucosamine hydrochloride (GH) and 1200 mg of chondroitin sulfate (CS) daily	May ameliorate symptoms of osteoarthritis.	39
Glutamine	Increases immune function.	6–10 g	May be more effective as immune function supporter in times of severe stress (exercise).	11
HMB	May alleviate the exercise-induced proteolysis and/or muscle damage; may increase muscle mass/function.	3 g/day	May work best in untrained individuals.	18
Myostatin blockers	Purported to block the action of myostatin, which is a negative regulator of skeletal muscle mass.	1200 mg/day of cystoseira canariensis	Research does NOT support the supplementation of purposed myostatin inhibitors.	47
Pre- and postworkout supplements	Increase muscle mass; increase muscle glycogen repletion; increase recovery.	Supplement containing 80 g CHO, 28 g Pro, 6 g fat immediately after exercise (10 minutes) and two hours post-exercise; as little as 100 calories may help; 6 g of essential amino acids consumed pre-workout effective	Timing of ingestion is critical. Need to consume a carbohydrate-protein beverage immediately post-exercise.	14,44

(continued)

TABLE 23.2 (continued)

Nutrient/ supplement	Actions	Dosage	Comments	References
Prohormones	Proposed to increase testosterone levels and have effects on anabolism.	Dosage varies based on individual prohormone.	May increase testosterone, but NO evidence to support that they have an effect on muscle mass. No ergogenic effect, and may also increase estrogen levels.	16
Sodium bicarbonate	Buffers the increase in H+ ions which increase acidity (lowers pH) and impact fatigue.	0.3 g/kg body weight	Potentially effective in maximal exercise lasting 2–5 minutes; may improve sprint performance.	21,24
Sports drinks	Carbohydrates necessary to maintain blood glucose to delay fatigue; electrolytes (sodium) help with absorption and complete fluid restoration.	4–8% carbohydrate solution	Dehydration causes decrease in performance; may be only effective when exercise duration exceeds 1 hour; fluid and electrolyte loss due to sweat is variable and dependent upon individual sweat rates; sports drinks without added protein are inadequate for promoting skeletal muscle recovery.	12,22

MAXING OUT

1 A football running back for a division 1 college football team asks for your advice regarding his nutrition and supplementation program. He currently eats two to three very large meals each day (lunch and dinner). He often skips breakfast because he is not hungry, and he drinks coffee. His meals are mainly fast food (i.e., burgers, fries, and regular cola) as well as pizza and beer on late-night binges. At 5 ft 10 in tall, weighing 200 lb, and 18 years of age, he consumes approximately 3,000 cal per day. His workouts for football are quite rigorous, and the day after a game he feels extremely lethargic. He wants to know how he can improve his diet as well as whether supplements might improve his performance and help him gain LBM.

2 There are literally thousands of purported ergogenic aids, all of which cannot be covered in a single chapter. Using the Internet or a library resource, investigate a familiar substance that is a purported ergogenic aid. Answer the following questions relative to the substance:

a   Is there a logical "mechanism of action" by which this substance may have a positive effect on human performance?

b   If this substance were to improve performance, what sports or events would be most likely to be improved?

c   What information can you find regarding the effectiveness of this ergogenic aid? Positive/negative results? Dosing requirements?

d   What information can you find regarding the safety of this ergogenic aid? Adverse events? Specific side effects? Any long-term health consequences?

3   It is difficult to address the ethical considerations of using ergogenic aids. Most will agree that there is a line we should not cross in recommending ergogenic aids. Write your own definition of an ergogenic aid. Then make a determination of whether or not these substances should be allowed to be used by athletes under your definition:

a   Amino acids
b   Creatine monohydrate
c   Concentrated glucose replacement beverage
d   Testosterone and related compounds
e   Insulin
f   Insulin-like growth factor
g   Growth hormone
h   Vitamin concentrates
i   Mineral concentrates
j   Coffee and concentrated caffeine beverages or tablets
k   Vitamin B12 injections
l   Protein bars

CASE EXAMPLE

Professional boxer

Background

You are a sports nutritionist who has been asked by a professional boxer how to best enhance his performance. He fights in the heavyweight division at 200 lb (he is 6 ft tall and 26 years old). He is preparing for an upcoming fight in three months and needs advice on how to improve his punching power/speed with new nutrition strategies. He is currently working with a top strength and conditioning specialist to improve his conditioning. This upcoming fight is ten rounds (three-minute rounds), with one minute of rest between rounds.

Recommendations/considerations

Because he is a heavyweight, he can add extra LBM and not worry about exceeding a weight limit. Also, he is "light" for a heavyweight boxer and likely needs to maintain his body weight while gaining more LBM.

(continued)

(continued)

Implementation

Descriptive information. Gathering basic information such as height, weight, body fat percentage (using skinfolds), age, and training history is essential. Examine past fights to see how he fared at different body weights and to determine at what rounds his strength/power subsided. Determine, if possible whether he has an "ideal" boxing weight.

Diet analysis. Have the subject keep a record of his food intake over the next seven days to assess whether he is currently meeting his energy needs as well as macronutrient requirements. It is important to ensure an adequate intake of protein and essential fatty acids.

Supplements. Is this athlete taking any supplements? Again, you can determine this from the interview and his food diary. Perhaps creatine monohydrate supplementation is needed.

Rest. How much rest is the athlete getting?

Conditioning program. Is he training properly for the fight? Is his training program periodized, matching up with his competition schedule? Does his regime include core training, and are his workouts sports specific? Work with his strength and conditioning coach to answer these questions.

Results

Based on the information obtained from this process, you make the following recommendations:

1   Increase daily caloric intake to 4,000 kcal a day, utilizing a weight gain supplement if needed to obtain the desired intake.
2   Maintain a protein intake of 1 g per lb body weight – 1 d-1.
3   Consume a preworkout beverage containing EAAs plus carbohydrate.
4   Consume a postworkout protein shake to expedite recovery and promote gains in LBM.
5   Consume 3 to 5 g of creatine monohydrate as a daily supplement.
6   Get seven to eight hours of sleep every night.

REFERENCES

1. **Acheson KJ, Gremaud G, Meirim I, et al.** Metabolic effects of caffeine in humans: lipid oxidation or futile cycling? *Am J Clin Nutr* 2004; 79:40–46.

2. **Antonio J, Sanders MS, Van Gammeren D.** The effects of bovine colostrum supplementation on body composition and exercise performance in active men and women. *Nutrition* 2001; 17:243–247.

3. **Armstrong LE.** Caffeine, body fluid-electrolyte balance, and exercise performance. *Int J Sport Nutr Exerc Metab* 2002; 12:189–206.

4. **Bell DG, McLellan TM.** Effect of repeated caffeine ingestion on repeated exhaustive exercise endurance. *Med Sci Sports Exerc* 2003; 35:1348–1354.

5. **Bermon S, Venembre P, Sachet C, et al.** Effects of creatine monohydrate ingestion in sedentary and weight-trained older adults. *Acta Physiol Scand* 1998; 164:147–155.

6. **Blomstrand E, Saltin B.** BCAA intake affects protein metabolism in muscle after but not during exercise in humans. *Am J Physiol Endocrinol Metab* 2001; 281:E365–E374.

7. **Borsheim E, Tipton KD, Wolf SE, Wolfe RR.** Essential amino acids and muscle protein recovery from resistance exercise. *Am J Physiol Endocrinol Metab* 2002; 283:E648–E657.

8. Braham R, Dawson B, Goodman C. The effect of glucosamine supplementation on people experiencing regular knee pain. *Br J Sports Med* 2003; 37:45–49, discussion 49.

9. Buckley JD, Brinkworth GD, Abbott MJ. Effect of bovine colostrum on anaerobic exercise performance and plasma insulin-like growth factor I. *J Sports Sci* 2003; 21:577–588.

10. Buford TW, Kreider RB, Stout JR, Greenwood M, Campbell B, Spano M, Ziegenfuss T, Lopez H, Landis J, Antonio J. International Society of Sports Nutrition position stand: creatine supplementation and exercise. *J Inter Soc of Sports Nutr* 2007; 4:6. DOI:a10.1186/1550-2783-4-6.

11. Candow DG, Chilibeck PD, Burke DG, Davison KS, Smith-Palmer T. Effect of glutamine supplementation combined with resistance training in young adults. *Eur J Appl Physiol* 2001; 86(2):142–9.

12. Coggan AR, Coyle EF. Carbohydrate ingestion during prolonged exercise: effects on metabolism and performance. *Exerc Sport Sci Rev* 1991; 19:1–40.

13. Goldstein ER, Ziegenfuss T, Kalman D, Kreider R, Campbell B, Wilborn C, Taylor L, Willoughby D, Stout J, Graves BS, Wildman R, Ivy JL, Spano M, Smith AE, Antonio J. International society of sports nutrition position stand: caffeine and performance. *J Inter Soc of Sports Nutr* 2010; 7:5. https://jissn.biomedcentral.com/articles/10.1186/1550-2783-7-5.

14. Ivy JL, Res PT, Sprague RC, Widzer MO. Effect of a carbohydrate-protein supplement on endurance performance during exercise of varying intensity. *Int J Sport Nutr Exerc Metab* 2003; 13:382–395.

15. Jowko E, Ostaszewski P, Jank M, et al. Creatine and beta-hydroxy-beta-methylbutyrate (HMB) additively increase lean body mass and muscle strength during a weight-training program. *Nutrition* 2001; 17:558–566.

16. King DS, Sharp RL, Vukovich MD, Brown GA, Reifenrath TA, Uhl NL, Parsons KA. Effect of oral androstenedione on serum testosterone and adaptations to resistance training in young men: a randomized controlled trial. *JAMA* 1999; 281(21):2020–2028.

17. Kraemer WJ, Volek JS. Creatine supplementation. Its role in human performance. *Clin Sports Med* 1999; 18:651–666, ix.

18. Kreider RB, Ferreira M, Wilson M, Almada AL. Effects of calcium beta-hydroxy-beta-methylbutyrate (HMB) supplementation during resistance-training on markers of catabolism, body composition and strength. *Int J Sports Med* 1999; 20:503–509.

19. Kreider RB, Melton C, Rasmussen CJ, et al. Long-term creatine supplementation does not significantly affect clinical markers of health in athletes. *Mol Cell Biochem* 2003; 244:9–104.

20. Layman DK, Baum JI. Dietary protein impact on glycemic control during weight loss. *J Nutr* 2004; 134:968S–973S.

21. Lindh AM, Peyrebrune MC, Ingham SA, Bailey DM, Folland JP. Sodium bicarbonate improves swimming performance. *Int J Sports Med* 2008; 29(6):519–523.

22. Maughan RJ, Leiper JB. Limitations to fluid replacement during exercise. *Can J Appl Physiol* 1999; 24:173–187.

23. Mayo Clinic. *Caffeine Content of Common Beverages.* Available at www.mayoclinic.com/health/drug-information/DR202105.

24. McNaughton L, Thompson D. Acute versus chronic sodium bicarbonate ingestion and anaerobic work and power output. *J Sports Med Phys Fitness* 2001; 41:456–462.

25. Mourier A, Bigard AX, de Kerviler E, et al. Combined effects of caloric restriction and branched-chain amino acid supplementation on body composition and exercise performance in elite wrestlers. *Int J Sports Med* 1997; 18:47–55.

26. Nissen S, Sharp RL, Panton L, et al. Beta-hydroxy-beta-methylbutyrate (HMB) supplementation in humans is safe and may decrease cardiovascular risk factors. *J Nutr* 2000; 130:1937–1945.

27. Piattoly T, Welsch MA. L-Glutamine supplementation: effects on recovery from exercise. *Med Sci Sports Exerc* 2004; 36:S127.

28. Poortmans JR, Francaux M. Long-term oral creatine supplementation does not impair renal function in healthy athletes. *Med Sci Sports Exerc* 1999; 31:1108–1110.

29. Rae C, Digney AL, McEwan SR, Bates TC. Oral creatine monohydrate supplementation improves brain performance: a double-blind, placebo-controlled, cross-over trial. *Proc R Soc Lond B Biol Sci* 2003; 270:2147–2150.

30. Ramazov Z, Jimenez del Rio M, Ziegenfuss T. Sulfated polysaccharides of brown seaweed Cystoseira canariensis bind to serum myostatin protein. *Acta Physiol Pharmacol* 2003; 27:1–6.

31. Rennie MJ. Glutamine metabolism and transport in skeletal muscle and heart and their clinical relevance. *J Nutr* 1996; 126:1142S–1149S.

32. Rennie MJ, Low SY, Taylor PM, et al. Amino acid transport during muscle contraction and its relevance to exercise. *Adv Exp Med Biol* 1998; 441:299–305.

33. Richy F, Bruyere O, Ethgen O, et al. Structural and symptomatic efficacy of glucosamine and chondroitin in knee osteoarthritis: a comprehensive meta-analysis. *Arch Intern Med* 2003; 163:1514–1522.

34. Rietveld A, Wiseman S. Antioxidant effects of tea: evidence from human clinical trials. *J Nutr* 2003; 133:3285S–3292S.

35. Rowlands DS, Thomson JS. Effects of beta-hydroxy-beta-methylbutyrate supplementation during resistance training on strength, body composition, and muscle damage in trained and untrained young men: a meta-analysis. *J Strength Cond Res* 2009; 23(3):836–846.

36. Sale C, Saunders B, Harris RC. Effect of beta-alanine supplementation on muscle carnosine concentrations and exercise performance. *Amino Acids* 2010; 39(2):321–333.

37. Schoffstall JE, et al. Effects of dehydration and rehydration on the one-repetition maximum bench press of weight-trained males. *J Strength Cond Res* 2001; 15:102–108.

38. Schedl HP, Maughan RJ, Gisolfi CV. Intestinal absorption during rest and exercise: implications for formulating an oral rehydration solution (ORS). *Med Sci Sports Exerc* 1994; 26:267–280.

39. Segal L, Day SE, Chapman AB, Osborne RH. Can we reduce disease burden from osteoarthritis? *Med J Aust* 2004; 180:S11–S17.

40. Smith, AE, Walter, AA, Graef JL, Kendall KL, Moon JR, Lockwood CM, Fukuda DH, Beck TW, Cramer JT, Stout JR. Effects of beta-alanine supplementation and high-intensity interval training on endurance performance and body composition in men: a double-blind trial. *J Inter Soc Sports Nutr* 2009; 6(5).

41. Tarnopolsky MA, Beal MF. Potential for creatine and other therapies targeting cellular energy dysfunction in neurological disorders. *Ann Neurol* 2001; 49:561–574.

42. Terjung RL, Clarkson P, Eichner ER, et al. American College of Sports Medicine roundtable. The physiological and health effects of oral creatine supplementation. *Med Sci Sports Exerc* 2000; 32:706–717.

43. Tipton KD, Borsheim E, Wolf SE, et al. Acute response of net muscle protein balance reflects 24-h balance after exercise and amino acid ingestion. *Am J Physiol Endocrinol Metab* 2003; 284:E76–E89.

44. Tipton KD, Rasmussen BB, Miller SL, et al. Timing of amino acid-carbohydrate ingestion alters anabolic response of muscle to resistance exercise. *Am J Physiol Endocrinol Metab* 2001; 281:E197–E206.

45. Volek JS, Rawson ES. Scientific basis and practical aspects of creatine supplementation for athletes. *Nutrition* 2004; 20:609–614.

46. Watsford ML, Murphy AJ, Spinks WL, Walshe AD. Creatine supplementation and its effect on musculotendinous stiffness and performance. *J Strength Cond Res* 2003; 17:26–33.

47. Willoughby DS. Effects of an alleged myostatin binding supplement and heavy resistance training on serum myostatin, muscle strength and mass, and body composition. *Int J Sports Nutr Exerc Metab* 2004; 14(4):461–472.

48. Willoughby DS, Rosene J. Effects of oral creatine and resistance training on myosin heavy chain expression. *Med Sci Sports Exerc* 2001; 33:1674–1681.

49. Willoughby DS, Wilborn C, Taylor L, Campbell W. Eight weeks of aromatase inhibition using the nutritional supplement Novedex XT: effects in young, eugonadal men. *Int J Sport Nutr Exerc Metab* 2007; 17(1):92–108.

50. Ziegenfuss TN, Rogers M, Lowery L, et al. Effect of creatine loading on anaerobic performance and skeletal muscle volume in NCAA Division I athletes. *Nutrition* 2002; 18:397–402.

51. Chromiak JA, Antonio J. Use of amino acids as growth hormone-releasing agents by athletes. *Nutrition* 2002; 18(7–8):657–661.

52. Isidori A, LoMonaco A, Cappa M. A study of growth hormone release in man after oral administration of amino acids. *Current Medical Research Opinion* 1981; 7(7):475–481.

53. Lambert MI. Failure of commercial oral amino acid supplements to increase serum growth hormone concentrations in male body-builders. *Int J Sports Nutr* 1993; 3(3):298–305.

54. Corpas E, Blackman MR, Roberson R, Scholfield D, Harman SM. Oral arginine-lysine does not increase growth hormone or insulin-like growth factor-I in old men. *J Gerontol* 1993; 48(4):M128–M133.

55. Trudeau F. Aspartate as an ergogenic supplement. *Sports Med* 2008; 38(1):9–16.

56. Maughan RJ. The effects of oral supplementation of salts of aspartic acid on the metabolic response to prolonged exhausting exercise in man. *Int J Sports Med* 1983; 4:119–123.

57. Nielsen FH, Hunt CD, Mullen LM, Hunt JR. Effect of dietary boron on mineral, estrogen, and testosterone metabolism in postmenopausal women. *FASEB Journal* 1987; 1:394–397.

58. Green NR, Ferrando AA. Plasma boron and the effects of boron supplementation in males. *Environmental Health Perspectives* 1994; 102:73–77.

59. Ferrando AA, Green NR. The effect of boron supplementation on lean body mass, plasma testosterone levels, and strength in male bodybuilders. *Int J of Sport Nutr* 1993; 3:140–150.

60. Wildman REC, Medeiros DM, eds. Nutraceuticals and nutrition supplements. In: *Advanced Human Nutrition*. Boca Raton, FL: CRC Press, 2000.

61. Smith W, Fry A, Tschume L, Bloomer R. Effect of glycine propinoyl-L-carnitine on aerobic and anaerobic exercise performance. *Int J Sport Nutr Exerc Metab* 2008; 18(1):218–223.

62. Lukaski HC, Bolonchik WW, Siders WA, Milne DB. Chromium supplementation and resistance training: effects on body composition, strength, and trace element status of men. *Am J Clin Nutr* 1996; 63(6):954–965.

63. Campbell WW, Joseph LJ, Davey SL, Cyr-Campbell D, Anderson RA, Evans WJ. Effects of resistance training and chromium picolinate on body composition and skeletal muscle in older men. *J Appl Physiol* 1999; 86(1):29–39.

64. Kaikkonen J, Tuomainen TP, Nyyssonen K, Salonen JT. Coenzyme Q10: absorption, antioxidative properties, determinants, and plasma levels. *Free Radical Research* 2002; 36(4):389–397.

65. Ylikoski T, Piirainen J, Hanninen O, Penttinen J. The effect of coenzyme Q10 on the exercise performance of cross-country skiers. *Molecular Aspects of Medicine* 1997; 18(suppl):S283–S290.

66. Bonetti A, Solito F, Carmosino G, Bargossi AM, Fiorella PL. Effect of ubidecarenone oral treatment on aerobic power in middle-aged trained subjects. *J Sports Med Physic Fit* 2000; 40:51–59.

67. Vasankari TJ, Kujala UM, Vasankari TM, Vuorimaa T, Ahotupa, M. Increased serum and low-density-lipoprotein antioxidant potential after antioxidant supplementation in endurance athletes. *Am J Clin Nutr* 1997; 65:1052–1056.

68. Balerdinelli R, Mucaj A, Lacalaprice F, et al. Coenzyme Q10 and exercise training in chronic heart failure. *European Heart Journal* 2006; 27(22):2875–2681.

69. Tarnopolsku M, Zimmer A, Paikin J, et al. Creatine monohydrate and conjugated linoleic acid improve strength and body composition following resistance exercise in older adults. *PLoS One* 2007; 2(10):e991.

70. Pinoski C, Chilibeck PD, Candow DG, et al. The effects of conjugated linoleic acid supplementation during resistance training. *Med Sci Sports Exer* 2006; 38:339–348.

71. Kreider RB, Wilborn CD, Taylor L, et al. ISSN exercise & sport nutrition review: research & recommendations. *JISSN* 2010; 7:7–49.

72. Nestler JE, Barlascini CO, Clore JN, Blackard WG. Dehydroepiandrosterone reduces serum low density lipoprotein levels and body fat but does not alter insulin sensitivity in normal men. *J Clin Endocrin Metabol* 1988; 66(1):57–61.

73. Lyons T. Effects of glycerol-induced hyperhydration prior to exercise in the heat on sweating and core temperature. *Med Sci Sports Exerc* 1990; 22:477–483.

74. Scheadler C, Garver M, Kirby T, Devor S. Glycerol hyperhydration and endurance running performance in the heat. *J Exerc Physiol Online* 2010; 13(3):1–11.

75. Knight C, Braakhuis A, Paton C. The effect of glycerol ingestion on performance during simulated multisport activity. *Res Q Exerc Sport* 2010; 81(2):233–238.

76. McNaughton L, Dalton B, Tarr J. Inosine supplementation has no effect on aerobic or anaerobic cycling performance. *Int J Sport Nutr* 1999; 9(4):333–344.

77. Starling RD, Trappe TA, Short KR, Sheffield-Moore M, Jozsi AC, Fink WJ, Costill DL. Effect of inosine supplementation on aerobic and anaerobic cycling performance. *Med Sci Sports Exerc* 1996; 28(9):1193–1198.

78. Beis L, Yaser M, Easton C, et al. Failure of glycine-arginie-a-ketoisocaproic acid to improve high intensity exercise performance in cyclists. *Int J Sport Nutr Exerc Metab* 2011; 21(1):33–39.

79. Jeukendrup AE, Saris WH, Schrauwen P, Brouns F, Wagenmakers AJ. Metabolic availability of medium-chain triglycerides

coingested with carbohydrates during prolonged exercise. *J Appl Physiol* 1995; 79(3):756–762.

80. Van Zyl CG, Lambert EV, Hawley JA, Noakes TD, Dennis SC. Effects of medium-chain triglyceride ingestion on fuel metabolism and cycling performance. *J Appl Physiol* 1996; 80:2217–2225.

81. Angus DJ, Hargreaves M, Dancey J, Febbraio MA. Effect of carbohydrate or carbohydrate plus medium-chain triglyceride ingestion on cycling time trial performance. *J Appl Physiol* 2000; 88:113–119.

82. Goedecke JH, Elmer-English R, Dennis SC, Schloss I, Noakes TD, Lambert EV. Effects of medium-chain triacylglycerol ingested with carbohydrate on metabolism and exercise performance. *Int J Sport Nutr* 1999; 9:35–47.

83. Goedecke JH, Clark VR, Noakes TD, Lambert EV. The effects of medium-chain triacylglycerol and carbohydrate ingestion on ultra-endurance exercise performance. *International J Sport Nutr Exerc Metab* 2005; 15(1):15–27.

84. Dunne L, Worley S, Macknin M. Ribose versus dextrose supplementation, association with rowing performance: a double-blind study. *Clin J Sport Med* 2006; 16(1):68–71.

85. Kreider RB, Melton C, Greenwood M, Rasmussen C, Lundberg J, Earnest C, Almada A. Effects of oral d-ribose supplementation on anaerobic capacity and selected metabolic markers in healthy males. *Int J Sport Nutr Exerc Metab* 2003; 13:76–86.

86. Kerksick C, Rasmussen C, Bowden R, Leutholtz B, Harvey T, Earnest C, Greenwood M, Almada A, Kreider R. Effects of ribose supplementation prior to and during intense exercise on anaerobic capacity and metabolic markers. *Int J Sport Nutr Exerc Metab* 2005; 15:653–664.

87. Wilborn CD, Taylor LW, Campbell BI, Kerksick C, Rasmussen FA, et al. Effects of methoxyisoflavone, ecdysterone, and sulfo-polysaccharide supplementation on training adaptations in resistance-trained males. *JISSN* 2006; 3:1550–2783.

88. Fawcett JP, Farquhar SJ, Walker RJ, Thou T, Lowe G, Goulding A. The effect of oral vandyl sulfate on body composition and performance in weight-training athletes. *Int J Sport Nutr Exerc Metab* 1996; 6(4):382–390.

89. Brilla LR, Conte V. Effects of a novel zinc-magnesium formulation on hormones and strength. *J Exerc Physiol Online* 2000; 3:26–36.

90. Wilborn CD, Kerksick CM, Campbell BI, Taylor LW, Marcello BM, Rasmussen CJ, Greenwood MC, Almada A, Kreider RB. Effects of zinc magnesium aspartate (ZMA) supplementation on training adaptations and markers of anabolism and catabolism. *JISSN* 2004; 1(2):12–20.

91. Ostojic SM, Calleja J, Jourkesh M. Effects of short-term dehydroepiandrosterone supplementation on body composition in young athletes. *Chin J Physiol* 2010; 53(1):19–25.

92. ACSM. Position stand. Exercise and fluid replacement. *Med Sci Sports Exerc* 2007; 39(2):377–390.

93. Gleeson M, Bishop NC. Elite athlete immunology: importance of nutrition. *Int J Sports Med* 2000; 21 Suppl 1:S44–S50.

94. Singh A, Failla ML, Deuster PA. Exercise-induced changes in immune function: effects of zinc supplementation. *J Appl Physiol* 1994; 76(6):2298–2303.

INDEX

Figures are not indexed separately but are included in text page spans and referenced within the text.